Dignified Retreat

Robert A. Schneider received his undergraduate degree from Yale University and his PhD from the University of Michigan. He has taught at Brandeis University, the Catholic University of America, and, since 2005, at Indiana University Bloomington. He has been a visiting professor at the National University of Ireland, Maynooth, Bristol University, and the Ecole des Hautes Etudes in Paris. He has received fellowships from the Simon Guggenheim Foundation, the National Endowment for the Humanities, the American Council of Learned Societies, and the French Government (the Chateaubriand Fellowship), and he has been a visiting scholar at All Souls College and Oriel College in Oxford. He has published several books on early modern French history, and was the editor of the *American Historical Review* from 2005 to 2015.

Frontispiece *Bene qui latuit bene vixit,* Otto van Veen, 1683. Printsandprinciples.com

The Hidden Life Is Best

If it were enough to be content in order to be truly happy, our painter would not have added this image to the four preceding ones. But with this one, he shows us what he could not convey in the others. He has demonstrated the advantages and delights that can edify our character. He now wants to teach us that to be completely happy, we must acknowledge our good fortune by savoring it, one might say, by recalling it, and to make this kind of reflection the main and most assiduous task of our life. This is why he depicts a perfect sage in the depths of a dark and isolated valley. In his reflective and still guise, he conveys the meditations of his soul and seems to be telling us that in examining his past life, he is trying to discover in the depths of his heart if he has or has not strayed from the principles which he established for himself as the guide of his actions and whether these same actions have conformed to the terms he set out to govern them. For those of us who are not engaged in this sort of reflection, let us cast our eyes elsewhere in this illustration and look carefully at what is happening above him. There are boulders high up. But they are being dislodged by a terrible storm. There are towers of enormous heights. But their foundations are soon to crumble. There are pine trees whose tops reach almost to the heavens. But they are being ripped out by the roots by the angry wind. All of these marvelous and disastrous images are lessons from nature, teaching us to avoid excess and to persuade us to understand that great ambition is a great evil and that the transgressions of the mind are no less criminal than those of the body.
—From Marin Le Roy de Gomberville, *La Doctrine des Moeurs tirée de la Philosphie des Stoiques: Representée en cent tableaux et expliquée en cent discours pour l'instruction de la jeunesse* (Paris, 1646), 34.

Dignified Retreat

*Writers and Intellectuals in the
Age of Richelieu*

ROBERT A. SCHNEIDER

OXFORD
UNIVERSITY PRESS

Great Clarendon Street, Oxford, OX2 6DP,
United Kingdom

Oxford University Press is a department of the University of Oxford.
It furthers the University's objective of excellence in research, scholarship,
and education by publishing worldwide. Oxford is a registered trade mark of
Oxford University Press in the UK and in certain other countries

© Robert A. Schneider 2019

The moral rights of the author have been asserted

First published in 2019
First published in paperback in 2022

All rights reserved. No part of this publication may be reproduced, stored in
a retrieval system, or transmitted, in any form or by any means, without the
prior permission in writing of Oxford University Press, or as expressly permitted
by law, by licence or under terms agreed with the appropriate reprographics
rights organization. Enquiries concerning reproduction outside the scope of the
above should be sent to the Rights Department, Oxford University Press, at the
address above

You must not circulate this work in any other form
and you must impose this same condition on any acquirer

Published in the United States of America by Oxford University Press
198 Madison Avenue, New York, NY 10016, United States of America

British Library Cataloguing in Publication Data

Data available

Library of Congress Cataloging in Publication Data

Data available

ISBN 978-0-19-882632-3 (Hbk.)
ISBN 978-0-19-286316-4 (Pbk.)

Links to third party websites are provided by Oxford in good faith and
for information only. Oxford disclaims any responsibility for the materials
contained in any third party website referenced in this work.

For Sarah, Kate, and Laura

Preface

When our daughters were little, one of their favorite books was *We're Going on a Bear Hunt*. The story is simple enough: a young family sets out to track down a bear, declaring, "We're going on a bear hunt! We're going to catch a big one!... We're not scared!" But along the way, they meet a series of obstacles: "long wavy grass," "a deep cold river," "thick oozy mud," and so forth; and at each turn they exclaim, "We can't go over it! We can't go under it! Uh-oh! *We have to go through it!*"

This children's book comes to mind as I recall the long process that led me to produce the present study. It started out simply enough as a quest to excavate fundamental features of the "political culture" (a relatively new concept for historians at the time) of absolutism during the ministerial reign of Cardinal Richelieu. And so I began by reading works of *raison d'état* by such writers as Jean-Louis Guez de Balzac, Jean de Silhon, Gabriel Naudé, and others whose texts figure prominently in the history of the political thought of the period. But as I was especially interested in the cultural dimensions of their political views, I began to look further into their backgrounds, their other writings, and their social milieu. And this plunged me into a rabbit hole of discovery, revealing (to me) unexpected depths—a cultural world of *gens de lettres* that literary scholars had long explored but that historians, I was and remain convinced, had not adequately taken the measure of. Despite the perils of trespassing on foreign disciplinary terrain, I decided that I had no choice: *I had to go through it*!

At the same time, I encountered the work of a group of French scholars in Paris led by Alain Viala and Christian Jouhaud, the Groupe de recherches interdisciplinaires sur l'histoire du Littéraire (GRIHL) at the Ecole des hautes études en sciences sociales, which has established the study of literature as a truly historical phenomenon of the Ancien Régime. Their work, along with the many studies of Hélène Merlin-Kajman, have been crucial to my thinking, informing this study at virtually every turn. My references in the footnotes to these Parisian scholars only partially convey my indebtedness to their remarkable work.

A book that took longer to complete than I care to admit affords me the opportunity to discharge the accumulated debts that I am happy to acknowledge. Like many others, I am struck by how much I have depended upon the riches of older scholarship, much of it bibliographic, documentary, or even antiquarian in nature; in particular, my reliance on the monumental works of erudition by the likes of Antoine Adam and Philippe Tamizey de Larroque should be evident in the references to their publications that fill the footnotes of these pages. And what scholar of the seventeenth century is not indebted to René Pintard's *Le libertinage érudit dans la première moitié du dix-septième siècle* (1943), an inexhaustible source for the intellectual history of the early decades of the century? Along with Pintard, I must acknowledge Marc Fumaroli's magisterial study *L'âge d'éloquence: Rhétorique et "res literaria" de la Renaissance au seuil de l'époque classique* (1980), a work that more than any other has forced literary scholars and historians alike to recognize the centrality of "eloquence" for the culture of the period.

Many institutions supported my research and writing over the years. The Simon Guggenheim Foundation, the American Council of Learned Societies, the National Endowment for the Humanities, as well as the Catholic University of America and Indiana University Bloomington, all subsidized time away from teaching duties. At Indiana I am happy to acknowledge a grant from the College Arts and Humanities Institute. I am grateful to All Souls College and Oriel College for residential fellowships at Oxford University. I was very pleased to be able to spend a month in my favorite French city in 2011 as a visiting lecturer at the Université de Toulouse II le Mirail, thanks to my favorite Toulousain, Jack Thomas. Likewise, I am indebted to the Ecole des hautes études en sciences sociales, Paris, for invitations on three different occasions to serve as *directeur d'études invité*. In particular, I thank Robert Descimon and Christian Jouhaud for their graciousness and generosity.

Like other scholars, I have profited enormously from the comments—or merely the forbearance—of audiences at conferences, universities, and seminars in the UK, Ireland, France, Germany, Switzerland, Canada, and the US. The experience of giving talks and presenting papers over the years served as a much-needed runway without which this book would never have gotten off the ground.

In ways I can barely hope to acknowledge, friends and colleagues provided invaluable help and moral support over the years. In Bloomington, I am daily grateful for its extraordinary intellectual community—the many seminars, workshops, conferences, study groups, and the like, as well as the chance encounters and conversations that make this quintessential "college town" such a stimulating place in which to live and work. As an early modernist, I have been happily stretched between two flourishing interdisciplinary groups at IU, Renaissance Studies and the Center for Eighteenth-Century Studies, which have nourished me over the years, both intellectually and socially. In particular, without, I hope, slighting many friends and colleagues, I would like to thank Massimo Scalabrini, Hall Bjørnstad, Dror Wahrman, and Rebecca Spang, successive directors of these groups. I cannot fail to acknowledge another community of colleagues and friends: those who gathered daily in the rickety converted bungalow at 914 Atwater in Bloomington, home of the *American Historical Review*, my second home from 2005 to 2015 (and beyond). I will always cherish the camaraderie and support of the *AHR* team over the years: Cris Coffey, Kon Dierks, Sarah Knott, Lara Kriegel, Alex Lichtenstein, Jane Lyle, Jessica Smith, and the many graduate students who served as editorial assistants.

Several friends and colleagues read portions of the manuscript or earlier drafts. I thank Phil Benedict, Robin Briggs, Barbara Diefendorf, and Peter Shoemaker for their comments. Jonathan Dewald, Mark Greengrass, and Rebecca Wilkin offered their expertise and time in reading the entire manuscript. I hope they realize how grateful I am for their generosity, their candor, and their critical acumen. (Mark deserves special thanks for an impromptu session of "manuscript therapy" in the courtyard of Oriel College, Oxford, in 2015.) An earlier version of this book was also read by Orest Ranum. I certainly benefited from his comments, but my gratitude to him goes beyond his careful reading. From the very start, Orest has been a source of knowledge, inspiration, and support. As several generations of scholars of the Ancien Régime will attest, Orest's reservoir of erudition is matched only by his generosity. I am blessed to have been the beneficiary of both. I can truly say that without his guidance, this study would not have gotten beyond folders in file cabinets and several gigabytes of data on my hard drive. I alone am responsible for any and all errors and excesses.

I am grateful to Oxford University Press for taking this project on; special thanks go to Stephanie Ireland, who first proved receptive to the manuscript, and then to Cathryn Steele, who expeditiously ushered it through the editorial process. Sathiyavani Krishnamoorthy led the production team with great dispatch and efficiency.

I owe OUP another debt of gratitude for assigning, at my request, the copyediting task to Jane Lyle, whose day job is Articles Editor at the *American Historical Review*. Readers of the *AHR* in the last fourteen years have benefited from her meticulous labor and unerring eye; she has made many, many authors look very, very good, as many of them have testified. Now I have joined their ranks.

In our household, this book project has been something like a long-term tenant whose lease should have expired long ago. I'm very sorry it overstayed its welcome. It took up residence not long after we were reading books like *We're Going on a Bear Hunt* and remained even as our daughters, now young women, left for wider vistas. And now that it too has finally left, it remains for me to thank Sarah, Kate, and Laura for their forbearance, support, and love.

Contents

List of Illustrations   xv

   Introduction   1

1. Reforming French: The Making of a Movement   40
2. Aristocrats and Writers: The Emergence of a Parisian "World"   85
3. A Culture of Discretion   123
4. Richelieu and Writers   163
5. The Rambouillet Salon: "A Purified World"   212
6. The Dupuy Cabinet: "An Innocent Refuge"   247
7. Writing *Otium*: Retreat as a Mode of Engagement   299

   Conclusion   336

Selected Bibliography of Primary Sources   345
Index   349

List of Illustrations

1. Groups, Associations, Academies, circa 1620–1648   13
2. Title page from *Of Wisdome: Three Bookes Written in French by Peter Charro[n], Doctr of Lawe in Paris*, translated by Samson Lennard. Courtesy of the Folger Shakespeare Library Digital Image Collection.   137

Introduction

OVER SEVERAL DAYS in 1628, during the time of the siege of the Protestant stronghold of La Rochelle, a small group of officials, lawyers, and a priest reputedly met in Paris in the *cabinet* (an office or quasi-private room for study and conversation) of a high magistrate in the Parlement. Their discussions considered the nature of eloquence, a burning question of the day, especially since a well-regarded writer had defiantly challenged the traditional standards of rhetorical excellence. But as much as they remained fixed on their subject, the participants were also keenly aware of the momentous events taking place in the Protestant fortress city on the Atlantic. Crucial matters of state and religion hung in the balance, casting their own discussions as somewhat trivial in comparison. Indeed, one remarked that because of the battle, Paris was virtually empty, deprived of its king and nobility. "There are hardly any more swords in this great city, except in the shops where they are sold, everyone whose calling is to carry one having fled on this honorable occasion in order to serve God and Prince together." But here they were in Paris, and here they would remain, acknowledging somewhat wistfully the great conflict raging to the south of them, but aware, too, that their professions excluded them from joining the ranks. They turned then to the question at hand, that is, to consider "the styles, the ways of expression, the good and bad diction, the correctness of terms, the usage of speaking our language; its clarity, force, purity, sweetness, polish... majesty and ceremony of discourse, in short, the perfections and faults of our language."[1]

In fact, we have no idea whether this gathering actually took place: all we have is a text, *Conférence académique*, published in 1630, which purports to represent it. Its author was Jean-Pierre Camus (1584–1652), a priest, a friend and confidant of the well-known Catholic spiritualist François de Sales, and a prolific author of potboilers. He was also a major player in the contemporary debate over rhetoric and eloquence, in which this work was a significant intervention. We shall shortly learn more about him. But beyond the subject matter of eloquence, his text resonates with an appreciation for the privileged leisure enjoyed by these learned gentlemen, a privilege rendered all the more precious by their awareness of the military encounter taking place elsewhere in their country. Their "cabinet" is a retreat dignified by the subject matter of their discussion, the nature of eloquence, but still somewhat diminished when viewed in the wider perspective of affairs of state.

---

[1] Jean-Pierre Camus, *Conférence académique, sur le différent des belles lettres de Narcisse et de Phyllarque, par le sieur de Musac* (Paris, 1630), 4.

Conférence académique thus illustrates two of the prominent themes in this study. The first considers a set of values, modes of behavior, indeed an entire ethos embraced by several generations of privileged French men and women, especially in the late sixteenth and early seventeenth century. This was an appreciation of a withdrawal from the travails of public life, of finding solace and edification in the company of kindred souls. The second is a concern for language—the nature of "eloquence" in a time when traditional notions of public discourse, especially the oratorical mode, had fallen into disrepute.

As for the first theme, it is virtually omnipresent in learned and literary discussions of the period. A perennial consideration, nourished by a stream of classical texts, it vaunted the desirability and moral value of retreat from the world. It was understood in many ways: as leisure, *otium*, and retirement; solitude, meditation, and repose; retreat, flight, and withdrawal. There were havens such as the cabinet, *ruelle*, garden, desert, bower, promenade, cloister, or *stoa*. Some were associated with particular writers: Petrarch's perch atop Mount Ventoux, Rabelais's (fictional) Abbaye de Thélème, Montaigne's "tower" study, Descartes's barren room (the enigmatic *poêle*). Others were metaphorical, evoking a psychological refuge, such as Montaigne's *arrière boutique* (back room) of the self, Saint Theresa of Avila's interior castle, or the Jansenist Antoine Arnauld's "inner library." To pursue this theme in all its variety would take us through the entire literary and humanistic corpus of the Renaissance and beyond. Short of that, one could do no better than Montaigne, an ideal source and exemplar here; reading his essays "On Solitude" and "On Vanity" with this theme in mind offers a tutorial in the ancients' handling of *otium*—from Socrates as a model and the ethics of Aristotle, to Cicero and Pliny, to Seneca's critique of Cicero's blending of *otium* and *negotium*, a critique that Montaigne apparently shared.[2] In 1571, on his thirty-eighth birthday, Montaigne did—famously—retire to his tower library, inscribing on its walls this declaration, which crystallizes his embrace of the virtues of *otium*: "Michel de Montaigne," it reads, "long weary of the servitude of the court and of public employment, while still whole, retired to the bosom of the learned virgins, where in calm and freedom from all worries, he will spend what little remains of his life, now more than half run out. If the fates permit, he will complete this abode, this sweet ancestral retreat; and he has consecrated it to his freedom, tranquility, and idleness."[3]

---

[2] Which the literary scholar Virginia Krause has ably done: Krause, *Idle Pursuits: Literature and Oisiveté in the French Renaissance* (Newark, NJ, 2003).

[3] Virginia Krause, "Montaigne's Art of Idleness," *Viator*, 31 (2000), 364, quoting from Pierre Villey, *Les essais de Montaigne* (Paris, 1914), xxxiv. For the theme of *otium* across the early modern period, see Bernard Beugnot, *Le discours de la retraite au xviie siècle* (Paris, 1996); Peter Burke, "The Invention of Leisure in Early Modern Europe," *Past and Present*, no. 146 (Feb. 1995), 136–50; Juliette Cherbuliez, *The Place of Exile: Leisure Literature and the Limits of Absolutism* (Lewisburg, PA, 2005); Marc Fumaroli, "Académie, Arcadie, Parnasse: Trois lieux allégoriques du loisir lettré," in Fumaroli, *L'école du silence: Le sentiment des images au XVIIe siècle* (Paris, 1998), 23–48; Alain Génetiot, *Poétique du loisir mondain: De Voiture à la Fontaine* (Paris, 1997); *Le loisir lettré à l'âge classique: Essais réunis par*

Despite a long and varied pedigree stretching back to antiquity, it was especially during the Wars of Religion of the sixteenth century that a withdrawal from the affairs of the world—from the passions that disturbed public life, the wayward proclivities of the people, or the intractable, obviously insoluble religious quarrels—marked the dispositions of a whole range of humanists and *gens de lettres*. This is why I choose here to think of *otium* in terms of retreat or withdrawal, rather than as "leisure," which is how it is more generally understood. For, in the sixteenth and seventeenth centuries, I argue, this ethos was seen as appealing, even necessary, for the pursuit of virtue precisely because the conditions of public life were so vexed. Justus Lipsius, the major exponent of Neo-Stoicism, fashioned his philosophy in the midst of the bitter sectarian conflict in the Low Countries; his *Two Books of Constancy* consists of a dialogue on the subject of what a virtuous man should do in the face of such disastrous circumstances and ends with an enthusiastic endorsement of the garden as both a metaphorical and a real place of retreat (quoting here from a contemporary English translation of his Latin text): "So soone as I put my foote within that place, I bid all vile and servile cares abandon me, and lifting up my head as upright as I may, I contemne the delights of the prophane people, & the great vanitie of humane affaires. Yea I seem to shake off all things in mee that is humaine, and to be rapt up on high upon the fiery chariot of wisdome." He concludes, referring to rival confessional identities, "Doest thou thinke when I am there that I take any care what the Frenchmen or Spaniards are in practising?"[4] Montaigne, too, wrote under the pressures of the wars, expressing incomprehension at his countrymen's willingness to engage in mutual slaughter over essentially unfathomable mysteries of religious dogma; and his decision to withdraw from public life was clearly linked to his exasperation, not only with the demands of court politics and royal service, but more particularly and urgently with the increasingly violent state of his country. Even in more tranquil times, he served notice that his willingness to enter into public life was not tantamount to bringing his whole self to the task. "The mayor and Montaigne have always been

---

Marc Fumaroli, Philippe-Joseph Salazar et Emmanuel Bury (Geneva, 1996); Marc Fumaroli, "*Otium, convivium, sermo*: La conversation comme 'lieu commun' des lettrés," in *Le loisir lettré*, 29–52; Bernard Beugnot, "Loisir, retraite, solitude: De l'espace privé à la littérature," in *Le loisir lettré*, 173–95; Alain Génetiot, "*Otium literatum* et poésie mondaine en France de 1625 à 1655," in *Le loisir lettré*, 213–31; Krause, *Idle Pursuits*; Krause, "Montaigne's Art of Idleness"; Brian Vickers, ed., *Arbeit, Musse, Meditation: Betrachtungen zur "Vita activa" und "Vita contemplativa"* (Zurich, 1985), especially Paul Oskar Kristeller, "The Active and Contemplative Life in Renaissance Humanism," 133–52; Daniel Gordon, *Citizens without Sovereignty: Equality and Sociability in French Thought, 1670–1789* (Princeton, 1994); Domna C. Stanton, "The Ideal of 'repos' in Seventeenth-Century French Literature," *L'Esprit créateur*, 15/1–2 (1974), 79–104; and Stanton, *The Aristocrat as Art: A Study of the Honnête Homme and the Dandy in Seventeenth- and Nineteenth-Century Fiction* (New York, 1980).

[4] *Two Bookes of Constancie Written in Latine by Justus Lipsius, Englished by Sir John Stradling*, ed. Rudolf Kirk (1596; New Brunswick, NJ, 1939), 136. Lipsius apparently began cultivating a real garden upon his arrival in Leiden. Harold J. Cook, *Matters of Exchange: Commerce, Medicine, and Science in the Dutch Golden Age* (New Haven, 2007), 111.

two, with a very clear separation," he famously declared.[5] His disciple Pierre Charron had himself direct experience in the civil conflict, even joining at one point the militant Catholic League, a passage that taught him the consequences of allowing himself to become ensnared by the passions of the many. His 1601 publication *De la sagesse* is infused with the memory of the Wars of Religion and concludes with the prescription of a divided moral code: one external, what one owed to one's community, nation, and prince, and in accordance with prevailing customs and conventions; the other internal, what one held to be true and important for oneself and among like-minded friends. This allowed the virtuous man to live in society while not truly being a part of it, or rather to be insulated from its excessive claims or the passions of the many by a kind of internal or psychological withdrawal. As Charron wrote (again from a contemporary English translation): "We must know how to distinguish and separate our selues from our publike charges: euery one of vs playeth two parts, two persons; the one strange and apparent, the other proper and essentiall: we must discerne the skinne from the shirt."[6] This reading of Montaigne, Lipsius, and Charron—and there are many others who could be cited—suggests that the embrace of the virtues of *otium*, while undoubtedly buttressed by a corpus of writings that endorsed its virtues, was as much the result of the unpleasant, dangerous, stressful, or otherwise compromising circumstances of life as its positive appeal.

An emphasis on the Wars of Religion and absolutism alike as promoting the move toward withdrawal or rupture briefly described here has shaped our understanding of much of the Ancien Régime. As with our general sense of "absolutism," many commentators tend to frame the historical process in terms of loss, decline, or negation. In this larger sense, "rupture" or "dissociation" defined its very nature. Lucien Goldmann in *Le dieu caché* (1955) argued that the effect of absolute rule on the class of Robe nobility—those who held positions in the monarchy's high judiciary—was to tragically compromise their position. These magistrates experienced a loss of power as the crown increasingly usurped their authority and undermined their autonomy, but they were powerless to contest the monarchy precisely because it—and it alone—ensured their legitimacy, status, and prestige, as well as the incomes derived from their offices and the significant investments they represented (offices were private property in the Ancien Régime). They were thus caught in a tragic situation of powerlessness and discontent, a situation that prompted them to take refuge in a worldview most prominently represented by

---

[5] "Of Husbanding Your Will," in *The Complete Essays of Montaigne*, ed. Donald Frame (Stanford, CA, 1958), III: 10, on 774. On this theme in Montaigne, see Timothy Hampton, "Private Passion and Public Service in Montaigne's Essays," in Victoria Kahn, Neil Saccamano, and Daniela Coli, eds., *Politics and the Passions, 1500–1800* (Princeton, 2006), 30–48. For a recent biography that emphasizes the active and engaged aspect of Montaigne's life, see Philip Desan, *Montaigne: A Life*, trans. Steven Rendall and Lisa Neal (Princeton, 2017).

[6] Pierre Charron, *Of Wisdome: Three Books Written in French by Peter Charro[n], Doctr of Lawe in Paris*, trans. Samson Lennard (London, 1608), 252.

Jansenism, which consoled them with a religiosity at once ambivalent about this world, elitist, and Augustinian—in other words, perfectly consonant with the necessity of living ethically in a fallen world. For Goldmann, writers like Pascal and Racine, both of whom were heavily influenced by Jansenism, most eloquently expressed this tragic view of being in the world while ethically maintaining an unworldly stance. And this was a stance that effectively meant a disengagement from politics and a withdrawal from the public realm.[7] This interpretation finds an interesting echo in the work of Reinhart Koselleck, whose *Critique and Crisis* was published just a few years after *Le dieu caché*. Like Goldmann, Koselleck sees the relationship between the absolute state and intellectuals as crucial, but takes a longer historical view of the matter. The sixteenth century, with its religious disputes, conflicts, and wars, saw an excess of what he terms "critique"—the voluble, often radical contesting of the established religious and political order. Order was restored in the seventeenth century with the emergence of strong "absolute" monarchies, but its restoration had a cost: the retreat of critique into the private realm and a politics guided by *raison d'état*, based on interest, not morality, which in fact ensured both order and de facto religious toleration. While for Goldmann the dialectical result of this dynamic was the creation of a tragic worldview, for Koselleck it yielded an ethics that, because of its removal from the realm of actual political practice, was utopian in vision and unrealistic in its critique, asking more ethically of politics than it could possibly bear. The result was, ultimately, the disaster of the French Revolution during its Jacobin phase, with its Rousseauist critique that thrust private and personal values into the political arena.[8]

In mentioning Goldmann and Koselleck, I mean to underscore the larger stakes and relevance of my topic—it has implications beyond the history of early modern France. Indeed, it seems to me that insofar as a historical understanding of the changing perspective on *otium* hinges upon a rupture, a breakdown, or a movement of withdrawal, it relates to a common observation on the advent of the modern world: that it is characterized by a loss of wholeness, by the dissolution of common forms of life and culture, the atomization of society, and the like. This critique, which has informed the discourse on "modernity" throughout the nineteenth and twentieth centuries, at least since Romanticism (if not before), is a familiar one. All these interpretations share in what might be called the "tragic" view of modernity as a sort of secular fall.

This book is mostly about the seventeenth century; it will not explore this larger theme, as tempting as that may be. Instead, it will focus on the problem of the

---

[7] Lucien Goldmann, *Le dieu caché: Etude sur la vision tragique dans les Pensées de Pascal et dans le théâtre de Racine* (Paris, 1955); English translation by Philip Thody, *The Hidden God: A Study of the Tragic Vision in the Pensées of Pascale and the Tragedies of Racine* (London, 1964).

[8] Reinhart Koselleck, *Critique and Crisis: Enlightenment and the Pathogenesis of Modern Society*, ed. and trans. Thomas McCarthy (Cambridge, MA, 1988); original German edition *Kritik und Krise: Eine Studie zur Pathogenese der burgerlichen Welt* (Freiburg, 1959).

relationship between this phenomenon and so-called absolutism. It asks the question, If there was in fact a withdrawal from public life, what did this mean for the larger terms of political culture in the Age of Richelieu?

In a sense, the answer has already been supplied by those commentators who see the relationship largely in negative terms—as a matter of a consolidated monarchy emerging in the wake of the Wars of Religion which, by virtue of the implicit terms of pacification, put an end to the kind of meaningful participation in public life that was seen as the source of the conflict itself. In what might be called the "absolutist pact," this process was accomplished with the willing acquiescence of various intellectual figures, especially those associated with the *politiques*, who saw the virtue of conceding dominant political authority to a monarch who would guarantee domestic tranquility in exchange for a certain degree of liberty they would enjoy in private. This was assumed to be the deeper meaning of the Edict of Nantes (1598), which, in granting French Calvinists limited rights to practice their faith, acknowledged that religious belief could remain a personal, private matter as long as it did not intrude into the public or political realm. Koselleck and those who follow him draw rather categorical conclusions about the nature of "absolutism" from this arrangement: that it fostered a separation of public and private spheres, implying as well an effective end to what in any meaningful sense could be described as "politics." It is a view, of course, that conforms to rather textbook views of "absolutism."[9]

This book will challenge this view. I will only sparingly, and with some hesitation, use the terms "absolutism" or "absolute state," for it is clear from recent work that these are imprecise, misleading, and simply inaccurate as descriptions of the actual effectiveness and extent of royal authority, and they are overloaded with more modern expectations of the deployment of state power as well.[10] That said, the historical significance of the consolidation of royal authority in the first part of the seventeenth century cannot be denied; and in this book I strive to understand how various intellectual and cultural developments relate to that process. What I do not accept is the view that the crown, Richelieu, or something we might

---

[9] Koselleck, *Critique and Crisis*. Koselleck based this analysis on Carl Schmitt, *The Leviathan in the State Theory of Thomas Hobbes* (Westport, CT, 1996), chap. 5. See especially the important essay by Marcel Gauchet, "L'État au miroir de la raison d'État: La France et la Chrétienté," in Y. Ch. Zarka, ed., *Raison et déraison d'État au XVIe et XVIIe siècles* (Paris, 1994), 193–244. Also Nannerl O. Keohane, *Philosophy and the State in France: The Renaissance to the Enlightenment* (Princeton, 1980), for a sustained analysis along these lines. For the "absolute pact," see Sylvio Hermann De Franceschi, "La genèse française du catholicisme d'Etat et son aboutissement au début au ministériat de Richelieu: Les catholiques zélés à l'épreuve de l'affairie Santarelli et la clôture de la controverse autour du pouvoir pontifical au temporal (1626–1627)," *Annuaire-bulletin de la Société de l'Histoire de France* (2001), 19–63.

[10] For a forceful critique of the concept of absolutism, see Nicolas Henshall, *The Myth of Absolutism: Change and Continuity in Early Modern European Monarchy* (London, 1992). James Collins' indispensable *The State in Early Modern France* (Cambridge, 1995), is a measured account of the role of the monarchy in Old Regime France.

generally understand as monarchical authority controlled these developments: just as we must be skeptical about claims for the "absolute state," so too for "cultural absolutism."[11] The consensus behind the need for a strong monarchy did not come into being at the command of the crown; rather, it emerged from a variety of sources, cultivated by a variety of contributors to the political discourse of the late sixteenth and early seventeenth century. Given the deep roots of the *politique* position in the sixteenth century, this much is clear from many accounts. Less clear is the place of the vast and varied output of writers in this period in the political culture of the era. What was the relationship between other cultural and intellectual developments and the consolidation of royal authority?

I pose the question because one of the striking features of this period is the disjuncture between its political and cultural (or intellectual) histories. The former recounts a process of consolidation, consensus, and concentration of authority. This process also encountered opposition and resistance; but while challenges to royal policies and especially Richelieu's dominant authority were frequent and varied in their origins—from peasants and great aristocrats to Louis XIII's mother and brother—rarely did they contest the need for a strong, if not necessarily "absolute," monarchy. On the other hand, when we turn to the cultural or intellectual history of the period, there, instead of a focused perspective, we have a kaleidoscope of tendencies emanating from an extraordinarily wide range of humanists, *gens de lettres*, and other contributors to contemporary discourse.

Nowhere is this range more apparent than in two monumental works of modern scholarship, published nearly forty years apart, that have been crucial in the origins of this study, René Pintard's *Le libertinage érudit dans la première moitié du dix-septième siècle* (1943) and Marc Fumaroli's *L'âge de l'éloquence* (1980).[12] Pintard's book reveals in teeming detail an intellectual climate of enormous variety, demonstrating that if conformism appeared to define the period intellectually and religiously, it was, in many respects, in appearance only, disguising many heterodox trends and strikingly original intellectual positions. Even if his overall characterization of these as "erudite libertinage" is problematic, he nevertheless conveys a sense that erudition and creativity, as well as the willingness to challenge religious and intellectual conventions, characterized this so-called Age of Absolutism. In Fumaroli's work, the range and variety of figures is just as impressive. And while he devotes part of his book to antiquity, the bulk of it describes a similarly varied range of writers who were not so much heterodox as engaged with the terms of "eloquence"—with the nature of language and how to understand

---

[11] Despite the fact that I used this term as a chapter title in Robert A. Schneider, *Public Life in Toulouse, 1463–1789: From Municipal Republic to Cosmopolitan City* (Ithaca, NY, 1989), chap. 8.

[12] René Pintard, *Le libertinage érudit dans la première moitié du XVIIe siècle* (Paris, 1943); Marc Fumaroli, *L'âge de l'éloquence: Rhétorique et "res literaria" de la Renaissance au seuil de l'époque classique* (Geneva, 1980).

its different rhetorical modes, limitations, and possibilities—in a period defined by the Counter-Reformation and a newly furbished French monarchy.

How, then, are we to understand the relationship between these two seemingly contradictory views of the Age of Richelieu, one of royal consolidation and a consensus behind its necessity, the other of a richly varied, often contentious, even heterodox intellectual field cultivated by a remarkable range of figures? More than anyone, it seems to me, the literary scholar Hélène Merlin-Kajman has supplied the means to answer this question. Across a range of challenging but fundamental works, she has gone beyond Koselleck, for one, by fixing her gaze on the breach between public and private that he and others have posited as something of a void. The mystical unity of crown and society celebrated as one body (following Ernst Kantorowicz here) was put asunder by the Wars of Religion; its foundering was codified by the Edict of Nantes and then translated into reason of state, which represented politics as the pragmatic expression of interests, superseding the "nostalgia for the mystical incorporation of the members in a present body."[13] But rather than simply acknowledging the negative space created by a broken mystical corporation—the gulf between individuals and monarch—she argues for the emergence of new modes of association and civic participation, especially evident in developments in language and "literature." In essence, she discovers the elements of civil society in the aftermath of a disintegrated mystical unity following the religious wars and the Edict of Nantes. This was a society of individuals who themselves experienced a kind of microcosmic division, mirroring that of the body politic, between inner conscience and outward behavior. But isolation, alienation, or anomie—or other such more modern notions that might be projected back onto this period—did not characterize these "particulars," even as they were barred from any meaningful participation in the "public" of political life. Instead, Merlin-Kajman points to cultural, especially literary, activities under the rubric of the Republic of Letters—an alternative "space" not to be confused with a "public," but a realm in which *gens de lettres* could aspire to contribute to, and indeed shape, the collective culture of France.

In following Merlin-Kajman, I explore the variety of interests, commitments, values, and activities that characterized "writers and intellectuals"—those "particulars" now detached from a mystical body—in the first part of the seventeenth century. But I do so, in part, at least, by keeping in view a withdrawal from public life—a rupture between the public or political and the private or personal—as fundamental to their culture, a withdrawal that, in its various modes, was

---

[13] Hélène Merlin, "Fables of the 'Mystical Body' in Seventeenth-Century France," *Yale French Studies*, no. 86 (1994), 135. See especially Hélène Merlin-Kajman, *Public et littérature en France au XVIIe siècle* (Paris, 1994), *L'absolutisme dans les lettres et la théorie des deux corps: Passions et politique* (Paris, 2000), and Merlin-Kajman, *L'excentricité académique: Littérature, institutions, société* (Paris, 2001).

characterized by the ethos of *otium*. It would seem important as a first step, then, to look at the nature of *otium* in this period.

Otium cum dignitate

When considered more broadly, it is only partially the case that *otium* was merely a recourse taken under dire or oppressive circumstances, as a sort of last refuge for the cultivation of virtue in a morally compromised world. It is true that writings on this theme also bore the traces of the worldly pressures and burdens that colored this choice, something evident in texts from Seneca to Montaigne and his many followers. But *otium* is also endowed with a positive valence that frames it as a spiritual mode of rare privilege, not a second-best resort or a mere consolation of the mind. As Seneca writes in *De otio*, an oft-cited text in the sixteenth and seventeenth centuries: "Even in retirement we can be servants of that greater republic, indeed, we can perhaps serve it better, so that we inquire about the nature of virtue...or whether nature or art makes men good."[14] Cicero's own understanding of the phrase, which is, after all, primarily associated with him, implied a conception of leisure as a means of self-development, especially for the *optimates* entrusted with the cares of authority in Rome. The most widespread practice of *otium*, the pious monastic life of retreat from worldly entanglements and desires, promised spiritual rewards that far surpassed anything that ordinary society could offer. The counsel to withdraw from the pressures or cares of the world—whether narrowly conceived as the "court" or more broadly as public life—might be seen as a secularization of the monastic ideal. Certainly, the delights of withdrawal into the refuge of one's study or library were proclaimed throughout the period. Seneca declared, "Idleness without letters is death."[15] Machiavelli wrote rhapsodically how at the end of each day he would change out of his normal attire, don his scholar's robes, and pass the night communing with the ancients and other sages of the past in order to fashion his political wisdom. Jean-Louis Guez de Balzac, a major figure in the literary history of the period, whom we shall consult many times in this study, likewise described a privileged place for scholarly retreat in terms reminiscent of Montaigne's tower library. "Beyond the cabinet where we normally gather," he writes in the *Socrate chrétien*, ushering us into an even more secluded place, "there is a little gallery overlooking the river, separate from the rest of the house. One gets there by a hidden staircase; the master of the house might call it his library, if he wanted to use the name for it used by most

---

[14] This phrase was often cited in contemporary texts. See, for example, Pierre Bardin, *Le lycée du Sr. Bardin, ou, En plusieurs promenades il est traité des connoissances des actions et des plaisirs d'un honneste homme* (Paris, 1632), Preface (unpaginated).

[15] See Beugnot, *Le discours de la retraite*, 97, on many citations in the period.

people. In this gallery there are only good and holy books."[16] Elsewhere, Balzac extols the lures of withdrawal from public affairs in terms that sound strikingly modern. Imagining Romans in the time of Augustus "at home," he writes, addressing the *salonnière* Catherine de Rambouillet, herself the mistress of a renowned place of retreat, that it was only there that they could be their "true selves." Balzac practiced what he preached: after he failed to secure Richelieu's support for promotion to high office in 1630, he withdrew to his ancestral home in provincial Charente, only to return to the capital on one or two occasions to polish his literary reputation.[17] His contemporary and friend René Descartes famously scorned Paris for Holland, retreating even further into his barren room (*poêle*). When he went out into the world, he proclaimed, "I come forth masked."[18]

With these sorts of comments by humanists and other *gens de lettres*, it easy to forget that this ethos largely conformed to a particular aristocratic ideal, that of conspicuous idleness. When we think of *otium*, in other words, even before we invest it with classical and humanistic values, which have a tendency to detach it from its social associations, we should also acknowledge that we confront a deeply ingrained ethos constituting the quintessence of aristocratic privilege. There are, of course, several ways of defining and establishing aristocracy: blood, lineage, virtue, the profession of arms, or other service to the crown.[19] But alongside the traditional understanding of the aristocracy in the context of the three orders of society as "those who fight" was another, based not upon what aristocrats did but upon what they were: here aristocracy is a matter of being, not doing.[20] And what aristocrats did, in essence, was nothing: they were idle; they did not work; their honorable status, their distinctiveness among the great wash of humankind condemned to earn its bread by the sweat of its brow, was exhibited in a life of conspicuous leisure. Although this feature of noble identity was well established by the late Middle Ages, in the early modern period it was, like the nobility as a whole, subject to various challenges. Changes in military technology and organization and the rise of a so-called Fourth Estate of Robe or legal noblemen meant that the aristocratic ethos of privileged idleness remained unstable, constantly interrogated in terms of its meaning, nature, legitimacy, and value. Nevertheless, the fundamental association of aristocracy with the privilege of *otium* remained

---

[16] Jean-Louis Guez de Balzac, *Socrate chrestien* (1652), ed. Jean Jehasse (Paris, 2008), 90.

[17] Jean Jehasse, *Guez de Balzac et le génie romain, 1597–1654* (Saint-Etienne, 1977).

[18] Jean-Luc Marion, "The Essential Incoherence of Descartes' Definition of Divinity," in *Essays on Descartes' Meditations*, ed. Amélie Oxenberg Rorty (Berkeley and Los Angeles, 1986), 338 n. 83. On Descartes's sense of solitude, see Kevin Dunn, "'A Great City Is a Great Solitude': Descartes' Urban Pastoral," *Yale French Studies*, no. 80 (1991), 93–107.

[19] For masterful summaries of this question, see Robert Descimon, "Chercher des nouvelles voies pour interpreter les phénomènes nobilaires dans la France moderne: La noblessse, 'essence' ou rapport social?," *Revue d'histoire moderne et contemporaine*, 46/1 (1999): *Les noblesses á l'époque moderne*, 5–21; and Jonathan Dewald, *Aristocratic Experience and the Origins of Modern Culture, 1570–1715* (Berkeley and Los Angeles, 1993).

[20] This is Virginia Krause's turn of phrase, from *Idle Pursuits*, 34.

firm—reasserted and refurbished in the course of the period. Appreciating how well the ethos of *otium* was attuned to aristocratic self-conceptions serves as a reminder of the close relationship between most *gens de lettres* and the social elite in this period, something that is too often forgotten in remaining fixed on its intellectual or literary history alone.

Still, in the hands of humanists and other writers, *otium* takes on a range of meanings, some positive, some negative, some merely peripheral to their attitudes to the world, others crucial in defining their moral and intellectual postures. It could define an entire literary work, such as pastoral novels, the most notable one in the period being Honoré d'Urfé's *L'Astrée*, a true best-seller of the time. A dominant feature of this sprawling tale is not only its pastoral milieu and geographical remoteness in the *pays* of Forez, but also its distance from monarchical authority and its unreal remove from all physical cares of the world. *L'Astrée* is situated in an aristocratic paradise—in fifth-century Gaul surrounded by, but isolated from, a Roman world at war. It was a whole country devoted to *otium*. In this sense, D'Urfé's novel embodied what Norbert Elias appositely called a sort of "aristocratic romanticism."[21] Likewise, François de La Mothe le Vayer, an important erudite skeptic, saw the privilege of *otium* as a marker of a particular kind of elite, the *esprit fort*, whose very distance from the world, even an indifference to its cares and demands, defined the only philosophy worthy of the name. La Mothe le Vayer conceives of retreat as a means of self-knowledge and what Foucault would call "care for the self." "Nothing strips us bare and forces us to acknowledge who we are more than retreat and the movement from the pressures of the world to solitude and the care of ourselves."[22] For Pierre Gassendi, the philosopher-priest and major proponent of Epicureanism, *otium* was a key term. Like others, he embraced it as restorative and edifying. The truly wise man recognizes tranquility (Epicurean *ataraxia*), and not sensual delights, as the highest form of pleasure. But this is an inner state, which those schooled in its cultivation can preserve even as they confront the challenging vicissitudes of the world. Gassendi, then, brings *otium* and *negotium* together, as two moments in the virtuous man's life.[23] Other writers framed the ethos of *otium* differently: for someone like Gabriel Naudé, an astute political commentator, it meant looking upon the theater of the world, "where some play comedies, others tragedies," as if from a distant vantage point of a "donjon in a high tower."[24] And followers of the Catholic spiritualist François de Sales were urged to cultivate both "mental solitude," even "in the

---

[21] Norbert Elias, *The Court Society* (Oxford, 1983), chap. 8.
[22] François de La Mothe le Vayer, "De la conversation et de la solitude," in *Opuscules, ou, Petits traitez*, in *Oeuvres*, I: 580, 36, as cited by and quoted in Sophie Gouverneur, *Prudence et subversion libertines: La critique de la raison d'Etat chez François de La Mothe le Vayer, Gabriel Naudé et Samuel Sorbière* (Paris, 2005), 326. See also La Mothe le Vayer, "De la vie privée," in La Mothe le Vayer, *Dialogues faits à l'imitation des anciens* (1606), ed. André Pessel (Paris, 1988), 157–8, 169.
[23] Lisa T. Sarasohn, *Gassendi's Ethics: Freedom in a Mechanistic Universe* (Ithaca, NY, 1996), 74, 73.
[24] Gabriel Naudé, *Considérations politiques sur les coups d'état* (1639), ed. Louis Marin (Paris, 1988), 81.

midst of the most engrossing conversations," and "real places of physical solitude... so that you spend more time in your room, in your garden, and other places, where you can more freely turn inward in your heart and refresh your soul in good reflections and holy thoughts or in edifying reading."[25]

Beyond these prescriptive ruminations, we might imagine an ethnography of *otium*—actual places of retreat that marked the Parisian cityscape: gardens, libraries, so-called cabinets, salons, academies, and other venues characterized by a privileged, private mode of sociability such as represented in Camus's *Conférence académique*. In fact, early seventeenth-century Paris experienced a remarkable blossoming of associations, conventicles, societies, and other groups, most of a literary or erudite nature. In subsequent chapters we shall take a closer look at these and their role in recasting contemporary culture. For now it is sufficient to note that though different, they possessed common features that defined them as self-consciously removed from public life, or as spaces, in short, of *otium*. Most obviously, they were detached from such official, institutional, or corporate venues as the university, the bar, the Church, or the royal court, thus marking them as informal associations, lacking in any formal status or identity. They had no "official" existence, no corporate status, no public presence in the ceremonial display that still marked city life. They were also exclusive, but with an informal selection process—often dictated by the discernment of a *salonnière* or the collective judgment of habitués—not determined by status, title, or other formally recognized or pre-established criteria. As well, they were defined by certain implicit restrictions—not only elitism and exclusivity, but also the observance of discretion, self-censorship, even secrecy.

If early seventeenth-century Parisian culture was characterized by both figurative and real spaces of *otium cum dignitate*—by both this ethos and the social practices guided by it—the question then becomes, in line with our overall inquiry, What were the sorts of concerns that "filled" these spaces? In other words, if we want to understand the relationship between cultural and intellectual life and the emergent royal authority, we simply need a better sense of what, in essence, "dignified" them. And we need not assume that escape, disengagement, or other essentially negative conditions defined this culture. This, then, is the prospectus of this book. For now I will simply introduce a series of concerns and commitments that weave in and out of *Dignified Retreat*—the values, interests, and activities that engaged writers and intellectuals in the Age of Richelieu.

---

[25] François de Sales, *Introduction to the Devout Life*, quoted in John D. Lyons, *Before Imagination: Embodied Thought from Montaigne to Rousseau* (Stanford, 2005), 77. Lyons makes the astute point that even before the Jansenists vaunted the virtues of "refusing the world from within the world," this was promoted by de Sales.

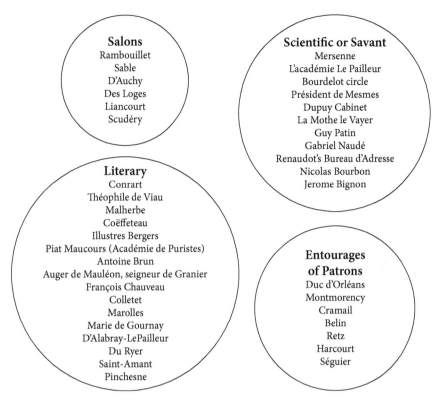

Figure 1 Groups, Associations, Academies, circa 1620–1648

The Cause of Language Reform

Perhaps the most pressing concern was for the development and refinement of the French language, a transformation driven by the efforts of a whole generation of men of letters, led in part by the poet François de Malherbe, who called for a refashioned French that would have as its hallmarks clarity and regularity of expression. Significantly, it was in the informal academies and salons that proliferated in the period, and not in the traditional venues of Church, university, and Parlement, where this new "eloquence" was cultivated. Rather, these bodies were seen as obstacles to language reform insofar as they were bastions of that most dreaded of seventeenth-century intellectual sins—pedantry.[26] Paradoxically, then, language, a quintessentially public aspect of human society, was cultivated in spaces defined by an ethos of retreat. To trace the influence of Malherbe and his

---

[26] For a survey of the critique of pedantry in the period, see Jocelyn Royé, *La figure du pedant de Montaigne à Molière* (Geneva, 2008).

language reforms in the first half of the century is to enter into the thicket of associations that made up Parisian social life; ultimately it explains as well the makeup of the Académie française, whose members were largely recruited from among the many disciples of Malherbe.

These *gens de lettres* committed to language reform confronted several obstacles apart from the established institutions that traditionally cultivated "eloquence." Perhaps the most daunting was the model of the public orator as the supreme embodiment of rhetorical power. In the Renaissance, this model was endowed with mythic authority from the emergence of a somewhat refurbished image of Hercules—not the superhuman figure of legendary strength, but a god whose powers were deployed through eloquence, illustrated by golden chains running from his tongue to the ears of his followers. While originating in antiquity, this particular Herculean image was in fact rarely evoked until the sixteenth century, when a number of chroniclers, historians, and poets promoted it as a serviceable motif to vaunt the persuasive power of rhetoric over sheer brawn. Erasmus, for example, "saw in it a timely device for reviving the ancient ideal of eloquence and claimed that the labors of Hercules should be regarded as works of the spirit."[27] And it was most enthusiastically embraced by the French, for Lucian, the Greek sophist, probably the main source of the myth, claimed to have seen a portrait of Hercules with the golden chains in Gaul. The image of the Gallic Hercules thus figured prominently in the emerging French national discourse in the sixteenth century; and while several writers, including Jean Bodin and Etienne Pasquier, expressed skepticism about its historical legitimacy, others continued to write about his sojourn in ancient Gaul as a matter of historical fact—a foundational myth for both French kings and the French themselves. Throughout the sixteenth century, the image was deployed as an emblem of French eloquence; Henri IV was celebrated as the "Gallic Hercules."

If this myth did not disappear entirely in the seventeenth century, it was certainly evoked less frequently. For one thing, it was undermined by those who, rather than celebrating the image of a haranguing figure capable of moving the masses, looked upon it fearfully as epitomizing everything that led France into the disastrous Wars of Religion. In the *Six Books of the Republic*, Bodin argued that one of the "causes of unrest" was the freedom "which proceeds from the freedom which is allowed to orators, who play upon the emotions and fan the desires of the people as they choose."

> There is nothing which has greater influence over men's souls than the art of eloquent speech. Our forefathers portrayed the Celtic Hercules as an old man,

---

[27] Robert E. Hallowell, "Ronsard and the Gallic Hercules Myth," *Studies in the Renaissance*, 9 (1962), 247. See also Michael Wintroub, "Civilizing the Savage and Making a King: The Royal Entry Festival of Henri II, Rouen 1550," *Sixteenth-Century Journal*, 29/2 (1998), 465–94, especially 480ff.; and Mark Greengrass, *Governing Passions: Peace and Reform in the French Kingdom, 1576–1585* (Oxford, 2007).

> trailing after him a crowd of people fastened by the ears with chains issuing from his mouth. They thus intimated that the powers and armed forces of kings and princes are not so potent as the vehemence of an ardent and eloquent man. He can excite the most cowardly to overcome the bravest, he makes the proudest cast aside their arms, turns cruelty into gentleness, barbarity into humanity, revolutionizes a commonwealth, and plays upon the people at will. I don't say all this in praise of eloquence, but to show what force it has, for it is a force more often used for ill than good ends. It is nothing more than disguising the truth, an artifice to make that which is evil seem good, that which is right, wrong, make a mountain out of a molehill and an elephant out of a mouse. In other words it is the art of successful lying.[28]

Beyond this critique, a new conception of the nature of eloquence and language also challenged the myth of the Gallic Hercules, crystallized by a sort of countermyth, drawn from a work by Tacitus discovered in the later part of the sixteenth century, *Dialogue on Orators*, which was edited by Lipsius and printed in Antwerp by Christopher Plantin. In this text the Roman historian provides a historical account of the decline of eloquence under the Empire, an account that was easily transposed to the European present. Under the Republic, which gave rise to civil strife and fractiousness, his account goes, eloquence flourished, for endemic discord between various parties, families, and factions, political violence, and other forms of conflict provided opportunistic orators the pretext to seize the public stage. Just as the conditions of war produce great generals, so civil war occasions the emergence of talented orators. With peace guaranteed by imperial rule, however, such license came to an end, and so too ended the reign of the orator; eloquence retreated from the public space into more discreet venues. The decline of eloquence might be mourned, but in Tacitus's view the exchange of dangerous license for tranquility and security was well worth the loss. Tacitus's text gave support to the growing suspicion of oratory expressed by Bodin, as we have seen, but also by Montaigne and others, fueled by the noxious fumes of incendiary preaching during the religious wars. They nodded in approval at his critical assessment linking unchecked speech with disorder: "the great and famous eloquence of old is the nursling of the license which fools called freedom; it is the companion of sedition, the stimulant of an unruly people." In the seventeenth century, Tacitus's text is oft-cited, serving as a warrant for the view that the peace ensured by

---

[28] Jean Bodin, *Six Books of the Commonwealth*, ed. M. J. Tooley (Oxford, [1955]), 145. Bodin goes on to acknowledge the positive use of eloquence in "converting a people from barbarism to humanity...reforming manners, improving laws, expelling tyrants, banishing vice, and strengthening virtue." He adds, "in brief, the issues of peace and war, arms and laws hang upon the words of orators. On the other hand there is nothing that the tyrant has to fear more than a popular orator, if his tyranny is hated" (145–6).

strong monarchical rule meant a welcome curtailment of certain kinds of public expression.[29]

Tacitus's account addressed the issue of rhetoric, challenging the image of the orator as the supreme embodiment of eloquence, contributing to the conviction that other rhetorical ideals were in order. It thus became the remit of *gens de lettres* to take up the cause of language reform. But what about the king, for the "Gallic Hercules" surely remained the alpha and omega of true eloquence? Interestingly, a turn away from oratory also meant a diminution of the royal authority in this domain—a limitation on monarchical responsibility in this so-called absolute age. For, asserted such stalwarts of language as Malherbe and Vaugelas, not even the king had the authority to meddle in this realm. In an anecdote recounted by his seventeenth-century biographer, Malherbe scolded Henri IV for wanting to use a word that was not acceptable by the standards of northern France, prompting the king to quip, when Malherbe threatened him with a 100 franc fine: "You are the most absolute king who ever governed France."[30] This anecdote epitomizes what others have noted, and which I will echo throughout this study: despite the much-evoked "absolutism" as the defining feature of this period of French history, language, as well as kindred aspects of the cultural realm, was largely under the jurisdiction of a new literary establishment whose emergence was equally a feature of this period.

Granted this power, *gens de lettres* committed to the elevation and reform of French still faced other problems. One of their greatest obstacles was the fragmented nature of readerships or publics. How, they asked, could a robust French language be fashioned that could appeal across so many different groups—magistrates, noblemen and ladies, savants, churchmen, *gens de lettres*, courtiers, and others? Jean Chapelain, another leading figure in the literary establishment whom we shall encounter many times in this study, worried aloud in the preface to his epic novel about Joan of Arc, *La pucelle*, that a balkanized readership—he lists eight different kinds of readers, each with different interests—would appreciate only a portion of this work, a work that was touted as the French *Aeneid*.[31] And Nicolas

---

[29] On this text of Tacitus, see Fumaroli, *L'âge de l'éloquence*, 63–70; Peter Shoemaker, *Powerful Connections: The Poetics of Patronage in the Age of Louis XIII* (Newark, NJ, 2007), 80–91; Mathilde Bombart, *Guez de Balzac et la querelle des* Lettres: *Ecriture, polémique, et critique dans la France du premier XVIIe siècle* (Paris, 2007), 125–6. The author of the preface to Balzac's *Lettres* essentially reproduced this account, transposing it to the present, in asserting that "we are no longer in a time when one criticizes publicly the government of the state, when orators make clear the orders to the Lieutenant Generals of the army, and consequently there is no longer the need for eloquence of this sort." "Préface sur les Lettres de Sieur de Balzac par le Sieur de La Motte Aigron," in *Les premières lettres de Guez de Balzac*, 2 vols., ed. H. Bibas and K.-T. Butler (Paris, 1933), I: 238.

[30] Honorat de Bueil, seigneur de Racan, *Vie de monsieur de Malherbe*, ed. Marie-Françoise Quignard (Paris, 1991), 41. See also Hélène Merlin-Kajman, "Vaugelas politique?," *Langages*, no. 182 (June 2011): *Théories du langage et politique des linguistes*, 111–22.

[31] "I am certain that *gens de lettres* will seek in this work only passages derived from old books, and that they will esteem only those parts that are not by its author; that courtiers will enjoy only that which depicts the *moeurs* of our times; that the *beaux esprits* only the clever and refined turns of

Faret, best known as the author of *L'honnête homme, ou, L'art de plaire à la cour*, in his brief for the French Academy turned the problem on its head, asserting that language reform had not only to "enrich our Language with the ornaments that it lacks," but, more urgently, to "cleanse it of the filth that it has collected, whether from the mouth of the People, or from the crowd at the [Parlementary] Palace, and the impurities of chicanery, or from the bad usage of ignorant Courtesans, or from the abuse of those who corrupt it in writing, or from those who say what they should from the pulpit but who say it otherwise than they should."[32] All of this recalls the earlier point of a corporate union of the French body politic having been shattered in the course of the religious wars, leaving in its wake only the crown and "particulars." Could language bridge this gap?

If so, it had to be a different genre of "eloquence"—not the elevated rhetoric of the orator, but a more worldly and varied register of expression. For one thing, as the academician Guillaume Colletet argued, it meant a different medium of expression. For the eloquence cultivated by the Athenians and Romans in their "public places and frequent assemblies" did not meant a "cooling" of its "spirit." Rather, speaking of his contemporaries, it has "been channeled into their pens, and we shall see it with the same grandeur in their writings as it was once superb from their mouths."[33] What Colletet marks with this commentary is not only the elevation of "writing" over "speaking" but a privileging of the *writer*—the *gens de lettres* of the new literary field.

For another thing, this new register of eloquence had to be calibrated to the men and women who made up the French public of "court and city"—a cultivated, mostly aristocratic elite of what then began to be referred to as *le monde*. This, then, suggests viewing the changing linguistic field as defined by both openness and innovation, on the one hand, and constraints, on the other. Following other commentators, we can appreciate language in this period as having been liberated from at least two sets of constraints: traditional rhetorical models and the limitations of the professions.[34] This, in turn, gave rise to a range of discursive

---

phrase; the inventors only the greatness of the design and the rightness of its order; the grammarians only the number and meter of the verses; pious people only the saintly matters; the brave only the scenes of combat; women only the passionate ones; the politicians only the advice; and that all, if they cannot find on each page something related to their interests, will regard the work as boring and slow-moving." Chapelain, *La pucelle, ou, La France délivrée*, 2 vols., ed. Emile de Molènes (Paris, 1891), I: cxiv.

[32] Nicolas Faret, *Projet de l'Académie pour servir de préface à ses statuts*, ed. Jean Rousselet (Saint-Etienne, 1983), 52.

[33] Guillaume Colletet, *Discours de l'éloquence, et de l'imitation des anciens* (Paris, 1658), 10ff. Though published in 1658, this "discourse" was delivered at the Académie française in the mid-1630s. On this, see the important work by Christine Zabel, *Polis und Politesse: Der Diskurs über das antike Athen in England und Frankreich, 1630–1760* (Berlin, 2017), chap. 4.

[34] Again, the work of Merlin-Kajman is fundamental here. See also "Gilles Siouffi, "Langue française et questions d'identité: Quelques propositions sur le XVIIe siècle," in Wendy Ayres-Bennett and Mari C. Jones, eds., *The French Language and Questions of Identity* (London, 2007), 14–22. Richard Scholar's important book *The Je-Ne-Sais-Quoi in Early Modern Europe: Encounters with a Certain*

possibilities, with writers experimenting in different modes of expression. Often this led to quarreling—disputes that arose precisely because of the greatly expanded latitude of the linguistic field. But this hardly meant a lack of constraints, for writers still had to attend to the tastes and values of their public: the aristocratic elite that made up the Parisian *monde*.

Indeed, most of the writers we will meet in the following chapters sought out this world, pandered to its denizens, craved their company, approval, and support. Their savant contemporaries, on the other hand, were not happy with how they were willing to accommodate the tastes and educational level of their aristocratic, often female, interlocutors, fearing that such pandering gave too much away in terms of the richness, history, and erudition of French expression. But while accommodation perhaps describes their attitude, it certainly did not mean a disavowal of learned or literary traditions, nor an absence of literary creativity. As always, the "art of pleasing" required considerable ingenuity; or rather, finding modes of pleasing through language leads to what must be called "literature."

The Literary Field

The movement for linguistic reform is thus linked to the development of French classicism, which for some literary historians amounted to the emergence not only of a particular style of literature but of literature *tout court*. In Alain Viala's view, it was in the seventeenth century that a literary "field" emerged, with many attributes that endowed it with a degree of autonomy as a sphere of cultural practice. Viala's book *La naissance de l'écrivain* (1985), a pathbreaking work, launched a whole school for the social and cultural study of literature in the Ancien Régime.[35] In it he sets out what amounts to a sociology of literature, presenting a kind of infrastructure of groups, patronage networks, publications, and the like that created and sustained the literary field.[36] And he strenuously argues against the traditional notion of "classicism"—a triumphalist consensus on the rhetoric and style that supposedly characterized French literature in this period—evoking a much more contentious and fraught literary field. Like anyone interested in the wider context of literature in this period, Viala confronts the question of the relationship of established authority, both royal and aristocratic, to this literary field. How much did it depend on patronage, and thus to what degree did it serve the

---

Something (Oxford, 2005) is also relevant here insofar as it argues for a rise in subjectivity along with a concomitant indeterminacy that characterized various intellectual and literary realms, including "polite society," largely in the period covered by this book.

[35] Alain Viala, *La naissance de l'écrivain: Sociologie de la littérature à l'âge classique* (Paris, 1985).
[36] Timothy Reiss's *The Meaning of Literature* (Ithaca, NY, 1992) should also be noted as a comparable work in terms of general thesis, although across a vastly larger canvas of literary works and time.

interests and reflect the values of the regime and traditional elites? The conclusion he draws from his study is interestingly mixed: writers were necessarily Janus-faced, both beholden to their patrons and endowed with a margin of autonomy. Their situation, accordingly, was ultimately fraught with inhibitions, for whatever freedom they might exercise had to be carefully restrained; as a result, their writings were characterized by duplicity, indirection, and an often tortured discursive mode that is a feature of much of the literature of the period.

In a powerful riposte, *Les pouvoirs de la littérature* (2000), Christian Jouhaud argued that the literary autonomy Viala ascribes to these writers is illusory.[37] True, they were "freed" from the corporate constraints of university, Church, and magistracy, a move that defined them as *mondain*, which is to say at large in the social world of the mostly Parisian cultivated elite. "Fundamentally, their status was not to have one," he writes.[38] But this very position—Jouhaud characterizes it as being "delocalized"—was hardly a source of autonomy. On the contrary, their lack of status pushed them into the arms of protectors—either royal or aristocratic—for both security and legitimacy. Jouhaud concludes that the literary field was established not despite aristocratic or royal authority, as Viala would have it, but rather *because* of it. The relationship went both ways. Writers sought legitimacy in the "power" of political rulers, who in turn saw the potential of this new *mondain* breed of *gens de lettres* as an instrument of control over the traditional bastions of cultural and intellectual power.[39]

It is not clear whether either Viala's or Jouhaud's analysis holds true across the entire literary culture of the period. On the one hand, Jouhaud is more precise in examining individual cases, thus calibrating his argument to suit particular circumstances, allowing considerable variation on the theme of how writers either were attracted to or were pulled into the force field of "power." On the other, however, it does not seem plausible to deny rather categorically the possibility that certain contexts and relationships created the conditions for a degree of autonomy. Likewise, as I will stress repeatedly in the chapters that follow, a measure of duplicity that Viala has discovered—or at least a sense of dividedness evoked by Charron and others—seemed to characterize the outlook of many writers and intellectuals. Finally, Jouhaud's focus on mainly the upper echelons of the literary world, where the relationships between Richelieu and writers were most stark, tends to obscure the wider, more varied terrain of literary and intellectual

---

[37] Christian Jouhaud, *Les pouvoirs de la littérature: Histoire d'un paradoxe* (Paris, 2000).
[38] Jouhaud, *Les pouvoirs de la littérature*, 20.
[39] "Writers were used to domesticate—the term is not necessarily pejorative—a cultural field that the rulers did not wish to see emancipated. They thus upset the norms of comportment and limited the authority of the 'learned' [*doctes*], scholars, jurists, orators, all while giving lessons on pleasure and good taste," he writes. Jouhaud, *Les pouvoirs de la littérature*, 368. For a somewhat critical but also very appreciative assessment of Jouhaud's book, see Robert A. Schneider, "Political Power and the Emergence of Literature: Christian Jouhaud's Age of Richelieu," *French Historical Studies*, 25/2 (2002), 357–80.

sociability, where, for example, *gens de lettres* managed to carve out spaces for themselves at a remove from the pull and influence of "power."

But Jouhaud's analysis receives qualified support in Peter Shoemaker's very fine study *Powerful Connections: The Poetics of Patronage in the Age of Louis XIII* (2007).[40] Shoemaker focuses on the patronage of writers in the same period, arguing that these relationships not only provided them support and legitimacy but also infiltrated the very nature of the texts they produced, even the genres they worked in. The patron-writer relationship was particularly suited to the new rhetorical mode of the period. "A particularistic system, patronage required not the tools of public oratory, but rather a particularistic rhetoric, narrowly targeted to an 'audience of one,'" he writes. "This rhetoric was necessarily *ad hominem* in that the success or failure of a given performance was not a function of swaying the opinions of a broad public, but rather of seducing a single individual."[41] In Shoemaker's book, the literary field is rich in relationships between writers and their patrons. Richelieu does loom large in this world, but it is also populated with aristocrats and their client-writers, reminding us of the Parisian *monde* that flourished largely outside the precincts of either the Louvre or the cardinal's palace.

Despite these different approaches, then, we return to the *mondain* quality of literature—its grounding in a particular social context—which had fundamental consequences for the very nature of literary discourse, both its appeal and its rhetoric. In our asserting its *mondain* quality, of course, its aristocratic nature goes without saying as well, for this "world" was a tidy, elite one indeed. And this suggests another possible criticism of Jouhaud's interpretation, which hinges on the claim that because writers flourished outside the traditional bastions of "eloquence," and thus were "delocalized," their "art of persuasion ... was emptied of its civic, moral, or apologetic purposes that justify recourse to it."[42] The implication here is that the new literary discourse was, in a sense, value-neutral, eligible for appropriation by any interest or force, and particularly suitable for the needs of "power" guided by that quintessentially situationist discourse, "reason of state."

But when we look at writers themselves, this analysis seems excessively severe. Were they so bereft, so rootless, so purposeless as this formulation seems to imply? As Shoemaker argues, the "space" of patronage provided writers with a "locale" that, *pace* Jouhaud, they inhabited, if not necessarily socially then at least metaphorically. But we can enlarge on Shoemaker's critique by pointing to the *monde* of literary sociability, which, sometimes in the presence of aristocratic patrons, other times among writers alone, also offered a space for literature, as well as an ethos of *otium cum dignitate*. Indeed, is not retreat itself, especially when it is socially padded and freighted with intellectual and spiritual associations, a meaningful locale? And was their "art" so devoid of meaningful ends? There is, to be

---

[40] Shoemaker, *Powerful Connections*.   [41] Shoemaker, *Powerful Connections*, 22–3.
[42] Jouhaud, *Les pouvoirs de la littérature*, 329.

sure, something about modern literature—its dialogic quality, its malleability, its susceptibility to a virtually limitless range of perspectives, values, ideologies, and the like—that jibes with Jouhaud's formulation. There are no fixed ends to literary discourse, at least in the way that such purposes guide the professional discourses of, say, law or theology. But this does not then mean that certain writers, sometimes whole schools of them, do not share values, even worldviews, that color their works, even sometimes compelling them to take up their pens. Like many contemporary studies of culture, both Viala's and Jouhaud's works are marked by a focus on form rather than content; the subtitle of Jouhaud's book, "The Terms of Exchange," conveys this interest in relationships and formal qualities at the expense of ideas or values.

In this study, however, I try to remain alert to the intellectual positions, prejudices, and sentiments of writers, even if obliquely expressed and seemingly governed by the demands of conformism. Several are most prominent and will surface in the following pages. Most obvious and widespread is a concern that the excesses and depredations of the last century's religious wars not be repeated. An acknowledgment of the early seventeenth century as a profoundly "post-bellum" period is something absent from Viala and Jouhaud's studies; significantly, it does play a role in Merlin-Kajman's overall analysis. While for the most part my study presents literary and intellectual life as a series of portrait studies, with little attention to movement across time, I do attend to the historicity of the period by factoring in an awareness of the wars as a fundamental element in contemporaries' attitudes. For one thing, it was crucial in the shift away from the oratorical model of eloquence and the embrace of more discreet, less public registers of expression. For another, the wars were important in fashioning a social vision that held the "people" in contempt as an ever-threatening, turbulent, wayward force whose proclivities can only be described as mindless. (See Chapter 3.) Without an appreciation of this basic prejudice of writers and savants, it is difficult to understand their readiness to identify and ally themselves with the emerging political order. Another legacy of the religious wars was a growing "national consciousness," which only developed further in the seventeenth century with the fear of Habsburg encirclement and especially the threat from Spain, seen to embody all that nearly destroyed France during the conflict. Writers expressed patriotic sentiments that we cannot discount merely because they were congenial to received opinion.

Gallicans and "Good Frenchmen"

This suggests several lines of development. As in the literary field, retreat and withdrawal defined religion in many, even in more obvious, ways. Here the lessons learned from the disasters of the Wars of Religion clearly played a role in instructing even the most devout and militant that the public airing of issues of doctrine or confessional partisanship was ill-advised. The nature of religious commitment—or rather its display and public assertion—largely changed direction. One example illustrates this change quite dramatically. In 1627, a group of elite laymen and high clerics founded a secret society, the Compagnie du Saint-Sacrement, an organization made up of militant Catholics who never accepted the terms of the Edict of Nantes. In spirit and doctrine they were the heirs to the Catholic League of the period of the religious wars. But their modus operandi could not have been more different: instead of taking to the streets, they worked behind the scenes as an influential pressure group at court, among the magistracy, and within the Church; instead of issuing inflammatory pamphlets or preaching incendiary sermons to the masses, they were discreet, secret, and publicly conformist while privately sometimes subversive (at least as far as the particularities of the Edict of Nantes were concerned).[43] This redirection of religious militancy into more discreet channels was also a feature of Jansenism, which in fact prompted those converted to this austere form of Catholicism to withdraw from public life. But, contrary to what Goldmann's thesis would lead one to conclude, this very act often amounted to an eloquent, though certainly oblique, commentary on the religious and secular politics of the day, not a tragic turn away from all engagement.[44]

This sort of religious austerity and severity held very little appeal for most men of letters and savants.[45] Rather, they were mostly Gallican in spirit. Gallicanism is probably the most overlooked aspect of the intellectual and religious history of the seventeenth century. Traditional accounts emphasize Gallican elements in the precincts of the university, the Parlement, or the clergy, for these were corporate bodies formally threatened by ultramontanism, and in particular by the Tridentine Reforms and the Society of Jesus. But it was the cause of men of letters and savants as well. And for good reason: with their fear of Rome's encroaching influence on French life, especially at the hands of the Jesuits, their concern for ultramontanism can only be compared to the anxieties of the Protestant English about the dreaded and ubiquitous agents of the Counter-Reformation, or the Dutch Arminians as they tried to hold a resurgence of hardline Calvinism at bay. They looked upon Venice during the papal interdict and saw that France, too,

---

[43] On the Company, see Raoul Allier, *La cabale des dévots, 1627–66* (Paris, 1902); Alain Tallon, *La Compagnie du Saint-Sacrement, 1629–67* (Paris, 1990). On their work in a provincial city, see Schneider, *Public Life in Toulouse*, chap. 6.

[44] See the case of the Jansenist Arnauld d'Andilly, who managed to maintain his profile as a writer while in self-imposed retreat. Rémi Mathis, "'Une trop bruyante solitude': Robert Arnauld d'Andilly, solitaire de Port-Royal, et le pouvoir royal (1643–1674)," *Papers on French Seventeenth Century Literature*, 37/73 (2010), 337–52.

[45] Although it is interesting to note that both Chapelain and Balzac expressed their admiration for Le Maistre's withdrawal; they were both quite close to the Arnaulds. See Chapelain, *Lettres de Jean Chapelain, de l'Académie française*, ed. Philippe Tamizey de Larroque, 2 vols. (Paris, 1880–2), I: 182, 184, 190, on this.

might find itself under the heel of a militantly aggressive and intolerant Church that targeted moderate Catholics and Protestants alike. They feared that the domestic forces of militant Catholicism would undermine the "absolutist pact" embodied by the Edict of Nantes.

There were several species of Gallicanism, some quite doctrinaire, some more critical of Rome than others, much of it increasingly erudite. And it was a stance tailor-made for the more discreet, less public orientation that characterized religious discourse in this post-civil war environment. For since the sixteenth century, erudition, even antiquarianism, had defined Gallican publications. In the early seventeenth century, the cabinet led by the Dupuy brothers, Pierre and Jacques, nephews of the great Gallican historian Jacques-Auguste de Thou, was the headquarters of Gallicanism. For them and their associates, the depredations of Rome represented only the most recent wave of a centuries-old assault on the "liberties of the Gallican Church," which they energetically defended with the only weapons they had—erudition and documentation.[46] But Gallican sentiments extended beyond this savant circle. Many other *gens de lettres* shared in the general suspicion of the Rome-Habsburg-Jesuit axis, especially as the forces of the Counter-Reformation were gaining strength and a European war loomed. If they were not card-carrying Gallicans like the Dupuys, they nevertheless harbored deep concern in the face of these threats both for themselves as *gens de lettres* and *esprits forts* and for their country. Writers like Guy Patin and Chapelain, for example, were haunted by the specter of legions of Jesuits undermining the very fabric of France's religious and intellectual life.

This fear fed a growing sense of national identity that had been developing at least since the Wars of Religion. There is a direct line from the *politiques* of that period to the *bons français* of the early seventeenth century, a line toed by most of the *gens de lettres* we shall encounter. Their opponents were the "*dévots*," who identified with a unified Catholic Europe, wishing to see France aligned with the Habsburgs in pursuit of this goal. In keeping with their religious and political orientations, the *bons français* were supportive of Richelieu's foreign policy, which placed France in alliance with Protestant powers and princes against the Catholic Habsburgs. And they thus largely subscribed to the doctrine of *raison d'état*, which served to justify this policy on the grounds of national interest. But their endorsement of this form of political reasoning—which is often depicted as guided by cold-blooded interest if not a caricatured form of "Machiavellianism"—was not purely servile or craven. Here we must acknowledge that "conformity" has never been simply that; nor is it less sincere or deeply felt merely because it

---

[46] See especially Donald Kelly, *The Foundations of Modern Historical Scholarship: Language, Law and History in the French Renaissance* (New York, 1970). More recently, see Jotham Parsons, *The Church in the Republic: Gallicanism and Political Ideology in Renaissance France* (Washington, DC, 2004). And more generally on the religious history of this period, especially in relationship to political developments, see Joseph Bergin, *The Politics of Religion in Early Modern France* (New Haven, 2014).

places one in line with the views of others, and in particular those in power. While most *gens de lettres* in this period agreed with both how Richelieu was conducting France's foreign policy and the political reasoning that justified it, they had their own ways of understanding, articulating, and, within limits, even criticizing both.

One feature of an emerging national identity was particularly prominent among savants and writers. Like the Gallican and *bon français* positions, this too had its origins in the sixteenth century, when, as Claude-Gilbert Dubois demonstrated, the historical recovery of ancient Gaul became something of a scholarly fashion.[47] It was in this period that "*nos ancêtres les Gaulois*" became a trope of French identity. The seventeenth century was heir to these scholarly labors, in this and so many other respects. An interest in Gaul in particular and in France's medieval past more generally is evident in a whole range of texts. D'Urfé's *L'Astrée*, perhaps the best-known, or at least the most widely read, seized upon the historical moment of ancient Gaul to fashion a veritable *lieu de mémoire*. It was then, this pastoral epic asserted, that France was born. Others delved into this particular past to revive a historical memory that could rival Roman antiquity as a source of French culture. Many vaunted the natural eloquence of the Gauls, as well as their martial prowess, as a source of France's unique virtues among the nations. Gallicans saw the special nature of French Christianity—the "eldest daughter of the Church"—as rooted in its ancient past; and they also focused their attention on the Middle Ages, when the "liberties of the Gallican Church" were time and again asserted and defended. And those interested in the long and venerable genealogy of both the French monarchy and aristocracy were keen to extend their line of descent into the deepest recesses of the past. In short, writers in seventeenth-century France cultivated their country's medieval past as an act of national identity formation.

To this should be added something that might easily be overlooked, probably because it seems to be based on less than elevated concerns. When it comes to understanding the interests and motivations of writers—what got them out of bed in the morning—there was also a competitive drive at work: the desire to equal or surpass the literary and cultural accomplishments of the Italians. Something of an inferiority complex had a strong hold on French *gens de lettres* and savants in the early seventeenth century, even as most deeply appreciated Italian achievements. For many, Italy was a second homeland; and, of course, Italian influences had been a part of French culture for centuries, borne by a constant flow of artists, literati, savants, students, and religious figures of various stripes, not to speak of the popularity and prestige of literary and scholarly works from the peninsula. But as early as the sixteenth century, *gens de lettres* had had enough, so to speak. Those interested in the fortunes of the French vernacular,

---

[47] See especially Claude-Gilbert Dubois, *Celtes et Gaulois au XVIe siècle: Le développment littéraire d'un mythe nationaliste* (Paris, 1972).

from Henri Estienne to François de Malherbe, strove to eliminate "Italianisms" from the language. As much as they were impatient with these foreign linguistic influences, they wanted nothing less than to have French attain the stature and currency of Italian. Critics of Henri III and Catherine de Medici often took aim at the Italian presence at court, and well into the seventeenth century unfriendly commentators noted that the French spoken at court was "Italianate," and thus not only inadequately French but effeminate to boot. The historical interest in the ancient Gauls, which, as just noted, took hold in the sixteenth century and continued into the seventeenth, was driven by a desire to imagine a truly national French past distinct from Roman sources.[48] That most Italian of Frenchmen in the seventeenth century, Gabriel Naudé, who was responsible for editing and publishing many works by Italian authors, nevertheless gave voice to the sentiment shared by most of his contemporary savants that France deserved its share of the glory of letters and erudition. His *Addition à l'histoire de Louis XI* is, in part, a brief for the claim that the rebirth of learning in the fifteenth century took place in France as much as in Italy.[49] The Republic of Letters, to be sure, took little account of political borders and encouraged a cosmopolitan spirit that united men of learning across Europe, despite considerations of religion and nationality. But in an era when France was locked in a diplomatic and military contest with the Habsburgs and otherwise troubled by the ambitions of a Counter-Reformation Rome, men of letters saw the chance to wrest from Italy the glory of letters and learning as another front in that European-wide campaign for dominance.

All of this is to suggest that even in an era when engagement was no longer the fashion, when the model of the Ciceronian orator no longer prevailed, when, in short, a retreat from public life was the reigning ethos, there still were important and profound ways in which French *gens de lettres* promoted values and interests that mattered to their countrymen. In various ways, they were in search of what it meant to be French.

Modes of Self-Presentation: Dissimulation, *Honnêteté*, and Libertinage

While writers' interest in vaunting "Frenchness" in a variety of ways suggests their qualified engagement with public concerns, they were as much, or perhaps even more, driven to define their own status and identities, especially as they mostly

---

[48] Philippe Desan, "The Worm in the Apple: The Crisis of Humanism," in Desan, ed., *Humanism in Crisis: The Decline of the French Renaissance* (Ann Arbor, 1991), 15.

[49] Gabriel Naudé, *Addition à l'histoire de Louis XI: Contenant plusieurs recherches curieuses sur diverses matières* (Paris, 1630). For an important analysis that demonstrates the skewed nature of Italian thinking that made its way into the French mainstream, see Paul Oskar Kristeller, "Between the Italian Renaissance and the French Enlightenment: Gabriel Naudé as an Editor," *Renaissance Quarterly*, 32 (1979), 41–72.

occupied positions outside traditional institutions of learning. And one curious aspect of their ambiguous status seems to have been the invention or deployment of names or ascriptions to identify themselves.[50] Those associated with the *mondain* world of the salons were known as *beaux esprits*, a tag the Jesuit Father Garasse also used, with vicious sarcasm, for the so-called "libertines" he calumniated in his *Doctrine curieuse des beaux esprits*.[51] Of course, "libertines" and "libertinage" were also terms bandied about, usually as terms of reproach.[52] But this is a problematic, hopelessly pejorative label: even those subsequently identified as "erudite libertines" by Pintard in his great book would be loath to accept this ascription.[53] They would, however, happily identify with the label *esprits forts*, a designation marking them as members of a hardy elite—but really understandable only when juxtaposed against its opposite, *esprits faibles*, for the term connotes a sense of tough-mindedness that distinguishes those disabused of the illusions and lies that keep the masses in their place. All writers saw themselves as *honnêtes gens*, which, it must be noted, described an ideal for French elites in general, not only *gens de lettres*. But it was writers who fashioned *honnêteté*, translating elements of classical learning into an accessible ethos for their privileged contemporaries.

As I will discuss in Chapter 2, *honnêteté* implied a mode of self-presentation and a value system that cannot be reduced to civility or politesse or subsumed by Elias's "civilizing process." Indeed, it usually prescribed prudence and often cautioned guardedness in social interactions, especially at court or in otherwise fraught company, suggesting that a measure of deception, even dissimulation— the necessity to disguise or hide one's true feelings or reactions—was often incumbent on the *honnête* man or woman. For the so-called *esprits forts*, there was rarely any question that they needed to be extremely cautious about disclosing their true beliefs. Writers like La Mothe le Vayer and Naudé embraced the dictum associated with the Italian natural philosopher Cesare Cremonini, "*Intus ut libet, foris ut moris est*"—"In private think what you wish, in public behave as is the custom." The practice of dissimulation is usually associated in this period with

---

[50] Richard Scholar calls them "lexical signs." Scholar, *The Je-Ne-Sais-Quoi in Early Modern Europe*, 190.

[51] François Garasse, *La doctrine curieuse des beaux esprits de ce temps, ou prétendus tels, contenant plusieurs maximes pernicieuses à l'Estat, à la Religion et aux bonnes moeurs* (Paris, 1624).

[52] Denise Leduc-Fayette, "Les 'esprits forts' au 'grand siècle,'" *Revue philosophique de la France et de l'étranger*, 126/1 (2000), 55–60.

[53] In the 1983 edition of his book, Pintard modified his view of "libertinage erudite." See also Paul Oskar Kristeller, "The Myth of Renaissance Atheism and the French Tradition of Free Thought," *Journal of the History of Philosophy*, 6/3 (1968), 233–43 for a skeptical view of the importance of atheism or "libertine" thought in this period. The question of the so-called libertines has been reopened most copiously by Jean-Pierre Cavaillé in a series of works: *Dis/simulations: Jules-César Vanini, François La Mothe le Vayer, Gabriel Naudé, Louis Machon, et Torquato Accetto: Religion, morale et politique au XVIIe siècle* (Paris, 2002); *Postures libertines: La culture des esprits forts* (Toulouse, 2011); and *Les deniaisés: Irréligion et libertinage au début de l'époque moderne* (Paris, 2013). Also, see Gouverneur's important work *Prudence et subversion libertines*.

raison d'état, which allowed for stratagems that ignored religious or moral norms. Contemporaries often cited the phrase attributed to Louis XI, "He who does not know how to dissimulate, knows not how to rule."[54] Looking at prescriptions governing elite personal behavior, however, and specifically *gens de lettres*, reveals that there was not such a large gap between statesmen and courtiers, on the one side, and *honnêtes gens* and *esprits forts*, on the other. All endorsed prudence as a necessary virtue, which in practice often meant shades of dissimulation, deception, duplicity, self-censorship, secrecy, or other forms of guardedness in the interest of either self-preservation or self-advancement. This is why mention of these stratagems, in both the public and private realms, will surface throughout this book: they were features of writers' and intellectuals' understanding of how one negotiated the tricky terrain of a vexed social world. And with this we return full circle to the ethos of retreat.

* * *

Dignified Retreat moves thematically in a series of chapters that together offer a portrait of literary and intellectual life across the period. "Portraiture" aptly describes my approach, for many of the chapters are sprinkled with capsule intellectual portraits of those writers and intellectuals whose lives and works not only embody the argument at hand but also demonstrate its variations.

Chapter 1, "Reforming French: The Making of a Movement," sets out ways in which the expressive capacities of French were expanded, largely in reaction against the perceived pedantry and excessive erudition associated with the sixteenth century. A range of writers participated in the move to reform French, with the view to expanding its appeal to a minimally educated elite—to transform it, in other words, into a truly robust vernacular capable of rivaling Italian, or even ancient Greek and Latin, as a language of eloquent but accessible expression. While focusing on individual writers, I emphasize that their efforts were part of a widespread movement—and it was perceived as such. It thereby provoked opposition from some writers who saw venerable notions of language and eloquence under attack. Here, too, I map out the various associations that sprang up in Paris in the early part of the seventeenth century, groups of writers and intellectuals, some devoted to cultivating the new literary "field," others invested in more erudite concerns. All of them, however, flourished outside the traditional bastions of knowledge—the university, the Church, the magistracy—as well as beyond the royal court. In this chapter as well I look at the translation of mostly ancient texts as another facet of this movement to fashion a literary discourse that appealed to a wider public beyond the learned. The second chapter, "Aristocrats and Writers: The Emergence of a Parisian 'World,' " builds on the first, turning from language

---

[54] Adrianna E. Bakos, "'Qui nescit dissimulare, nescit regnard': Louis XI and Raison d'état during the Reign of Louis XIII," *Journal of the History of Ideas*, 52/3 (1991), 399–416.

and literature to the social conditions in post-religious wars Paris that gave rise to a culture that brought *gens de lettres* and an aristocratic elite in close proximity. Without an appreciation of these relationships, I argue, it is difficult to understand the origins of the movement to transform the nature of French eloquence, for this aristocracy comprised the writers' public. And here it will become apparent that while *gens de lettres* were "in charge" of language, there were constraints on their custodianship, mostly having to do with the social environment in which they operated. This was the Parisian *monde*—the urban world of cultivated elites who colonized the city in the generation following the Wars of Religion. *Gens de lettres* were virtually in constant contact with these elites. And nothing embodies this relationship more than the development of the ethos of *honnêteté*, a discourse fashioned by writers out of ancient sources, but calibrated for the moral sensitivities and worldly demands of contemporary aristocrats and those who aspired to this elevated status.

Chapter 3, "A Culture of Discretion," changes direction. After describing the modalities of a worldly culture, open to new influences, here I look at the other slope of the culture—the variety of ways it was governed by discretion, self-censorship, and in general a concern for the dangerous consequences of unguarded public discourse. And I argue that this concern was less a matter of repression or the constraints of patronage and more an aftereffect of the Wars of Religion and the consequent fear of inflaming the people—the "many-headed beast"—by airing potentially provocative subjects in public. This long chapter looks at this profoundly discretionary culture as largely the work of *gens de lettres*, who had their own reasons for fashioning it in these terms, but ultimately suggests that it supports our view of seventeenth-century France as a fundamentally aristocratic society, with writers bringing to this social formation their own values and interests. As much as "openings" and a relative lack of restraint characterized language and the new literary culture, the imperatives of discretion, in part in keeping with an identification with privileged elites, in part the result of writers' own sensitivities and concerns, meant that significant constraints were operative as well.

Chapter 4, "Richelieu and Writers," is in two parts. The first gives an account of the pre-history and founding of the Académie française. Here I emphasize the fact that this institution, which is most often identified as the embodiment of "cultural absolutism"—an imperious intrusion into the cultural realm if ever there was one—was actually at most an act of cooptation of a well-established movement among men of letters. Their focus on the expressive capacities of French, which defined the academy's activities in its first years, was not imposed upon them but rather grew out of their own concerns. The second part looks at the relationships between a range of different writers and savants and the cardinal, highlighting in some cases how these men managed to maintain ties with others, some elite patrons, some fellow *gens de lettres*, while serving him; in others how they bore the stamp of their own intellectual and literary interests into service at this stratospheric level.

Chapters 5 and 6 are complementary, looking at what have been called the two poles of Parisian culture in this period. Chapter 5, "The Rambouillet Salon: 'A Purified World,'" offers a portrait of this most famous literary salon, emphasizing it as an arena rich in literary activity. In Chapter 6, "The Dupuy Cabinet: 'An Innocent Refuge,'" this library, which served as something of a headquarters for the emergent European Republic of Letters, reveals a somewhat different set of preoccupations, more Gallican, more savant, and ultimately more critical of Richelieu and his policies.

Chapter 7, "Writing *Otium*: Retreat as a Mode of Engagement," looks at four texts, two classed as works of the "reason of state" genre, two large-scale literary works. While quite different, each of these, I argue, illustrates a major theme of this book—that "retreat" and "engagement" were not necessarily contradictory in this period; that, indeed, the stance of retreat often served as a useful strategy for discreet, though perhaps oblique, interventions into public matters.

* * *

While not a collective biography, this book rests on a prosopography of over approximately 130 *gens de lettres* who were active roughly from 1620 to 1648. Most were born circa 1600, and thus comprise what we might identify as the "generation of 1630." For the most part, then, they shared the experiences of a cohort born after the conclusion of the Wars of Religion in 1594 but still affected by the memory of this prolonged period of civil strife while also imbued with the hope of a restored France under the tutelage of a strong monarchy. These "writers" did not all publish, for publication was not the distinguishing feature of this identity in the Ancien Régime. I culled their names from a variety of sources,[55] which mostly privilege those individuals who were successful in establishing themselves as *gens de lettres*, recognized by their peers or otherwise acknowledged in the sources as having a presence in literary and intellectual circles. There is a degree of arbitrariness in this sort of research; some figures stand out more than others for reasons that can only be explained by the nature of the sources consulted and the way I read them. Other sources or a somewhat altered perspective would undoubtedly have revealed a very different universe of figures. The most obvious liability of this approach is that it inevitably fails to acknowledge those less successful or mainstream *gens de lettres*—those who wrote "from the margins" or otherwise harbored less conformist values and more critical sensibilities. It must

---

[55] Including: members of the first generation of the Académie française; writers discussed in Gédéon Tallemant des Réaux, *Historiettes*, ed. Antoine Adam, 2 vols. (Paris, 1960); as well as those mentioned in Michel de Marolles, *Mémoires de Michel de Marolles, abbé de Villeloin* (Paris, 1656). For others, I remained alert to those figures who were active between circa 1620 and 1648.

Table 1 The Generation of 1630: Writers and Intellectuals Who Figure in This Book

Name and (Date of Birth)	Background: Family Status/Father's Occupation	Occupation/Status	Académie française	Rambouillet Salon	Dupuy Cabinet	Illustres bergers	Conrart Circle
Ablancourt, Nicolas Perrot d' (1606)	magistrate	lawyer	X				
Arnauld, Antoine (1612)	magistrate	lawyer		X			
Arnauld, Pierre Isaac de Corbeville (?)	magistrate	royal officer, soldier		X			
Arnauld d'Andilly, Robert (1588)	magistrate	intendant to Gaston d'Orléans		X			
Aubignac, François Hédelin, abbé d' (1604)	magistrate	lawyer, priest, tutor					
Balzac, Jean-Louis Guez de (1597)	noble	noble	X	X	X		
Barclay, John (1582)	professor, jurist	writer	X		X		
Bardin, Pierre (1590)	noble	tutor	X				
Baro, Balthazar (1590?)	professor	writer	X				
Baudoin, Jean (1590)	?	servant to royal ministers	X				
Bautru, Guillaume (1588)	noble	count, diplomat	X				
Boisrobert, François Le Metel de (1592)	lawyer	lawyer, servant to royal ministers	X	X			X
Boissat, Pierre de (1603)	?	soldier	X				
Bouchard, Jean-Jacques (1606)	secrétaire du roi	secretary in Vatican			X		
Boulliau, Ismaël (1605)	notary	librarian			X		
Bourbon, Nicolas (1574)	physician	professor, priest			X		
Bourdelot, Pierre (1610)	?	physician			X		
Bourzeys, Amable de (1606)	?	theologian	X				
Brun, Antoine (1599)	?	magistrate					
Camus, Jean-Pierre (1584)	noble	priest					

Cerisiers, René de (1603)	?	priest				
Chapelain, Jean (1595)	notary	tutor, client of several great nobles	X	X	X	X
Charron, Pierre (1541)	bookseller	priest				
Chevreau, Urbain (1613)	glass painter (artisan)	tutor and secretary				
Coëffeteau, Nicolas (1574)	?	priest				
Colletet, Guillaume (1598)	lawyer (*procureur*)	lawyer	X		X	
Colomby, François de Cauvigny de (1588?)	?	priest	X			
Conrart, Valentin (1603)	merchant	royal officer	X	X		X
Corneille, Pierre (1606)	magistrate, royal officer	playwright	X			
Costar, Pierre (1603)	?	priest				
Cotignon de la Charnaye, Pierre (1582 or 1588)	?	priest			X	
Cramail, Adrien de Montluc (1571)	noble	noble				
Croisilles, Jean-Baptiste de (1593?)	?	priest				
Cureau de la Chambre, Marin (1596)	?	physician	X			
Descartes, René (1596)	magistrate	soldier				
Desmarets de Saint-Sorlin, Jean (1595)	?	*conseiller du roi*	X			
Diodati, Eli (1576)	noble	lawyer, diplomat		X		
Du Bosc, Jacques (1600?)	?	priest				
Du Chastelet, Paul Hay (1592)	minor noble	magistrate, lawyer	X			
Duchesne, André (1584)	?	royal historiographer				
Du Duc, Fronton (1559)	?	priest (Jesuit)				

Continued

Table 1 *Continued*

Name and (Date of Birth)	Background: Family Status/Father's Occupation	Occupation/Status	Académie française	Rambouillet Salon	Dupuy Cabinet	Illustres bergers	Conrart Circle
Dupleix, Scipion (1569)	minor noble	lawyer, royal historiographer					
Dupuy, Jacques (1591)	magistrate	royal librarian			X		
Dupuy, Pierre (1582)	magistrate	lawyer, royal librarian			X		
Du Ryer, Pierre (1600?)	?	historiographer of France	X				
Du Vair, Guillaume (1556)	?	royal magistrate					
Fancan, François Langlois, sieur de (1576)	minor noble	church canon, Richelieu's confidant					
Faret, Nicolas (1596)	shoemaker	lawyer, secretary	X	X			X
Ferrier, Jérémie (1576)	?	royal historiographer			X		
Fortin de la Hoguette, Philippe (1585)	noble	soldier					
Frénicle, Nicolas (1600)	?	royal officer				X	
Furetière, Antoine (1619)	employee of royal household	abbot					
Gaffarel, Jacques (1601)	physician	theologian, librarian			X		
Garasse, François (1585)	?	priest (Jesuit)					
Garnier, Claude (1583)	?	?	X				
Gassendi, Pierre (1592)	peasant	priest			X		
Giry, Louis (1596)	magistrate	lawyer	X				X
Godeau, Antoine (1605)	royal official	priest	X	X		X	
Godefroy, Théodore (1580)	jurist	historiographer of France			X		
Gombauld, Jean Ogier de (1570?)	?	courtier	X				X
Gomberville, Marin Le Roy de (1600)	minor official	writer	X				
Goulu, Jean (1576)	professor, humanist	priest					
Gournay, Marie de (1566?)	minor noble	writer					
Grotius, Hugo (1583)	jurist, mayor, university rector	jurist, ambassador			X		

Name	Status	Occupation			
Guyet, François (1575)	noble	preceptor			
Habert, Germain (1615)	royal official	aumônier du roi and abbot		x	x
Habert, Philippe (1605)	royal official	?	x	x	x
Habert de Montmor, Henri Louis (1600)	royal official	royal official, maître des requêtes	x		
Hardy, Alexandre (1570?)	?	member of Comédiens du roi			
Holstenius, Lucas (1596)	?	librarian		x	
Jacob de Saint-Charles, Louis (1608)	?	priest		x	
La Mesnardière, Hippolyte-Jules Pilet de (1610)	?	physician and royal official	x	x	
La Milletière, Théophile Brachet de (1596)	royal official	lawyer			
La Mothe le Vayer, François de (1588)	magistrate	magistrate	x	x	
Le Bret, Cardin (1588)	noble	jurist			
Lesclache, Louis de (1620)	?	philosopher			
L'Estoile, Claude de (1597)	notary and royal secretary	writer	x		
Luillier, François (16??)	minor noble?	magistrate		x	
Lusson, Guillaume (?)	physician, professor	royal officer		x	
Mairet, Jean (1604)	?	playwright, diplomat		x	
Malherbe, François de (1555)	magistrate, noble	secretary, courtier		x	x
Malleville, Claude (1596)	officer in household of Cardinal de Retz	secretary to nobleman	x		x
Marbeuf, Pierre (1596)	?	royal officer			
Marcassus, Pierre de (1584)	?	professor			
Marolles, Michel de (1600)	minor noble	priest, abbot	x	x	
Mauduit, Louis (?)	royal musician	poet			
Maynard, François (1582?)	magistrate	secretary, servant of nobles, royal official	x	x	

Continued

Table 1 Continued

Name and (Date of Birth)	Background: Family Status/Father's Occupation	Occupation/Status	Académie française	Rambouillet Salon	Dupuy Cabinet	Illustres bergers	Conrart Circle
Ménage, Gilles (1613)	lawyer	priest		X	X		
Mersenne, Marin (1588)	laborer	priest			X		
Mézeray, François Eudes de (1610)	surgeon	royal official in army, historian	X				
Méziriac, Claude-Gaspar Bachet de (1581)	counselor to the Duke of Savoy	priest (Jesuit)	X				
Molière d'Essertines, Hugues Forget (1600)	minor noble	minor noble					
Montausier, Charles de Sainte-Maure (1610)	noble	duke, soldier		X			
Morel, Fédéric (1558 or 1559)	printer	royal printer					
Morgues, Mathieu de (1582)	municipal official	priest, preacher				X	
Naudé, Gabriel (1600)	official in Bureau des finances	physician, librarian			X		
Ogier, François (1597)	officer in royal court	priest				X	
Patin, Guy (1601)	?	physician, professor			X		
Patru, Olivier (1604)	lawyer	lawyer	X				
Peiresc, Nicolas-Claude Fabri de (1580)	noble	noble, magistrate			X		
Pellisson Fontanier, Paul (1624)	?	lawyer	X				
Pétau, Denys (1583)	?	Jesuit theologian					
Pinchesne, Etienne Martin de (1616)	merchant	?					

Poirier, Hélie (?)	?	court poet, professor of theology	
Porchères-d'Arbaud, François de (1590)	?	court office	X
Porchères-Laugier, Honorat de (1572)	lawyer	minor noble	X
Racan, Honorat de Bueil (1589)	minor noble, soldier	noble, official in army	X
Renaudot, Théophraste (1586)	?	physician, editor	
Revol, Louis de (?)	?	priest, professor	
Rigault, Nicolas (1577)	physician	magistrate, royal librarian	X
Rotrou, Jean de (1609)	?	magistrate	
Saint-Amant, Antoine Girard (1594)	merchant	secretary	X
Sarasin, Jean-François (1614)	municipal and royal official	secretary	X
Saumaise, Claude (1588)	royal magistrate	professor	X
Scarron, Paul (1610)	royal magistrate	priest, abbot	
Scudéry, Georges de (1601)	noble, soldier	noble, soldier	X
Scudéry, Madeleine de (1608)	noble, soldier	writer, *salonnière*	X
Serisay, Jacques de (1590)	?	officer in a noble household	X	X
Servien, Abel (1593)	noble	officer, magistrate, diplomat	X
Silhon, Jean de (1596)	?	secretary, magistrate	X
Sirmond, Jacques (1559)	?	Jesuit, royal confessor	
Sirmond, Jean (1589)	?	royal historiographer	X
Sorbière, Samuel (1615)	?	physician	X
Sorel, Charles (1599 or 1602)	magistrate	historiographer of France	
Tallemant des Réaux, Gédéon (1619)	banker	banker?	X

Continued

Table 1 *Continued*

Name and (Date of Birth)	Background: Family Status/Father's Occupation	Occupation/Status	Académie française	Rambouillet Salon	Dupuy Cabinet	Illustres bergers	Conrart Circle
Thou, François-Auguste de (1607)	royal magistrate	royal magistrate			X		
Thou, Jacques-Auguste de (1553)	royal magistrate	royal magistrate			X		
Tristan l'Hermite, François (1600)	minor noble	in entourage of nobles	X				
Urfé, Honoré d' (1567)	noble	noble, soldier					
Valois, Adrien de (1607)	minor noble	royal historiographer		X	X		
Vanini, Lucilio (1585)	merchant	priest, Carmelite					
Vaugelas, Claude Favre de (1585)	noble (baron)	noble (baron)	X	X			
Viau, Théophile de (1590)	minor noble	court poet		X			
Villeneuve, Jean César de (?)	noble	noble				X	
Vion, Charles, sieur Dalibray (1600)	minor official	soldier					
Voiture, Vincent (1598)	wine merchant	official in royal household	X	X			

be said that writers and intellectuals who defied conventions or otherwise expressed heterodox ideas and views are apparent to anyone who merely wades into the teeming waters of French culture in the first part of the seventeenth century. Figures such as Théophile de Viau, Lucilio (or Giulio Cesare) Vanini, Paul Scarron, Charles Sorel, and others certainly left their mark on their contemporaries; and posterity has, for the most part, rewarded them (Vanini excepted) with considerable attention. But to see this period in terms of "libertinage," which has been the unfortunate result of Pintard's great book, is not terribly helpful, and conveys the misleading impression that intellectual adventurism and non-conformism characterized the period. On the contrary, I argue, the inclination to defy established conventions and challenge orthodoxies, though certainly present in various quarters of intellectual life, remained covert, muted, or otherwise expressed only with great care and discretion.

One thing to note from Table 1 is the indication of a particular profession or at least professional background of these writers and savants. For many these point to an early law career, although there are several notable instances of physicians (Naudé, Patin, Renaudot). What this shows is that a significant number of young men left careers for which they had been educated in favor of a commitment to a life of letters. In most cases, it was a move that entailed finding support from a high-born patron, usually an aristocrat, thus suggesting a group migration from the legal Robe milieu, with its particular intellectual and linguistic orientations, to the privileged society of the aristocracy, whose values and interests were quite different. Théophile de Viau, for example, who was the son of a lawyer, began his spectacularly successful, though fatally doomed, literary career by way of attaching himself to the Duc de Montmorency. His two *compagnons de route*, Guillaume Colletet and Nicolas Frénicle, were debutant lawyers when they collaborated with him and others in the publication of the notorious *Parnasse satyrique*. Despite these examples, this affiliation with the legal establishment characterizes less literary men than the savants associated with the Dupuy cabinet, which makes sense as the brothers were themselves scions of a renowned Robe dynasty. But here too we can detect another variation on a migratory dynamic that also reflects the ethos of *otium*. For, as we shall see, a commitment to a life of letters often entailed a retreat from involvement in a profession, something embodied by the Dupuy brothers themselves.

My selection process clearly favors literary "writers" over "intellectuals" or savants, at least in terms of numbers. Does this accurately reflect the demographic complexion of Parisian literary and intellectual culture in the Age of Richelieu? Without a firm sense of the total population of writers and intellectuals, it is, of course, impossible to tell. Implicit in my presentation in what follows, however, is the claim that an understanding of the cultural history of the period derived mostly from the activities of notable *érudits* misses the main action in the (perhaps less intellectually compelling) community of literati. From the perspective of posterity and the canon of intellectual history, it is certainly true that Descartes and Gassendi, for example, merit the attention conventionally accorded to them. But in this book, the concern is for the most part neither with canonical figures nor with the major figures in the history of ideas; rather, I seek to assess the dynamics of contemporary culture from the perspective of contemporaries themselves. In this sense, at least, what stands out in relief more than Cartesian metaphysics or the scholarship of antiquarian humanists is the community of *gens de lettres* who devoted themselves to the concerns of language reform and literature.

Unlike most literary scholars and intellectual historians, I have been guided by a desire to corral as many writers and savants as I could into my field of analysis; for my goal has been to discover meaningful patterns of commonality and division that could help explain the literary and intellectual culture of the period.[56] Some of these are ultimately connected to the aftermath of the Wars of Religion and a concern on the part of writers and savants to avoid contributing to a recurrence of that disastrous experience. The many references to this universally lamented chapter in recent history, and in particular the more pointed evocations of the role of the Catholic League in aggravating the conflict, demonstrate the vitality of this historical memory into the seventeenth century. But the role of this memory in fashioning the literary and intellectual culture of the day is not always so apparent. As usual when one is thinking about history in this way, the long-term effects of even cataclysmic events are difficult to trace across several generations, for they are filtered by selective memory and forgetfulness, deformed by subsequent developments, eclipsed by more immediate concerns and threats, or otherwise transformed by the thousands of imponderable mediations that operate in what we call "collective memory." To assert the primacy of the memory of the Wars of Religion in the literary and intellectual culture of the Age of Richelieu would, then, be merely that—an assertion that, while plausible, does not work very well as a convincing historical explanation.

Nevertheless, several features of this literary and intellectual culture not only stand out in what follows but also, I believe, allow us to see through them ultimately to the impact of the religious wars. The first is the turning inward of writers and savants, away from direct engagement in public affairs in favor of an intense sort of sociability that gave rise to a cityscape of private and informal associations—a fellowship of kindred spirits. As noted, and as we shall further see, this associational life was often constituted by a mix of noblemen and women and these *gens de lettres*, giving rise to a city culture that rivaled the royal court in its appeal, dynamism, and creativity. A concern with reforming the French language represents, in my estimation, a second aftereffect of the religious wars. Implicit in both is a downgrading of the oratorical model of public expression in favor of more discreet,

---

[56] Although Viala's foundational work *Naissance de l'écrivain* is obviously similar in this respect.

indeed less public modes. The connection between this project and the trauma of the wars might seem strained, but, as with the importance of scientific investigations at about the same time, especially in England, language was a comparatively safe pursuit, far from the confessional and theological matters that ensured conflict. Moreover, in seizing upon linguistic concerns, *gens de lettres* were not only claiming an area of expertise all their own, they were also addressing the question of how modes of expression could be reformed and mastered so as to avoid the kind of voluble indiscretion that fueled the confessional conflict of the last century. Finally, the prominence of Gallicanism, which was embraced by a wide range of writers and savants, is perhaps the most obvious result of the Wars of Religion in the first part of the seventeenth century. While derived from sources deeply rooted in France's past and largely refashioned by the erudition of the sixteenth century, it flourished as an ideology which, while Catholic, stood in stark opposition to the kind of ultramontane Catholic militancy that both threatened the peace of the realm and risked undoing the "absolute pact" embodied in the Edict of Nantes. Especially as cultivated in libraries and "cabinets"—the privileged haunts of savants—its impact was limited and only rarely spilled over into the public realm where it could risk fomenting controversy.

The importance of Gallicanism leads to another theme in what follows in these chapters. To focus solely on the desire to avoid a repeat of the religious wars is to frame contemporary culture in purely negative terms, when, in fact, a flip side of this disposition, as Gallicanism suggests, is a strong identification with the fortunes of France and their hopes for the continued stability and unity of the realm. *Gens de lettres* identified with their country, its culture, and especially its language, and readily rallied in praise and support of their king. While for some this identification may have been qualified either by Neo-Stoicism, which vaunted cosmopolitanism over patriotism, or simply by cynicism disguised as conformism, they nevertheless often lent their pens to the project of celebrating and promoting France as it confronted the forces in Europe, both political and religious, that challenged it in this era of the Thirty Years' War.

1
Reforming French
The Making of a Movement

ANTOINE FURETIÈRE IS remembered mostly for his French dictionary, published posthumously in 1690, and for the conflict with his fellow members of the Académie française over its preparation, which ultimately led to his exclusion from their ranks in 1685. But four years before his election, he published *Nouvelle allégorique, ou, Histoire des derniers troubles arrivez au royaume d'éloquence* (1658), which not only celebrates the academy but also offers an imaginative, somewhat fanciful depiction of France's literary culture in the first part of the century.

Furetière's narrative divides the literary world into two rival camps. The country of "Rhetoric and Eloquence," led by the Queen of Good Sense, is at war with the land of "Pedantry," ruled by Galimatias (a term that can be translated as rubbish or balderdash). Furetière lists virtually every contemporary literary figure of note, certainly every academician, among partisans of the former camp—writers like Balzac, Chapelain, Scarron, Malherbe, Vincent Voiture, Jean Ogier de Gombauld, Valentin Conrart, and others, most of whom we will meet in the following pages. And he includes men like François de La Mothe le Vayer and Nicolas-Claude Fabri de Peiresc, who, though certainly not pedants, were eminent *érudits*, tending to keep their distance from these fashionable *gens de lettres*. In Furetière's allegory, however, the inhabitants of Pedantry remain nameless. Their ranks include "Arabs and Rabbis, Greeks and Romans"; they are associated with "all kinds of nations"; their capital is called "Gymnasie," where "all sorts of languages are spoken." In Furetière's mind, the country of Pedantry is clearly the realm of erudition, both scholastic and humanistic.[1]

Furetière's allegory contains several features of interest, not the least of which is how it abounds in references to actual writers and institutions constituting the literary culture of the first half of the seventeenth century. But it also provides a retrospective brief for the *mondain*, or worldly, culture that took root in a public of lay readers. The writers Furetière places at the center of his allegory were the prime fashioners of a literary movement that subsequent scholars have identified as classicism (or sometimes with the qualification pre-classicism). In most cases,

---

[1] Antoine Furetière, *Nouvelle allégorique, ou, Histoire des derniers troubles arrivez au royaume d'éloquence* (Paris, 1658). This text is also discussed by Alain Viala in *Naissance de l'écrivain: Sociologie de la littérature à l'âge classique* (Paris, 1985), but used differently than I use it here. See also the recent edition with commentary by Mathilde Bombart and Nicolas Schapira (Toulouse, 2004).

Dignified Retreat: Writers and Intellectuals in the Age of Richelieu. Robert A. Schneider, Oxford University Press (2019).
© Robert A. Schneider. DOI: 10.1093/oso/9780198826323.001.0001

they were disciples of François de Malherbe and followers of his so-called doctrine, which vaunted clarity, order, and *bienséance* as the supreme values for literary French. Their critics called them "purists," a label that, while somewhat misleading, has stuck. In the larger context of seventeenth- and eighteenth-century intellectual history, they stand out as "moderns," as opposed to those who hewed to the tradition of the "ancients." Whatever we call them, these writers dominated the literary scene: they were responsible for the enormous literary productivity that marks the early part of the century; they formed the core of the first generation of the French Academy; they furthered the progress of the French vernacular as a language capable of literary excellence, equal to the standards of the ancients or the Italians; and they also engaged in a series of very public and quite contentious "quarrels," most of which had something to do with establishing common understandings regarding the rules for literary expression. The more learned discussions and commentaries gave rise to what in retrospect can be seen as the first moves toward literary criticism. For Alain Viala, it was this generation of writers that witnessed the creation of a literary "field." It might be said as well that literature, conceived as a self-sustaining cultural sphere, with its own traditions and its own patrons and public, was then born.

That Furetière should enshrine the Queen of Good Sense as the heroine of his allegory and represent her enemies as partisans of Pedantry speaks to the whole literary culture he strove to characterize. For this antinomy was fundamental; it was part and parcel of the emerging code of *honnêteté*, which increasingly defined the ethos of elite culture. Whatever else the *honnête homme* was, he was certainly not a pedant. The attack on pedantry was one of the persistent themes among men of letters of the period. Faret asserted that the *honnête homme* should rather study from the "great book of the world than from Aristotle." Malherbe defined his literary project in direct opposition to those who limited their appeal to a learned audience, which he identified as the strategy of the poets of the last century. "I do not prepare my meats for chefs," he sniffed. His disciple and biographer, the poet Honorat de Bueil, siegneur de Racan, declared that he meant his verses to be read "in the King's cabinet and the *ruelles* [salons], rather than in his study or in those of other savants in poetry."[2] Virtually every writer and even many savants managed to get around to casting scorn on that least desirable of figures, the pedant; it may have been the one characteristic everyone could agree upon of a true man or woman of letters. And the nature of their condemnation makes clear that pedantry is not only undesirable or ridiculous but noxious, an obstacle to a more appealing, engaged type of learning and letters. In his *Projet de l'Académie*, Faret barred savants from the ranks of the French Academy, because "the most learned are often the least able to express their thoughts and to judge correctly works of

---

[2] Both quotations from Racan, *Vie de Malherbe*, ed. Marie-Françoise Quignard (Paris, 1991), 44.

Eloquence."[3] Balzac went even further, banishing them from civil society; in *Le Prince* he declared, "I scorn those savants who only know things that are never used.... I disapprove of Doctors who use their doctrine as much as misers their wealth... who take the means for the end and the paths for the towns. Those sorts of people are ill-suited for civil life.... They should be purged from common society... as superfluities of the Republic."[4] The attack on pedantry was a theme of perhaps the most successful comic novel of the early part of the century, Charles Sorel's *Francion*. One of the major characters, Hortensius, is mocked for his useless knowledge and lack of true understanding of the world. When he responds to some advice offered by Francion, he defends his ignorance of practical matters by claiming that he "had never noticed it in any book." Francion replies, "the best book you could consult is the experience of the world." "I only commit fashionable blunders," Hortensius responds. "I conduct myself according to the ancients."[5] Francion himself bitterly complains about his stilted and useless education at the hands of a teacher whose idea of pedagogy was endlessly to pose questions to his young charges regarding words. A free and irreverent spirit, Francion is usually thought of as the prototypical libertine, but he also embodied the new spirit of learning and letters that saw language and literature as aspects of aristocratic culture.

The attack on pedantry was broad-based, cutting across various literary and intellectual camps; it even drew the *érudits* of the Dupuy cabinet into its ranks. It was a fundamental and telling trope of the early seventeenth century. More than a pointed assault on erudition and the learning of the schools, it was a defining element of a literary and intellectual movement that strove to transform language, with profound implications for elite culture as a whole.

But was the early part of the seventeenth century really the crucial moment in this movement? In terms of a critique of pedantry, one problem is immediately apparent: it was a commonplace of the sixteenth century. Montaigne's essays "Of Pedantry" and "Of the Education of Children" are two of the best-known expressions of this sentiment, but he himself notes that in his youth "the finest gentlemen were those who held teachers most in contempt," and then adds, "witness our good Du Bellay [who wrote]: 'But I hate above all pedantic learning.'"[6] Even a cursory knowledge of humanistic literature, from Erasmus to Rabelais and others, reveals a perennial concern with meretricious erudition, the unsociable ways of scholars, and the stultifying, soporific effects of knowledge for knowledge's sake. Erasmus's *Ciceronianus* was a humanistic critique of humanism, which bemoaned

---

[3] Nicolas Faret, *Projet de l'Académie, pour servir de préface à ses statuts*, ed. Jean Rousselet (Saint-Etienne, 1983), 48.

[4] Balzac, *Le Prince*, 2nd ed. (Paris, 1632), 130.

[5] On this, see F.-E. Sutcliffe, *Le réalisme de Charles Sorel* (Paris, 1965), 176. Hortensius, however, was seen as a send-up of Balzac.

[6] "Of Pedantry," in *The Complete Essays of Montaigne*, trans. Donald Frame (Stanford, 1958), I: 25, on 97.

the strict adherence to Cicero's style as a pedantic exercise that failed to revive the Roman writer's spirit.[7] Humanist erudition, of course, was itself forged in the teeth of a critique of scholastic teaching, a critique that plays on the antinomy between erudition for the schools and learning that engages with life in the city.

Was there, then, nothing new to the seventeenth-century attack on pedantry, or was it merely a continuation of the humanistic campaign against the same enemy? In fact, pedantry here should be seen as a stand-in for a larger critique that struck at the heart of a campaign to reform the French language, a campaign ultimately understood under the mantle of "purism." It amounted to a concerted effort to elevate French to the level where it would rival or equal the expressive capacities of Latin and Greek and surpass Italian, the reigning European vernacular in terms of prestige. And it strove for more, as we shall see. The reform of language, then, is one of the basic strands in the history of this period—to be placed alongside the emergence of so-called absolutism as fashioning its master narrative. I would insist, however, that we should view them as proceeding along separate, perhaps parallel, tracks—but not intersecting. For one of my arguments here and elsewhere in this book is that a reformed French vernacular in this crucial period of its history emerged from a literary culture that, if not necessarily autonomous, had little to do with the efforts of the crown and royal court.

One might be forgiven for thinking otherwise, for there are powerful reasons for seeing language in general, and the French language in particular, as following an inexorable historical logic. Generally, linguistic evolution over time appears to be characterized by convergence, homogenization, standardization, and in general many, many more losers than winners in the fight for survival. And for French, it is usually assumed that the centralized state guided it along this same course of development. Across the centuries, this development might be seen in three moments: The first was the promulgation of the Villers-Cotterets Ordinance in 1539, which stipulated that all "decrees and other proceedings" be "spoken, written, and given to the parties [concerned] in the French mother tongue, and not otherwise"—which is to say, not in Latin. A century later, in 1635, the preamble of the constitution of the new Académie française explains its creation as the culmination of a process of France's triumphant transformation ever since the Wars of Religion. The king has been preoccupied with "remedying the disorders created by the civil wars that long afflicted us." Now, however, he is ready "to ensure that Sciences and Arts flourish," chief among them "eloquence." The new academy was thereby charged with the "perfection" of the French language. Finally, a century and half later, it became one of the Revolutionary government's main tasks to impose French on its polyglot population, an aspect of an effort—radical and widespread in its compass—that the French historian Mona Ozouf

---

[7] See Richard Waswo, "Theories of Language," in Glyn P. Norton, ed., *The Cambridge History of Literary Criticism*, vol. 3: *The Renaissance* (Cambridge, 1999), 25–35.

calls "the homogenization of mankind."[8] To these moments we might add the more prolonged process, fundamental to the political culture of the Third Republic, of turning peasants into French-speaking Frenchmen and women.[9]

If we were to accept this historical account, then, it follows that the Académie française, and through it the monarchy, played a crucial role in the "perfection" of the French language. It did not.[10] Instead of celebrating the academy as the promulgator of this development, we should see this institution rather as its *result*. In other words, the reform of language was not *dirigiste*—or *Colbertist avant la lettre*—in origin. A movement of linguistic reform was set in motion well before the founding of the academy in 1635, creating the conditions, both discursive and social, for the successful transformation of French. This movement was broad-based and varied, animated by a cohort of writers featured in Furetière's parable: Malherbe, Balzac, Chapelain, Conrart, Antoine Godeau, and many others. These were *gens de lettres* who by circa 1630 had not only made a convincing case for their view of language but also, in securing the support of a public of Parisian aristocrats, managed to legitimize their status as "writers," or what Nicolas Schapira, in his study of Valentin Conrart, calls "professionals of letters."[11] Many of these writers were also attached to Cardinal Richelieu in one way or another, and a good portion of the forty original members of the Académie française were recruited from their midst when it was founded in 1635.

The story has been told many times, from the fundamental accounts by Ferdinand Brunot and Antoine Adam, to Fumaroli's magisterial study, to Viala's Bourdieu-inspired analysis, to the more recent works by Merlin-Kajman, Jouhaud, and others. There can be no attempt to duplicate those studies here.[12] Rather, in what follows I want to demonstrate that this was indeed a movement—that it drew upon a host of fellow travelers, and that it was socially organized in a range of associations, many entailing the participation of aristocratic men and women. A small but formidable group of ambitious *gens de lettres* galvanized this movement—men who not only shared a commitment to the "purist" vision of

---

[8] Quoted by David A. Bell, "Lingua Populi, Lingua Dei: Language, Religion, and the Origins of French Revolutionary Nationalism," *American Historical Review*, 100/1 (1995), 1403–37.

[9] On attempts to promote French under the Third Republic, see Eugene Weber, *Peasants into Frenchmen: The Modernization of Rural France, 1870–1914* (Stanford, 1976), chap. 18.

[10] For a sustained argument along these same lines, see Paul Cohen, "Courtly French, Learned Latin, and Peasant Patois: The Making of a National Language in Early Modern France" (PhD diss., Princeton University, 2001). For a recent example of the analysis associating the development of French with the monarchy (or the state), see Jacques Derrida, "If There Is Cause to Translate I: Philosophy in Its National Language (Toward a 'licterature en françois')," in Derrida, *Eyes of the University: Right to Philosophy 2*, trans. Jan Plug et al. (Stanford, 2004), 1–19.

[11] Nicolas Schapira, *Un professionnel des lettres au XVIIe siècle: Valentin Conrart, une histoire sociale* (Paris, 2003).

[12] Ferdinand Brunot, *Histoire de la langue française: Des origines à nos jours*, vol. 3: *La formation de la langue classique (1600–60)* (Paris, 1909); and Ferdinand Brunot, *La doctrine de Malherbe, d'après son commentaire sur Desportes* (1891; reprint, Paris, 1969). Antoine Adam, *Histoire de la littérature française au XVIIe siècle*, 3rd ed., 3 vols. (Paris, 1997). See also the works already cited by Fumaroli, Viala, Merlin-Kajman, and Jouhaud.

French but who were also linked by friendship, common endeavors, and various modes of association and interaction.[13]

Turning to this movement, let us first look at several leading "purists": Malherbe, Balzac, and Vaugelas. Pairing each with a critic—respectively, Marie de Gournay, Jean-Pierre Camus, and François de La Mothe le Vayer—I want to suggest that one indication of this movement's force and novelty is that it gave rise to a robust opposition. The purist movement, then, occasioned a sustained "quarrel"—only one of several during the century—over its merits and legitimacy. "Movement" and "quarrel" are thus key terms, one giving rise to the other. For the latter, it has been noted that for those involving participants with no formal status and which transpired outside an academic or judicial setting where disputations were both routine and highly regulated, there was always the risk of the contest spinning out of control.[14] And it was precisely this concern that prompted an

---

[13] Lest one conclude that what I am calling a movement was monolithic and entirely cohesive, it should be noted that several figures contributed to the reform of French but did so from somewhat different positions than Malherbe, Chapelain, and their confreres. For example, Guillaume du Vair, the eminent Gallican magistrate and royal officer, endorsed a sort of revised Ciceronianism. While he criticized the style of oratory practiced in the Parlement of Paris for its showy erudition and excessive reliance on citations, he still vaunted the oratorical mode. His *De l'éloquence françoise* (1594) advocated a speech that was clear and unmannered, capable, in a Platonic sense, of promoting harmony among its auditors. In his idealistic view, the Gallican magistrate could once again don the mantle of the philosopher-orator whose healing speech would spread like harmonious music over the people, fostering a city of "well-ordered assemblies and communities united under the banner of holy and just laws." Du Vair, *De l'éloquence françoise et des raisons pourquoy elle est demeurée si basse*, in *Les oeuvres de messire Guillaume du Vair* (Paris, 1641 ed.), 395. Honoré d'Urfé, the author of *L'Astrée*, also contributed to a reformed French, especially evident in the successive volumes of his pastoral epic. In a painstakingly close study of the more than five thousand pages of the epic, literary scholar Anne Sancier-Chateau has documented the myriad changes d'Urfé made between the first edition and subsequent versions, changes not merely on the order of corrections, elisions, or additions. She finds a consistent pattern in favor of eliminating "embarrassing and incoherent passages" in order to make the text more reader-friendly. In point of fact, she finds that "there were no changes to the text that went in the other direction." Although d'Urfé was never the master of a school, ready to indoctrinate his students like Malherbe, it nevertheless seems that he was a precocious practitioner of a reformed vernacular style whose impact, given the legion of readers of *L'Astrée*, cannot be underestimated. Anne Sancier-Chateau, *Une esthetique nouvelle: Honoré d'Urfé, correcteur de* L'Astrée *(1607-25)* (Geneva, 1995). See also Wendy Ayres-Bennett, "Enfin D'Urfé vint?," *Seventeenth-Century French Studies*, 18 (1996), 177–80. Finally, perhaps the most surprising advocate for a new kind of French vernacular was Pierre Dupuy, who with his brother Jacques presided over their "cabinet," a prestigious center of savant life. On one level, the Dupuys were at ground zero of the opposition to the purists. Certainly this was the case during the quarrel over Balzac's *Lettres*. But in a short biography written in 1651, after his death, Nicolas Rigault, an intimate of the cabinet, made very clear that Pierre's choice of the vernacular placed him among his contemporaries who understood that linguistic reform was the order of the day. According to Rigault, he came to believe that it was a "detestable habit for both preachers and lawyers to corrupt their discourses in sprinkling their sentences with Latin and Greek words." Rather, "he judged it suitable so as to be understood more easily and quickly by our fellow citizens, to conceive and fashion his works in our language," judging Latin "ineffective...to directly reach the ears of the least accustomed." All quotes from Marc Fumaroli, "Aux origines érudites du grand goût classique: L'*Optimus stylus gallicus* selon Pierre Dupuy," in Pierre Aquilon, Jacques Chupeau, and François Weil, comps., *L'intelligence du passé: Les faits, l'écriture et le sens: Mélanges offerts à Jean Lafond par ses amis* (Tours, 1988), 185–95.

[14] Antoine Lilti, "Querelles et controverses: Les forms du désaccord intellectuel à l'époque moderne," *Mil neuf cent: Revue d'histoire intellectuelle*, 1/25 (2007), 13–28.

imposed closure of the "Querelle *Le Cid*." It is interesting to note, however, that apart from the dust-up over Balzac's *Lettres*, a sustained, intractable quarrel was not occasioned by this opposition. Indeed, the purists' critics were not dogmatic; as we shall see, they too were in many respects open to the spirit of language reform, an indication that in this quarrel—as in many—the argument was joined precisely because the opposing disputants shared some fundamental convictions.

As important as such key figures as Malherbe and Balzac were, it is imperative to look beyond them in order to appreciate the wide support behind the drive to reform French, which is especially evident in the various associations devoted to this cause. And this further supports the view that it was indeed a movement. The Parisian cityscape was distinguished by a plethora of groups, some composed only of *gens de lettres*, others a mixed assortment of aristocrats and other elites and writers, that characterized the urban sociability of the period. This constituted a sort of infrastructure that enabled this movement. Finally, I will look at a particular aspect of this movement—the effort to translate (mostly) ancient texts into French as a concerted attempt to render these important writings accessible to those educated, literate French men and women whom *gens de lettres* saw as their principal public.

Purists and the Opposition

François de Malherbe and Marie de Gournay

François de Malherbe (1555–1628) spent most of his life trying to gain a foothold in the princely and royal circle of literary patrons, with only mixed success.[15] The son of a *conseiller* in the *présidial* court in Caen, he spent a formative period in Aix, where he gained the friendship of both Guillaume du Vair and Peiresc. It was probably under the influence of these two *érudits* that he immersed himself in Neo-Stoicism. He translated several texts of Seneca, thus aligning himself with a new trend that saw the transmission of ancient wisdom to a readership ignorant of ancient languages as an important task for an erudite *homme de lettres*. In 1605 he accompanied Du Vair and Peiresc to Paris, where he remained, with some periods of absence, mostly in pursuit of various patrons, for the rest of his life. He died in 1628, embittered by his lack of royal support and exhausted by his futile attempts to have the man who killed his son in a duel brought to justice.

Malherbe's published poetic output during his lifetime was rather meager; his most significant writings reached the public in a serious of *recueils* (collections), which featured other poets who were largely his followers.[16] Rather, his reputation

---

[15] On Malherbe, see Brunot, *La doctrine de Malherbe*; Claude K. Abraham, *Enfin Malherbe: The Influence of Malherbe on French Lyric Prosody, 1605–1674* (Lexington, KY, 1971); Renée Weingarten, *French Lyric Poetry in the Age of Malherbe* (Manchester, 1954).

[16] On Malherbe's reluctance to have his verses printed, reflecting an "aristocratic amateurism" and disdain for that mode of publicity, especially in contrast to Balzac's strategy with his *Lettres*, see

stems from his "Doctrine," and his importance, most famously and pithily captured by Nicolas Boileau's "Enfin Malherbe vint," as the progenitor of French classicism and the founder of modern French. This so-called "Doctrine," however, is encrusted with myths and misconceptions. Malherbe was hardly the single-handed reformer that commentators have made him out to be; other contemporaries shared in his convictions on how to refashion the French language. His "Doctrine" was nothing of the kind, at least if understood as a set of coherent principles and prescriptions. Rather, it has been reconstructed post hoc from his various comments and criticisms, and especially from the extensive "corrections" scrawled on the texts of poems of his rival at court, Philippe Desportes. It is from this commentary that Ferdinand Brunot, the great early twentieth-century historian of the French language, managed to put together a deceptively coherent doctrine that in retrospect appears like the ideology of a premeditated literary campaign.[17]

Nevertheless, Malherbe's impact as a reformer cannot be denied; his reputation as a dogmatic corrector is well earned. The poet saw French literary discourse of his time as riddled with foreign and antiquated words, vocabularies that were technical in nature, inconsistencies in grammar, spelling, and verb formation, obscure references and formulations, and vulgar and "provincial" expressions. He took the attack on "pedantry" to new levels; not only did he scorn the mythological allusions that abounded in the humanistic poetry of the previous generation, but in his correspondence he even condemned the likes of Erasmus and Lipsius as pedants. According to his disciple and biographer, Racan, he had no respect for the Greeks, and thought that Pindar was nothing more than a "Galimatias." As much as the previous century's poets had emulated the Italians, he was dismissive of the literary traditions across the Alps. Even Petrarch's sonnets were hardly worthy of his consideration.[18] More than anything, he maintained his insistence on clarity and regularity in poetic diction, even at the price of inspiration. Or even accuracy: critics attacked his translations for lack of faithfulness to the original meaning of the text. His response was that he failed to see the purpose of writing for two or three experts. "He wrote his verses to be read in the bedroom of the king and in the *ruelles* of ladies rather than in his room or in those of other savants in poetry," writes Racan.[19]

Mathilde Bombart, *Guez de Balzac et la querelle des* Lettres: *Ecriture, polémique, et critique dans la France du premier XVIIe siècle* (Paris, 2007), 204–5. For his life and career, see Antoine Adam, "Introduction," in *Oeuvres de François de Malherbe*, ed. Adam (Paris, 1971), x–xxvi.

[17] Malherbe's teachings did not represent such a dramatic break with the literary traditions of the sixteenth century, especially that of Ronsard and the Pléiade, as it is sometimes claimed. Malherbe's "triumph" was not total; nor were his supposed followers of one mind as to the virtue of his prescriptions. Shortly after his death, in fact, many reacted against the severity and rigidity of his teachings, finding that they went too far in emphasizing form and regularity at the expense of inspiration. Brunot, *La doctrine de Malherbe*.

[18] Racan, *Vie de Malherbe*, 21. [19] Racan, *Vie de Malherbe*, 44.

His influence was probably felt less through his poems and other writings than in the sessions at his Paris house, where, in the company of an assortment of aspiring poets, he held forth nightly. Racan, who was always present, left an account of these soirees, which suggests that if Malherbe had anything approaching a doctrine, it was largely oral and demonstrative in nature. He seems to have been an inveterate pedagogue. Sometimes he would read aloud from poets both ancient and modern, including Desportes and Pierre de Ronsard, savagely pointing out the excesses, obscurities, and inconsistencies that marred their texts. Other times he would instruct his acolytes by punctiliously combing through their own literary efforts, filling the margins with his comments and corrections. Malherbe was imperious intellectually but also in manner. He brooked no opposition, complaining to Balzac about those "barn owls" who dared to criticize his views—even more, who "expend all efforts to deny me the public voice that has long been conferred upon me."[20] This was a man convinced of his mission.[21]

The other avenue of Malherbe's influence was in the *recueils* that were popular publishing ventures of the time. Malherbe's works begin to appear in various *recueils* soon after his arrival in Paris. In 1609, two years after his exit from the court and his greater identification with the city, François de Rosset published *Nouveau recueil des plus beaux vers de ce temps*, a collection of poems by Malherbe and his disciples, including Racan, François de Cauvigny de Colomby, Charles de Pyard Touvant, and François Maynard, the whole volume dedicated to Malherbe's mistress, the Vicomtesse d'Auchy.[22] In a publication of 1627, *Recueil des plus beaux vers*, Malherbe's dominance is striking: the volume features sixty-two of his works. The editor notes that the collection consists of poems by the master and "those he acknowledges as his students."[23]

Racan famously recorded what posterity has taken to be the essence of Malherbe's doctrine: that when asked about a particular question of usage, he answered that one should ordinarily consult the street porters (*crocheteurs*) of Paris, who in his estimation were the real masters of the French language. He did not mean by this that lower-class workers should actually serve as the arbiters of linguistic usage; but he did mean that *usage*, and present-day usage, as opposed to foreign or ancient sources, should be the touchstone of correct speech and writing. Pierre de Deimier, a writer who very likely was within Malherbe's orbit, gave

---

[20] Quoted in René Winegarten, "A Neglected Critic of Malherbe: Jacques Favereau," *French Studies*, 6/1 (1952), 33.

[21] One evening, when François Maynard, a major poet and president in the Parlement of Toulouse, was present, someone began banging on the door asking, "Monsieur le président, is he here?" Malherbe barged outside and yelled at the poor man, "What president are you looking for? Learn this, there is no other president here than me!" Racan, *Vie de Malherbe*, 21–2.

[22] Adam, *Oeuvres de Malherbe*, 13.

[23] Unpublished paper by Deborah Blocker, Deborah Blocker. "Une négligence etudiée: ordres et recompositions dans le *Recueil de lettres nouvelles*," presented at the annual meeting of the Society for the Study of French History, 2004, Paris. on the *recueils*, see Bombart, *Guez de Balzac*, 36–7.

voice to his sentiments in *L'académie de l'art poétique* (1610). For him, obscurity is the enemy, which means that clarity must be the poet's watchword. "This is why to write obscurely and not to wish to be understood are the same thing. It would be better... to produce nothing than to write amidst clouds of obscurity."[24] While subsequent generations would judge Malherbe severely as only constraining the boundaries of expression with his dogmatic emphasis on regularity and propriety, for contemporaries he participated in fostering a liberating trend that served to enlarge French literary expression to accommodate the interests and understanding of aristocratic men and women, who were largely bypassed by the erudite humanism of the previous century.

A poet to his bones, Malherbe nevertheless maintained a rather diminished status for poetry, at least compared to his celebrated predecessors of the Pléiade. For them, poetry was a sacred calling; the true poet was possessed of an esoteric wisdom, combining encyclopedic knowledge with mystical understanding, which he then channeled through his verses. Poets like Ronsard and Clément Marot were visionaries who not only embodied humanism at its best but also were bearers of the hermetic tradition, which, Frances Yates argues, offered a combined intellectual and spiritual way out of the bloody impasse of religious and sectarian warfare.[25] For these poets, the "word" had a sacred quality, a power and majesty conferred, of course, by the Christian tradition but with pagan roots as well. In sixteenth-century France, as noted, the myth of the Gallic Hercules was frequently deployed to elevate the role of the orator, king, or poet—that is, those authorized to stir the assembled to virtuous action. For a poet like Ronsard, this myth vaunted not only kingship but more generally eloquence, and thus the status of the poet as the vehicle for true and virtuous eloquence.[26]

Compared to this elevated conception of the poet, Malherbe seemed to embrace a rather debased notion of their vocation. But this only highlights a self-conscious rejection of his predecessors, giving rise to the worldly, or *mondain*, orientation of the writer. Malherbe demonstrated his disapproval of Ronsard's poetry by blackening out half the text of his collected verses and filling the margins with scathing commentary on those left untouched.[27] He famously, and rather facetiously, gave voice to this devalued sense of his own calling, proclaiming "that it was silly to make verses and hope for any other reward than one's own amusement, and that a good poet was no more useful to the State than a good skittles player."[28]

As is often the case with those who take it upon themselves to promote significant changes, Malherbe's success as a reformer was undoubtedly due in large part to his strong convictions and uncompromising attitude, something borne out in Racan's biography. He was an irrepressible critic of anything and anyone who

---

[24] Pierre de Deimier, *L'académie de l'art poétique* (Paris, 1610), 258.
[25] Frances Yates, *French Academies of the Sixteenth Century* (London, 1947), chap. 12.
[26] On Hercules, see the Introduction.   [27] Racan, *Vie de Malherbe*, 37–8.
[28] Racan, *Vie de Malherbe*, 36–7.

offended his linguistic convictions. But for all his misanthropy and general unpleasantness, when it came to his friends and disciples, he was loyal and generous to a fault. They were the faithful, devoted foot soldiers in his campaign to transform the language of the realm. And a campaign it was; the reform of French did not simply happen—it was waged by a generation of *gens de lettres* of sundry stripes. But it undoubtedly benefited from being spearheaded by such a single-minded crusader.[29]

* * *

Malherbe was certainly not without critics, and chief among them was his near-contemporary Marie le Jars de Gournay (1566–1645).[30] One of the most original writers of her day, she is largely remembered as the *"fille d'alliance"* of Michel de Montaigne. It is true that Montaigne made her his literary executor; she was responsible for editing the posthumous editions of the *Essays*, which alone would reserve her a place in literary history. But her importance goes well beyond a privileged relationship with the famous essayist. Sorel referred to her as "la Docte et Vertueuse Demoiselle de Gournay."[31] She published many works in her lifetime; she was a conspicuous figure on the literary scene, the animator of her own "academy," and a forceful commentator on and critic of contemporary literary trends. And while she certainly admired Montaigne's writings, she identified as much with the Pléiade poets and a few later *gens de lettres*, including the Cardinal Du Perron, whose example she continued to celebrate in the face of the "purist" fashion.[32]

Born in Paris to a family of minor nobles and officers in 1566, Gournay was almost completely self-taught, learning Latin and even some Greek on her own. When she was barely 20, she conceived a passion for Montaigne's *Essays*, which ultimately led to a meeting between the 55-year-old writer and his young acolyte. After his death she became his literary executor. The first posthumous edition of the *Essays* (1595) was published under her supervision; she also supplied a preface. For the ten editions that followed, she continued her editorial care, amending the text and, in 1617, translating the many passages by ancient authors. In 1594 she

---

[29] Marc Fumaroli, "Sous le signe de Protée," in Jean Mesnard, ed., *Précis de littérature française du XVIIe siècle* (Paris, 1990), 91: "La 'doctrine de Malherbe' n'est pas une fiction de Ferdinand Brunot, mais un point de ralliement des forces vives de la culture française impatiente de se donner à l'Europe comme la nouvelle 'culture classique' pour les modernes."

[30] On Marie de Gournay, see Michèle Fogel, *Marie de Gournay* (Paris, 2004); Margaret Ilsley, *A Daughter of the Renaissance: Marie le Jars de Gournay, Her Life and Works* (The Hague, 1963); Carol Pal, *Republic of Women: Rethinking the Republic of Letters in the Seventeenth Century* (Cambridge, 2012), 78–97; Alan M. Boase, *The Fortunes of Montaigne: A History of the Essays in France, 1580–1669* (London, 1935), 48–76; Rebecca M. Wilkin, *Women, Imagination and the Search for Truth in Early Modern France* (Burlington, VT, 2008), 177–82.

[31] Charles Sorel, *La bibliothèque française* (1667), édition critique, ed. Filippo d'Angelo, Mathilde Bombart, Laurence Giavarini, Claudine Nédelec, Dinah Ribard, Michèle Rosellini, and Alain Viala (Paris, 2015), 140.

[32] For her relationship with Montaigne as well as contemporaries' views of Gournay, see especially Maryanne Cline Horowitz, "Marie de Gournay, Editor of the *Essais* of Michel de Montaigne: A Case-Study in Mentor-Protégée Friendship," *Sixteenth-Century Journal*, 17/3 (1986), 272–84.

published *Le proumenoir de M. de Montaigne*, a tragic love story that served as a vehicle for her mentor's ideas. She continued to write, publish, and edit many works until her death in 1645. Two collections of her writings appeared in her lifetime, *L'ombre de la damoiselle de Gournay* (1626) and *Les advis ou les presens de la damoiselle de Gournay* (1634 and 1641).

A writer to be reckoned with for the originality of her writings and her unfashionable opinions, she was notorious for her strong and, it seems, somewhat contentious personality. Sometimes celebrated, sometimes ridiculed, she surfaces in many contemporary observations and letters, including several satires on the creation of the Académie française. While she is often singled out both for her views and for her gender, suffering from the typical misogynistic resentment one would expect for an accomplished woman in her day, she was hardly isolated. She maintained personal ties with a range of French *gens de lettres*, including Théophile de Viau, Balzac, François Le Metel de Boisrobert, Michel de Marolles, and Colletet, as well as others outside France, such as Antoine Rivet, Anna Maria van Schurman, and especially Justus Lipsius, with whom she conducted a long correspondence. One could easily place her in the ranks of the emerging Republic of Letters. Comfortable in the world of the *grands* and at court, she is reputed to have received a pension from Richelieu, although this is not certain.[33] She wrote on a number of different subjects, from court affairs and current events to poetry, language, and religion. Unlike most of her fellow writers, who tended to identify with Gallicanism, she was a staunch supporter of the Jesuits.

While Gournay was a forthright advocate for the education of women and the legitimacy of female writers, it was not her proto-feminist views that caused waves among her fellow writers. Rather, she was one of the first both to register the success of the purists' reforms and to push back with vigorous critique. Gournay's attack on the "*nouvelle Bande*," as she called Malherbe and his disciples, was sustained and vigorous—she was hardly coy or oblique in her criticisms. In her eyes, their efforts amounted to nothing less than demoting poetry to something ordinary, tasteless, and weak, lacking in the nobility and inventiveness that characterized the poets of the Pléiade. For her, it came down to juxtaposing a rhetorically rich sixteenth century, with Montaigne, Rabelais, Ronsard, and the other Pléiade poets as well as Du Perron in the forefront, against their paltry successors of her day. After a visit to one of the city's leading salons, she commented with disgust, "I have just left a house where I saw thrown to the winds the precious ashes of Ronsard and his contemporary poets with as much impudence as these ignorant people could manage."[34]

---

[33] Fogel, *Marie de Gournay*, 275.

[34] Marie de Gournay, "Deffence de la poesie et du langage des poëtes," in Gournay, *Oeuvres complètes*, ed. Jean-Claude Arnould, 2 vols. (Paris, 2002), I: 1081. See also Jean-Philippe Beaulieu and Hannah Fournier, "'Les interests du sexe': Dédicataires féminins et réseaux de sociabilité chez Marie de Gournay," *Renaissance and Reformation*, no. 1 (2004), 54.

But her critique was not limited to poetic diction; her concern was for the very health and vitality of language itself. And, as was her wont, her critique was full-throated, especially when it came to her charge that these "doctors in the art of speaking" were intent on impoverishing the French language. "They want to kick language in the stomach in order to cause an abortion."[35] Their reforms would only deprive it of the "of its bold and generous expression," yielding a language merely "sweet and soft."[36] She described her forebears' language with an assortment of qualities—"abundance, generosity, genius, and the hope of enrichment."[37] The purists' efforts were "impotent and weak." She preferred stronger stuff: "Works that shine with vivid descriptions or images, with invention, with boldness, with generosity, and whose lively, florid, and poetic richness would allow for three times as much freedom as [the purists] want to deny it."[38]

Marie de Gournay's own use of language is striking in its aggressive and conversational tone: she confronts the reader directly with her palpable outrage and impatience. Interestingly, there is a gendered quality to her critique, a critique, however, that does not conform to the terms one might expect. Unusual among her contemporaries as a visible female writer—and certainly not hesitant about demanding the recognition she knew she deserved—Gournay was scathing when it came to the influence of women, especially the *salonnières* and their hangers-on. Moreover, her sense of language is virile, with an emphasis on strength, vitality, majesty, and the like, while the purists' preferences yield "impotence" and "sweetness." This is not unconnected to what she sees as the real source of the pitiable state of the French language at the present. Indeed, she blames less Malherbe (whom she names only once) and the small-minded "grammarians" than the courtiers and (especially) ladies who frequent the Louvre and the salons: "the tender Nymphes and their pampered *ruelles*," "the lilies of the court," the "baby-doll teachers," who presume to lay down the law about language and books.[39]

In Gournay's view, poetry had fallen from the exalted position it once occupied with the Pléiade. Referring to the purists, she lamented their cavalier debasement of the "furious" inspiration of the gods, "that great, magnanimous, powerful Empress of Poetry." "Would they prefer that we become their disciples, after being those of Apollo? Or rather that he himself should become their pupil, for they have erased his laws and imposed others on us."[40] Her summary of the purists' views is not inaccurate, though somewhat tendentious: "Excellence and perfection in the principles of language consists, according to their opinion, in fleeing certain words and phrases that the ordinary speakers of the court do not use;

---

[35] Gournay, "Deffence de la poesie," 1106.   [36] Gournay, "Deffence de la poesie," 1154.
[37] Marie de Gournay, "Du langage françois," in *Oeuvres completes*, I: 696.
[38] Gournay, "Deffence de la poesie," 1176.
[39] Gournay, "Deffence de la poesie," 1101, 1112–13, 1117, 1138, for these and other similar quotes. See also Linda Timmermans, *L'accès des femmes à la culture (1598–1715)* (Paris, 1993), 134–5.
[40] Quoted in Giovanna Devincenzo, *Marie de Gournay: Un cas littéraire* (Paris, 2002), 67.

words borrowed from Latin, or old words, or those derived from other terms, or those of principal origins—these too they reproach."[41] For the sake of clarity and consistency, they were willing to sacrifice innovation and creativity.[42]

From the purists' perspectives, Gournay's views were outdated and old-fashioned—what we might call conservative. In this context, however, the "conservative" position was on the side of experimentation and novelty, of inventiveness and daring in formulating new metaphors. She finds particularly objectionable the Malherbians' general disapproval of metaphorical language, so much so that she provides a list of metaphors, culled from one of her favorite writers, Cardinal Du Perron, which are "indigestible to the vulgar," that is to say the purists.[43] And she refuses to accept their categorical prohibition against borrowing from other languages simply because some ancient writers were also of this opinion. Her reasoning here identifies her as an "ancient" with regard to the relative richness of French as compared to Latin and Greek. Yes, she admits, these ancient writers were of this opinion, but "the circumstances are completely opposite: the imperfection of our language and the perfection of theirs, that is, Latin and Greek, means that innovation and additions are necessary for our French, but not so for these two ancient idioms." Moreover, she adds, "I do not know of any language that has attained such a level as to renounce all amplification and culture."[44]

In truth, the purists were not so rigid about linguistic change as Gournay makes them out to be. As we shall see with Vaugelas, in resorting to the authority of "usage," she conceded that French would naturally evolve and change with time. And while she rarely had a good word for works of her contemporary *gens de lettres*, Gournay still was welcome in their company;[45] some undoubtedly harbored similar misgivings regarding the more doctrinaire strictures of the purists. Balzac found much of value in Gournay's critique; he praised her learning and wisdom, as well as her longevity, confiding his own doubts about some aspects of current literary fashion. Gournay herself was not so dogmatic as to fail to recognize that the cherished works of her sixteenth-century heroes were in some respects in need of editorial care in order to render them readable for contemporaries. After all, it was she who decided to translate the many Latin quotations in Montaigne's *Essays*. She even suggested editing Ronsard's poems, eliminating the anachronisms and infelicities that rendered his verses less

---

[41] Gournay, "Du langage françois," 694–5.
[42] See Bombart, *Guez de Balzac*, 195–7, for an interesting exchange between Balzac and Gournay, where she criticizes purists for their extremism, and seems to take Balzac's side in the quarrel over his letters.
[43] Peggy P. Holmes, "Mlle de Gournay's Defence of Baroque Imagery," *French Studies*, 8/2 (1954), 124.
[44] Gournay, "Du langage françois," 697, 698.
[45] Her "Deffence de la poesie et du langage des poëtes" was dedicated to Mme des Loges, Malherbe's mistress, in whose salons were to be found his disciples such as Chapelain and Conrart, along with Marie de Gournay. Clearly the lines of linguistic partisanship and literary sociability did not always line up. See "Deffence de la poesie," 1081 n. c.

accessible to a contemporary readership.[46] While averse to fashion and pandering to a public made up of *salonnières* and courtiers, she still wanted readers. And she strove to influence the course of literary culture with all the energy and persistence of Malherbe or Balzac, but with much less success.

More than anything else, her insistence that both poetry and the poet belonged to an exalted sphere was what separated her from most of her contemporary *gens de lettres*, who, if they did not necessarily embrace Malherbe's rather debased view, still agreed that theirs was a worldly profession bound up with the needs and tastes of their society and their time. Marie de Gournay could not have disagreed more. This is to betray the true mission of the poet, which is to appeal only to "superior beings," not the denizens of the salons or *gens de la cour*. This is why poetry cannot be hemmed in by rules or doctrines or other restrictions that might be appropriate for ordinary speech and ordinary language—because it deals with extraordinary things. In an image that summarizes her almost mystical conception of poetry—and which has interesting resonance in a period when the so-called witch-hunts were at their height—she compares the true poet to a magician who has demons at his beck and call, while the "grammarians" are like witches obliged to obey them.[47]

Guez de Balzac and Jean-Pierre Camus

Balzac called Malherbe his "intellectual father." In the nineteenth century, Charles Augustin Saint-Beuve referred to Balzac as the "Malherbe of prose."[48] There is no doubt that this deeply learned and supremely ambitious man of letters, who at once aspired to literary greatness and political heights, or at least influence, knew exactly what he was doing when he published the first edition of his *Lettres de Monsieur de Balzac* in 1624. Balzac's first venture into print, it contained sixty-one letters, some addressed to leading *grands*, such as Richelieu, the Duc d'Epernon, and his son, Louis de Nogaret de La Valette, others to various high churchmen, fellow writers, a couple of rivals, and several anonymous figures. The publication was a veritable *succès de scandale* and initiated one of the great "quarrels" in a century known for its contentiousness in literary matters. The reception of the *Lettres*—there were sixteen editions in eight years, and the quarrel generated over

---

[46] On this, see Boase, *The Fortunes of Montaigne*, 60, 65; Claude Blum, "Les principes et la pratique: Marie de Gournay éditrice des Essais," in Jean-Claude Arnould, ed., *Marie de Gournay et l'édition de 1595 des Essais de Montaigne: Actes du Colloque organisé par La Société des Amis de Montaigne, les 9 et 10 juin, en Sorbonne* (Paris, 1996), 33–6.

[47] Danielle Trudeau, *Les inventeurs du bon usage (1529-1647)* (Paris, 1992), 150–1. Hélène Merlin-Kajman, *La langue est-elle fasciste? Langue, pouvoir, enseignement* (Paris, 2003), 134.

[48] Peter Shoemaker, *Powerful Connections: The Poetics of Patronage in the Age of Louis XIII* (Newark, NJ, 2007), 57; E. B. O. Borgerhoff, *The Freedom of French Classicism* (Princeton, 1950), 21. On Balzac and Malherbe, see especially Bombart, *Guez de Balzac*, 141ff.

thirty publications in the space of six years—demonstrated the existence of a reading public that not only appreciated their literary merits but also understood the issues that were at stake.[49] Sorel's assessment conforms to the general view: "Never before have any letters been so sought after and so valued."[50] "It is certain that we had seen nothing similar in France," wrote Gédéon Tallemant des Réaux of the publication, "and that all those who have written well in prose since then, and who will write well in the future in our language, will be obligated to him."[51] One of the most brazen literary self-promoters of his time, Balzac blithely exaggerated the novelty of his letters, comparing them with nothing less than Galileo's recent discoveries.[52] This obscured his debts to others. The *Lettres* owe much to Cicero, the letter writer, not the orator; they surely were inspired by the success of Justus Lipsius's letters, which, while in Latin, provided a living model for the epistolary genre within the Republic of Letters. And, despite Balzac's critique of the "rudeness" of Montaigne's style, they were inspired by the intimacy and vivacity conveyed in the *Essays*.[53] Finally, of course, and here Balzac never disavowed his inheritance, the *Lettres* applied Malherbe's reforms to the realm of prose. Malherbe, as we have seen, propagated his views before a rather limited group of acolytes. Balzac's *Lettres* were broadcast to the world of readers; they demonstrated what Malherbe tended only to preach. Moreover, in the quarrel that erupted in the publication's wake, Balzac and his opponents and supporters made explicit, in polemical and often violent tones, the issues regarding language, rhetoric, eloquence, and public discourse that were at stake.

Fundamentally, these had to do with whether true eloquence was possible, not only in French vernacular, but in the private mode of the letter. Balzac's *Lettres* were meant to demonstrate its possibility that private or domestic "space," as opposed to the public venue of the oration, the traditional context of eloquence in the eyes of the ancients and most humanists. Much of the controversy over their publication, therefore, was not necessarily about the *Lettres* themselves, but rather what his critics insisted was his exalted claim that this domestic form, usually associated with trivial or merely personal matters, could embody true eloquence. It was in fact true that Balzac wanted to entirely transform the criteria for judging eloquence; in insisting that the epistolary form was just as suited for conveying great and grave matters, he argued that "modern" eloquence should be natural in style, tailored to the tastes and dispositions of contemporary French men and women, rather than to the standards and criteria established by ancient authors,

---

[49] For a meticulous recounting of its publishing history, see Jean Jehasse, *Guez de Balzac et le génie romain, 1597–1654* (Saint-Etienne, 1977).
[50] Sorel, *Bibliothèque française*, 177.
[51] Gédéon Tallemant des Réaux, *Historiettes*, ed. Antoine Adam, 2 vols. (Paris, 1960), II: 42.
[52] Bombart, *Guez de Balzac*, 158.
[53] On Balzac's critique of Montaigne, see Sorel, *Bibliothèque française*, 150; Bombart, *Guez de Balzac*, 58–9. See also Alan M. Boase, *The Fortunes of Montaigne: A History of the Essays in France, 1580–1669*, 2nd ed. (New York, 1970), 297–8.

"schoolmasters," magistrates, and other "pedants." To his friend and fellow *homme de lettre* Boisrobert, he wrote, with a degree of exaggeration that was characteristic of his writing, "I try as much as possible to disclose all of my secrets [*rendre tous mes secrets populaires*] and to make them understandable to women and children even when the things I speak about are not within their scope of knowledge."[54] His ideal reader was that ubiquitous figure of the *honnête homme*, a figure he not only rhetorically addressed but also helped to create. In 1628, Descartes, one of the *gens de lettres* enlisted to endorse Balzac's *Lettres*, responded with his enthusiastic approval. The terms of his approbation reveal an appreciation for Balzac's success in fashioning an accessible but also intellectually elevated style. Balzac, Descartes wrote, "does not abuse the simplicity of the reader; but generally uses arguments that are so clear that they are easily accepted by the public, and nevertheless they are so solid and so true that the better the reader's mind, the more likely he is to be convinced."[55]

The emphasis on Balzac changing the terms of eloquence tends to obscure something even more fundamental about his dramatic entry into public life with the publication of his letters. Here a word should be said about the status of Balzac in present-day scholarship on French literature in the first half of the seventeenth century: there simply is no more important figure, as work by Jean Jehasse, Jouhaud, Merlin-Kajman, Shoemaker, Mathilde Bombart, and others attests.[56] These and other studies have plumbed the depths of Balzac's writings with brilliance and erudition. It is difficult to escape the conclusion that he warrants elevation to the canonical position of his contemporary Pierre Corneille; or at least that he is an endlessly rewarding source for insights into the nature of French culture in the Age of Richelieu.

There can, in short, be no attempt on my part to do justice to the kind of analyses produced by these scholars. Rather, I would point to something quite basic about Balzac's letters, which underscores their impact in shaping the worldly culture that is the theme of this chapter. This is the form of the letter itself as the vehicle for his intervention as the fashioner of a new eloquence. His appropriation of this form, as noted, was not unprecedented, but he did exploit it in ways that capitalized on its apparent novelty as an accessible mode of self-expression at once literary and worldly. Balzac was nothing if not ambitious, but he deliberately chose a genre that, in the context of his literary forebears and the long tradition of

---

[54] Jehasse, *Guez de Balzac*, 137.

[55] See Jean Pierre Cavaillé, "'Le plus éloquent philosophe des derniers temps': Les stratégies d'auteur de René Descartes," *Annales: Histoire, sciences sociales*, 49/2 (1994), 383; and Stephen Gaukroger, *Descartes: An Intellectual Biography* (Oxford, 1995), 181–2.

[56] Jehasse, *Guez de Balzac*; Christian Jouhaud, *Les pouvoirs de la littérature: Histoire d'un paradoxe* (Paris, 2000); Shoemaker, *Powerful Connections*; Bombart, *Guez de Balzac*; also Marc Fumaroli, *L'âge de l'éloquence: Rhétorique et "res literaria" de la Renaissance au seuil de l'époque classique* (Geneva, 1980).

Renaissance and even ancient literature, was second-best to the elevated status of poetry. Even Malherbe, despite his professed rupture with the tradition of Ronsard and Marot, never thought of himself or presented himself as other than a poet. Balzac, however, went further in breaking with this tradition, and with this he might have been successful in surpassing Malherbe, his avowed master. For the letter as a form was, of course, more accessible, more personal, and thus more appealing to a wider readership than the odes and other verses that Malherbe and others continued to produce, largely for the limited public of the court. By its very mundane nature, it stripped the writer of his sacral aura, transforming literature, in Benichou's terms, from a calling to a profession.[57] But the "professional" man of letters was then, as Balzac demonstrated and as Christian Jouhaud has asserted, better positioned to address a range of concerns and a range of readerships.

The appeal of the letter as a form was affirmed shortly after the publication of Balzac's *Lettres*. In 1627, under the editorial direction of Nicolas Faret, there appeared the *Recueil de lettres nouvelles*, which included letters from a range of *gens de lettres*, among them Malherbe, Jean de Silhon, Godeau, Boisrobert, Racan, Balzac, and Faret.[58] Recall that that same year saw the publication of the *Recueil des plus beaux vers*, which showcased Malherbe's poetry and gathered poetic contributions by writers who were identified as his "students." In the *Recueil de lettres nouvelles*, Malherbe, too, had pride of place, with ten letters at the very beginning of the collection. But these show a man in decline, expressing an increasing estrangement from the court as well as a world-weariness that presaged his death just a year later. In his letter to Balzac he darkly quips, "I am not yet buried, but those who are dead are not more so than I."[59] Balzac, on the other hand, dominates the collection: not only are his twelve letters a kind of keystone of the *Recueil*, but letters by others, either to him or about him, serve as an "echo chamber" of praise for his prose style as well as announce their support for him in the continuing quarrel. In a letter to Pierre de Marca, Silhon, whom we will meet later, calls him the "first to endow our language with the eloquence of which it was capable."[60] Unlike other authors, even those who wrote well, he alone had the courage to go beyond the narrow straits and explore the open waters in search of the "grandeur" he knew existed. If "men had remained content to navigate land to land and did not dare to explore the seas beyond the shore, they would never have left their state of poverty, and the treasure that we have taken and the riches we have transported across the world would still be in the Indies or in those places where nature placed them." Balzac might have opened himself up to ridicule when he

---

[57] Paul Bénichou, *The Consecration of the Writer, 1750–1830*, trans. Mark K. Jensen (Lincoln, 1999).
[58] Nicolas Faret, *Recueil de lettres nouvelles* (Paris, 1627). There is a modern critical edition of this text, *Recueil de lettres nouvelles, "dit" Faret*, ed. Eric Méchoulan (Paris, 2008).
[59] *Recueil de lettres nouvelles*, 62.   [60] *Recueil de lettres nouvelles*, 441–2.

compared his writings to Galileo's discoveries, but his supporters seemed to believe that they were epoch-making nevertheless.[61]

* * *

Though they shared a measure of antipathy toward the "worldly" purists in the camp of Malherbe and Balzac, there could be no two more different writers than Marie de Gournay and Jean-Pierre Camus.[62] This is especially true in their contrasting views of an ideal readership. While the celebrated "Damoiselle" scorned the common reader, reserving her rich works for the spiritual elite alone, the Bishop de Belley was a veritable publishing machine, unleashing a stream of moralizing potboilers designed to appeal to the widest possible literary public. In a treatise he published in 1609, "Traittant des Passions de l'Ame," Camus made explicit the readership he strove to reach: "it is the simple, unlearned people for whom I toil."[63] Elsewhere he talks about leading readers along like children through the maze of rooms in a castle.

But in another respect they were quite similar: it is hard to find two more eccentric individuals in a literary landscape teeming with compelling figures. Jean-Pierre Camus was a priest, a close companion and disciple of François de Sales, a writer of many devotional texts and sermons, and the author of numerous fictional works. Like Gournay, he was older than most of his contemporary *gens de lettres*, which, as with her, might account for his preference for the style and sensibility of the sixteenth century. In his youth, he too was taken with Montaigne.[64] But Camus certainly wrote with a present-day readership in mind. He was particularly energetic in promoting the spiritual model of his mentor and edited de Sales's works. In his own religious treatises and published sermons, which are numerous, he shows himself to be a learned theologian. Elevated to bishop in 1608, he engaged in numerous polemics, especially against the mendicant orders and as a champion of the Jesuits.

But Camus is best known as a writer of fiction, probably the most prolific author of his generation. His publications in this genre take up sixty volumes, including one thousand short stories and, astonishingly, thirty-five novels published in the decade 1620–30 alone. Although he took as his model the immensely popular *Histoires tragiques* of François de Rosset, Camus's fiction is difficult to

---

[61] Paul Pellisson and Pierre-Joseph Thoulier d'Olivet, *Histoire de l'Académie françoise, par Pellisson et d'Olivet*, 3rd ed., revised and enlarged, 2 vols. (Paris, 1743), II: 79.

[62] For Camus, see Sylvie Robic-de Baecque, *Le salut par l'excès: Jean-Pierre Camus (1584–1652), la poétique d'un évêque romancier* (Paris, 1999); Boase, *The Fortunes of Montaigne*, 114–34; Peter Shoemaker, "Violence and Piety in Jean-Pierre Camus's histoires tragiques," *French Review*, 79/3 (2006), 549–60; Jean Dagens, "L'écrivain et l'orateur chrétien suivant Jean-Pierre Camus," *Studi Francesi*, no. 6 (Sept.-Dec. 1958), 379–94.

[63] Richard Scholar, *The Je-Ne-Sais-Quoi in Early Modern Europe: Encounters with a Certain Something* (Oxford, 2005), 131.

[64] But see Mathilde Bombart, "La parole et le livre: Camus orateur et auteur selon le 'Jugement des Essais de Michel de Montaigne' et le Conférence académique," *XVIIe siècle*, 2/251 (2001), 279–85, on his turning away from Montaigne.

classify. He disavowed writing "novels," disapproving of such books as frivolous and corrupting. Indeed, he called his works "anti-novels," offered as a cure to readers, like "the Pharmacist who had discovered the secret of having his patients take bitter drugs as if they were sweets."[65] His genre was the *histoire dévote*, tales to edify and instruct in the perils of passion and sin. And in this sense, he was writing as a true Salesian, immersing his characters in a world of myriad pleasures and pitfalls that they might enjoy and resist in different measure, but which were the stuff of ordinary Christian lives nevertheless. In fact, his stories are not entirely fictional, for they were often based on true accounts, which he embellished and elaborated upon to create tales of astonishing variety and violence, usually dealing with themes of thwarted love, family discord, village rivalries, and moral turpitude. While his master François de Sales embodied the "sweetness" in tone and language found in the writings of d'Urfé, Camus's stories were fast-paced and crudely plotted. He admitted that he wrote quickly, never revising, and dismissed any efforts to achieve elegant, finely crafted prose, judging such efforts meretricious and vain.[66] Peter Shoemaker has suggested that these stories were the first "pulp fiction." Camus not only wrote about violence, he himself likened his writing style to the act of evisceration, striking the body quickly and deeply.[67] Despite the sensational nature of his works—which certainly attracted the criticism of many *dévots*—he insisted that they were meant only for the spiritual edification of his readers.[68]

It is perhaps strange, then, that this author of the seventeenth-century equivalent of potboilers, who may have coined the term "belles-lettres,"[69] failed to identify with the "purists" who were responsible for opening up the literary field to precisely the kinds of texts he produced in such plenitude. But Camus's position was a complex one. In the *Issue aux censeurs* (published in 1625 as a kind of afterword to his novel *Alcime, relation funeste, ou, Se descouvre la main de Dieu sur les impies*), he refuses to target individual writers, pointing rather to unnamed "Censors." These "little minds" have arrogantly assumed a large goal—to impose a "tyrannical" rule over the "Republic of Letters," he writes. "They wish to be taken for Oracles and have accepted without contradiction their prohibitions as sovereign laws."[70] Like Marie de Gournay, he is incensed at their apparent readiness to

---

[65] Barbara R. Woshinsky, *Imagining Women's Conventual Spaces in France, 1600–1800: The Cloister Disclosed* (London, 2016), 81.
[66] Eugene Griselle, "Camus et Richelieu en 1632," *Revue d'histoire littéraire de la France*, 21/3–4 (1914), 682–3. On the disavowal of "writer" status and his belittling of French, see Fumaroli, *L'âge de l'éloquence*, 548–9.
[67] Shoemaker, "Violence and Piety," 552.
[68] One writer called him "Le Rabelais des êveques." From Gabriel Joppin, *Une querelle autour de l'amour pur: Jean-Pierre Camus, évêque de Belley* (Paris, 1938), 21; as quoted by Alexander T. Pocetto, OSFS, "Jean-Pierre Camus (1584–1652) as Disseminator of the Salesian Spirit," http://hosted.desales.edu/w4/salesian/icss_de/artikel/english/pocetto08.pdf, 5.
[69] Fumaroli, *L'âge de l'éloquence*, 573. But Bombart disputes this: *Guez de Balzac*, 447.
[70] Douglas Kibbee, "Continuités et discontinuités dans l'histoire du prescriptivisme français," *Collection des Congrès mondiaux de linguistique française*, July 12, 2010, 58, https://doi.org/10.1051/cmlf/2010264; Jean-Pierre Camus, *Issue aux censeurs* (Paris, 1625), 603.

purge French of old or foreign words—simply one more egregious example of their "tyranny." Their "laws" are capricious and unfounded. He scoffs at their claims to "reason" as the basis for their reforms; he has even less confidence in their reliance on "usage," which he says they cite only in order to make up for the "weakness" of their position, which amounts to discarding established "authority and usurping common and generally accepted rules."[71] Under their arrogant domination, he asks, what is to become of "that France, mother of arts and especially of the liberty of speaking naively and without affectation, which is its pure and natural voice [*ramage*]"?[72]

In 1625, it may have been that Camus was reacting not so much to the likes of Malherbe, Balzac, and their acolytes, but rather to the more severe strictures of another camp on the literary scene.[73] Five years later, however, there is no mistaking his concern. *Conférence académique sur le différent des belles-lettres de Narcisse et de Phyllarque* (1630) is an explicit intervention into the quarrel over Balzac's *Lettres*: "Narcisse" is Balzac; "Phyllarque" is Dom Goulu, the Feuillant monk who was the first to go on the attack against Balzac. The protagonists are not present in the text, however; rather, the *Conférence académique* presents an assortment of magistrates, officials, and churchmen in the library of "Critobule," a *conseiller* in the Parlement of Paris, who have gathered to discuss the controversy between the two, principally Narcisse's claim to have fashioned a new sort of eloquence. Critobule largely remains silent throughout the discussion, rendering an opinion—measured, judicious, and learned, as befitting an august magistrate—only at the end.

The protagonists are evenly divided between advocates for Narcisse and Phyllarque. The discussion, then, conveys an even-handed approach to a quarrel that had been characterized by polemics, personal attacks, and intractable positioning. The three partisans of Narcisse/Balzac are fulsome in their praise. A young *secrétaire du roi* Nector extols the *Lettres* for their eloquence in language that might have made even Balzac blush. "Canonization is too little a thing" for this man, proclaims Nector. "There should be an apotheosis, a divination.... His book should be the model, the standard, the rule for perfect eloquence, and those who fail to imitate this language should be banished from the empire of speaking well."[74] Critobule, too, in the discourse that ends the conference, offers his own ringing accolade: "France will owe him an immortal obligation for having elevated its language above that of the Greeks and Romans and for having enriched it with so much luster and in so many noble and illustrious ways of expression unknown in past times."[75] On the other hand, some of the comments by the

---

[71] Kibbee, "Continuités et discontinuités," 59; Camus, *Issue aux censeurs*, 611–12.
[72] Kibbee, "Continuités et discontinuités," 58; Camus, *Issue aux censeurs*, 598.
[73] This is the Piat Maucors group. On them, see later in this chapter.
[74] Jean-Pierre Camus, *Conférence académique sur le différent des belles-lettres de Narcisse et de Phyllarque, par le sieur de Musac* (Paris, 1630), 95.
[75] *Conférence académique*, 310.

supporters of Phyllarque/Goulu are scathing, echoing the often personal nature of the quarrel. He is declared "healthy in mind but sick in body," thus implying a lack of vitality, which leads to the aspersion, also voiced in the text, that for all his attempts to appeal to fashionable society, he is nothing more than a pedant. This, of course, nimbly turns the tables on Balzac and his acolytes, who, as we have seen, were quick to tar their opponents with the broad brush of pedantry.

But the most convincing criticism of Balzac in the *Conférence académique*, which is not balanced by an opposing view, comes from Critobule at the very end. While deftly refusing to adjudicate between the two parties, he nevertheless declares that, whatever other virtues they may embody, Balzac's *Lettres* (or any letters) do not achieve the level of eloquence. "Someone who expresses himself only with his pen might be worthy of the name elegant, but not eloquent, nor that of orator."[76] This struck at the heart of the quarrel, and at Balzac's very *raison d'être* as a writer—the man his contemporaries came to call the "*unico eloquente.*" Indeed, Critobule acknowledges that François Ogier, Balzac's main champion in the quarrel over the *Lettres*, conferred upon him the title *Dieu de l'Eloquence*. If he wants to truly deserve this ascription, comments Critobule, "he has to write something other than letters."[77] He fully acknowledges that Balzac's writing was stylish, vigorous, and accomplished, which is say elegant, but these were merely meretricious qualities capable of giving pleasure but nothing more. More to the point, a mere writer like Balzac could not embody the eloquence of an orator because he failed to enter the public arena and put his language to the test. "For after all, action is the touchstone of the true and perfect orator. It is for him to appear at the bar or in the pulpits, places open to everyone."[78] Elsewhere Camus casts scorn on the very status of a "writer," ranking it only slightly above actors, cooks, jewelers, and hairdressers—those devoted to amusement or serving our superficial needs.[79]

More than an attack or an intervention in a contemporary quarrel, then, the *Conférence académique* was Camus's attempt to put Balzac and other writers in their place, so to speak; to acknowledge their talents and accomplishments, but to remind everyone that there was another register of language—venerable and engaged—to which they might aspire. But herein lies the paradox of Camus, the author of hundreds of works of what we might call "popular" fiction: that, his dearly held views about writing to the contrary, his stories and novels were much of the same genre as those of the worldly *gens de lettres* he seemed to scorn. Like them, he contributed to the expansion of a vernacular literature, and thus to the "opening up" of French culture. Following his master François de Sales, he consciously fashioned his works to appeal to the tastes, sensibilities, and intellectual capacity of a wide readership, translating his considerable theological and philosophical knowledge into stories that could both edify and entertain. He regarded

---

[76] *Conférence académique*, 302.　　[77] *Conférence académique*, 306.
[78] *Conférence académique*, 306–7.　　[79] Fumaroli, *L'âge de l'éloquence*, 573.

his readers with sympathy, if also with a touch of condescension, as wanting to "be led by the hand, as in a superb palace, through many porticos, passages, long galleries, through a great multiplicity of halls, rooms, closets and contours."[80] And he too was impatient with pedantry. "Instead of filling us with the knowledge of things," he writes, "and endowing us with understanding, we are sent in pursuit of silly words and phrases.... What a thought, to call a man learned because he babbles in Latin and can spit out a few words in Greek."[81] In a sense, he was as much a fellow traveler of the purists as their critic.[82]

Claude Favre de Vaugelas and François de La Mothe le Vayer

In Moliere's *Les femmes savantes* (1672), a character comments on the advisability of "speaking Vaugelas [*parler Vaugelas*]," a sure sign that Claude Favre de Vaugelas's *Remarques sur la langue françoise*, first published in 1647 and subsequently reissued many times over the next decades, had lodged itself as a colloquial reference point among Parisian audiences. Vaugelas's book, which he worked on for much of his adult life, represents a kind of summa of much that had changed in the French language in the course of the first half of the century. (In the 1650s, even Corneille took to revising his plays according to the standards set by this text.[83]) If Malherbe's status as a promulgator of a "doctrine" is open to question, there is little doubt that Vaugelas intended to prescribe the guidelines for proper French for his contemporaries and posterity alike. Following Malherbe, along with others interested in the literary and expressive possibilities of the French vernacular, such as Du Perron, Nicolas Coëffeteau, and François de Sales, he formulated an extensive and deceptively simple brief for *usage* as the guide to correct French. He was so wedded to the principle of usage that he refused to undertake the drafting of a French grammar, conceding what generations of writers, from Dante down to his contemporaries, had feared: that vernacular languages, unlike Latin and Greek, were unstable, subject to constant change, and thus ran the risk of proving incomprehensible to successive generations. For Vaugelas, however, such concerns meant that "usage" must be not simply followed but monitored and critiqued as well.

Vaugelas was the product of Savoy and its remarkably fertile cultural climate, part Italian, part French, part all its own, which contributed so much to the

---

[80] Quoted in Woshinsky, *Imagining Women's Conventual Spaces*, 83.
[81] Scholar, *The Je-Ne-Sais-Quoi in Early Modern Europe*, 130.
[82] See also Mark Bannister, "Free Will, Determinism and Providence: The Ideological Context of the *Histoires tragiques* of Jean-Pierre Camus," in Sarah Alyn Stacey and Véronique Desnain, eds., *Culture and Conflict in 17th-Century France and Ireland* (Dublin, 2004), 117–27.
[83] Wendy Ayres-Bennett, "From *l'usage* to *le bon usage* and Back: Norms and Usage in Seventeenth-Century France," in Gijsbert Rutten, Rik Vosters, and Wim Vandenbussche, eds., *Norms and Usage in Language History, 1600–1900: A Sociolinguistic and Comparative Perspective* (Amsterdam, 2014), 193.

literary and linguistic history of the period. He came from a long line of prominent Savoyard magistrates. His father, Antoine Favre, an eminent judge and learned humanist, published several books on legal and religious subjects as well as a collection of poems. He also helped found, along with François de Sales, a close friend, the Académie florimontane. The young Claude Favre was nurtured in this academic, humanistic environment. As a young man, he was placed in service to the Duc de Nemours, a well-known Maecenas, who took him to Turin and finally Paris. Once installed in the French capital, Vaugelas immediately entered the orbit of Malherbe and his disciples. He gained entry into the "cabinet" of Nicolas Coëffeteau and attended his rather exclusive weekly sessions, where language and literature were the central concerns, rubbing shoulders with the likes of Racan, Faret, and, of course, Malherbe.[84] He was among the first generation of habitués of the Hôtel de Rambouillet, and was instrumental in ushering foreign *hommes de lettres*, most notably Giambattista Marino, into that privileged milieu.

Vaugelas was the author of several works besides the *Remarques*, most notably a translation of the *Life of Alexander the Great* by Quintus Curtius, the product of more than thirty years' labor, which was finally published posthumously by a group of his friends, most of them academicians, in 1653. The academy also commissioned him to produce a French dictionary, a project that encountered great logistical difficulties, only to be completed late in the century and well after Vaugelas's death. But it is *Remarques sur la langue françoise* for which he is primarily remembered. Twenty editions were published between 1647 and 1738.[85]

Perhaps the best-known sentence in the *Remarques*—a passage that invites consideration as something of a "sound bite"—is Vaugelas's definition of "good usage": "It is the manner of speaking of the most intelligent members of the Court, in conformance with the most intelligent authors of the time." Lest one conclude from this that Vaugelas means to restrict his reference to the courtiers of the Louvre—which *bien-pensant* Parisians judged pitifully lacking in cultivation— he immediately expands his definition of the "court" to include "the women as well as men and many people of the city where the Prince resides who through the communications they have with the people of the Court share in its polite society."[86] But he makes sure to provide another qualification to a reliance on usage: the stipulation that the best authors serve as guides or arbiters in establishing the standards for correct usage. Indeed, the prescription of usage as the touchstone for correct French is hemmed in at virtually every turn. Later, he emphasizes the

---

[84] In the *Remarques*, he notes that his views on language were derived not only from the many years spent at court but also from his "apprenticeship" to Cardinal du Perron and Coëffeteau, as well as his "continual conversation and conferral with all those excellent men of that sort in Paris." Claude Favre de Vaugelas, *La preface des "Remarques sur la langue françoise,"* ed. Zygmunt Marzys (Neuchâtel, 1984), 9.

[85] In general on Vaugelas, see the fundamental work by Wendy Ayres-Bennett, *Vaugelas and the Development of the French Language* (London, 1987).

[86] Vaugelas, *La preface des "Remarques,"* 40–41.

point: "The approval of good authors is like a seal or a verification which authorizes the language of the Court and stamps good usage."[87] Unlike Malherbe, who provocatively, and certainly facetiously, commented that he referred to the "street porters of Paris" for his understanding of correct French, Vaugelas was careful to designate the elite of court and city as his informants. He echoed the conviction, voiced, as we have seen, by a whole range of commentators, that pedantry and a slavish obeisance to the ancients were to be avoided at all cost: "in all languages it is ordinarily better to consult women and those who have not studied at all than those who are very learned in Greek and Latin."[88]

Throughout the *Remarques*, Vaugelas ultimately returns to usage as the fundamental guide to proper French. He raises it above all other arbiters, in particular specialists such as grammarians, who traditionally had been conferred authority in matters of language. Usage even trumps reason. "In a word," he writes in the preface to the *Remarques*, "usage renders many things according to reason, many without reason, and many contrary to reason."[89] He likens a reliance on usage to religious faith, for it too is above, and sometimes contrary to, reason: "Usage [is] like faith, which obliges us to believe simply and blindly, without our reason providing its natural light."[90] For this he was attacked by one contemporary, who saw it as a descent into an unthinking bestial state. And as an authoritative assertion, it certainly strikes one as a self-conscious alternative to Descartes's rationalist method, unleashed on the world just a decade before. Vaugelas allows himself to wonder about the wisdom of following willy-nilly the dictates of usage. For example, he virtually throws up his hands in bemused incomprehension at the aversion for the word *poitrine* simply because of its unsavory association with the phrase *poitrine de veau*.[91] Nevertheless, he concedes, here as elsewhere, to a fundamental deference to "usage"—the only true sovereign in the realm of language.

In asserting the "sovereignty" of usage, Vaugelas might be seen as embracing an almost republican understanding of the basis of language. Here again, however, he qualifies his formulation in ways that reveal an awareness of its radical implications. It has been argued that Vaugelas derived his concept of usage from the discourse of customary law, which he learned from his father and the legal milieu in which he was raised.[92] If so, this implies a formal authority derived from usage, suggesting a political aspect of Vaugelas's formulation. At one point, he

---

[87] Vaugelas, *La preface des "Remarques,"* 41.
[88] See Trudeau, *Les inventeurs du bon usage*, 175.
[89] "En un mot, l'usage fait beaucoup de choses par raison, beaucoup sans raison, et beaucoup contre raison." Vaugelas, *La preface des "Remarques,"* 50.
[90] Claude Favre de Vaugelas, *Remarques sur la langue françoise utiles à ceux qui veulent bien parler et bien escire*, ed. J. Streicher (Geneva, 1934), 503; Trudeau, *Les inventeurs du bon usage*, 184.
[91] Ayres-Bennet, *Sociolinguistic Variation in Seventeenth-Century France: Methodology and Case Studies*, (Cambridge, 2004), 153.
[92] Harald Weinrich, "Vaugelas et la théorie du bon usage dans le classicism français," in Weinrich, *Conscience linguistique et lectures littéraires* (Paris, 1989), 189–217.

makes a comment that certainly confronts the political nature of language, even implying a fundamental limit on royal authority. "It is not permitted for anyone to create new words," he proclaims, "not even the sovereign, such that Pomponius Marcellus was correct in taking the Emperor Tiberius to task for making one, saying he could justly confer the right of the bourgeoisie of Rome over men but not over words; his authority did not extend that far."[93]

To deny the king's authority over language was one thing; to declare that this implies a "republican" understanding of language is quite another. To be sure, the identification of French eloquence with the ancient Gauls, a theme evoked by many contemporary commentators on language, approaches a proto-nationalist sentiment rooted in the assumption of a common linguistic heritage for the French people. Vaugelas, and other purists, however, refused to conceive of language in such socially capacious terms. On the contrary, he made a point of framing usage as restrictive and elitist; the fact that he insisted on this point in a variety of ways in the *Remarques* underscores how crucial it was to his overall understanding. He certainly wanted to avoid being misunderstood as endorsing the speech and linguistic practices of "the people." His fundamental dictum underscores its restrictive quality: his reference is to the "most intelligent" among the courtiers and writers, he insists—that is, the most refined of an already constituted elite. He also asserts the rule that "bad usage" can always be identified with the "majority," while "good usage" is found among the few. Moreover, the purpose of his work was not simply or even primarily to instruct readers in the banal aspects of common speech and writing—not to correct "gross errors"—but rather to aim for a refined understanding of the subtleties of French usage. "Purity of language is thus not such an easy acquisition to attain."[94] As Trudeau has suggested, in this sense the project outlined in the *Remarques* begins to look like the travails of the saints, whose quest for spiritual perfection becomes more difficult the closer they approach it.[95]

If Vaugelas's conception of language had a social aspect, it had a temporal quality as well. One of the perennial concerns of those interested in language across the centuries was for the assumed mutability of spoken vernaculars, of their inevitable transformation over time, such that what was written in one generation risked being misunderstood or unreadable in the next. This was Dante's worry, despite the fact that he staked his literary reputation on the Tuscan language. And it was also Montaigne's, even though his writings were a milestone in the development and acceptability of French as a literary language. This concern buttressed the prestige of Latin: it was better suited to resist the fortunes of time.

---

[93] This echoes the anecdote recounted by Racan regarding Malherbe's proscription against the king intervening in matters of language (mentioned in the Introduction). *Vie de Malherbe*, 41.
[94] Quoted in Trudeau, *Les inventeurs du bon usage*, 174–5.
[95] Trudeau, *Les inventeurs du bon usage*, 174–5.

Vaugelas's lack of anxiety regarding the mutability of the vernacular is probably the trait that most distinguishes him from others, especially in the humanist tradition, who had seriously considered the relative virtues of French and Latin. While he acknowledged this concern, he did not share it. He fully conceded that his prescriptions might well prove "outmoded" in twenty or thirty years. But he also hoped, like many of his contemporaries, that French was poised to achieve the level of perfection, expressiveness, and eloquence that Latin had in Cicero's day. This is why Cicero remained so prominent as an example: not as a writer to be imitated, but rather as a stylist to be equaled. With Vaugelas's *Remarques*, one has the sense that the French language had arrived.[96]

* * *

François de La Mothe le Vayer (1588–1672) was a leading skeptic, an intimate of the Dupuy cabinet, and one of the most erudite men of his day, known as the "French Plutarch." Though groomed to follow in the career footsteps of his father, who was a lawyer in the Parlement of Paris, he found that after a period spent indulging his wanderlust, which only seemed to heighten his Montaignian appreciation for the variety of human experience and indeterminacy of all things, he could no longer confine his intellectual energies to the study of law. Most of his writings, published under the pseudonym Orasius Tubero, consisted of dialogues on a range of topics, conversations among like-minded *esprits forts* that tended to illustrate a skeptical approach to knowledge, truth, and faith. (We shall look further at La Mothe le Vayer and his other writings and associations in Chapters 4 and 6.) Despite his somewhat heterodox views, which he was careful, however, to publish under only the most discreet, even obscure, conditions, he gained acceptance in the highest circles. In 1639 he was elected to the Académie française, over the objections of Balzac, who correctly saw "Orasius" as an opponent of the literary movement he aspired to lead.[97] Before he died, Richelieu designated him as the young Louis XIV's preceptor, a choice overruled by Anne of Austria, presumably because of La Mothe le Vayer's uncertain views on matters of faith.

La Mothe le Vayer conceived of his treatise *Considérations sur l'éloquence française* (1638) as a riposte to Vaugelas's *Remarques*, then circulating in manuscript.[98] With regard to his position in the controversy over Balzac's *Lettres*, La Mothe le Vayer, as a savant identified with the Dupuy cabinet, could only have been at one

---

[96] Cohen, "Courtly French, Learned Latin, and Peasant Patois," 459: "Montaigne feared that composing his *Essais* in a rapidly evolving vernacular like French, rather than a grammatically fixed idiom like Latin, would condemn them to be incomprehensible to readers within fifty years. His concern was not entirely misplaced. French had evolved sufficiently in the years since the *Essais*' first appearance that Marie de Gournay felt obliged to warn readers of this fact in her preface to the 1595 edition of her uncle's essays." See Marie de Gournay's "Preface" to the *Essays*, reprinted in Olivier Millet, *La premiere reception des Essais de Montaigne (1580–1640)* (Paris, 1995), 89–90.

[97] Fumaroli, *L'âge de l'éloquence*, 650.

[98] Pellisson and d'Olivet, *Histoire de l'Académie française*, I: 101.

with other learned men who objected to the new "worldly" concept of eloquence. But by the late 1630s, after almost fifteen years during which the purists' conquest of the world of letters and, especially, the milieu of the salon was virtually complete, the savants had largely retreated from the field of battle. Clearly, however, Vaugelas's efforts to present the purist position in the summa of the *Remarques* provoked a renewed counterattack.

But for an attack, La Mothe le Vayer's text is mild-mannered, even generous, especially compared to the sharp, often vicious polemics that had characterized the quarrel over Balzac's letters. Dedicated to Richelieu, *Considérations sur l'éloquence françoise* amounts to a brief for humanistic learning, including a justification for the study of ancient languages, especially Greek. He defends the authority of the *doctes*, whose erudition was grounded in knowledge of the ancients. Of the many writers who commented on eloquence and the literary possibilities of the vernacular—including Camus, Balzac, and Malherbe—La Mothe le Vayer cites only Du Vair, who shared his learned conception of eloquence in the Ciceronian mode. Without deigning to name them, he takes several swipes at the contemporary *mondain* writers, ridiculing them for their superficial understanding of eloquence and their frivolous fixation on style.

There is, in short, no mistaking where La Mothe le Vayer stands in the divide between the *érudits* and the writers of the new literary culture. He is not very happy with the vogue of translating ancient writers, arguing that just as the flavor of wines passed from vessel to vessel tends to "evaporate," so ancient texts in translation lose the better part of their "sharpness and significance," the "force and grace" found in the original.[99] Knowing Greek is not essential, he concedes, but it does provide more insight into the nature of French than even Latin.[100] He likens an excessive attention to style to courtesans who wear too much makeup.[101] The supposed eloquence in the writings of his contemporary rivals struck him as nothing but "spider webs full of subtlety and artifice but which are only good for attracting gnats."[102] Eloquence is not merely a matter of glibness (*un beau parleur*) but the "explication of the thoughts of a wise man."[103] This is why there have always been very few eloquent men—because wisdom, unlike the mere capacity of speaking well, is rare.[104] The fashionable writers of the day are successful not because they are wise or truly eloquent, but because they are "popular." They are promoted by their "counterparts" in the "cabinets" and "*ruelles...* far beyond what is due to them."[105] His scorn for the literary fashions of the day, as well as

---

[99] François de La Mothe le Vayer, *Considerations sur l'éloquence françoise de ce tems* (Paris, 1638), 144.
[100] *Considérations sur l'éloquence françoise*, 104.
[101] *Considérations sur l'éloquence françoise*, 85–6.
[102] *Considérations sur l'éloquence françoise*, 124.
[103] *Considérations sur l'éloquence françoise*, 120.
[104] *Considérations sur l'éloquence françoise*, 120.
[105] *Considérations sur l'éloquence françoise*, 134.

his resentment at the prominence of those writers, such as Voiture, Balzac, and others of their camp, is palpable throughout his text.

But La Mothe le Vayer adds something more to the critique of the purists. His defense of erudition and his opposition to a literary culture that prized accessibility and clarity above all were not rooted solely in his belief in the virtues of learning and an allegiance to long-standing humanist traditions. He had other concerns. Like others, even many of the fashionable writers he looked upon condescendingly, he was anxious lest undue clarity and accessibility prove dangerous; some knowledge is too sensitive, or unpredictable in its implications, or otherwise risky in how it might be misunderstood or irresponsibly deployed, to be disclosed indiscriminately. Hence the necessity of obscuring the true meaning of these texts to unlearned minds. He writes that Aristotle assured Alexander that while his writings were made available to the people, he was careful not to render them too easily understood.[106] The problematic nature of knowledge, especially knowledge of an esoteric sort, was a constant concern of La Mothe le Vayer, as it was for a range of *gens de lettres* of the period (as we shall see in Chapter 3). Even poets, he asserts, "have invented the better part of their fables only to disguise the truths that they think should not be divulged to everyone."[107] In the *Considérations sur l'éloquence françoise*, he raises this concern as one aspect of his critique of the emerging literary culture.

For all his criticism of the followers of Malherbe, Balzac, Vaugelas, and other champions of this culture, however, La Mothe le Vayer also finds common ground with them in their repeated call for clarity and appeal to "good sense." La Mothe le Vayer has some nice things to say about the "books about shepherds"—meaning d'Urfé's *L'Astrée* and its many imitations—which, he readily concedes, "are written with such art, grace, and judgment that one cannot deny them a high ranking among the eloquent *pièces* of our time."[108] And he acknowledges that many "Ladies and Cavaliers" today speak very well. Even more, he cannot endorse learned treatises that vaunt their obscurity as a virtue, and finds repugnant the notion, shared by too many writers and some readers alike, that "nothing seems spiritual or well-said if their mind does not have great difficulty in understanding it." Toward the end he proclaims: "God, who is called the father of light, created it the first day, so that it would illuminate the rest of his works, has taught us by this to do nothing without the greatest clarity possible."[109] Despite his identification with the privileged milieu of the Dupuy cabinet, a sanctuary of learned elites if ever there was one, he asserts his opposition to "those who wish to establish over the Republic of Letters a kind of tyranny of the few, who alone possess the books and thus make themselves absolute masters of riches all the more valuable the

---

[106] *Considérations sur l'éloquence françoise*, 161–2.
[107] *Considérations sur l'éloquence françoise*, 162.
[108] *Considérations sur l'éloquence françoise*, 128.
[109] On this aspect of La Mothe le Vayer, see Adam, *Histoire de la littérature française*, I: 308–9.

fewer who can share in them." Faithful to Cicero, he writes, "For we only speak and write in order to be understood, following from which an Oration's first perfection consists in being clear and intelligible, it likewise follows that its principal failing will proceed in any ambiguities that occur, as it is likely when we use terms that are little known."[110]

Like some of his predecessors, most notably Guillaume du Vair, La Mothe le Vayer presents himself as the champion of the Roman model of the orator, sprinkling his text with references to Cicero, Quintilian, Aristotle, and other ancients. And, unlike his other writings, which were deliberately fashioned as esoteric texts, bristling with Latin citations and obscure references, *Considérations sur l'éloquence françoise* is notably open in its address. "My intention is to say simply what I think about the language of today, to communicate to the public some reflections I have made on the subject and to expose my sentiments to the judgments of those who can correct them, if they do not approve of them," he states at the outset.[111] Like the orator, he strives "to please in order to persuade."[112] He clearly would like to revive those Ciceronian virtues—clarity, appropriate language, measured and pleasing discourse—that were, in his mind, overlooked in the meretricious fixation on style and clever turns of phrase of his rivals, the fashionable *gens de lettres*. But despite this somewhat rear-guard exercise, there is also something wistful about his brief. For like many, he acknowledges that the waning of eloquence—at least the eloquence of the orator—had less to do with the decline of learning or the literary fashions of the day, and more with contemporary political circumstances. Others had cited Tacitus's view that eloquence cannot thrive under monarchies, as there was then less need for debate and discussion, unlike in a republic. La Mothe le Vayer takes a similar tack, noting that in republics there is more contention among the people and a greater need often to pacify the populace. Just as "excellent Captains" are more likely to emerge in the face of "those violent agitations that sometimes trouble Republics," so it is with orators. And just as fewer physicians are needed when there is less sickness, so the "number of Orators is very little under governments less likely to be shaken by seditious movements."[113] La Mothe le Vayer cites ancient Persia and Macedonia, as well as Crete and Sparta, but he also clearly has in mind the French monarchy under the Bourbons. While La Mothe le Vayer's *Considérations sur l'éloquence françoise* is a defiant critique of the dominant literary and linguistic trends of his time, in this sense, at least, he is forced to undercut the very position he defends.[114]

---

[110] La Mothe le Vayer, *Considérations sur l'éloquence françoise*, 159, 17–18.
[111] *Considérations sur l'éloquence françoise*, 3. [112] *Considérations sur l'éloquence françoise*, 17.
[113] *Considérations sur l'éloquence françoise*, 187.
[114] For La Mothe le Vayer's later critique of Vaugelas, see François de La Mothe le Vayer, *Lettres touchant la nouvelle remarques sur la langue française* (Paris, 1658), addressed to Gabriel Naudé. On this, see Isabelle Moreau, "Polémique libertine et querelle du purisme: La Mothe le Vayer ou le refus d'un 'art de plaire' au service du vulgaire," *Revue d'histoire littéraire de la France*, 103/2 (2003), 377–96.

The Sociability of Language Reform

A remarkable feature of post-bellum Paris—the generations following the end of the Wars of Religion—was its vibrant intellectual and literary sociability. Whatever differences in intellectual orientation divided savants and *gens de lettres*, they were as one in embracing the ethos of *otium cum dignitate*, evident in the forms of association in which they congregated. These "cabinets," private academies, salons, and other types of groups, many informal or ephemeral, had no corporate status or institutional basis; yet, for all the ways they embodied the spirit of retreat, they were still engaged in some of the most crucial issues of the day.

While there were many groups devoted to other interests, by far the dominant form of sociability consisted of groups of writers who met to cultivate their particular approach to language and literature, an indication that this concern was indeed widespread. And most of these groups flourished without the support of aristocratic patronage, suggesting that this kind of legitimation was not always necessary as an organizing force in contemporary culture. There were nearly twenty associations whose existence can be documented in the three decades before the outbreak of the *Fronde*. One of the earliest was a sort of academy presided over by Malherbe, whose disciples gathered every evening in his cramped room from 1610 until his death in 1628. As I suggested above, Malherbe was a determined pedagogue and proselytizer; he used these séances to create disciples—a generation of purists.

Nicolas Coëffeteau, a Dominican priest, hosted his own academy in the early twenties, at which many of the same writers could be found. Coëffeteau himself was part of a movement among religious writers to bring theological matters to a reading public of laypeople.[115] Like Malherbe's, Coëffeteau's sessions were devoted to discussions of proper French usage, only here the interest was largely in prose rather than poetry. Another group concerned itself with introducing notions of *bienséance* into the theater; in particular, they were critics of the "baroque," often excessively violent dramatic style as represented by the many plays of the enormously productive Alexandre Hardy.[116]

---

[115] Jean-Pascal Gay, "Les 'Théologies françoises' au XVIIe siècle: Remarques sur l'histoire d'un échec," in Gay and Charles-Olivier Stiker-Métral, eds., *Les métamorphoses de la théologie: Théologie, littérature et discours religieux au XVIIe siècle* (Paris, 2012), 210–14.

[116] On these groups, see Josephine de Boer, "Men's Literary Circles in Paris, 1610–1660," *Proceedings of the Modern Language Association*, 53/3 (1939), 730–80; Harcourt Brown, *Scientific Organizations in Seventeenth-Century France* (1934; reprint, New York, 1967); Adam, *Histoire de la littérature française*, vol. I; Wendy Gibson, *Women in Seventeenth-Century France* (London, 1989); Simone Mazauric, *Savoirs et philosophie à Paris dans la première moitié du XVIIe siècle* (Paris, 1997); Mesnard, *Précis de littérature française*; Carolyn C. Lougee, *Le Paradis des Femmes: Women, Salons, and Social Stratification in Seventeenth-Century France* (Princeton, 1976); Viala, *Naissance de l'écrivain*; Orest Ranum, *Paris in the Age of Absolutism: An Essay* (University Park, PA, 2002).

The existence of these groups is one measure of the impact of Malherbe and his approach on the Parisian literary life of the day; their emergence suggests a veritable movement far outstripping the reformist labors of a handful of literati. Perhaps the best-known group of Malherbians was the informal assembly of literati that met in the late 1620s at the townhouse of Valentin Conrart, which included Faret, Chapelain, Godeau, Gombauld, Jacques de Serisay, and four others. Writing years afterward, Pellisson evoked the ethos of *otium* that governed their sessions: "in total innocence and liberty...without publicity and without ceremony, and without any laws other than those of friendship, they together savored all that can be had that is sweet and charming in the meeting of reasonable minds."[117] It was the "discovery" of this group's periodic meetings—which they attempted to keep secret—that led to the founding of the Académie française.

But the Malherbians or purists held no monopoly over literary sociability; other groups, with somewhat different perspectives, also seized the terrain, indicating that a concern for the state of the vernacular was not limited to partisans of one approach. Before it was apparent that Malherbe's "doctrine" had prevailed, there were other coteries of writers already meeting with language and literature as their main agenda. One was the "Académie de Piat Maucours," also known as the "Académie des puristes," whose members harbored rather severe, restrictive views on linguistic purity. In his *Mémoires*, Michel de Marolles, a member of the group, provides an account of the reaction to their sessions of a young man from Languedoc, newly arrived in Paris in 1619:

> He could not prevent himself from expressing his astonishment at finding us examining certain ways of speaking our language, which he considered of little importance compared to other things, on which he thought it would have been better for us to employ our time. Perhaps he is right, but there was not one among us who was not convinced that for the perfection of the Sciences, nothing should be neglected, particularly with regard to eloquence and the purity of language, so necessary for clear expression and which can only be learned after much practice and with particular care.[118]

Marolles was an abbot, a savant, and an omnipresent figure on the literary scene, who managed to maintain ties with fashionable writers and *érudits* alike. He was joined in this informal academy by a handful of aspiring writers, including François de Molière d'Essertines, a promising writer associated with Théophile de Viau and the Duc de Montmorency, who was murdered in 1624; Guillaume Colletet, a future member of the French Academy; and Jean-Baptiste de Croisilles

---

[117] Freely translated, from Pellisson and d'Olivet, *Histoire de l'Académie française*, I: 13.
[118] Michel de Marolles, *Mémoires de Michel de Marolles, abbé de Villeloin*, 3 vols. (Amsterdam, 1755), I: 77–8.

(sometimes Croisille), another priest, who spent the last ten years of his life in prison for being secretly married. In Marolles's account, the academy's sessions resembled a study group or seminar: "Beyond the language and ways of speaking, we also examined the economy of the pieces, and each of us tried to write something on the subjects that were proposed."[119] They maintained a conservative attitude toward literature: while they were advocates of linguistic reform and the cause of "purism," they also insisted on preserving ancient forms and models. It is likely that Sorel had them in mind when he commented disparagingly on those writers who "do nothing but translate books, which is something quite servile; and when they wish to compose something for themselves, they only create ridiculous grotesques [*grotesques ridicules*]."[120]

The Illustres bergers were another group of mostly young writers, whose existence seems to date from the mid-1620s to around 1632. These "shepherds" lived up to their name by meeting in a pastoral setting on the banks of the Seine on the outskirts of Paris. There was meaning to their choice of venue, for, like many of their contemporaries, literati and aristocrats alike, they were followers of d'Urfé's *L'Astrée*, and strove to emulate the virtuous simplicity of the novel's characters. Their literary agenda inclined as much toward Ronsard as Malherbe; they celebrated the sixteenth-century court poet's birth every year. Still, they were not doctrinaire: Malherbe supposedly attended their earlier meetings, and he was included (posthumously) in the published dialogues that emerged from their rustic colloquies. Included in their ranks were writers who ultimately figured in the mainstream of French classicism, such as Colletet, Claude Malleville, Godeau, François Ogier, Nicolas Richelet, and Philippe and Germain Habert. Godeau, the Haberts, and Malleville were also members of the Conrart circle.[121]

It some cases, it seems as though to be a "writer" meant attracting or entertaining an entourage. Théophile de Viau, perhaps the greatest champion of a literary alternative to Malherbe, formed the center of another group, a kind of confraternity, possibly of a clandestine nature, which attracted such figures as Antoine Girard, sieur de Saint-Amant, Boisrobert, Maynard, Colletet, Pierre de Boissat, and Tristan l'Hermite, among others.[122] Colletet animated his own group in the early 1620s, a collection of poets who disavowed any allegiance in the partisan conflict between Malherbians and their critics. As one of the members of his group announced in the preface to a collective publication, *La muse champêtre*, "I am aware that these works are not fashioned according to the Laws of Modern Poetry that reign at Court. I know that those who have set themselves up as sovereign Judges in this domain entirely condemn this manner of writing."[123] A circle of

---

[119] Marolles, *Mémoires*, I: 78.
[120] Quoted in Antoine Adam, *Théophile de Viau et la libre pensée française en 1620* (Paris, 1935), 232.
[121] Maurice Cauchié, "Les églogues de Nicolas Frénicle et le groupe littéraire des 'illustres bergers,'" *Revue d'histoire de la philosophie et d'histoire générale de la civilisation*, no. 30 (Apr.-June 1942), 115–33. On a skeptical view of this group, see Schapira, *Un professionnel des lettres*, 63, 64.
[122] Adam, *Théophile de Viau*, 128, 138.   [123] Adam, *Histoire de la littérature française*, I: 343.

friends of the poet Saint-Amant also seemed to resist the purist movement and perpetuated, in their own discreet fashion, the bacchanalia tradition in the city's taverns.[124] In 1620 there is evidence of a small group that circulated around one Antoine Brun, whose confreres mostly hailed from the southeast. What seemed to distinguish this group was its deliberate and self-conscious embrace of archaic expressions and an outmoded poetic diction, despite the presence in their midst of such future "moderns" as Faret, Colletet, and Marin Le Roy de Gomberville. In a similar vein, but unusual because of the prominence of a female writer as animator of her own academy, Marie de Gournay hosted a group of *hommes de lettres* whose inclinations, in keeping with the taste of their hostess, ran contrary to the Malherbian trend of the day.[125]

The conjoined interest in language reform and the rejection of pedantry found other enthusiasts, even in the usually academic domain of philosophy. Of course, it was Descartes—especially the Descartes of the *Discours sur la méthode* (1637)— who famously strove to appeal to people of "good sense" with his "clear and distinct" ideas, and to that end wrote in French. As he writes in the preface, "If I write in French, the language of my country, rather than Latin, the language of my teachers, it is because I hope that those who use their purely natural reason will be better able to judge my views than those who believe only in ancient books."[126] But Descartes was a loner, a notorious recluse who stayed far away from Paris for most of his adult life. Others, if they were not as revolutionary in their thinking, also saw the cause of philosophy served by reaching out to a wider public, and did so directly.

A good example is the rather obscure figure of Louis de Lesclache (1600?–71) who from 1633 to 1669 offered public lessons in philosophy in his Parisian rooms to both men and women, apparently with great success. In a journal entry from 1643, someone in attendance recorded this observation: "On Saturday...after dinner, rue Quinquepoix, I was at M. Lesclache's, who gave three French lectures at the start of his lessons on philosophy in French. There were many present, including some Jesuits and other people of wit. He spoke of God according to Aristotle and pleased all those present." (Note the emphasis here on the ascription "French," mentioned twice in one sentence.) Lesclache apparently also held forth

---

[124] On Saint-Amant's group, see Adam, *Histoire de la littérature française*, I: 376–7.

[125] On Gournay's gatherings, see Marolles, *Mémoires*; Fogel, *Marie de Gournay*; Ilsley, *Daughter of the Renaissance*; Adam, *Histoire de la littérature française*, vol. I. On the Brun group, see Adam, *Histoire de la littérature française*, vol. I. The writer Pinchesne had a sort of *bacchique* academy with Costar and others: *Dictionnaire des lettres françaises: Le XVIIe siècle* (Paris, 1951) [hereafter *DLF*], 993.

[126] On this aspect of Descartes's approach to philosophical discourse, see Cavaillé, "'Le plus éloquent philosophe'"; and Marc Fumaroli, "Ego Scriptor: Rhétorique et philosophie dans le *Discours de la méthode*," in Henri Méchoulan, ed., *Problématique et réception du "Discours de la méthode" et des "Essais"* (Paris, 1988), 31–46; Elaine Limbrick, "To Write in Latin or in the Vernacular: The Intellectual Dilemma in the Age of Transition; The Case of Descartes," *History of European Ideas*, 16/1–3 (1993), 75–80; Alain Viala, "Le Discours de la méthode comme récit génétique," *Paragraphes*, 9 (1993), 153–63.

at the salon of Madame d'Auchy—known as something of an "academy" for its savant tone—before a mixed group of men and women.[127] In 1660, a contemporary left an account of Lesclache's influence over the years, an account that underscores his effort to bring philosophy to a lay audience of well-born men and women. "He was the first to purge philosophy of its barbarous terms and civilized this body of knowledge so necessary for the conduct of the lives of men who wish to distinguish themselves from the common sort. For twenty-five years and more he has made this his public duty, but in a manner quite different from that of the schools. He has rendered it so easy that women and young children find themselves capable of learning it, so clear he is in his method and his speech."[128]

Acknowledging these various groups of writers helps us understand how young men and at least one woman (Gournay) of this generation accumulated the requisite cultural capital to establish themselves as "writers" when publication was hardly the norm, nor even necessary. As well, Lesclache's public philosophy lessons show that *gens de lettres* were not simply talking among themselves; many took on the task of instructing and appealing to a certain "public."

Interactions between writers and aristocratic men and women were most sustained in the context of the salon, perhaps the most conspicuous and important informal association of the period. There were several in this period. The gatherings at the townhouse of Madame de Loges, Malherbe's mistress, attracted the leading literary lights of the day, including Chapelain and Balzac; but the *salonnière*, a Protestant, was persuaded to leave the capital in 1629 by Richelieu, who feared her association with a religiously inspired opposition. The Vicomtesse d'Auchy presided over another salon, which, however, gained a reputation for the dreaded pedantry, and thus was shunned as a sort of academy. The townhouse built by Roger du Plessis, marquis de Liancourt, in 1631 was more in keeping with the *mondain* spirit so congenial to aristocrats and fashionable writers. Chapelain, Gomberville, Saint-Amant, and several members of the Arnauld family were often in attendance. The most celebrated salon of the period was undoubtedly the Hôtel de Rambouillet, which flourished as a center of literary life and polite sociability for more than three decades. (In Chapter 5 we shall look more closely at this salon.) It may be, as has been argued, that its historical stature is as much a result of deliberate mythmaking on the part of *gens de lettres* who attached their reputations to its prominence.[129] In any case, its importance in the careers of numerous *gens de lettres* cannot be denied.

---

[127] Tallemant des Réaux, *Historiettes*, I: 135–6.

[128] This paragraph is based on Charles Urban, "Louis Lesclache (1600?–1671)," *Revue d'histoire littéraire de la France*, 1/3 (1894), 353–8. See also Sorel, *Bibliothèque française*, 97–8 on Lesclache: "un célèbre Professeur, qui depuis si longtemps enseigne la Philosophie en notre Langue, et qui a eu un si grand nombre d'Ecoliers. Il a maintenant fait des Livres sur toutes les Parties de la Philosophie."

[129] See Schapira, *Un professionnel des lettres*, chap. 4, and Antoine Lilti, *Le monde des salons: Sociabilité et mondanité à Paris au XVIIIe siècle* (Paris, 2005) on this.

The Rambouillet salon loomed large on the Parisian cityscape, but it shared the urban stage with a very different association, the Dupuy cabinet; indeed, they could be considered as constituting two poles in the cultural life of the capital.[130] In a subsequent chapter we shall look more closely into the life of this group, which really amounted to an institution—a sort of early modern think-tank that served as the informal headquarters of the Republic of Letters, attracting scholars from throughout Europe. But with the Dupuys we cross over into another world of letters and sociability—the savant milieu of Paris.

Here, too, as with the literary landscape, several private and informal associations, marked by the ethos of *otium*, flourished. The Minim monk Marin Mersenne presided over a sort of academy from his cell at the monastery of the Annonciade, an institution that had a virtual existence embodied in his wide correspondence with savants from throughout Europe. In a letter to Peiresc written in 1635, he boasts that when their common friend Gassendi comes to Paris, "he will see the most noble academy in the world which has just recently been established in that city, for it is entirely devoted to mathematics."[131] Another group met under the wide-ranging impresario Théophraste Renaudot, whose "conferences" at the Bureau d'adresse were held each Monday afternoon from 1633 to 1642. Unlike the other literary and intellectual conventicles, which limited their memberships, these were open to the public. Renaudot himself emphasized the public nature of his institution: "[I]t may well boast...of having given publicity to several wits who had previously held themselves hidden and buried in the dust of the schools."[132] And there is also the "academy" of Nicolas Bourbon, a scholar of Latin and Greek. The grand-nephew of his namesake, a well-regarded Greek poet, he was appointed professor of Greek Eloquence at the Collège Royale, but around 1620 retired to the Oratoire Saint Honoré, where, according to Pellisson, his gatherings were attended by "a great concourse of people of all sorts."[133] Although Bourbon intervened on the side of Balzac in the quarrel over his *Lettres*, the discussions were devoted to erudite, not worldly, concerns, suggesting the vitality of traditional scholarship and letters. His academy met until 1644. Another "academy" came about through the efforts of a medical man, Pierre Michon

---

[130] Jouhaud, *Les pouvoirs de la littérature*, 195; and Peter N. Miller, *Peiresc's Europe: Learning and Virtue in the Seventeenth Century* (New Haven, 2000), 68.

[131] P. J. S. Whitmore, *The Order of Minims in Seventeenth-Century France* (The Hague, 1967), 151. See also Jean-Robert Armogathe, "Le groupe de Mersenne et la vie académique parisienne," *XVIIe siècle*, no. 175 (Apr.-June 1992), 131-9; Adam, *Histoire de la littérature française*, I: 297.

[132] Brown, *Scientific Organizations*, 23-4. Howard Solomon emphasizes the public nature of the conferences and how the Bureau d'adresse departed from the norm of intellectual sociability of the day: "Renaudot's academy broke all the rules that were followed by the Académie Française, the circles of Dupuy or Rambouillet. It was public, and not private; it sought publicity, rather than fleeing from it; it was directed to rhetorical ends, as much as to informational and scientific ends." Solomon, *Public Welfare, Science, and Propaganda in Seventeenth-Century France: The Innovations of Théophraste Renaudot* (Princeton, 1972), 66. See also, more recently, Kathleen Wellman, *Making Science Social: The Conferences of Théophraste Renaudot, 1633-1642* (Norman, OK, 2003).

[133] Pellisson and d'Olivet, *Histoire de l'Académie française*, 245-6.

Bourdelot (1610–85), who earned his entry into the milieu of Parisian savants through his closeness to Mersenne's circle and also enjoyed the patronage of Henri II, prince de Condé (he was the physician to the Condé family). His sessions, convened every other week on Tuesday, were "conferences" covering a range of topics but somewhat skewed toward medical and scientific interests.[134]

Whatever differences and particularities characterized these groups, together they fostered an exchange of ideas, novel cultural patterns, and the circulation of people, creating a nexus of venues that both rivaled the royal court as the cultural center of the realm and signaled a robust intellectual and literary life in the generation following the Wars of Religion. We should not limit our sense of these groups to their status as institutions or associations, but rather appreciate them as porous byways that facilitated the movement of writers and savants across the Paris cultural cityscape. This can be illustrated by looking at the career of one well-connected writer as he made his way in this world, noting not only his many affiliations but also his several *compagnons de route*.

Guillaume Colletet (1598–1659) published several learned treatises on poetic theory and also accumulated a vast archive on the history of French poetry. He was a member of the first generation of the French Academy and also belonged to Richelieu's private academy of writers. In the course of his career, we find him circulating through a number of groups. In the 1620s, perhaps even earlier, he was part of the circle of young writers around Théophile de Viau.[135] About the same time, Colletet could be found in the private academy of Nicolas Bourbon.[136] Despite this association with an erudite group, Colletet was not entirely of this camp; indeed, his association with Théophile would seem to indicate an aversion for such "pedants." Like many of his generation, he ultimately identified with the *mondain* literary movement. Although he was somewhat critical of Malherbe's so-called doctrine, he did join the handful of devotees who crammed into Malherbe's small room each evening to hear the master propound his views, where he rubbed shoulders with future stalwarts of the literary establishment. On the other hand, he was not within Conrart's "circle"—that germ of the French Academy. Indeed, his literary loyalties remained interestingly skewed, for he was a leading member of the Illustres bergers. Likewise, his place among the *gens de lettres* who met in the home of Marie de Gournay allied him with the writer

---

[134] Anita Guerrini, *The Courtiers' Anatomists: Animals and Humans in Louis XIV's Paris* (Chicago, 2015), 44.

[135] Other boon companions of the beleaguered writer were Saint-Amant, Godeau, Nicolas Frénicle, and the Luillier brothers, who were both associated with the Dupuy cabinet.

[136] Adam, *Histoire de la littérature française*, I: 286. Among the other members were François Guyet, a well-known *érudit*; Adrien de Valois, the historiographer; Charles Garnier, a court poet; Gilles Ménage, an important savant and author of *Les origines de la langue françoise*; Naudé; Balzac; Chapelain; and François Ogier, who wrote in defense of Balzac during the controversy over his *Lettres*. Guy Patin, who was also a habitué of the group, gives the impression that their discussions sometimes touched upon sensitive topics, especially with regard to the Jesuits, for he advised Bourbon's son to burn the records of their meetings; de Boer, "Men's Literary Circles," 738.

probably most identified with the opposition to modern literary styles; it was a group that included Malleville, the Ogier brothers, Claude de L'Estoile, and Boisrobert. He was also among the young *gens de lettres* who gravitated to Antoine Brun, a group that included Frénicle, Boissat, Faret, and Malleville. Starting in 1632, Colletet animated his own private academy in the confines of his extensive library, which was apparently well stocked with the help of his friend Gabriel Naudé. Several of the Illustres bergers were usually in attendance, joined by others including Naudé, Saint-Amant, Faret, Marolles, and Tristan l'Hermite. Although not known as a playwright, Colletet is mentioned as having a place in the ranks of a group of young dramatists meeting around 1628. He was also a member of the so-called "Académie de Piat Maucours." It is likely that he was part of the entourage of *gens de lettres* attached to Chancellor Séguier, which met from 1633 to 1643, for he is mentioned as a translator of a work by Séguier's grandfather, which was edited by a known attendee. Finally, Colletet definitely figured among the select few, including Patin, Gassendi, Eli Diodati, and other so-called *libertins*, who were invited to Naudé's country home.[137]

Colletet's march through the thicket of Parisian sociability shows a man of varied tastes and associations. While he certainly ranks as an establishment "insider," given his proximity to Richelieu, he still maintained ties with a range of *gens de lettres* and savants, some outside the literary mainstream. In this sense he was, in fact, typical, for, like most other writers and savants, he cultivated ties running along two axes—both the vertical link to the cardinal, or to some other *grand*, and his horizontal associations with his "friends" in the many subgroups that made up the literary culture of the early seventeenth century.

The New Translators

In 1635, shortly after the Académie française was officially established, Vaugelas read before the assembly a manuscript written by an absent colleague, Claude-Gaspar Bachet de Méziriac's *De la traduction*, one of the first theoretical considerations of the art of translation. In particular, the treatise criticized Jacques Amyot's version of Plutarch (1559), long considered an exemplary text, for its many errors and infelicities, asserting that "no one would deny that there is much that needs to be revisited regarding Amyot's style, and that it is far removed from the purity of language that one finds in the works of those who are considered the best writers today."[138] Vaugelas's interest in translation was not incidental to his

---

[137] For the information in this paragraph, see de Boer, "Men's Literary Circles"; Adam, *Histoire de la littérature française*; Cauchié, "Les églogues de Nicolas Frénicle"; DLF.

[138] Quoted in Dinah Ribard and Hélène Fernandez, "Histoire," in Yves Chevrel, Annie Cointre, and Yen-Maï Tran-Gervat, eds., *Histoire des traductions en langue française: XVIIe et XVIIIe siècles, 1610–1815* (Lagrasse, 2014), 780–1. See also Julie Candler Hayes, *Translation, Subjectivity, and Culture in France and England, 1600–1800* (Stanford, 2009), 36. See Sorel, *Bibliothèque française*, 274–5 n. 10.

general concerns; as we have seen, he worked for thirty years on producing a French version of *The Life of Alexander* by Quintus Curtius. Translation was an important aspect of the literary culture of the early seventeenth century; many *gens de lettres*, even if they were not translators themselves, took an active interest in the project of rendering Greek and Latin texts into correct and stylish French. The aim was not only to make accessible these important works, works that opened up the world of classical learning and literature to French men and women who lacked the requisite education and linguistic preparation to read and appreciate the originals, but also to demonstrate that the French language, if sufficiently refined and perfected, had the capacity to express the ideas and spirit of the ancients. As several commentators noted, translation was as much about French eloquence, about demonstrating the stylistic capacity of the contemporary vernacular, as it was about actually translating texts from other languages.

The fact that Valentin Conrart was so active in patronizing translation projects is an indication of their importance for contemporary *gens de lettres* and the *mondain* reading public alike. Conrart did not work as a translator himself—he was competent in neither Greek nor Latin; but he used his considerable power and influence in the literary world to encourage others to undertake translations. The permanent secretary of the Académie française, Conrart was connected to virtually everyone and every venue of importance in literary and social circles. He was close to Chapelain, an intimate of the Rambouillet salon, a protector and sponsor of a whole range of men of letters, as well as the host to the group of writers meeting in 1629 who formed the core of the Académie française. Most of the writers who undertook translations were associated with him, such as Louis Giry, Guillaume Colletet, Olivier Patru, and Nicolas Perrot, sieur d'Ablancourt. And in the letters of dedication they offered him, Conrart embodied, as Nicolas Schapira writes, "the man of letters as *honnête homme*, desirous of reading in French the masterpieces of the Ancients: an ideal image of the public imagined for these translations."[139]

The most significant translation of the day, the *Huit oraisons* of Cicero, published in 1638, was dedicated to Conrart, who organized and sponsored the project, securing the services of Jean Camusat, the printer most closely connected with *mondain* publications as well as the official printer of the academy. Although the translators of this volume remained anonymous, they were all members of Conrart's circle and already well known for their translations. D'Ablancourt was the author of four of the orations; Giry, Patru, and Pierre Du Ryer were responsible for the rest. Soon after the publication appeared, Gilles Ménage, a savant and outspoken critic of the *mondain* writers, sarcastically christened these translations "*les belles infidèles*," or "the beautiful but unfaithful." It was a label that stuck.[140]

---

[139] Schapira, *Un professionnel des lettres*, 164.

[140] Ménage explains that this is the same name "he gave when he was young to one of his mistresses." Yen-Maï Tran-Gervat, "Penser la traduction," in Chevrel, Cointre, and Tran-Gervat, *Histoire des traductions*, 369–432, on 382. More generally, see especially Roger Zuber, *Les belles infidèles et la formation du goût classique* (Paris, 1995).

And "unfaithful" their translations were, for the authors abandoned the time-honored feature of scrupulously transposing the ancients into French in a word-for-word fashion, preferring, rather, to fashion texts that were readable and eloquent. In a preface to one of his translations, d'Ablancourt explained that his intent was to present the ancients as if they lived in the seventeenth century. In his translation of Tacitus, for example, he replaced proper names, which he deemed unimportant or potentially confusing to contemporary readers, with general terms; and he also eliminated vulgar passages that risked offending the sensitivities of his refined readership. For him, faithfulness to the original wording was nothing more than a "Jewish superstition."[141]

D'Ablancourt did not hesitate to edit, modify, or even rewrite the original, as long as it achieved its goal of conveying the essential meaning of the texts to his *mondain* readers. And this, like the efforts of the "purists," attracted the scornful commentary of savants, who were generally quite critical of the whole alignment of literary culture with the tastes and intellectual capacities of the gentlemen and ladies of the court and salon. As with the movement for language reform, this reaction is proof of its significance. La Mothe le Vayer's comment on the value of venerable texts in translation was typical of the traditional view: the difference from the original is like the difference between the front and back of a tapestry.[142] Ismaël Boulliau, an astronomer who was close to the Dupuys, was scathing when it came to these new translators: "Do you know why I am so angry when I look at all these translations?" he wrote to Jacques Dupuy. "These interpreters are corruptors. Each wants to refashion into French this beautiful literature, and those who drink only from the muddy cisterns and crevices want to impose it upon those who draw from the clear and pristine original fountains. In the end you will see that this will produce dummies, not savants," he concludes, "for it is impossible to understand things perfectly in a translation rather than the original."[143]

In an earlier work, d'Ablancourt emphasized the imperative of rendering his translations into eloquent, not merely serviceable, French: "I believe that two works resemble one another more when both are eloquent than when one is eloquent and the other not.... After all, we only render an Author in part, if we rob him of his eloquence."[144] Elsewhere he insists on the necessity of taking liberties in translation, otherwise "we will end up with a carcass with all its beauty gone." The translator must consider the "purpose" of the original work, not simply its words; the idea was to make it "French," not to teach young readers Greek or

---

[141] *DLF*, 1226.
[142] François de La Mothe le Vayer, *Mémorial de quelques conférences avec des personnes studieuses* (Paris, 1669), 100–1. But see Sorel's critique of La Mothe le Vayer's criticism, citing his analogy without acknowledging the source: *Bibliothèque française*, 285.
[143] Henk J. M. Nellen, *Ismaël Boulliau (1605–1694): Astronome, épistolier, nouvelliste et intermédiaire scientifique* (Amsterdam, 1994), 110.
[144] Hayes, *Translation, Subjectivity, and Culture*, 31.

Latin.[145] In a later work, a translation of Lucian published in 1654, d'Ablancourt made explicit his method: "I do not always remain faithful to either the words or the thoughts of the author; and while adhering to his purpose, I convey things in our air and in our fashion. Different times require not simply different words but also different thoughts." As a translator, he likens himself to ambassadors who "are accustomed to dress in the manner of the country to which they are sent, for fear of being ridiculed by those they try to please."[146] In all of this, as Emmanuel Bury points out, d'Ablancourt and his associates were convinced they were merely emulating the ancients. Did not Cicero and Virgil do the same in "translating" Plato and Homer? Indeed, the contemporary discussion over the modalities of "imitation" only confirmed their approach to translating. Colletet, for example, spoke for his literary peers when in a discourse pronounced at the Académie française in 1636 he asserted that "imitation" never demanded slavish attention to the words or style of the original, but rather an appreciation of its "conception." The goal, in fact, was not merely to reproduce the original but to improve upon it.[147] The desire to accommodate contemporary readers is underscored by Du Ryer, who provided the preface to Vaugelas's translation: "Here is the celebrated Quintus Curtius, appearing in all his pomp and with every advantage on the Stage of France." Vaugelas, he continued, " "sought always the clearest, the simplest, and altogether the most concise French."[148]

This approach was not limited to texts in ancient languages; translators of recent or contemporary literature in English, Italian, or Spanish also followed suit. Jean Baudoin, who was one of the most prolific translators of the day, normally began his work with previous translations, if they existed, and then strove to produce a text in a "modern" French, which, he asserted, was actually an improvement on the original.[149] In the preface to his translation of the works of Tacitus, he declared his intention "to liberate [French] from a dependence on other languages, especially Greek, Latin, and Italian."[150] For this he was severely criticized by Charles Sorel, who nevertheless recognized that translations should be updated every twenty years. For Baudoin, guided by the purist vogue, the "bad taste" of foreign authors had to be supplanted by the "clarity" and "cleanness" of modern French.[151] In a preface to one of his translations, he acknowledged his strategy of eliminating phrasing and references that smacked of "Galimatias." Galimatias, recall, was a dreaded figure in Furetière's allegory that began this

---

[145] Emmanuel Bury, "Traduction et classicism," *Littératures classiques*, 19 (1993), 129–43, on 133.
[146] Bury, "Traduction et classicism," 134.
[147] Bury, "Traduction et classicism," 133–4. See Guillaume Colletet, *Discours de l'éloquence et de l'imitation des anciens* (Paris, 1658).
[148] Hayes, *Translation, Subjectivity, and Culture*, 33, 43.
[149] On Baudoin, see Fritz Nies and Yen-Maï Tran-Gervat, "Traducteurs," in Chevrel, Cointre, and Tran-Gervat, *Histoire des traductions*, 103–85, here 151–4.
[150] Nies and Tran-Gervat, "Traducteurs," 153.
[151] Nies and Tran-Gervat, "Traducteurs," 152; Emmanuel Bury, "Trois traducteurs français au XVIe siècle et XVIIe siècle: Amyot, Baudoin, d'Ablancourt," *Revue d'histoire littéraire*, 3/97 (1997), 367.

chapter. The act of translating, in both the literal and the more general sense, was a weapon in the campaign against this prime enemy of "Good Sense."[152]

* * *

Whether purists, their critics, or savants, *gens de lettres* in this period gravitated to their own associations. Thus, whatever distinguished them, and despite their differences in size, social profile, and cultural commitments, these groups all stood outside the established institutions and professions that made up the traditional landscape of French public life. And by and large, they were animated by people who participated in these associations not by virtue of their formal status—as, for example, a member of the clergy or an officer of state—but rather as writers or savants, despite the fact that these lacked a formal "dignity." In other words, the ethos of retreat—of *otium*—defined this associational culture.

But *otium* did not mean quiescence or the disavowal of contention, certainly not in matters having to do with language, as we have seen. The period was marked by a series of notable "quarrels" pitting different camps of writers and their partisans against one another. In Chapter 3 I will look at the one involving Théophile de Viau in 1623-4, which was, of course, much more than a quarrel: it was a real life-and-death campaign against the poet for blasphemy, heresy, sodomy, and other "crimes." The quarrel over Balzac's *Lettres*, at about the same time, as also already noted, gave rise to a remarkably acrimonious spat among a range of commentators, some using the occasion to make clear their basic contempt for the new linguistic and literary positions Balzac represented. Perhaps the most famous quarrel of the period—certainly the one that has most interested posterity to this day—broke out over Pierre Corneille's *Le Cid* in 1637, a controversy that provided an occasion for the newly founded Académie française to establish its bona fides in literary matters. Though certainly contentious, unlike the quarrels provoked by Théophile's writings and Balzac's *Lettres*, it remained largely an intramural affair, involving writers who, while they differed on the virtues of Corneille's play and the way he promoted himself as a playwright, were still of the same literary camp. It might be said that the quarrel was joined precisely because the various factions were of one mind about something more fundamental than the issues dividing them. And this was that the theater, and the literary culture that generated it, was legitimate and important—indeed, an element of culture worth fighting for.

Without denying the many differences that marked seventeenth-century literary culture and intellectual life, there was one even more fundamental difference. This was the division between those who remained wedded to erudite humanism, with little concern to appeal to a wider readership of minimally educated elites, and those committed to fashioning French into a literary vernacular distinguished

---

[152] Pellisson and d'Olivet, *Histoire de l'Académie française*, 298 on Baudoin: "Baudoin's style in translating was 'natural, easy [*facile*], and French [*français*].'"

by clarity, regularity, and accessible eloquence. As noted, there were some who associated with both camps and freely circulated along the byways of contemporary literary and intellectual culture without any sense that they were crossing significant boundaries. But the divide was considered fundamental nevertheless. In *Le lycée* (1632), an important text on the emerging code of *honnêteté*, Pierre Bardin, a member of the first generation of the Académie française, framed the division in rather categorical terms. "Two kinds of writers now dominate all the presses," he writes. "One is inventive in exercising the imagination; the other displays all the riches of memory. The first are poets and the writers of novels... who have at least succeeded to a degree that their writings have found a place in the 'cabinets' of ladies. The others are those who, in order to gain the approval of knowledgeable men, study languages, the opinions of the first authorities, relating to the greatest difficulties in the sciences, on the illumination of obscure passages in old books."[153] To focus on this division is to shift our attention away from the dominant theme in the cultural history of seventeenth-century France. For the common narrative in this respect, in keeping with an obsession with "absolutism," recounts the monarchy's relentless and total monopolization of patronage and the steady imposition of royal authority over the arts, a process symbolized in the Age of Richelieu by the founding of the Académie française. But there is another narrative that, in the realm of "letters," at least, tells a somewhat different story, of the emergence of a *mondain* French literature deliberately fashioned by a generation of *gens de lettres* who strove to appeal to a wider public of noblemen and ladies, those of the "Court and City."

Toward an Explanation

Why were *gens de lettres* so intent on rendering their texts in ways that would appeal to a broad readership? Why did they go to such great lengths to avoid even the semblance of pedantry? Was the crown the force behind this movement to purify the French language? In fact, the links between this movement and the monarchy are weak at best. While the ambition to elevate the French vernacular was often rhetorically linked to the crown's interests and efforts, in actual fact its sources were largely autonomous of the court's influence and example. Balzac, though he certainly curried Richelieu's favor, aimed his epistolary texts at a whole range of aristocrats and *gens de lettres*. The new translators were connected, through Conrart, to the Académie française, but the trend to translate ancient texts for *mondain* contemporaries was set in motion long before the founding of this royal institution. Of all these writers, Malherbe most energetically pursued

---

[153] Pierre Bardin, *Le lycée du Sr. Bardin, ou, En plusieurs promenades il est traité des connoissances des action et des plaisirs d'un honneste homme* (Paris, 1632), "Au Lecteur" (unpaginated).

royal patronage, but the active proselytizing for his "doctrine" took place not at court but in the salons and private assemblies of Paris. And while Vaugelas pronounced that one should follow the "usage of the court" in establishing the standards of correct French, he clearly meant a very capacious understanding of the Parisian elite and was careful to add that in any case the advice of the best-known writers should be sought. In short, the partisans of "modern" French did not depend on the crown for support; they did not see themselves as primarily serving the monarchy's interests; they were not identified with the court; and they certainly did not believe that the king should or, in the case of either Henri IV or Louis XIII, could serve as a model for purified French expression. Neither was seen as an exemplar of French eloquence; nor was the Louvre under these first two Bourbons a beacon of refinement.

If not the monarchy, then what promoted the purist movement? Was it the *gens de lettres* themselves, guided by their own sense of language and literature? Given the tricky task of explaining transformations of a cultural nature, especially something as unstable and difficult to trace as linguistic change, I think a certain measure of speculation—and tentativeness—is in order. I would suggest, however, that speculating along these lines takes us back to the sixteenth century.

But not the sixteenth century of humanism and the poets of the Pléiade. Although writers like Joachim du Bellay, author of *La deffence et illustration de la langue francoyse* (1549), certainly celebrated French and its literary possibilities, and went a long way toward yoking a commitment to a national language to a sense of nationhood itself, they remained wedded to traditional humanism.[154] Their ambitions for French could not disguise their clear preference for Greek, Latin, and even Italian as superior languages, with historically proven expressive capabilities. In their view, French, "a language so poor and denuded" (Du Bellay), needed "ornaments" borrowed from these more esteemed languages.[155] Moreover, writers in the seventeenth century made clear their opinion of their predecessors by their persistent belittlement of Ronsard as a literary model. Ronsard's reputation plummeted; after 1631, his works were not reprinted until 1781. As noted, Malherbe demonstrated his disapproval of Ronsard's poetry by blackening out half the text of his collected verses, and filling the margins with scathing commentary on those left untouched.[156] Chapelain found his that his tastes smacked more of a schoolboy than a man of the court.[157] Though he acknowledged the Pléiade poets

---

[154] On Du Bellay and other sixteenth-century poets serving the cause of the "nation," see Timothy Hampton, *Literature and Nation in Sixteenth-Century France: Inventing Renaissance France* (Ithaca, NY, 2001). See also Cohen, "Courtly French, Learned Latin, and Peasant Patois," for the mixed attempts of sixteenth-century humanists and poets to elevate the cause of French.

[155] Jacques du Bellay, *La deffence et illustration de la langue françoyse* (1549), ed. Henri Chamard (Paris, 1904), 3.

[156] Racan, "Vie de Malherbe," 37–8.

[157] *Lettres de Jean Chapelain, de l'Académie française*, ed. Philippe Tamizey de Larroque, 2 vols. (Paris, 1880–2), I: 635.

for rescuing French letters from "barbarism and savagery," Balzac criticized them for squandering their talents by cravenly imitating the ancients. Writing to Jean de Silhon, he noted that there was much that was praiseworthy in Ronsard's verses, but "far more to disgust you."[158]

Rather than the poets of the sixteenth century, I think we should look to religious writers of that period who, more than their secular-minded contemporaries, understood the virtue and necessity of addressing a public at their own level. The agenda was set by Ignatius Loyola in one of the articles in the Constitution of the Society of Jesus: "They will exercise themselves in preaching and in delivering sacred lectures in a manner suitable for the edification of the people, which is different from the scholastic manner, by endeavoring to learn the vernacular language well, to have, as matters previously studied and ready at hand, the means which are most useful for this ministry."[159] Fumaroli's magisterial study copiously documents the intense involvement of churchmen from the middle of the sixteenth century, especially Jesuits but certainly not exclusively, in cultivating registers of eloquence designed to reach the laity. While, unlike the new *mondain* writers, they insisted on the superiority of an *éloquence orale* over texts—the "pulpit" over the "pen"—their commitment to vernacular expression was if anything historically more sustained.[160] And with their re-admission to the realm in 1603 through their curriculum, the Jesuits conveyed this linguistic commitment to a generation of young men, for many of the *mondain* writers were educated in the society's *collèges*.[161]

An appreciation of several generations of clergymen who thought about the nature of language in their education and evangelizing, then, helps to explain the "push" toward a reformed French. But to understand the "pull" returns us to a consideration of the social context that nurtured the new literary and linguistic culture. It was primarily the French nobility, especially the Parisian elite, that constituted a "public" for this new generation of *gens de lettres*—"*la cour et la ville*." Their literary and intellectual commitments were forged in their relationship with those noblemen and other elites who, in the generations following the Wars of Religion, began to identify with a literary culture that, in turn, was largely fashioned in their image. In order better to understand the relationship between *gens de lettres* and the aristocratic Parisians who found their company so congenial and advantageous, we need next to look more closely at the social context of the city itself and the intellectual and literary sociability that characterized it in the generations following the Wars of Religion.

[158] H. Frank Brooks, "Taste, Perfection and Delight in Guez de Balzac's Criticism," *Studies in Philology*, 68/1 (1971), 82.
[159] Saint Ignatius of Loyola, *The Constitution of the Society of Jesus*, trans. George E. Ganss (St. Louis, MO, 1970), 201.
[160] Fumaroli, *L'âge de l'éloquence*, 357 and *passim*.
[161] On the intense involvement of French theologians in adapting their teaching and preaching to the contours of an accessible vernacular, see Gay, "Les 'Théologies françoises,'" 197.

2
Aristocrats and Writers
The Emergence of a Parisian "World"

It might be said that the Paris we know today—that is, the *centre ville* of old buildings and thoroughfares inside and between the boulevard corridors created by Haussmann's urbanism in the late nineteenth century—was largely a product of the early part of the seventeenth.[1] Whether or not Henri of Navarre actually said "Paris is well worth a mass," his actions as king certainly proved his appreciation for its value. Upon assuming power, he took the unusual measure of appointing himself governor of the city, and his subsequent actions suggest that he understood the position as more than symbolic. In 1601 he announced his intention "to stay and live in this city for many years...and to make this city beautiful and full of all the conveniences and ornaments that are possible."[2] He was true to his word. After his assassination in 1610, a pamphlet reflected, "as soon as [Henri IV] became the master of Paris, you could see construction workers all over the city."[3] The results were soon apparent. In his play *Le menteur* (1644), Corneille enthused that Paris had been "miraculously" raised as if from a ditch, offering viewers a spectacle of a city that could only be inhabited by "Gods and Kings."[4]

The Paris Henri conquered was certainly in need of attention. For much of the second half of the sixteenth century, it had been the scene of conflicts and uprisings, of massacres and assassinations, leaving whole parts of it neglected and derelict. Buildings were crumbling, institutions underfunded, whole neighborhoods abandoned.[5] From 1589 to 1594, Paris was under siege, leaving vast areas of rubble, the remnants of a war zone. But as is often the case in history, wartime devastation provided an opportunity for renewal and renovation. The city's recovery was in fact remarkably swift. Part of the story can be told in numbers, in a rapid demographic resurgence. After the last phase of the conflict, the population

---

[1] For a recent study that emphasizes the importance of the seventeenth century as creating modern Paris, see Joan DeJean, *How Paris Became Paris* (New York, 2014).
[2] Quoted in René Pillorget, *Nouvelle histoire de Paris: Paris sous les premiers Bourbons, 1594–1661* (Paris, 1988), 273.
[3] From the *Mercure françois*, 1612, as quoted by DeJean, *How Paris Became Paris*, 6.
[4] Quoted in Elizabeth Kugler, "Spectacular Sights: The Promenades of Seventeenth-Century Paris," *L'Esprit créateur*, 39/3 (1999), 38.
[5] On the challenges facing Henri IV following the Wars of Religion in Paris, see Roger Chartier, "Power, Space and Investments in Paris," in James L. McClain, John M. Merriman, and Ugawa Kaoru, eds., *Edo and Paris: Urban Life and the State in the Early Modern Era* (Ithaca, NY, 1994), 137.

Dignified Retreat: Writers and Intellectuals in the Age of Richelieu. Robert A. Schneider, Oxford University Press (2019).
© Robert A. Schneider. DOI: 10.1093/oso/9780198826323.001.0001

bounced back, regaining its 1560 level of 300,000 by 1600. With this, the size of the cityscape grew as well, nearly doubling by 1680.[6]

The post-bellum city experienced a facelift. Under Henri's impetus, the Pont Neuf, languishing in a half-built state since work had abruptly stopped in 1588, was finally completed, providing the city with an impressive and convenient pathway across the Seine, which in addition opened up other spaces for traffic and congregating. Royal initiatives were responsible for two important projects of urban renewal and beautification. The Place Royale (today's Place des Vosges), a great space in the heart of the Marais, was originally conceived for manufacturing. But once reclaimed, after having been largely abandoned since the jousting accident there that cost the life of Henri II in 1559, it proved irresistible to the property lust of noblemen, high officials, financiers, and royal officials seeking new abodes in an exclusive neighborhood. The development of the Marais and elsewhere was in keeping with the king's conviction that it was "more necessary than ever to increase the size of Paris so as to accommodate the seigneurs, gentlemen, and other officials of our entourage."[7] Richelieu purchased a property there in 1615.[8] The Place Dauphine was a smaller area, and attracted less prominent property owners, but it still offered the opportunity for spacious residences "previously unknown in Paris to all but kings and princes." Other areas, such as the Isle Saint-Louis and the Faubourg Saint-Germain, also proved ripe for development. This was the golden age of private hotels, which foreign visitors, impressed by their size, if not necessarily their architectural style, referred to as "palaces." Mme de Rambouillet's townhouse, which she designed herself, was only the most famous of these.[9]

A feature of the city's renewal was the return of the nobility. After the religious wars, an enlarged portion of this class established a presence in the capital, a presence that endowed the city with a titled elite that would prove crucial to the period's character. One explanation for this reflux into the capital—apart from the post-religious wars period of domestic peace—was the relative physical stability of the royal court. Although the king's entourage was still peripatetic, its peregrinations were largely limited to palaces in the Paris region; and in the seventeenth century, the Louvre was more often the royal domicile of choice. As a result, the

---

[6] For the demographic and physical transformation of Paris in this period, see Jean-Nöel Biraben and Didier Blanchet, "Essay on the Population of Paris and Its Vicinity since the Sixteenth Century," *Population*, 11/1 (1998), 155–88; Philip Benedict, "French Cities from the Sixteenth Century to the Revolution: An Overview," in Benedict, ed., *Cities and Social Change in Early Modern France* (London, 1989), 7–68; Chartier, "Power, Space and Investments in Paris"; Hilary Ballon, *The Paris of Henri IV: Architecture and Urbanism* (Cambridge, MA, 1991).

[7] Quoted in Pierre Lavedan, *Histoire de l'urbanisme à Paris*, 2nd ed. (Paris, 1993), 146. On the aristocratic character of the Marais, see Joan DeJean, "The Marais: 'Paris' in the Seventeenth Century," in Anna-Louise Milne, ed., *The Cambridge Companion to the Literature of Paris* (Cambridge, 2013), 24.

[8] Pillorget, *Nouvelle histoire de Paris*, 278.

[9] Orest Ranum, *Paris in the Age of Absolutism*, 2nd ed. (University Park, PA, 2002), 96 and *passim*.

realm's nobility increasingly settled in the capital in order to be within the orbit of royal preferment and splendor. The case of the Rohan family illustrates the point: while in the sixteenth century their main residences as well as sources of income were in Brittany and Poitou, by the early years of the seventeenth their base had shifted to Paris and its environs.[10] The same could be said for the realm's governors: by this time, this supposedly provincial corps of authorities was no longer so provincial; they resided virtually year-round in Paris. After 1605, governors were more likely to live out their lives in the capital than in previous times.[11] Paris attracted them for many reasons: it offered proximity to the king and access to credit, and it was the place to conduct legal affairs, the prime marriage market, the source of military commissions, and more generally where people acquired the trappings and insider knowledge of a new elite culture—urban, literate, sophisticated. In short, a large portion of France's privileged classes were becoming not only more urban but in particular more Parisian.[12]

It was an elite exposed to new intellectual and cultural trends, especially the virtues and advantages of educating young men. Of course, the traditional nobility's openness to intellectual cultivation was hardly universal; its reputed resistance to education and learning was an oft-repeated trope. Faret commented incredulously on "the ill-formed souls who, as a result of their beast-like stupidity, cannot conceive that a nobleman might be both learned and a soldier."[13] From the sixteenth century, however, this combination of traits was not only possible but increasingly viewed as desirable. What ultimately explains this embrace of "letters" by men of "arms" is a complex of factors, not the least of which was increased competition from the Robe class of nobles, and a perception, voiced by various reform-minded spokesmen, that the aristocracy had to change to meet the demands of the day. Charles Loyseau asserted that the traditional nobility's "scorn for letters and embrace of idleness" was to blame for its relative decline vis-à-vis the "fourth estate" of educated magistrates.[14] Montaigne might have disparaged

---

[10] Jonathan Dewald, *Status, Power, and Identity in Early Modern France: The Rohan Family, 1550–1715* (University Park, PA, 2015), 155–60.
[11] Robert Harding, *Anatomy of a Power Elite: The Provincial Governors of Early Modern France* (New Haven, 1978), 171 and *passim*.
[12] As DeJean notes for the neighborhood surrounding the new Place Royale, "In the 1630s, the Marais introduced Parisians to a novel urban experience—life in an upscale enclave, a privileged space that afforded residents both easy access to the city's amenities and the sense of living in their own private haven." *How Paris Became Paris*, 62. From a reading of the memoirs of Saint-Simon, a historian has calculated that over 1,000 marriages were "arranged, contracted and inevitably gossiped about at the court of Louis XIV." John Adamson, "Introduction: The Making of the Ancien Régime Court, 1500–1700," in Adamson, ed., *The Princely Courts of Europe: Ritual, Politics and Culture under the Ancien Régime, 1500–1750* (London, 1999), 8.
[13] Nicolas Faret, *L'honnête homme, ou, L'art de plaire à la cour* (1630), ed. Maurice Magendie (1925; reprint, Geneva, 1970), 24.
[14] Quoted by Virginia Krause, *Idle Pursuits: Literature and Oisiveté in the French Renaissance* (Newark, NJ, 2003), 70. See Gabriel Naudé, *L'addition à l'histoire de Louys XI* (Paris, 1630), for additional comment on the need of nobility to seek education.

the effeminizing effects of school learning, but in the seventeenth century the conventional wisdom among his disciples was that one of the liabilities of the French aristocracy was that it lagged behind its Italian and Spanish rivals in the appreciation for letters.

Such an attitude was once considered symptomatic of the nobility's atavism in the face of social and cultural changes—further proof that the titled and privileged elite was mired in its "feudal" ways, unable to adapt to the challenges of a developing society, threatened at once by a centralizing monarchy bent on depriving it of its traditional powers and a rising "bourgeois" class of educated Robe families with their own pretensions to leadership and privilege. This view is hardly tenable now. The ground had indeed shifted under the feet of the nobility in the period following the Wars of Religion. The wars themselves had instructed them on their own limitations, both military and political. Transformations in military technology and organization challenged their supremacy as unrivaled leaders on the battlefield. Venality of office had promoted many new families into the elite, as had the "inflation of honors," another result of the religious wars. The upper ranks of society were more crowded and competitive than ever, with families jostling for preference and position, both at court and in the wider *monde*. In addition, the advent of Catholic Counter-Reformation piety, combined with more secular value systems, some rooted in humanism, some stemming from newer intellectual trends, meant that aristocrats were increasingly confronted with new, more refined, or at least more demanding models for behavior and self-fashioning.

We now can appreciate that many aristocrats not only readily adapted to the changing and challenging developments but also managed to turn them to their own advantage. Indeed, it is remarkable, especially in the face of older assumptions about a "crisis of the aristocracy," how the titled elite continued to dominate seventeenth-century French society, especially culturally. And it is clear as well that this class did not have to wait until Louis XIV's Versailles to experience the "civilizing process"; changes in the *moeurs*, behavior, and values of a significant portion of the aristocracy were apparent long before the Sun King's reign. This is not to say that this transformation was seamless, or that it was accomplished without stress and anxiety. One has only to look at the "epidemic" of dueling during the first part of the century to acknowledge that there were many ways to meet these challenges; for many noblemen, the most satisfying way was in defiance, "libertinage," or even revolt. But even many of those who preferred to assert their traditional autonomy and license still embraced the new intellectual and cultural challenges with aplomb. Witness the case of the Duc de Montmorency, one of the most prominent patrons of letters, a veritable Maecenas, who kept company with the likes of Vanini, Théophile, and Sorel, while also ultimately embracing the *devoir de révolte*,[15] which led him to an ill-fated rebellion in 1632.

---

[15] Arlette Jouanna, *Le devoir de révolte: La noblesse française et la gestation de l'Etat moderne, 1559-1651* (Paris, 1989).

In all of this, as the case of Montmorency suggests, *gens de lettres* were at aristocrats' beck and call, often acting as agents, mediators, and translators of those new forces that challenged their patrons' traditional world.

* * *

One aspect of the cultural and intellectual rebirth of Paris following the years of religious warfare was the reestablishment of a Jesuit college in the capital in 1603. Gallicans decried the re-admission of this order, the spear-point of the Counter-Reformation, as a disastrous concession to the ultramontane forces that threatened to undermine the "liberties" of the French Church. Nevertheless, the dramatic spread of their schools in the early part of the century was important in meeting a rising demand for education, especially as the Jesuits seemed to recognize the strong desire of noble families to turn their sons into accomplished gentlemen, not scholars. From its establishment at the beginning of the century, the Jesuit *collège* La Flèche attracted many among the upper reaches of the aristocracy. In the 1607 yearbook, the names of five hundred sons of dukes, marquis, or counts are inscribed, out of a student body of twelve hundred.[16] The influence of the Jesuits cannot be underestimated, especially for those families aspiring to promote their sons into the officialdom. And many, if not most, of those who succeeded in securing a foothold in the emerging world of letters also owed their intellectual formation to the Jesuit fathers, whose emphasis on classical learning, and especially rhetoric, had a lasting effect on the literary and intellectual culture of the period.

The increasing interest on the part of aristocratic families in sending their sons to college, however, did not supplant the tradition of home schooling for the young. Many scorned the newer institution, associating it with upstarts—especially their competitors of the Robe.[17] Tutors were thus to be found in virtually every aristocratic household. And in this way, many budding *gens de lettres* first earned their livelihoods as instructors to the privileged youth of France. Chapelain, for example, began his Parisian career as a "preceptor" for the children of the Marquis La Trousse, as did many other young men with literary aspirations. But there were other pathways for integration into a noble household. Many became librarians, most famously Gabriel Naudé, who, while trained as a physician, served a series of patrons in this capacity.[18] Pierre Michon Bourdelot, another medical man who animated a private academy, was long the house physician

---

[16] Roger Chartier, Dominique Julia, and Marie Madeleine Compère, *L'éducation en France du XVIe au XVIIIe siècle* (Paris, 1976), 179.

[17] See Mark Motley, *Becoming a French Aristocrat: The Education of a Court Nobility* (Princeton, 1990), 18ff. for the persistent practice of home-schooling children of noblemen.

[18] More generally, in an inventory of writers from the period, Viala finds that 20 out of 256 served as preceptors, with several others serving as librarians in various families, although many more occupied this position in the earlier part of their careers. Alain Viala, *La naissance de l'écrivain: Sociologie de la littérature à l'âge classique* (Paris, 1985), 249.

for the Condé family.[19] The poet Tristan l'Hermite wrote in his autobiographical *Page disgracié* of his "profession of secretary," while Marie de Gournay noted how common personal secretaries had become "among the servants of households of middling status and less than this," and another writer declared that there was "not a gentleman with one hundred crowns income who does not have one."[20] The integration of writers into the households, entourages, and clientages of aristocrats, then, was both a cause and a symptom of the new literary and intellectual culture, creating a situation where few leading men or families were not linked in some fashion to the world of letters. Aristocrats had long enjoyed, and needed, the services of men with skills who could fill positions of tutor, preceptor, governor, secretary, librarian, historiographer, and the like. But the fact that aristocrats now more likely resided in Paris and maintained permanent residences there made relationships with *gens de lettres* more a part of their normal experience.

Even beyond this, aristocrats turned to *gens de lettres* as friends and counselors as they attempted to hold their own in the evolving urban milieus of court and city, where correct speech and a smattering of culture were increasingly expected. A nobleman on the rise would do well to have in his entourage someone who could draw upon the wisdom of the ancients as a source of advice, who could tutor him in the necessities and pitfalls of witty conversation, or who could simply correct his garbled French. Writers and savants were thus useful in the project of noble self-fashioning, especially as many gentlemen were beginning to appreciate the limitations of a strictly martial background and bearing. In Sorel's *Francion*, when the protagonist first encounters his future patron, Clérante, Francion meets his reluctance to be instructed with the argument that those who wish to command need "more wisdom, not more force."[21] Later, Francion proves his worth by penning a response to a libelous satire written by Clérante's chief enemy.[22] In the new age of print, it was often imperative for noblemen to enter the fray, not only as combatants jousting for power on the battlefield or in the Louvre, but also in the court of public opinion. As Jonathan Dewald points out, throughout the 1620s, Henri II de Condé (the Great Condé's father) proved adept or at least assiduous as a publicist, engaging men of letters to magnify his various exploits in printed pamphlets that might be seen as the early modern equivalent

---

[19] On Bourdelot, see René Pintard, "Autour de Pascal: L'Académie Bourdelot et le problème du vide," in *Mélanges d'histoire littéraire offerts à Daniel Mornet* (Paris, 1951), 73–81.

[20] For Tristan, see Viala, *Naissance de l'écrivain*, 53; for the quotes from Gournay, see George Hoffmann, *Montaigne's Career* (Oxford, 1998), 41.

[21] Charles Sorel, *Histoire comique de Francion* (1623), in Antoine Adam, ed., *Romanciers du XVIIe siècle* (Paris, 1958), 251; F. E. Sutcliffe, *Guez de Balzac et son temps: Littérature et politique* (Paris, 1965), 68.

[22] Sorel, *Histoire comique de Francion*, 249.

of press releases.[23] Several of the *Lettres de Monsieur de Balzac* were in fact originally drafted in the name of Balzac's patrons, the Epernons, as missives in the pamphlet war between sparring aristocrats in the earlier part of the century.[24] Writers could even be of service in their patrons' love lives. Malherbe wrote love sonnets for Henri IV's campaign to win the heart of Charlotte de Montmorency. Isaac La Peyrère was the go-between for Condé in his courtship of the Queen of Sweden.[25] Théophile's efforts were more down-to-earth: he more or less acted as Montmorency's smooth-talking pimp.[26] For those noblemen with literary pretensions, a writer could serve as a ghostwriter or an editor of their texts. Adrien de Monluc, who in fact published several anonymous works, benefited from the collaboration of his literary servant Charles Sorel. The early seventeenth century was a period that saw a veritable outburst of noble *mémoires*, which were almost always written with the help of an educated scribe or secretary.[27] Valentin Conrart was instrumental in providing the genealogical documentation necessary for proving the nobility of several families.[28]

* * *

Men of letters were thus equipped to provide a range of services to their aristocratic patrons. Some of these services were virtually menial, on the order of a hired pen; others suggest the position of a confidant, advisor, and all-purpose aide-de-camp. The latter roles are illustrated by the case of Jean Chapelain, who drew upon both his literary skills and his connections in aid of several aristocrats, in particular warriors on the front with whom he corresponded regularly.

Chapelain was a prominent figure in French literary life who managed to balance service to Richelieu with intense involvement in the Parisian *monde*. Despite his service to the cardinal, he assiduously maintained a wide correspondence with fellow *gens de lettres* and aristocrats alike. His letters to the Duc de Longueville, one of his main patrons, reveal a twofold mission on the part of the writer and cultural impresario: he kept the duke informed of Parisian political and social affairs, and he also served as a conduit for the letters the duke sent back from the front in Piedmont. These Chapelain would edit, rewrite, and then circulate in manuscript or have published in the *Gazette*, consequently enhancing the duke's martial, and literary, reputation.

---

[23] Jonathan Dewald, *Aristocratic Experience and the Origins of Modern Culture: France, 1570–1715* (Berkeley and Los Angeles, 1993), 189.

[24] Christian Jouhaud, *Les pouvoirs de la littérature: Histoire d'un paradoxe* (Paris, 2000), 232–40.

[25] Richard Popkin, *Isaac La Peyrère: His Life, Work and Influence (1596–1676)* (Leiden, 1987), 12.

[26] Antoine Adam, *Théophile de Viau et la libre pensée française en 1620* (Paris, 1935), 280.

[27] Joan Davies, "History, Biography, Propaganda and Patronage in Early Seventeenth-Century France," *Seventeenth-Century French Studies*, 13/1 (1991), 5–17.

[28] Nicolas Schapira, *Un professionnel des lettres au XVIIe siècle: Valentin Conrart, une histoire sociale* (Paris, 2003), 255.

Christian Jouhaud has documented Chapelain's service to a trio of aristocrats—two of them warriors—as they attempted to maneuver in particularly delicate situations.[29] In 1640 the young Jean de Montreuil found himself on a diplomatic mission in London; because the French ambassador, Pomponne de Bellièvre, was absent, Chapelain took pains to advise him on how to act in such a conspicuous and politically sensitive post. "I believe you should speak little and consider well what you do say," he writes. His instruction takes on a schoolmasterly tone: "it is extremely important to be perfectly familiar with the map of Germany where currently the quarrel over liberty is taking place and to be fully apprised of the interest of each of its Princes." For the Marquis de Gesvres, his service went beyond good counsel and entailed calling upon a whole network of friends and patrons to rescue him from a potentially ruinous situation. Though entirely guiltless, the marquis was implicated in a military scandal that ultimately led to the downfall of his commander, the Duc de La Valette, Epernon's son; at his wits' end, he appealed to his friend to help protect his reputation and career. Chapelain immediately turned to the milieu of the Hôtel de Rambouillet, where both he and Gesvres were well-known habitués, producing an outpouring of letters attesting to the marquis's courage and probity from such luminaries as the Condés, the Arnaulds, La Trousse, and the Duc de Longueville, among others. Here Chapelain's unique position as a man of letters with widespread contacts in the Parisian *haute société* proved instrumental for his aristocratic friend. In the case of the Marquis de Montausier, another aristocrat-warrior, his *crédit* served not only this even closer friend but his troops as well. In 1638 Montausier was posted as governor of Alsace, where his most pressing responsibility was the provisioning of the French army on a war footing. But difficulties abounded, most involving the resistance of several cities in coming through with supplies. Chapelain set to work in Paris, contacting through Jean de Silhon, a fellow academician and *créature* of Richelieu, the Alsatian agent at court, who in turn agreed to act on the army's behalf and apply pressure to the cities to get them to cooperate. The matter was not resolved without Chapelain engaging in some further deft maneuvering on his friend's, and the troops', behalf.[30] In all of these cases, it was Chapelain as factotum and man of letters who gave proof of his indispensability to his noble patrons.

Chapelain was unique among his peers, not least because of his political astuteness, considerable stature, and proximity to the likes of Richelieu, which made him an ideal intermediary and agent for aristocrats, especially those far from Paris. But even others less advantageously positioned could provide similar services. Nicolas Faret, for example, who was in the entourage of Henri de Lorrain,

---

[29] Christian Jouhaud, "Sur le statut d'homme de lettres au XVIIe siècle: La correspondance de Jean Chapelain (1595–1674)," *Annales: Histoire, sciences sociales*, 49/2 (1994), 311–47.

[30] All from Jouhaud, "Sur le statut d'homme de lettres," 335–9.

the count of Harcourt, offered his patron some astute if unconventional career advice. As a member of the Lorraine family, who were Richelieu's enemies, Harcourt was out of favor; but he apparently was open to a rapprochement with the cardinal in order to better his prospects at court. Faret was able to intervene on his behalf because he had access to Boisrobert, a fellow man of letters who was Richelieu's literary pet. As a remedy, it was proposed that Harcourt offer himself to Richelieu as a marriage partner for whomever the cardinal desired. The offer was accepted, and Harcourt ended up with both a new wife and a new military command.[31] Comments Pellisson, "Faret, who had always lived quite familiarly with [the count], rather as a friend than as a domestic, played a part in his new prosperity."[32]

There was thus certainly an instrumental, pragmatic aspect to the ties between men of letters and noblemen, but some relationships went beyond this. In some cases, writers participated in the rather intimate project of "self-fashioning"—constructing idealized portraits for the great that could both flatter and challenge them with better versions of themselves. With an aristocrat who had the ambition or self-confidence to engage in this mode of interaction—and who was fortunate to have found a writer equal to the task—the game could be a subtle, complex one indeed, sometimes entailing a remarkable degree of frankness, intimacy, and intrusiveness. And here the rhetoric of counsel—the muted, personal, and confidential tone of one person both listening to and advising another—characterized the exchange.

Balzac, Voiture, and La Valette

No publication exemplified this more than the *Lettres de Monsieur de Balzac*. These letters to prominent figures, many of them noblemen, demonstrate the power and eloquence of Balzac's rhetoric while also evoking an intimacy that cannot fail to impress with its authenticity. (Of course, to impress his readers with his intimacy and ease with the great was precisely the point.) They include a series of letters to his patron, Cardinal La Valette, who, though a great church prelate, was mostly committed to the warrior life. Although the letters are often about himself, Balzac manages to tear himself away from his favorite subject to attend to the interests and concerns of his interlocutors, especially when they are of the stature of La Valette. In his case, they flatter, cajole, and idealize—holding up a mirror reflecting an image of a better self.

---

[31] Gédéon Tallemant des Réaux, *Historiettes*, ed. Antoine Adam, 2 vols. (Paris, 1960), II: 237.
[32] Paul Pellisson and Pierre-Joseph Thoulier d'Olivet, *Histoire de l'Académie française, par Pellisson et d'Olivet*, 3rd ed., revised and enlarged, 2 vols. (Paris, 1743), I: 250.

He begins his correspondence by asserting the cardinal's nobility in the most generous terms, taking care to frame it appropriately. Family ranks first: "You come from the most beautiful source in the world and are born of a Father whose life is full of miracles"; then country: "You have been made Prince of a State which is limited neither by the seas nor by the mountains."[33] In Balzac's version of La Valette, he is possessed of qualities that set him above even those of high birth:

> Indeed...to have a great following, some striving to satisfy your pleasures, others worrying about your business, that you will always have in common with many people you despise. But to do good deeds, when you are sure they will never be acknowledged by the world; to fear only those things that are dishonest; to believe that death is neither good nor bad in itself, but if the occasion to receive it is honorable, it is always better than a long life; to have a reputation for holding your tongue when the most credulous know no better than to parrot common belief; this is what I value about you, My Lord, and not your Red Hat, and your fifty thousand *escus* in rent.[34]

Time and again he reminds La Valette of his superiority, of those qualities that distinguish him even from those of his own class. "You are elevated above the things of this world," Balzac informs him on an occasion when the death of a friend (or relative, it is not clear) seemed to trouble the cardinal's peace of mind.[35] Being of stronger stuff than most, La Valette, though mourning as only a great soul can, must realize that others look to him to provide an example of how one should deal with death. The subject of mortality surfaces several times in the letters, providing Balzac an opportunity not only to extol La Valette's superior abilities to meet and overcome misfortune, but also to coax him to a better understanding of what is expected of a truly great man. Here Balzac writes not precisely as a writer-cum-factotum but rather as a philosophical tutor. And his tone is less obsequious than challenging, even stern. To be sure, he disguises his counsel with disingenuous disclaimers about La Valette already being possessed of "all human wisdom," needing the precepts of "neither Seneca nor Epictetus."[36] Several passages in his letters read as Neo-Stoic lessons in the virtues of constancy, duty, and reason. He must learn to steel himself against the sufferings of others whose fate cannot be prevented by his efforts.[37] Though burdened by the travails of the world as only a great soul can be, he nevertheless should "taste a little the fruits which [this world] produces and reward yourself with something for all the success that continually comes to you."[38] Above all, he must remember that his exalted position binds him to a higher calling to serve king and country. After suggesting that it is time for

---

[33] *Les premières lettres de Guez de Balzac, 1618–1627*, ed. H. Bibas and K. T. Butler, 2 vols. (Paris, 1933–4), I: 11.
[34] *Lettres de Balzac*, I: 12–13.   [35] *Lettres de Balzac*, I: 16.   [36] *Lettres de Balzac*, II: 33.
[37] *Lettres de Balzac*, I: 88.   [38] *Lettres de Balzac*, II: 33.

him to set aside his grief over the death of his friend, Balzac challenges La Valette with the imperative of self-abnegation in favor of the life of duty to which he is destined. "It is to the public that you owe your cares and your passions, and it is not permitted for you to afflict a spirit that is no longer yours."[39]

Not all his counsel is of such an elevated nature; on occasion Balzac offers La Valette advice on more mundane matters—for example, how to handle himself amidst all those crafty Italians at the papal conclave in Rome. Here and elsewhere his discourse can be likened to that of a coach delivering a pep talk: his aim is to instill confidence by reminding his "player" of his strengths. "I have no doubt that you will maintain over the minds of the Italians the same advantage you have over ours, and that their tricks will be as useless in your presence as the charms of magicians are weak before divine things."[40]

Coach or sycophant? Balzac, to be sure, is a bit of both in these letters. But they should be more properly understood as exercises in the rhetoric of counsel, with all the features of intimacy and privilege entailed in the relationship between counselor and counseled. His "coaching," however, was done from the sidelines. And in this sense, Balzac's self-positioning in the *Lettres* is crucial. For he explicitly takes himself "out of the game," rhetorically distancing himself from the arena of action to which his great interlocutor is committed by birth and vocation. Often his expressions of recusal are couched with excuses of his weak health and medical condition, a theme running throughout the letters. "As for me," he writes in the context of counseling La Valette on his trip to Rome, "who does not have these concerns, and have put myself under the care of doctors, I must flee even the shadow of danger, living as I do in the world with as much fear as in a land of enemies or in a forest of wild beasts."[41] This stance of retreat fosters what might seem paradoxical—an intimacy of distance. But it also allowed Balzac to cast his relationship to the great on his own terms, that is, as a man of letters at once removed from and profoundly interested in the affairs of the world. The *Lettres de Monsieur de Balzac* was performative, advertising not only his new form of eloquence but also his proximity to the great, his ease and self-possession in their presence.

In the 1630s, it was Voiture's turn to serve La Valette in an epistolary capacity. The son of a wine merchant, Vincent Voiture was educated, like most of his confreres, by the Jesuits. Long in service to Gaston d'Orléans, he became a fixture in the Hôtel de Rambouillet: the salon was his main public, for he never ventured into print. His letters were not published until after his death, although they were likely passed around and read among the frequenters of the Rambouillet *hôtel*.

---

[39] *Lettres de Balzac*, II: 33.   [40] *Lettres de Balzac*, I: 22.
[41] *Lettres de Balzac*, I: 24. On this see Mathilde Bombart, *Guez de Balzac et la querelle des* Lettres: *Ecriture, polémique, et critique dans la France du premier XVIIe siècle* (Paris, 2007), 49.

Like Balzac, Voiture sounds the theme of distance: his warrior/patron is far away on the battlefront while the poet makes a point of representing himself as ensconced in the Parisian salon, and especially among the "ladies" eagerly awaiting the cardinal's return. Voiture appeals to La Valette's vanity in celebrating both his martial and amorous conquests—come home, he writes, adding, in reference to the women, that there he "will find a few enemies quite braver and prouder than the Germans."[42] Continuing in this vein throughout the letters, he constructs an ideal image of a fully virile man, accomplished in both domains. This is highlighted by the fact that Voiture's self-representation entirely lacks this warrior dimension—the poet usually places himself as the sole male in the privileged society of women. He does not precisely emasculate himself, for he also flaunts his own gallantry and (hetero)sexual prowess. (According to Tallemant, Voiture fought in at least four duels.[43]) This is indeed part of his bond with La Valette: they are both *galants*, presumably sharing the favors of those women of the Rambouillet milieu whose participation in the highly ritualized flirtation was not always chaste. But while in this sense he is able to meet La Valette "man-to-man," so to speak, he also takes on the attributes of his female companions—like them, he is marooned in civilian Paris, caught up in the life of endless aristocratic *divertissements*, fearful of their hero's safety, gushing with admiration at his martial exploits, and eager to have him return to their midst. Voiture, in short, represents an androgynous figure, serving as the perfect go-between for the manly La Valette and the female habitués of the Rambouillet salon.[44] Voiture was no doubt speaking for the Rambouillet ladies here and elsewhere. But he was also writing as a man whose declared affections for his patron, and his ambiguous position in the sexual hierarchy, allowed him to address La Valette in frank and intimate terms.

Despite this, his letters affirmed his essential inferiority to La Valette. As a mere writer, moreover, this certainly was his place, just as it was for others in the cardinal's extensive entourage. But unlike other underlings or clients, writers like Voiture had the advantage of being able to cast their dependent relationships in a currency they had mastered—language. He arguably, therefore, had a measure of control in the process of defining his relationship to his patron. This surely was one reason why Voiture and other *gens de lettres* were appreciated as insiders in this aristocratic milieu: they were a relief from the sycophantic attentions proffered by most other servants or clients. Voiture thus knew what he was doing when his letters suggest a certain degree of sexual rivalry vis-à-vis the ladies of the salon, however muted and ultimately undermined it was by his acknowledgment of the cardinal's superior prowess. He was not above including an original passage from Cicero in one letter, fully realizing that La Valette would have difficulty reading it; for this allowed him to assert his superiority in this domain by

---

[42] *Oeuvres de Voiture: Lettres et poésies*, ed. M. A. Ubicini (1855; reprint, Geneva, 1967), I: 254.
[43] Tallemant des Réaux, *Historiettes*, I: 495.   [44] *Oeuvres de Voiture*, 289, 323.

offering to tutor his patron on his Latin authors: "[I] will teach you the secret graces and the most hidden beauties of these writers; in a word, I will return to you all that you have lent me."[45]

But all of this banter and subtle gamesmanship ends when La Valette proves in desperate need of consolation, having suffered a career setback. And here it is most evident that his relationship with both Voiture and the Rambouillet milieu served as a kind of counterbalance against the demands and dangers of the world that a great aristocrat like him often encountered—as a sort of refuge of *otium* from the tribulations of *negotium*. It is not clear whether his failure to raise the Spanish siege at Verceil in Italy in 1638 was perceived at court as a personal debacle. La Valette, in any case, seemed to take it that way, and clearly others were murmuring against him. Voiture's letters at this difficult moment for his warrior friend are filled with solicitude and the kind of sage advice that only a man of letters schooled in Neo-Stoicism could offer. He begs him to be reasonable: "[Y]ou are hardly making use of your reason if this displeasure has continued this long."[46] He offers a logical rebuttal to his fears: "However, you speak as though you have lost, because of your mistakes, ten battles and a hundred cities; and it seems that you have been in despair for having lost a place which from the beginning everyone knew could not be saved."[47] He counsels moderation and prudence, cardinal stoic virtues: "Please take more moderate resolutions…and not being in a position to strike fear into your enemies, don't do it to your friends. You who have taught me everything I know, you certainly know that prudence is a general virtue that mixes with all others."[48] He reassures him, perhaps disingenuously, that his reputation has not been seriously damaged by the affair. And he agrees to pay court to Anne of Austria on his behalf.[49] Like Balzac, Voiture could play the coach as well as the sycophant.

Pierre Gassendi and His Patrons

Pierre Gassendi, the priest and philosopher, wrote hundreds of letters, almost all of them in Latin, to a wide range of friends and patrons. Between 1638 and 1653, he addressed almost five hundred—more than he wrote to any other single person during that period—to his patron, Louis-Emmanuel de Valois-Angoulême, son of Charles d'Angoulême, the illegitimate offspring of Charles IX.

Valois was the count of Alais, the governor of Provence, a prince of the realm, and a military commander on the front in both Italy and Lorrain. He also maintained a keen interest in books and philosophy; Mersenne's seventeenth-century

---

[45] *Oeuvres de Voiture*, 266–7. [46] *Oeuvres de Voiture*, 308.
[47] *Oeuvres de Voiture*, 309. [48] *Oeuvres de Voiture*, 310.
[49] *Oeuvres de Voiture*, 319 n. 2. She apparently was not terribly disappointed about the loss of Verceil, since it hurt Richelieu, her rival.

biographer described him as a "prince who strokes savants no less than warriors."[50] The association between Gassendi and Valois had many of the attributes of a typical patron-client relationship, with mutual service at its heart: Gassendi organized Valois's library, while Valois was instrumental in securing the philosopher-priest a high position in France's ecclesiastical establishment. But their relationship was really much more. Like the exchanges between Balzac or Voiture and La Valette, their correspondence shows Gassendi playing the role sometimes of tutor, sometimes of coach, sometimes of confidant. Except here, Valois also submitted himself to a sort of philosophical apprenticeship, with the learned Gassendi serving as master sage, patiently instructing his student in the teachings of Epicurus. Hundreds of his letters are long-winded expositions on Epicurus and his philosophy. In fact, they are less letters than written lectures; some even begin the way many professors today begin theirs: "As I was saying in my last letter," or "I left off my last letter to you with the discussion of such and such," or variations thereof.

This was, of course, Gassendi's major intellectual contribution: more than anyone else in the seventeenth century, he was responsible for recovering this ancient and controversial philosophy for Christian savants. Gassendi's letters to Valois dwell on this life-long project, which, in fact, he found it prudent to suspend in print after an initial publication in 1624.

The letters are in Latin. Valois was apparently up to speed, capable of reading them, and, if necessary, he undoubtedly had tutors in his household who could help him out. But the style of Gassendi's letters-cum-lectures is far from pedantic or technical or otherwise obscure; they conform to the rhetoric of the letter—intimate, personal, mannered only in the sense that they sometimes exhibit the sycophancy typical in the address of a client to a great patron. Valois's greatness is acknowledged, but there is no mistaking who has, intellectually, the upper hand here. Gassendi is the master. In fact, he uses Valois as a vehicle—a conduit for the articulation of a philosophy that, if disclosed publicly and in an academic discursive form, would likely have attracted censure. These letters, then, were a safe form of legitimation of a controversial subject.

Their focus, however, is not so much the "scientific" aspect of Epicureanism, that is atomism, but rather Epicurean moral philosophy. Gassendi's letters are heavily leavened with personal advice and counsel in the spirit of steeling the prince to the demands of his birth and position; more than anything, he hammers away at the point that study and philosophical meditation are not only the way to virtuous living but even more necessary for a great ruler. Gassendi is Valois's tutor and coach, urging him to stay on course, waste not a minute, keep to the narrow path of work, study, and duty. He expresses his satisfaction on learning that Valois

---

[50] Sylvie Taussig, *Pierre Gassendi: Introduction à la vie savante (1592–1665)* (Turnhout, 2003), 404.

is careful to spend part of every day reading and writing.[51] Contrary to its critics, he notes, the philosophy of Epicurus did not encourage rest but rather constant vigilance and study, even in moments of repose. Has Valois doubts about his moral mettle? "You say that you do not possess true virtue," Gassendi begins a letter from August 1641, apparently in response to his patron's qualms. "But that you wish to possess it: that thought derives from virtue itself." When Valois's only son dies, Gassendi's words of consolation amount to a philosophical meditation on misfortune, mortality, and grief. He reminds Valois that "human frailty" is incapable of pushing away such suffering—just as it should be: "It is not in vain that the author of nature himself wanted us to have such great attachment to our children." Nevertheless, he writes, "Wisdom, that divine gift, is not entirely useless in tempering the vehemence of our emotions, sweetening all our bitterness, and inclining our hearts to the decrees of nature's author." Gassendi reminds Valois of his forebears who also lost sons, but whose greatness was based not on their progeny but on their virtuous deeds. "The law of succession of everything now alive will continue to play its role," he concludes; "it will transform kingdoms into republics, republics into kingdoms and states of anarchy."[52]

Gassendi's correspondence with Valois was intense, but the relationship itself remained epistolary in nature; the philosopher-priest managed to resist the prince's overtures to join his patron's household, much to his relief. Indeed, his interactions with him were characterized by a distinct caginess, with Gassendi often playing hard to get, the prince in hot pursuit. Gassendi was intent, however, on not becoming Valois's "man." He even refused the prince's gift of a house in Provence, and wielded the strategy of avoidance with consummate skill, making sure that when Valois was in Paris, he was in Provence—and vice versa. Gassendi prized his freedom, something that, if deftly managed, a patron's support and protection could ensure. He also was intent on clarifying the emotional terms of the relationship, insisting—contrary to Valois's wish, it seems—that they were not "friends." In response to an overture, Gassendi asks, in effect, why Valois wants to label his affection for him as friendship, reminding him of the inequality of their "conditions." "As if you had forgotten the right you have to exercise your will over me, not only immediately but as often as you wish."[53]

In fact, Gassendi maintained a series of complex relationships with patrons throughout his career. Early on he established ties with both Mersenne and Peiresc, two figures who ensured his entry into the highest circles in both Paris and the wider Republic of Letters. In the late 1620s, Gassendi fell in with a very different sort of patron: François Luillier, a wealthy magistrate and officer. Like Peiresc, Luillier was close to the Dupuy brothers. There had to be some risk

---

[51] *Pierre Gassendi (1592–1655): Lettres latines*, 2 vols., ed. and trans. Sylvie Taussig (Turnhout, 2004), I: 193.
[52] *Gassendi: Lettres latines*, I: 365.   [53] *Gassendi: Lettres latines*, I: 347.

in Gassendi's relationship to Luillier, for the latter's lifestyle was notoriously disordered. But his wealth and wherewithal—including his extensive library—were at Gassendi's disposal. And he subsidized the publication of Gassendi's *Life of Epicurus*, something that apparently brought him great satisfaction. He also made possible the philosopher's trip to Holland, where he established contact with Isaac Beeckman, among others.[54]

After Valois's death in 1653, Gassendi found other patrons, and others sought him out. In the years just before his death, like many other French and European savants, Gassendi was courted by Queen Christina of Sweden, but he managed to deflect her invitation, preferring the virtual contact of letter-writing to taking up residence in the dangerously frigid climes of Stockholm. Gassendi died in the apartment of the Parisian nobleman Henri Louis Habert de Montmor, the last of his patrons, a wealthy official and an accomplished Latinist who in subsequent years would convene his own private academy. After his death, Montmor edited Gassendi's complete works in six volumes, adding a Latin preface in his own hand. Gassendi left him a telescope—a gift from Galileo.

Perhaps as interesting as this string of patrons are those whose advances Gassendi resisted. His refusal of Christina of Sweden's rather insistent overtures is easily explained by his dislike of travel and his age and health, compounded by the terrible experience of his friend Naudé, who, like several other savants, found her court not only unpleasant but deadly—he died there in 1653. But she was not the only potential patron Gassendi put off; indeed, fending off solicitous overtures seems to have been a pattern in his career. Séguier's invitation of protection apparently fell flat; the royal chancellor even failed to entice Gassendi to visit his library. He declined the patronage of such powerful men as Alphonse de Richelieu, the cardinal-minister's brother, and Henri de Mesmes, a president in the Parlement of Paris—even though both of them offered him attractive conditions: a library, a guarantee of complete independence, and the like.

Gassendi's career was thus bound up with patrons. He was, of course, hardly unique in this respect; most *gens de lettres* and savants found support not only in patronage but also amidst the dense network of literary and intellectual societies that abounded in early seventeenth-century Paris. Except for the Dupuys, Gassendi seemed to keep aloof from these. By all accounts, including his own, he was an inveterate loner—disdaining the company of others, although deeply attached to such men as Peiresc, Naudé, Mersenne, and Luillier. While Gassendi clearly

---

[54] Luillier has left testimony that speaks to the symbiotic relationship often embodied in patronage. Writing to Peiresc in 1634 on the occasion of the publication of Gassendi's *Life of Epicurus*, Luillier acknowledges his own role in making this "very lovely and useful work" public, and then confides, "Despite my retreat from public affairs, I am so happy that my life has rendered such a good service not simply to my country, which I believe I have done, but to all of Europe... even though I know I am not worthy of all that it means." François Luillier, "Lettres inédites écrites de Paris à Peiresc, 1630–1636," in Philippe Tamizey de Larroque, ed., *Les correspondants de Peiresc*, vol. XVI: François Luillier, *Lettres inédites, écrites de Paris à Peiresc, 1630–1636* (1889; reprint, Geneva, 1971), 29.

valued his protectors, just as clear is how valuable he was to them, so valuable that several important figures were willing to risk having their overtures rejected. Gassendi was obviously a "catch." But just as obvious is that he cleverly augmented his value by playing hard to get. For someone like Luillier, he represented the fulfillment of a desire to contribute something to the Republic of Letters. For Valois, he was an attentive and demanding tutor. Gassendi himself, beyond the support and protection, seemed to use his relations with his patrons and potential patrons as a means to assert his identity as an autonomous, even solitary, savant.

An Age of Maeceneans?

Beyond the one-to-one relationships many *gens de lettres* maintained with aristocrats and other elites, most were also immersed in the Parisian *monde* as members of various groups, private academies, cabinets, salons, and other gatherings that proliferated in the early seventeenth century. The sociability of that period was a feature of a revived city after nearly a half-century of religious warfare and urban strife. Contributing to this revival, as we have noted, was the influx of aristocrats and their colonizing of whole neighborhoods, along with a building boom that transformed the cityscape. The royal court at the Louvre was an important feature of post-bellum Paris, of course, drawing elites to the city because of its presence. It did not, however, function as a cultural beacon. It is sometimes assumed that until the eighteenth century the royal court exercised a sort of cultural hegemony over French, or at least Parisian, cultural life, leaving very little space for the emergence of an independent "city" culture. Certainly the court looms large under the Valois in the sixteenth century, and again in the latter part of the seventeenth with Louis XIV's creation of the supremely courtly venue of Versailles. But it cannot be said that the reigns of the first two Bourbons, whatever their other achievements, were distinguished by efforts to establish a court culture that could both represent the monarchy and appeal to a wider elite public.[55]

Commentators noted the dissolute, abandoned state of the Louvre during Louis XIII's reign, when the king's energies were more often claimed by war and his obsession with hunting. Richelieu himself frankly acknowledged, if only posthumously, the pitiful state of the French royal court, and despaired at ever

---

[55] To be sure, Henri IV mounted a series of impressive ballets that rivaled those spectacles for which his English counterparts are better known. He was also known for taking an interest in various building projects, and especially for the significant steps he took in refurbishing the Louvre. Louis XIII continued the tradition of his father, but outside the realm of the dance he showed little interest in culture, and certainly not in the world of letters, whose refashioning would forever be associated with his reign. Even the dance seemed to be inspired by Richelieu's efforts; according to Margaret McGowan, from 1635 most court ballets were performed at his behest. Margaret M. McGowan, *L'art du ballet de cour en France* (Paris, 1963), 184; and Edric Caldicott, "Richelieu and the Arts," in Joseph Bergin and Laurence Brockliss, eds., *Richelieu and His Age* (Oxford, 1992), 203–35.

being able to impose a measure of order on a king who seemed, like his father, constitutionally incapable of disciplining either himself or his household. The cardinal-minister was not the only one to bemoan the state of the French court: the *salonnière* Mme de Rambouillet's disgust at the lack of decorum in Henri IV's court is legendary; and she never was persuaded that conditions had improved enough under his son to warrant her return. Compared to the impressive palaces of Whitehall and the Escorial, or that of the Barberini in Rome, graced with the work of such artists as Titian, Velázquez, and Rubens, the Bourbon court appeared shabby indeed.[56] "Foreigners who have visited France in my time," Richelieu wrote in his *Political Testament*, "have often been astounded to see a state so grand combined with a household so mean."[57] As for Louis XIII's indifference to the world of letters, nothing bears this out more than his dismissive comment scrawled at the bottom of a list of writers whom the just-deceased Richelieu had favored with pensions: "We'll have no more of this."[58] While hardly moribund, the other traditional centers of the city's intellectual life, the Sorbonne and the Parlementary Palace, still suffered from the neglect and divisions of generations of religious and civil strife, as well as the professional, specialized languages that branded them as bastions of "Galimatias."

Rather, the city's cultural vitality was derived from a range of venues and associations that were defined precisely by their private, unofficial nature (as we have already seen in Chapter 1). This was a Parisian *monde* characterized by the ethos of *otium cum dignitate*. One historian has noted the "just right" quality of Parisian sociability in this period: neither too close to the court nor far-flung in some outlying country district, these groups occupied a middle ground of proximity to the center while escaping the force field of the Louvre's pull.[59]

Many of those venues were in fact alternative courts—the entourages of great princes and aristocrats who, among their servants and factotums, found the company of *gens de lettres* interesting or advantageous. Chief among these "courts" was that of Gaston d'Orléans, the king's brother and, until the birth of the future Louis XIV in 1638, the presumed heir to the throne. The true beginnings of his *Mécénat* can be detected by 1626, but even before then he was active in attracting poets and other writers into his entourage.[60] Tristan l'Hermite had been in his

---

[56] Though the first two Bourbons went to great lengths to physically upgrade the Louvre. See Ranum, *Paris in the Age of Absolutism*.

[57] *The Political Testament of Cardinal Richelieu*, trans. Henry Bertram Hill (Madison, WI, 1961), 49–50.

[58] Tallemant des Réaux, *Historiettes*, I: 344.

[59] Emmanuel Bury, *Littérature et politesse: L'invention de l'honnête homme, 1580–1750* (Paris, 1996), 84. On the lack of support for writers, see Antoine Adam, *Histoire de la littérature française au XVIIe siècle*, 3rd ed., 3 vols. (Paris, 1997), I: 24–6. See also Malherbe's complaint in the *Recueil* of 1627.

[60] On the definition of a Maecenas and some discussion of the specificity of its status and meaning in relationship to a patron and "clientelism," see Viala, *Naissance de l'écrivain*, chap. 2; Peter Shoemaker, *Powerful Connections: The Poetics of Patronage in the Age of Louis XIII* (Newark, NJ, 2007), 36ff. An important consideration of this topic is Christian Jouhaud and Hélène Merlin, "Mécènes, patrons et clients: Les médiations textuelles comme pratiques clientélaires au XVIIe siècle," *Terrain*, 21 (1993), 491–504.

service for at least five years, Malherbe for two. In a letter of 1626 to Vaugelas, Faret claimed that "Everyone hopes to see henceforth flourish with him a century of honorable men."[61] Pellisson testified that he "loved cultivated spirits and… hosted learned conferences where the participants were to arrive ready to discuss subjects that he himself had chosen."[62] His literary entourage was extensive and varied, including both writers who were in line with the emerging conventions of classicism and those who were unconventional, even "libertine," in their orientation. Voiture was a particular favorite and boon companion, who demonstrated his loyalty by following his patron into exile in 1630.[63]

Henri II, duc de Montmorency, maintained another court in the early seventeenth century, attracting an impressive literary clientage that included the likes of Théophile, François Maynard, Boissat, Hardy, Jean Mairet, Sorel, and Balthazar Baro. Saint-Amant called him *"mon unique Mécène."*[64] He was also a supporter of the pantheist philosopher from Naples, Giulio Cesare (or Lucilio) Vanini, who was burned at the stake in Toulouse in 1619; and the Toulousain poet Peire Godolin, the most accomplished Occitan writer of his day.[65] Tallemant des Réaux confirms this prince's appreciation of his entourage: he surrounded himself with "men of learning in his pay who wrote verses for him, who discussed millions of things with him, and who told him what to think about what was being discussed at the time."[66] Montmorency's clientele overlapped with that of another nobleman, Adrien de Monluc, grandson of the warrior and memoirist Blaise, and himself a minor literary figure of the day. His several works, published anonymously, were characterized by an unconventional, somewhat surreal style and licentious content. He was close to Sorel and supported both Godolin and Vanini. He also was patron of the poet Mathurin Regnier, who won the praise of Marie de Gournay for resisting the purist vogue.[67]

Not all patrons were as elevated as Montmorency or Gaston. François de Bassompierre, a noble courtier, offered protection to Maynard, Malleville, Vanini, and Gombauld. His career as a patron was curtailed by his imprisonment in the Bastille in 1631, where he remained until the cardinal's death in 1642.[68] This was, of course, also true for Gaston and Montmorency, both of whom ultimately

---

[61] Claude K. Abraham, *Enfin Malherbe: The Influence of Malherbe on French Lyric Prosody, 1605–1674* (Lexington, KY, 1971), 12.
[62] Pellisson and d'Olivet, *Histoire de l'Académie française*, II: 81.
[63] Emile Magne, *Voiture et l'Hôtel de Rambouillet*, 2 vols. (Paris, 1929).
[64] Adam, *Histoire de la littérature française*, I: 93.
[65] See sources cited in Robert A. Schneider, *Public Life in Toulouse, 1463–1789: From Municipal Republic to Cosmopolitan City* (Ithaca, NY, 1989), 139ff. On Vanini, see Didier Foucault, *Un philosophe libertin dans l'Europe baroque: Giulio Cesare Vanini (1585–1619)* (Paris, 2003).
[66] Tallemant des Réaux, *Historiettes*, I: 362–3. See also Marc Fumaroli, *L'âge de l'éloquence: Rhétorique et "res literaria" de la Renaissance au seuil de l'époque classique* (Geneva, 1980), 533.
[67] Alain Niderst, "Mécènes et poètes à Toulouse entre 1610 et 1639," in Christian Anatole, ed., *Pèire Godolin* (Toulouse, 1982), 36, 42; Véronique Garrigues, *Adrien de Monluc, 1571–1646: D'encre et de sang* (Limoges, 2006). On Marie de Gournay and Regnier, see Giovanna Devincenzo, *Marie de Gournay: Un cas littéraire* (Paris, 2002), 213.
[68] Adam, *Histoire de la littérature française*, I: 49, 222, 335, 347, 356, 358.

disappeared from the scene, the former by banishment, the latter by means of the executioner's axe. Other aristocrats remained active as literary patrons, however, even after Richelieu's offensive in the world of letters. Henri de Lorrain, the count of Harcourt, maintained a household of writers who periodically met for convivial conversation. Known as the "Confraternity of Monosyllables," its members gave each other nicknames, suggesting a measure of intimacy: Harcourt was "the Round," Faret "the Old," and Saint-Amant "the Fat."[69] Louis de Bourbon, the future Condé, surrounded himself with a coterie of writers with decidedly skeptical and epicurean leanings: Jean-François Sarasin, Roger de Bussy-Rabutin, Chevalier de Rivière, and Charles de Saint-Evremond.[70] He also served as the princely patron of an academy animated by his house physician Bourdelot, which inclined toward medical and scientific interests.

It may even have been that literary patronage of this sort was an act of compensation for finding oneself at a remove from the arena of the royal court and the centers of power; the *otium* of privileged retreat was thus sometimes a matter of a privileged choice, sometimes a situation of forced retirement, and sometimes, too, merely part and parcel of an era that had grown wary of public engagement. Gaston's court was a sort of alternative to the Louvre—a more culturally vibrant venue than the royal court. This could be said of François II de Faudoas-Averton, the count of Belin, another great nobleman who courted men of letters. Banished from the court for his failure to serve adequately Marie de Medici in her contest with the king, Belin retired to his ancestral home in the Maine, where he divided his time between his chateau in Averton and his townhouse in Mans. In league with the Bishop of Mans, who employed Scarron as part of his household, Belin hosted, according to the playwright Mairet, "a true academy of *beaux esprits*." The count was known as learned, or at least interested in matters of language: Mathurin Regnier called him "the father provider of good speech" and granted him "authority over their language," while Chapelain, whose advice he solicited, approved of his views on correct word usage.[71] Writers such as Balzac, Boisrobert, Germain Habert, Georges and Madeleine Scudéry, and especially Scarron, Mairet, and Jean de Rotrou were recipients of his hospitality and support. Belin was especially interested in the theater, and not only because he was in love with an actress: to further her career, he threw his support behind the Mondory troupe of the Marais.[72] He inherited from Montmorency, after the prince's execution in 1632, the playwright Mairet, Corneille's rival and one of the

---

[69] Tallemant des Réaux, *Historiettes*, II: 236. See also Faret, *L'honnête homme*, for Faret's own mention of this group.

[70] Magne, *Voiture et l'Hôtel de Rambouillet*, II: 158–9. See also Katia Béguin, *Les princes de Condé: Rebelles, courtisans et mécènes dans la France du Grand Siècle* (Seyssel, 1999).

[71] *Lettres de Jean Chapelain, de l'Académie française*, ed. Philippe Tamizey de Larroque, 2 vols. (Paris, 1880–2), I: 93–4.

[72] See Tallemant des Réaux, *Historiettes*, II: 774.

most well-regarded writers of the theater of his generation. Rotrou, another playwright, was his constant companion.[73]

In many cases, the relationship between men of letters and their aristocratic patrons was simply a matter of service, if not necessarily servitude—the former were merely workers in a great man's household. Even so, these were desirable positions in a time when the literary marketplace, such as it was, rarely generated enough revenue to sustain a writer without recourse to patronage. Such relationships should not, however, be seen solely as a means of material support or protection, or as fundamentally restrictive of creative possibilities. As Jouhaud has argued (contra Viala), it was through patronage that writers secured both legitimacy and autonomy. Only by ensuring the protection and support of the great, whether aristocrats, high officers, or royal ministers, could *gens de lettres* establish themselves outside the corporate structures of Parlement, Church, or magistracy. While the association of freedom with personal service might seem contradictory to a modern, liberal sensibility, in the Old Regime it was more often gratefully acknowledged. "[B]ecause of your resources [*moyens*]," Balzac writes in July 1621 to La Valette, "I have two things that rarely go together, a master and liberty, and the great leisure that you give me is not the least gift you have granted."[74] (He was actually quoting Tacitus.[75]) The sentiment was echoed by the playwright Rotrou in a dedication to his patron, the Count of Belin: "Though a great lord, and of a condition to rule me as master, I would mention, among the gifts he bestows, that of the liberty which he confers upon me."[76]

Patronage not only was a source of freedom but also served as an impetus for creativity and innovation, something established by Peter Shoemaker as a key element in the literary culture of the seventeenth century. Through a careful reading of a number of texts, he demonstrates that "the social energies created by the patronage system could be productive.... Precisely because it does not depend upon existing institutional hierarchies, patronage can in fact be a force for cultural and intellectual dynamism."[77] This is evident, for example, in Balzac's seizing upon the letter as a means of appealing to various elites in an era when the oratorical mode had been discredited: his publication elevated this genre, endowing it with a literary validity and prestige it had often lacked. But this choice was largely the result of his rhetorical strategy dictated by the demands of patronage.

---

[73] Daniel Aris, "Le mécénat dans la Maine (1630–1645)," *Cahiers de littérature du XVIIe siècle*, 6 (1984), 23–32; see also Deborah Blocker and Elie Haddad, "Protections et statut d'auteur à l'époque moderne: Formes et enjeux des pratiques de patronage dans la querelle du *Cid* (1637)," *French Historical Studies*, 31/3 (2008), 381–416; Shoemaker *Powerful Connections*, 167; and especially Elie Haddad, *Les comtes de Belin: Fondation et ruine d'une maison* (Limoges, 2005).

[74] *Lettres de Balzac*, 94–5.   [75] Sorel, *Bibliothèque française*, 185.

[76] Aris, "Le mécénat dans la Maine," 31. See the fundamental work by Mario Biagioli, *Galileo, Courtier: The Practice of Science in the Culture of Absolutism* (Chicago, 1993).

[77] Shoemaker, *Powerful Connections*, 56. For a complementary analysis of patron-writer relationships, see Blocker and Haddad, "Protections et statut d'auteur."

It is also evident, as Pellisson notes, in the career choice of playwright for so many men of letters: theater was simply the best way to appeal to the *grands*.[78] Moreover, as Mario Biagioli has suggested, aristocrats often sought out and encouraged men of letters and savants known for their novel or innovative literary or scientific work precisely so they could distinguish themselves among their peers as patrons.[79]

For their part, writers rarely stayed monogamous when it came to patrons, for they frequently maintained multiple ties with aristocratic supporters, moving rather easily in a social world of elites, a milieu they served as much by their presence and company as by the specific tasks they could fulfill. We can see evidence of this plurality of patrons in a range of *gens de lettres*. Balzac's disclosure to La Valette that his patron had rivals apparently caused some concern. "It is very true," he writes in a tone that is meant to assuage, "that having testified that you do not wish to restrict my liberty...I have sometimes used it, and have imagined that without violating that first commitment that I vowed to your service, it was yet permitted for me to maintain other [*secondes*] affections."[80] But in fact moving from patron to patron was a common strategy, hardly considered a betrayal of an exclusive bond. Théophile de Viau is a case in point. He went through a string of patrons—Marie de Medici, the Duc de la Roche-Guyon, the Comte de Candale, Charles d'Albert, duc de Luynes, Montmorency, and others.[81] Gassendi, as we have just seen, also attached himself to several patrons in his career. Chapelain managed to serve a number of noblemen, while at the same time maintaining his attachment to Longueville, as well, of course, as his place close to Richelieu. Saint-Amant had at one time or another ties to Paul de Gondi, Harcourt, Marie de Nevers, the Marquise de Rambouillet, Liancourt, the Maréchal de Crequi, and Louise-Marie de Gonzague. Malherbe's trajectory among his supporters traversed the likes of Du Vair, Peiresc, Henri d'Angoulême, the Duc de Bellegarde, Marie de Medici, and the Princesse de Conti; he also dedicated works to both Luynes and Richelieu.[82] Boisrobert, Richelieu's literary confidant, who probably maintained the closest relationship with the cardinal, also established ties with a range of *grands* and others in the course of his career, both at court and in the city. Likewise, Tristan l'Hermite, while he enjoyed the support of the Duc d'Orleans, Richelieu, and the Duc de Guise, also benefited from the patronage of two *robins*, Nicolas and Scévole de Saint-Marthe.[83]

---

[78] Pellisson and d'Olivet, *Histoire de l'Académie française*, I: 104.
[79] Biagioli, *Galileo, Courtier*, 38, 49, 105, 306.   [80] *Lettres de Balzac*, II: 36–7.
[81] Adam, *Théophile de Viau*.
[82] Dedications were not necessarily proof of a relationship, but they still indicate a strategic desire to address the great and influential. For evidence on the multiple dedicatees of writers, see Wolfgang Leiner, *Der Widmungsbrief in der französischen Literatur, 1580–1715* (Heidelberg, 1965).
[83] Blocker and Haddad, "Protections et statut d'auteur," 384. That contemporaries were aware of this richly varied social context—and its importance for the pursuit of "literature"—is suggested by Pierre Corneille's riposte to his critics. In *Excuse à Ariste* he boasts that his success rests solely on the merits of his work: "my verses in every respect are my only supporters [*mes vers en tous lieux sont mes*

All of this allows us to take the measure of the importance of the nobility for writers—not only as patrons, nor even as merely a public, but perhaps more fundamentally as defining the world and the values that both lived in and aspired to. Emmanuel Bury notes the pedagogical function performed by writers as "theoreticians" in the art of social advancement for aristocrats, and those who aspire to that status, in the competitive and fraught world of courtly Paris.[84] The "imaginary" of writers, asserts Deborah Blocker, was colored by the "lifestyles" (*manières de vivre*) of the nobility. For someone like Chapelain, literature was "essentially an idealized representation of the noble *savoir-vivre* which should mark all the texts produced [*nobiliaire qui devait trouver à s'inscrire partout dans les textes produits*]."[85] The "art of pleasing" is seen as defining the culture of the period. But it is crucial to underscore what was obvious to contemporaries: those to be pleased were the noblemen and women of the Parisian *monde*. Here too we should note other elements of the elective affinity between writers and the nobility: a shared embrace of the virtue of *otium* and an aversion for pedantry.

Female Aristocrats and Writers

Given the appeal to a female readership of such texts as *L'Astrée* and François de Sales's *Introduction à la vie dévote*, and the prominent role of the *salonnière* as a cultural arbiter, there can hardly be any question of the importance of women to the emerging literary and linguistic trends. The very concept of the *monde* as an ascription of the Parisian elite implied a community of well-born of both sexes, as opposed to the male-only preserves of the professions or the university. Even Descartes was viewed as appealing particularly to women. "For educated, upper-class women, his philosophy was like a university without walls," writes Erica Harth.[86] If there is one element that distinguishes literary from erudite circles, it is the presence of women: there were none in the orbit of the Dupuy cabinet. And contemporary opinion mostly characterized their presence in morally positive terms. Voiture expressed the common view that women had achieved a level of

---

seuls partisans]." Not so those who deign to attack him: they rely upon "*réduits*," "*appuis*," and "*amis*," which is to say on their friends, their patrons, and the influence of *mondain* circles, such as the salons, in order to get their works performed. While Corneille's observations are proffered critically, to say the least, they also describe the literary field, which was characterized by overlapping ties of patronage, protection, and support, even friendship. Quoted in David Clarke, *Pierre Corneille: Politics and Political Drama under Louis XIII* (Cambridge, 1992), 46. See also Deborah Blocker, *Instituer un "art": Politique de théâtre dans la France du premier XVIIe siècle* (Paris, 2009).

[84] Bury, *Littérature et politesse*. See also Viala, *Naissance de l'écrivain*, 261–4, on what he calls a "*tropisme nobiliaire*" among *mondain* writers.
[85] Blocker, *Instituer un "art,"* 75.
[86] Erica Harth, *Cartesian Women: Versions and Subversions of Rational Discourse in the Old Regime* (Ithaca, NY, 1992), 3.

discernment that made them worthy arbiters of literary taste.[87] Vaugelas pointedly advised listening to cultivated women in matters of language; this was certainly preferable to consulting with pedants steeped in Greek and Latin tomes, cut off from the world of polite conversation. Daniel Huet, a man of letters somewhat younger than those examined in this book, explained that the remarkable appeal of the novel in France, as opposed to Italy or Spain, lay in "the great freedom in which Frenchmen live with women."[88] In Huet's interpretation, the mixed sociability that characterized the French was a sign of a level of sophistication and civility that other countries, which felt compelled to keep their women out of sight, simply had not achieved. This echoed Chapelain's argument that conversation between the sexes could only be edifying—for men, that is: in this way, they "learn to make their pronunciation less harsh."[89] And a result of this freedom— this advanced state of development, so to speak—was a "modern" literary genre characterized by the need to please women and men alike.

But it was more than the presence of women that mattered. The linguistic and literary styles championed by the *mondain* men of letters were infused with the values and tastes associated with women in more profound ways. Women were seen as embodying the natural graces over the artificial and learned. "By their mere presence," writes Faret, "our spirits are awakened."[90] It is true that the commentary often cut the other way: women were also ridiculed for being weak, mindless, and, in the context of salon society, given to the excessively mannered behavior characteristic of *préciosité*. In treatises aimed at women, such as Du Bosc's *L'honnête femme*, affectation, or *coquetterie*, was seen as the opposite of *honnêteté*.[91] Bardin remarks rather snidely to his young male charge that *bienséance* ought not to be understood in the manner of women, who are capable of regarding it only in terms of their appearance.[92]

Whatever women were, however, they normally were not pedants— notwithstanding Molière's *Femmes savantes*. As Pierre Bourdieu points out, the "ideology of good taste," a hallmark of aristocracies, vaunts the "natural" acquisition

---

[87] Alain Génetiot, *Poétique du loisir mondain, de Voiture à La Fontaine* (Paris, 1997), 23.

[88] Maurice Magendie, *La politesse mondaine et les théories de l'honnêteté en France au XVIIe siècle, de 1600 à 1660* (1925; reprint, Geneva, 1970), 89; Pierre-Daniel Huet, *Traité de l'origine des romans* (Paris, 1670), 208. On this, and on Huet more generally, see especially April G. Shelford, *Transforming the Republic of Letters: Pierre-Daniel Huet and European Intellectual Life, 1650–1720* (Rochester, NY, 2007), 108–13.

[89] *Lettres de Chapelain*, II: 169. On this, see Peter Burke, *Languages and Communities in Early Modern Europe* (Cambridge, 2004), 35.

[90] Faret, *L'honnête homme*, 98.

[91] Jacques Du Bosc, *L'honnête femme: The Respectable Woman in Society and the New Collection of Letters and Responses by Contemporary Women*, ed. and trans. Sharon Diane Nell and Aurora Wofgang (Toronto, 2014), 114–5ff.

[92] Pierre Bardin, *Le lycée du Sr. Bardin, ou, En plusieurs promenades il est traité des connoissances des action et des plaisirs d'un honneste homme* (Paris, 1632), 517.

of culture over the acquired and scholastic.[93] Cultivated naturalness—Castiglione's *sprezzatura*—is a class ideal, which distinguishes the true aristocrat from the parvenu or outsider, who can only hope to approximate, through effort and study, the natural grace of his betters. Insofar as women were usually denied the possibility of formal study and professional formation, this ideal turned a liability into a virtue. Anthony La Vopa identifies the distinctiveness of this view of women, which departed from the terms that framed the *querelle des femmes*, a staple of philosophical conversation since the Renaissance. That prolonged debate hinged on the question of whether women could ever equal men. Accordingly, women were assessed in masculine terms. With the ethos of *honnêteté*, however, the equation was reversed. "As the discourse of *honnêteté* put a premium on the distinct kind of social intelligence required in polite conversation, qualities considered 'natural' to women became normative for men."[94]

The importance ascribed to women, in both social and discursive terms, should not obscure the essential limitations on female power and, especially, publicness. As Erica Harth has argued, to see the salon and *salonnière* in the light of feminism, and thus to congratulate this aristocratic subculture for supposedly promoting female authority and self-expression, is to ignore the ways in which women even among the elite in the seventeenth century were restricted both physically and expressively and demeaned and devalued by their male counterparts.[95] A *recueil* of letters by women, published in 1635, illustrates the point. Du Bosc, the editor of this collection, declared in the preface that he wanted to make up for the lack of letters by women in recent *recueils*. In the sixteenth century, there had been publications of this sort in which the female writers were identified by name. In Du Bosc's collection, however—despite his proclaimed intent to act as their publicist—all of the authors were shrouded in anonymity, while the identities of male writers in the same genre of publications are almost always revealed.[96] There were important female authors in the early seventeenth century, including Marie de Gournay and Madeleine de Scudéry. But while the latter

---

[93] Pierre Bourdieu, *Distinction: A Social Critique of the Judgment of Taste*, trans. Richard Nice (Cambridge, MA, 1984), 69–71; see also Aurora Wolfgang, *Gender and Voice in the French Novel, 1730–82* (Aldershot, 2004), 33.

[94] Anthony J. La Vopa, "Sexless Minds at Work and at Play: Poullain de la Barre and the Origins of Early Modern Feminism," *Representations*, 109/1 (2010), 65. I was not able to incorporate the findings of La Vopa in his recent important book, *The Labor of the Mind: Intellect and Gender in Enlightenment Cultures* (Philadelphia, 2017).

[95] Harth, *Cartesian Women*. See also Richard Scholar, *The Je-Ne-Sais-Quoi in Early Modern Europe: Encounters with a Certain Something* (Oxford, 2005), 91: "salon culture itself excluded many more women than it ever included, since its criterion of selection reflected the interests of a dominant class more strongly than those of an oppressed gender."

[96] Janet Gurkin Altman, "Espace public, espace privé: La politique de la publication de lettres sous l'ancien régime," *Revue belge de philologie et d'histoire*, 70/3 (1992), 619–20. On Du Bosc, see especially Aurora Wolfgang and Sharon Diane Nell, "The Theory and Practice of Honnêteté in Jacques Du Bosc's *L'honnête femme* (1632–36) and *Nouveau recueil de lettres des dames de ce temps* (1635)," *Cahiers du dix-septième: An Interdisciplinary Journal*, 13/2 (2011), 56–91.

sometimes published under her own name—and was certainly acknowledged as an important figure in the Parisian literary world—she often resorted to the cover of a pseudonym or her brother's name. And the Marquise de Rambouillet wielded her considerable cultural power—deliberately and theatrically—not only behind the closed door of her salon but even more meaningfully from the deep recesses of her *chambre bleue*.

Many writers were comfortable among women—singing their praises as a sex, appealing to their presumed tastes and sensibilities, gently tutoring them in the virtues of appropriate learning, happily engaging in the conversational badinage that characterized the salon. It is not clear, on the other hand, that all of them were entirely pleased with being identified with a feminized milieu. To follow the provocative line of analysis offered by Anthony Grafton and Lisa Jardine, it may have been that in mixing with women, these men of letters ultimately realized that they were "taking themselves out of the game"—forsaking their role as independent humanists in favor of the comforts of high society, catering to its needs and tastes.[97] *Mondain* writers of the seventeenth century did not have to imagine this sort of humanist: they only had to look upon the savants of the Dupuy cabinet, that all-male bastion of no-nonsense erudition, whose members regarded the salon culture and its "literature" with disdain.

In fact, both Balzac and Chapelain, who saw the salon as their primary public, were scathing when it came to learned women. And this reflected a larger concern. They worried that their own authority over literary matters was slipping away from them, increasingly usurped by the half-educated denizens of the *ruelles*, where, they often complained, the tastes and opinions of women were all that counted. They and their fellow travelers had fought to establish a literary life outside the precincts of "Galimatias"—the court, the magistracy, the university, and the Church. But the fear, then, was that things had gotten out of hand (as we shall see in Chapter 5). Chapelain ruminated to Balzac about the power of women as "savants or judges of knowledge, such that one cannot consider oneself successful unless one appeals to their taste and accommodates their abilities." His misgivings are evident, especially when it comes to "serious matters." In such cases, he declares, "we must have enough courage to stand up to the judgments of these new sort of 'long robes,'... and think about posterity, which is not subject to the weaknesses of the times and which, sooner or later, renders to each what it deserves."[98] To Antoine Godeau, another frequenter of the Rambouillet salon, he confided: "I know from experience that in the company you find yourself in [referring to the salon] one cannot do as one pleases... its orders are absolute, if

---

[97] Anthony Grafton and Lisa Jardine, "Introduction," in Grafton and Jardine, *From Humanism to the Humanities: Education and the Liberal Arts in Fifteenth- and Sixteenth-Century Europe* (Cambridge, MA, 1986). I am indebted for this to Constance Furey, *Erasmus, Contarini, and the Religious Republic of Letters* (Cambridge, 2006), 117.

[98] *Lettres de Chapelain*, I: 381.

not to say tyrannical."⁹⁹ A set of dialogues among reputed members of a French "academy"¹⁰⁰ confronted the issue of female influence squarely. One participant first rejoices that philosophy is no longer the exclusive property of the university ("School") but now the stuff of civilized conversation, such that "even...women themselves both understand it, and handle it, in a mild, and gentle way of argumentation, and discourse." But no sooner are women evoked approvingly than the concern is raised that such conversational pursuits risk becoming "the Play of wonders, which is used amongst Women, at Wakes, and other petty Pastimes... in those petty Divertissements and gossiping of Women." The objection is met with a categorical ruling: Lacking in "profundity, and the universality of the Sciences," women fail to handle philosophy "regularly and dexterously," proving unable "to maintain and defend any such argument as may be started by curiosity."¹⁰¹ Thus, even among those who embraced new venues for literary and intellectual activities, shunning the traditional confines of the university or other scholarly precincts, there was a reluctance to accept the conversation and company of women.

What was the source of this anxiety? Was it merely a reflection of the more generally held misogyny that, like racism and other social prejudices, was simply part and parcel of their worldview? Certainly. But perhaps there was another factor, which takes us again to the element of privileged *otium* that characterized this aristocratic, feminized milieu—the milieu infused with the air of *L'Astrée*, that pastoral retreat so cherished by contemporaries. Women were at home in this world, just as more generally they were limited to the domestic sphere that traditionally confined them. But while the men of this milieu clearly found the ethos of retreat appealing, and thus abided in and profited from the company of women, they also may have seen it as a problem. For not only were women "already there"; they were *only* there.¹⁰² Men, on the other hand, understood retreat as a choice or the result of circumstance; they had—or at least were supposed to have—the liberty of moving from one realm to another. Following the celebrated ideal of Cincinnatus, they could, at a moment's notice, re-engage with the active life of service and commitment. It is notable, for example, that Bardin's *Lycée* instructs how to behave in a whole gamut of venues, under the assumption that his student will naturally find himself at court and on the battlefield as well as in the company of other men and women, both virtuous and not.¹⁰³ To dwell in the feminized world of *otium* without recourse to this modal option was thus not only to forsake a masculine prerogative, it was to admit defeat. This is perhaps why men of

---

⁹⁹ *Lettres de Chapelain*, I: 80. See also Lewis C. Seifert, *Manning the Margins: Masculinity and Writing in Seventeenth-Century France* (Ann Arbor, MI, 2009), 79.
¹⁰⁰ Monsieur de Marmet, Lord of Valcroissant, *Entertainments of the Cours; or, Academical Conversations, Held upon the Cours at Paris, by a Cabal of the Principal Wits of That Court* (London, 1658).
¹⁰¹ *Lettres de Chapelain*, I: 142, 148, 149.
¹⁰² Furey, *Erasmus, Contarini, and the Religious Republic of Letters*, 116.
¹⁰³ Bardin, *Le lycée*, 624ff. I stressed this point in the Introduction.

letters, along with their assiduous participation in the life of the salon, also were careful to maintain the vitality of their all-male groups. It may even explain why these same men, who otherwise were so protective of their liberty, accepted with very little demurral the "yoke" of royal protection in the creation of the Académie française, an institution that explicitly prohibited women from its ranks.[104]

Inventing *Honnêteté*

The relationship of men of letters with women, then, was complex, characterized by a mix of solicitude and condescension, identification and ambivalence. But in a sense, their attitude to their male patrons and supporters was not all that different; for however closely they identified with the Parisian elite, aspiring to live among them as virtual equals, most were not. A significant number of writers were noble, or at least socially privileged. D'Urfé, Malherbe, Balzac, Conrart, Racan, Maynard, Georges and Madeleine Scudéry, and Montausier are among the more prominent *gens de lettres* who came from the upper ranks of society.[105] Most, however, were commoners, eager to find a foothold among the titled elite. They were ambitious, educated, and talented—attributes their social betters for the most part lacked. But in order to leverage this intellectual capital, they had to invest it in a currency that was, in a sense, marketable to the nobility. Indeed, they had to invent a new currency. And this meant translating their humanistic knowledge and values into a discourse that the nobility could at once understand, appreciate, and profit from. That discourse was *honnêteté*.

It is one of the most misunderstood concepts in the history of French culture, yet few are as ubiquitous or as fundamental. One of the problems is that it is often conflated with kindred notions, such as politesse and civility, or even with Elias's "civilizing process." It shares values and dispositions with these "lexical signs,"[106] but it is both more complex and more precise than these concepts: while there is certainly a psychological dimension to civility and politeness, for the most part these qualities focus on behavior and self-presentation, while *honnêteté* emphasizes more questions of character, personal development, and virtue. And while *honnêteté* has its origins in ancient writings as well as in Montaigne's *Essays* and in Italian texts, as a term it emerges only in the first decades of the seventeenth century. Thus unlike Elias's "civilizing process," a concept retrospectively imposed

---

[104] See Robert A. Schneider, "Friends of Friends: Intellectual and Literary Sociability in the Age of Richelieu," in Lewis C. Seifert and Rebecca M. Wilkin, eds., *Men and Women Making Friends in Early Modern France* (Burlington, VT, 2015), 135–59.

[105] See Viala, *Naissance de l'écrivain*, 262–4, for writers with a noble background and what he calls the "*héroïsme littéraire*."

[106] The term is Scholar's, *The Je-Ne-Sais-Quoi in Early Modern Europe*, 190.

upon a long-term historical development, *honnêteté* belongs to contemporary culture, and emerges at a particular time.[107]

Many different writers had a hand in formulating this ethos as part of their ambition to appeal to their less educated social betters. The "appealing" tone of this discourse was not only a tactical means toward effectively conveying the ethos but a demonstration of *honnêteté* itself. As both a literary discourse and a social ideal, then, it exemplifies perhaps more than anything else the melding of literature and society; in other words, it was both an ethical code and an ideal that guided writers as they strove to appeal to a certain readership of discerning elites.[108] One might say that *honnêteté* was both a rhetoric of speech and a rhetoric of behavior.[109]

The ethos of *honnêteté* was generated by the process of translation, distilling considerable erudition into usually tidy manuals for moral guidance. Beneath the surface of texts on *honnêteté* lie ancient sources, which, however, barely cause a ripple. Little is entirely new, as it was ultimately derived from the rhetoric of Aristotle, Cicero, and Quintilian, with a concern for the apt and measured means of addressing an audience. Thus the Ciceronian notion of "decorum," originally conceived in the context of oratory, implied appropriateness and polish as well as propriety, placing the emphasis on outward appearance and appealing to others, while holding fast to the ideal of the orator as embodying high moral qualities. Implicit in *honnêteté* was something of a paradox: in a period that witnessed the demotion of oratory as a mode of rhetoric, its emphasis on performance as an aspect of this ethos was preserved.

Its ancient roots are apparent in several publications. Nicolas Faret brought considerable learning to what was probably the most important work in its history, *L'honnête homme, ou, L'art de plaire à la cour*, but it rests lightly upon his text.[110] This only underscores the point: for a signature feature of *honnêteté* was an avoidance of pedantry at all cost. Faret insisted that the *honnête homme* should rather study from the "great book of the world than from Aristotle."[111] Nevertheless, his text is laced with references to ancient authors, and he also

---

[107] This can be illustrated in its appearance in *L'Astrée*. In the first book (1607) the terms *courtoisie* and *civilité* are used, but in the fourth book d'Urfé more often resorts to *honnêteté* to signify a virtuous and pleasing self-presentation. See Anette Höfer and Rolf Reichardt, *Honnête homme, Honnêteté, Honnêtes gens* (Munich, 1986), 11; Hans Krings, *Die Geschichte des Wortschatzes der Höflichkeit im Französischen* (Bonn, 1961).

[108] Emmanuel Bury, one of the most astute commentators on *honnêteté*, has observed that it is rare among ideals in being fundamental for both literature and society, "to the extent that all 'literature' only thus seems able to speak of society." *Littérature et politesse*, 127. See also Elena Russo, *La cour et la ville, de la littérature classique aux Lumières* (Paris, 2002), 86.

[109] On the melding of rhetoric and action, see the brilliant article by Victoria Kahn, "*Virtù* and the Example of Agathocles in Machiavelli's *Prince*," *Representations*, no. 13 (Winter 1986), 63–83.

[110] On contemporaries' acknowledgment of the importance of Faret's book, see Sorel, *Bibliothèque française*, 127.

[111] Faret, *L'honnête homme*, 26 and, for Faret's further elaboration on this, 30.

114 DIGNIFIED RETREAT

includes several pages under the rubric "Those Sciences of Which a *Honnête Homme* Should Not Remain Ignorant" (Des sciences qu'un honneste homme ne doit pas ignorer), providing a reading list of ancient historians—Herodotus, Thucydides, Xenophon, Polybius, Plutarch, Tacitus, Sallust, Titus-Livy, Caesar, Quint-Curse, and others—where the severe brevity of his annotations merely serves to call attention to the author's aversion to pedantry.

Faret's competitor in the publication of early works on *honnêteté*, Pierre Bardin, a member (like Faret) of the first generation of the French Academy (who was also the first to die, in the course of trying to rescue one of his students from drowning), made a greater show of ancient sources in his own guide to *honnêteté*, *Le lycée*, published in 1632, two years after *L'honnête homme*. Like Montaigne's *Essays*, it is filled with references to classical authors. But in contrast to Montaigne, there are virtually no passages in Latin and none in Greek; all of the sources are translated into French. Moreover, as has been noted more generally for the period, the text consists of a compendium of "commonplaces" (*lieux communs*) that pithily manage to convey the learning of ancients simply, accessibly, and practically—without a trace of erudite commentary. *Lycée* is a sort of seventeenth-century "Ancients for Dummies."[112]

Balzac's own version of *honnêteté*, what he called "urbanity," evokes Augustus's Rome as a foil for valorizing private virtues in a discourse addressed to Mme de Rambouillet, "De la conversation des romaines."[113] As he acknowledges, his discussion draws upon the fourth book of Aristotle's *Ethics*. In fact, throughout these essays, Balzac's erudition is more on view than in previous writings, referring to his Roman sources on virtually every page. But the Roman cast of these discourses was evident in more than the references: an imagined ancient Rome also serves as a model for his description of the private pastimes—the pleasures cultivated at a remove from the public realm—that gave rise to his notion of urbanity. Similarly, Bardin cited episodes and warriors from Greek and Roman history as examples of the martial virtues that a true *honnête homme*—in his view, preferably a nobleman—should embody. Tellingly, of all the ancient figures, it is Socrates whom he vaunts as the ideal *honnête homme*.[114]

Despite these gestures toward the ancient world and ancient learning, most authors tended to qualify their reliance on erudition as a precondition for *honnêteté*. Reading "good" books and conversation—in the case of Faret, in the company of cultivated women—and other edifying activities were just as or more important. And this is a point of distinction between these texts on *honnêteté* and those dealing primarily with politesse and civility: an emphasis on personal

---

[112] Bury, *Littérature et politesse*, 33, 88.
[113] Jean-Louis Guez de Balzac, *Oeuvres diverses (1644)*, ed. Roger Zuber (Paris, 1995), 59–94.
[114] On the importance of Socrates in this period, and more generally in early modern French intellectual life, see George Huppert, "Under the Shadow of Socrates," in Gerald Sandy, ed., *The Classical Heritage in France* (Leiden, 2002), 281–95.

cultivation and development that underscores the aspirational feature of this ethos. A Franciscan monk, Jacques Du Bosc, unique in addressing the *honnête femme*, argued for education as essential. Those objecting "want women to sail through the most treacherous seas on a leaky raft, so to speak, and to protect themselves from the storm with a bit of plank or only by floating on some remaining debris," he writes. He did not, however, endorse their reading novels, preferring history or religious texts. Some novels are excellent, even edifying, he concedes. "I also grant that there likewise is pleasure in novels: but is there not sometimes a pleasing taste in poisoned meat?"[115]

While Du Bosc's conception of the skill set for *honnêtes femmes* was rather narrow, mostly limited to conversation and reading, men were expected to master a wider range, especially those in keeping with a noble calling. Faret assumes that one should be an accomplished horseman, capable in all the chivalric and martial arts, but also be able to play the lute and guitar because these are things that "please our masters and mistresses." One should also be familiar with "games of chance," which "take place among the Great," providing, he adds, that one does not play oneself.[116] Here, as elsewhere, Faret counsels a certain distance between the aspiring *honnête homme* and other courtiers and aristocrats.[117] Bardin advises occasionally taking refuge in the "Empire of Letters, which is bounded by no seas nor mountains." But he also stresses bodily needs and pleasures and the practical side of living. To ignore this aspect of our being is not only to limit ourselves to a truncated knowledge of who we are; it also leads to unwarranted and unnatural expectations of the limits of our passions and appetites. Bardin acknowledges those who strive to "overcome themselves," obviously thinking of mystics and saints whose heroic acts of self-abnegation were the stuff of Christian hagiography. As much as he wants to frame *honnêteté* as an aspirational goal for a virtuous elite, he also defines it in conformance with universal expectations: "Thus, I do not want to propose rules for *honnêteté* that cannot be observed by all men."[118]

These sorts of prescriptions and comments suggest seeing *honnêteté* as an ethos that might be embraced by those outside the traditional nobility. Faret, like others, acknowledges an aristocratic pedigree as a decided advantage, especially for those attempting to make their way at court. But he does equivocate on the matter: "a good birth [*une bonne naissance*] is not sufficient."[119] Beyond this, his prescriptions are "precepts," which, if followed diligently, can produce an *honnête homme*. Du Bosc asserts that learning can compensate for a non-noble birth. More generally, the very nature of texts on *honnêteté*, which tend to emphasize skills and qualities that could be acquired with practice and study, seemed to open the door

---

[115] Du Bosc, *L'honnête femme*, 54.   [116] Faret, *L'honnête homme*, 16, 17.
[117] Seifert notes "the courtier" as "the figure who precedes and competes with the honnête homme." *Manning the Margins*, 25.
[118] Bardin, *Le lycée*, 57.   [119] Faret, *L'honnête homme*, 12.

to an expanded elite based less on birth and title and more on cultivation. *Honnêteté* was aspirational, implying in theory an elite open to outsiders.

The trick, however, was that any evidence of aspiration or effort had to be well hidden, which suggests an innate talent that could not be learned. Beyond the many skills—practical, intellectual, martial—that might enhance *honnêteté*, several authors ultimately resort to the *je ne sais quoi* of ineffable qualities that could not be spelled out. *Honnêteté* combined high standards for artful self-presentation with the demands of virtue; and yet the behavior it prescribed was supposed to seem effortless, unstudied, and natural—the "negligence" or "nonchalance" that Faret, following Castiglione's neologism *sprezzatura*, placed at its very heart. The *honnête homme*, he writes, "knows how to employ a kind of negligence that disguises any artifice, demonstrating that he seems to act without thinking and without any sort of effort."[120] Whatever learning or cultivation went into *honnêteté*, it was not to show; indeed, in Balzac's view it should leave "an imperceptible impression that is recognizable only by accident," revealing "nothing that appears studied or learned; which is not felt or seen, and is inspired by a 'genie' that is lost in looking for it." As Richard Scholar writes, "It is in the very act of heaping one insufficient definition upon another that Balzac places the quintessence of *urbanité* beyond definition or explanation."[121]

This, then, leads to the question of how far one was to take this this emphasis on appearing and accommodating, the "art of pleasing," which, as the subtitle of Faret's book ("The art of pleasing at court") makes clear, was as much a part of *honnêteté* as virtue. Could it also entail degrees of deception? For the literary scholar John Lyons, *honnêteté* and dissimulation were kindred concepts. "In the language [*langue*] of the seventeenth century...honnêteté is not incompatible with dissimulation; it is rather the *result* of dissimulation."[122] It was difficult, however, for writers to acknowledge this compatibility. Philippe Fortin de la Hoguette, a cultivated military man associated with the Dupuys who wrote his *Testament* to guide his sons as they came of age, recognized dissimulation as a necessary recourse in statecraft, "which has need of this covering like a second night"—a common enough assumption. But practiced by the courtier, it is "a disguise that travesties a man so completely that the whole course of his life is nothing but a continual lie." It is even worse than lying, for at least with a liar there are moments of truth, whereas the dissimulator's life is like a permanent Carnival, where the masked revelers couldn't care less whether they recognize others or not.[123]

---

[120] Faret, *L'honnête homme*, 20.

[121] Scholar, *The Je-Ne-Sais-Quoi in Early Modern Europe*, 204.

[122] John D. Lyons, "La rhétorique de l'honnêteté: Pascal et l'agrément," in François Cornilliat and Richard Lockwood, eds., *Ethos et pathos: Le statut du sujet rhétorique* (Paris, 2000), 360, emphasis in the original.

[123] Philippe Fortin de la Hoguette, *Testament, ou, Conseils fidèles d'un père à ses enfans* (Paris, 1648), 235.

Faret certainly does not endorse dissimulation or other morally dubious stratagems of self-presentation, but he does advise an accommodating disposition that suggests the necessity of hiding or disguising one's true reactions to others. "Someone with a well-formed character," he writes, "knows how to adjust to every encounter and, as was said of Alcibiades, is so accommodating and does everything in a certain way such that he seems to have a particular inclination [for it].... There are no humors so extreme that he cannot live without contesting, nor so bizarre that he cannot find a way of sympathizing with."[124] The successful courtier, it is clear, knows how to disguise his true feelings even in the face of "extreme" or "bizarre" situations; in his capacity to adapt to any situation, his ethical stance is not very different from that of the statesman guided by reason of state, a subject we shall return to in Chapter 7.

The moral qualms of the "art of pleasing" as a feature of *honnêteté* are evoked most directly by Du Bosc in his *L'honnête femme*. In one of the longest chapters in the book, "On Having a Compliant Temperament," he considers the expectation for women—imposed, to be sure, much more on them than on men—to calibrate their behavior to suit others.[125] He acknowledges the danger of excessive "compliance" (which in this context might be understood as amenability combined with affability), not merely because it might mean tolerating or accepting bad behavior or forsaking the scruples of conscience for the sake of simply "getting along," but also because it leaves one vulnerable, inviting the importunate or evil overtures of others who might mistake amiability for passivity, or worse. And if compliance means being coquettish, he wants nothing of it. But after cataloguing its perils, he then turns to its virtues and advantages, even its necessity for the smooth functioning of society. Du Bosc understands compliance as the opposite of incivility. In a passage that underscores the worldly bent of *honnêteté*, its tendency to demarcate, like other contemporary moral prescriptions, a distinction between one's inner life and the exigencies of living in the world, he acknowledges that Christian conscience and polite sociability operate in different registers. Faced with disagreeable or morally vexed circumstances, "women always owe their conscience to God, while sometimes they owe their outwardly appearances to the world and to custom."[126] While the *honnête femme* would never countenance sinful or threatening behavior, discernment is the watchword. "Compliance is not a blind virtue.... There are faults that it corrects while there are others that it tolerates. It endures what it cannot prevent."[127] Again, Du Bosc posits a distinction between the inner self and the demands of society. "And truly, besides the brotherly discipline required of us by Christianity, what does it matter if some people stray or have bad feelings if they do not concern either conscience or salvation?"[128] There is no question of duplicity in Du Bosc's counsel; but his notion of

---

[124] Faret, *L'honnête homme*, 139.   [125] Du Bosc, *L'honnête femme*, 114ff.
[126] *L'honnête femme*, 133.   [127] *L'honnête femme*, 130.   [128] *L'honnête femme*, 130.

compliance invites the conclusion that feigning, muting, or otherwise hiding one's true feelings—which is to say a measure of dissimulation—has a place in the sociable arsenal of his *honnête femme*.

If outright dissimulation is rarely endorsed in manuals on *honnêteté*, it does figure in probably the most widely read literary work that served as one of the Ur-texts for this ethos, *L'Astrée*. The world d'Urfé created is "a dream image of peaceful and simple pastoral existence for war-weary people."[129] But there is a disturbing trait apparent throughout. Dishonesty and dissimulation, doubt and insecurity characterize virtually every relationship in the novel. The response of one character when challenged on why she has no pity for her love-struck suitor expresses this well: "Sister... the shepherds in this country are so devious their hearts usually contradict what their mouths promise; if we reflect on the actions of this one we shall see there is nothing but artifice in them."[130] People continually deceive one another, feign love or indifference, profess one thing and mean another; in short, they remain suspended in a constant state of doubt, suspicion, and confusion that propels the novel forward as they negotiate the countless contretemps that ensue.[131] *L'Astrée* presents a world where virtually everyone in the novel is engaged in some sort of deception; they are at the same time subject to a nearly constant regime of surveillance and prying. When characters are not in pursuit of love, they are spying on one another.[132] In this novel constructed around intimate matters of the heart, privacy is virtually nonexistent. One is never really alone, or at least unobserved: Jacques Ehrmann notes the deeply constraining effect of this pattern: "the most profound sense of illusion... results from the characters becoming spectators of their own spectacle. Their subjugation is then complete."[133] Endemic deception, panoptic surveillance—even in this aristocratic paradise, far from court and country, the stratagems of dissimulation, caution, and secrecy are hardly unknown.

While writers of works explicitly addressing *honnêteté* did not represent reality as deeply troubled, as D'Urfé does in what is, after all, a work of imagination, they did not shy away from describing the pitfalls of the social world and the myriad challenges to maintaining one's virtue. Faret's book provides a sustained anatomy of the difficulties confronting the virtuous man at court at every turn: it is a minefield of deception, fear, ambition, flattery, falsehood, avarice, and more. "It is

---

[129] Norbert Elias, *The Court Society* (Oxford, 1983), 246–50.

[130] Honoré d'Urfé, *Astrea, Part One*, trans. Steven Rendall (Binghamton, NY, 1995), 99, 101.

[131] The narrative explanation for this feature is that the Fountain of Love, which in Forez traditionally serves to reveal the identity of one's true love, has been bewitched, thus leaving the shepherds and shepherdesses to their own imperfect, often devious devices in their quest for love.

[132] "The so-called idyllic world is penetrated by lookers and listeners whose role it is to deny all that is secret and intimate, in favor of public revelation," observes Louise Horowitz, whose astute reading of *L'Astrée* I follow here. Horowitz, *Honoré d'Urfé* (Boston, 1984), 81.

[133] Jacques Ehrmann, *Un paradis désespéré: L'amour et l'illusion dans "L'Astrée"* (New Haven, 1963), 80–1.

certainly true that there are an infinite number of reasons to turn those people away who are aware of its perils.... Everyone can see that corruption generally reigns there," he declares.[134] *L'honnête homme* belongs to the anti-court literature that flourished in the sixteenth and early seventeenth century.[135] But Faret does not reserve his moralistic disapprobation to courtly life. Unlike many of his contemporaries, especially savants who viewed themselves as *esprits forts* or *déniaisés*, Faret unabashedly vaunted the importance of piety for the *honnête homme*.[136] He rails against "that arrogant sect of *esprits forts*," the mention of which was probably meant to signal in readers' minds his distance from those whom Garasse had vilified just a few years earlier.[137] In this he is joined by Bardin, whose *Lycée* conveys a dark side of the world, filled with moral challenges, social snares, and general uncertainty. "Would we see anything other than disorder in the world," he asks, "if evil-intentioned men were not restrained, for in order to avail themselves of all the pleasures they fancy, they would not hesitate to ruin the happiness of others nor to break the sacred bonds of society?"[138] Like Faret, he is alarmed at the recent rise of atheism, especially among those who pretend to justify its precepts with "philosophy," which he identifies, perhaps thinking of Vanini and others who were influenced by Paduan philosophy, as a form of "libertinage."[139] And like Faret as well, he sees the royal court as a place where menacing impulses abound. There, he counsels, in an obvious nod to Machiavelli's *Prince*, one must be both the lion and the fox; one must be practiced in the subtle arts of secrecy and dissimulation; there, one can never distinguish friend from foe.[140] And he also presents a bellicose depiction of relations between nations, scoffing at the ideal of peace as a natural or even desirable state of affairs. Rome is a constant reference point for this humanist preceptor, who is filled with admiration for its martial conquests and its renowned military discipline. Bardin extols Caesar's ruthless measures against a rebellious populace. He endorses the principle that a citizenry accustomed to peace cannot hope to preserve itself.[141] Du Bosc, not surprisingly, acknowledged the obstacles confronting the *honnête femme*, especially the deceitfulness rampant even, or especially, among the privileged elite. "There is so much falseness in worldly society!" he writes. "Those who have admiring faces sometimes have murdering souls. Often those who praise us in their speech blaspheme against us in their thoughts."[142]

What recourse does the *honnête* man or woman have in such a world? For the women Du Bosc advises, it is largely a matter of avoidance, tempered by the measured "compliance" just noted. For men the counsel is more complicated. On the one hand, withdrawal, repose, and other strategies of retreat are on offer.

---

[134] Faret, *L'honnête homme*, 33.
[135] The anti-court theme was also prominent in several of the contributions to the 1627 *Recueil*.
[136] Different from *The Courtier* in this respect; see Magendie, *La politesse mondaine*, Introduction.
[137] Faret, *L'honnête homme*, 32.   [138] Bardin, *Le lycée*, 33.   [139] *Le lycée*, 232.
[140] *Le lycée*, 477ff.   [141] *Le lycée*, 130.   [142] Du Bosc, *L'honnête femme*, 133.

Faret counsels leaving the court and seeking the company of cultivated ladies in the "city." Bardin evokes the privilege of "repose," citing Seneca's oft-quoted line "*Otium* without letters is death, a death like being buried alive." He refers as well to the double nature of man, body, and spirit, which in turn conforms to the two aspects of life—the active and the contemplative. Moments of *otium* are necessary in the life of the *honnête homme*, just as they are for kings, whose enemies are often vanquished more by the efforts expended in their "cabinets" than by those on the battlefield.[143] La Hoguette, in good Neo-Stoic fashion, cautions his sons against too closely identifying with the world, or trying to change those things beyond one's power. "You will work in vain if the wheels of your spirit are concentric with those of your times; their movement, which is swift, will carry you away despite yourself."[144] And here his counsel for withdrawal is inflected with the theme of a divided self: "It is sufficient for the wise man to withdraw into himself and away from the crowd, and to preserve the freedom of judgment within himself of things as they really are; but as for things beyond him, publicly he should participate in conventional ways."[145]

But, on the other hand, the counsel of retreat is qualified: it is not permanent but merely a moment in the life of the *honnête homme*, who ultimately must enter this vexed world. Bardin, while extolling the virtues of *otium*, concludes that the tranquil life is a privilege that cannot be abused at the expense of others. The Pythagoreans and Epicureans enjoyed the spiritual and intellectual pleasures of their calm retreat; still, Bardin adds, they never went as far as preaching against the common good. Plutarch wrote that service to one's country was a pleasure, not simply a duty.[146] Real philosophers were never so ensconced in the solitude of their studies that they would fail to come to the aid of their fellow citizens. And if they did, it was probably because the government had fallen into the hands of the "people," in which case the corruption was already so great that their remedies would prove useless.[147] La Hoguette couples his endorsement of retreat with a warning that this does not preempt the obligation of sociability, although he poses it in somewhat quiescent terms: "Do not cut yourself off from people.... Live civilly with your inferiors, familiarly with your equals, respectfully with those who are above you, with total obedience and submission toward your Prince, and charitably with all kinds of men."[148] Faret went beyond merely criticizing court life—and advising flight from its noxious precincts—but also proclaimed, "Every man of quality is obliged to attend court." Permanent retreat, then, hardly receives his approval. To hide his gifts, to share them with "rude and timid minds," is unworthy of a true gentleman. For Faret, "the *honnête homme*...should strive to be useful to his country; in making himself

---

[143] Bardin, *Le lycée*, 245. [144] La Hoguette, *Testament*, 261. [145] *Testament*, 263.
[146] *Testament*, 248, 250. [147] *Testament*, 250–1. [148] *Testament*, 383.

agreeable to everyone, he not only profits himself but also the public and especially his virtuous friends."[149]

Designed by men of letters for an aspiring elite, *honnêteté* embodies their relationship at its most discursive. The invention of *honnêteté* entailed translating ancient wisdom into an accessible ethos. It not only avoided any hint of pedantry but also taught that an *honnête* man or woman was anything but a pedant. It not only meant accommodating this elite but also instructing it in how to maintain the traditional values of virtue and honor in a world where, so it was acknowledged, this was often difficult. But writers on this ethos also challenged tradition in suggesting that noble birth did not guarantee *honnêteté*; that self-cultivation was a pathway to *honnêteté*, a path that was created by the *gens de lettres* who committed themselves to serving their social betters, with whom they identified, in this way.

* * *

Contrary to Elias's formulation of the "civilizing process," where the court plays the leading role in fostering new standards for conduct and self-presentation, *honnêteté* was fashioned in "the city"—"in the secrecy of intimate space or the heart of the salons."[150] Ever since Jean de La Bruyère, and then Ernst Auerbach's foundational essay "La cour et la ville," this antinomy has served as a reference point for parsing the contours of seventeenth-century Parisian culture.[151] Here I prefer *le monde* to "the city" and certainly to "the public," with all its problematic, Habermasian associations. For it not only suggests a socially limited environment but also evokes the *mondain* literary culture that gave rise to it. This chapter has offered a portrait of this world, focusing on relations and associations between aristocrats and *gens de lettres*. Some of these ties were personal and individual; some arose in social settings such as the salon or other groups; some involved service or employment; others were more intimate, entailing instruction, collaboration, even companionship. Certainly writers and savants gained recognition and a measure of respect from this elite milieu. Working outside the institutions of the magistracy, the Church, or the university—those strongholds of "Galimatias"—they welcomed the favor and company of the well-born as a source of both protection and legitimacy. This was their readership, their audience, and their interlocutors, whom they addressed in terms that appealed and conformed to this public's sensibilities and intellectual capacities. But all was not limited to "the art of pleasing." Writers and savants were not entirely craven. Channeling the humanist tradition that most of them had imbibed, they offered their betters a distilled and palatable version of this tradition in the discourse of

---

[149] Faret, *L'honnête homme*, 68–9, 71.   [150] Russo, *La cour et la ville*, 21.
[151] Erich Auerbach, "La cour et la ville," in Auerbach, *Scenes from the Drama of European Literature: Six Essays* (Minneapolis, 1984), 133–82.

honnêteté, which both instructed and challenged them to aspire to the mixed, not always compatible, values of virtue and *bienséance*. Strictly speaking, however, this was an elite that, precisely because of its exalted breeding and position, should not have required tutoring in the ways of a virtuous life. In this sense, then, the discourse of *honnêteté* opened a window to others who aspired to live according to its elevated values, tempting them to view this "sign of quality" as a model for their self-cultivation.

The Parisian *monde* emerged from a re-settled post-bellum Paris infused with a literary and intellectual culture rooted in varied forms of sociability. Whatever its dimensions, this was a world still governed by assumptions and concerns that militated against the sort of "publicness" that reputedly began to characterize the eighteenth century, at least according to the well-known formulation associated with Habermas. Thus what might seem paradoxical—a culture characterized by worldliness—was at the same time regulated by constraints, limitations, and self-censorship in modes of public discourse. A worldly culture was also a culture of discretion.

3
A Culture of Discretion

"*I Go Forth Masked*"—Descartes

In *The Misanthrope* (1666), Molière presents two characters embodying radically different styles of self-presentation. Alceste, the Misanthrope himself, is misanthropic not really because he is mean (although he is), but mostly because of his uncompromising honesty, his brutal frankness, which renders him both ridiculous and hurtful. He is honest to a fault, with an unrestrained openness that undermines the very fabric of society. Philinte, on the other hand, is the model *honnête homme*, whose discretion merely greases the wheels of social intercourse. But it takes the foil of Alceste to bring out the more problematic aspects of Philinte's suave discretion, which, he is forced to reveal, ultimately depends upon a readiness to disguise and dissimulate. Philinte, to be sure, justifies his practice as socially necessary: "It's often best to veil one's true emotions. / Wouldn't the social fabric come undone / If we were wholly frank with everyone?"[1] Increasingly exasperated by Alceste's rude honesty, at one point he cries out, "If only you could be politic!"[2] As with many of his contemporaries, Philinte's outlook seems to be deeply Augustinian, and thus he presents himself as at once resigned and pessimistic but also eager to conform to the ways of a fallen world:

No, all you say I'll readily concede;
This is a low, dishonest age indeed;
Nothing but trickery prospers nowadays,
And people ought to mend their shabby ways.
Yes, man's a beastly creature; but must we then
Abandon the society of men?[3]

The implication is clear: given the fallen nature of society, Philinte's dissimulating *honnêteté* was more "politic" than Alceste's honesty.

All of this is by way of acknowledging what, following on the first two chapters, might be understood as simply axiomatic: All cultures are defined not only by their inclusiveness but by their boundaries and limits as well. Thus, if the code of *honnêteté* represented a widening of elite culture, it also implied a commensurate

---

[1] Molière, *The Misanthrope*, in *The Misanthrope and Tartuffe*, trans. Richard Wilbur (New York, 1965), 19.
[2] *The Misanthrope*, 74.   [3] *The Misanthrope*, 132.

Dignified Retreat: Writers and Intellectuals in the Age of Richelieu. Robert A. Schneider, Oxford University Press (2019).
© Robert A. Schneider. DOI: 10.1093/oso/9780198826323.001.0001

consciousness that it *was* a code—that is, an ethos that both prescribed and proscribed. As will be argued in this chapter, there was another aspect to this "worldly" culture—that as much as it was characterized by a measure of expansiveness, it was also bounded by restrictions and inhibitions that were just as fundamental to the practices and understandings governing it.

To start with the most conspicuous feature of this code, we can point to the emphasis, not only on frankness and unmannered eloquence, but also on discretion, reticence, and even self-censorship. Advice of this sort is found in countless texts. Like the critique of pedantry, it might be seen as a commonplace of the Renaissance and post-Renaissance, hardly specific or particularly characteristic of the Age of Richelieu. And its pedigree is long. In *The Book of the Courtier* (1528), Castiglione has Federico argue that the courtier should "consider well whatever he does or says, the place where he does it, in whose presence, its timing, why he is doing it, his own age, his profession, the end he is aiming at, and the means that are suitable; and so, bearing all these points in mind, let him prepare himself discreetly for all he wishes to do or say."[4] As long as there were princely and royal courts, there was awareness that caution, in both speech and behavior, was paramount; that a slip of the tongue could prove degrading or even fatal; that frankness was an invitation to ridicule or worse. Stephen Greenblatt has made the concept of "self-fashioning" a defining feature of Renaissance court culture, and one technique of this highly self-conscious mode of self-presentation was in one's ability to adapt to the linguistic fashions, the unwritten speech and conversation codes, of the court.[5] A hundred years after Castiglione's popular book appeared, Faret echoed—and partially plagiarized—the Italian's advice, only in blunter terms. In a section of his *L'honnête homme* entitled "On the Difficulty of Keeping Silent," he writes: "There seems to be no virtue easier to acquire than this one, and yet one could say that there is none more difficult or rare. There are many more people who are brave, generous, chaste, and moderate in their violent passions than there are those who know how to keep silent as one should."[6]

This would seem to point to a fairly venerable notion, a veritable commonplace of the early modern period. There are reasons, however, to conclude that its importance and meaning measurably deepened in the decades from the end of the sixteenth century to the early seventeenth. For one thing, the language reforms discussed in Chapter 1 were explicit in banning inappropriate, crude, or vulgar words from the discourse of the *honnête homme*, just as it rejected foreign words, ancient terms, or provincial expressions from the vocabulary of proper French. The

---

[4] Baldesar Castiglione, *The Book of the Courtier*, trans. George Bull (New York, 1976), 115. The importance of prudence in the early modern period is discussed in a very important article by John Martin, "Inventing Sincerity, Refashioning Prudence: The Discovery of the Individual in Renaissance Europe," *American Historical Review*, 102/5 (1997), 1309–42.

[5] Stephen Greenblatt, *Renaissance Self-Fashioning: From More to Shakespeare* (Chicago, 1980).

[6] Nicolas Faret, *L'honnête homme, ou, L'art de plaire à la cour* (1925; reprint, Geneva, 1970), 73.

notion of *bienséance*—which is to say "propriety" or what is socially proper—was as fundamental to the emerging code for speech and behavior as *honnêteté*. Malherbe and Vaugelas, who both strove to purge French of all that was improper, were especially assertive in their proscriptive measures, even when, in the case of the former, it meant limiting language's expressive possibilities. Malherbe even famously quipped that he would happily sacrifice an idea if he could not find the proper way of expressing it. And they were in turn criticized by the likes of Marie de Gournay, François de La Mothe le Vayer, and Jean-Pierre Camus precisely because these defenders of an older humanist tradition saw the reformers as constraining the creative possibilities so valued in the works of Rabelais, Ronsard, and Montaigne. But while Montaigne continued to be read and valued by the seventeenth-century modernists, his style was found by many of these admirers to be prolix, shapeless, and indulgently self-referential.[7] Even Gournay, his "adoptive" daughter, who in other respects bucked the tide of linguistic and literary reform in the seventeenth century, as we have seen, confessed that she felt moved to distance herself from the great essayist's "frankness" of expression.[8] While some so-called libertine writers continued to cultivate the Rabelaisian tradition in a literature that circulated mostly in the tavern culture and low-lying precincts of the Parisian scene, Rabelais never had a seventeenth-century counterpart; nor were his writings in favor among the *bien-pensants*. The most successful "libertine" novel of the period, Sorel's *Francion*, while audacious in mocking a whole range of conventional views and icons, carefully skirted the bounds of religious criticism and was marked by a prose style that was surprisingly tame.[9]

For another thing, the ethos of Neo-Stoicism, which gained a remarkable purchase on a wide range of European elites in the period, certainly espoused restraint, in both behavior and speech, as crucial for the virtuous individual. "Governing passions" was the watchword of Neo-Stoicism: striving for that much-vaunted goal of "constancy" in the face of the vicissitudes of a chaotic world that could not be controlled but only endured. And one of the strategies for enduring its misfortunes, which were never more apparent than during the Wars of Religion, was to attain mastery over oneself—to know when and how to act and when and how to speak. Such mastery was apparent in the reticence and discretion that the virtuous man exhibited, especially in contrast to the volubility and lack of control ascribed to the common sort. Justus Lipsius was most responsible for the popularization of Neo-Stoicism, and his own writings not only

---

[7] See Charles Sorel, *La bibliothèque française* (Paris, 1667), 80ff.

[8] Alan Martin Boase, *The Fortunes of Montaigne: A History of the Essays in France, 1580–1669* (London, 1935), 60ff. Richard L. Regosin, "1595: Marie de Gournay Publishes the Posthumous Edition of Montaigne's *Essais*," in Denis Hollier, ed., *A New History of French Literature* (Cambridge, MA, 1989), 249.

[9] This is true for the first edition, but even more so for the edition of 1626, in which Sorel eliminated some of the more controversial passages in the original.

embodied its principles but also demonstrated them in the very writing itself. For one of the features of texts influenced by Neo-Stoicism was their crisp, epigrammatic, even elliptical style, often understood as a shift from the Ciceronian model, which prized oratorical eloquence and ornamentation, to the so-called "plane" style, "characterized by brevity, wit, archaism, and innuendo, paradox, and suggestive density."[10] Guillaume du Vair, the leading French exponent of Neo-Stoicism, wrote in his *Philosophie morale des stoïques*, "The best precept we can offer is to remain silent. To know how to keep silent is a great advantage in speaking well. Silence is the father of discourse and the fountain of reason."[11] While recent scholarship has complicated the view of a simple turn away from Cicero, the consensus is still that one of the dominant prose styles to emerge in the latter part of the sixteenth century conformed to this "Attic" mode. It was a style most suited to erudite or savant exchanges and less appropriate to the *mondain* milieu, where *bienséance*, rather than Neo-Stoicism, governed the nature of expression. But its importance cannot be denied: an indication that the imperative to transform discursive modes could take different forms.

* * *

When it comes to the reticence and discretion of men of letters and savants, however, it might be argued that these virtues had less to do with *bienséance*, Neo-Stoicism, and other cultural or philosophical influences and more with the threat of persecution. The case is a strong one. Many were convinced that France under Richelieu was becoming a dangerous place, a land haunted by surveillance, repression, and outright tyranny. For most, it was the Church and its agents, not the monarchy, that posed the greater threat. Gallican liberties were under assault by the papacy; the Jesuits had recently re-established themselves in Paris and were re-asserting their control over the education of the young. Influential clerics railed against the many "libertines" and atheists who, they insisted, abounded in Paris. France looked as though it could go the way of Venice, once a haven of republican liberty, now suffering under a papal interdict. In 1638, Grotius reported to Oxenstierna (inaccurately) that Gallicans were being thrown into prison, that informing monks haunted the city.[12]

---

[10] The classic work on this is by Morris W. Croll. See his two collections of essays, *Style, Rhetoric, and Rhythm: Essays by Morris W. Croll*, ed. J. Max Patrick and Robert O. Evans (Princeton, 1966), and *"Attic" and Baroque Prose Style: The Anti-Ciceronian Movement: Essays by Morris W. Croll*, ed. J. Max Patrick and Robert O. Evans (Princeton, 1969). But Marc Fumaroli offers a sustained argument for the persistence and renewal of Ciceronian rhetoric in *L'âge d'éloquence: Rhétorique et "res literaria" de la Renaissance au seuil de l'époque classique* (Geneva, 1980). For a useful survey, see Deborah Shuger, "Conceptions of Style," in Glyn P. Norton, ed., *The Cambridge History of Literary Criticism*, vol. 3: *The Renaissance* (Cambridge, 1999), 176–86.

[11] Guillaume du Vair, *Philosophie morale des stoïques* (Paris, 1585), 109.

[12] Henk J. M. Nellen, "*Disputando inclarescet veritas*: Grotius as a Publicist in France (1621–1645)," in Henk J. M. Nellen and Edwin Rabbie, eds., *Hugo Grotius, Theologian: Essays in Honour of G.H.M Posthumus Meyjes* (The Hague, 1994), 138.

In fact, the early years of our period saw a series of repressive measures against philosophers and poets who were targeted for their heretical or impious views. In 1619, the Neapolitan philosopher Vanini, whose writings reveal a Paduan strain of pantheism, was burned at the stake in Toulouse, despite the fact that he had powerful protectors both in the royal court and in the provincial city where his life ended. In 1622, a mystic named Jean Fontainier met the same fate in Paris. In these years Paris was apparently the scene of several gatherings that attracted students to lectures delivered by chemists or alchemists espousing anti-Aristotelian views, which provoked repressive measures by the Parlement. In August 1624, a group of three—a student, a university teacher, and a physician/alchemist— announced a public disputation in which they promised to refute the philosophy of Aristotle and defend a variety of atomism. They too were convicted and exiled.[13] In 1624, this period of "crisis" came to a head with the prosecution and imprisonment of the poet Théophile de Viau, an episode that would cast a long and baleful shadow over Parisian intellectual and literary life for the next several decades.

Théophile's trial marked a turning point in the attitudes and latitude of expression for a generation of writers, inducing them to see the wisdom of caution, discretion, and conformism. Although tried and convicted by the Parlement of Paris, Théophile was first pursued by the Jesuit François Garasse, who had already earned a reputation as a fierce hater of Protestants and Gallicans alike. Garasse was a formidable figure, headstrong and passionate, hell-bent on smoking out the masses of "atheists, blasphemers, and libertines" who were comfortably and dangerously ensconced, he believed, in the highest circles. For him, the Wars of Religion had not ended; he saw no distinction between Calvinists and Catholic *politiques*. In his earlier polemics, he took aim at such well-known Gallican writers as Louis Servin, Pierre Dumoulin, and especially Estienne Pasquier. In 1623 he unleashed a diatribe of over one thousand pages, taking special aim not only at Gallicans but at all those *beaux esprits* who, he declared, were nothing less than secret atheists and enemies of Christianity. And he named names. Charron and Vanini were dead, but Théophile was very much alive and at the height of his powers, with highly placed patrons in the aristocracy, friends in the royal court, boon companions in the city's taverns, and legions of admirers among Paris's poets. When the magistrates picked up Garasse's charges, he first fled, seeking the protection of Montmorency, but the patronage of the great counted for only so much, especially with the Counter-Reformation in full swing. The beleaguered

---

[13] Daniel Garber, "On the Frontlines of the Scientific Revolution: How Mersenne Learned to Love Galileo," *Perspectives in Science*, 12/2 (2004), 135–63; and Garber, "Defending Aristotle/Defending Society in Early 17th Century Paris," in Wolfgang Detel and Claus Zittel, eds., *Wissensideale und Wissenskulturen in der frühen Neuzeit: Ideals and Culture of Knowledge in Early Modern Europe* (Berlin, 1969), 135–60.

poet spent nearly a year in prison, an ordeal that weakened him so much that death came shortly after his release in 1627.[14]

Théophile's demise also implicated others. Among those who published suspect verses along with him in the *Parnasse des poètes satyriques*, which attracted Garasse's prurient attention, were Colletet, Frénicle, and Berthelot; all were condemned, like Théophile, in absentia. There were other close friends of Théophile who were not implicated in the publication that led to his demise, but who nevertheless took advantage of the occasion to distance themselves from the victimized poet. Most notably, Balzac, who at precisely that moment was on the brink of publishing his *Premières lettres*, a collection devised to mark his triumph as the master of French prose, made sure to enter the fray as a critic of his former friend and companion.[15] Nicolas Schapira writes that the Théophile affair served as a warning to writers not to get involved in "theological-political controversies," prompting them to "retreat into the space [*espace*] of belles-lettres."[16]

While a fear of religious persecution and watchdog zealots like Garasse haunted men of letters, this did not mean that they were unconcerned about the depredations of the secular authorities. Many cast a wary eye on Richelieu, especially as censorship, summary justice, and the heavy hand of ministerial patronage were becoming features of his rule. Mathieu de Morgues, Richelieu's one-time pamphleteer, now in the service of the Queen Mother, was not alone in concluding that the French Academy was really a gilded cage for writers.[17] Mersenne, writing to Descartes, seems to confirm the existence of a beefed-up surveillance regime: "Never have they been more strict than at the present in examining books, for Monsieur le Chancelier [Séguier] has several faithful agents to judge those of theology, others for politics, the Academy of Paris for both those works in prose and poetry, and some mathematicians for the rest."[18] The three Campion brothers, noblemen bitterly opposed to Richelieu, had a more extreme view of things, which, if it reflected their rhetorical inclination to make matters seem as dire as possible, still echoed a widespread sentiment: "We can scarcely discuss our own misfortunes in our own house and with our own family; I hardly am able to recognize France in this altered state."[19] It is, however, curious, given these

---

[14] Antoine Adam, *Théophile de Viau et la libre pensée française en 1620* (Paris, 1935). See also Joan DeJean, *The Reinvention of Obscenity: Sex, Lies, and Tabloids in Early Modern France* (Chicago, 2002); Stéphane Van Damme, *Épreuve libertine: Morale, soupçon et pouvoirs dans la France baroque* (Paris, 2008).

[15] I will have more to say about Balzac's role in the Théophile affair later in this chapter.

[16] Nicolas Schapira, *Un professionnel des lettres au XVIIe siècle: Valentin Conrart, une histoire sociale* (Paris, 2003), 64.

[17] Paul Pellisson and Pierre-Joseph Thoulier d'Olivet, *Histoire de l'Académie française, par Pellisson et d'Olivet*, 3rd ed., revised and enlarged, 2 vols. (Paris, 1743), I: 64.

[18] H. J. Martin, *Livre, pouvoirs et société à Paris au XVIIe siècle (1589–1701)* (Paris, 1962), I: 445–6.

[19] *Mémoires d'Henri Campion (1613–1663), suivis de trois entretiens sur divers sujets d'histoire, de politique et de morale*, ed. Marc Fumaroli (Paris, 1967), 246–7.

fearful expressions, that royal instruments for book censorship were rather late in developing. Although there had long been legislation calling for the scrutiny of printed matter, as well as effective bouts of severe censorship and repression, especially during the religious wars, it was not until the 1630s that these efforts were solidified in royal hands.[20]

Whatever its source—secular or religious—caution was the byword among writers and savants in these decades. If in the 1630s the fate of Théophile was only half-remembered, the protracted case of Galileo certainly served as a worrisome reminder of the very real threat of persecution. The obvious circumspection exercised by Descartes, who carefully avoided religion and politics in his writings, postponed publishing some of them, and took the additional precaution of remaining in Holland, demonstrates that the most important philosopher of the day was keenly aware of the lurking dangers.[21] He was hardly alone. Gassendi, too, agonized over publishing his anti-Aristotelian, Epicurean writings, waiting many years before allowing them to see the light of day.[22] The published dialogues of the so-called Tetrade, a coterie of intellectuals including La Mothe le Vayer, Naudé, Diodati, and Gassendi, illustrates another set of defensive strategies. A quasi-clandestine publication containing some bold professions of religious skepticism, it was printed under the pseudonym Orasius Tubero, with a false date, a fictitious imprimatur, and the participants' names disguised as well. Even letters reveal a concern with official scrutiny. When Gassendi wanted to write to console the imprisoned Galileo, Peiresc cautioned him to be discreet in choosing his words: "I advise you to conceive them in terms so reserved and so appropriate that there will be a way to understand a good part of your intentions without the literal meaning being specified."[23] The use of codes—and not just in official correspondence regarding matters of state—was common among writers, indicating a concern for surveillance. When Naudé was in Rome serving as Cardinal Bagni's secretary, he corresponded with the Dupuy brothers on a range of matters; his letters were carefully coded to disguise the identities of various figures, and in one

---

[20] Alain Viala, *La naissance de l'écrivain: Sociologie de la littérature à l'âge classique* (Paris, 1985), 115–22; Nicolas Schapira, "Quand le privilège de librarie publie l'auteur," in Christian Jouhaud and Alain Viala, eds., *De la publication: Entre Renaissance et Lumières* (Paris, 2002), 121–37; Schapira, *Un professionnel des lettres*, chap. 2; and especially Alfred Soman, "Press, Pulpit, and Censorship in France before Richelieu," *Proceedings of the American Philosophical Society*, 120/6 (1976), 439–63. See also DeJean, *The Reinvention of Obscenity*.

[21] Stephen Gaukroger, *Descartes: An Intellectual Biography* (Oxford, 1995), 290–2; Antonio Negri, *Political Descartes: Reason, Ideology and the Bourgeois Project*, trans. Matteo Mandarini and Alberto Toscano (London, 2007), 140ff. Descartes had firsthand knowledge of Séguier's interest in monitoring the publication of books; when his *Discourse* was about to be published, the chancellor asked to examine the work personally. See Robert Mandrou, *From Humanism to Science, 1480–1700*, trans. Brian Pearce (Atlantic Highlands, NJ, 1979), 214; and Schapira, *Un professionnel des lettres*, 111.

[22] On Gassendi, see especially Sylvie Taussig, *Pierre Gassendi (1592–1655): Introduction à la vie savante* (Turnhout, 2003), 17 and *passim*.

[23] Quoted in Joan DeJean, *Libertine Strategies: Freedom and the Novel in Seventeenth-Century France* (Columbus, OH, 1981), 25.

of them he expresses alarm over the possible development of a "leak" within the Dupuys' Parisian circle.[24]

But while the fear of persecution should not be underestimated, we must not assume that *gens de lettres* uniformly saw themselves as beleaguered; many, in fact, were just as concerned about the rise in atheism or "libertinage" as the more zealous guardians of faith and morals. In other words, we must not jump to the conclusion that all writers were simply opportunistic or cowardly, making sure to keep their heads down while some of their confreres were threatened with prosecution. (Although Balzac's behavior certainly makes us think otherwise.) Most were surely devout, undoubtedly in their own way, and many obviously worried about the seductive influence of their more freethinking fellow writers. The two major architects of *honnêteté*, for example, Faret and Bardin (as we have seen), both warned against the snares of "libertinage" and the pernicious example of *esprits forts*. And Jean de Silhon, a servant of Richelieu and another defender of the cardinal's controversial policies, left his mark early in his career as a pious critic of skeptics like Montaigne and Charron. Even Guy Patin, something of a freethinker himself, lumped "bigots and libertines" together, "which are two odious extremes."[25] Some *gens de lettres* believed that the responsibility for policing the moral and religious rectitude of literary culture and intellectual life was primarily theirs.

Neither should we assume that persecution was the only or even the most urgent concern of writers and savants as they cast about for proper modes of expression. As just noted, the threat, such as it was, certainly should not be seen as originating from one single source, and thus for some writers and thinkers, casting their lot with the monarchy or attaching themselves to powerful patrons was not a mode of servitude but a source of freedom. For one thing, despite the close identification between the monarchy and the Roman faith—an identification only heightened by the elevation of a cardinal to the position of chief minister—it is clear that many saw the crown as a traditional bulwark against the more militant tendencies of the Counter-Reformation, especially as the persecutory arm of the Church was seen as a foreign threat to the "liberties" of the Gallican Church.

For another thing—and more generally speaking—"freedom" in this period did not necessarily mean independence, for in a corporate and hierarchical society, to be independent entailed vulnerability. This was especially true for the *mondain* writers, who for the most part lacked an affiliation with an institution like the Church, the university, or the magistracy, and for whom royal or aristocratic

---

[24] *Lettres de Gabriel Naudé à Jacques Dupuy (1632–1652)*, ed. Phillip J. Wolfe (Edmonton, AB, 1982), 13. On Boulliau's use of *"chiffres"* in his correspondence of a political nature, see Henk J. M. Nellen, *Ismaël Boulliau (1605–1694): Astronome, épistolier, nouvelliste et intermédiaire scientifique* (Amsterdam, 1994), 348.

[25] René Pintard, *Le libertinage érudit dans la première moitié du XVIIe siècle* (Paris, 1943), 322.

patronage conferred not only status but protection as well. *Gens de lettres* were rarely outsiders, loners, or otherwise alienated from the institutions and hierarchies of power and authority: this is a modern conception of the writer or artist inherited from Romanticism. Many writers, even those with somewhat unconventional or non-conformist views on religion, were servants of the state. They thus might be counted as "outsiders" vis-à-vis the Church, while quintessential "insiders"—members of Richelieu's personal team of writers, for example—among the power elite. It is remarkable that in this period of the Counter-Reformation and the active campaign on the part of the crown to convert important Protestants, dismantle Huguenot fortresses and protected cities, and in general undermine the provisions of the Edict of Nantes, many Calvinists managed to thrive and even enjoy great privileges and important positions in various inner circles, even at court. Richelieu's publicist, Théophraste Renaudot, the man to whom he entrusted the direction of the *Gazette de France* as well as the Bureau d'adresse, was a Protestant. Valentin Conrart, the first secretary of the Académie française, remained a Protestant, as did Pierre d'Ablancourt, a prominent translator and early member of the academy; the Marquis de Montausier, another royal servant who was also prominent in the world of letters, converted only late in his career. Richelieu energetically courted the self-exiled Protestant savant Claude Saumaise to join his entourage, as well as the Dutch Calvinist Hugo Grotius while he lived in Paris.

While tolerated, these Protestants were still a minority among *gens de lettres*. Most were Gallicans: sincere Christians who nevertheless feared the growing influence of the Jesuits and the repressive power of the ultramontane Church. In either case, it is not clear that fear of official repression was the primary factor in their disposition toward reticence, discretion, even self-censorship. Other concerns preyed upon their minds, concerns having more to do with lessons learned from the Wars of Religion, with the potentially deleterious effects of disclosure of controversial ideas on the public, than with a threat to their personal liberty. To illustrate the problem, I turn now to Pierre Charron, an emblematic and influential figure of the period.

Pierre Charron and the "Many-Headed Beast"

No writer was more important to the generation of *gens de lettres* of the 1620s and '30s than Pierre Charron, the literary disciple of Montaigne and a major exponent of philosophical skepticism. Naudé gave him pride of place among modern writers in his ideal library,[26] while Gassendi praised Charron's *De la sagesse* as one of

---

[26] *La bibliographie politique du sieur Naudé* (Paris, 1642), 17: "Je l'estime en cela plus sage que Socrate."

his favorite books. Charron's popularity exceeded that of his master well into the century. *De la sagesse* went through forty editions in the seventeenth century, and the abridged version, *Petit traicté de sagesse*, enjoyed twelve re-editions in the first half of the century alone. Garasse attacked him as chief of the libertines, second in perniciousness only to such Italian atheists as Pietro Pomponazzi and Vanini.[27]

But herein lies what might be called the "Charron problem." One interpretation sees him as an intellectual libertine, whose views, though somewhat cryptically presented, are nevertheless clear to the astute and knowing reader. For at times Charron seems to assert that wisdom, which he sees as a combination of worldliness and morality limited to the few, is more fundamental than, even superior to, religion. "Religion is posterior to prudence," he writes.[28] Not only does he argue, somewhat obliquely but unmistakably, for a set of values transcending particular religions, he also embraces a relativistic view of religion in general, using comparative history to demonstrate that religious identity comes from human, not divine, sources. Echoing Montaigne, he writes, "Nation, region, and place bestow religion...we are circumcised, baptized, Jewish, Moslem, or Christian before we know we are men."[29] His scorn for religious practices and beliefs as practiced by the multitude—whose faith is polluted by superstition, fanaticism, and ignorance—is barely contained. But his critique goes even farther, underscored by his judgment that religion is essentially contrary to natural reason. "All religions have this in common, that they are strange and horrible to common sense."[30] It is these views that provoked the critical reading of *De la sagesse* upon its publication, leading to its condemnation by the Sorbonne in 1604 and its placement on the Index in 1605.

There is, however, another view of Charron that sees him as a Christian Pyrrhonist whose skepticism was primarily cast as a defense of Catholic orthodoxy, as opposed to the dogmatism and false reasoning of Protestantism. This position, most forcefully presented by Richard Popkin, places him in the company of other so-called libertines who, rather than attack the faith, embraced Pyrrhonism as a means of intellectually discrediting Protestantism.[31] Charron and his disciples were thus not freethinkers or non-conformists, but sincere though perhaps somewhat lukewarm Catholics, whose faith, based on pure belief, eschewed the support of reason.

---

[27] On Charron, see Renée Kogel, *Pierre Charron* (Geneva, 1972); Tullio Gregory, "Pierre Charron's 'Scandalous Book,'" in Michael Hunter and David Wootton, eds., *Atheism from the Reformation to the Enlightenment* (Oxford, 1992), 87–109; Eugene F. Rice Jr., *The Renaissance Idea of Wisdom* (Cambridge, MA, 1958), chap. 7; Maryanne Cline Horowitz, *Seeds of Virtue and Knowledge* (Princeton, 1998), chap. 10; Nannerl O. Keohane, *Philosophy and the State in France: The Renaissance to the Enlightenment* (Princeton, 1980), 135–44.

[28] Pierre Charron, *De la sagesse, trois livres* (Paris, 1604), II, 5: 463–4.

[29] *De la sagesse*, II, 5: 451.

[30] *De la sagesse*, II, 5: 451; see Gregory, "Pierre Charron's 'Scandalous Book,'" 99.

[31] Richard H. Popkin, *The History of Scepticism from Erasmus to Spinoza*, 3rd ed. (Berkeley, 1979), chap. 3.

Although Popkin is not able to cite many passages from *De la sagesse* to support his interpretation, it is certainly true, for one thing, that Charron was not an atheist: informed by Neo-Stoic thinking, he saw wisdom as the pathway to God. For another, there is circumstantial evidence suggesting that contemporaries had little trouble with Charron's writings. Despite the objections that initially met the first edition of his book, his subsequent revisions merely toned down some of the more offending passages; the text was not significantly altered. Charron also was and remained a priest, enjoying the friendship and support of such respected clerics as the eminent Cardinal Du Perron. Finally, and perhaps most telling for Popkin's view, Charron's book received an unambiguous endorsement from the well-known, deeply pious Saint-Cyran, who took it upon himself to study *De la sagesse* carefully while preparing a riposte to Garasse's *La doctrine curieuse*, which excoriated Charron as a libertine atheist of the worst kind. Saint-Cyran found nothing objectionable; quite the contrary: he discovered in Charron a kindred spirit whose own doubt and belittlement of human reason suggested the Augustinian understanding of man as irredeemably lost without God's grace. Likewise, Jean de Silhon, who had criticized Charron in his *Les deux vérités*, was moved, upon further considerations of the priest's views, to retract his judgment.[32]

There is no point in trying to determine here Charron's true view of Christianity, even if that were possible—there are good arguments for either interpretation. But one thing is clear: Charron himself went to some lengths to ensure that his readers would be forced to work hard to decipher his views, for not only did he include ambiguous and mutually contradictory passages, he also supplied contradictory guides to how his book should be read. As David Wootton brilliantly argues, the reader of *De la sagesse* must know how to "read between the lines" in the Straussian sense, for Charron's text conveys both a conventional and an esoteric set of instructions. These are contained in the prefaces to books I and II of *De la sagesse*. In the preface to the first book, Charron warns the reader not to confuse his descriptions and musings, which might be interpreted as supporting unbelief, with his true values and sentiments. Here he acknowledges an incorrect way to interpret his book, one leading to impious conclusions; and by underscoring this way as incorrect, he fulfills the requirement of warning the reader against it. In the preface to the second book, however, he boasts that he is going to write bluntly in praise of true wisdom while also attacking folly. As Wootton concludes: "When the discussions of reading and writing contained in the two prefaces are juxtaposed, the tension between them can only be resolved by concluding that his description of how *not* to read his book in the first preface is in fact a description

---

[32] On Saint-Cyran's view of Charron, see Kogel, *Pierre Charron*, 153–4; Jean Orcibal, *Les origines du Jansénisme*, 3 vols. (Paris, 1947), III: chap. 5. On Silhon, see Popkin, *The History of Scepticism*, chap. 8.

of how we *should* read it: only then will he seem blunter and bolder than all those who have gone before."[33]

These messages—cryptic keys to his text—were included in the second edition of *De la sagesse*, clearly in response to the critical reception of the book in certain devout circles. They allowed Charron to preserve the essence of his text while disclaiming responsibility for its more dangerous implications. What was behind this strategy? Was Charron himself fearful of persecution? In fact, there is very little evidence to indicate that this was the case. As noted, he altered the substance of the text very little in the second edition. And though it was placed on the Index after his death, it had a flourishing publishing history throughout the century. Charron was never personally threatened; nor did he have anything less than an entirely conventional and successful clerical career. It seems quite plausible, then, to conclude that Charron was motivated not by fear but by responsibility—not out of a concern for his own persecution but because, like many of his contemporary writers, he was profoundly alert to the danger of exposing controversial and potentially subversive matters to the light of day.

Like others of his generation, Charron was deeply influenced by the Wars of Religion, and in particular by the emergence of the Catholic League. He understood the League's seductive power, for following Henri III's order to assassinate the Guise brothers in 1588, he flirted with joining the Catholic militants, and "even put a foot inside." He soon realized his folly, but the experience taught him the danger of giving rein to his passions: "I was always angry, in a continual fever and agitation; when I have learned, at my own expense, that is impossible to be both moved and wise at the same time."[34] Charron was candid enough to admit his own susceptibility to the excesses of passion, and writes of emerging from his anger "completely changed," suggesting that the awakening was instrumental in bringing him to the insight that the prudent individual keeps passions in check. But in *De la sagesse*, this concern is largely projected upon the lower classes, who are excoriated for their waywardness and excitability. And it is this social element that provides the key to Charron's real fears.

An entire chapter of the book, "Peuple ou vulgaire," consists of a veritable tirade against them. The people are changeable and of several minds, he writes. They are capricious and easily aroused. They are herd-like and conformist, and petty-minded, envious, and malicious. They are immoral and intemperate, child-like and fickle. And they are prone to indiscipline and rebellion: "Always muttering and murmuring against the State, always belching out slanders and insolent

---

[33] David Wootton, "New Histories of Atheism," in Michael Hunter and David Wootton, eds., *Atheism from the Reformation to the Enlightenment* (Oxford, 1992), 39.

[34] Charron, *Discours Chrestien, qu'il n'est permis ny loisible au subiet, pour quelque cause et raison que ce soit, de se liguer, bander et rebeller contre son roy* (Paris, 1606), quoted in Kogel, *Pierre Charron*, 20.

speeches against those that govern and command." Though they are hopelessly dependent on leaders, they lack all judgment in choosing them: "They prefer those that have hot heads and active hands, before those that have a settled and temperate judgment, and upon whom the weight of the affairs must lie; boasters and prattlers before those that are simple and staid." Their stunted intelligence and lack of discernment do not prevent them from being voluble and opinionated: "They have nothing but a mouth, they have tongues that cease not, spirits that budge not; they are a monster whose parts are all tongues, they speak all things, but know nothing; they look upon all, but see nothing; they laugh at all, and weep at all." "To conclude," Charron ends his tirade,

> the people are a savage beast, all that they think is vanity; all they say is false and erroneous; that they reprove is good; that they approve is naught; that which they praise is infamous; that which they do and undertake is folly.... The Vulgar multitude is the mother of ignorance, injustice, inconstancy, idolatry, vanity, which never yet could be pleased: their motto is, *Vox populi, vox Dei: The voice of the people is the voice of God:* but we may say, *Vox populi, vox stultorum: The voice of the people is the voice of fools*.[35]

Charron was by no means alone in conveying this particular image of the lower orders, but *De la sagesse* contains perhaps the most ample and spirited exposition in the period of their supposed noxious tendencies. Moreover, his social vision led to a wider concern permeating his writings and pointing to the fears that governed his general outlook. What he lamented most among the people was their propensity to act without thinking, their inconstancy, their susceptibility to being aroused. Thus, according to his instructions, a frontispiece was added to the 1604 edition to illustrate the guiding tenets of *De la sagesse*. A female figure, Wisdom, stands alone on a pedestal gazing at a mirror, with the words "Know Thyself" engraved below. Four other figures are chained at the base of the pedestal, signifying the lower aspects of human nature: Passion, Opinion, Superstition, and Pedantry. Passion appears as deformed and demanding. Opinion stands on the heads of the popular crowd. Superstition is possessed by fear. And Pedantry reads from a book of "yes" and "no." Once again we see the scorn for pedantry, but here as a source of division and pernicious sophistry. The illustration stands for a central feature of Charron's outlook: the division between the wise individual, the *esprit fort*, whose constancy and fortitude allow him special insight into the nature of wisdom; and the multitude of others who, ever prone to their passions, must remain in the thrall of custom and convention.[36]

---

[35] *Of Wisdome: Three Books Written in French by Peter Charro[n], Doctr of Lawe in Paris*, trans. Samson Lennard (1608; London, 1630), 208–11; Charron, *De la sagesse*, I, 51: 335–8. I have modernized the spelling of this English translation.

[36] See Horowitz, *Seeds of Virtue*, 225.

This division is reflected in the overall organization of *De la sagesse*. The first book anatomizes the human condition, describing the customs and foibles that govern ordinary people. The other two books address the question of prudence in a wide range of contexts and aim to explain how the wise man can manage to accommodate himself to a world of such inconstancy and folly while preserving a sense of rectitude and tranquility of soul. One part of *De la sagesse* thus deals with the nature of the "*sottes multitudes*"; the other was a breviary for the *esprits forts*. The latter understood not only how to live in this world, but how it must be governed. Indeed, a wise ruler was the quintessential *esprit fort*, and in this context it is worth noting that Richelieu owned a copy of *De la sagesse* and was accused by the Spanish minister Olivares of trying to impose Charron's impious "wisdom" on the French.[37]

While not primarily a political tract, *De la sagesse* addressed political concerns, endorsing an understanding of political expediency that places it within the reason of state tradition. "The greatest thing this world can show is authority," Charron writes in Book II. "This is the image of the divine power.... Nothing but authority can prevail with fools, to make any tolerable advances toward wisdom."[38] Charron advocated a "pliable justice" in the face of worldly, political matters, a kind of justice that was distinct from the divine or natural guides to conduct. "Political justice" allowed the prince to violate certain moral and religious tenets for the sake of preserving order, putting down rebellions, or thwarting attempts at usurping legitimate authority. That he had in mind mainly the Wars of Religion is made clear from his examples and a chapter in Book III entitled "Civil Wars," in which he declares that "there is no evil more miserable, nor shameful; it is the sea of misfortunes." Citing Cicero, he writes, "properly speaking it is not a war but a disease of the state, a hot and frenzied sickness."[39]

All of this allows us to appreciate Wootton's insight regarding the esoteric nature of *De la sagesse*. It was, in short, a text written for the *esprit fort* who could appreciate that, just as there were two types of justice, there were two different kinds of morality, one conventional, largely religious in nature, the other exclusively based upon the dictates of reason. And just as the *arcana imperii* were, as the concept implies, to remain secret, so Charron's wisdom had to be conveyed obliquely, with provisos attached to veil the text's true meaning from the eyes of the uninitiated. Discretion was needed not out of fear for oneself, but because of a sense of responsibility for maintaining the order of things.

* * *

---

[37] Peter Burke, "Tacitism, Scepticism, and Reason of State," in J. H. Burns, ed., *The Cambridge History of Political Thought, 1450–1700* (Cambridge, 1991), 496.

[38] Quoted by Paul F. Grendler, "Pierre Charron: Precursor to Hobbes," *Review of Politics*, 25/2 (1963), 216.

[39] Eugene Rice, *The Renaissance Idea of Wisdom* (Cambridge, MA, 1958), 201.

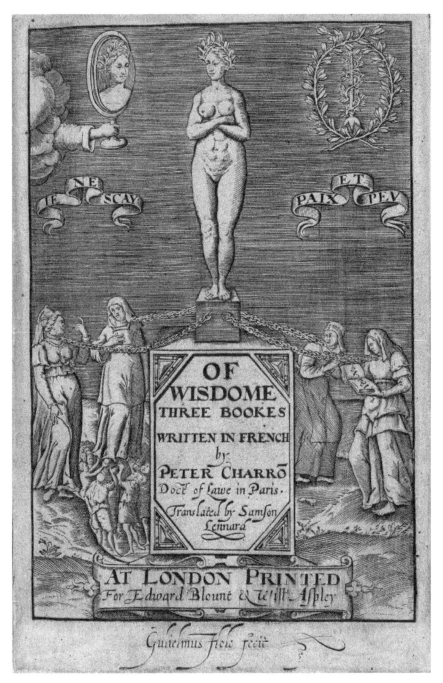

Figure 2 Title page from *Of Wisdome: Three Bookes Written in French by Peter Charro[n], Doctr of Lawe in Paris*, translated by Samson Lennard. Courtesy of the Folger Shakespeare Library Digital Image Collection.

Charron was by no means alone in conveying this threatening image of a populace—one with "many heads." Indeed, it was something of a trope. In the sixteenth century, the author of *Vindiciae contre tyrannos* railed against "a populace... that beast which sports a million heads."[40] A seminal text published in the wake of the League takeover in Paris in 1588 blames the people "who like a ferocious animal wanted to shake off the yoke of royal dominion in order to secure I don't know what kind of imaginary liberty."[41] A commentator on the Catholic militants during the Wars of Religion described the "Party of the League" as a "monster having been formed of many members... it is no wonder if it has been seen to have several heads, like a serpent engendered out of the earth's putrescence."[42] Estienne Pasquier often cited Horace, apparently his favorite author, denouncing the threatening presence of the "many-headed beast."[43] Jean Baudoin, in his *Discours politiques* of 1619, asserted that "the *ville populaire* is a terrifying monster."[44] John Barclay, in his Latin novel *Argenis* (1621), a fictional treatment of the Wars of Religion aimed primarily at a French readership, depicts the people as "a many-headed monster" responsible for inflaming the conflict.[45] Likewise, in his *Ministre d'Estat* of 1632, Jean de Silhon drew upon the image to explain the sorry fate of Henri III during the wars. Henri, he claimed, mistakenly put his trust "in the will of the people and on the inclinations of this beast, which arouses itself as it is pushed and... dared to wage war against him."[46] Naudé in his *Considérations politiques sur les coups d'état* (1639) also evoked the image, and in doing so rivaled Charron in the prolixity and viciousness of his critique: "a beast with many heads, vagabonds, wayward, crazy, thoughtless, rudderless, mindless, without judgment," he writes.[47] Georges de Scudéry contemptuously described spectators in the *parterre* section of the theater as "an animal with so many heads..., half man, half goat, all beast."[48] Another writer interested in the theater, Hippolyte-Jules Pilet de

---

[40] Quoted in Hélène Merlin, *Public et littérature en France au XVIIe siècle* (Paris, 1994), 79.

[41] *Le dialogue d'entre le Maheustre et le Manant* (1593), quoted in William F. Church, *Constitutional Thought in Sixteenth-Century France: A Study in the Evolution of Ideas* (Cambridge, MA, 1941), 304.

[42] Timothy Reiss, *The Meaning of Literature* (Ithaca, NY, 1992), 55.

[43] Both quotes from George Huppert, *The Style of Paris: Renaissance Origins of the French Enlightenment* (Bloomington, IN, 1999), 30, 67.

[44] Quoted in Etienne Thuau, *Raison d'Etat et pensée politique à l'epoque de Richelieu* (Paris, 1966), 19.

[45] *John Barclay, His Argenis, Translated out of Latine into English*, trans. Robert Le Grys (London, 1628), 286.

[46] Jean de Silhon, *Le ministre d'Estat, avec la véritable usage de la politique moderne* (Paris, 1641 ed.), 177.

[47] Gabriel Naudé, *Considérations politiques sur les coups d'état* (1639), ed. Louis Marin (Paris, 1988), 138. On the next page he qualifies his assessment: "I say that [the populace] is inferior to beasts, worse than beasts, and a hundred times more stupid than beasts."

[48] Georges de Scudéry, *Apologie du théâtre* (Paris, 1639), cited in John Lough, *Paris Theatre Audiences in the Seventeenth and Eighteenth Centuries* (London, 1965), 65; and Jeffrey S. Revel, "Définir le parterre au XVIIe siècle," in Roger Duchêne and Pierre Ronzeaud, eds., *Ordre et contestation au temps classique* (Paris, 1992), 228. See also Pierre Ronzéaud, *Peuple et représentations sous le règne du Louis XIV* (Aix-en-Provence, 1988), 221–2. On this imagery in the English context, see Christopher Hill, "The Many-Headed Monster in Late Tudor and Early Stuart Political Thinking," in

La Mesnardière, anatomized audiences in similar terms, arguing that "the vulgar masses [*multitude grossière*] cannot obtain any pleasure from a serious, solemn, chaste, and truly tragic discourse; and that this many-headed Monster can at best only understand the superficial ornaments of the Theatre."[49] The writer who wrote the preface to Balzac's letters refers to the Roman populace in Caesar and Cicero's time as an ignorant "hundred-headed beast," easy to manipulate.[50] In his dictionary, Furetière defines "hydra" by explicitly referring to "popular seditions and other things that pullulate and multiply such that one is forced to destroy them.... The people are a hydra with a hundred heads."[51]

Now, it would be misleading to assert that these expressions of contempt and fear for the people as some kind of beast or monster were new to the period. Clearly they were not. The expression "the many-headed beast" has ancient sources, and was oft-evoked in humanist texts. In this earlier period, however, along with complaints about the people's waywardness and ignorance, there was a certain measure of hopefulness regarding their potential for wisdom, or at least their susceptibility to reason and moral suasion, despite the acknowledgment of popular threats and the capriciousness of the lower orders. Pasquier, for example, extolled the qualities of the common people, especially when it came to language, and vociferously defended their ways against his friend Petrus Ramus. Writing to one of his sons in the course of the religious wars, he urges him to spare the civilian population while campaigning, reminding him that "These poor people bore no responsibility for the bloody conflict."[52] In a poem written to Charles IX in the late 1560s on the "Four Estates of France," Joachim du Bellay speaks favorably of the lower orders, referring to "the great providing people" whose labors support the crown and cultivate the land.[53] Montaigne, too, though he certainly bemoaned the superstition and deleterious passions of the common sort, also demonstrated a real appreciation for their unpretentious ways and solid knowledge. In fact,

---

Charles H. Carter, ed., *From the Renaissance to the Counter-Reformation: Essays in Honor of Garrett Mattingly* (New York, 1965).

[49] Reiss, *The Meaning of Literature*, 81.
[50] *Les premières lettres de Guez de Balzac, 1618–1627*, ed. H. Bibas and K.-T. Butler, 2 vols. (Paris, 1933–4), I: 240.
[51] Quoted in Ronzéaud, *Peuple et représentations*, 222. In 1637 Gassendi wrote to Galileo regarding his house arrest as a "most desired and fortunate retirement," adding that "wise men desire nothing more than to be removed from the turbulence of the court and the tumults of the city, and... from the profane crowd, which like a many-headed beast knows nothing human, and hopes for nothing but lying, invidiousness, perfidy and other such things." Lisa Tunick Sarasohn, "Epicureanism and the Creation of a Privatist Ethic in Early Seventeenth-Century France," in Margaret J. Osler, ed., *Atoms, Pneuma, and Tranquillity: Epicurean and Stoic Themes in European Thought* (Cambridge, 1991), 175. See also Corneille's *Cinna, ou, La clémence d'Auguste* (Paris, 1641) for mention of people as a hydra-headed beast.
[52] Huppert, *The Style of Paris*, 67.
[53] Timothy Hampton, *Literature and Nation in the Sixteenth Century: Inventing Renaissance France* (Ithaca, NY, 2001), 157.

the *Essays* exhibit a revealing shift from the first edition to subsequent versions. In "Of the Inequality That Is between Us," in Book I, he writes of "the mass of men nowadays, senseless, base, servile, unstable, continually bobbing about in a storm of conflicting passions which drive them hither and thither, men totally dependent upon others: they are farther apart than earth and sky."[54] In Book III, however, both his tone and his view change, based upon a Neo-Stoic appreciation of strength of character, resolve, and calm in the face of misfortune rather than learning or social status. There he praises the rustic sort for their simple wisdom and unthinking strengths, even, at one point, comparing peasants to Socrates, the ultimate encomium. Even Machiavelli, whose political wisdom seemed to hinge on the people's fickleness, harbored a respect for them, evident, most notably, in his preference for a popular militia; he even cited with approval the adage "Vox populi, vox dei."[55] The constitutional tradition of political thought, which largely disappeared in the seventeenth century, acknowledged the lower classes, at least theoretically, as legitimate elements of the social order. Bodin's commonwealth certainly includes all citizens, even the most humble; likewise, Loyseau's *Traité des ordres* offered a portrait of France as a sort of social great chain of being, connecting the highest to the lowest of its inhabitants.[56]

In the late sixteenth and early seventeenth century, however, this disposition to look favorably upon the lower orders was rarely in evidence. On the contrary, the people were almost universally seen as threatening, ignorant, and beyond redemption. Chapelain could only express contempt at any attempt to please "these idiots and this riff-raff [*racaille*]." Colletet echoed the commonplace that "the people are a poor judge...if they happen to deliberate correctly, it is only by accident and not from reason, because, in effect, they are deprived of that quality which is characteristic of *honnêtes gens*."[57] What are the reasons for this—why was a fearful, disparaging view of the lower orders invoked more readily and with greater political significance in the early seventeenth century than previously?

First, and most obviously, the Wars of Religion seemed to offer graphic proof of the people's wayward and violent proclivities. Many tended to blame the excesses of the conflict on the populace, conveniently forgetting that such forces as the League and the nobility had played a role in arousing passions. Barclay and

---

[54] "Of the Inequality That Is between Us," in *The Complete Essays of Montaigne*, trans. Donald Frame (Stanford, 1957), I: 42, on 191. In "Of Glory," II: 16, on 473, he writes, "we refer to the voice of the common people and of the mob, the mother of ignorance, injustice, and inconsistency. Is it reasonable to make the life of a sage depend on the judgment of fools?...Whoever aims to please them has never done; this is a shapeless and elusive target."

[55] *The Essential Writings of Machiavelli*, ed. and trans. Peter Constantine (New York, 2007), 218. See also his statement in the *Discourses*, 217: "I propose that a populace is more prudent, more stable, and has better judgment than a prince." See Alfredo Bonadeo, "The Role of the People in the Works and Times of Machiavelli," *Bibliothèque d'Humanisme et Renaissance*, 32/2 (1970), 351–77.

[56] Church, *Constitutional Thought in Sixteenth-Century France*.

[57] René Bray, *La formation de la doctrine classique en France* (Paris, 1927), 133, 134.

Silhon, as just noted, cast the people as culprits; so too did Guillaume du Vair, who pointed to the Parisian crowd—"a tempestuous sea"—as responsible for the League takeover and the Day of the Barricades.[58] During the wars themselves, while the Leaguers used the word "people" in laudatory terms, meaning Catholics righteously united against heresy, the *politiques*' use was solely disparaging. The *politique* diarist Pierre de L'Estoile voiced a common analysis when he recorded: "The people, instead of murmuring against the League, murmur against the King, so stupid are they."[59] Guy du Faur de Pibrac, writing under the influence of Tacitus, blamed the Parisian mob for the Saint Bartholomew's Day Massacre.[60] An anti-League pamphlet excoriated the "*base population parisienne*" which, "with an extreme contempt for all the Estates, and the Nobility more than anything," had made Mayenne (a leader of the Holy League) "the People's Tribune."[61] As Robert Descimon has shown, during the League takeover of Paris, the people then, too—not the princes and priests—were deemed the truly culpable agents.[62] Henry Heller claims that the fear of popular rebellion first surfaces in print in the 1590s, citing a pamphlet by Pierre Constant, *La cause des guerres civiles de la France*, which blames "artisans and 'mechanics'"—"their pride, gluttony, drunkenness, defiance of the sumptuary laws, impatience in adversity, and felony against the king had helped to unleash the tempest of the wars."[63] In short, the "people"—the many-headed beast—became a common explanation for the conflict's excesses, and even for the wars themselves, an explanation that not only doubled as an exculpating process for those truly responsible, but also provided a basis for a rapprochement between previously warring elites. It is relevant to note that for Hobbes, too, the many-headed beast represented the danger of civil war.[64]

A fixation on the dangerous and wayward nature of the lower orders did not stem solely from the experience of the Wars of Religion, however; it was an outgrowth of certain intellectual orientations as well. Stuart Clark has reminded us of the ubiquity of binaries—opposites, inversions, contrarieties, and the like—in

---

[58] Guillaume du Vair, *De la constance et consolation és calamitez publiques*, in *Les oeuvres politiques, morales et meslées du sieur Du Vair, premier président au Parlement de Provence* (Cologny, 1614), 1005–6, 1009.

[59] Nancy Roelker, *One King, One Faith: The Parlement of Paris and the Religious Reformation in the Sixteenth Century* (Berkeley and Los Angeles, 1996), 340.

[60] Richard Tuck, *Philosophy and Government, 1572–1651* (Cambridge, 1993), 42.

[61] Myriam Yardeni, *La conscience nationale en France pendant les guerres de religion (1559–1598)* (Paris, 1971), 260; *Le manifeste de la France: Aux Parisiens, et à tous les François* (Tours, 1590).

[62] Robert Descimon, *Qui etaient les Seize? Mythes et réalités de la Ligue parisienne (1585–1594)* (Paris, 1983), 43; Merlin, *Public et littérature*, 86 n. See Descimon, *Qui etaient les Seize?*, 19–20, 27–33, for royalists blaming the people for sedition.

[63] Henry Heller, *Iron and Blood: Civil Wars in Sixteenth-Century France* (Montreal, 1991), 187.

[64] Hobbes's Behemoth was a multi-headed monster of rebellion. See Royce MacGillivray, "Thomas Hobbes's History of the English Civil War: A Study of *Behemoth*," *Journal of the History of Ideas*, 31/2 (1970), 184–5. In the context of Rouen during the religious wars, Philip Benedict states that "[t]he metaphor of the populace as a many-headed monster was used so often it would be tedious to cite all cases." Benedict, *Rouen during the Wars of Religion* (Cambridge, 1981), 41 n. 1.

sixteenth- and seventeenth-century thought.[65] To cast the people as irredeemably irrational and capricious was also to suggest opposing terms. But here there were, in fact, two possibilities. The first was the king. Opposed to the many-headed beast—indeed, the instrument of its control and domination—is the royal "One," whose authority is both demonstrated and secured in its conquest. It might be suggested that the image of the king slaying the hydra of rebellion captures so-called absolutism at precisely its genesis. During the religious wars, Innocent Gentillet, in his *Anti-Machiavel* of 1576, yearned for a monarch who "will extinguish the fires of our civil wars in the countryside and the cities: And like a French Hercules cut off the heads of this monster who still today shows itself sworn enemy to our laws."[66] For many, that monarch was Henri IV. In a poem dedicated to Henri, Mathurin Regnier recounts a vision of a horrible hydra in pursuit of a nymph, who is saved by an armed knight, Henry of Bourbon. The grateful nymph rewards Henri with a prophecy of a peaceful and fruitful reign.[67] Malherbe praised Louis XIII for slaying the "*hydre feconde* of rebellion."[68]

Standing opposed to—and above—the hydra-headed beast of the people was another figure, or rather a category of individuals characterized by a set of virtues, moral and intellectual qualities that deemed them superior in every way. Unlike the king, who was duty-bound to engage this beast and overcome it, these individuals kept their distance. They were the *esprits forts*, the strong-minded few. The concept of the *esprit fort*, while not as ubiquitous as the *honnête homme*, is a common designation of the period, especially prevalent in the writings of the so-called erudite libertines. As noted, Charron's *De la sagesse* was, it seems, primarily written for the *esprit fort*; the text itself was deeply structured in terms of the distinction between the strong-minded few and the hopelessly benighted masses. (Charles Sorel called Charron "the patriarch of the so-called *esprits forts* of his time."[69]) This, then, suggests a rather schematic view of the social order, largely configured in terms of the binary *esprit fort* and wayward masses, which is, to be

---

[65] Stuart Clark, *Thinking of Demons: The Idea of Witchcraft in Early Modern Europe* (Oxford, 1997), 43–68.

[66] Reiss, *The Meaning of Literature*, 55.

[67] Corrado Vivanti, "Henri IV, the Gallic Hercules," *Journal of the Warburg and Courtauld Institutes*, 30 (1967), 192; Kathleen Wine, *Forgotten Virgo: Humanism and Absolutism in Honoré d'Urfé's "l'Astrée"* (Geneva, 2000), 85–6.

[68] Quoted in Catherine Randall, "Possessed Personae in Early Modern France: du Bellay, d'Aubigné and Malherbe," *EMF: Studies in Early Modern France*, 3 (1997), 13. As Stephen Holmes reminds us, in Hobbes's writings, "Behemoth," the monstrous incarnation of rebellion, can only be slain by Leviathan, the embodiment of supreme state power. Stephen Holmes, *Passions and Constraint: On the Theory of Liberal Democracy* (Chicago, 1995), 70–3. The image of the king slaying a beast was prominent in royal iconography, especially in the latter part of the sixteenth century and throughout the seventeenth. However, as David El Kenz points out, the beast only occasionally represents general disorder or anarchy; more often it embodies the threat of the Huguenots, the Catholic League, or foreign enemies. David El Kenz, "Le roi de France et le monstre dans les gravures: Genèse et déclin politique d'une image au XVIe et XVIIe siècles," *Matériaux pour l'histoire de nostre temps*, 18/1 (1992), 3–7. I am grateful to Peter Sahlins for this reference.

[69] Sorel, *Bibliothèque française*, 155ff.

sure, a somewhat tendentious understanding of society, contrasting markedly with the constitutional vision of the social order as articulated by Bodin or Loyseau. But the sort of savants and writers we are examining were not inclined to pen this genre of learned text; rather, their interests were more polemical and partisan, more in keeping with their desire to promote an ethos that combined moral and intellectual elitism with an appreciation of prudence, self-censorship, and circumspection in the realm of public discourse.[70]

* * *

Charron stands as both an illustration and a model of a pattern of exposition that characterized several generations of men of letters in the period following the Wars of Religion. Indeed, the insight that caution, discretion, and reticence were cardinal virtues seems to have been learned in the course of the wars themselves. As noted, this style of self-presentation and discourse had a long pedigree, especially in Italian texts of the sixteenth century, which vaunted dissimulation and "holding one's tongue" as necessary skills for the successful courtier. But in France, I argue, this inheritance was endowed with particular urgency primarily because of the religious wars. In the fourth book of the *Republic*, Jean Bodin expressed approval of the Peace of Augsburg (1555) for stipulating "That no man should upon pain of death dispute of the religions," and counseled for France a similar prohibition against those who would open up matters of faith to public discussion. "They are not only mad with reason," he writes, "but weaken also the foundations of all sorts of religion."[71] For Bodin, "the eloquent tongue of a mutinous orator is like a dangerous knife in the hand of a madman."[72]

Montaigne echoes Bodin's concern for the uncontrollable effects of oratory, unmonitored discourse, and the rage of publication, especially in a volatile context where "opinion" reigns unchecked. Throughout the *Essays* he bemoans the volubility and indiscretion of his contemporaries, especially with regard to sensitive matters. As Timothy Reiss has pointed out, this critique is linked to his larger concern for the potential excesses and abuses inherent in speech, as opposed to the law, as the governing mechanism of the people. The danger of speech is that it could "manipulate and agitate a crowd and a disorderly populace." For Montaigne,

---

[70] On the figure of the *esprit fort*, see Charron, *De la sagesse*, Preface. See also Silhon, *Le ministre d'Estat* (1641 ed.), 154. All of "Discourse IV & V" of this work is largely derived from the humor theories of the Spanish physician Huarte. See the section on Silhon in the following chapter for more on this subject.

[71] Jean Bodin, *The Six Bookes of a Commonweale*, ed. Kenneth Douglas McRae (Cambridge, MA, 1962), IV, 7, 535–6. This aspect of Bodin's thought is also discussed by Stephen Holmes in his *Passions and Constraint*, chap. 4, which I have found very helpful.

[72] *Les six livres de la république* (Paris, 1583), IV, 661–2. See also Ellen M. McClure, *Sunspots and the Sun King: Sovereignty and Mediation in Seventeenth-Century France* (Urbana, IL, 2006), 24, 25. In Book IV of the *Heptaplomeres*, Coronaeus asks: "Is it proper for a good man to discuss religion?" All seven speakers, in fact, agree that discussions of religion can be dangerous. When public debate is forbidden, many other worthwhile activities are made possible for the first time.

writes Reiss, speech "appealed precisely to the constant oscillation of the private being and not to the loyalty and obedience of the public one. Either it sparked anarchy... or it was of use only where anarchy already reigned, for instance in the Rome of the civil wars."[73] Despite the prolixity Montaigne displayed in his *Essays*, he was quite circumspect when it came to the problematic nature of some writings, something borne out in his decision not to publish his late friend Etienne de La Boétie's "On Servitude," a text that expressed potentially subversive views, precisely because he feared that it would be read by "men without understanding."[74] Montaigne's contemporary Justus Lipsius, also writing in the shadow of the religious wars, insisted that his books appear only in Latin, and opposed those who wrote in the vernacular for profaning the mysteries of philosophy.[75] In his *Histoire universelle*, published shortly after the wars, Agrippa d'Aubigné, like others, blamed the conflict on the plague of publications: "All of France was filled with pamphlets and treatises" dealing with matters of the greatest importance and sensitivity.[76] François de la Noue was not alone in citing Thucydides' account of civil strife in Athens, which, according to the ancient historian, was fueled by a kind of rhetorical escalation: "As soon as an insolent remark was made somewhere, everyone else found the nerve to say something worse, either in order to do something new or to show that they were more assiduous than the others, or more insolent and eager to avenge themselves.... Today I ask if in similar actions we have not equaled the Greeks."[77]

History and Forgetting

In the last phase of the Wars of Religion and their aftermath, this concern to temper the passions that fueled them found its way into legal and official discourses, crystallized in royal edicts that ordered memories of the conflict cast into oblivion. Ultimately it was codified in the Edict of Nantes (1598), which essentially made it illegal to write about the events of the Wars of Religion, or at least those that occurred after 1585, except in official documents. The second article of the edict makes clear the connection between *oubliance* and peace, and asserts as well

---

[73] Reiss, *The Meaning of Literature*, 58.
[74] Patrick Moser, "Montaigne's Literary Patrons: The Case of La Boétie," *Sixteenth-Century Journal*, 31/2 (2000), 381–97; Keohane, *Philosophy and the State*, 93.
[75] Mark Morford, *Stoics and Neo-Stoics: Rubens and the Circle of Lipsius* (Princeton, 1991), 112.
[76] Giovanni Dotoli, "Politique et littérature en France au XVIe et au XVIIe siècle," in Dotoli, ed., *Politique et littérature en France aux XVIe et XVIIe siècles: Actes du Colloque international, Monopoli, 28 septembre–1 octobre 1995* (Paris, 1977), 27.
[77] François de la Noue, *Discours politiques et militaires du Seigneur de la Noue* (Basel, 1587), 55–6, quoted in Reiss, *The Meaning of Literature*, 54. See Bardin, *Le lycée du Sr. Bardin, ou, En plusieurs promenades il est traité des connoissances des action et des plaisirs d'un honneste homme* (Paris, 1632), 253, on Athenians and how they succumbed to the dangerous harangues of orators.

a restriction on speech: "We forbid our subjects... to renew the memory thereof, attack, resent, injure or provoke each other with reproaches for what is past, for any cause or pretext whatsoever, to dispute, contest, quarrel, insult or offend each other by deed or word; but to contain themselves and live peaceably together."[78] But the imperative to forget was long in the making. As early as 1570, the Edict of Saint Germain, which called a truce after the third round of warfare, ordered that "the memory of... them be extinguished and dulled as of things that never happened."[79] In 1582, a well-known jurist, Antoine Loisel, published his speech before the *chambre de justice* at Agen, in which he argued that peace could come only with deliberate forgetting. Quoting the wisdom of Cicero on the title page, "Optima belli civilis defensio, oblivio est," he advocated that a sort of legal amnesia was necessary to overcome the passions that had perpetuated the religious conflict.[80] "The only thing left is the remedy of forgetting and of abolition of injuries and offenses suffered on both sides, to erase everything as soon as possible, and proceed in such a way that nothing remains in the minds of men on either side, not to talk about it, and never to think about it."[81] In other writings, Loisel identifies the connection between *oubliance*—which was the French translation of the Greek word for amnesty—and the mindless violence engendered by opinion: "there is no other remedy but to smother and extinguish it as swiftly as possible.... Whoever does anything else will only reactivate and increase the evil, and make it more bitter."[82] In the *Republic*, Bodin praised an ancient emperor who issued a "law of forgetfulness."[83] As Mark Greengrass comments, "The magistrate who could 'forgive' and 'forget' the past was the individual who mastered his own passion and was swayed uniquely by reason and prudence."[84]

In her remarkable study of the history of this process, *Forgetting Differences: Tragedy, History and the French Wars of Religion*, the literary historian Andrea

---

[78] Diane C. Margolf, "Adjudicating Memory: Law and Religious Difference in Early Seventeenth-Century France," *Sixteenth-Century Journal*, 27/2 (1996), 401; quoting text of edict from Roland Mousnier, *L'assassinat d'Henri IV, 14 mai 1610: Le problème du tyrannicide et l'affermissement de la monarchie absolue* (Paris, 1963), 319. On the general subject of the memory of the religious wars among both Protestants and Catholics, see Elizabeth Labrousse, "Les guerres de religion vues par les Huguenots du XVIIe siècle," in Philippe Joutard, ed., *Historiographie de la Réforme* (Neuchâtel, 1977), 37–44; and Philip Benedict, "Divided Memories? Historical Calendars, Commemorative Processions and the Recollections of the Wars of Religion during the Ancien Régime," *French History*, 22/4 (2008), 381–405, which is, in part, a response to Labrousse's article.
[79] Andrea Marie Frisch, *Forgetting Differences: Tragedy, Historiography and the French Wars of Religion* (Edinburgh, 2015), 38.
[80] Mark Greengrass, *Governing Passions: Peace and Reform in the French Kingdom, 1576–1585* (Oxford, 2007), 199–200.
[81] Frisch, *Forgetting Differences*, 39.
[82] Mark Greengrass, "An Edict and Its Antecedents: The Pacification of Nantes and Political Culture in Later Sixteenth-Century France," in Ruth Whalen and Carol Baxter, eds., *Toleration and Religious Identity: The Edict of Nantes and Its Implications for France, Britain and Ireland* (Dublin, 2003), 134–5, 139. On Loisel, see also Jotham Parsons, "The Political Vision of Antoine Loisel," *Sixteenth-Century Journal*, 27/2 (1996), 453–76.
[83] Bodin, *The Six Bookes*, III, 7, 382.   [84] Greengrass, *Governing Passions*, 199.

Frisch begins with the important insight that early in the wars, royal clemency, as the preferred mode for putting public misdeeds aside, had to give way to the imperative to forget, or *oubliance*. It simply became apparent that a royal pardon or clemency was a paltry mechanism for dealing with the cycle of violence, recrimination, and resentment engendered by the wars. But this change had two implications. First, it displaced the king from this process: while it was his royal edict that mandated *oubliance*, the command was hardly sufficient to make forgetting happen. And second, stemming from this, the imperative to forget, while clear enough as articulated in royal edicts, opened up a host of questions that subsequent commentators explored with varying success. *Oubliance* was hardly a simple matter. How could the wars be forgotten when the issues that provoked them remained unresolved? The very attempt to forget, Montaigne astutely observed, creates an even stronger memory (something akin to the conundrum of not thinking about something that you've been told not to think about).[85] The great Gallican historian Jacques-Auguste de Thou, who wrote volumes on the Wars of Religion, simply declared to Casaubon that *oubliance* is "not possible."[86] Frisch's book is a detailed account of the struggle to come to terms with the intractable problems with forgetting, a struggle that yielded interesting innovations especially in the writing of history and the shape of French tragedy. Ultimately, she argues, "the policy of *oubliance* necessarily implicated the broader question of the relationship between the past (or a past) and the present."[87]

Nowhere was this a greater issue than in the writing of history, which in the course of the seventeenth century was increasingly valued as a crucial element in the creation of a French monarchical tradition able to compete with ancient models.[88] As conceived by erudite critics, history implied the obligation to record a truthful account of what happened in the past without embellishment or comment. But this very formulation suggested difficulties: how to deal with state secrets, unflattering material, or unsavory episodes? The issue was given urgency with the placing on the Index of Jacques-Auguste de Thou's *History of Our Own Time* in 1609, which was judged to have treated the Wars of Religion too candidly. The solution was for the historian to exercise discretion, of course, which in practice led to the contradiction of being less than truthful. De Thou's nephew Pierre Dupuy argued, following the venerable example of Tacitus, that a candid treatment of history, revealing both the faults and the good deeds of princes, would be necessary if it were to be truly instructive. And he had the temerity to cite the Bible, in which, he asserted, God showed us Thomas as a doubter, Paul as a persecutor, and Mary Magdalene as a fallen woman: "Why can we not say, if not with

---

[85] Frisch, *Forgetting Differences*, 11.   [86] Frisch, *Forgetting Differences*, 66.
[87] Frisch, *Forgetting Differences*, 9.
[88] See especially Orest Ranum, *Artisans of Glory: Writers and Historical Thought in Seventeenth-Century France* (Chapel Hill, NC, 1980).

the same authority then with the same liberty, what the great and small have done that is both good and bad?"[89]

Dupuy's argument, however, was decidedly a losing one; and relying upon Tacitus as a precedent was hardly likely to convince his opponents, given the widespread assumption that the Roman historian was merely a stand-in for Machiavelli. Most writers of history preferred to exercise circumspection, forsaking completeness for acceptability. In the early years of the seventeenth century, it was commonly conceded that no historian could be found who did not bring a degree of partisanship to his account of the Wars of Religion.[90] Even later events proved problematic. When it came to the Day of Dupes, Scipion Dupleix, in his history of the reign of Louis XIII, which had been ordered by Richelieu, simply let this embarrassing episode fall between the cracks separating two chapters.[91] Chapelain, who gave much thought to the writing of history, acknowledged that any account worthy of the title must contain state secrets. Ever mindful of the fate of de Thou's book, he recommended that such histories be withheld from publication until the time when they could do no harm to the king or his allies.[92] In a critique of an Italian history of the sixteenth-century wars in Flanders, he endorsed a position of "general indifference" on the part of historians, especially when dealing with religious matters. Matters of faith were simply too controversial. Rather, the "judicious historian who wants to be of public service ought simply to restrict himself to those matters beyond dispute such as the safety, repose, wealth, and flourishing of the state."[93] The concern for discretion, even secrecy, evidenced by seventeenth-century historians can be contrasted with the aspirations of François Eudes de Mézeray, a royal historiographer, whose attempted innovations serve as an exception that proves the rule. Mézeray found previous histories of France lacking in appeal; among other lacunae, they failed to include "state secrets, intrigues, and war plans."[94] But when he circulated his own version among Parisian critics, they faulted it for excessive disclosure. "The historian is not obliged to say everything that is true," commented one. "It is sufficient if everything he says is true, and there are many things that he is obliged to dissimulate as long as that does not insult the truth or the historian's intelligence."[95] Here we find not only the evocation of self-censorship,

---

[89] Pierre Dupuy, *Apologie pour Monsieur le président de Thou sur son Histoire* (Geneva, 1620).

[90] Christophe Angebault, "L'historiographie officielle des guerres de religion sous Richelieu entre censure et droit d'inventaire: Jean de Serres par Scipion Dupleix," in Jacques Berchtold and Marie-Madeleine Fragonard, eds., *La mémoire des guerres de religion: La concurrence des genres historiques (XVIe–XVIIe siècles)* (Geneva, 2007), 156.

[91] Christian Jouhaud, *Le Main de Richelieu, ou, Le pouvoir cardinal* (Paris, 1991), 56–7.

[92] Ranum, *Artisans of Glory*, 188.

[93] *Lettres de Jean Chapelain, de l'Académie française*, ed. Philippe Tamizey de Larroque, 2 vols. (Paris, 1880–2), I: 15; Thuau, *Raison d'Etat*, 217. See also Christian Jouhaud, *Les pouvoirs de la littérature: Histoire d'un paradoxe* (Paris, 2000).

[94] Ranum, *Artisans of Glory*, 204.   [95] Quoted in Ranum, *Artisans of Glory*, 222.

but also the strains and contradictions that emerged as it confronted the dynamic of an evolving literary culture.[96]

Even Pierre Dupuy ultimately acknowledged the necessity for self-censorship that his uncle had failed to accept. In 1621, Pierre de L'Estoile's *Journal* covering the reigns of Henri III and Henri IV was published, anonymously, without a date, the place of publication, or the name of the printer. It has long been a mystery how this publication found its way into print. We know now from Jérôme Delatour's research that Dupuy was responsible for the publication of the diary of the Parisian Gallican, whose partisan comments, and especially his attacks on the Jesuits and the Catholic League, are apparent on virtually every page. But, as Delatour also shows, Dupuy imposed a heavy editorial hand on the edition. He softened L'Estoile's attacks on the Jesuits and took the edge off his many sarcastic asides on the clergy. For example, in a passage in which L'Estoile had claimed that the leader of the Catholic League, the Cardinal of Lorraine, had "called out for the devil with his last breath," Dupuy simply allowed that he had died "in great pain and troubled in spirit."[97] Most importantly, as a good royalist, Dupuy rescued Henri III from the imprecations against the king's piety—and sexual proclivities—that were widespread at the time and copiously documented in the journal. What readers were presented in 1621, then, was a publication that, to be sure, still conveyed a Gallican version of the last phase of the religious wars and its aftermath, but, thanks to Pierre Dupuy, was significantly less strident than the L'Estoile journal that modern scholarship has given us.[98]

Theatrical Contradictions

The writing of history was torn in two directions: between the humanist goal of a "perfect" history, on the one hand, and a more prudential approach to the past, on the other. Another area marked by a similar tension was the theater, perhaps the most innovative cultural venue in the seventeenth century. French theater was largely reborn under Richelieu, but its rebirth created problems concerning the functioning of a necessarily public forum in a culture uneasy with the unpredictable

---

[96] La Mothe le Vayer, like Chapelain, understood that the writing of history must be done with one eye on the sensitivities and interests of the powerful; his *Discours de l'histoire* (1638), dedicated to Richelieu, contains a justification for the historian not to reveal all that he might know. See Philippe-Joseph Salazar, "La Mothe le Vayer ou, l'impossible métier d'historien," *Seventeenth-Century French Studies*, 13/1 (1991), 55–70.

[97] Jerôme Delatour, "Les frères Dupuy (1582–1656)" (thèse pour le diplôme d'archiviste paléographe, Ecole nationale des Chartes, 1996), I: 210.

[98] Delatour, "Les frères Dupuy," I: 208–13. See also Tom Hamilton, *Pierre de L'Estoile and His World in the Wars of Religion* (Oxford, 2017), 200. See Chapelain defending Guido Bentivoglio's history against Richelieu's criticism in *Lettres de Chapelain*, I: 13–17.

nature of dramatic display.⁹⁹ François Hédelin, abbé d'Aubignac, whose treatise *Pratique du théâtre* (published in 1657 but written much earlier) represents a quasi-official view of theatrical decorum according to Richelieu, sets out the limits of theatrical license: religious "truths" and political "maxims" are not to be broached.¹⁰⁰ "There are many truths which ought not to be seen, and many that cannot be represented publicly."¹⁰¹ Unlike the Athenians, he writes, we cannot look with sympathy upon an attempted assassination of a tyrant, because, "living in a Monarchical State, we hold kings sacred, even when they are unjust."¹⁰² Commenting on Corneille's *Oedipus*, he goes further, suggesting that such a play risked provoking the people's untoward curiosity. "It is to encourage them, in case of political misfortune, to examine all the actions of their Princes, to wish to penetrate into the secrets of their *cabinet*, to make them judges of their opinions, and to blame them for all the ills they suffer," he writes. Rather, he continues, "we must maintain them in that pious belief that kings are always blessed with heaven's particular favor, that they are everywhere innocent, and that no one has the right to judge them guilty."¹⁰³

Corneille's theatrical innovations were indeed at the center of the matter, for he rejected the view that the public had to be shielded from the dangers of a frank presentation of life and valued verisimilitude over political expediency or moral edification.¹⁰⁴ "I satisfy at once both populace and courtiers," he proclaimed in *Excuse à Ariste*.¹⁰⁵ Whatever else was at stake in the "Quarrel of *Le Cid*"—and there was, notoriously, much on the disputants' minds—this was one issue that clearly emerged in the course of the controversy. Corneille, charged his critics, violated not only dramatic conventions but also prudence in appealing to public taste by exposing the passionate caprices and dangerous contretemps among royalty and noblemen. Despite his overall caution in drafting his assessment of the play, Chapelain did not mince words when it came to taking its author to task for irresponsibly attempting "to divert the people with pleasures that one day might produce public ills." A poet must first think of edifying his public with the proper

---

⁹⁹ On the growth of the theater in various parts of Europe in this period, see the classic article by Hans Koenigsberger, "Republics and Courts in Italian and European Culture in the Sixteenth and Seventeenth Centuries," *Past & Present*, no. 83 (May 1979), 32–56.

¹⁰⁰ On d'Aubignac's relationship to Richelieu and the genesis of *La pratique du théâtre*, see Hans-Jörg Neuschäfer, "D'Aubignacs Pratique du théâtre und der Zusammenhang von *imitatio*, *vraisemblance* und *bienséance*," in François Hédelin, abbé d'Aubignac, *"La pratique du Théâtre" und andere Schriften zur "Doctrine classique"* (Munich, 1971), VII–XXVIII.

¹⁰¹ D'Aubignac, *La pratique du Théâtre* (Amsterdam, 1715 ed.), reproduced in *"La pratique du Théâtre" und andere Schriften*, 1–325, on 66.

¹⁰² D'Aubignac, *La pratique du théâtre*, 304.   ¹⁰³ Quoted in Merlin, *Public et littérature*, 281.

¹⁰⁴ David Clarke, *Pierre Corneille: Poetics and Political Drama under Louis XIII* (Cambridge, 1992), 45–56.

¹⁰⁵ Pierre Corneille, *Excuse à Ariste*, in Georges Scudéry, *Observations sur le Cid, ensemble l'Excuse à Ariste et le Rondeau* ([Paris], 1637).

values and sentiments. "All truths are not fit for the theater," he writes. "And there are some like those horrible crimes in which judges burn the trial records along with the criminal. There are monstrous truths...which one should suppress for the good of society."[106]

More generally, theatrical representations, according to the emerging rules that governed them, were to be purged of displays of violence or other excesses that might offend or otherwise stir the passions of audiences. This was especially relevant to religious drama, which often exploited the physical and emotional travails of the saints. Here, of course, these rules, with their concern for *bienséance*, ran up against a prevalent stylistic feature of Counter-Reformation Catholicism across Europe, which positively reveled in the depiction of the physical agonies of holy figures. But in France, at least, as was more broadly the case with early seventeenth-century art, a desire to moderate and refine the excesses of the Baroque in favor of "classicism" largely prevailed. In the theater, this meant banishing the kinds of displays that were a specialty of Alexandre Hardy, the enormously successful playwright whose prodigious output—it is said that he wrote more than five hundred plays, although only thirty-four were published[107]—was often characterized by scenes of violence, both emotional and physical. Again, d'Aubignac presented the official case: "[W]ithout doubt it was he who suddenly halted the progress of the theater in giving a bad example of the disorders that we have seen prevail in our times."[108] French theater was to be sanitized, with discretion and refined speech, not passion and excess, as its hallmark.[109] To return to the case of *Le Cid*, this is precisely what Corneille's critics charged: that the climactic scene where Rodrigue appears before his lover Chimène, his sword dripping with the blood of her father, whose body lies within, was not only "implausible" but simply shocking—an offense to the moral sensibilities of the audience.[110]

These same audiences were also to be spared revisiting not only the religious wars but any and all episodes from French history as well. If contemporary historians tread lightly over the disquieting past, the stage was marked by its total absence. During the wars themselves, it was quite common for playwrights to seize upon the civil and religious strife as the stuff for their tragedies, some attempting to further one side or the other, using drama as a polemical or political tool,

---

[106] Jean Chapelain, *Les sentimens de l'Académie françoise sur la tragi-comédie du Cid* (1638), ed. Georges Collas (1912; reprint, Geneva, 1968), 21. Jean-Marc Civardi, *La querelle du Cid (1637–1638): Edition critique intégrale* (Paris, 2004), 958.

[107] Antoine Adam, *Histoire de la littérature française au XVIIe siècle*, 3rd ed., 3 vols. (Paris, 1997), I: 191.

[108] D'Aubignac, *La pratique du théâtre*, 105.

[109] Marolles testifies to the shift: "Hardy had composed more than 800 plays for the theater, whose verses were so hard [*dur*] as to render it disagreeable." Adam, *Histoire de la littérature française*, I: 198. On this, see especially Katherine Ibbet, *The Style of the State in French Theater, 1630–1660* (Farnham, 2009).

[110] See on this Hélène Merlin-Kajman, "Les guerres de religion et l'interdit de la mort sur scène," in Berchtold and Fragonard, *La mémoire des guerres de religion*, 247.

others aspiring to enact testimonies to the current miseries as exercises of public grief. Robert Garnier, perhaps the most published dramatist of this period—there were at least fifty-three reissues of his collected tragedies between 1585 and 1626—held back nothing when it came to the horrors of the wars. In his plays, comments Georges Forestier, "the more unbearable the violence of the events recounted the stronger the moral efficaciousness of tragedy seemed."[111] By the early decades of the seventeenth century, however, this characteristic had been effaced. French tragedy drew almost exclusively upon ancient history for its themes, eschewing revisiting the recent tragic history of France. It was not merely a matter of avoiding the excesses and disagreeableness of "baroque" displays of bloodshed and torment; it was also a decisive move away from the rhetoric of exemplarity, central to sixteenth-century drama and other forms of literature, which often graphically depicted episodes of civil strife and violence on the stage.[112]

What forces stood behind these sorts of transformations? The case of theatrical culture suggests that the more general move toward discretion primarily resulted neither from the efforts of the crown nor from a fear of official repression. As Sara Beam demonstrates, in fact, the farcical tradition embodied by the young law clerks of the *Basoche*, long a staple of urban culture both in Paris and in the provinces, waned in the early seventeenth century despite Louis XIII's personal enthusiasm for this genre. She further argues that, contrary to previous histories of French theater, it was not Richelieu who was responsible for forcing the farceurs "off the stage." Rather, they were motivated to change their repertoire because of shifting tastes among Parisian theatergoers, who voted with their ticket purchases in favor of a more refined, less vulgar form of dramatic presentation.[113]

The Terms of Quarreling

Another look at the "crisis" provoked by Garasse's attack on Théophile offers further insight into the governance of language and self-expression in this period. One effect of this episode was to force men of letters to choose sides in what appeared to be a well-coordinated campaign against "libertinage." Several writers who had once been close to the beleaguered poet now denounced him, including

---

[111] Quoted in Frisch, *Forgetting Differences*, 129.

[112] Frisch, *Forgetting Differences*, 156: "In sharp contrast to what we saw in the latter part of the sixteenth century, the tragedies of Corneille and his contemporaries shun the rhetoric of exemplarity that targets specific historical individuals and situations, and that made sixteenth-century tragedy decidedly 'moins agréable' than its seventeenth-century counterpart. There is, in sum, no claim that the tragedies played out in the theater have a special connection to French history; consequently, the historicity of the French public that watches them remains unacknowledged."

[113] "By the mid-1620s, professional actors had to adapt to the new fashion for neoclassical plays or risk being eclipsed by other troupes." Sara Beam, *Laughing Matters: Farce and the Making of Absolutism in France* (Ithaca, NY, 2007), 158.

Balzac, Boisrobert, and Saint-Amant.[114] And while a few attacked Garasse and his supporters for their fanaticism, evoking the fear that the Inquisition was about to be established in the French capital, it is interesting to note that the ripostes to the Jesuit's offensive did not primarily focus on the substance of his charges. Rather, they objected to the rhetorical excess, the overkill and exaggeration that even partisans of his campaign like Mersenne could agree characterized his text. The sheer scope of his invective granted his opponents an opening, allowing them to take the offensive against the style, if not the substance, of his attack, and thus to use the occasion to assert the bounds of public discourse.

The main figure in this counterattack was François Ogier, a friend and defender of Balzac, who in 1623 published anonymously his *Jugement et censure du livre de la Doctrine curieuse, de François Garasse*. Ogier was a priest, a well-regarded preacher, and a man of letters. In this tract, he takes care not to disassociate himself wholly from Garasse, joining him in condemning "those persons so furiously unnatural that, inspired by a diabolical audacity, they even want to dethrone Jesus Christ." He even has some good words to say about the Jesuits.[115] It is rather Garasse's style—the venom, violence, and general lack of restraint—that draws Ogier's fire. How can a priest be pious, he asks, if his words are so unseemly? Where is the Christian decorum that ought to be inseparable from true Christian piety? Garasse, he charges, has committed the very outrages he denounces by employing the terms and language of the "libertines," thus offending the "chaste ears" of his readers. A year later, *Jugement et censure* was followed by Balzac's entry into the fray in the form of a "Lettre à Hydaspe." The master of French eloquence echoed Ogier's reproach against the Jesuit's style, condemning him for the violence, illogic, and hideousness of his writing. Though Ogier and Balzac ultimately reconciled with Garasse, he never really recovered from the critical response to his invective. In 1626 the Sorbonne censured his *Somme théologique* (1625), a work that tried to shore up *La doctrine curieuse* by placing its claims on a firm theological footing.

Other clerics followed Garasse in continuing to rail against impiety and "libertinage," but none matched his hyperventilated style. In this respect, the notable case of Mersenne is instructive. Garasse and Mersenne are often lumped together as constituting a formidable, even coordinated assault on "free thought" in this period. It is true that following closely on the heels of Garasse's broadside, the Minim monk published his own *L'impiété des déistes, athées et libertins de ce temps*, which, like *La doctrine curieuse*, sounded the alarm about a city supposedly teeming with atheists and heretics. But though Mersenne was just as exercised

---

[114] Adam, *Théophile de Viau*, 366. On this subject of quarrels in this period, see especially Antoine Lilti, "Querelles et controverses: Les formes du désaccord intellectuel à l'époque moderne," *Mil neuf cent: Revue d'histoire intellectuelle*, 1/25 (2007), 13–28.

[115] François Ogier, *Jugement et censure du livre de la Doctrine curieuse, de François Garasse* (Paris, 1623). Ogier prefaces his text with a letter, "Aux révérends Pères de la Compagnie de Jésus."

by the threat to the faith as Garasse, his approach differed from the Jesuit's in several important respects. Mersenne took care to revise and modify his text in a second edition, all in the direction of moderating several of his claims and charges. For example, he conceded that there was much of value in Charron's book *De la sagesse*; his main worry was only that it would mislead the ignorant.[116] He asserted that "deists" could receive the Eucharist, something unthinkable for Garasse, whose denunciations were sweepingly indiscriminate. Unlike Garasse, too, Mersenne makes no mention of Montaigne, one of the Jesuit's many targets. More generally, Mersenne's tone is measured throughout, especially in comparison to Garasse's inflammatory prose, marked by qualifications and some avowal of the intellectual merits of his doctrinal enemies. Mersenne, in short, despite his deep commitment to Counter-Reformation orthodoxy and patent fear of so-called libertinage, seemed to share an understanding of the implicit limits of public discourse with those writers and savants who were hardly his fellow travelers in a religious sense. Mersenne, to be sure, was a man of great intellect and curiosity, who remained open to new developments in science, such as Galileo's discoveries, which certainly distinguished him from the likes of Garasse. What separated them, then, was not so much their beliefs as the fact that one, recognizing that the age of confessional combat was over, understood that discretion must govern public discourse, while the other, for whom the religious wars had not ended, deployed language as a weapon to injure and inflame.[117]

Failure or unwillingness to accept prevailing codes extended to others. In any culture, the lines separating permitted from illicit discourse are fluid and often imprecise—shifting barriers that often confound even insiders. Garasse's excesses were in all likelihood willful, audacious expressions of someone for whom extremism in the defense of the true faith was no sin.[118] Balzac's attack on Théophile

---

[116] Garber, "Defending Aristotle/Defending Society."

[117] For the evolution of Mersenne's position, see Garber, "On the Frontlines of the Scientific Revolution." On Garasse, see Fumaroli, *L'âge de l'éloquence*, 329–33; Jouhaud, *Les pouvoirs de la littérature*, 150–65.

[118] Théophile, however, may have been laboring under a very different understanding of the meaning of poetic expression, and indeed language, from most of his contemporary men of letters. In his "Apologie," written from the depths of his imprisonment, he mounts a defense that seems nothing more than the commonplace and predictable plea from an accused that "I didn't really mean it," but which actually asserts something quite principled. "To speak of the sweetness of revenge is not the same as assassinating one's enemy," he writes. "To write verses on sodomy does not make a man a sodomite: poet and pederast are two different things." Following Hélène Merlin-Kajman's astute analysis of this episode, we can see that Théophile's defense rests on a particular conception of the public sphere and how a poet might represent himself in this realm. To disclose the self remains a matter of the fiction of poetry—mere words. Théophile concedes that his verses could be judged; that is his "honor" as a poet. But he insists that they are "merely a bunch of fantasies which I present...less to increase my honor than to preserve it." Théophile was a writer who constantly tested the limits of poetic diction, and his literary adventurousness was based less on a very modern notion of "freedom of expression" and more on his own perception that there now existed a literary "space" in which the poet could represent himself freely and with impunity. While, as Viala has demonstrated, a literary "field" emerged in this period, the persecution of Théophile illustrates the problematic and uncertain dynamics governing this space, which at once seemed to invite self-expression but also proved

154 DIGNIFIED RETREAT

seems to acknowledge that his transgression was more a matter of failing to recognize these implicit prescriptions than it was his particular beliefs. Balzac, in fact, avers entertaining "impious ideas" himself, but then, deftly shifting attention to the accused, declares that the poet should have kept his to himself, "so as to reconcile himself with the people and not to appear their enemy for the sake of a few words."[119] Théophile failed to understand that the role of the poet was no longer that of the "legislator," as it was in the sixteenth century with the Pléiade, but rather a more worldly calling with limited aspirations and possibilities. The great master of French prose was thus able, at this critical juncture in his career, to strike blows both left and right, at Garasse and Théophile alike, and essentially on the same grounds. As he writes of Garasse, he "speaks an unknown language even though he seems to be speaking French."[120]

But Balzac, too, would be "called" on a similar count. For critics of his *Lettres* accused him of a lack of discretion, an exaggerated self-regard, and self-absorption that was simply inappropriate in public discourse, even in the supposedly private genre of the letter. His most flagrant misstep came in 1630, when he published two letters to Richelieu as an addendum to his political treatise *Le Prince*—letters that aired the cardinal's contretemps with the king's mother in the recesses of the Louvre during the Day of Dupes. "Your friend is a fool," Richelieu is known to have said, probably to Boisrobert. "Who told him that I was not on good terms with the Queen Mother? I thought him a man of sense; but he is just a coxcomb."[121]

Interestingly, one of the last interventions in the controversy over Balzac's *Lettres* provided an occasion for an important figure on the literary scene to make a case for discretion rather than conflict, for moderation over dogmatism. Again, Camus's *Conférence académique* is the pertinent text. There Critobule, the acknowledged moderator, concludes the discussion—where advocates for both Balzac and his main opponent, Dom Goulu, exchange views—on a conciliatory note, refusing to rule in favor of one or the other. Rather, he prefers to "preserve the propriety of modesty, to praise that which is good in both, without criticizing what is undesirable in either."[122] He generously sees enormously appealing qualities in both. But he asserts as well that these discussions are not like the deliberations of law courts, where a decision has to be rendered by a vote one way or another.

---

sensitive to possible excesses and transgressions. Théophile de Viau, "Apologie de Théophile" (1624), in *Théophile en prison et autres pamphlets: Texte etabli sur les editions originales*, trans. Albert Bianchi and Robert Casanova (Paris, 1967), 104; quoted in Hélène Merlin-Kajman, *L'excentricité académique: Littérature, institution, société* (Paris, 2001), 80. For an astute analysis of the trial, see Joan DeJean, "Une autobiographie en procès: L'affaire Théophile de Viau," *Poétique*, 48 (1981), 431–48.

[119] Quoted in Merlin-Kajman, *L'excentricité académique*, 103.
[120] Quoted in Merlin-Kajman, *L'excentricité académique*, 123.
[121] Quoted by Pierre Watter, "Jean Louis Guez de Balzac's *Le Prince*: A Revaluation," *Journal of the Warburg and Courtauld Institutes*, 20/3–4 (1957), 219.
[122] Camus, *Conférence académique*, 320.

Here, in the confines of their cabinet in discussions among friends, "when as many heads harbor as many different opinions, that matters little. On the contrary, it can serve to make conversation more delightful because of the great variety of thoughts."[123] Camus, through his mouthpiece Critobule, clearly meant to target Balzac, as well as others, for stirring up contention over matters unsuited for such treatment, rather than consigning them to the gentle discussions in private quarters where they belonged.

A note of moderation was sounded in order to put an end to another notable conflict. The "Quarrel of *Le Cid*," begun in 1637 with the initial salvo by Georges de Scudéry, had dragged on for several months. Its contentiousness and length and the voluble comments of its participants were beginning to worry Richelieu and others, who were not pleased that certain *ignorants* were exercising the right to make public their particular opinions. Jean Chapelain was tasked to draft the French Academy's opinion of Corneille's play. The result was *Les sentimens de l'Académie française*, a document that was rewritten several times, in part with Richelieu's marginalia and critical eye as a guide. As its first intervention in a literary affair, it was seen as defining the French Academy, founded just two years previous, an institution that troubled many by its ambiguous and potentially imperious position in the realm of language and literature, as well as its intimate relationship with the powerful cardinal. The document was intended to put an end to the quarrel over the merits and propriety of Corneille's play.

Given the verdict of posterity, which remembers the quarrel as an episode in which a beleaguered genius was bullied by an authoritarian minister served by a bunch of narrow-minded critics, it is not surprising that the *Sentimens de l'Académie* has not been looked upon very sympathetically. While a committee of academicians was convened to draft the text, and while it was reviewed, edited, and redrafted several times with the input of several members, as well as Richelieu, the primary author was Chapelain (something confirmed by Pellisson in his account of the quarrel).[124] His task was not an easy one, for it entailed more than pleasing the cardinal. Given Richelieu's distaste for the play, the conclusion was forgone. At the same time, Chapelain, like other academicians, realized that this first intervention on the part of the just-born academy would define it in the public's eyes. And, given their obvious enthusiasm for *Le Cid*, the theater public would only have been insulted by a judgment that impugned their taste by categorically condemning a play that was packing the house. Finally, unlike Scudéry, whose *Observations* dismissed Corneille's play as crude, brutal, and simply implausible, Chapelain appreciated its appeal to audiences, who could not help but be moved by the scenes of inner turmoil and conflicting affection on display.[125]

---

[123] *Conférence académique*, 313.
[124] Pellisson and d'Olivet, *Histoire de l'Académie*, I: 119.
[125] Chapelain, *Sentimens de l'Académie françoise*, ed. Collas, 5.

Indeed, the *Les sentimens de l'Académie* is a virtuoso balancing act. It conveys Richelieu's displeasure with the play while at the same time acknowledging its virtues. It both draws upon learned sources of poetic judgment, from Aristotle to Scaliger, and expresses its critique in a language accessible to unlearned readers. And it put an end to a prolonged quarrel while avoiding terms that consigned one party to the position of vanquished.

In an insightful and far-reaching essay, Orest Ranum focuses on the quarrel's "terms of the exchange," suggesting that at the heart of the controversy, beyond the character of Corneille's play or his position as a playwright, lay concerns central to the very nature of aristocratic culture and public discourse.[126] He points to Scudéry's use of legal language, his call for a "judgment" on the play, and in general the rather intemperate language he employs and the often personal nature of his attack, "in which the frame of bienséance is broken." "By couching his 'Observations' in legalese and Aristotelian criticism, Scudéry set the terms of the exchange."[127] In a subsequent intervention, Scudéry refers to the academy as a tribunal, again confirming the legal paradigm of his attack. In drafting the academy's response to the quarrel, Chapelain might have adopted Scudéry's legal vocabulary, thus affirming the new institution's authority in no uncertain terms. But he did not. Pellisson reports that Richelieu, upon reading a first draft, found it lacking in severity. Here, at least, Chapelain showed that he was not entirely the compliant courtier, for in this instance he was willing to push back against his master. The title of his text was not "Judgment," but *Sentimens*, a title that was maintained even through successive drafts. In a letter to Balzac, he notes the distinction in meaningful terms: "I do not pretend at all to give you judgments but sentiments, naively and without ambition, as usual."[128] And this attitude informs his document on *Le Cid*. Chapelain confided to Boisrobert that a frontal attack on the play would risk provoking the "public's hatred."[129] Comments Ranum: "The challenge was how to quiet things down and return theater-goers to reading rather than writing."[130]

But getting there entailed a deft deployment of a discursive tradition that sought "Concordia" rather than debate, the model of the conference or salon rather than the courtroom, appreciative commentary rather than criticism. Chapelain was guided by his knowledge of the ancients, especially Aristotle, as well as the Italian school of sixteenth-century literary criticism, the terms of which he deployed throughout *Les sentimens*. Unlike Scudéry, who was categorical and judgmental,

---

[126] Orest Ranum, "Imposing Discordant Harmony on the Quarrel over *Le Cid*," in Benoît Bolduc and Henriette Goldwyn, eds., *Concordia Discors I: Choix des communications présentées lors du 41e congrès de la North American Society for Seventeenth-Century French Literature* (Tübingen, 2011), 19–42. See also Hélène E. Bilis, *Passing Judgement: The Politics and Poetics of Sovereignty in French Tragedy from Hardy to Racine* (Toronto, 2016), 23ff.
[127] Ranum, "Imposing Discordant Harmony," 23. [128] *Lettres de Chapelain*, I: 147.
[129] See Chapelain to Boisrobert, *Lettres de Chapelain*, I: 160.
[130] Ranum, "Imposing Discordant Harmony," 24.

as well as polemical in tone, "It was not his intention to stifle debate about *Le Cid* but to uplift that debate and encourage others to read the ancients, in order to create a modern perspective on the moral and the pleasurable in literature," concludes Ranum.[131] Comments Chapelain's early twentieth-century biographer: "We detect here a tone that is serious, moderate and polite, which is hardly recognizable among *érudits* in the sixteenth century and is rarely encountered among those of the seventeenth."[132] Chapelain, who at one point wrote to Balzac, "I am no longer a man. I am a Courtier," here at least demonstrated a measure both of independence and of prudence in smoothing the waters of a quarrelsome public.

* * *

Writers and savants, who for the most part earned their keep, or at least their status, with their pens, were, however, quite ambivalent about the act of publication. Several notable writers never published at all—Conrart, Voiture, Peiresc, François Guyet—reminding us that being a man or woman of letters did not depend upon entering into print. For some, their reputations depended on personal contacts and associations, the circulation of their letters and writings in manuscript, or their work as custodians and cultivators of archives, libraries, or other repositories of knowledge. In general, the same ambivalence about disclosure and the danger of volubility served to inhibit their readiness to publish via print. As we have noted, this ambivalence was fueled by the experience of the religious wars, which many blamed on the inflammatory pens of "scribblers." Such was the diagnosis of Montaigne: "Scribbling seems to be a sort of symptom of an unruly age," he writes in "Of Vanity." "When did we write so much as since our dissensions began? When did the Romans write so much as in the time of their downfall?"[133] In the early seventeenth century, in the wake of the pamphlet wars initiated by warring noblemen, Naudé asserted that these *libelles* would, like the sorcerer's apprentice, one day prove to be their undoing by stirring up the passions of the unruly crowd.[134] Although he did not necessarily see publication as a provocation, Gassendi did express a similar impatience with "the multitude of scribblers," "the uncontrollable itch to write in the men of our day."[135]

Faced with the demands of discretion but also the lure of publication, many writers resorted to the time-honored traditional strategies to disguise or veil their texts—to make them less accessible to the prying eyes and curious minds of the ill-informed and uninitiated. A display of erudition was probably the most venerable of these. Some publications, especially those from erudite libertines, were covered in "a shower of citations" from ancient authors. La Mothe le Vayer's

---

[131] Ranum, "Imposing Discordant Harmony," 35.
[132] Chapelain, *Sentimens de l'Académie françoise*, ed. Collas, 142.
[133] "Of Vanity," in *The Complete Essays of Montaigne*, III: 9, on 721–2.
[134] Gabriel Naudé, *Le marfore, ou, Discours contre les libelles* (Paris, 1620).
[135] *The Selected Works of Pierre Gassendi*, ed. and trans. Craig B. Brush (New York, 1971), 15.

dialogues favored Latin citations and seemed to be put together in a deliberately convoluted and cryptic manner: he advised his interlocutors that they should "imitate animals that efface their tracks."[136] Lipsius, as noted, opposed the whole enterprise of translation into the vernacular, and attacked Dirck Volckertszoon Coornhert, who wrote in Dutch, for profaning those mysteries that should be divulged only to the knowing few. Publishing in Latin, of course, was perhaps the most usual means to limit a readership; and the early seventeenth century—a period when a purified, reformed vernacular French emerged—also witnessed a kind of renaissance of Latinate literature. Théophile resorted to Latin phrasing in the more licentious verses that circulated among his friends.[137] But on occasion, Latin provided insufficient cover: although he enjoyed the protection of several noblemen and magistrates, and his two Latin books the approval of the Sorbonne theologians, Vanini was still convicted of blasphemy and atheism, and was burned at the stake in 1619.

Perhaps the major difficulty with prudential self-censorship was generated by the need to circulate knowledge and foster the exchange of information in an era when the state and savants alike increasingly acknowledged this imperative. Indeed, it was at the heart of the Republic of Letters, but here again, private correspondence and other discreet modes of communication, rather than print, were the medium of choice. For someone like Théophraste Renaudot, however, publication meant entering into print. His *Gazette*, an official newspaper, and the Bureau d'adresse, a clearinghouse for the gathering and dissemination of information of all sorts, were both established with the aid and sponsorship of Richelieu. They were thus, in part, instruments of royal propaganda and policy; the *Gazette*, in particular, regularly presented its readers with the official "spin" on the events of the day, with some of its articles edited and rewritten by the cardinal-minister or even the king himself. But Renaudot also served the interests of a growing city culture of savants and amateurs alike who participated in the "conferences" held weekly at the Bureau. Unlike other literary and intellectual conventicles, which limited their memberships, these were open to the public, and the proceedings were published. Renaudot himself celebrated the public nature of his institution, but he also proclaimed that the conferences would observe strict limits on the nature of their conversations, referring all discussions on religion to the Sorbonne, "for fear of aggravating those spirits easily provoked about religious affairs," and those concerning government to the king's consul, "because the mysteries of state are of the nature of divine things; those who speak of them best speak of them the least."[138]

---

[136] *Quatre dialogues faits à l'imitation des anciens, par Orasius Tubero* (1606), in La Mothe le Vayer, *Dialogues faits à l'imitation des anciens*, ed. Andre Pessel (Paris, 1988), 136.

[137] Lewis C. Seifert, *Manning the Margins: Masculinity and Writing in Seventeenth-Century France* (Ann Arbor, MI, 2009), 203.

[138] Quoted in Gilles Feyel, "Renaudot et les lecteurs de la Gazette, les 'mystères de l'Etat' et la 'voix publique,' au cours des années 1630," *Les Temps des médias*, 1/2 (2004), 163–75, on 165.

Like the London Royal Society, founded in the wake of England's Civil Wars, Renaudot embraced the practice of self-censorship. Interestingly, however, his projects drew the criticism of the Dupuy cabinet, and Naudé in particular, precisely because they objected to the kind of publicity these vehicles gave to questions of policy.[139] Other demurred as well. In particular, in 1630 the Faculty of Medicine led a "cabal" against his *Gazette* for supposedly violating the "rule of secrecy" that ought to govern all aspects of "Authority."[140]

The question might be turned around: Rather than focusing on the obstacles and contradictions embodied in print and publication, we might think of this relatively new medium as an appealing outlet for writers and savants who were otherwise reluctant about going public. Was publication via print a way of remaining in a state of retreat while participating in the public realm?[141] Insofar as it was, we should acknowledge this dynamic as exemplifying another way *otium* was compatible with the *vita activa*. These years were marked, as Stéphane Van Damme writes, "by the emergence of a whole new economy of the book in Paris, linked significantly to the scandalous dimension of libertine culture."[142] As Sophie Gouverneur has noted, the so-called libertines hardly limited their works to the circulation of manuscripts or to publication via clandestine byways.[143] *Esprits forts* like La Mothe le Vayer, Naudé, Jacques Gaffarel, and others published extensively. True, they rendered their texts accessible only to the educated few, and their publicness was often couched in expressions of great reluctance, even temerity, regarding their entering into print. But these strategies ensured that their engagement with a public was on their own terms—indeed, that it would be a public after their own fashion.

No one embodied the contradiction created by the simultaneous need for the circulation of knowledge and the fear of its consequences more than Gabriel Naudé. His early publication *Le marfore, ou, Discours contre les libelles* (1620) was a reasoned plea for restraining the *grands*' penchant for authorizing the publication of pamphlets as weapons in their political campaigns. These publications, filled with intemperate, inflammatory criticisms of kindred noblemen, would, he predicted, ultimately prove their collective undoing. His best-known publication, *Considérations politiques sur les coups d'état* (1639), was one of the purest expressions of reason of state in the seventeenth century. Its recurring motif evokes the

---

[139] Harcourt Brown, *Scientific Organizations in Seventeenth-Century France* (1934; reprint, New York, 1967), 20.
[140] Joel Cornette, *La mélancolie du pouvoir: Omer Talon et le procès de la raison d'état* (Paris, 1998), 101; Feyel, "Renaudot et les lecteurs de la Gazette." In general, see Kathleen Wellman, *Making Science Social: The Conferences of Théophraste Renaudot, 1633–1642* (Norman, OK, 2003).
[141] On this, see Lisa Jardine, *Erasmus, Man of Letters: The Construction of Charisma in Print* (Princeton, 1993).
[142] Stéphane Van Damme, "Libertine Paris," in Anna-Louise Milne, ed., *The Cambridge Companion to the Literature of Paris* (Cambridge, 2013), 43.
[143] Sophie Gouverneur, *Prudence et subversion libertines* (Paris, 2005), 317ff.

arcana imperii, the mysteries of state, which can be comprehended only by the few *esprits forts*. Like others, however, he frankly acknowledged that his very writing on the subject was to violate them. In several of his writings, Naudé proves to be one of the earliest and most astute commentators on the printing press, but his comment focuses precisely on its double-edged, contradictory nature.[144] He celebrates it as a marvelous instrument ensuring the spread and conservation of knowledge, while bemoaning its role in serving to fuel the masses' appetite for frivolous pamphlets, scandalous libels, and a whole industry of fantastic literature. Another of his publications, *Advis pour dresser une bibliothèque* (1627), adds to the image of Naudé as embodying this cultural contradiction of his day. Here the sage advocate of secrecy and a restrained public discourse turns champion for a library that would be truly accessible to the public. It would house a "universal" collection of books and manuscripts that cut across the boundaries of Christian and pagan, orthodox and heterodox. "Libraries can be compared to nothing better than to the meadow of Seneca, where every living creature finds that which is most proper for it."[145] The collections would be open to everyone: "to devote them to the public use and never to withhold them from the humblest of those who may reap any benefit thereby."[146] He conceived of it as a Baconian instrument of learning that would serve as a corrective to credulity and the inherent weaknesses of the human mind.[147] Readers might even borrow books to take them home with them.[148] Naudé criticizes the library of a certain "Monsieur de T.," undoubtedly a reference to the de Thou cabinet, for its inaccessibility. No wonder the Dupuy brothers disapproved of Naudé's scheme, for it violated the very foundation of the privileged cabinet that served as the model for their own library.[149]

* * *

---

[144] Gabriel Naudé, *Apologie pour tous les grands personnages qui ont esté faussement soupçonnés de magie* (Paris, 1625).
[145] Gabriel Naudé, *Advice on Establishing a Library*, ed. Archer Taylor (Berkeley and Los Angeles, 1950); on this aspect of Naudé's thought, see especially Robert Damien, *Bibliothèque et état: Naissance d'une raison politique dans la France du XVIIe siècle* (Paris, 1995). For some astute comments on Naudé in this context, see Jacob Soll, *The Information Master: Jean-Baptiste Colbert's State Secret Intelligence System* (Ann Arbor, MI, 2009), 40–42.
[146] Naudé, *Advice on Establishing a Library*, 74.
[147] On the ways Naudé both followed and differed from Bacon's conception of the institutional instruments of knowledge, see Paul Nelles, "The Library as an Instrument of Discovery: Gabriel Naudé and the Uses of History," in Donald R. Kelley, ed., *History and the Disciplines: The Reclassification of Knowledge in Early Modern Europe* (Rochester, NY, 1997), 41–57. See also Jacques Revel, "Entre deux mondes: La bibliothèque de Gabriel Naudé," in Marc Baratin and Christian Jacob, eds., *Le pouvoir des bibliothèques: La mémoire des livres en Occident* (Paris, 1996), 243–50. John F. Boitano, "Naude's *Advis pour dresser une bibliothèque*: A Window into the Past," *Seventeenth-Century French Studies*, 18/1 (1996), 5–19.
[148] Naudé, *Advice on Establishing a Library*, 79.
[149] Fabienne Queyroux, "Recherches sur Gabriel Naudé (1600–1653), érudit et bibliothécaire du premier XVIIe siècle" (thèse doctorat, Ecole des Chartes, 1990), 60, 301; see also Damien, *Bibliothèque et état*, 48.

Naudé's intellectual career serves as a reminder that in practice the tendencies toward openness and discretion were hardly distinct and separate, and that the attempt to follow both imperatives created strains and contradictions. Discretion and openness should be seen as conjoined in the *honnête homme*. They are not contradictory aspects of a paradoxical culture, but rather part and parcel of a common disposition—a habitus—that marked the period.

This should prompt us to question some assumptions about the now well-established concept of an emerging public in the eighteenth century. In Habermasian terms, the public sphere represents the negation, the undoing of absolutism. The opposition between the public and the royal court is sharpest in the contrast between the secrecy of the king's cabinet and the publicity that exposes political decision-making to rational scrutiny. Publicity and reason stand opposed to secrecy and will. "Just as secrecy was supposed to serve the maintenance of sovereignty based on *voluntas*, so publicity was supposed to serve the maintenance of sovereignty based on *ratio*," writes Habermas.[150] The opposite of the public—the royal court or absolute power—is characterized by contrary elements: secrecy and unreason. Roger Chartier has taken Habermas's formulation and used it to characterize the seventeenth-century "public" in ways that only affirm this opposition. "In the age of 'baroque' politics," he writes, meaning the seventeenth century, "the traits that defined the public were the same as those that typified the theater public: heterogeneous, hierarchized, and formed into a public only by the spectacle that they were given to see and to believe.... It was...a public to be 'led by the nose'; to be 'seduced and deceived by appearances,' according to Naudé."[151]

But appreciating the paradoxical nature of seventeenth-century elite culture suggests a different public—not a public "led by the nose," but rather one *in the know*. This "knowing public" was the *monde* referred to in the previous chapter. Naudé and his savant fellow travelers wrote for an even more select readership: the *esprits forts*—the strong-minded few—those who thought themselves worthy of sharing and generating potentially inflammatory "insider" knowledge. These were limited publics constituted in the circumscribed circulation of ideas and people, the tacit appreciation of which was a sign of admission. It was a public whose fundamental stance was conformist, not critical; and in this sense it contrasts markedly with the Habermasian public of the eighteenth century. Not only was the element of secrecy not in contradiction to disclosure, it was part of the very process that created a discreet public.

Fashioners of a "worldly" culture, writers, savants, and their aristocratic patrons constituted a discreet yet dynamic and, in many ways, autonomous public. Unlike

---

[150] Jürgen Habermas, *The Structural Transformation of the Public Sphere: An Inquiry into a Category of Bourgeois Society*, trans. Thomas Berger (Cambridge, MA, 1989), 53.

[151] Roger Chartier, *The Cultural Origins of the French Revolution*, trans. Lydia G. Cochrane (Durham, NC, 1991), 33.

that of the eighteenth-century, this public did not function as the negation of the absolute monarchy and the royal court. But neither was it simply the court writ large (despite the fact that habitués of the Rambouillet salon and others were often called *gens de la cour*). This public was the vehicle for elite participation in the wider political culture in several ways: in creating an accessible literary culture, in expanding the expressive possibilities of the vernacular, in creating sociable venues, in circulating ideas and fashions, and in exploring the variety of modes of political conformism, among others. On the most fundamental level, this public, characterized by a tension between openness and discretion, ultimately served the interests of a monarchy that could not have functioned with a cultural base simply of its own making—the royal court or such royal institutions as the Académie française. As we shall see next, Richelieu's move to create an academy was an act of virtuoso cooptation, the harnessing of a literary movement that he had the astuteness to recognize, but which was in the making long before he took power. Men of letters were drawn into the orbit of this remarkable master of the "state as a work of art," but they often entered on their own terms.

4
Richelieu and Writers

When Hippolyte-Jules Pilet de La Mesnardière, a minor poet who had been Richelieu's personal physician, was inducted into the Académie française in 1655, his "Discours de réception" included a remarkable disclosure. La Mesnardière claimed that in several conversations toward the end of his life, Richelieu had mused about founding a "*grand collège*" in Paris with 100,000 *livres* a year for the study of "*les belles sciences*," which would attract "the most dazzling" writers from throughout Europe. The cardinal did not envision the college supplanting the academy. Rather, it would provide a permanent home for the still-itinerant academicians, supporting them with pensions derived from its abundant foundation. They would, in addition, be charged with its direction: they would "be the arbiters of competence, merit, and reward for all the Illustrious Professors" called to serve the college. La Mesnardière referred to his colleagues in this elevated role as "Pyrtanes," an allusion to the fifty elite men in ancient Athens who served as the executive council of the ruling "Council of Five Hundred."[1] With such a grand institution, Paris would become what so many contemporary literati and savants had hoped: the new Rome, the cultural capital of Europe, surpassing in prominence such rival intellectual centers as Padua and the Low Countries.

It is unlikely that La Mesnardière could have found a better way to flatter the "immortals" whose ranks he had just joined, nor to celebrate the memory of the academy's founder and his patron. And for a writer whose claim to importance was supported by a thin corpus of dubious value,[2] he certainly cannot be faulted for exploiting his privileged relationship with Richelieu, especially when that relationship was the means of bringing such grandiose visions for the academy to light. Unfortunately, there is no way to confirm whether Richelieu was serious about these plans. Still, this vision for the academy-college epitomizes a common view of the role of Richelieu and the academy in the cultural life of seventeenth-century Paris. It is that of the monarchy, through Richelieu, as the prime mover in

---

[1] Gédéon Tallemant des Réaux, *Historiettes*, ed. Antoine Adam, 2 vols. (Paris, 1960), I: 274. A. H. T. Levi, "What Was the Querelle du *Cid* about?" (paper presented at Trinity College, Oxford, October 15, 1996). I am grateful to Mr. Levi for letting me have a copy of his unpublished paper. See also Paul Pellisson and Pierre-Joseph Thoulier d'Olivet, *Histoire de l'Académie, par Pellisson et d'Olivet*, 3rd ed., revised and enlarged, 2 vols. (Paris, 1743), I: 90.

[2] La Mesnardière contributed a pamphlet to the controversy over *Le Cid*. See David Clarke, *Pierre Corneille: Politics and Political Drama under Louis XIII* (Cambridge, 1992), 57–61.

the organization, centralization, and standardization of culture, all for the sake of service to the state. In this view, aristocratic patronage gave way to royal, or at least ministerial, monopoly; baroque gave way to classicism; heterodoxy gave way to orthodoxy; and everything provincial gave way to Paris.

There is some truth in much of this; certainly the "Quarrel of *Le Cid*" demonstrates the subtle means by which the cardinal managed to orchestrate the culture of his day. But there is also a tendency both to exaggerate Parisian centralization and royal monopoly and to simplify what was an exceedingly complex cultural history. And even if one were to concede a decisive role in the evolution of culture to Richelieu and the crown, it does not explain how cultural trends and actors converged to serve the interests of the state. This chapter will look at two aspects of this process: first, the formation of the Académie française, and then, Richelieu's relationships with a range of writers. I am interested less in what the academy did over the long run than I am in its founding and its first years. The Académie française was not created out of thin air, but rather drew upon already well-established literary, linguistic, and even associational developments, developments that had the reform of the French language as their purpose, which also was the charge of the new academy. Likewise, though Richelieu managed to lure writers with the prospect of considerable prestige and reward—setting aside his strong-arm recruiting methods—their service cannot be explained by his subtle mix of seduction and coercion alone. Most gravitated to him because they identified with his cause and his policies, and his vision for France. They thus bore into service their own ideas and ideals, as well as often complex, even contradictory, allegiances and orientations. These savants and *gens de lettres*, and the literary and intellectual traditions they drew upon, were the real fashioners of the culture of their day. In this respect, the great Armand, however deft he was at reading, manipulating, and even co-opting it, does not entirely deserve the reputation posterity has conferred upon him.

*   *   *

Evidence supporting Richelieu's central role in the cultural sphere is, to be sure, abundant, for he was enormously successful as a sponsor, patron, reformer, and founder of cultural institutions and enterprises. As a statesman he belongs in the tradition of the Renaissance prince, the artist behind the "state as a work of art."[3] No one in his day understood better the value of propaganda, and none of his contemporaries was more deft and energetic in the political uses of the printing press. His legacy is prodigious: his initiative in launching Renaudot's *Gazette de France*, his reform and expansion of the Sorbonne, the rebirth under his tutelage

---

[3] Jacob Burckhardt, *Civilization of the Renaissance in Italy*, trans. S. G. C. Middlemore (1878; reprint, London, 1990), chap. 1.

of French theater, the founding of the Académie française, the installation in the Louvre of the Imprimerie royale, his recruitment of writers to serve as propagandists for the regime and its policies, as well as his more ad hoc and personal efforts as art patron, theologian, critic, and playwright. Indeed, one of the problems in making sense of his cultural patronage is in differentiating between those efforts that were primarily personal in nature and those pursued on behalf of the state. As a man who strove for grandeur in his three roles as prince of the Church, royal minister, and aristocrat, Richelieu appreciated the utility of art, and he had a personal passion for collecting and building as well. Hence his vast building campaigns; at one time or another he owned or had constructed four chateaux, a Parisian hotel, and the Palais-Cardinal—even an entirely new town, Richelieu, in his native Poitou. But while these were "private" residences, they were also princely venues that served as alternative cultural sites to a royal court that as yet fell short of constituting the "charismatic center" it would become in the next reign.[4]

He made a point of cultivating his ties to men of letters, especially the generation of writers who, born at the turn of the century, were coming of age just as he rose to power. These disciples of Malherbe were poised to become the architects of the vernacular literature that came to be known as classicism. They were, as we have seen, quite self-conscious of their position in society as writers—or at least as custodians and artisans of literary forms and French literary expression—something evident in their engagement in an intense associational life. Richelieu was somewhat older than most of these writers, but in some respects he thought of himself as a master of French prose as well. His rise to power has been well documented, especially his use of his ecclesiastical position as a vehicle for ascending into the ranks of royal favorites.[5] His exploitation of the literary scene was a factor as well, not necessarily in terms of gaining him advancement at court, but more as a way of attracting the support and respect of some of the most interesting and creative young authors of the day. It is hard not to conclude, in fact, that he deliberately associated himself with Malherbe's disciples as a calculated move to place himself at the head of a literary movement.

This can be seen in two crucial steps. First was his willingness to accept the dedication of Balzac's *Lettres*, a move that was engineered by Jean de Silhon, an important man of letters himself. Balzac had included three letters to Richelieu in

---

[4] C. E. J. Caldicott, "Richelieu and the Arts," in Joseph Bergin and Lawrence Brockliss, eds., *Richelieu and His Age* (Oxford, 1992), 228. Christian Jouhaud, *La Main de Richelieu, ou, Le pouvoir cardinal* (Paris, 1991). See also the essays in Roland Mousnier, ed., *Richelieu et la culture: Actes du colloque international en Sorbonne* (Paris, 1987). For the "charismatic center," see Clifford Geertz, "Centers, Kings, and Charisma: Reflections on the Symbolics of Power," in Sean Wilentz, ed., *Rites of Power: Symbolism, Ritual, and Politics since the Middle Ages* (Philadelphia, 1985), 13–38.

[5] Joseph Bergin, *The Rise of Richelieu* (New Haven, 1991).

the first edition of the *Lettres* of 1624, many fewer than to others, especially the three members of the Epernon family, his patrons. The subsequent edition, however, published three years later, began with a dedication written by Silhon to Richelieu, followed by a letter from Balzac to the cardinal-minister. The dedication combined with the letter as the leadoff piece of the volume signaled Richelieu's prominence in the publication, both as an addressee and as its patron. Whereas in the 1624 edition he was merely one among many, in the 1627 edition he occupied a place of singular honor. Coming after an intense period of controversy over the *Lettres*, Richelieu's patronage amounted to an endorsement of both Balzac's literary enterprise and the movement it was meant to affirm. But in aligning himself with this movement, he was also exploiting it for his own purposes, riding the crest of a rising tide of literary figures at a crucial early moment in his own rise to power.[6]

In that same year, 1627, he accepted the dedication of a collection of writings edited by Nicolas Faret, the *Recueil de lettres nouvelles*, writings that, like Balzac's *Lettres*, were the product of men of letters who were followers of Malherbe. (This collection was discussed in Chapter 1.) Malherbe himself contributed several letters. Others were by writers such as Racan, Faret, Boisrobert, Silhon, Balzac, and Godeau—all of whom eventually became members of the Académie française. While most were "private" in nature, that is, dwelling on personal matters having to do with love, thwarted ambition, loss, and the like, several focused on affairs of state, in particular the happy circumstances of Richelieu's ascension to power. In the dedication, Faret offered a typically fulsome homage to Richelieu's virtues and talents, referring to the "confused" state of France before his rule and his miraculous successes toward its recovery: "You have made foreigners understand that the illnesses of France were not as incurable as they believed." But Faret also addresses the cardinal in the tone of one *honnête homme* to another, confiding that "the greatest pleasure of a free soul is to meet others to whom one can tell the truth without blushing." (This was in order to explain that his praise was not mere flattery.) He notes as well the "ardent love that you have for good letters."[7] In the context of this important collection by up-and-coming *gens de lettres* of the day, Richelieu was thus both a man of state and a man of letters, at once the king's most trusted advisor, France's savior, and their man as well. Many of these same writers would ultimately sour on the cardinal, even as they readily fell in line with his policy to establish a royal monopoly over the world of letters with the founding of the French Academy. Eight years before, Richelieu had already begun to collect the writers who would form the core of his academy.

---

[6] On this, see, most recently, Mathilde Bombart, *Guez de Balzac et la querelle des* Lettres: *Ecriture, polémique, et critique dans la France du premier XVIIe siècle* (Paris, 2007), 221ff.

[7] Nicolas Faret, *Recueil de lettres nouvelles* (Paris, 1627), dedication.

The Académie française and the Cause of French Eloquence

Although it appears that Richelieu was particularly proud of his reform and reconstruction of the Sorbonne—"a superb palace of theology and a mausoleum for his ashes," one panegyrist called it[8]—his most famous institutional legacy was undoubtedly the founding of the Académie française. There are several ways to approach the founding of the academy. One way is to appreciate its distinctiveness in the history of academies in France and elsewhere. Another is to see it, as Frances Yates argued, as the successor to the sixteenth-century court academies of Charles IX and Henri III.[9] This is doubtful. The sixteenth-century academies were situated at court and thus created an arena where artists, poets, and musicians interacted with the king and his courtiers in a manner commensurate with Renaissance, and especially Neo-Platonic, ideals concerning the edifying effects of the arts. In contrast, the Académie française was not housed in the Louvre; nor did its patron, Richelieu, ever attend its sessions.[10] In fact, he made a point of defining the new company of writers as an institution that would not function in a panegyric, personal mode, for one of his first acts was to eliminate a proposed statute stipulating an annual ode to the academy's protector. The Académie française was designed, not to educate the monarch, but to add to his glory and that of the realm.[11]

The story of the academy's establishment is well known, recounted initially by its first historian, Paul Pellisson, and serves as its founding myth. "Around 1629"—Pellisson is imprecise about the date—a group of young writers began to meet at the home of Valentin Conrart, a rich *officier* who had acquired the charge of councilor-secretary to the king and his finances in 1627. Their meetings were informal; there were no great noblemen or noblewomen present. Their group had none of the qualities either of a salon or of a nobleman's cabinet. There was even an air of secrecy about them. Nevertheless, word of their meetings reached Richelieu, probably through François Le Metel de Boisrobert, who, though not a regular member of the group, had been admitted as a visitor. The occasion of Boisrobert's visit was Faret's reading of the text of *L'honnête homme* (1630), which reveals something about the interests of Conrart and his friends: they were men of letters interested not only in literature but in the broader cultural concerns of Faret's text. Informed of the group's existence by Boisrobert, who was the cardinal's advisor on literary matters, Richelieu offered them the opportunity to "become a *corps*, and to meet regularly under public authority." It is quite evident,

---

[8] Quoted in Robert J. Knecht, *Richelieu* (London, 1991), 199.
[9] Frances Yates, *The French Academies of the Sixteenth Century* (London, 1947).
[10] Pellisson and d'Olivet, *Histoire de l'Académie*, I: 92.
[11] See on this Roland Mousnier, *L'homme rouge, ou, La vie de cardinal de Richelieu (1685–1642)* (Paris, 1992); and more recently, Mark Greengrass, *Governing Passions: Peace and Reform in the French Kingdom, 1576–1586* (Oxford, 2007), 44ff.

however, that Conrart and his friends were not entirely pleased with this offer, having grown accustomed to the tranquility and privacy of their meetings; some undoubtedly harbored fears that in accepting the cardinal's patronage, they risked angering their own aristocratic patrons. After the academy's founding, they would look upon their pre-academic gatherings as a kind of "golden age." But Richelieu's will was not to be denied. As Chapelain warned his confreres, he "was not accustomed to meeting resistance or to accepting it with impunity." In March 1634 the academy began to meet regularly, with Conrart serving as permanent secretary. In February 1635 its *lettres patentes* were submitted to the cardinal for approval, although the Parlement of Paris delayed their registration for two years, fearing that the new institution represented a challenge to its authority.[12]

Despite their hesitancy, it is not likely that Conrart and his friends really wanted to disappoint the cardinal. For by the early 1630s, most had already established ties to Richelieu, or at least had publicly acknowledged their allegiance to him. Desmarets and Boisrobert were already part of his immediate entourage. Chapelain, Godeau, and Faret had written verses singing the cardinal's praises, with the latter also having dedicated the 1627 *Recueil* to him. The Habert brothers' place in Séguier's household identifies them as close to official circles. Gombauld had been in service to Marie de Medici, but upon the Queen Mother's forced exile, he quickly dedicated an ode to Richelieu, which earned him a pension of 400 pounds. Thus, in fishing in Conrart's circle for the core of his new academy, Richelieu could be reasonably certain he was in friendly waters. And yet, the view of these writers as already snugly in his pocket is not entirely accurate either. Gombauld, for example, was still willing to declare his affection for the Queen Mother: the second edition of his *Amarante*, published after the Day of Dupes, bore her name prominently as the dedicatee. Philippe Habert, though an officer in the artillery and a loyal soldier in Richelieu's campaigns, was also a member of the Company of the Holy Sacrament, a secret society that had ties to the *dévot* party; while his brother Germain demonstrated his independence of mind by siding with Corneille in the "Quarrel of *Le Cid*." Faret, though allied to Richelieu, also maintained a connection to one of his chief enemies: he dedicated his *L'honnête homme* to Gaston d'Orléans, and elsewhere declared, "Everyone hopes to see henceforth flourish with him a new era of virtuous people [*honnestes gens*]."[13] Conrart was, and remained, a Protestant. Several were tied to important patrons. Jacques de Serisay was the intendant in the house of La Rochefoucauld; the Habert brothers served in Séguier's entourage; Malleville was Bassompierre's secretary.[14]

---

[12] Pellisson and d'Olivet, *Histoire de l'Académie*, I: 48–53.

[13] Faret, *Recueil de lettres nouvelles*, II: 100.

[14] Orest Ranum, *Artisans of Glory: Writers and Historical Thought in Seventeenth-Century France* (Chapel Hill, NC, 1980), 153. Antoine Adam, *Histoire de la littérature française au XVIIe siècle*, 3rd ed., 3 vols. (Paris, 1997), I: 222ff.

Conrart and his friends were mostly young writers, with reputations largely limited to the Parisian milieu of literary conventicles. Most displayed a concern with language and the proper use of the vernacular. Conrart never disguised the fact that he was entirely ignorant of Latin, exhibiting a much keener interest in Italian, Spanish, and, of course, French. Several had personal ties to Malherbe, such as Malleville, Gombauld, and Faret, while Faret, Godeau, and Boisrobert contributed to the *Recueil de lettres nouvelles*.[15] Gomberville was a well-known "purist" in matters of language. Desmarets, Conrart, Gombauld, Malleville, Chapelain, the Habert brothers, and Godeau were all habitués of the Hôtel de Rambouillet; five of them (Conrart, Malleville, the Haberts, and Godeau) would contribute to the celebrated homage to the marquise's daughter, the "Guirlande de Julie," further proof of their intimate connection to this salon. Indeed, in numerical terms, the Hôtel de Rambouillet furnished more members to the nascent academy than Conrart's group. In addition to those just named, these include Balzac, Racan, Maynard, and Voiture. The strong links between these founding members of the Académie française and the Rambouillet salon confirm the view that the academy itself was an outgrowth of a vibrant city culture that flourished independently of the court.

And this reflects another important feature of the new academy. As Richelieu surveyed the intellectual landscape of his city in the mid-1630s, he undoubtedly perceived—as we have in our own survey—a division between two somewhat distinct groups. In one camp were the Dupuys and their associates, whose intellectual proclivities were erudite, encyclopedic, and humanistic, and who maintained various ties to Richelieu and the crown. He might have fashioned the Académie française from this milieu; after all, the "cabinet" had all the attributes of a serious intellectual enterprise that could easily be harnessed for various political ends. The Dupuy brothers often did just that, lending their scholarly expertise and archival resources to several of the monarchy's causes. But he did not. Rather, he recruited the bulk of his new academicians from the *mondain* society of the salons, from those writers committed to the vernacular, whose interests were primarily linguistic and literary. His choice not only signaled an embrace of French as the official language of eloquence, but also amounted to a rejection of both an older humanist tradition and, of course, the primacy of Latin. In this sense, the academy's founding was less a beginning than a culmination of a movement that started with Malherbe and others, a movement, as we have seen, that helped

---

[15] Hugh Gaston Hall, *Richelieu's Desmarets and the Century of Louis XIV* (Oxford, 1990), 119, does not see a connection between the contributors to the 1627 *Recueil* and the initial group that formed the Académie française. In 1630 Godeau wrote a *Discours sur les oeuvres de Mr de Malherbe*. (See Chapter 5.) He also professed great admiration for Malherbe in the preface to his *Paraphrase des Pseaumes de David* (Paris, 1648); see Claude K. Abraham, *Enfin Malherbe: The Influence of Malherbe on French Lyric Prosody, 1605–1674* (Lexington, KY, 1971), 88.

define the sociability of literary and intellectual life in the early decades of the seventeenth century.[16]

The charge to the new academy conformed to this concern with language in no uncertain terms. The preamble to its statutes explains the academy's creation as the culmination of a process of France's triumphant transformation ever since the Wars of Religion. The king, it states, has been preoccupied with "remedying the disorders created by the civil wars that long afflicted us." Now, however, he is ready, through his chief minister, Cardinal de Richelieu, to ensure that the "Sciences and Arts flourish and that Letters, like Arms, are honored, because they are the principal instruments of virtue."[17] But of all the arts and sciences, "eloquence" is declared the noblest. The new academy not only was charged with the "perfection" of the French language, it was forbidden from taking up other concerns. To its critics, then and now, this is proof only of the narrowness of its authority and its prescribed interests, especially as compared to the encyclopedic breadth of the sixteenth-century academies with their humanistic scope of intellectual and literary concerns. As Frances Yates concludes, "When Richelieu lays his hand upon the academic tradition, that tradition hardens into something unlike its former self."[18]

Indeed, contemporary critics delighted in pointing to the new institution's pitifully narrow purview. Several satires mocked the academy as a den of pettifoggery, with its members tied up in knots over silly linguistic concerns. The *Comédie des académistes* (1650), which circulated in manuscript as early as 1637, depicts various writers—most members of the academy, some not—as self-important buffoons bent on exercising a tyrannical authority over the French language. They are shown as mean-spirited hacks, given to quarreling among themselves, frequenting taverns, and concocting some truly dreadful verses. The figure of Théophile de Viau seems to haunt the characters, who clearly have self-doubts about their own literary worth, especially when compared to the near-martyred poet, whose greatness was universally acknowledged.[19] The short play ends with the pronouncement by Serisay that anyone denying the company's authority should be considered "worse than a heretic."[20] But more than anything else, the satire targets the academicians' supposed mission to purify the French language, represented as a caricature of the Malherbian project. Act III opens, for example, with Boisrobert and Silhon at loggerheads over the word *or*. Then intervenes the "sibyl," Marie de Gournay, cast, appropriately, as the stout defender of the old ways.

---

[16] Alain Viala, *La naissance de l'écrivain: Sociologie de la littérature à l'âge classique* (Paris, 1985), emphasizes this point.

[17] Pellisson and d'Olivet, *Histoire de l'Académie*, I: 39–40.

[18] Yates, *The French Academies*, 292.

[19] See Saint-Evremond and Comte d'Etelan, *La comédie des académistes*, ed. Paolo Carile (Milan, 1976), 180, 182. On this and other satires on the new academy, see Pellisson and d'Olivet, *Histoire de l'Académie*, I: 64ff.

[20] *Comédie des académistes*, 219.

In a blatantly misogynistic stroke, she is represented as quite eccentric, even slightly mad; nevertheless, she proves the voice of common sense, which makes the academicians look more ridiculous by comparison. Displaying a cavalier logic as silly as it is arbitrary, Godeau expresses his contempt for both "*or*" and "*d'autant*": "The first has the odor of the schools.... The second is too old."[21] Other academicians voice their objections to a string of words, which are instantly dispatched. The prize for pedantry goes to Chapelain, who insists that the phrase "*fermer la porte*" be deemed improper. "Vous 'poussez' vostre porte et 'fermez' vostre chambre," he reasons.[22] Other satires also ridiculed the academy's reputed zeal for purging French of its older stock of words and phrases, reflecting a concern among many men of letters.[23]

Criticism of the new academy was not limited to rival *gens de lettres* of the *mondain* camp. The savants of the Dupuy cabinet also regarded the institution with contempt, targeting precisely its authority in matters of language as most troublesome. At first Chapelain was convinced that the Adelphes approved of the enterprise, for they advised him in launching the academy's project of a French dictionary. Ultimately, however, their critical views came to the surface, probably as it became increasingly apparent what the charge of the academy actually was. In a letter to Jacques Dupuy, the cabinet's librarian, Ismaël Boulliau, who was also an important astronomer, did not mince words: "This stupid rabble with its reformed dictionary presumes to judge things that it does not understand." He homes in on exactly the area of difference between savants like him and the fashionable writers who filled most of the academy's ranks. "You will see that this Academy," he writes, "will be a seminar of barbarism, and as much as it can it will stifle the knowledge of languages and '*bonnes lettres*,' and this along with the fact that today there are few people who care to take the trouble of studying them." The talent of these men, he continues, "consists of the ability to turn a phrase, make up a *rondeau*... or some other trifle, which can be done in three weeks or a month and then be paraded around the *ruelles* of the coquettes of Paris, who grant their approval to these men according to their whims." Boulliau thus sounds themes dear to the savant camp, in particular a concern with the narrowing of intellectual life in ways that essentially cut off the legacy of humanism, conferring authority on a new breed of *gens de lettres* who, moreover, are in thrall to the

---

[21] *Comédie des académistes*, 214.   [22] *Comédie des académistes*, 215.
[23] Ménage's *Requête des dictionnaires (ou, La Parnasse alarmé)* (Paris, 1649), which circulated as early as 1639, imagines a dictionary petitioning the academicians to preserve those words they are on the brink of discarding. And *Rôle des présentations faites aux grands jours de l'Eloquence françoise* (1634), attributed to Sorel, also sets the academy up as a capricious tribunal bent on linguistic parsimony. Marguerite de Gondi, sister of the Cardinal de Retz, appears before the academicians to beg for the suppression of *concevoir* as a synonym for *penser*—out of a concern for the prurient meaning of the word. Interestingly, in this case, too, Marie de Gournay plays the role of defender of the old order, with its richer, more robust vocabulary.

"coquettes of Paris." Interestingly, he closes his letter with a request for discretion: "Everything that I have said here is under the seal of confession," he writes.[24]

Contemporaries, then, were certainly not of one mind regarding the French Academy. There were obstacles and doubters in many quarters, including among its members. Its progress was first blocked by the Parlement, which approved its statutes only after gaining assurances that its purview would be limited to language and literature. Many academicians themselves were less than faithful to their new charges. Absenteeism was so great that Chapelain suggested the company be known as "l'Académie des Fainéants" (the Academy of Slouches).[25] Voiture almost never attended its sessions, and Balzac kept his distance in his Charente retreat. Early on, Richelieu became so angry at the desultory pattern of attendance that he ordered members to attend the weekly meetings or resign. More serious than indifference, the new academy also provoked concern that it was designed as an instrument of the cardinal's "tyranny." It is no surprise that the pamphleteer Mathieu de Morgues, who regularly vented his hatred for Richelieu from the safety of Brussels, mocked the academy as nothing but a cabal of literary henchmen, "this rabble that has turned on the truth for some bread."[26] But Balzac, too, ruminated about the pernicious possibilities of the new institution. "It has been suggested to me," he wrote, "that a tyranny over minds is about to be established."[27] The academicians themselves were sensitive to this charge. When the prospect of deliberating over the merits of Le Cid was raised, several wanted to demur, acknowledging that there were those who suspected the new institution "of presuming a kind of empire over our language."[28]

Pellisson's history certainly provides evidence supporting the view that the academy was fundamentally a creation of state. In his account of the predicament of Conrart's group as they were confronted with Richelieu's "invitation," he makes it plain that they had no choice, explicitly noting, "by the laws of the realm, all sorts of assemblies which occur without the authority of the Prince are prohibited." Accordingly, he adds, "it would be quite easy, despite them, to stop them from meeting, and in this way to destroy a society that each of them wished to be

---

[24] Jerôme Delatour, "Les frères Dupuy (1582–1656)" (thèse pour le diplôme d'archiviste paléographe, Ecole nationale des Chartes, 1996), II: 332. See also Henk J. M. Nellen, *Ismaël Boulliau (1605–1694): Astronome, épistolier, nouvelliste et intermédiaire scientifique* (Amsterdam, 1994), 340.

[25] See Chapelain on Voiture's neglect of his academic duties: "Le nom académique de Mr Voiture est *il Negligente* ou, si vous voulez, *il Trascurato*. Jamais homme ne fut moins à l'Académie que luy, et la vostre des Humoristes se peut vanter de l'avoir plus veu en trois jours qu'il a esté à Rome que la nostre en quatre ans qu'il ya que nous l'y avait recue." *Lettres de Jean Chapelain, de l'Académie française*, ed. Philippe Tamizey de Larroque, 2 vols. (Paris, 1880–2), I: 357.

[26] Adam, *Histoire de la littérature française*, I: 225, 229; Pellisson and d'Olivet, *Histoire de l'Académie*, I: 63–4.

[27] Both quotes from Adam, *Histoire de la littérature française*, I: 225.

[28] In the preface to the first edition of the academy's dictionary, it is acknowledged that there existed a "false opinion among the people in the first years of the academy that it had invested in it the authority to create new words and to reject others at its whim." Pellisson and D'Olivet, *Histoire de l'Académie*, I: 69.

eternal."[29] Thus is affirmed a general view of the French Academy: established by Richelieu—whose intentions for the institution were made crystal-clear with his behind-the-scenes intervention in the notorious "Quarrel of *Le Cid*"—it was an instrument of cultural absolutism if ever there was one.

But Pellisson himself gives us another view of the academy's creation. Later in his history, he speaks of it in very different terms: "If it is true what the jurists say, that the temples, the city squares, the theaters, the stadiums, in a word all the public places, are as like powerful ties of civil society, which join and unite us together, it cannot be doubted that a certain place assigned to the Academy, and shared by all those who compose it, would embrace in some way this sweet society and contribute to its long life."[30]

Which passage from Pellisson defines the academy—the one warning of the power of the prince to control, or even crush, independent gatherings, or the one that seems to evoke an image—in fact a rather modern one—of it as having a place in a robust civil society comprised of a range of assemblies?

For Marc Fumaroli (himself a contemporary immortal), it is this second understanding that seems telling. Focusing on the formal status of the institution, he writes, "In order to attach men of letters to the state, Richelieu had no other instrument at his disposal than the medieval concept of corporation, which Jean Bodin tried to restrain but which he could not dream of replacing." Fumaroli footnotes Bodin's passage in his *Six Books of the Republic* where the sixteenth-century political philosopher vaunts "communities, corps, and colleges," that is, a civil community, situated between the natural community of the family on the one side, and the political entity of the Republic on the other.[31] Accordingly, while the academicians hardly exercised any real initiative or independence, they were nevertheless insulated from monarchical or ministerial interference by virtue of this status. As an illustration, Fumaroli points out that Boisrobert, though dismissed from Richelieu's private cabinet of writers in 1641 for his scandalous behavior, remained a member of the French Academy until his death in 1661.

Along these same lines, we have the interpretation of Hélène Merlin-Kajman. In her book *L'excentricité académique*, she argues that the seventeenth-century academy, unlike those of the previous century, was concerned merely with "elocution" rather than "eloquence," and thus detached from royal sovereignty.[32] As opposed to eloquence, mere language, or elocution, is not a matter of state. Language in this sense, in contrast to its understanding for humanists, had only to do with words—with usage, diction, style—and not things. It thus escaped monarchical control—not even the king, commented Malherbe on one occasion

---

[29] Pellisson and d'Olivet, *Histoire de l'Académie*, I: 18.
[30] Pellisson and d'Olivet, *Histoire de l'Académie*, I: 88.
[31] Marc Fumaroli, "Les intentions du Cardinal de Richelieu, fondateur de l'Académie française," in Mousnier, *Richelieu et la culture*, 73.
[32] Hélène Merlin-Kajman, *L'excentricité académique: Littérature, institution, société* (Paris, 2001).

to Henri IV, had the right to dictate correct usage. Merlin-Kajman takes a common critique of the French Academy, voiced by commentators from Charles Sorel in the seventeenth century to Frances Yates in modern times ("When Richelieu lays his hand upon the academic tradition, that tradition hardens into something unlike its former self"), and turns it on its head: what was once seen as a loss can now be appreciated as a gain for men of letters, who were granted a bailiwick all their own. In an era of so-called absolutism, it turns out that the founding of the institution seen as the embodiment of absolute power in the cultural realm actually entailed the creation of a free zone in that most fundamental of areas— language. The new academy was accorded custodianship of nothing less than the French language.

* * *

Pellisson's history cites and partially summarizes a text by Nicolas Faret entitled "Projet de l'Académie,"[33] which was to serve as a preface to the academy's statutes, though his account conveys the impression of a rather modest text. Recently, however, the original text has been discovered, and it can now be appreciated fully as a justification of the new academy by a man of letters intimately involved in its founding—someone, moreover, who had been entrusted by his confreres to fashion a formal text to serve as their company's birth certificate. Faret played a central role in the founding of the academy. Conrart and his friends had invited him to their semi-secret meetings. He served as a bridge between the group and Richelieu's entourage, for it was he whose extravagant praise of Faret to Boisrobert led to the cardinal-minister's offer to form an academy. He was the editor of the *Recueil de lettres nouvelles*, published in 1627, whose importance we have already noted, and, most famously, the author of *L'honnête homme, ou, L'art de plaire à la cour* (1630).

A theme running through Faret's literary projects is the need for reform. The precise object of reform shifts somewhat from text to text, but consistent throughout is the sense that it is a necessary prelude to French greatness. He thus acknowledges, like many of his contemporaries, those aspects of culture and politics that have suffered from neglect and corruption, whether as a result of the religious wars or from more secular trends.[34] In addition, Faret frequently evokes the principle of virtue in ways that recall an earlier humanist tradition. His political treatise *Des vertus nécessaires à un prince pour bien gouverner ses sujets* (1623), for example, addresses the question of kingship in a way that is clearly opposed to

---

[33] The "Projet" was not published until the twentieth century. See Nicolas Faret, *Projet de l'Académie, pour servir de préface à ses statuts*, ed. Jean Rousselet (Saint-Etienne, 1983).

[34] On the issue of reform, see Robin Briggs, "Richelieu and Reform: Rhetoric and Political Reality," in Bergin and Brockliss, *Richelieu and His Age*, chap. 3; and J. H. Elliott, *Richelieu and Olivares* (Cambridge, 1984).

the dominant political discourse of reason of state. He espouses love between a king and his subjects as essential to proper rule: "It is impossible for him to be loved if he himself does not love.... You who are born to rule, live with your Citizens like your children, and incite their love with good actions [*courteoisie*], without, of course, undermining your dignity, for respect born of terror is undesirable."[35] And in another passage he explicitly attacks a fundamental tenet of the statecraft associated with Machiavelli, Tacitus, and Lipsius. Recalling the dictum supposedly voiced by Louis XI, "He who cannot dissimulate, cannot rule," Faret counsels rather the opposite strategy of kingly rule. "A good Prince much prefers to be virtuous than merely to seem so," he writes.[36] The example of Louis XI was a stock motif in reason of state writings; in espousing its rejection, Faret self-consciously cast his conception of proper statecraft in an older tradition that saw even dissimulation as contrary to the exercise of true virtue.[37]

In the "Projet de l'Académie," this idealism is transferred to the new academy and its founder. For there Faret presents a vision for the Académie française as the instrument for a refurbishment of the French language far surpassing the narrow concerns of correct usage and "elocution," one that links a revival of eloquence with the cultural renewal of France. His text opens with a patriotic excursus, reaching far back into history. Faret cites Greece and Rome as past models whose exploits in arms and letters France is now poised to surpass. But he also notes that these ancient empires feared Gaul more than any other of their enemies. Faret thus sounds a motif that had found many exponents in the sixteenth and early seventeenth centuries: the myth of the Gauls as a source of French pride and independence and as a means of constructing an ancient history that could rival Rome in its longevity. The problem with the Gauls, Faret explains, is that they lacked the means to celebrate their exploits and preserve their memory for posterity.[38] Instead, it was the Greeks and Romans who left us their accounts of the past, which naturally slight and even defame the Gauls. But now things have changed. These ancient empires have vanished; even their languages, Faret adds in a passage that reveals his "modernist" bias, are "counted among dead things."[39] Today, alone among nations, France stands prepared to perform a dual revival: of both the ancient vigor of its ancestors the Gauls, and that eloquence once thought buried with Greece and Rome.[40] Faret's views are not only patriotic; they are frankly imperialistic. Letters complement arms; after so many victories and conquests,

---

[35] Nicolas Faret, *Des vertus necessaires à un prince pour bien gouverner ses sujets* (Paris, 1623), 31.
[36] Faret, *Des vertus necessaires*, 40.
[37] Adrianna E. Bakos, "'Qui nescit dissimulare, nescit regnare': Louis XI and Raison d'état during the Reign of Louis XIII," *Journal of the History of Ideas*, 52/3 (1991), 399–416.
[38] "If these Valliant men could have coupled their natural ardor to conquer with the art of rendering them illustrious through their Writings, who could doubt that their glory would have shone forth to our day with more brilliant and finer rays than those of their Enemies?" Faret, *Projet de l'Académie*, 20.
[39] *Projet de l'Académie*, 22.   [40] *Projet de l'Académie*, 22.

there remains only the task of rendering them celebrated. The language spoken by the king "should be spoken by all who fear him."[41]

To make the French language worthy of such heights is the goal of the new academy. Men of letters can accomplish this task, but they need the support of a powerful sovereign.[42] In this context, Faret offers a remark that provides one view of the changing conception of the public in the seventeenth century: the "approbation" of princes "takes the place today of what the applause of a whole people provided in other times," he writes.[43] This comment suggests not only the dramatic collapse of a public and its replacement by the singular figure of the prince, a rather remarkable, if implausible, representation of an absolutist literary field, but also the existence, or imagined existence, of a public in some bygone era. In any case, he calls for attention to be paid to the "language spoken by [the] king, that bears his commandments and should make known his glory." For, laments Faret, today it is "treated respectfully by only a few people, endlessly violated by ignoramuses, and shamefully disfigured, without anyone, until the present, offering to rescue it from their hands."[44] This, of course, is the mission taken up by Richelieu.[45] Moreover, though he predicts that the language of the king will soon be spoken throughout Europe, it is the cardinal-minister himself whose effortless eloquence serves as a model to which all of France, indeed all of Europe, should aspire.

Faret observes how well French has survived over the centuries, though, unlike the "dead" languages or the sciences, which have been taught in schools and graced with "masters" who have ensured their progress, it suffered from neglect like naturally fertile fields left uncultivated. He calls for a French rhetoric, with an emphasis on "elocution," which, more than the invention of ideas or the ordering of one's thoughts, is the skill that ensures an orator's success.[46] Elocution endows the art of rhetoric with all that makes it "sublime and divine": "the stateliness of sentences, the richness of images, the magnificence of words, the harmony and cadence."[47] Not everyone, however, recognizes its importance; many are those who are ignorant of it altogether. Some think it well "to banish all ornament from their speech and try to have their gruffness and barbarism pass for virile beauty and natural grace."[48] Here, no doubt, he has in mind those aristocratic warriors whose tendency to behave as if they were still on the battlefield drove the likes of Mme de Rambouillet from the court. But others, too, remain obtuse to the true worth of elocution. There are "those who wear themselves out and consume themselves with doing nothing else but selecting and ordering words."[49] The trouble with this enterprise, especially if pursued immoderately, is that it fails to

---

[41] *Projet de l'Académie*, 24.
[42] *Projet de l'Académie*, 26.
[43] *Projet de l'Académie*. 26.
[44] *Projet de l'Académie*, 32.
[45] *Projet de l'Académie*, 28.
[46] *Projet de l'Académie*, 36.
[47] *Projet de l'Académie*, 38.
[48] *Projet de l'Académie*, 38.
[49] *Projet de l'Académie*, 38.

appreciate that vigorous speech is a marriage of words and meaning.[50] Words must be infused with the matter of the things they express. "Those who love words excessively become their slaves.... [T]hey burden [their speech] with an infinite multitude of circumlocutions... which only corrupts and smothers."[51] Faret clearly aims this critique at the "Ronsardists," who, despite the success of Malherbe and his disciples, still were energetic in their appeal for a language that preserved the ornate imagery and richness of expression of a bygone era. But does not this critique fit the strict purists as well, who were ridiculed by their opponents for attending to words without a concern for things?

Having delivered blows left and right—both at those who ignore language and those who pay it excessive attention—Faret proceeds to discuss what kinds of men of letters should be entrusted with the enterprise of raising the French language to new heights, which is to say, who should be included in the academy. All kinds of "minds" (*esprits*) are not suited to this task. In particular, he notes that "the most learned are often the least able to express their thoughts and to judge correctly works of Eloquence."[52] True eloquence is more rare than great knowledge; experience and diligence might produce excellent philosophers, but a good orator is born, not made. The genius of true eloquence is refined, subtle, and beyond understanding—certainly far beyond the grasp of those trained in physics, geometry, or philosophy. This is why savants, though well trained and learned, should be excluded from the academy; they lack the spark of imagination and natural discernment necessary for the custodians of the nation's eloquence. Like other *mondain* writers, Faret was alert to the fact that many traditional humanists were contemptuous of their literary pretensions, especially since this "modern" approach seemed to eschew the classics and Latinate culture. In claiming true eloquence as their domain, Faret and his confreres were indeed challenging the humanists on their own grounds.

Faret summarizes the charge of the academy in a passage also cited by Pellisson. It is essentially twofold. The first is to "enrich our Language with the ornaments that it lacks." The second is to "cleanse it of the filth that it has collected, whether from the mouth of the People, or from the crowd at the [Parlementary] Palace, and the impurities of chicanery, or from the bad usage of ignorant Courtiers, or from the abuse of those who corrupt it in writing, or from those who say what they should from the pulpit but who say it otherwise than they should."[53] Here again, Faret demarks the academic purview as distinct from, and superior to, other competing realms: those of the populace, the magistracy, the court, and the clergy. Above all, he defines the academy's founding as a patriotic, indeed imperialistic, mission, and a difficult one at that, given the long history of corruption and

---

[50] *Projet de l'Académie*, 40.
[51] *Projet de l'Académie*, 40.
[52] *Projet de l'Académie*, 48.
[53] *Projet de l'Académie*, 52.

neglect and the range of social and institutional obstacles—a veritable campaign on several fronts to purify and elevate the French language.[54]

* * *

It must be said that despite Faret's vision, at once patriotic and imperialist, the new academy did not meet with great success in its first years. The academicians were charged with undertaking three fundamental works: a dictionary, a guide to French grammar, and a treatise on rhetoric and poetry. But these were long in coming. It was not until 1694 that the dictionary appeared, while only the first part of the grammar ever saw the light of day. According to Pellisson, Richelieu let it be known that "he expected something more grand and solid from the body."[55] He did not care for the practice, which some academicians apparently enjoyed, of holding "conferences" at which various "discourses" were presented. These, notes Pellisson, seemed too much like "youthful spouting" rather than the serious task of an official academy.[56] Indeed, it was precisely the desultory nature of the early sessions—which seemed to reproduce the *otium* of a private conventicle—that prompted Richelieu to charge the academy with deliberating on the merits of *Le Cid*.

Thus, the "Quarrel of *Le Cid*," the controversy that forced the Académie française to go public, has been seen as defining its very nature and mission. But the academicians were, in fact, of several minds regarding Corneille's play. And from the start they were clearly reluctant to intervene in the quarrel, which in fact began with a critique of the play by a writer, Georges de Scudéry, who was not even a member of the academy. According to Pellisson, the "most judicious in this body gave evidence of their great repugnance for this project." Quoting an unattributed document, he notes a whole series of objections, including the concern that the academicians would risk displeasing "a great part of France...in undertaking [to rule] over a work that has pleased and won the approval of such a great number of people." Moreover, the document continues, this intervention will only mean a "delay of its principal aim," whose completion has already been long in coming.[57] This undoubtedly referred to the drafting of a French dictionary, which, alas, did not have an auspicious beginning. The academicians spent nine months on the letter "A," and work was further hampered when creditors seized the papers of the editor, Vaugelas, who had died suddenly, heavily in debt. The academy was able to take possession of his research and notes only in 1651, after a protracted legal struggle.[58]

---

[54] See Hélène Merlin-Kajman, "La langue, 'compagne de l'empire,'" in Merlin-Kajman, *La Langue est-elle fasciste? Langue, pouvoir, enseignement* (Paris, 2003), 69–93.
[55] Pellisson and d'Olivet, *Histoire de l'Académie*, I: 103.
[56] Pellisson and d'Olivet, *Histoire de l'Académie*, I: 103.
[57] Pellisson and d'Olivet, *Histoire de l'Académie*, I: 112.
[58] Pellisson and d'Olivet, *Histoire de l'Académie*, I: 141–4. On the history of the academy's various editions of a French dictionary, see Michael P. Fitzsimmons, *The Place of Words: The Académie française and Its Dictionary during an Age of Revolution* (New York, 2017).

But the academicians were also busy with other activities. In a sense, they never stopped thinking of themselves as a group of gentlemen writers devoted to the eclectic discussions—"conferences"—that had characterized the literary and intellectual sociability of their informal circles in years past. Thus, the meetings of the first couple of years of the Académie française were taken up with a series of "discourses." At least twenty academicians expostulated on a range of subjects. Boisrobert spoke on "The Defense of the Theater"; Honorat de Porchères-Laugier on "Praise for the Academy, Its Protector, and Its Members"; Racan on "Against the Sciences"; and François de Porchères-d'Arbaud on "The Love of the Sciences." Chapelain, Desmarets, Boissat, and Porchères-Laugier conducted a running debate about the spiritual and physical properties of love, while Gombauld offered a discussion "On the *Je ne sais quoi*."[59]

But one subject attracted more attention than any other: the question of eloquence in general and the potential greatness of the French language in particular. This was to continue in the vein outlined in Faret's "Projet," although it is clear that here, too, there were differences among the academy's members. Over half of the discourses adhered to this theme. Godeau spoke "Against Eloquence," but by that term he meant the meretricious language associated both with the royal court, with its excessive, "Italian" turns of speech, and with the Jesuits, with their well-known sophistry and ornate imagery that appealed to so many. Rather, Godeau, who had recently reinvented himself from a house poet of the Rambouillet salon (*le nain de Julie:* "Julie's dwarf") into a model bishop, a follower of Charles Borromeo and François de Sales, called for a sober brand of Ciceronianism appropriate to a France that had achieved the greatness of the ancients. Paul Hay du Chastelet, a writer in service to Richelieu, approached the subject somewhat differently. Unlike Godeau, who seemed to narrow the range of desirable expression, his "On French Eloquence" addressed the difficulty of establishing a linguistic standard in the face of the variety, and validity, of different styles of eloquence. This variety is evident across history, among different sorts of people, with their different humors, and even in the multiplicity of publics that confront the orator in present-day Paris. The kind and level of eloquence, therefore, must be tailored to its audience, asserts Hay du Chastelet, who concludes his discourse on a somewhat pessimistic note. Given that ignorance and frivolous expression reigned in the only public that mattered, which is to say the court, the academicians must resign themselves to the fact that true eloquence was probably beyond their charge. "It is for you, Messieurs, to find a just mean between reason, if it must be said, and the passions of our language, in order to satisfy the judgment and usage of everyone," he declaimed. He endorsed, however, the practice of "conferences"—again a reference to the sociability that

---

[59] Pellisson and d'Olivet, *Histoire de l'Académie*, I: 95.

characterized the informal Parisian literary circles—as a means of arriving at this "just mean."[60]

More in keeping with the optimistic tone of Faret's "Projet" was Guillaume Colletet's *Discours de l'eloquence et de l'imitation des anciens*. The theme of his discourse, which echoed Erasmus's *Ciceronianus*, was that imitation of the ancients, while natural and necessary, ought not to limit the French in the quest for true eloquence. We should, he acknowledges, "enrich the poverty of our language with the abundance of theirs."[61] Appropriate imitation, however, looks not only at style, the effects of genius, but at its source, in hopes of learning how to surpass it. To be sure, eloquence is based in the "knowledge of ancient books," Colletet admits; but he also asserts that "we know things that were hidden from [the ancients], that time has uncovered and seemingly saved only for us."[62] He is Baconian in his insistence on the superiority of moderns over ancients, citing the art of printing, the use of cannon in warfare, and the discovery of new stars and new continents as recent advances that disprove the ancient adage that "there is nothing new under the sun."[63] And now France's time has arrived to achieve in eloquence what Virgil and Cicero secured for Rome. Colletet's appreciation is broad: he cites Malherbe and Du Perron, but also Amyot and Ronsard, who together have "rendered their language so stately and so flourishing that there is very little to add."[64] Nevertheless, vigilance and effort are still required, especially from the academicians. Indeed, says Colletet, it is the task of the Académie française to "snatch it from the hands of the barbarians who profane its mysteries and corrupt its purity."[65] He ends his discourse with an expression of homage to Richelieu: "Is not this name alone capable of elevating our spirits and making you conceive of thoughts as noble as he is generous?... [H]e was born for the resurrection of belles-lettres and the fine arts."[66] But he couples this with a patriotic exhortation to his confreres: "Thus work seriously on this wonderful task; you owe this glory to your country [*Païs*]."[67]

Other academicians echoed this concern for language in general and modern French as a rival to ancient eloquence in particular. Amable de Bourzeys (or Bougeis) was an abbot, a relative of the king's confessor, and himself a famous preacher who delivered the funeral oration for Louis XIII.[68] A man of letters, he presented his "Discours sur le dessein de l'Académie et le différent génie des

---

[60] Marc Fumaroli, *L'âge de l'éloquence: Rhétorique et "res literaria" de la Renaissance au seuil de l'époque classique* (Geneva, 1980), 651–7. These texts can be found in Bibliothèque nationale, MS fr. 645.

[61] Guillaume Colletet, *Discours de l'éloquence et de l'imitation des anciens* (Paris, 1658), 43. Though published in 1658, this discourse was delivered in the late 1630s.

[62] Colletet, *Discours de l'éloquence*, 47. [63] Colletet, *Discours de l'éloquence*, 49.
[64] Colletet, *Discours de l'éloquence*, 56. [65] Colletet, *Discours de l'éloquence*, 50.
[66] Colletet, *Discours de l'éloquence*, 52. [67] Colletet, *Discours de l'éloquence*, 51.

[68] Adam, *Histoire de la littérature française*, I: 225. See also Jean Lesaulnier, "Antoine Arnauld et la société littéraire des années 1630," in Jean-Robert Armogathe, Jean Lesaulnier, and Denis Moreau, eds., *Antoine Arnauld: Trois études* (La Rochelle, 1994), 9–31.

langues" in February 1635. Bourzeys begins his address where Colletet left off, with a panegyric to Richelieu, "that great Cardinal who ought to be the object of your most perfect productions." Certainly, he continues, Richelieu would never allow a history of his government to be recited in a foreign language. It must be admitted, however, that at present "the French language is not worthy of his incomparable actions." Why its lamentable state? he asks. It is because it has been under the control of "particulars," he answers. It has been "hidden" among them like a "fugitive," "covered with dust in the study or library." Here Bourzeys targets savants—the pedants and professors whose narrow concern for texts and citations has prevented the French vernacular from attaining its potential eloquence and clarity. It is Richelieu's great merit to have saved French and placed it before the public, "in the heart of the temple of Eternal Peace which he has brought to France." Alas, he continues, one man cannot achieve perfect eloquence; moreover, the contrary passions, the various affections and humors and men's different tastes, are always obstacles in the path toward the majesty and beauty of language. This is why we need "well-ordered conferences," which is to say discussion and conversation in an established company, to realize a truly eloquent discourse. It is only in conversation that timeless reason can be applied to ephemeral passions and where individual caprice can be moderated by collective wisdom. Like others, in particular Hay du Chastelet, Bourzeys recognizes that the way of speaking of a people is also determined by the nature of their government. "It is certain that a republic does not speak the same language as a monarchy; usually their inclinations are contrary.... The court is content with a mediocre vigor ... while the people are satisfied with common beauty." Fundamentally, however—and beyond all other considerations with regard to governments or different milieus—it is always conversation that engenders eloquence. And it is in this sense that Bourzeys sees the Académie française: as a series of conferences or conversations that can serve as a laboratory for true French eloquence.[69]

It would be a mistake to discount these sentiments as merely rhetorical statements that academicians felt moved to mouth as so many pieties. True, we know that more than a couple remained cynical about the academy, and especially Richelieu. Certainly this was true of Balzac, arguably the most important man of letters of his day. But while others, both inside and outside the company, might have harbored doubts about its ultimate mission—whatever that was—and the political exploitation of their literary talents, most also shared in some of its goals, especially the development of French eloquence. This had been the concern evident in the majority of the "discourses" pronounced in the academy's first sessions. It was also evident in the literary movement associated with Malherbe, which began

---

[69] James Dryhurst, "Les premières activités de l'Académie française: Le *Discours sur le dessein de l'Académie et sur le différent génie des langues*, de Bourzeys," *Zeitschrift für französische Sprache und Literatur*, 81 (1971), 225–42, gives the text.

long before the founding of the Académie française. Richelieu co-opted this movement, harnessing a Parisian literary culture that had for a generation made the cultivation of the vernacular its main business. Edric Caldicott summarizes the founding of the academy in the following terms: "it was an invention of Richelieu's to link...the genteel concept of the academy, traditionally a refuge in polite society for the pleasures of a cultured *otium*, with the more overtly political notion of national prestige."[70] This is certainly correct, indeed astute, especially insofar as it appreciates the central ethos of early seventeenth-century literary culture. But we should not thereby underestimate the degree to which the writers themselves shared in the quest for "national prestige" even in the reclusive venues of their "cultured *otium*." The Académie française certainly emerged from a convergence between Richelieu's appreciation of the political uses of culture and men of letters' own literary activities, but the convergence was not as asymmetrical as is sometimes thought.

A Gallery of Writers for the Cardinal

Well before the founding of the Académie française, Richelieu had established ties with a range of writers who served him in a variety of capacities. Some were his secretaries, his constant companions, who were often roused from their beds in the middle of the night to transcribe the thoughts and dictations of their master, a notorious insomniac; whence the transcriptions that resulted in the *Mémoires* and the *Testament politique*, his two most important writings. These faceless servants were so adept at copying Richelieu's hand that historians have never been able to conclude which manuscripts are autograph. Richelieu liked the company of writers and fancied himself a man of letters. He wrote several theological treatises and at least one anonymous political pamphlet, and collaborated in the drafting of several plays. Naudé claimed that he "was pulled from the depths of his library to govern France."[71] Like French statesmen in more recent times, Richelieu went to great lengths to cultivate his image as a man of intellect and letters, and astutely monitored the currents of contemporary literary culture.[72]

Upon his entry into the king's council in 1624, Richelieu immediately called upon the services of a team of writers to engage in the pamphlet war with the

---

[70] Edric Caldicott, "Richelieu and the Arts," in Bergin and Brockliss, *Richelieu and His Age*, 229.
[71] Gabriel Naudé, *Considérations politiques sur les coups d'état* (1639), ed. Louis Marin (Paris, 1988), 158.
[72] A still useful study of Richelieu and the men of letters he recruited is Maxime Deloche, *Autour de la plume du Cardinal de Richelieu* (Paris, 1920).

Habsburgs and their supporters over the direction of French foreign policy. Chief among them were two especially skilled at invective, Mathieu de Morgues and François Langlois, sieur de Fancan, both of whom ultimately fell from favor. A former Protestant, Jérémie Ferrier, Hay du Chastelet, and others joined them in producing a stream of pamphlets, many hastily written and distributed on the Pont Neuf to provide the maximum effect in parrying the charges of the pro-Spanish press. Two of Richelieu's most exalted advisors, Pierre Bérulle and Father Joseph, were not beneath lending their efforts to this campaign: in 1625 they collaborated with Ferrier in producing *Le catholique d'Estat*, an important defense of the crown's foreign policy and a major expression of reason of state. After the Day of Dupes, in 1630, when Richelieu consolidated his power, he turned to more established writers. Jean Chapelain became the quasi-official poet of the crown and functioned something like a minister of culture for the regime. Jean de Silhon wrote in defense and praise of Richelieu and served him as a secretary. Daniel Priézac, a noted law professor at Bordeaux who was part of Séguier's entourage, penned a refutation in Latin to Jansen's *Mars gallicus*, an effective attack on Richelieu's alliance with Protestant powers against the Habsburgs. In addition, Richelieu assembled a stable of playwrights known as the "*cinq auteurs*," composed of Boisrobert, Colletet, Corneille, L'Estoile, and Rotrou, who collectively were responsible for a series of plays performed at his Parisian palace. These literary offerings not only signaled the revival of French theater; they were themselves dramatic missiles in the cardinal's propaganda campaign.[73]

Richelieu's skill at recruiting talented writers was unequaled.[74] But an aspect of his skillfulness lay in realizing that compliancy and a ready pen were not sufficient. Even those closest to him, who might be mistaken as mere mouthpieces, clearly harbored their own views; sometimes these views came between them and the cardinal. Beyond those in his inner circle, he attracted, engaged, recruited, or attempted to recruit a remarkable range of writers and savants. What follows is a sample "gallery" of these *gens de lettres*: those of his inner circle; those who served him with their scholarly skills; those whose literary efforts were panegyric in nature; those whom he tried and failed to woo to his service; and those who, while serving him, expressed views that challenged conventional opinion. In each case, my aim is to raise these figures from the purely sycophantic, servile position that "service" to the cardinal is often assumed to entail.

---

[73] Deloche, *Autour de la plume de Richelieu*. See also Etienne Thuau, *Raison d'Etat et pensée politique à l'époque de Richelieu* (Paris, 1966), 214–22; Adam, *Histoire de la littérature française*, I: 213–20.

[74] For an analysis that emphasizes the ways Richelieu acted much like any great patron, see especially Elie Haddad, "Politique nobiliaire du patronage à l'époque de Richelieu: L'exemple du comte de Belin" (paper presented at annual meeting of the Society for the Study of French History, Montreal, April 2014).

Three from the Inner Circle: Fancan, Boisrobert, and Chapelain

François Langlois, sieur de Fancan (1576–1628) entered Richelieu's entourage as early as 1621, three years before the cardinal entered the royal council: it was then that he wrote a pamphlet against Luynes and the royal favorite's pro-Spanish foreign policy. Fancan's effectiveness as a pamphleteer derived in part from his ability to place the Spanish and their apologists on the defensive, throwing their accusations against France for betraying the Catholic cause back in their faces. He dwelled, for example, on the excesses and crimes of the Spanish, especially in the New World, proving himself one of the most adept perpetrators of the Black Legend in France. But there was another side to his anti-Spanish position that, though largely covert, still informed his writings. He was not only a fierce Gallican—a position that underscored many of his contemporaries' antipathy to Spain and Rome—but also likely pro-Protestant. He certainly was opposed to the policy of forcible conversion. "Sometimes it's better to let a snotty child go than to yank at his nose," he commented.[75] If he was not precisely a sympathizer, he nevertheless readily defended the Huguenots' political interests, both at home and abroad, and sharply resisted any attempts to limit their power. In Richelieu's *Mémoires*, written after Fancan's imprisonment and death, the judgment is categorical and severe, if also vague: "The Huguenot party was so high in his estimation... that he exchanged information with foreign Protestants, for whom he served as a faithful spy."[76] Richelieu's worst suspicions might have been justified, for Fancan may have been acting somewhat covertly in his service, as a kind of inside agent for extreme Gallicanism. While in the Bastille, he occupied a room next to another prisoner, who testified that Fancan had confided to him that he, his brother Dorval-Langlois, Ferrier, and the Maréchal d'Effiat had formed a kind of cabal around Richelieu. They deliberately fed the cardinal information, presented well-chosen arguments and views, and generally coordinated efforts among themselves to ensure that their position prevailed. With such evidence, Fancan would certainly have been executed if he had not soon died while in prison.[77] In any case, like others, he saw service to Richelieu in larger terms that transcended the narrow relationship of writer to patron, regardless how grand. He was serving France and a certain view of its destiny.

* * *

Another member of Richelieu's inner circle of writers was François Le Metel de Boisrobert (1592–1662), who passed many hours in consultation with Richelieu,

---

[75] Thuau, *Raison d'Etat*, 177 n. 2.

[76] *Dictionnaire des lettres françaises: Le XVIIe siècle* (Paris, 1951) [hereafter *DLF*], 467.

[77] On this episode, see Léon Geley, *Fancan et la politique de Richelieu de 1617 à 1627* (Paris, 1884). See also Gustave Fagniez, "Fancan et Richelieu," *Revue historique*, 107/1 and 107/2 (1911), 59–78, 310–22.

seemingly on a daily basis.[78] When one accounts for the time Richelieu apparently spent in the company of Boisrobert and Fancan—the former his counselor on literary affairs, the latter his *consigliore* on European politics—it is difficult not to conclude that the cardinal was rarely alone. But unlike Fancan, Boisrobert did not seem to harbor any strong political views. He was primarily Richelieu's literary servant and his boon companion. (In Pellisson's account of the founding of the French Academy, the historian notes that his "greatest task was to relax the spirits of his Master," a service endorsed by Richelieu's personal physician. "Monseigneur," the doctor supposedly confessed, "we will do as much as we can for your health, but all of our drugs are useless unless you mix with them a bit of Boisrobert."[79]) He was the cardinal's agent in the world of letters, acting as a kind of broker, furnished with the credit of his great patron and his writer-clients both. "You are particularly necessary to the savant world and to the Republic of *belles-lettres*," Balzac wrote him. "The good services that you have offered [writers] with His Eminence have softened their bad spirits and rendered their thoughts less violent.... [T]oday there is neither a panegyric nor an ode of which you are not the first author."[80] Richelieu referred to him as the "Advocate of Distressed Muses."[81]

Though an abbot, Boisrobert was widely considered an unbeliever. His behavior was suspect: Tallemant asserts that his involvement in several homosexual affairs was well known; in 1641 he was banished from the court for a time for escorting an actress of dubious character to the theater.[82] Given this reputation, why did Richelieu keep him around for so long? Certain evidence suggests that the question should be reversed: How did Boisrobert manage to preserve the cardinal's favor in the face of such seemingly credible and widely circulated charges against him? A clue lies in a letter written by Boisrobert and published in Faret's *Recueil de lettres nouvelles* of 1627. Most of his letters in this collection are to women, with whom his relations are evidently quite complex, if not tortured. One, however, is straightforward: it is to the *salonnière* Mme des Loges, thanking her for her "*bienveillance*," which, he asserts, is the reason why he now receives "the caresses of Monsieur le Cardinal de Richelieu, accompanied by the most dependable reassurances he has ever uttered." The letter somewhat cryptically refers to a recent "disgrace." Because of her support, he exclaims, he "will never

---

[78] On Boisrobert, see *DLF,* 168–9; René Pillorget and Suzanne Pillorget, *France baroque, France classique,* 2 vols. (Paris, 1996), I: 130–1; Adam, *Histoire de la littérature française,* I: 217ff.; Tallemant des Réaux, *Historiettes,* I: 392–417; Emile Magne, *Le plaisant abbé de Boisrobert* (Paris, 1909).

[79] Pellisson and d'Olivet, *Histoire de l'Académie,* I: 15.

[80] Guez de Balzac, *Oeuvres complètes,* 2 vols. (Paris, 1665), II: 716, quoted in Ranum, *Artisans of Glory,* 153–4. The translation is mine.

[81] See Tallemant des Réaux, *Historiettes,* I: 397; and Fumaroli, "Les intentions du Cardinal de Richelieu," 77 n. 10.

[82] Tallemant des Réaux, *Historiettes,* I: 392–418. On Boisrobert's sexuality, see especially Lewis C. Seifert, *Manning the Margins: Masculinity and Writing in Seventeenth-Century France* (Ann Arbor, MI, 2009), 173–81.

have to worry about a second reversal of fortune."[83] Clearly, Boisrobert got himself in trouble with Richelieu, in all likelihood because of his scandalous behavior, which at some point became simply too flagrant to ignore. He then turned to Mme des Loges, whose reputation among the Parisian *bien-pensants* made her intervention count for something in the eyes of the cardinal. It is hardly surprising that a man like Boisrobert should have cultivated the protection of powerful figures, even if his primary allegiance and the source of his own power was his relationship to Richelieu. It is merely instructive to see how crucial it was for Boisrobert, a sycophant if ever there was one, to keep those various ties alive if he was to survive in the parlous world of Richelieu's entourage.

* * *

"I am no longer a man," Jean Chapelain wrote to Balzac, his favorite interlocutor; "I am a Courtier."[84] A year later, in a letter to Boisrobert, he recalled his first encounter with Richelieu in terms that suggest nothing less than a swooning sycophant-to-be:

> I was thinking of explaining the violent passion I had to please him and the rapture created in me by the marvels with which he has glorified our times. I did not know how it happened, however, but with his warm welcome and the charming discourse with which he anticipated mine, I remained as if under a spell and lost the memory of what I should have said in order to enjoy the excellent things he was saying to me.... [T]he thought I had was not to lose a single one of his words, and it seems to me that I would lose less if I lost my reputation.... I confess to you that his voice seemed to me sweeter than any harmonious thing I have ever heard. I have no shame in repeating it, and I will announce it everywhere.... I feel myself elevated to the highest heights since I have been inspired by his presence and hold myself capable of writing heroically since he strengthened my hand in pressing it in his.[85]

It is certainly true that Chapelain had served Richelieu unswervingly in several capacities, ever since his *Ode à Monsiegneur Cardinal de Richelieu* of 1633 had earned him a ministerial gratification, which in 1636 became an annual pension. He was a member of the cardinal's literary cabinet; at Richelieu's behest, he took the lead in drafting the *Sentiments de l'Académie*, which was to put an end to the "Quarrel of *Le Cid*"; he was Richelieu's agent among his literary peers in the machinations leading to the founding of the Académie française, and drew up the

---

[83] Faret, *Recueil de lettres nouvelles*, I: 267.   [84] *Lettres de Chapelain*, I: 58.
[85] Quoted from an unpublished letter in Christian Jouhaud, "Sur le statut d'homme de lettres au XVIIe siècle: La correspondance de Jean Chapelain (1595–1674)," *Annales: Histoire, sciences sociales*, 49/2 (1994), 325–6.

new institution's statutes as well; he occasionally produced texts that would aid the cardinal in the pursuit of his policies; and in general, he served as Richelieu's ombudsman in the new literary field. After Richelieu's death, he maintained his prominence both in the corridors of power and among his literary peers, becoming under Colbert a sort of minister of culture, the André Malraux of his day.

But Chapelain sells himself short, for his engagement with contemporary literary and intellectual life extended well beyond Richelieu's orbit. He was a fixture in the Rambouillet salon and had access to the Dupuy cabinet, somewhat unusually, then, maintaining close personal associations with a host of writers in the *mondain* and savant camps alike. His privileged relationship with Balzac, constructed through a steady stream of letters, created an axis of complicity whereby the two *gens de lettres* surveyed the literary scene, authoritatively evaluating and criticizing their fellow writers. Along with Richelieu's favor and material support, he enjoyed a pension from the Duc de Longueville and the patronage of other aristocrats, including Jean-François Paul de Gondi (the future Cardinal de Retz), in whose household he resided at least part-time. He began his career as a tutor in the household of the La Trousse family, serving subsequently as secretary and then intendant. But even after his formal service ended, he continued to play a role in this great noble family's affairs, as not so much a client as a trusted advisor, educating the sons in the ways of an *honnête homme*. And throughout his career, his erudite, sure-footed critical commentary on the writings of his contemporaries established him as the premier literary critic of his day—perhaps one of the first in history.

However, this man, so clearly in the thick of things, saw himself quite differently, as operating on the sidelines. Like Balzac he relished a position of retreat, or rather the pretense of this stance. "All my life I have been immersed in affairs as if I were not, and I have lived alone and in retreat even amidst them," he wrote to Balzac.[86] According to Christian Jouhaud, he was attentive to public affairs as well as to those of his patrons, all the while protective of his position somewhat at a remove. To one of his aristocratic patrons whose importunate demands he found ill-conceived, he wrote, referring to himself: "This is the sentiment of a man who while zealous for the well-being of your family…is by inclination and the kind of life he leads removed from the business [of the world]." "The fiction of retreat from the world," writes Jouhaud, "…is a topos which Chapelain wields deftly in

---

[86] Chapelain to Balzac in 1633: "Toute ma vie, j'ay esté dans les affaires comme n'y estant pas et ay vescu particulier et retiré au milieu du monde." *Lettres de Chapelain*, I: 29. When Hugo Grotius, who was well known in various Parisian circles, accepted the appointment of Swedish ambassador to France, Chapelain lamented that his transformation from "savant" to "*politique*" had "made a mediocre man from the extraordinary one he was." Grotius, in his view, had lost more than he gained in taking up his public charge; even his personality had been transformed, with a certain arrogance never displayed in his previous incarnation, though his considerable erudition had certainly warranted it. *Lettres de Chapelain*, I: 677.

the midst of so much worldly activity."[87] It is, he argues, a fundamental attribute of the emerging status in the early seventeenth century of a man of letters.

While insightful, this depiction, in keeping with the general approach of Jouhaud, Viala, and others, tends to privilege the forms and relationships that characterized the new literary culture. And in the case of Chapelain, this comes at the cost of slighting what he actually believed and espoused; for he was more than a virtuosic impresario, craftily negotiating the uncharted landscape of the new literary field. If he was something of a courtier, his service was neither craven nor unprincipled. He was especially exercised when it came to France's place in the European cultural hierarchy. To Balzac he confided his concern that their compatriots were not capable of the political wisdom found especially among the Italians, expressing the fear that "our country will let itself be surpassed by foreigners in the knowledge of its own affairs."[88] He bristled when he learned that many of the contributors to the tribute to a well-known French savant (Peiresc) were Italians, proclaiming, "it would be shameful if the magnanimous Italy were to glorify the name of a Frenchman with so many demonstrations of esteem, while the French themselves neglect to honor him."[89] But he also frequently expressed optimism about the prospects of a French renewal. "In thirty years at the very latest," he wrote to Balzac in 1638, "France will rid itself of its barbarism [*se debarbarezera*]."[90] On a more general level, his letters are sprinkled with emotional expressions of concern for the fate of France's armies, and his country's fortunes in the geopolitical arena of Europe. *Patrie* is a word that flowed easily from his pen. And like many men of letters of his day, he harbored a Gallican distrust of the forces of Tridentine Catholicism, especially the monks and Jesuits—those "*crabrons*" (hornets) whose insidious influence he saw threatening French liberties, and his own. To be sure, in all of these matters, he saw Richelieu as the best hope and defense.

Chapelain's Gallicanism found expression in his most ambitious literary effort, a work thirty years in the making, eagerly awaited by the new literary establishment as a masterpiece that would enshrine him as the French Virgil. This was the epic poem *La pucelle, ou, La France délivrée*, the first part of which was published in 1656. While it hardly lived up to contemporaries' expectations, it nevertheless stands as a major statement from this quintessential insider in early seventeenth-century France.[91] It told a story intended to appeal to all who identified with

---

[87] Jouhaud, "Sur le statut d'homme de lettres," 344.
[88] *Lettres de Chapelain*, I; 529; Thuau, *Raison d'Etat*, 217.
[89] *Lettres de Chapelain*, I: 464.   [90] *Lettres de Chapelain*, I: 433.
[91] Nicolas Boileau, his successor as the arbiter of French classicism, savaged him with a devastating couplet that quickly made the rounds: "*La pucelle* is a very gallant song / Then why when reading it do I yawn?" "Satire III," in *Satires et oeuvres diverses De M. Boileau Despreaux* (London, 1769), 22. Even Chapelain's twentieth-century biographer has very little good to say about his subject's lifework. Georges Collas, *Jean Chapelain, 1595–1674: Etude historique et littéraire d'après des documents inédits* (Paris, 1912), 223ff.

France, its history and destiny; which is to say that Chapelain's aspirations conformed to the highest goal of the epic genre: to create an imaginary space capacious enough to contain the nation. On the most superficial level, the story of Joan of Arc as refashioned by Chapelain serves as a moral lesson on the cost of political evils that readers could only have understood in very specific, timely, and relevant terms: the role of foreign powers in fomenting civil conflict and weak kingship.

Beyond this, his depiction of Joan of Arc approximates as much a saint as a warrior—indeed, a female saint-cum-warrior whose heroic exploits appealed especially to the salon culture, this venue of "women triumphant," which was Chapelain's primary constituency.[92] In his hands, she emerges as the handmaiden and prophet of French kingship down to the seventeenth century. Her martial strength, for example, comes from the discovery of Charles Martel's sword, which not only explains how this young maiden could be endowed with such military prowess but also connects her to the origins of the French monarchy. In Book VIII of the epic, Joan reveals to Charles VII after his coronation at Reims the future of his line: if he defeats the English and liberates his country, then "jealous Iberia will see your descendants increase their states by entire countries."[93] She then appears to Clermont, duc de Bourbon, and assures him that his family will ascend to the throne with the future triumph of Henri IV and achieve glory with the continued conquests of his successors. Louis XIII will be "monarch of the world, sovereign arbiter of earth and seas." And through the efforts of his son, a savior not just of France but of the whole continent, Europe will finally be free.[94] Joan is thus France's savior and protector. Like Christ for humanity, she enters history in order to save France. Her entry comes about through the entreaties of Charles, who appeals to heaven to rescue France from the abyss. Mary, moved by her prayers, intercedes on France's behalf. To honor the Virgin, "and her sex," God chooses the humble maid for this mission, and her advent signals that the French are chosen as well. Joan approaches Charles as God's messenger and as a soldier for France: "I will be his warrior, He will be your savior."[95] Chapelain, then, was

---

[92] Though clearly aiming his work at this *mondain* milieu, Chapelain himself was on the defensive about having a woman as the subject of his epic: he devoted much of his preface to justifying his choice, citing both biblical figures and stories of warrior women in the "Republic of Women." But his most convincing defense is in fact rather weak, and conveyed, it must be said, with very little conviction: Joan of Arc existed. Chapelain, *La pucelle, ou, La France délivrée*, ed. Emile de Molènes, 2 vols. (Paris, 1891), I: lvi.
[93] *La pucelle*, II: 113–21.   [94] *La pucelle*, II: 114.
[95] *La pucelle*, I: 34. Despite her cloak of heroism, Joan is a sacrificial figure from the start. Her death is foretold, and she accepts it with Christ-like resignation. Supernatural agents regularly intervene to move the story. An army of "demons" fight alongside the English, while the French have the support of a bevy of angels. At one point, Joan—and only she—witnesses a celestial battle between brigades of devils and godly soldiers. At another, Satan nearly succeeds in turning the French army away from its noble destiny. In Book IV, the evil Duke of Bedford, fighting hand to hand with Joan, is prompted by Satan to push her off a wall. His soldiers then rain whole sections of the wall down upon her. But she is

one of the first writers to emphasize the saintly aspect of Joan of Arc.[96] But was she a *Gallican* saint? She certainly committed herself to France's protection and destiny—more so, at least explicitly, than to Christ or the Church. Indeed, the Catholic clergy do not come off very well in Chapelain's epic. In Georges de Scudéry's *Cabinet* (about which more later in this chapter), "La pucelle d'Orléans" receives her own tableau: there she is called "la sainte pucelle."[97] Prominent Gallicans had, in fact, recently embraced the maid. Chapelain based his account on the researches of the well-known Gallican scholar Estienne Pasquier. In 1630 the important Gallican clergyman Edmond Richer wrote a defense of Joan of Arc as the supporter of Charles VII.[98] But Chapelain himself seemed to consider her a somewhat ecumenical figure—saintly, to be sure, but as much French as Catholic, capable of appealing to Huguenots and Catholics alike. In a letter of 1633 to Montausier, then deployed in the taking of Nancy, he urges his friend to visit the nearby place of her birth, a spot that "even the Huguenots, if they are truly French, could venerate without reproach."[99] If she is a Gallican saint, then, Chapelain's image of her conforms to a rather mild, hardly doctrinaire Gallicanism, as much accommodating toward French Protestants as it was hostile to the pretensions of Rome. In this sense, it was in keeping with the religious posture of many of his confreres in the literary and intellectual circles in which he traveled.

It would, of course, take almost three centuries and the aftermath of the slaughter of the Great War for her to be canonized by Rome. Then she was enshrined as France's saintly savior, and subsequently captured by French nationalists, who elevated her to a symbol of the cherished unity of Church and Nation. In the seventeenth century, in Chapelain's French *Aeneid*, her ideological valence, while certainly different, conveyed a particular sense of French identity and history.

---

saved by the intervention of a guardian angel, who swoops down and shields her from being crushed, turning the stones into powder as they break harmlessly upon her. *La pucelle*, I: 160.

[96] Françoise Michaud-Fréjaville has done an inventory of the terms Chapelain used to describe Joan; the 203 references in the first twelve books (the only ones published in the seventeenth century) fall into three categories: "warrior," "*pucelle* or girl," and "saint." By Michaud-Fréjaville's count, the allusions decisively favor the saintly ascription: 96 or 47% for saint; 71 or 35.2% for *pucelle/fille*; 35 or 17.3% for warrior. Françoise Michaud-Fréjaville, "Personne, personnage: Jeanne d'Arc en France au XVIIe siècle," *Cahiers de recherches mediévales (XIIe-XVe s.)*, 12 spécial (2005), 245. On historical investigation into the history of Joan of Arc, see George Huppert, *The Idea of Perfect History: Historical Erudition and Historical Philosophy in Renaissance France* (Urbana, IL, 1970).

[97] Georges de Scudéry, *Le cabinet de Monsieur de Scudéry* (1646), ed. Christian Biet and Dominique Moncond'huy (Paris, 1991), 141–2.

[98] Edmond Richer, *Histoire de la pucelle d'Orléans: La première histoire en date de Jeanne d'Arc, 1625-1630*, ed. Philippe-Hector Dunand, 2 vols. (Paris, 1911).

[99] *Lettres de Chapelain*, I: 47. In an exchange of letters over the merits of celebrating the Maid of Orleans, Chapelain's friend Conrart, himself a life-long Protestant, expresses his support, though in qualified terms: "As for me, Monsieur, I would neither have her pass as a saint, nor swear that her calling was miraculous. But I certainly find admirable her worth, her conduct, and her actions." Ed. de Barthélemy and René Kerviler, eds., *Un tournoi de trois pucelles en l'honneur de Jeanne d'Arc* (Paris, 1878), 17. This exchange is also discussed in Nicolas Schapira, *Un professionnel des lettres au XVIIe siècle: Valentin Conrart, une histoire sociale* (Paris, 2003), 352–64.

Her uniqueness in this respect suggests that she was meant to embody a fidelity to both crown and faith that others had forsaken, an attachment to something deeply French but lost in the power politics and, most importantly, the foreign occupation that was the Hundred Years' War. Through her, Chapelain also asserts the divine origins of the French monarchy, its favored status in the eyes of God, and its mission, ultimately borne out across the centuries, to prevail over all other nations. While not a card-carrying Gallican like the Dupuys—and eminently discreet when it came to his political views—Chapelain invested his major life's work, a national epic, with a sentiment that was congenial to the general Gallican sentiments of *bien-pensant* French men and women. And the fact that it *was* his life's work serves to round out the profile of this supremely devoted of Richelieu's servants.

Scholars in Service: The Dupuy Brothers

While at the same time presiding over their cabinet and library, the informal headquarters of the European Republic of Letters, Pierre and Jacques Dupuy also labored for years as conventional and dutiful servants of the crown. They were scholars willing to apply their expertise to the documentary front in France's multiple contests with Rome, Spain, and the Empire. The skills they brought to their service were forged by the legal humanists of the sixteenth century, whose advances in scholarship endowed them with a legacy of historical and linguistic expertise that had already proven useful in the course of the religious contests of the period. As early as 1615, the brothers were recommended by the *procureur général*, Mathieu Molé, for the daunting task of reorganizing and inventorying the documents in the Trésor des Chartes, transforming it into an arsenal for making French territorial claims. Such was the prestige of legal documents in this age of humanism that the mere existence of charters, decrees, and other legal texts could make a case that held weight before a European public.[100] When Richelieu came to power in 1624, he appointed Pierre Dupuy and Théodore Godefroy, himself a member of a dynasty of archivists, to work under the jurist Cardin Le Bret as members of a commission to discover "the usurpations and acquisitions made by foreigners of the lands, *seigneuries*, and houses that are in the areas of the King's obedience and protection," in this case in the bishoprics of Metz, Toul, and Verdun.[101] In 1630 and 1631 they produced a series of treatises and reports asserting French claims over a variety of disputed lands in Habsburg and Italian

---

[100] Delatour, "Les frères Dupuy," I: 168.
[101] Quoted by William Farr Church, *Richelieu and Reason of State* (Princeton, 1972), 362. On the Godefroy dynasty of scholars in service to the crown, see Caroline R. Sherman, "The Genealogy of Knowledge: The Godefroy Family, Erudition, and Legal-Historical Service to the State" (PhD diss., Princeton University, 2008).

territories. Their labors at his behest suggest, as William Church argues, that the cardinal sincerely believed that France's claims to contested territories were not simply a matter of might but were based on fundamental and historically verifiable legal rights. As excavators, conservers, and exegetes of these documents, Pierre and his confreres fashioned the documentary weapons in the crown's war against rivals, both internal and external.[102] In Michelet's words, "the conquering archivist marched ahead of the army."[103]

Michelet also characterized their work as "intrepid servitude" (*servilisme intrépide*),[104] an interesting oxymoron that captures the complex nature of their work on the crown's behalf. In one sense, there is no doubt that the Dupuys (especially Pierre) willingly served as all-purpose scholars, happy to lend their expertise to any task that promoted the interests of state, just as generations of humanists had often ransomed whatever independence they had by serving princes, emperors, kings, and high churchmen. For example, Pierre wrote a justification for the annulment of the marriage of Gaston, the king's brother, to Marguerite of Lorraine, in the face of Louis XIII's refusal to grant him permission for an alliance with the sister of a rival prince, Charles IV, duke of Lorraine. There he asserted that the issue was not open to debate or discussion, and that personal sentiment or loyalty had no place in the decision-making. All that counts is reason of state: it is the king's right and duty to defend the realm as he sees fit.[105] In 1636, Richelieu sent Pierre along with Godefroy to represent France at a peace conference in Cologne. Pierre argued that having documentary proof for territorial claims and the like was necessary to rebut "excuses for these usurpations"; it allowed one "to be better prepared and informed when it comes to entering into discussions and peace negotiations and agreements on a particular subject." But he added another reason that suggests a more nuanced understanding of his expert service as mitigating bellicose state power rather than propitiating it. Knowing precisely what territorial claims and rights France legitimately possessed could also be a source of caution—for determining "to what degree His Majesty is well-founded or not, and thus what difficulties might be encountered, so that we do not enter too easily into ill-conceived wars and make the same mistakes as in the past."[106] In arguments such as these, we see evidence not of servility but of wisdom—reason of state tempered by prudence.

Ultimately, however, the Dupuys would go beyond offering prudential advice. In 1638, they published two volumes of Gallican texts, *Traitez des droits et libertez de l'Eglise gallicane* and *Preuves des libertez de l'Église gallicane*, both of which appeared anonymously and without permission. With this, they brought the

---

[102] Church, *Richelieu and Reason of State*, 363 and *passim*.
[103] Jules Michelet, *Histoire de France* (Paris, 1833), II: 699.
[104] Jules Michelet, *Histoire de France*, new ed., revised and enlarged (Paris, 1876), III: 230.
[105] Delatour, "Les frères Dupuy," II: 318.
[106] Quoted in Delatour, "Les frères Dupuy," II: 312.

Gallican case before a public in ways that threatened the fragile truce that Richelieu had arranged between partisans of that cause and their ultramontane enemies. It may have been that the cardinal actually approved of this publication as a way of increasing his pressure on Rome for reasons of his own. (This event will be explored further in Chapter 6.) Historians are divided on the question. In any case, it is clear that they capitalized on their position close to the cardinal, as privileged savants whose intellectual skills had been recognized in service to the state, to unleash a publication that had dramatic consequences far and wide. Like others, then, these servants served on their own terms and according to their own lights. In this case, as in others, these lights were Gallican.

Two Panegyric Authors: Silhon and Scudéry

Many authors found ways to praise Richelieu. As we saw, both Balzac's *Lettres* and the 1627 *Recueil des lettres nouvelles* were dedicated to him, and many of the texts included in each of these collections were panegyric in nature. Chapelain confirmed Richelieu's favor with an "Ode." Antoine Godeau, a priest and a frequenter of the Rambouillet salon, dedicated his *Oeuvres chrestiennes* (1633) to him and continued to sing his praises long after his death. Many more textual panegyrics could be cited.

In his *Ministre d'Estat* (1631), Jean de Silhon offers a full-bodied treatment of Richelieu as the supreme statesman. Silhon's interests and connections were many. He was close to Balzac, writing the preface for the sixth edition of his *Lettres*. And he was known to frequent the Rambouillet salon. Like Balzac, he was a friend of Descartes. He secured Richelieu's patronage with the publication of his *Panegyrique à monseigneur le cardinal de Richelieu* (1629), which praised Richelieu's role in the pivotal Siege of La Rochelle. He continued to benefit from ministerial favor even after the cardinal-minister's death, serving as Mazarin's secretary from 1642 to 1661. While he is best known for his political writings, his main intellectual interest was combating skepticism and defending Catholicism, the first being, in his mind, necessary to accomplish the latter.

In his preface to *Le ministre d'Estat*, Silhon apologizes in advance for dwelling so much on Richelieu's qualities, and assures his readers that he does not mean to slight the king, whom he acknowledges as the fountainhead of all that is good for France.[107] But the cardinal occupies center stage in his text; he is the Neo-Stoic hero, whose reason, strength, and prudence are exemplary. Indeed, Silhon breaks off his search in philosophy or the past for singular virtues of rulers by declaring

---

[107] Jean de Silhon, *Le ministre d'Estat, avec la véritable usage de la politique moderne* (Paris, 1641 ed.), a4v.

that such efforts are now needless: "we have them so clearly and so visibly in the person of Monsieur le Cardinal de Richelieu."[108]

What is unusual about Silhon's panegyric is that he exploited up-to-date "science" to fashion it. Like many contemporary thinkers, Silhon was influenced by the Spanish physician Juan Huarte's treatise *L'examen des esprits*, which appeared in twenty-two French editions before 1675, ranking as probably the most important work of its kind in the century.[109] Huarte's approach was based on the relationship between bodily humors and temperament, and provided the basis for a typology of personalities. Chief among his concerns was establishing a hierarchy of character types in order to distinguish psychologically between an intellectual and moral elite and those intrinsically less worthy or competent. For Silhon, Huarte's schemata allowed him to write more precisely about the kinds of men who should be recruited into serving as minister, the subject of Discourse IV, the second book of *Le ministre d'Estat*. But his real purpose here is to buttress his ongoing apotheosis of Richelieu with the psychology of the day. Four different categories of men are proposed, each composed of different balances of humors. Beyond these four types, Silhon adds, is a fifth category of men, one that in all likelihood is a set with only a single member. Its characteristic temperament is the sum of all the good qualities, "most rare and pure," of the other four. Their "bodies...are not prisons of the soul but very spacious palaces, not rebellious slaves but tractable servants or obedient subjects." The sole exemplar of this type is Richelieu, whose "desire for glory is the sole passion which makes itself violently felt." Silhon displays some ambivalence in proclaiming Richelieu's virtues in such extravagant terms, or at least professes a need for maintaining a degree of reticence: "I will not speak here of the constitution of Monsieur le Cardinal.... There are truths which should not always be published." Still, his desire to praise ultimately gets the better of his sense of discretion: in his eyes, Richelieu deserves comparison with Christ himself. "The constitution of which we speak," he writes, "covers his face with majesty. It puts into his eyes a fire which is brighter than that of ordinary men, and gives him, in a word, some of the beauty which Jesus Christ did not refuse to be praised for."[110]

Richelieu occupies center stage in Silhon's book. But there was something else on his mind that offered something of a distraction from his panegyric. Silhon was a vehement Gallican, revealed for the most part in long passages dilating on

---

[108] *Le ministre d'Estat*, 17.

[109] On Huarte, and especially his influence on French thinking, see Gabriel A. Pérouse, *L'examen des esprits du Docteur Juan Huarte de San Juan: Sa diffusion et son influence en France aux XVIe et XVIIe siècles* (Paris, 1970); Fumaroli, *L'âge de l'éloquence*, 127–34; Emmanuel Bury, *Littérature et politesse: L'invention de l'honnête homme, 1580–1750* (Paris, 1996), 71; Bombart, *Guez de Balzac*, 112; Jean Jehasse, *Guez de Balzac et le génie romain, 1597–1654* (Saint-Etienne, 1977), 49; and Henry C. Clark, *La Rochefoucauld and the Language of Unmasking in Seventeenth-Century France* (Geneva, 1994), 29–31.

[110] *Le ministre d'Estat*, 157–8.

his fear of ultramontane forces. Silhon certainly gives vent to his hatred of Spain, like any "good Frenchman" of this part of the century, but as far as he was concerned, ultramontanism was the greatest threat to France. Whole sections of *Le ministre d'Estat* are devoted to criticizing the papacy, the Church, and the clergy in a manner so severe that one would be tempted to brand Silhon a Calvinist if it were not for his equally pronounced Gallican views. Silhon was aware that his opinions might be considered extreme: In the "Advertissement" he acknowledges that his judgments on the pope and Rome might seem "too free," but these, he adds, "are only the conclusions which follow from the examples cited."[111] He attacks the Church for venality, nepotism, excessive worldliness and wealth, and corruption, and blames it for various crimes and unfortunate episodes of the past. The popes especially come in for heavy criticism in terms reminiscent of the Reformers; "they have trafficked in the merit of Jesus Christ," he accuses.[112] Their ill-advised actions, in conjunction with the equally inappropriate policies of the emperors, served only to magnify Luther's threat; in his view it would have been better to leave the heretic alone.[113] Silhon is a moderate on religious matters: he refuses to pronounce on the ultimate wisdom of the Saint Bartholomew's Day Massacre, but believes that it was an act of cruelty and excess that redounded to the detriment of Catholics themselves.[114] And he is also a wistful partisan of religious reform, expressing the desire "to purify the ecclesiastical order and to return it to its first beauty and its original innocence." Here and elsewhere Silhon professes Gallican sentiments regarding clerical reform, but regretfully notes that such an effort would be "to jump from one extreme to the other."[115] He concludes with resignation, "whatever the state of the Church, anyone can find salvation there if he wants, and outside it no one can avoid being lost."[116]

As with others in Richelieu's orbit, the strongly held Gallican views of this trusted servant risked pulling him toward its outer reaches.

* * *

Another author offered a panegyric that was also distinctive in a different way, in part because it appeared several years after Richelieu's death. Georges de Scudéry, noble soldier, prolific playwright, and a fixture in *mondain* circles—Chapelain called him the "Apollo of the Marais" —published the first part of his *Cabinet* in 1646 (the second never appeared).[117] This was a characteristic publication of the age, a textual representation of a series of objects, here paintings by a range of artists, French, Italian, and Flemish, both living and dead. The paintings, however, were pure fiction: Scudéry takes the reader through an imagined gallery of

---

[111] *Le ministre d'Estat*, a2–a2v.   [112] *Le ministre d'Estat*, 216.
[113] *Le ministre d'Estat*, 205.   [114] *Le ministre d'Estat*, 202–3.
[115] *Le ministre d'Estat*, 231.   [116] *Le ministre d'Estat*, 232.
[117] Georges Scudéry, *Le cabinet de Mr de Scudéry, gouverneur de Nostre Dame de la Garde* (Paris, 1646). The subsequent page numbers in the notes refer to this edition.

representations evoked solely by the author's verses. Based on Giambattista Marino's *La galeria* of 1620, the *Cabinet* was composed of little more than a hundred of these "paintings." As with most such texts, disorder rather than order seems to prevail; the arrangement of images strikes one as more arbitrary than meaningful.

Scudéry's *Cabinet* conformed to type: mythological stories, genre paintings, and still lifes compete for space with "images" of real personages of note. Most of the paintings are taken from Roman myths or history, in keeping with his belief that antiquity is the "mother of the most ingenious fables,"[118] but others portray a gamut of images and themes, some of individuals, others merely scenes of life. Scudéry appeals to the reader, "hoping that such a great diversity of tableaux will give you some pleasure, as long as you are curious." "For myself," he continues, "I am hopelessly stricken by this pleasant malady of the mind, which has me looking all over the earth for things to satisfy me, driving me to gather in the same place all the rarities of art and nature."[119] This expressed the essence of the gentleman savant's prerogative: the privilege of indulging his curiosity in a sort of intellectual *flânerie*, the seemingly purposeless accumulation of objects representing a nobleman's deep and learned engagement with "art and nature," but decidedly, even eccentrically, on his own terms.

The reader of Scudéry's *Cabinet* thus enters his carefully constructed world, a world, in short, characterized by *otium cum dignitate*. The intimate and personal nature of the text is underscored by comparison with Marino's *La galeria*, its model. That work of 1620 was much longer, composed of more than 300 pieces as compared to Scudéry's 110. Unlike the Italian's work, Scudéry's did not strive for encyclopedic completeness, eschewing an attempt to compose a panorama of great men from antiquity to the present in all domains—war, the arts, philosophy, medicine, and so on. Marino's projection was, as named, a "gallery"—an open, quasi-public space where one could presumably wander at will. Scudéry's text, on the other hand, explicitly evokes the enclosed confines of a cabinet, a term that almost always conveyed a sense of privacy, or at least limited access. The *Cabinet de Monsieur de Scudéry* invites us into one person's world.[120]

Interestingly, however, a portion is also France's world. While for the most part the range of images was dictated by Scudéry's tastes and whims, a careful selection is reserved for important figures such as royalty and great aristocrats. These reside in his "imaginary" not by virtue of his curiosity or whimsy; they are there because of their objective stature as great personages, indispensable to the very order of things. Two are of Louis XIII, the first "painted" by the king himself, "because no mortal but he could do justice to his image."[121] These are followed by

---

[118] *Le cabinet de Mr de Scudéry*, Preface (unpaginated).

[119] *Le cabinet de Mr de Scudéry*, "Au Lecture" (unpaginated).

[120] See Richard Crescenzo, *Peintures d'instruction: La postérité littéraire des "Images" de Philostrate en France de Blaise de Vigenère à l'époque classique* (Geneva, 1993), 211ff.

[121] *Le cabinet de Mr de Scudéry*, 22.

the queen, members of the royal family, Henrietta Maria (the queen of England, Louis's sister), then Condé, Richelieu, Mazarin, and various nobility, some chosen because of their prominence, some because of their connections to Scudéry.

In all of this, what strikes the reader—and what endows *Le cabinet de Monsieur de Scudéry*, despite its personal nature, with a panegyric accent—is the prominence and space dedicated to Richelieu. His placement just after the royal family and Condé underscores his prestige; even more significant is the fact that far more text is devoted to him—210 lines, twelve pages—than to any other figure, dead or alive, royal, aristocratic, historical, or mythological. (Mazarin, by comparison, gets only six lines and a single page.) Scudéry's homage comes by way of imagining him delivering instructions to the French artist Philippe de Champaigne, who in fact had already painted the cardinal's portrait: "Renowned painter, it is in this place / that the great Richelieu / Like a brilliant star should shine," reads the first verse. He guides Champaigne step by step in the crafting of the portrait, noting his pleasure with the result, but ultimately confesses that no painting, however faithful and scrupulously rendered, can convey the magnificence of the man. "Though it be charming / I must avow (without insulting you) / That it is hardly a shadow of Armand."[122] Scudéry proceeds to evoke Richelieu in terms of what cannot be depicted, the ineffable qualities that made him France's savior and a hero among the French. Vanquisher of the English, Spanish, and Austrians, he is likened to Hercules in the grandeur of his victorious labors.

Scudéry fills out his *Cabinet* with a handful of other figures—not for the most part royalty and aristocrats, but still important to his world, and certainly prominent in the recent cultural history of France. Catherine de Rambouillet is accorded the distinction—which she shares only with Louis XIII—of two portraits, one depicting her gazing at the body of her son, who fell in battle ("It is Thetis mourning Achilles"). Another image acknowledges Chapelain by way of depicting "La pucelle d'Orléans," Joan of Arc, the subject of his epic poem, at the time still a work in progress. The balance of his *Cabinet* is inhabited by the portraits of a discreet selection of contemporary or recent writers: Godeau, d'Urfé, Théophile, Malherbe; only Ronsard, tellingly, is worthy of inclusion from among the previous century's poets. His homage to Théophile refers scornfully to the "blind, unjust, and envious" who persecuted him. His portrait of d'Urfé is something of a self-portrait: the author of *L'Astrée* is shown holding both a pen and a sword, a reference to his two roles as writer and warrior, a dual identity that Scudéry vaunted for himself.

The cumulative impression of this aspect of Scudéry's *Cabinet* is to re-create the world he in fact inhabited, the overlapping realms of court, nobility, salon, the Marais, and the literati. Scudéry thus reveals himself as a man with multiple

---

[122] *Le cabinet de Mr de Scudéry*, 70.

connections and allegiances: to *grands*, such as Condé and Montmorency; to the feminized salon culture; to the outdated or non-conformist literary traditions associated with Ronsard and Théophile; to the martial life of a noble soldier; to Richelieu. To conclude that the last claimed his greatest affection and energies is not to deny the importance of the others, for there is no evidence that Scudéry saw them as mutually exclusive. He lived, rather, in the cultural world of a *galant* aristocrat, where the values of heroism and urbanity, despite their differences, were celebrated and cultivated. There were those of this cultural milieu who never overcame their suspicion of Richelieu, just as the cardinal tended to look upon the Rambouillet salon, for example, with a wary eye. But this was not Scudéry's experience. This noble soldier and writer saw Richelieu as the greatest of heroes in a world ideally populated with heroic figures, himself included—this "Apollo of the Marais."[123] The world Scudéry identified with was thus not the rarefied space created by Richelieu's ministry, but rather a wider world of the Parisian nobility and men of letters.

Two Who Got Away: Saumaise and Grotius

Richelieu was not always successful in wooing men of letters into his service, despite the considerable resources he could offer, as well as the heavy hand of persuasion he was not shy about using. Among those who resisted his overtures were two Protestants, one a Frenchman who found the Low Countries more to his liking, Claude Saumaise (1588–1653), and the other the renowned Dutch scholar Hugo Grotius, who spent many productive years in Paris. Their cases shed some light on both the process and the interests that were in play when men of letters and a man of power danced to the tune of service.

The son of a magistrate in the Parlement of Dijon, Saumaise had deep roots in France and maintained ties with many French savants throughout his life, especially the Dupuys and their associates. One of the most learned men of his times, in 1632 he succeeded the great Joseph Scaliger as professor at Leyden University, where he remained, despite Richelieu's best efforts, for all but one year of the rest of his life. His linguistic virtuosity was indeed impressive, including mastery not only of Latin, Greek, and Hebrew, but also of Arabic, Syriac, Persian, and Coptic. Most of his scholarly career was devoted to the study, editing, and annotating for publication of Latin and Greek texts, but he hardly shied away from controversy, writing, for example, against the primacy of the papacy and in defense of Charles I of England, for which he was attacked by Milton.

---

[123] *DLF*, 1166.

Saumaise was not in principle opposed to serving the great: he applied his scholarly skills in service to Charles II, Queen Christina of Sweden, and Prince Frederick Henry of Nassau.[124] The difference between these rulers and Richelieu, of course, was that they shared his faith, something that remained a sticking point in the negotiations between Saumaise and the French cardinal. While his Calvinism was somewhat liberal, he was not for that any less devout, something that was borne out in his negotiations with the cardinal. Conversion was out of the question. As a Calvinist living in the Dutch Republic, however, Saumaise was already religiously and politically disposed to look upon Richelieu somewhat favorably, as the pivotal figure in France's turn toward a European policy of opposing the Habsburgs and fighting alongside Protestant powers in the Thirty Years' War.

There is an important point to raise here—relevant to both Saumaise and Grotius—a subject that has always been shrouded in obscurity but nevertheless loomed large in the minds of contemporaries. In the late 1630s, speculation was rife throughout Europe that Richelieu intended to provoke a schism in Catholicism by establishing a Gallican Church, which would rally all those fearful of the growing power of ultramontanism and the Habsburg-Roman axis. It was even rumored that he intended to set himself up as the "Patriarch" of this schismatic church. Its potential followers would include not only Gallican Catholics, who of course would form its core, but also those Calvinists who were increasingly challenged by a hardening of attitudes in their own confessional camp. The most promising source of such recruits was the Netherlands, especially as the victory there of the strict Counter-Remonstrants provoked the forced exile of Grotius and others of his persuasion who chafed under a Dutch Reformed Church in the hands of militant Calvinists. Whether Richelieu's plans were ever more than sheer speculation he found it useful not to discourage cannot be determined. At the very least, he clearly set out to woo prominent Calvinists who might be encouraged to convert as a means of bolstering a Catholic position that could resist the imperial intentions of ultramontanism while still playing a role in the campaign against hardline Calvinism. Hence his courtship of the likes of Grotius and Saumaise.[125]

So when Saumaise returned to France in 1640 to attend to family business,[126] he was subject to a full-court press on Richelieu's behalf. No sooner had he arrived in Paris than he received word, passed through several intermediaries, that the cardinal wanted to see him—that, indeed, he wanted "to keep him." The path of this summons is itself interesting: from the cardinal to François-Auguste de Thou, the

---

[124] Henk J. M. Nellen, *Hugo Grotius: A Lifelong Struggle for Peace in Church and State, 1583–1645*, trans. J. C. Grayson (Leiden, 2015), 503 (especially on Frederick of Nassau).
[125] On this, see Jean Orcibal, *Les origines du Jansénisme*, 3 vols. (Paris, 1947), III: 108–46.
[126] Saumaise's letters in this period have been published in Pierre Leroy, *Le dernier voyage à Paris et en Bourgogne, 1640–1643, du réformé Claude Saumaise* (Amsterdam, 1983), 9.

historian's son (who in two years would perish on the scaffold for his involvement in the Cinq-Mars conspiracy against Richelieu), on to the Dupuy brothers, and then to Saumaise. This was in July. In November he had his first "interview" with Richelieu. They appear to have made a favorable impression on each other. Saumaise reports having been charmed by the cardinal, while Richelieu made a great show of his esteem for the Protestant savant. On one occasion he greeted him very publicly in front of his courtiers, audibly praising him as "the ornament of our times." As Saumaise wrote to a friend, "the King and His Eminence have absolutely resolved to hold me and reclaim me from foreign countries, asserting that it would be a shame and a dishonor for France to let me return."[127]

Despite this flattering attention, Saumaise apparently found it easy to resist the offer. This did not, however, put an end to Richelieu's efforts. In 1642 Saumaise met with Condé, who continued the campaign to win him over to ministerial service. His letter to his fellow savant and co-religionist Antoine Rivet describes the encounter, and hints at the stakes. Saumaise says that they spoke "mainly of religion," and "especially of this reconciliation that they wanted to effect," a clear allusion to Richelieu's reputed plan to unite like-minded Christians in a new camp. Apparently, then, he and Condé went on to debate the conditions of this new venture. Saumaise insisted that the papacy was the sticking point: the plan could proceed only by removing the pope or occur with his approval, "one and the other being equally impossible." Condé agreed, but suggested there might be a "third way for us to recognize the truth of Catholic dogmas." Unfortunately, Saumaise does not divulge the substance of their discussion of this proposition, but merely notes that they continued their "dispute." Finally, Condé asked him what points of belief he could not concede. Saumaise listed what were, in essence, four non-negotiable obstacles in Roman Catholic doctrine: the power of the pope, transubstantiation, the sacrificial aspect of the Mass, and purgatory, adding that any one of these would be sufficient to "withdraw from the communion of a church which believed in it or forced us to believe in it." Despite this rather intransigent declaration of principles, Condé ended their meeting by declaring that he wanted Saumaise to have a position "worthy of him," suggesting that entry into the Council of State would be suitable, which could be effected virtually immediately. And he insisted that he would see Saumaise the next time the savant came to Paris. To Rivet, Saumaise sighed, "Here's another stone in my path. I hope I can get around it."[128]

But that proved somewhat difficult. In August of 1642, he wrote Rivet that Richelieu had ordered him to stay in Paris until the first of the year. Pressures to accept an offer continued, "which might have been effective on someone with less resolve than me."[129] In November, Théophile Brachet de la Milletière, an

---

[127] Leroy, *Le dernier voyage*, 142, 145. [128] Leroy, *Le dernier voyage*, 207.
[129] Leroy, *Le dernier voyage*, 208.

important figure in the movement to reconcile the churches, wrote to Saumaise informing him that Richelieu still thought very highly of him, adding that the cardinal intended to entrust him with the task of creating a large and well-furnished library—a very tempting prospect for a scholar of Saumaise's stripe.[130] Clearly La Milletière was working at Richelieu's behest. Several weeks later, he received a letter from Gilles Ménage, another savant with ties to the Dupuys, repeating Richelieu's desire for him to remain in France, adding that he would receive a royal pension. But by then Saumaise's mind had long been made up. And when Richelieu died in late 1642, he wrote the Dupuys, "I can breathe." The worst fate would have been to lose his freedom—to be forced to write "contrary to my knowledge [*science*] and my conscience." "Better to have suffered the scaffold in Lyons."[131]

This last sentence is, of course, a reference to the recent execution of F.-A. de Thou, which took place in Lyons, an act of steely, if also needlessly harsh, political resolve on the part of Richelieu that sent shockwaves of fear and revulsion through various French and European aristocratic and humanistic camps. It crystallized for Saumaise, as it did for others, what was increasingly becoming apparent: that despite his impressive personal cultivation, his evident appreciation of men of letters and savants, and his ostensible desire to create a united front of well-meaning Christians against the depredations of Rome and the imperial intentions of the Habsburgs, service to this prince of state ultimately meant bending to the reason of state that guided him. This was something Saumaise knew in his bones when he confided to Pierre Dupuy in December 1641 that a reunion of Catholics and Protestants "would produce only neuters. They want to make a new religion that will be neither the one we hold nor that which you follow." It would, rather, be an instrument of state.[132]

* * *

Like other Christian humanists, Hugo Grotius believed that a correct understanding of early Christian sources would reveal the fundamental beliefs and rituals of the primitive Church, thus providing the basis for a faith that could be embraced by all believers. And during his years in Paris, from 1621 to 1625 and 1634 to 1645, the bulk of his efforts were devoted to promoting the irenic ideal, the belief that the schism in Christianity could be healed.[133] In these irenic efforts, he was aided by the Protestant scholar Heinsius, whose Bible annotations *Exercitationes*

---

[130] On La Milletière, see R. J. M. van de Schoor, *The Irenical Theology of Théophile Brachet de la Milletière (1588–1665)* (Leiden, 1994).
[131] Leroy, *Le dernier voyage*, 236.
[132] "Leur reunion ne produisoit que des neutres. Ils voudroient faire une nouvelle religion qui ne seroit ni celle que nous tenons, ni celle que vous suives." Leroy, *Le dernier voyage*, 234.
[133] On this, see Nellen, *Hugo Grotius*, especially 442ff.

ad Novum Testamentum (1639) he had recently consulted.[134] Grotius's efforts were not merely academic: his letters show that he believed that the moment for reconciliation was at hand. The current European conflict would eventually come to an end, providing an opening for the calling of a council of Christian churches to seek a rapprochement among them.[135]

Grotius, of course, was not alone in this vision; some Christians had long imagined a *via media* along the "neither Rome nor Geneva" path. While the Gallicans of the Dupuy cabinet never explicitly endorsed such a choice, their fear of ultramontane Catholicism and abhorrence of hard Calvinism placed them "objectively" in this camp. There is, however, evidence that Grotius received support in Paris, not so much from the Dupuys, but from a more prestigious source—that is, Richelieu, and the much-rumored suspicion that he was scheming to elevate himself as the patriarch of a Gallican Church: still Catholic, but no longer Roman.

Indeed, it seems that around 1638, Grotius was convinced that Richelieu had sent him encouraging signals that they were of one mind, leading him to believe that he could expect the powerful backing of France's most powerful man for his vision of a reconciled Christianity. That Grotius's views were well known is confirmed by those who looked upon them disapprovingly. Saumaise commented to Claude Sarrau that his friends found Grotius "insufferable" on the subject: "they say he refuses to talk about any other subject than the reconciliation of Religions."[136] Chapelain, who had long maintained a respectful correspondence with Grotius, gave vent in 1640 to his exasperation with the latter's religious schemes to Balzac: "I do not know by what peculiarity a jurist, a critic, a poet, a historian, an ambassador leaves the care of all these occupations in order to become a theologian and seek out Arminianism in the New Testament. There is no way to forgive him this fantasy." A few weeks later, he underscored Grotius's folly in striving to "fashion a Christian religion of his making which would be neither Catholic nor Huguenot, and to create a new church in refining Arminianism."[137] Chapelain's skepticism points to a fault line in the Gallican camp, a division between those whose commitment to reform was bathed in idealism and those who believed that, in the wake of confessional strife, lowered expectations and modest reforms were the order of the day. No fanatic and certainly no religious crusader, Grotius nevertheless held out for a Christendom healed of its doctrinaire divisions and sectarian squabbling. While the Dupuys were too discreet and probably too hardheaded to endorse his vision, their Gallicanism and his irenic Christianity were very close.

---

[134] On this, see Henk J. M. Nellen, "*Disputando inclarescet veritas*: Grotius as a Publicist in France (1621–1645)," in Henk J. M. Nellen and Edwin Rabbie, eds., *Hugo Grotius, Theologian: Essays in Honour of G.H.M Posthumus Meyjes* (The Hague, 1994), 136.

[135] Nellen, "*Disputando inclarescet veritas*," 130ff.; and René Pintard, *Le libertinage érudit dans la première moitié du XVIIe siècle* (Paris, 1943), 307–8.

[136] Leroy, *Le dernier voyage*, 127.   [137] *Lettres de Chapelain*, I: 677, 692.

Once Grotius was disabused of the hope of enlisting Richelieu as the godfather of a reconciled Christianity, however, his approbation turned bilious. He condemned the cardinal for his cynicism; he saw him as a veritable tyrant and an enemy of peace in Europe. He abhorred his power politics, and apparently was put off early in the relationship when the cardinal confided to him during a conversation in 1625 that "in matters of state, the weakest are always wrong."[138] "He was concerned only with his own ambition at the expense of everything else, whether it be for the State or Religion," he proclaimed to Guy Patin after Richelieu's death. "He had no other care than to preserve himself and to rule, to the detriment of the good of all of Europe.... This was a miserable man who troubled everything and ruined everything, and, after having devoured poor France down to the bone, God deemed that he himself should die all thin and completely dried up."[139] Grotius was not the only man of letters who placed his hopes in the cardinal only to have them precipitously dashed.

On the Fringes: Jacques Gaffarel and François de La Mothe le Vayer

The sheer range of intellectual and literary figures associated with Richelieu is striking, not only for the differences among them, but also insofar as several of them tested the bounds of religious orthodoxy in this age of the Counter-Reformation. The cardinal maintained ties with notable Protestants, such as Valentin Conrart, and courted others, as we have just seen. He welcomed the controversial Calabrian monk Tommaso Campanella into his company, and tolerated (until he went too far) the flagrantly misbehaving Boisrobert. He also protected savants whose views and interests attracted the censure of leading religious figures. One of these was Jacques Gaffarel.

One might easily dismiss Gaffarel as a scholar whose boundless enthusiasm for esoteric learning eclipsed any sense of criticism or discernment, rendering his enormous erudition essentially useless. Even Naudé and Sorel, who shared many of his interests and sympathies, found him lacking in intellectual judgment.[140] But Gaffarel was in fact one of the most accomplished "Orientalists" of his generation, a student of Arabic and Hebrew texts, especially the Jewish Kabbalah, and an advocate for enriching and strengthening Christianity by incorporating the wisdom of non-Christian traditions of the Middle East into its doctrines.

---

[138] Richard Tuck, *Philosophy and Government, 1572–1651* (Cambridge, 1993), 197.
[139] René Pintard, "Grotiana," in Pintard, *La Mothe le Vayer—Gassendi—Guy Patin: Etudes de bibliographie et de critique suivies de textes inédits de Guy Patin* (Paris, 1943), 75.
[140] Cecilia Rizza, "Les 'Curiositez inouyes' de Jacques Gaffarel," in Rizza, *Libertinage et littérature* (Paris, 1996), 215. Sorel even wrote a book as a reaction to Gaffarel's: *Des Talismans, ou, Figures faites sous certaines constellations, pour faire aymer et respecter les hommes, les enrichir, guérir leurs maladies, etc., avec des observations contre le livre des Curiositez inouyes de M. J. Gaffarel* (Paris, 1636).

He was born in Provence, in the town of Mane, in 1601. His father was a physician, but he studied for the priesthood, receiving degrees in theology and canon law from the Universities of Valence and Paris. He soon attracted the attention of Richelieu, who made him his librarian. The cardinal's favoritism meant that he was showered with ecclesiastical positions, despite his contretemps with the Sorbonne and conflicts with Mersenne; at the end of his career he was the dean of the canon law faculty at the University of Paris. He maintained close ties with a number of savants, including Naudé, his fellow Provençals Gassendi and Peiresc, La Mothe le Vayer, and Jean-Jacques Bouchard. While he does not seem to have been very close to the Dupuys, he definitely was within their orbit, managing, like others, to maintain one foot in the cabinet while also serving Richelieu.

Like most of his confreres, he spent several years in Italy, from 1626 to 1633, especially Venice. It was as Richelieu's agent that he made the journey, which ultimately took him to Greece and the Levant. His mission seems to have been to secure valuable manuscripts and books for the cardinal's library; he apparently returned with a trove of seventeen bales of works in Greek, Arabic, Hebrew, Chaldean, and Syrian.[141] Of special interest—whether his or Richelieu's, one cannot tell—were manuscripts of the most important Christian student of Jewish mysticism in the Renaissance, Pico della Mirandola. Gaffarel ultimately published a catalogue of three Kabbalistic manuscripts once in Pico's possession, or so he claimed.[142] In Venice, he served in the entourage of the French ambassador, who prized him as a learned companion.[143]

It is not clear where Richelieu's assignment ends and Gaffarel's own agenda for his research begins; it may have been that Gaffarel's particular interest in the Jewish occult was his alone. In any case, his pursuit of Kabbalistic lore was a life-long endeavor, which was evident in print well before he entered Richelieu's service, thus suggesting that the cardinal engaged him with full awareness that this servant harbored intellectual proclivities that would raise the hackles of many pious Parisians.

Gaffarel's first publication, *Codium cabalisticorum manuscriptorum*, has not survived. It was followed in 1625 by another work on the same theme, *Abdita divinae cabalae mysteria* (Profound Mysteries of the Divine Kabbalah), which offers a sustained brief for the study of the Jewish Kabbalah as a legitimate source for religious wisdom. On one level it is a response to those—most prominently Mersenne and Garasse—who saw the Kabbalah as nothing but a heretical work whose influence could only be dangerous if not demonic. Gaffarel devotes considerable effort to arguing that just as Christians have long read ancient pagan

---

[141] Pintard, *Le libertinage érudit*, 223.
[142] Yaacob Dweck, *The Scandal of Kabbalah: Leon Modena, Jewish Mysticism, Early Modern Venice* (Princeton, 2011), 158.
[143] Pierre Bayle, *Dictionnaire historique et critique*, new ed. (Paris, 1820), VII: 2.

fables and myths for their insights, interpreting them according to the superior wisdom of Christianity, so the Kabbalah and other Jewish sources should be similarly appreciated and studied.[144] A follower of such Renaissance scholars as Ficino, Pico, Guillaume Postel, and others interested in Neo-Platonism, hermeticism, and Jewish mysticism, he was dedicated to the proposition, shared by other humanists, that ancient learning, whether Jewish or pagan, contained sacred wisdom that could buttress Christianity, perhaps even establishing a theological basis for a rapprochement between Catholics and Protestants.

Gaffarel's defense of the Kabbalah did not go unanswered: Mersenne responded by insisting that it was simply magic by another name. But it is remarkable that, in 1625, Gaffarel remained entirely unmolested, despite his unorthodox views, while all around him those suspected of heresy, blasphemy, and even anti-Aristotelianism were on the run. (See Chapter 3.) Gaffarel had defenders and protectors, including Richelieu and Richelieu's brother, which clearly insulated him from these sorts of threats, despite the fact that Mersenne continued to attack him by name. It was different with his next work, *Curiositez inouyes, sur la sculpture talismanique des Persans, horoscope des Patriarches, et lecture des Estoilles*, published in 1629.[145] If anything, this text enlarged upon his appreciation for unconventional learning and rituals by considering not only the Kabbalah but also astrology and other ancient sacred traditions of the Middle East. Even more, here Gaffarel challenged fundamental teachings of the Church, likening the Bible to Aesop's fables, casting doubt on miracles and "demons" alike, defending rabbinical doctrines, and in general exhibiting a suspicious sympathy for Jewish traditions. In August, the Sorbonne condemned the text for teachings that were "false, erroneous, scandalous, opposed to Holy Writ, contumelious toward the Church Fathers, and superstitious." Gaffarel was given the opportunity to abjure his views, as long as he acted quickly. In October he signed a general retraction, stating that he never meant to teach or espouse condemned doctrines, but merely to report on the various views of the Hebrews and Arabs. He also pointed out that in the preface he had reminded readers that his belief in these views extended only to what was permitted by the Roman Catholic Church.[146] Despite the Sorbonne's actions, Gaffarel's interest in Jewish mysticism and occult philosophy never wavered. In the early 1630s—after this controversy—he could be found in Venice as Richelieu's agent and the French ambassador's companion. There he sought out the greatest scholar and critic of Kabbalistic literature of the period, Leon

---

[144] Rizza, "Les 'Curiositez inouyes' de Jacques Gaffarel," 219.

[145] Rizza, "Les 'Curiositez inouyes' de Jacques Gaffarel," 230. See also on this text Bérengère Parmentier, "Un 'libertin par mégarde'? Le cas Gaffarel: Réseaux érudits et prose du monde," in Patricia Harry, Alain Mothu, and Philippe Sellier, eds., *Dissidents, excentriques et marginaux de l'Âge classique: Autour du Cyrano de Bergerac* (Paris, 2006), 323–48.

[146] It has been noted, however, that Gaffarel's retraction never mentioned what portions of his text were condemned. Moreover, the work seems to have remained in circulation, never subjected to the normal draconian measures imposed on banned books.

Modena. Upon his return to Paris in 1637, he published the rabbi's apologia for Jewish customs and rituals, *Historia de gli riti hebraici*.[147]

Despite these contretemps, Gaffarel remained in Richelieu's service for the duration of the cardinal's life. And it is a last act of service that might provide a clue into the nature of their converging interests. There is no doubt that, like others who took an interest in hermeticism and mysticism, Gaffarel harbored the hope that these esoteric sources of ancient wisdom might provide the basis for the reconciliation of the churches. And it was here, it seems, that their plans overlapped. Whether he was sincere or not, during the later years of his ministerial reign, the cardinal at least liked to give the impression of fostering a French approach to Catholicism that might entice Protestants into the Gallican fold (as we have seen). In this spirit, it seems, he dispatched Gaffarel to the Church of Saint-André in Grenoble to preach during the Lenten season of 1641. Grenoble had a substantial Huguenot community. Gaffarel's sermons, in which he confronted systematically the central doctrines that divided Catholics and Protestants—the Eucharist, priestly celibacy, indulgences, purgatory, papal supremacy—ignited a storm of controversy, especially among local Catholic clerics. The simple fact that he cast his preaching in this confessionally divided city as—in the words of a sympathetic auditor—"an offering of Peace, Concord, Union... by attempting to find some principles of accord conforming to those already advanced by approved authors" was sufficient to provoke opposition.[148] While overall he defended the letter of orthodoxy, it seems as though he particularly cast doubt on the existence of purgatory. His reasoning and tone were accommodating in spirit. "He showed us by summarizing all forms of knowledge, whose secrets he revealed, supported by the cross and the mystery of Calvary, that what Jesus Christ taught on that sacred mount was the same as revealed by both the most admirable of our sciences and the purest of our love."[149] Nevertheless, his preaching on this occasion was so controversial that he avoided prosecution by the Parlement only because of the intervention of his powerful protectors, including, in all likelihood, Richelieu.[150]

This was not the last of his efforts toward reconciliation of the faiths. After Richelieu's death, he published *Quaestio pacifica, num orta in religione dissidia componi et conciliari possint per humanas rationes et philosophorum principia* (1645), a work that made a plea for the union of Christians based not on the Kabbalah or hermeticism, but on arguments that were "prudent, measured, and orthodox."[151]

* * *

---

[147] Dweck, *The Scandal of Kabbalah*, 157–8.
[148] *Lettre du sieur de St-Clément à monsieur d'Hozier... sur les prédications faictes à Grenoble, par le sieur de Gaffarel* ([Paris], [1642]), 8.
[149] *Lettre du Sieur de St-Clément*, 3.
[150] Parmentier, "Un 'libertin par mégarde'?," 343.
[151] Pintard, *Le libertinage érudit*, 274.

Another savant close to Richelieu whose views did not conform to the orthodoxy of the day was François de La Mothe le Vayer. We have already met him as the author of *Considérations sur l'éloquence française*, in which he argued for a revived Ciceronian eloquence that was at once rooted in the learned humanist tradition but purged of obfuscation, pointless citations, and unnecessary erudition. And we will again encounter him in Chapter 6 as a habitué of the Dupuys, as well as the center of a smaller group of savants somewhat misleadingly known as "erudite libertines." La Mothe le Vayer was indeed immensely erudite, and normally made few concessions in his writings to those readers not well versed in the ancients. He was also a steadfast skeptic, a disciple of Montaigne and Charron, as well as a prolific author best known for a series of dialogues purportedly recorded by Orasius Tubero, his rather ineffective sobriquet. If anyone deserved the ascription *esprit fort*, it was La Mothe le Vayer. A man of many parts, like many of his savant and literary contemporaries, he managed to be at home in several different worlds. His primary abode was the Dupuys', where discretion and, in his particular case, secrecy were prized. But he also had an official profile in high circles, gaining entry into the Académie française, and serving Richelieu with his pen. He wrote several tracts in support of the cardinal's policies, including *En quoi la piété des Français diffère de celle des Espagnols*, and another that asserted that the French and their enemies differed even in terms of their basic humors.[152]

In 1642 he drafted another text most certainly at Richelieu's request, although what La Mothe le Vayer actually produced may have served more his own interests, conforming more to his own intellectual orientations than those of his master. Here is an example of the unintended consequences that can result when powerful authorities recruit learned and creative writers to do their bidding: they may get more than they bargained for.

The context for this publication was the emerging Jansenist critique of mainstream Catholicism, which Richelieu feared had the potential not only to provoke another religious schism but also to undermine the support of France's elite, and especially the learned elite, for established orthodoxy. In the 1630s, sympathy for partisans of the Dutch bishop and theologian Cornelius Jansen was, in fact, quite strong among leading intellectual and literary figures. For one thing, insofar as they perceived a threat of a religious nature, it was not from latter-day followers of Saint Augustine but rather from the Jesuits; in this sense the Jansenists and many secular-minded writers, who were largely Gallicans, had a common enemy. There were also ties of friendship between them; they tended to live in the same cultural and intellectual Parisian world. Several members of the clan most intimately associated with Jansenism in France, the Arnaulds, were faithful habitués of the Rambouillet salon, boon companions of the likes of Chapelain and Voiture.

---

[152] François de La Mothe Le Vayer, *En quoi la piété des Français diffère de celle des Espagnols, dans une profession de même religion* (Paris, 1658).

As noted in an earlier chapter, Saint-Cyran, later to gain notoriety as perhaps Richelieu's most severe critic in the Jansenist camp, verified Charron's Christian bona fides in the face of Garasse's attack. Further demonstration of the overlap of these two groups comes from a round of letters between Chapelain and Balzac in which the two men discuss with great sympathy and concern the plight of their friend Antoine Le Maistre, a disciple of Saint-Cyran, who in 1638 dramatically resigned his official position in a move that was designed to publicize his Jansenist convictions.[153] It is likely, then, that Richelieu, who was remarkably astute in these matters, grew increasingly anxious about the possibility of sympathetic ties between notable Jansenists and men of letters. He may also have been fearful that the intellectual flower of France would prove susceptible to the appeal of Jansenism, despite its rigors, especially as it embodied a religious sensibility at once elitist, intellectually challenging, and, moreover, in step with the tendency toward *otium* that many embraced.

If so, La Mothe le Vayer was the man for him. For the cardinal certainly appreciated that a potential wedge between *gens de lettres* and Jansenists was the latter's total rejection of paganism, a position that, of course, not only denied Christianity what had been a venerable philosophical source for its theology since the early Church Fathers, but also, more immediately, would likely alienate anyone with humanist allegiances. And there was no one more steeped in the ancients than La Mothe le Vayer, who has been called the "French Plutarch."[154]

In *Augustinius*, published in 1640, Jansen asserted that the pagans lacked virtue, a claim that obviously challenged the legions of contemporaries who modeled their thinking and behavior on the likes of Cicero, Horace, and Seneca. It certainly offended someone of La Mothe le Vayer's ilk. His *De la vertu des payens*, dedicated to Richelieu, was published in 1642.[155] Although La Mothe le Vayer does not mention Jansen or his book, his own text is clearly designed as a response, at least with regard to its dismissive view of pagan virtue. On one level it adheres to a conventional understanding of Christianity's view of pagans and paganism, which accepted the possibility that some who lived before the Incarnation of Christ and the Evangelization of the Word, whether in Greece and Rome or in ancient Israel, were possessed of virtuous qualities, although they still were denied a place in heaven. To contest the claim that no pagans could be considered virtuous was, thus, not a controversial move on La Mothe le Vayer's part. As well, his book aimed to undermine the Augustinianism that was, after all, not only central to Jansenism but at the root of Luther's theology. La Mothe le Vayer devotes many

---

[153] *Lettres de Chapelain*, I: 151–2, 183–5, 192–3.

[154] Isaac Uri, *Un cercle savant au XVIIe siècle: François Guyet, 1575–1655, d'après les documents inédits* (Paris, 1886), 31. Balzac also indicated some sympathy for the emerging Jansenist position; see Jean Lesaulnier, "Antoine Arnauld et la société des années 1630," in Armogathe, Lesaulnier, and Moreau, *Antoine Arnauld*, 9–31.

[155] François de La Mothe le Vayer, *De la vertu des payens* (Paris, 1642).

pages to exposing passages in *The City of God* where pagans are discussed favorably: he cites Augustine to refute contemporary Augustinians. In this sense, he is one of Richard Popkin's Christian skeptics whose intellectual labors were meant not to undermine the faith but rather to support it against Protestants and other heretics whose intellectual certitudes led them into error.[156] There are indeed notes of skeptical fideism in the text, most notably at the conclusion of Part II, when, after marshaling a wealth of citations from canonical Christian authors to buttress his case, he "humbly" declares that "the ways which God employs to save men are not always apparent; that his counsels, as Saint Paul says, are unfathomable depths; and that no one can ever hope to comprehend his judgment."[157] Ultimately, his case is founded on the conception of a merciful God who, he virtually cries out, could not possibly consign so many to eternal damnation simply because they had the misfortune to be born before the advent of Christ or had never heard the Gospel. Several times he asks, uncomprehendingly, Who would have the "inhumanity" to countenance or believe in such a thing? These outbursts and his emphasis on God's mercy and goodness are clearly meant to contrast with the severity and rigor of Jansen's Augustinianism.

But for the most part in *De la vertu des payens*, La Mothe le Vayer is uncharacteristically less skeptical in tone and more positive in his assertions than in his other writings. He repeatedly alludes to notions such as the "light of reason," "natural light," "natural goodness," the "law of nature," and a kind of naive yet efficacious "faith" that endows some pagans with grace even though they lived their lives without the benefit of the Christian revelation. Accordingly, he insists on an optimistic assessment of infidels' moral inclination for virtue based upon their natural proclivity, guided by reason and not necessarily revelation. Again, the contrast with the Augustinian position, with its emphasis on the stain of original sin and the utter perversity of fallen man, is deliberate. He also posits a three-stage division of history: from Adam to Abraham was a state governed by nature; the Jewish period was ruled by law; the advent of Christ ushered in an age of grace. This, in turn, allows him to suggest a relativistic view of the threshold for salvation: God surely judges people only in terms of their awareness and understanding. Anything else would be the sign of a deity lacking goodness and mercy.

Michael Moriarty, in a very astute reading of *De la vertu des payens*, argues that it subtly moves from conventional to subversive positions, using irony and indirection to convey its more challenging message.[158] However, on one level, the potentially heterodox nature of the text hardly needs to be teased out "between

---

[156] Richard H. Popkin, *The History of Scepticism from Erasmus to Spinoza*, 3rd ed. (Berkeley, 1979), 90ff.
[157] *De la vertu des payens*, 52.
[158] Michael Moriarty, "Authority and How to Evade It: La Mothe le Vayer, *De la vertu des payens*," *Biblio*, 17/166 (2006), 99–113.

the lines"; it repeatedly strikes the reader in the face. Although the title of the work suggests that it will deal with the question of pagans' virtue, very early on the subject turns to their *salvation*. And there is no mistaking La Mothe le Vayer's meaning. He not only wants to rescue pagans from the eternal damnation to which his Augustinian opponents want to consign them; he argues that those who acted virtuously in their lifetime and acknowledged a single creator would enjoy the same heavenly rewards as virtuous Christians. He even rejects the suggestion of an archbishop that virtuous infidels might reside in a kind of halfway station, neither heaven nor hell. In short, throughout the first part of *De la vertu des payens*, La Mothe le Vayer unmistakably asserts that for some "Pagans, Gentiles, and Infidels," salvation was possible without Christ's sacrifice.

This in itself would seem to mark La Mothe le Vayer's book as going well beyond Richelieu's purposes, if not to risk associating the cardinal with views that skirted the edges of heterodoxy. Moriarty's interpretation takes us further into these dangerous waters. In the second part of the work, La Mothe le Vayer undertakes a biographical excursus into the lives of pagan philosophers, from Socrates to Seneca, adding portraits of Julian the Apostate and Confucius ("the Chinese Socrates") as well. "The biographical sketches," Moriarty argues, "serve to distract the reader, to blur the Christian perspective." Instead, our attention is directed to these virtuous pagans, to be judged not merely in comparison to Christianity or as precursors to the Christian revelation, but as valued exemplars in their own right, to be celebrated and admired for their wisdom and insight. "All this suggests that, while purporting to be settling a question within Christian theology, La Mothe le Vayer is in fact undermining the claim of orthodox Christianity to a unique divine revelation."[159] The second part of the book, so much longer than the first that one tends to lose sight of the original question, has the effect of plunging the reader into a deep and prolonged encounter with non-Christian lives and minds, such that an appreciation of their unique spiritual value is the likely result. Moriarty's interpretation of La Mothe le Vayer's particular treatment of Socrates and the Siamese philosopher Xaca endows the text with a truly Straussian twist. For these figures are presented as forced to disguise or otherwise obscure their teaching in order to prevent those less capable of appreciating it from perceiving its true meaning. And this is a likely tip for how La Mothe le Vayer, the quintessential *esprit fort*, wanted discerning readers to approach *De la vertu des payens*.

This interpretation is made more plausible when La Mothe le Vayer's other writings are considered: anyone familiar with those published by "Orasius Tubero" would be struck by the contrast between *De la vertu des payens*, with its emotional appeal, its profession of faith in human nature and reason, and its general

---

[159] Moriarty, "Authority and How to Evade It," 105.

lightness in tone, and the skeptical dialogues, which were shot through with erudition, cryptic in style, and generally contemptuous of the intellectual capacities of the mass of humankind. In short, *De la vertu des payens* is *not* by "Orasius Tubero," and that is sufficient to suggest that it should be read with discernment, that its purported defense of the virtue of pagans is really something else. As Jean-Pierre Cavaillé comments à propos of this publication, "Le Vayer always manages such that his orthodoxy is not entirely clear, or that his ideological zeal is often enough accompanied with serious reservations."[160]

* * *

It may seem nothing more than common sense to appreciate the mythic quality of the traditional image of the cardinal's role in fashioning the culture of his day, an image that depicts him and especially the Académie française as exercising almost tyrannical power over the world of letters—something of an early modern Stalin. Not only is this view patently false; it might be helpful to risk erring in the opposite direction—to see Richelieu as more a product than a master of cultural trends. Certainly the concern with linguistic reform and renewal, so central to the mission of the academicians, was well-entrenched long before his rise to power; likewise, the fertile soil of Parisian literary and intellectual sociability had long borne the fruit of a post-civil war society in the full bloom of cultural renaissance. So too with the Gallican spirit—in some quarters doctrinaire, in others merely a strong version of the *bon français* position—which virtually all *gens de lettres* of the period shared: this even more obviously was part of the legacy of the sixteenth century, if not earlier times. No one should dispute Richelieu's genius in reading and manipulating the culture of his day; indeed, to understand its complexity and autonomy is to gain an even greater appreciation of his talent and efforts. As with his place in Scudéry's imagined *Cabinet*, however, he loomed large, to be sure, but his prominence was rendered visible in the context of a "world" created by a man of letters out of his very personal and varied interests and allegiances.

---

[160] "Le Vayer se debrouille toujours pour que son orthodoxie ne paraisse pas entière, ou pour que son zèle idéologique s'accompagne, ici et la, de serieuses reserves." Quoted by Moriarty, "Authority and How to Evade It," 144.

5
The Rambouillet Salon
"A Purified World"

THE SUBJECT OF Faret's *L'honnête homme, ou, L'art de plaire à la cour* is not simply *honnêteté*, but, as the full title suggests, how this virtue can be maintained in the often immoral, frequently contentious milieu of the royal court, a place characterized by competition, duplicity, dissimulation, and just plain bad manners. One particular problem is the difficulty of simply carrying on conversations at court, indeed the very possibility of civil interactions in this vexed social space. In a chapter entitled "On the Conversation at the Louvre and Its Discomforts," Faret observes that there prevails such a "confusion of people...that the best sorts of encounters suffer." No sooner does a "good company" form than "straightaway it is sullied by an annoying somebody, or the pleasantness is troubled by some person of high station, or completely disturbed by the proximity of some spies of the Court, with mercenary ears, who are useful only in the way Physicians make use of blood-suckers." But Faret has a solution for those virtuous souls who want to perfect their conversational skills amidst virtuous company: leave the court. "It is necessary to go down into the City," he writes, "and seek out the most virtuous Ladies in whose homes are found the most appealing gatherings, and if possible, to place oneself in their care, in hopes that they interest themselves in helping all those who visit them."[1]

Faret published *L'honnête homme* in 1630. By then the Rambouillet salon was well established; and although there were other *ruelles* on the Parisian cityscape, he likely had this one in mind, especially as he was close to several intimates of the Rambouillet milieu, including Conrart and Chapelain. His prescription certainly serves to highlight the salon as a privileged place for the promotion of new modes of elite behavior and self-presentation in the seventeenth century—as specialized arenas that nurtured refinement, polite conversation, and in general those values and standards associated with the "civilizing process." And it does this by asserting not only its distance but also its difference from the royal court.

Contemporary historians and literary scholars have recovered Faret's appreciation of the salon's importance in contemporary life, and thus have moved it from the margins to the center of cultural history of the seventeenth and

---

[1] Nicolas Faret, *L'honnête homme, ou, L'art de plaire à la cour* (1630), ed. Maurice Magendie (1925; reprint, Geneva, 1970), 90.

eighteenth century.[2] Cultural historians of the eighteenth century especially see it as embodying, and fostering, some of the most important trends of the period. Like Faret, these historians identify it as a kind of refuge, an alternative to the noxious court. Whereas the court was characterized by a concern for rank and a tendency toward dissimulation, the salon fostered free discussion and an elite form of sociability that recognized habitués as equals. Thus a polarity is drawn in ways that have already been addressed in this study—between the political realm (the court) and one created by a withdrawal from this realm (that is, the salon). Faret's prescription marks this withdrawal as a self-conscious move and highlights as well the importance of women in this cultural space.[3]

Although the centrality of the salon to the culture of the Ancien Régime can hardly be contested, historians continue to argue about its nature, especially the degree to which it actually fostered comity and equality among members. For the seventeenth century, Nicolas Schapira offers a critique that calls into question any assertions regarding the activities of the salon as a whole. What we know comes by way of a celebratory historiography based on testimonies from *gens de lettres* alone, with little corroborating evidence from other sources, he argues.[4] These writers, who lacked an institutional identity in the corporate structure of the Ancien Régime, had everything to gain from promoting its importance and magnifying their own role in its life. This, of course, returns us to Jouhaud's fundamental insight concerning the "delocalized" feature of *mondain* literary culture, although here, it would seem, a new "locale" was constructed in the space—both discursive and real—of the salon. The salon was primarily a venue for writers that provided them with a cultivated "public" of well-born men and especially women whose approval was crucial in establishing their status as *gens de lettres*.

What follows, then, is based largely on the only informants we have, our *gens de lettres* who celebrated the Rambouillet salon; but this will not preclude inferences about the nature of the larger community of aristocrats and writers evoked by their writings. For evidence in fact exists beyond writers' self-regarding and self-interested testimonies, evidence that speaks to the activities and interests of the salon as a whole—both *gens de lettres* and the noble attendees who, after all, were the main reason for its existence. Thus, while cognizant of the limitations of

---

[2] For a comprehensive survey of the historiography of the French salon from the nineteenth century onward, see Nicolas Schapira, *Un professionnel des lettres au XVIIe siècle: Valentin Conrart, une histoire sociale* (Paris, 2003), chap. 4.

[3] Dena Goodman, *Republic of Letters: A Cultural History of the French Enlightenment* (Ithaca, NY, 1994); Daniel Gordon, *Citizens without Sovereignty: Equality and Sociability in French Thought* (Princeton, 1994). For a convincing argument for the importance of salons, and for the women who presided over them in the seventeenth century, see Faith E. Beasley, *Salons, History, and the Creation of Seventeenth-Century France: Mastering Memory* (Abingdon, 2006). Fundamental to the study of French salons and *salonnières* in the seventeenth century is Carolyn C. Lougee, *Le Paradis des Femmes: Women, Salons, and Social Stratification in Seventeenth-Century France* (Princeton, 1976).

[4] "Rien ne peut donc en etre deduit sur ces pratiques elles-mêmes: ce qui est produit dans ces texts n'est pas un savoir sur les 'salons', mais le sens que les écrivains entendent conférer à certains espaces sociaux." Schapira, *Un professionnel des lettres*, 230.

the evidence, I refuse to refrain from assuming that noblemen and ladies were part of the social mix that constituted the salon as an important cultural institution of its day. Rather, I will focus on the *relationships* between writers and the elite denizens of the salon. Whatever the limitations of our evidence, it cannot be denied that these relations existed. As we saw in Chapter 2, writers made themselves at home in the Parisian *monde* of the well-born; they cultivated relationships with aristocrats, whether as clients or within various associations. The salon was perhaps the foremost among these, an informal institution that, whatever the nature of the evidence, is inconceivable without acknowledging the aristocratic men and especially women attracted to its confines.

But one thing is clear: it is mistaken to define the salon primarily in terms of Elias's "civilizing process." This is not to say that values such as refinement, politesse, *civilité*, and the like were not central to its subculture—they certainly were. But these were very general values given expression primarily by writers; we have very little evidence to make claims about the actual behavior and values of the well-born ladies and gentlemen who frequented the salon. Moreover, these values hardly do justice to the specific activities and functions of the salon, where, most particularly, an interest in "literature" and various literary activities involving *gens de lettres* and its other habitués were so central. Likewise, it seems something of a stretch to frame the salon as a sort of countercultural venue embodying such virtues as comity, equality, and publicness, especially given the aristocratic, hierarchical society of which it was an integral part (as argued by Schapira and Antoine Lilti).[5] Certainly a degree of free play and badinage characterized the interactions of *gens de lettres* and the high-born men and women they courted. But this must be seen in the context of the spirit of *galanterie* that infused these interactions, a spirit that, while often refreshingly improvisational in nature, still preserved, even resurrected, essentially courtly, chivalric notions of how men and women should interact. Writers were instrumental in fashioning this spirit. Thus, I prefer to be guided by Domna Stanton's concept of the aristocrat as a "work of art"—with the important proviso that we recognize as "artists" the *gens de lettres*, their canvas (or perhaps studio) the salon.[6] The notion of the self as a work of art allows us to appreciate the importance of leisure or *otium* to aristocrats and *gens de lettres* alike; it thus not only entails self-fashioning but also presupposes a privileged space for that process. Working within both an aristocratic value system and aristocratic spaces, writers developed codes or ideals for their social superiors, holding up mirrors to better selves.

*　*　*

[5] Schapira, *Un professionnel des lettres*; Antoine Lilti, *Le monde des salons: Sociabilité et mondanité à Paris au XVIIIe siècle* (Paris, 2005).

[6] Domna C. Stanton, *The Aristocrat as Art: A Study of the Honnête Homme and the Dandy in Seventeenth- and Nineteenth-Century French Literature* (New York, 1980).

The beginnings of the Rambouillet salon date to around 1615. By then the Marquise de Rambouillet, Catherine de Vivonne, had established herself in Paris in a townhouse located on rue Saint-Thomas-du-Louvre, near the Palais Royal, a dwelling that she herself designed and had built on the site of their previous house in 1604. Her father was the Marquis of Pisani; her mother, Julia Savelli, was descended from Roman aristocracy. Roman by birth, in 1607 Catherine married Charles d'Angennes, who would have a long career as a royal servant—councilor of state, captain of the Hundred Gentlemen of the King's House, ambassador to Spain, and master of the King's Wardrobe. They had seven children: Julie, the oldest, played a principal role in the salon; one son would die in the aftermath of the Battle of Nordlingen in 1634. The marquise spoke Italian and Spanish fluently, and was one of the main conduits of Italian influences on Parisian culture in the early decades of the century, a time when the Italian presence was particularly strong at court, with both an Italian queen and a royal favorite, Concino Concini, and his wife.[7]

It is worth considering how a woman of foreign birth who, though graced with an impeccably distinguished noble pedigree, was not related to royalty managed to climb to such commanding heights. Here, if ever, the notion of "constructing" an identity would surely seem appropriate. Unlike her successor and emulator Madeleine de Scudéry, however—and unlike the not inconsiderable number of female authors and memoirists of the period—Madame de Rambouillet never published, nor did she ever present herself as a writer. Hers was an identity fashioned in the ephemeral, daily manifestations of her personality within the precincts of the *hôtel* she so assiduously managed—and thus it is largely beyond our reach.

But writers were clearly instrumental in this process. Certainly a degree of mythmaking was set in motion even in her lifetime. In Madeleine de Scudéry's novel *Artamène, ou, Le Grand Cyrus*,[8] the marquise, thinly disguised as "Cléomire," is vaunted for her many gifts: her beauty, to be sure, but also her composure, reason, and wisdom, attributes normally associated with a masculine temperament endowed with Neo-Stoic virtues.[9] Her relative Tallemant des Réaux, whose *Historiettes* is a rich source for the period—and who himself was part of the salon in its later years—probably contributed more than anyone to the fashioning of the reputation of salon and *salonnière* alike. In his pages the marquise comes off as commanding, demanding, exacting, and somewhat peculiar in her ways.

---

[7] On the Rambouillet salon, see Emile Magne, *Voiture et l'Hôtel de Rambouillet*, 2 vols. (Paris, 1929–30); Gédéon Tallemant des Réaux, *Historiettes*, ed. Antoine Adam, 2 vols. (Paris, 1960), I: 442–55; Maurice Magendie, *La politesse mondaine et les théories de l'honnêteté en France au XVIIe siècle, de 1600 à 1660* (1925; reprint, Geneva, 1970); Nicole Aronson, *Madame de Rambouillet, ou, La magicienne de la chambre bleue* (Paris, 1988); Beasley, *Salons, History*; plus other works cited below.
[8] M. de Scudéry, *Artamène, ou, Le Grand Cyrus*, 10 vols. (Paris, 1649–53).
[9] Victor Cousin, *La Société française au XVIIe siècle d'après le Grand Cyrus de Mlle de Scudery*, 2 vols. (Paris, 1858), I: 285–7.

Her health was precarious, forcing her to remain indoors, largely within the confines of her *hôtel*, which thus served not only as a haven for its chosen habitués but also as a personal refuge for her—something of a sanitarium. But she exploited her frailty in ways that only highlighted her sensitive nature. She proclaimed a horror for anything coarse, common, or vulgar; indeed, unlike some of the other frequenters of her salon, who often engaged in risqué bantering or allowed themselves to be entertained by a poet's mildly bawdy verses, she was something of a prude, displaying an intolerance for any reference to sex or bodily functions, violence, or anything that violated her rather strict notions of *bienséance*. Fundamental to the "myth" of the salon is its reputed genesis, which in Tallemant's telling was as a sort of anti-court. In her early years she had been raised at court; she and her husband belonged to the courtly milieu, those known as *gens de la cour*. And yet Mme de Rambouillet, put off by its rough-and-ready atmosphere, left Henri IV's Louvre, and never found much to her liking in the court of his son to tempt her to return.[10] In this account, then, her withdrawal from the royal court thus defined her *hôtel* as a kind of refuge. It was part of the city culture but insulated from the rudeness of both city life and the Louvre. It embodied, perhaps more than any other venue at the time, the ethos of *otium*—leisure, pleasant sociability, and conversation, self-consciously removed from the cares and demands of labor and commerce, office and court, battlefield and profession.

Writers found there a select public of well-born Parisians who constituted a discerning and influential public for their work. Chapelain called the salon "*le monde purifié*." Balzac, who probably never entered the salon, nevertheless declared, with characteristic hyperbole, "One day at the Hôtel de Rambouillet is worth more than several centuries elsewhere."[11] For an exclusive milieu, however, the Rambouillet salon turned out to be a very crowded place. Many of the great of the realm were among its denizens. While it cannot be known whether actual social interactions were hierarchically constrained, such frequenters as Gaston d'Orléans, Condé, La Valette, Henri de Schomberg, and other grandees, as well as Richelieu's niece, the Duchess of Aiguillon, had to make Mme de Rambouillet aware of her middling status vis-à-vis many of her guests, even if she managed to preside over the gatherings through the sheer force of her personality.[12] Others of lesser rank were surely cognizant of their place in the company of these *grands*. Montausier, a sword nobleman and warrior and a connoisseur of letters, was one

---

[10] Tallemant des Réaux, *Historiettes*, I: 442. Nicolas Schapira expresses skepticism with regard to this account, underscoring the fact that the Rambouillets were also part of the courtly milieu. He also speculates that the marquise's promotion of this "posture" of retreat into an alternative court, one marked by certain *"valeurs 'culturelles,'"* was "a response to the relative mediocrity of the career of the Marquis de Rambouillet, a means of regaining his position at court." *Un professionnel des lettres*, 237.

[11] Jean Lesaulnier, "Antoine Arnauld et la société littéraire des années 1630," in Jean-Robert Armogathe, Jean Lesaulnier, and Denis Moreau, eds., *Antoine Arnauld: Trois études* (Paris, 1994), 22.

[12] On the relationship of seventeenth-century salons to great aristocrats, see Schapira, *Un professionnel des lettres*, 239.

of the salon's most visible intimates, who managed to win the hand of Julie only after a prolonged campaign. It is said that Richelieu made an appearance in the early years of the salon; later, he would grow suspicious of its independence. James I's favorite Buckingham was hardly the only distinguished foreigner who made a point of dropping in while visiting the French capital. The renowned Italian poet Giambattista Marino graced the salon with his presence during the time he lived in Paris from 1615 to 1623. Great noble ladies such as the princesses of Condé and of Conty, the Duchess of Longueville, two Montmorency sisters, the marquises of Sablé and of Clermont d'Entragues, and the countesses of Moret and of Fargis were also regularly in attendance.

These great aristocrats gave the Rambouillets an impeccably elite profile. But they also rubbed shoulders with some *robins*, for the salon selectively opened its doors to certain high officers of distinction. In particular, the Arnauld family, best known for their role in the history of Jansenism, had deep and lasting ties to the *hôtel* on rue Saint-Thomas-du-Louvre. Robert Arnauld d'Andilly and his son belonged to the salon's inner circle, as did Arnauld de Corbeville and Arnauld de Briotte, the marquis de Pomponne. The presence of this Robe family as intimates of the Rambouillet salon suggests a feature of this subculture that has been observed for the culture of *honnêteté* in general: its expansiveness beyond the hereditary elite of the *noblesse de race*. This should not be exaggerated; nor, certainly, should it be taken as evidence of a growing "bourgeois" element in this aristocratic venue. The gate was still narrow, with admission only to the few. The Arnaulds, in fact, were very high in the Parisian pecking order, hardly bounders seeking entry into quarters beyond their station. The point is that rank or birth, though perhaps necessary, was not sufficient. We cannot know, of course, whether social distinctions counted for less than level of cultivation, refinement, and the ability to interact with men and women of wit, especially writers. Still, it is unlikely that the royal court could have managed the melding of these distinct, often contentious elements of the elite with such ease. As for the marquise herself, the salon's gatekeeper, she seemed to be more concerned with social skills and level of cultivation than with title or rank. She once told Tallemant that she would happily welcome an "Indian" into her salon as long as he acted and spoke correctly—that is, if he were an *honnête homme*—without knowing anything more about him.[13]

The Salon as a Home Front

Many of these aristocratic guests were also warriors. It is often claimed that because of the transformations in warfare stemming from the so-called Military

---

[13] Tallemant des Réaux, *Historiettes*, I: 444.

Revolution, European aristocrats in the sixteenth and seventeenth centuries were experiencing a range of challenges to their vocation as "those who fight." Whether these changes really amounted to a fundamental repositioning of elites on the battlefield or not, it is clear that aristocrats were called to combat more than ever. When it comes to the aristocrats of the Rambouillet salon, their profile as warriors is quite impressive—no cosseted courtiers these. Many were active combatants, often experiencing great hardship, imprisonment, or injury in the course of the near-incessant campaigns leading up to and during France's entry into the Thirty Years' War.[14]

The greatest casualty from among the Rambouillet aristocrats was the marquis and marquise's son, mortally wounded in the Battle of Nordlingen. The Marquis de Montausier, Julie's future husband, was often on active duty; his brother died in battle, and he himself was taken prisoner. Perhaps the most active warrior among the Rambouillet aristocrats was Cardinal La Valette, an important commander in the French campaigns in Alsace and Italy in the course of the 1630s, whose military experience and knowledge made him an indispensable advisor to Richelieu in his efforts to reorganize the French army. Philippe Habert, a writer and frequenter of the salon, perished in combat in 1637, at the age of 32, serving under Charles de la Porte, duc de la Meilleraye.[15]

These aristocrats thus led lives that had them shuttling from the battlefront, with its deprivations and danger, to the pampered, leisurely, and lettered environment of the salon. Their identities were, accordingly, divided between warrior and *galant*, with the salon as the context for the latter, and its men of letters sometimes acting as tutors in drawing out their *galanterie*.[16] Certainly Vincent Voiture served Cardinal La Valette in this tutorial context. While also linked in service to Gaston d'Orléans, Voiture was most closely identified with the Rambouillet *hôtel* and served as La Valette's informant on the activities of the salon during his absence from the battlefront (as we have seen in Chapter 2), using his literary

---

[14] Arlette Jouanna, *La France au XVIe siècle, 1483-1598* (Paris, 2006), 61-3, on the percentage of nobles who participated in battle as between 6% and 30%.

[15] Among the noble warriors who frequented the Rambouillet salon were La Tremouille, who was active as a commander, charged with levying two regiments of infantry, and Harcourt, who saw hard campaigning in Italy in the late 1630s. Some served not with French forces but as combatants in the armies of the Habsburgs, sometimes because of their sentiments, sometimes merely because they wanted to gain military experience. This was true for Bassompierre, who volunteered in the Habsburg armies in Hungary; and also for Gramont, who, while he began his military career fighting the Huguenots in 1621, shifted his service to the Dutch side in the Siege of Breda, but then joined Tilly's Catholic League army. Schomberg participated in the Siege of La Rochelle; Arnauld de Corbeville was present at the Siege of Dunkirk and was taken prisoner at Württemberg. See David Parrott, *Richelieu's Army: Government and Society in France, 1624-1642* (Cambridge, 2001), 30-1 and *passim*; Cousin, *La société française*, I: 306; René Pillorget and Suzanne Pillorget, *France baroque, France classique*, 2 vols. (Paris, 1996), I: 973.

[16] In a letter to Godeau, the marquise referred to Pierre-Isaac Arnauld, a *maître de camp*, as "my carbine-poet." Lesaulnier, "Antoine Arnauld et la société littéraire," 13. On the military aspect of aristocratic culture in this period, see the fine study by Brian Sandberg, *Warrior Pursuits: Noble Culture and Civil Conflict in Early Modern France* (Baltimore, 2010).

skills to bring textually alive what his correspondent was missing. His letters show the poet intimately involved in a project of aristocratic self-fashioning, as I have noted. But they also represent the salon as a refuge from the battlefront and reminded La Valette of that half of his personality that his role as warrior prevented him from realizing, at least at the moment.[17]

Writers, Literature, and the Rambouillet Salon

Tallemant commented that the *hôtel* was the "meeting place of those who were the most *galant* of the court and the most polished among the *beaux esprits* of the age."[18] By the latter he meant men of letters. The expansiveness of the *hôtel* was only affirmed in the presence of a platoon of writers who rivaled in number the aristocratic habitués. If anything distinguished the Rambouillet salon, it was its receptivity to budding and established writers alike and its role as a forum for literary works. Voiture's literary reputation was virtually synonymous with the salon. In its early years, Théophile's plays and poems were read aloud and even performed there.[19] Malherbe "conquered" the Rambouillet milieu both personally and with his views on poetry, which aided him in gaining support for his so-called doctrine. It was he who renamed the marquise "Arthénice," an anagram of Catherine, a name by which she has continued to be known. His disciple Racan was also among the writers welcomed in its precincts. Chapelain made sure to put in frequent appearances and played an important role throughout its history. Balzac understood the members of the salon as a discerning readership for his writings. Antoine Godeau, a member of the French Academy and a priest, was another favorite, especially to Julie d'Angennes: small in stature, he was known as "Princess Julie's midget," and officiated at her wedding to Montausier. Although not associated with the salon—nor with any other Parisian establishment, for that matter—Pierre Corneille submitted his play *Polyeucte* to the judgment of the Rambouillet habitués. Most of these writers were followers of Malherbe and his "doctrine" that sought to purge French of both its "Gascon" barbarisms and the mannered style of the Pléiade. As already noted, out of the forty members of the first generation of the French Academy, over half had ties to the Rambouillet salon.[20]

---

[17] *Oeuvres de Voiture: Lettres et poésies*, ed. Jean-Henri-Abdolonyme Ubicini, 2 vols. (Paris, 1855), I: 25, 44, 52–4, 75, 206, 252, 254, 260, 264, 287, 308, 322.
[18] Tallemant des Réaux, *Historiettes*, I: 443.
[19] Magne, *Voiture et l'Hôtel de Rambouillet*, I: 112.
[20] Other writers who frequented the Rambouillet salon include Valentin Conrart, Georges and Madeleine de Scudéry, Jean Mairet, Boisrobert, Malleville, Vaugelas, Isaac de Benserade, Jacques de Serisay, La Mesnardière, Saint-Amant, Gilles Ménage, Desmarets de Saint-Sorlin, Germain Habert, and Claude de L'Estoile. On frequenters of the salon, see Emile Magne, *La vie quotidienne au temps de Louis XIII* (Paris, 1942), 224 and *passim*.

The salon integrated men of letters into this essentially aristocratic milieu—the Parisian *monde*. But the integration was not without fissures and competition. Within the confines of the *hôtel*, at least, the male habitués formed bonds and subgroups; in fact, the salon seems to have been a rather complex society, hardly a cozy community of erstwhile courtiers. In this sense, while not as hierarchical or constrained as the royal court at the Louvre, the salon did not escape rivalries and divisions.

There were at least two recognized camps. The "corps" included Voiture, the Marquis de Pisani (Mme de Rambouillet's son), and the counts of Guiche and Vaillac. Except for Voiture, these were warriors on leave, who found the salon a welcome source for rest and recreation. They were opposed by a group that came to be known as the "anti-corps," composed of Montausier, Arnauld de Corbeville, Chapelain, Godeau, Conrart, and, by virtue of their association with him, the self-exiled Balzac. Mme de Rambouillet seems to have favored the corps, while her daughter Julie sided with their opponents. It is not always clear what principle divided these two camps. The corps had a decided martial bent; the anti-corps was mainly a group of men of letters. The "Guirlande de Julie," conceived and organized by Montausier, should probably be considered an expression of this latter camp, for no member of the corps participated, not even Voiture. (It is likely that Montausier deliberately excluded Voiture, whom he quite rightly saw as a rival for Julie's attention.) The division between the two camps might also reflect a difference running through the whole subculture of the Rambouillet salon, and perhaps even of aristocratic culture in general. For the corps was not only martial in bearing, it also was responsible for many of the more boisterous, even malicious antics that characterized many of the salon's pastimes. Its members' behavior was more carefree, less in conformance with Mme de Rambouillet's standards of *bienséance*, and womanizing, or at least badinage, as much as literature was their favorite pastime. Their opposing group, on the other hand, tended more to literary matters and, in the context of the salon, was considered learned. Chapelain's presence in the *hôtel*, for example, usually meant a reading of one of Balzac's letters or a discussion of literature or language. His tendency to leaven his conversations with learned citations irritated the marquise, it seems, and on one occasion his extended ruminations on *Medea*, in the context of a discussion about a mother who had killed her child, apparently did not endear him to the salon's habitués.[21] This division came to be embodied by the rival poets Voiture and Godeau. Voiture had been considered the salon's poet-in-residence since 1625 and used his privileged position not only to broadcast his writings before an audience of the great but also to establish a tone of light-hearted gallantry, in both verse and behavior. Around 1630, however, he was challenged by the arrival of

---

[21] Magendie, *La politesse mondaine*, 131.

Godeau, who soon became Julie's favorite. While a *galant* himself, Godeau, like his anti-corps comrades Chapelain and Conrart, was more inclined to the Malherbian tradition than Voiture, who self-consciously strove for a freer, less rule-bound style of versifying.[22]

These divisions and rivalries were played out in the context of several quarrels over literary and linguistic matters. The period, of course, was rife with disputes of this sort, those over Balzac's *Lettres* and Corneille's *Le Cid* being only the most prominent. The Rambouillet *hôtel* not only generated its own quarrels, it also functioned as a kind of tribune of judgment for those that broke out beyond its precincts. In the conflict over Balzac's *Lettres* and *Le Cid*, for example, the salon was appealed to for its opinion, which it offered in the form of support for both authors. In 1640, the salon demonstrated an avid interest in the academy's discussion over the usage of the word *car*. Julie and Voiture objected to the academicians' decision to banish it in favor of *pour ce que*, a decision Voiture mocked in a humorous letter he wrote to Julie.[23] In this and other quarrels, the Rambouillet salon carried out its self-appointed role as the "arbiter of Parnassus."[24]

This role is illustrated by another dispute that was generated by the intimates of the Rambouillet salon and divided its ranks, that over Ludovico Ariosto's early sixteenth-century comedy the *Suppositi*, which pitted Voiture against Chapelain along with their supporters, corps versus anti-corps. The quarrel started in 1639 when Chapelain sent the play in question to Voiture, who was in Rome, ostensibly so the poet could improve his Italian. Even before this, it seems that the two had often sparred over the relative merits of Italian and Spanish, with Voiture professing a marked preference for the latter. As for the *Suppositi*, Voiture responded with a dismissive critique, declaring it poorly constructed, even obscene. Chapelain answered with an outraged defense and offered to submit the matter to "Princess" Julie for a final judgment, adding that a pair of Spanish gloves should go to the victor. Though usually allied with the anti-corps, Julie took Voiture's side, claiming to be shocked by the realistic liberties of the play. Chapelain graciously and somewhat obsequiously handed over the gloves, but he

---

[22] *Dictionnaire des lettres françaises: Le XVIIe siècle* (Paris, 1951) [hereafter *DLF*], 1067; Alain Génetiot, *Poétique du loisir mondain, de Voiture à La Fontaine* (Paris, 1997), 121; Tallemant des Réaux, *Historiettes*, I: 492: "Le marquis de Pisani et lui [Voiture] étaient toujours ensemble: ils s'aimaient fort, ils avaient les mêmes inclinations; et quand ils voulaient dire: 'Nous ne faisons point cela, nous autres', ils disaient *Cela n'est point de notre corps*. Ils faisaient tous les jours quelque malice à quelqu'un; c'était un tintamarre perpetual à l'hôtel de Rambouillet." On corps and anti-corps, see also Antoine Adam, *Histoire de la littérature française au XVIIe siècle*, 3rd ed., 3 vols. (Paris, 1997), I: 269 n. 10, who quotes Voiture's *Lettres*, in *Oeuvres de Voiture*, I: 293.

[23] Alain Viala, *La naissance de l'écrivain: Sociologie de la littérature à l'âge classique* (Paris, 1985), 39; see also Benedetta Craveri, *The Age of Conversation*, trans. Theresa Waugh (New York, 2005), 58–9, on Voiture's letter to Julie, who defended *car*.

[24] In 1638, Voiture, Malleville, and Tristan l'Hermite competed to see who could write the most appealing verses on the theme from a poem by the Italian poet Annibale Caro. The competition, in fact, was instigated by the marquise, who seemed to want to invite challengers to Voiture's primacy as house poet. Aronson, *Madame de Rambouillet*, 228.

did not let the issue rest there. His letter of concession to Voiture is a masterpiece of double-talk, at once deferential to Julie's judgment and defiant on the merits of the case. It is full of interesting political allusions. He likens her to an absolute monarch "who is not above the laws but still superior to them." In expressing his hope that the gloves will please Voiture, he notes that they are at least "one conquest that we have made in Spain and the only advantage we have won over them this year."[25]

But his determination to pursue his case is evident. Chapelain proceeds to launch a campaign on several fronts to vindicate his judgment. Letters are posted to Godeau and Balzac, while the Scudérys—Georges and Madeleine—are likewise drawn into the controversy. The whole salon is in a state of "combustion" over the quarrel, comments Chapelain. He coaxes Godeau, now far from Paris in his bishopric, to offer his views, adding that he need not devote much time to the play—he might even fib a bit and merely endorse Chapelain's position without bothering to read it. Clearly this is a matter of great importance: "There are great battles to wage in this matter," he writes to Balzac.[26] The hermit of Charente indeed holds the key; he is the acknowledged arbiter. And when Balzac responds with a ringing endorsement of the merits of Ariosto's play, as well as his authority as a critic, Chapelain's joy is palpable. "Your letter honors me in the extreme and has lifted my party, which could not have been more dispirited." Never was a man more "trapped" than Voiture when he read Balzac's judgment, he gloats.[27] Balzac's text is read before the habitués of the salon, as well as the intimates of the Dupuy cabinet, to general approval. Even Voiture is forced to acknowledge its brilliance. Further support comes to the pro-*Suppositi* camp with the intervention of the Scudérys. In his text, Georges adopts the sobriquet "Adolphe," borrowed from Ariosto's more famous work, *Orlando Furioso*, while Madeleine's opinion earns her Balzac's praise as that "firm Amazon." The quarrel seems to conclude with a victory for Chapelain and his fellow partisans of the Italian comedy.

The quarrel over the *Suppositi* reveals what was often at stake in the salon. From Chapelain's perspective, at least, it was nothing less than the standards of artistic judgment—or rather whether the authority of those standards was to be maintained in a *mondain* culture of marginally educated ladies and gentlemen. "Most men are governed by nature and not by art," he writes to Balzac. "Each follows his own bent and accepts as preceptor only himself because it is easier and more indulgent, and as art is the only thing that can perfect human efforts, from that it follows that there are so many mediocre minds and so few that are sublime and excellent." Voiture, he claims, is guided merely by "good judgment" and not

---

[25] *Lettres de Jean Chapelain, de l'Académie française*, ed. Philippe Tamizey de Larroque, 2 vols. (Paris, 1880–2), I: 396.
[26] *Lettres de Chapelain*, I: 408, 405, 402.   [27] *Lettres de Chapelain*, I: 405.

by laws, "as if good judgment were not the father of laws."[28] And not only Voiture, but also his fellow travelers, Julie and other habitués of the salon, are gravely misled in thinking that they can judge a work of art by the standards of their own opinions and reactions alone. Because they cannot base their judgment on any "irregularity" in Ariosto's comedy, asserts Chapelain, they are forced to fall back on personal judgment. This "heresy" is the issue, according to the critic, which reveals the cleavages in the culture of the salon that this quarrel—and others like it—called into play. If Chapelain, Balzac, and the salon's other men of letters are not precisely enforcers of Malherbe's doctrine, they nevertheless stand for the principle that doctrine should guide literary judgment. They are thus the new *doctes*: not the erudite scholars scorned by them and others as pedants, but defenders of some standards of judgment against those who would dispense with them altogether in favor of the whims of personal taste. Having participated in the opening up of belles-lettres to the *mondain* society of court and salon, having fostered an accessible vernacular literature that required no particular expertise, Chapelain and Balzac now found themselves beating the bounds of contemporary culture in precisely the other direction.[29]

This quarrel, like others, serves as a warning against viewing the salon strictly in terms of civility, *honnêteté*, or the like, terms that tend to offer a quite impoverished view of both this institution and the slice of aristocratic culture it cultivated. While the values evoked by these terms were certainly in play—*bienséance* was *always* the touchstone of the marquise's judgments of individuals and literary works alike—there was obviously much more to the habitués' concerns. Here it was the very modalities of artistic or literary judgment.

Jean Mairet's Sophonisbe

Men of letters used the salon to preview their works, to try them out on this eminently discerning audience. Literary debuts were common at the Hôtel de Rambouillet. In 1636 Desmarets de Saint-Sorlin gave a reading of the *Visionnaires*; two years later he offered a rendition of his tragedy *Scipion l'Africain*. In 1638 Chapelain's presentation of the second part of his epic poem on Joan of Arc, *La pucelle*, was received with less than enthusiasm; associates of the corps predictably found his erudition pretentious and tiresome. As noted, in 1640 Corneille's

---

[28] *Lettres de Chapelain*, I: 403, 402.
[29] However, see *Lettres de Chapelain*, I: 417, on Guyet's attitude toward Balzac's letters, where the *érudit* (Guyet) is reported as expressing scorn for Balzac for precisely the same reasons that Chapelain and Balzac were critical of the literary tastes of the salon.

Polyeucte was met by a rather disapproving audience, who did not care for his mixing of the sacred and the profane.[30]

On occasion works were performed, not merely read. The *hôtel* was a theatrical venue of sorts, with the habitués themselves serving as actors. In 1627, days after Théophile's release from prison, his *Les amours tragiques de Pyrame et Thisbé* was staged at the Rambouillet salon, with Julie playing the title role.[31] Three years later, the Count of Belin persuaded the marquise to allow the theater group of the Marais, which he protected, to perform Jean Mairet's *Virginie* at her *hôtel*.[32] There was a kinship between Théophile and Mairet: Mairet was the beleaguered poet's literary executor, and they shared Montmorency as a patron. In 1636, Mairet's play *Sophonisbe* was performed by salon intimates two years after its debut.

Jean Mairet (1604–86), one of the most prominent playwrights of the period, has been overshadowed by the more enduring fame of Pierre Corneille. Contemporaries, however, recognized him as one of the founders of the modern French stage. Born in Besançon, he came to Paris as a young man to attend *collège*, but quickly announced his debut as an author with a series of tragicomedies and pastoral plays, culminating with his greatest success, *Sophonisbe*, first performed in 1634. After the execution of his patron, Montmorency, he entered the entourage of the Count of Belin, a great booster of the theater. Mairet is probably most remembered as one of Corneille's chief adversaries in the "Quarrel of *Le Cid*," to which he contributed four rather venomous tracts. After this episode, his fortunes as a writer waned, and in 1640 he began a new career as a diplomat, forever abandoning his calling as playwright.

Sophonisbe is considered the "first truly genuinely classical French tragedy"—the play that introduced the Roman theme to the French stage.[33] The moment of its staging by the Rambouillet salon, late summer 1636, was significant, especially for this particular play, which pitted the interests of state against amorous passion, the public versus the private. A pause in the Siege of Corbie had allowed such warriors as the Marquis de Pisani, the Count of Guiche, and two Arnaulds, all habitués of the salon, to return to Paris for three days. Anxiety, in fact, was rampant in France that August, with fears that imperial troops, having won a string of victories, might easily reach the capital in a matter of days. In his memoirs, Abbé Arnauld, the son of Robert Arnauld d'Andilly, noted that "[t]he alarm was great in Paris," with families

---

[30] See David Clarke, *Pierre Corneille: Politics and Political Drama under Louis XIII* (Cambridge, 1992), 238, citing Magendie, *La politesse mondaine*, 401. See *Lettres de Chapelain*, I: 339–40, for the occasion of an Italian play performed at the *hôtel* upon Montausier's return from the Siege of Brisach.

[31] Henry Carrington Lancaster, *A History of French Dramatic Literature in the Seventeenth Century* (Baltimore, 1929–42), pt. 1, 2 vols., I: 169; Adam, *Histoire de la littérature française*, I: 199, writes of salon members as actors.

[32] Lancaster, *A History of French Dramatic Literature*, pt. 1, II: 747–8.

[33] Lancaster, *A History of French Dramatic Literature*, pt. 1, II: 703.

fleeing the eastern provinces. Tallemant registered his disgust at the rich Parisians who "so cowardly" sought refuge south of the city.[34]

Among these refugees from the threatened capital, in fact, were members of the salon, who had regrouped at the Rambouillet country estate. Mairet's play was their chief entertainment. The actors, who included Julie, Mademoiselle de Clermont, and two Arnaulds, might have outnumbered the audience. Between acts, Mademoiselle de Paulet, the daughter of the magistrate who gave his name to the notorious tax on offices, appeared; dressed as a nymph, she sang and played the theorbo (a sort of long-necked lute developed in the late sixteenth century in Florence). "And that admirable voice, which has been often talked about as that of 'Angelique,' made us hardly miss the orchestra of violins that normally appear during these interacts," writes Arnauld.[35]

Arnauld's recollection of this event might serve to confirm the hackneyed image of the Rambouillet salon as a group of pampered aristocrats enjoying frivolous pleasures and banal pastimes, especially as they were safely removed from a Paris under threat of siege. But we should pause to consider that on this occasion, as on others, they were involved in a rather sophisticated literary exercise that had, in fact, political resonances. Mairet's play is a challenging text. Its appeal, on several levels, to the Rambouillet milieu seems clear, if also a matter of some speculation. The tragedy was scrupulous in observing the three "unities" of place, time, and action. It was the first French play to take as its plot a chapter from Roman history, a subject of great interest to Mme de Rambouillet, as is evident from Balzac's four texts on Roman themes dedicated to her. (See below in this chapter.) Mairet also took great care in sanitizing the original story, as found in Polybius and Appian of Alexandria, rescuing the play's heroine from the charge of bigamy and in general endowing the protagonists' relationships with more emotion and less political calculation than in the ancient accounts. Saint-Evrémond praised Mairet as having "recognized the taste of ladies and the true spirit of the *gens de la Cour*."[36] The title character also was a figure of obvious appeal to the *salonnière*, for although the combined forces of love and war ultimately proved her undoing, she nevertheless strove to become the mistress of her destiny.

Beyond these features of the play, there is the plot itself, which presents a clash of political and personal interests in a way that spoke to contemporary events and

---

[34] See Pillorget and Pillorget, *France baroque, France classique*, I: 294ff.; Magendie, *La politesse mondaine*, 127: "[P]endant le siège de Corbie par les Français, quelques membres de la famille Arnauld quittaient l'armée, où ils avaient, paraît-il, des loisirs, et venaient surprendre la Marquise; en trois jours, on apprit, on monta et l'on representa la *Sophonisbe* de Mairet: Mlle Paulet chantait entre les actes, vêtue en nymphe"; "C'est par une comédie que l'on célébrait, un peu plus tard, la prise de Brisach, et le retour de M. de Montausier." Magendie cites here Antoine Arnauld, *Mémoires de l'Abbé Arnauld* (Paris, 1838), 490, and *Lettres de Chapelain*, I: 339.

[35] *Mémoires de l'Abbé Arnauld*, 490; quoted in Jean Mairet, *La Sophonisbe*, ed. Charles Dédéyan (Paris, 1945), 129–30.

[36] Quoted in Lancaster, *A History of French Dramatic Literature*, pt. 1, II: 704.

concerns. It culminates with the tragic demise of its two protagonists: rather than submit to Rome's demand that he surrender Sophonisbe, the Numidian queen and his new bride, to his Roman commanders, Massinisse and she choose death by their own hand, which "Show[s] that the sternness of a pitiless Roman / Hath power o'er a lover, but not o'er love."[37]

As these lines suggest, the attitude toward Rome in the play is hardly favorable. Unlike Balzac's *Dissertations politiques*, for example, where Augustan Rome is vaunted as a model of urbanity and culture, and unlike the general view of Rome espoused by contemporary writers and artists, who tended to celebrate France as a latter-day incarnation of Roman virtues and glory, Mairet's play reveals deep misgivings about the Roman model. It prefigures *Horace*, in which Corneille offered a meditation on the tragic implications of the Roman commitment to the interests of state and imperial conquest. And it echoed other contemporary concerns about the moral cost of empire, both Rome's and France's. In Nicolas de Campion's *Entretiens* (probably written late in Richelieu's ministerial reign), a text that was quite critical of Richelieu's policies and methods of rule, the participants reflect on the cause of Rome's eventual downfall, speculating that its origins lie in the excesses and crimes of its history dating from Romulus's original usurpation.[38] Mairet was not identified with the opposition to Richelieu.[39] Nevertheless, *Sophonisbe* plays upon the theme of the cost of conquest, and its toll in terms of human affection and loyalty, by using Imperial Rome as a foil.

The calculus of this cost can be seen in the play's three male protagonists, for each embodies the elements of state interest and human affection in different measure. Siphax, the Roman general, and Scipio, the vanquished Numidian king, are mirror images of one another in each being deficient, but of opposing virtues. Siphax is fatally compromised by his love for his wife, Sophonisbe, which blinds him to the realities of war and the Roman threat until it is too late. In the first act he realizes how foolish he has been, how his love for her has unmanned him: "...when her beauty / Bereft me of all sense and liberty. / Ever since this mistake darkened my life / Ill fortune hath fast followed on its heels." It was for her sake, and not for his realm's, that he opposed Rome, "For which my ruin is my just reward."[40] On the other hand, the Roman general Scipio is nearly entirely lacking in human affection. Though he demonstrates real concern for Massinisse's well-being and fate, he is above all a warrior in unbending service to the state.

---

[37] Jean de Mairet, *Sophonisbe* (1634), in Lacy Lockert, ed. and trans., *The Chief Rivals of Corneille and Racine* (Nashville, TN, 1956), 3–54, on 54. Subsequent citations of *Sophonisbe* in the notes refer to this translation.

[38] *Mémoires de Henri de Campion (1613–1663), suivis de trois entretiens sur divers sujets d'histoire, de politique et de morale*, ed. Marc Fumaroli (Paris, 1967), 248.

[39] Although he had been a member of Henri II de Montmorency's entourage, the great nobleman was executed for raising an army against the crown in 1632.

[40] *Sophonisbe*, 10, 7.

He "knows not the mighty power of love," and, in chastising Massinisse for marrying Sophonisbe, he presents himself as the quintessential Roman stoic:

> True, I have always kept myself, heart-free,
> From falling into the snares that have ensnared thee,
> ...It is not that my breast
> Contains a heart of stone...
> The hand that fashioned thine, fashioned mine, too.
> And only manhood renders it impervious
> 'Tis with this shield one must protect oneself...[41]

Of the three male protagonists, only Massinisse combines the virtues of affection and martial strength: he is at once a *grande âme* and a *honnête homme.* Unlike Siphax, he has not let love cloud his reasoning: he is both effective and heroic on the battlefield, while recognizing the imperatives of war that have led to his tragic predicament. And he acknowledges his debt to Rome for giving him a command that promised to return him to his rightful place as ruler. But unlike Scipio, he has allowed himself to love. Being fully human, however, and not merely a stoic half-man, means not only that he will have to defy Rome, but that he is doomed as well. In a passage that can be read as a critique of Neo-Stoicism, Massinisse reflects on his fate: "How much the gods, perfect although they are, / Display inconstancy in the gifts they give us!"[42] *Sophonisbe* thus operates on several levels of commentary and critique. It suggests that the Neo-Stoic model, if taken to an extreme, could distort human virtues. It undermines a reliance on reason of state as the sole guide for statecraft. It definitely offers a highly distasteful image of Rome, and by implication any state, even France, that has imperial ambitions. Finally, in the doomed couple at the center of the play, it conveys a sophisticated appreciation of the inherent tragedy and human cost of war as an element of statecraft. Whether or not the play was meant as a critique of Richelieu, it certainly crystallized the concerns and reflections of many of the salon's habitués for whom war was an ever-present reality. Like Massinisse, they found their lives stretched between two worlds, the battlefield and the salon, which threatened them, too, with a clash of commitments they had difficulty resolving.

Montausier: Arms and Letters

War was never far from the salon's concerns, and returning warriors reminded the company of its cost. Some never returned. Especially in the dark years of the

---

[41] *Sophonisbe*, 37, 38.   [42] *Sophonisbe*, 42.

mid-1630s, when France's formal entry into the Thirty Years' War began so uncertainly, the spirit of the *hôtel* oscillated with the fortunes of France's armies on the battlefield. But when Gustavus Adolphus became the hero of the hour with his stunning string of victories in 1630, the Rambouillet salon embraced him in its own way. Princess Julie publicly proclaimed what can only be called a crush on the Swedish king, declaring that her heart was reserved for him alone. (Never mind that she had never seen him.) She erected a shrine in his honor in her rooms and inspired the poetic efforts of several writers of the salon in a competition to pen verses in praise of the royal general.[43]

Julie would eventually marry Charles de Sainte-Maure, marquis de Montausier (1610–90), an important patron of writers and a central figure in the salon.[44] A stalwart of the anti-corps, he was both a warrior and a man of letters, at home on the battlefield and in the salon. Born to a Protestant family, Montausier was educated at the Huguenot *collège* in Sedan, where he learned Greek and Latin. His grandfather and uncle had been loyal servants of the first two Bourbons, and he continued in this family tradition, remaining on the side of the crown during the *Fronde*, and ending his career with Louis XIV naming him a Knight of the Saint Esprit in 1662 and the Dauphin's governor in 1668. He was a constant campaigner, seeing action, along with his brother (who was killed in battle), during the Mantuan crisis, and in Alsace and Lorraine during the Thirty Years' War. In 1642–3 he was captured by imperial troops and spent ten months as a prisoner of war in Bavaria, during which time he produced a series of Latin epigrams. Upon his release, he converted to Catholicism and finally, as the culmination of a thirteen-year campaign, won the hand of Julie.

Though he was both a translator and a writer, Montausier never bothered to publish his work. Perhaps, like others of his class, he believed that publication was an indignity for a gentleman, for it smacked of needing to secure the attention and approval of a public, something unworthy of a true aristocrat. In any case, his name has entered the annals of literature as the animator of the "Guirlande de Julie" (Garland for Julie), the single work most associated with the Rambouillet salon and a curiosity of French belletristic culture in the seventeenth century. Assembled and produced in the course of a decade, from about 1633 to 1641, the "Guirlande" is a collective homage to Mme de Rambouillet's daughter in the form of a number of poems, each based on the conceit of a flower representing her charms and virtues. It was, notes a modern commentator, "one of the most exquisite productions of the flower mania" of the seventeenth century.[45] Nearly all the

---

[43] Magendie, *La politesse mondaine*, 132; Arnauld, *Mémoires*, 482, col. 2.
[44] On Montausier, see especially Denis Lopez, *La plume et l'épée: Montausier (1610–1690)* (Paris, 1987).
[45] Elizabeth Hyde, *Cultivated Power: Flowers, Culture, and Politics in the Reign of Louis XIV* (Philadelphia, 2005), 108. See also Elizabeth Hyde, "Flowers of Distinction: Taste, Class, and Floriculture in Seventeenth-Century France," in Michael Conan, ed., *Bourgeois and Aristocratic Cultural Encounters in Garden Art, 1550–1850* (Washington DC, 2002), 77–100.

verses were madrigals, a later medieval genre mixing poetry and voice that emerged in the fourteenth century and then was revived in the sixteenth. Its revival, in fact, can be ascribed to the Italian humanist Pietro Bembo, who is best known to posterity as one of the characters in Castiglione's *The Courtier*.[46] The appeal of this genre for Montausier was in keeping with the salon's general interest both in medieval genres and in all things Italian. But he had his own Italian connections. He probably encountered the madrigal during his campaigning in Italy and was likely influenced by the *La ghirlanda della contessa Angela Bianca Beccaria*, by the sixteenth-century poet Stefano Guazzo, which also celebrated a lady.[47] Montausier's knowledge of Italian letters and culture was deep, as attested by Balzac, who compared him to Castiglione.

Montausier used his connections in the salon and among French writers to good effect: there were over sixteen contributors to the "Guirlande," the vast majority of whom were associated with the Rambouillet milieu, including such prominent men of letters as Chapelain, Scudéry, Conrart, Malleville, Desmarets de Saint-Sorlin, Ménage, and Colletet, as well as the four Arnaulds and Julie's father. The collection included ninety-one poems and twenty-nine flowers, all introduced by "La couronne impériale," a set of verses written by Chapelain, Malleville, and Scudéry that, alluding to Julie's affection for Gustavus Adolphus, represented a crown of flowers figuratively placed on her head by the Swedish king.[48]

We should pause to appreciate the political dimensions of this public celebration of the Protestant warrior-king. In the early 1630s, before France had formally entered the European conflict that would be known as the Thirty Years' War, its policy of supporting Protestant powers such as Sweden in opposition to the Catholic imperial forces hardly met with universal approval, either within France or across Catholic Europe. While the *dévot* party had been dealt a serious blow in 1630 with the Day of Dupes, this did not mean that discontent and criticism of Richelieu's pro-Protestant, anti-imperial course was totally muted. Thus to have the most prominent Parisian salon publicly embrace a heretic monarch—the greatest Protestant sword in Europe—and extol his victories over Catholic forces was no small or inconsequential matter. It was a rare moment when the face of the Rambouillet *hôtel* took on a political guise, although one still shrouded with a theatrical mask.

Montausier's sustained labors in conceiving, organizing, and editing the "Guirlande," a work-in-progress that took several years to complete, show him to be a man of considerable concentration and entrepreneurial skills, skills that likely were honed by his service as a military commander responsible for the

---

[46] Lopez, *La plume et l'épée*, 133.   [47] Lopez, *La plume et l'épée*, 132ff.   [48] *DLF*, 571.

well-being of his troops.[49] He was aided in his labors, of course, by having the Rambouillet salon as a base for recruiting authors, and his friendship with Balzac and Chapelain provided him access to the best-known poets of his generation. The whole enterprise also captures in microcosm, and under rather unique circumstances, the close relationship between writers and aristocrats that we have already observed, and which was at the heart of literary culture in the seventeenth century. It was less a product of the love-struck Montausier, campaigning for the hand of the reluctant Julie, and more a group endeavor involving a cross-section of the salon habitués. In this sense, too, it should be seen as part of the movement of *mondain* writers to affirm the legitimacy both of their status as *gens de lettres* and of the literary discourse they cultivated. The very organization of the "Guirlande" reflected this movement's cohesion but also its allowance for authorial expression: the collection hewed to a single theme, addressed to one person, while featuring individual poems signed by their authors. It resembled in this sense the several *recueils* that were so instrumental in introducing *mondain* writers to the reading public. In presenting this collection to Julie, and with her ritualistically receiving it, Montausier and his confreres not only demonstrated their literary and linguistic virtuosity, they also asserted their identities as *hommes de lettres*. While Montausier was not a published "author" like others, his role as instigator and impresario—from recruiting the participants, selecting and editing their contributions, and finding the best artisans, to producing the tome, selecting the paper, and collating the madrigals and illustrations[50]—shows him to be a "professional of letters," in the sense demonstrated by Nicolas Schapira in the case of Valentin Conrart. Like Conrart, who also never published anything, he made "literature" possible outside the traditional bastions—Church, university, law—of knowledge and letters.

The "Guirlande de Julie" allows us to see Montausier for what he was, a warrior nobleman who embodied two aspects of elite culture, arms and letters, the relationship between which was often problematic. But Montausier did not have to be coaxed into learning, like some others of his class; he pursued it with as much energy and discipline as he did the enemy on the battlefield. He was quite learned, even erudite, and might have even been subject to that most dreaded of insults,

---

[49] On the Guirlande, see Irène Frain, *"La Guirlande de Julie": Suivie d'un dictionnaire du langage des fleurs aux fins de chiffrer et déchiffrer vos tendres messages floraux* (Paris, 1991); and Lopez, *La plume et l'épée*, chap. 6.

[50] The "Guirlande" was a beautifully bound volume; handcrafted and luxuriously appointed, it was an *objet d'art* ceremonially presented to Julie. For the calligraphy, Montausier secured the services of Nicolas Jarry, who under Louis XIV was granted the title of *écrivain et noteur de la musique du roi*. To paint the flowers, he hired Nicolas Robert, who served Gaston d'Orléans as painter and engraver. "Le Gascon," a well-known craftsman, was responsible for the work's binding and cover, which was in red Moroccan leather with a frangipani scent. Stephanie Bung, "Une *Guirlande* pour Julie: Le manuscrit prestigieux face au 'salon' de la marquise de Rambouillet," *Papers on French Seventeenth-Century Literature*, 38/75 (2011), 349.

pedantry, for his Latin verses give off a whiff of the schools. He was the author of a large collection of neo-Latin epigrams, self-consciously modeled after the Roman poet Martial. Molière seized upon him as a model, if not of a pedant, then of an antisocial prig, for it appears that he based his character Alceste, the Misanthrope himself, on Montausier. Whether or not this is true or fair, the "Guirlande de Julie" was precisely the kind of literary, chivalric exercise that an eminently erudite man of letters, let alone a misanthrope, might have looked upon as a merely meretricious attempt to win the approval of semi-educated noblemen and ladies. What was this erudite warrior doing spending a good part of a decade thinking about the supposed virtues of flowers? Rereading his Lipsius, Montausier might have felt chastened by the Dutchman's comment on his countrymen's rage for them, which "they preserve and cherish more carefully than any mother doth her child.... These men will bee more grieved for the losse of a newe-found flower, than of an olde friende."[51] But the "Guirlande de Julie" had, in fact, rather elevated features: "The Neoplatonic love poems in the form of madrigals employed the contemplation of the beauty of flowers to honor the physical, or outer, beauty of Julie d'Angennes that was symbolic of her inner beauty."[52] Moreover, the flowers were rendered realistically and faithfully, exhibiting not only an exquisite tastefulness and attention to sheer beauty but also an awareness of recent botanical studies. It was worthy of a man for whom learning and erudition were paramount.[53]

Still, the "Guirlande" embodies something else, another set of values that contemporaries were beginning to express in terms of *galanterie*. Tallemant des Réaux called it "one of the most illustrious *galanteries* ever produced," while Pierre-Daniel Huet echoed this praise in similar terms: "Love has never created a *galanterie* more ingenious, more polished, more novel than the Guirlande de Julie."[54]

Today "gallant" is rather casually, even facetiously, ascribed to any man who manifests an obsequious care for a woman's well-being, especially in trivial circumstances. In the middle decades of the seventeenth century, it was emerging as a distinct personality type, a sort of successor to the *honnête homme*, who combined virtue with the desire to please women and an ability to mix easily and playfully in their company.[55] Alain Viala has offered an analysis of *galanterie* that

---

[51] Anne Goldgar, *Tulipmania: Money, Honor, and Knowledge in the Dutch Golden Age* (Chicago, 2008), 36–7.
[52] Hyde, *Cultivated Power*, 109.   [53] Hyde, *Cultivated Power*, 109–10.
[54] *Huetiana, ou, Pensées diverses de M. Huet, evesque d'Avranches* (Paris, 1722), 103.
[55] There is a burgeoning literature on *galanterie*: see Stanton, *Aristocrat as Art*, 28–9, 51–2, 137–8; Alain Viala, *La France galante: Essai historique sur une catégorie culturelle de ses origines jusqu'à la Révolution* (Paris, 2008); Viala, "Les Signes Galants: A Historical Reevaluation of *Galanterie*," *Yale French Studies*, no. 92 (1997), 11–29; and Noémi Hepp, "La galanterie," in Pierre Nora, ed., *Les lieux de mémoire*, 3 vols. (Paris, 1992), III, pt. 2: 745–83; Lewis C. Seifert, *Manning the Margins: Masculinity and Writing in Seventeenth-Century France* (Ann Arbor, MI, 2009), 86–7 and *passim*.

aspires to anatomize its complex, even contradictory meanings, highlighting the subtle distinctions at play in the mid-seventeenth century, especially when moralists and other writers filled volumes with ruminations on the ethical pitfalls of living in a courtly, aristocratic, but also fallen world. Domna Stanton has explained the artful, ritualized nature of *galanterie*, an "art of loving" that derived from an insider's knowledge of how to please with expressions of love and courtliness without the potentially unpleasing excesses of passion or spontaneous physical expressions of affection.[56] Like *honnêteté*, *galanterie* is an ascription that resists being pinned down; it is necessarily fluid and indistinct, containing an element of that "je ne sais quoi" that ran through so much of contemporary commentary regarding aristocratic ideals. Vaugelas resorts to this concept in defining "*Galant, galamment*": "composed of that je ne sais quoi, or that gracefulness, that something of the Court, that wit, judgment, civility, courtesy, and gaiety, all without effort, without affectation, without vice."[57] It is unclear where *honnêteté* ends and *galanterie* picks up: they are kindred concepts, with the latter emphasizing both playfulness and, most crucially, a playful, solicitous regard toward women. While, according to most scholarly accounts, *galanterie* would become more prominent as an ideal personality trait later in the century, Montausier's supremely gallant gesture clearly contributed to its early history. That this warrior and *érudit* embraced *galanterie* and was responsible for producing a ritualized object that defined it for his contemporaries is perhaps surprising only if we refuse to acknowledge that an aristocrat of his ilk—a true *honnête homme*—was expected to move effortlessly in many circles.

There is no way to know, of course, whether Montausier's personality proved as protean as the range of contexts—battlefield, cabinet, salon—in which he moved might suggest. The fact that he was reputed to be the model for Alceste, the Misanthrope himself, casts some doubt on this sort of virtuoso versatility.[58] But if he was not an accomplished shape-shifter, he certainly made a great effort to perform according to the appropriate code, a code that cannot be reduced to the behavioral ideals of "civility," "politeness," or other terms that are commonly deployed to explain the emerging values of seventeenth- and eighteenth-century elites. He was, rather, an aspiring artist, or at least an impresario with an artistic bent, striving to create something of beauty and meaning that would embody all the virtues he saw in his love object. The "Guirlande de Julie" was, then, much more than a very expensive, very long, ostentatious, and certainly creative mash note. Beyond Montausier's personal interests—and perhaps even his awareness—it also amounted to a ritual act that affirmed and represented this quintessentially aristocratic, refined, "artful" community itself.

---

[56] Stanton, *Aristocrat as Art*, 137. [57] Viala, *La France galante*, 33.
[58] Lopez, *La plume et l'épée*, 9.

Voiture and the Art of Pleasing

The poet most identified with the Rambouillet salon was undoubtedly Vincent Voiture. Voiture had other important associations that raised his profile in the Parisian world of letters: he was close to Gaston d'Orléans, serving as his secretary and boon companion for years; he was also a member of the first generation of the French Academy, although hardly the most dutiful participant in its sessions. He never deigned to have his works printed, but the posthumous publication of his letters precipitated a quarrel over their merits, causing many, ultimately even Balzac, to reevaluate his stature as a writer. While he eventually gained recognition as a literary figure, in the salon his role seemed to be that of entertainer and impresario—a kind of master of ceremonies who was responsible for many of the divertissements that animated the assembled. To be playful and familiar with the aristocratic habitués—this was, above all, his modus operandi. Commented Tallemant, "He took care to amuse the company at the hôtel de Rambouillet. He had always seen things that the others had not seen; so, as soon as he arrived, everyone gathered around to listen to him.... In gatherings at the hôtel de Rambouillet and the hôtel de Condé, Voiture always amused people, at times with his ballads, at times with some foolish thing that came to his mind."[59] At no time was Voiture's frankness more apparent, even alarming, than when he publicly commented on Anne of Austria's affair with the Duke of Buckingham. The affair was common knowledge within the Parisian *monde*, but for the poet to have made reference to it, and in front of the queen herself, seemed to redefine the limits of indiscretion. (It turns out, however, that she enjoyed his sally and rewarded him with a long private conversation.) In short, Voiture both exemplified and promoted an aspect of the salon's ethos that was most apparent in relationships between aristocrats and men of letters: a certain freedom and openness of expression that contrasts sharply with the hierarchical, constrained relationships one usually associates either with the court or with a "society of orders." At one point, according to Tallemant, he managed to bring two bears into the *hôtel*. One of his poems, apparently reflecting an episode during an outing, was entitled "To a Lady Whose Skirts Were Raised While Falling from a Carriage in the Country."[60] Though he was of common birth—his father was a prosperous wine merchant—his talents and panache conferred on him a kind of honorary nobility. A friend of the marquise supposedly declared one day: "Monsieur, you are much too *galant* to remain in the bourgeoisie."[61]

For all Voiture's somewhat frenetic activity as conspicuous bon vivant and merrymaker, he was essentially a literary man, who, though unpublished, wrote

---

[59] Craveri, *The Age of Conversation*, 47; Tallemant des Réaux, *Historiettes*, I: 489–91.
[60] Monsieur de Voiture, *Lettres (1625–1648)*, ed. Sophie Rollin (Paris, 2013), 46.
[61] Tallemant des Réaux, *Historiettes*, I: 485.

prolifically. It has been said that his conception of poetry represented a departure from Malherbe's so-called purist doctrine, which strove to establish rules and standards for poetic diction, emphasizing order, regularity, and precision. Tallemant even commented that Voiture "is the first to have introduced libertinage into poetry," adding that "before him no one ever wrote stanzas of unequal length, either verses or measures."[62] Pellisson confirms his reputation as a rebellious stylist who "did not deign to be constrained to observe" rules.[63] Above all, Voiture's verses seem self-consciously crafted to avoid ponderousness. He was responsible for popularizing several poetic genres; some, like the *rondeau*, were deliberate revivals of older forms associated with the Old French of Marot and others. After reading Ovid, he came up with the prose form of the *metamorphose galant*, devised to sing the praises of the ladies of the Rambouillet salon. He also revived the ballad, the *chanson royale*, and other poetic genres distinguished by their brevity and lightness. Voiture had a special affection for the Old French of the Middle Ages and penned several letters and prose pieces in it. In this, of course, he went against the prevailing view of medieval literary genres as asserted by such figures as Joachim du Bellay, who in his *Deffence et illustration de la langue francoyse* (1549) condemned "such groceries [*epiceries*] which corrupt the taste of our language and serve only to advertise our ignorance."[64] But his efforts did not stem solely from his appreciation for these bygone literary forms; they were also suited to his self-appointed role as entertainer and animator, for his literary inventions and innovations were appropriate for the light love verses, poetic jousting, and other diversions that made literature part of the everyday pastimes of the salon's habitués. "All contributed to a collective game that produced unlimited verses year after year, continually enriching them with variations along the way."[65] Perhaps more than anyone else in his time, Voiture was the master of the "art of pleasing."[66] Of course, those he aimed to please were the denizens of the salon and others among the Parisian monde. Writes Tallemant, "He soon became the joy of the society of these illustrious persons."[67] In Voiture we have the quintessential example of the man of letters who conceived his literary production with the tastes and pleasures of his aristocratic public always in mind.

---

[62] Tallemant des Réaux, *Historiettes*, I: 490.

[63] Paul Pellisson and Pierre-Joseph Thoulier d'Olivet, *Histoire de l'Académie françoise, par Pellisson et d'Olivet*, 3rd ed., revised and enlarged, 2 vols. (Paris, 1743), I: 276.

[64] Quoted by Génetiot, *Poétique du loisir mondain*, 78.

[65] Craveri, *The Age of Conversation*, 51.

[66] On this paragraph see Y. Fukui, *Raffinement précieux dans la poésie française du XVIIe siècle* (Paris, 1964), 186ff.; Génetiot, *Poétique du loisir mondain*, 53, 62–3, 78–9; *DLF*, 1068. See Adam, *Histoire de la littérature française*, I: 266. See the testimony of Chapelain on the introduction of *enigmas* at the expense of *rondeaux*, and the triumph of abbé Cotin over Voiture in this respect: *Lettres de Chapelain*, I: 198.

[67] Tallemant des Réaux, *Historiettes*, I: 485.

One of his more spectacular pranks was not fundamentally literary but managed to combine a remarkable demonstration of *galanterie* with a message that was somewhat political in nature, or at least one that brought, once again, the realities of war home to the salon. This returns us to Julie's "crush" on Gustavus Adolphus. In 1632, Voiture capitalized on the public airing of her affections with a theatrical practical joke that must have taken all the resources he could marshal. One day the members of the salon were astonished to see a carriage pull up to the *hôtel*, from which descended several men in what was taken to be Swedish dress. Other costumed gentlemen bore a portrait of Gustavus Adolphus. With a flourish, a letter was presented to Julie, supposedly written by her beloved hero, but penned, of course, by Voiture, or so the assembled soon realized. It read, in part:

"Mademoiselle,
Here is the Lion of the North, the conqueror whose name has sounded throughout the world, who comes to place trophies from Germany at your feet and who, having defeated Tilly and crushed the power of Spain and the forces of the Empire, comes to join our ranks. Among the cries of joy and songs of victory that I have been hearing for many days, I have heard nothing so agreeable as the news that you wish me well, and since hearing it, I have changed my plans and limited my ambition, which embraced the whole earth, to you alone.... I would say more, Mademoiselle, but I am at this moment about to fight the imperial army and six days later to take Nuremburg. I am, Mademoiselle, your most passionate servant."
Gustav Adolphe[68]

Given the panache of this prank, it may have been that Montausier was inspired to set plans for the "Guirlande de Julie" in motion in part as a riposte to Voiture's *coup de théâtre*, especially as the two were rivals. In any case, his prank converged with Montausier's project in bringing the salon's celebration of the victories of Gustavus Adolphus to the public's attention.

Voiture himself was responsible for another of those moments. He was probably the least political of men of letters; the quintessential house poet, he happily continued to amuse the great as long as he remained comfortable and wanted in their midst. But he did make one notable intervention of a political nature, and here we can observe that his penchant for frankness allowed for the expression of sentiments that were common though rarely aired. Opposition to France's alliance with Protestant powers, grumbling about Richelieu's arrogation of so much power into his own hands, distress over the cost of war on the home front, and the likely prolongation of France's participation in the general European conflict—these objections were routinely the stuff of published tracts, usually from abroad, and

---

[68] Voiture to Mlle de Rambouillet, in *Oeuvres de Voiture*, I: 73–5; Craveri, *The Age of Conversation*, 57.

private conversations alike. Voiture was never suspected of harboring or expressing these sentiments, though his patron Gaston d'Orléans of course did. And undoubtedly they were common, though certainly not rampant, in the Rambouillet milieu. Interestingly, Voiture managed to acknowledge these sentiments precisely while endorsing Richelieu's war policy, in what was the only public political commentary of his life.

In the aftermath of the decisive victory at Corbie, when French troops retook this important fortress from the Spanish in November 1636, Voiture wrote an open letter addressed to an unnamed friend, an obvious critic of France's foreign policy. It is clear from the text of the letter itself that Voiture's interlocutor is French, and the tone of the text suggests a close relationship. In the letter Voiture celebrates the victory of France's armies, and mocks those who had belittled them as being composed of "our coachmen and our lackeys."[69] He calls to mind the cruelty of the Spanish forces, who "kill our peasants and burn our villages," but who prove themselves cowards when confronted with the resolve of a united and powerful France. Addressing his friend, he is sure that "even if this event will not make you become a *bon français*, at least it will make you angry at the Spanish."[70] The letter contains several expressions of patriotism. He writes, à propos of Richelieu: "If they have even a drop of French blood in their veins, some love for the glory of their country, can they read about his accomplishments without some heightened respect for him?"[71] And much of the text is devoted to Richelieu. "During these storms, has he not always held the rudder in one hand, the compass in the other?"[72] Like a dutiful subject, and like someone familiar with the strictures of *raison d'état*, he acknowledges the limits of his own knowledge, obsequiously deferring to the masters of state: "As for me...I have ceased judging. I realize that those who preside in the consuls have seen the same things I have seen and have seen other things I have not."[73]

Despite the fact that his letter is dripping with praise of Richelieu, Voiture attempts to make his case more convincing by emphasizing his abhorrence of exaggeration in the service of flattery. He clearly wants to preserve his reputation for frankness. And this leads to perhaps the most interesting feature of the text. In extolling Richelieu, Voiture also acknowledges those forces and sentiments arrayed against him; and if he does not endow them with any legitimacy—which he decidedly does not—he nevertheless reveals, even lingers over, the elements of opposition to the cardinal-minister. He takes these seriously; after all, they constitute the position of his friend, a Frenchman, and not some foreigner or paid hack. For example, in the construction of one argument, he acknowledges that there are those who despise Richelieu but begs that this sentiment be put aside for the good

---

[69] *Oeuvres de Voiture*, I: 267–8. [70] *Oeuvres de Voiture*, I: 270.
[71] *Oeuvres de Voiture*, I: 273. [72] *Oeuvres de Voiture*, I: 276.
[73] *Oeuvres de Voiture*, I: 271.

of France.[74] In another passage, he admits that Richelieu has not always succeeded, although, he adds, only in those things he has undertaken in conjunction with others. He admonishes his friend to "leave your party before it leaves you," the word "party" signifying the recognized opposition camp known as the *dévots*.[75] Finally, at the end of his open letter, Voiture speculates about what Richelieu will do after he has been victorious on the battlefield. And here the poet gives voice to the widespread view of those who suspected that the cardinal-minister's political goals could not be accomplished by a limited European campaign, who feared a protracted war and its deleterious effect on French society, but who hoped otherwise. Voiture confidently predicts that Richelieu will quickly end this war and then immediately "turn his designs to rendering his state the most bountiful of all." He asserts that the cardinal-minister realizes that "the most noble and most assured conquests are those of the heart and the affections." Like everyone, he knows that "laurels are infertile plants; better are the harvests and fruits of peace." He will lower the *taille* and return the land to its former richness and abundance. "He will make no more edicts except to control luxury and reestablish commerce."[76]

All of these, of course, were mere wishes harbored precisely by those who doubted their realization. And they were right: Richelieu's resolve was to pursue the war in Europe until it was safe from Habsburg domination, which meant a protracted struggle on all fronts. It was this resolve, inherited by his successor Mazarin, that disappointed those who expected an end to the campaign with the Peace of Westphalia in 1648. Voiture's letter of 1636 was not an expression of support from him alone.[77] A political commentary by a poet whose reputation was synonymous with the Rambouillet salon, it was seen as coming from this important milieu, representing its backing for Richelieu's foreign policy at a decisive moment, just a year after France formally entered the Thirty Years' War. But it also betrayed the doubts and fears harbored by many, including those associated with the salon, concerning the nature of France's commitment to war under Richelieu's leadership. In a sense, his open letter was the Rambouillet milieu speaking discreetly but publicly on political matters.

Antoine Godeau: A Malherbian Uses the Salon as His Support Group

Montausier was not Voiture's only rival for Julie's attentions: around 1632 another man of letters entered the orbit of the Rambouillet *hôtel*, threatening Voiture's privileged status for several years until he left Paris to take up a position as Bishop

---

[74] *Oeuvres de Voiture*, I: 270.   [75] *Oeuvres de Voiture*, I: 277–8.
[76] *Oeuvres de Voiture*, I: 278.
[77] He was rewarded with an office from Richelieu in 1637, *controleur des gages des officiers du présidial de Beauvais*, which was likely in recognition of his open letter. Voiture, *Lettres (1625–1648)*, 33.

of Grasse in far-off Provence. Like Voiture, Antoine Godeau cut a flamboyant figure in the ranks of the salon, combining a talent for the rapid-fire production of poetry with a refined sense of *galanterie* that was a crucial advantage in this competitive milieu. And like his rival, he was diminutive in stature, which was often—sometime cruelly—noted: "He is extraordinarily short and extraordinarily ugly," observed Tallemant.[78] But Godeau surpassed even Voiture in the breadth of his contacts and the range of his literary activities. His cousin was Valentin Conrart, who became secretary of the French Academy and was at the center of the new literary culture. As with Conrart, his early associates were the poets of the Illustres bergers. He published seven letters in Faret's *Recueil* of 1627, was a *créature* of both La Valette and Richelieu, corresponded frequently with Chapelain, and championed Malherbe with his 1630 *Discours sur les oeuvres de Mr de Malherbe*.[79] He even maintained cordial relations with intimates of the Dupuy cabinet. In 1633 he dedicated his *Oeuvres chrestiennes* to Richelieu, a work that signaled his embrace of the priesthood and his transformation from *galant* to *dévot*. He left Paris for his bishopric in Grasse in 1637 but managed an intense relationship with the salon even in his "exile."

It is likely that Godeau's cousin Conrart greased his path into the salon sometime around 1632. It was his *Discours sur les oeuvres de Mr de Malherbe*, however, that marked his true literary debut and announced his allegiance to the master "purist" as well. While clearly aimed at a *mondain* readership, it had been vetted by the new *doctes*—the men of letters, the vanguard of this literary movement— for Godeau had read it to the members of Conrart's circle in 1629. But, as Camille Venner argues in her analysis of the *Discourse*, Godeau offers a respectful if not quite fulsome rendition of Malherbe's views while appealing to the tastes and expectations of the men and women who comprised the Parisian *monde*, especially that of the salon.[80] Reading Malherbe, he fashions a notion of *le bon goût* as the ideal standard for literary French: "the most excellent poet knows the art of benefiting [*profiter*] and pleasing together both the learned [*doctes*] who have refined their minds from study, and those others equipped with only the light of their own natural judgment."[81] Malherbe is the model of this ideal, but in his *Discourse* Godeau expands upon the deceased poet's rather inchoate "doctrine" in a way that, three years after his death, might be seen as representing "Malherbianism" beyond Malherbe. And all the while he remains attentive to the interests and tastes of the salon. Indeed, the text might be seen as his passport to the Rambouillet milieu.

---

[78] Tallemant des Réaux, *Historiettes*, I: 550.

[79] In Antoine Godeau, *Oeuvres chrestiennes et morales en prose*, 2 vols. (Paris, 1658), II: 235–62.

[80] Camille Venner, "Les *Discours sur les oeuvres de Mr de Malherbe*, par Antoine Godeau: Creuset d'une définition du 'bon goût' classique?," *XVIIe siècle*, 3/260 (2013), 537–49.

[81] Godeau, *Discours sur les oeuvres de Mr de Malherbe* (1630), in *Oeuvres de Malherbe*, ed. Ludovic Lalanne (Paris, 1862), I: 365–85, on 376. For a thorough analysis of the place of taste (*goût*) in the seventeenth century, see Michael Moriarty, *Taste and Ideology in Seventeenth-Century France* (Cambridge, 1988), especially chap. 2.

There are several features of Godeau's brief that suggest a self-conscious attentiveness to this *mondain* readership. For one thing, he takes care to frame his praise of Malherbe in terms that would appeal to those who saw themselves as part of a discerning elite. Thus, he begins his *Discourse* with an energetic defense of his master, suggesting a beleaguered and maligned figure. Still, he writes, "all those ears that are not barbaric are charmed by the sweetness of his verses." As well, throughout the text he ultimately appeals to the ineffable standard of the "*je ne sais quoi*" as the touchstone of eloquent French, explicitly disavowing any recourse to doctrinal criteria. Commenting on Malherbe's letters, he hesitates to delve deeply into reasons for their appeal, "for this would require a separate discourse and a complete understanding of the secrets of rhetoric, about which I must confess my ignorance."[82] Throughout, he gestures toward the mysterious, hidden, and (again) ineffable nature of "*bon goût*," a style whose "artifice" remains "entirely hidden."[83] And refusing any hint of pedantry, he underscores Malherbe's distance from the ancients: "He loved the Greeks and the Romans, but he never was an idolater."[84]

Finally, Godeau enlarges upon a panegyric for Malherbe—and makes clear that his *Discourse* goes beyond an interest in poetry—in asserting the crucial relationship between proper eloquence and a "well-ordered republic." For just as magistrates are distinguished by clothing that others are not permitted to wear, "so in the state of Eloquence in order to prevent confusion, all subjects should not be ornamented the same way [*toutes les matières ne doivent pas paroître sous des ornements de pareil éclat*]."[85] Readers of his *Discourse* could be assured that their embrace of "good taste" in language was commensurate with a comforting image of a well-ordered society, with, of course, themselves as the worthy elite.

* * *

When Godeau left Paris for his bishopric in Provence, this did not mean estrangement from the Parisian salon—quite the contrary. Even in what he called his "exile," Chapelain kept him abreast of its activities. More than this, the Rambouillet milieu served as his base of support and source of advice as he negotiated some tricky business, for there were two occasions in particular that demanded deft maneuvering on his part as well as some pressure on his behalf from his Parisian friends.

In both cases, Godeau relied upon his correspondence with Chapelain, using him as a sounding board and confidant. As Sophie Fournier-Plamondon shows in her recent *thèse* on Godeau,[86] it is clear that Chapelain serves as a conduit for the

---

[82] Godeau, *Discours*, 371–2.   [83] *Discours*, 374.   [84] *Discours*, 383.
[85] *Discours*, 373.
[86] Anne-Sophie Fournier-Plamondon, "Pratiques d'écriture et exercice du pouvoir: Du centre aux marges. Localiser Antoine Godeau (1605–1672)" (thèse de doctorat, Université Laval, 2016).

collective views of the Rambouillet milieu. He repeatedly refers to discussions "among your friends in common," that is, with Arnauld, Conrart, and the intendant of the Hôtel de Rambouillet, as well as the Duchesse d'Aiguillon, an intimate of the salon, concerning Godeau's best course of action. In one case, Chapelain was able to secure information that apparently eluded Godeau, and which ultimately provided him useful leverage in his dealings. Still, Chapelain's letters show him having to coax the far-off bishop toward the desired solution, with indications that, speaking for Godeau's "friends," there was concern in Paris that he might not take the right path. The Rambouillet milieu thus served Godeau as a source of information and advice as well as a venue for some crucial negotiations. The "network" of the salon was mobilized on his behalf.[87]

Evidence of this network at work surfaces in the context of Godeau's dealings with the provincial estates of Provence in 1639, where resistance to the crown's new fiscal demands seemed intractable.[88] Godeau was Richelieu's man, and there was no doubt that he could be counted on to serve as an advocate for the royal position, despite his titular position as leader of the First Estate. Chapelain's letters are again the source (Godeau's have not survived). And here again, the bishop relied upon his Parisian friends to stiffen his backbone. In one letter, Chapelain rehearses the choice for the estates between "submission" and "liberty," leaving no doubt that the former was the only reasonable course. And he expresses both outrage and surprise that Godeau's support of the crown's demands was rejected by "Messieurs les Provenciaux"—surely a matter of some feigning on Chapelain's part, especially as he also blithely expresses the stereotypical view that these provincials are simply lacking in "judgment." In another letter, Chapelain reports having vetted Godeau's "harangue" to the estates presenting the case for the crown. If Godeau was not necessarily fishing for approval, this is nevertheless what he got, along with Chapelain's confirmation that the network of his Parisian friends, based in the Rambouillet salon, stood behind him. "We have seen," Chapelain writes, "the summary of your harangue, and all of us have approved and praised it," adding that his friends were pleasantly surprised by his ability to orate in secular as well as sacred matters.[89]

As with others, Godeau's admission to the Rambouillet *hôtel* served to confirm his status as a man of letters; and the relationships he formed in this privileged milieu were surely crucial in his promotion to the Church hierarchy. But this office, which he undoubtedly coveted, meant his exile from Paris and his friends in the salon, something sounded often in his letters. Indeed, the way Godeau played upon this trope is another expression of "retreat," only here it is adopted as

---

[87] On this episode, which involved a conflict between Godeau and the former Bishop of Grasse over the authority of the city of Antibes, see Fournier-Plamondon, "Pratiques d'écriture," 295–303.

[88] Fournier-Plamondon, "Pratiques d'écriture," chap. 7.

[89] Fournier-Plamondon, "Pratiques d'écriture," 388.

an element of his new identity: he is not only a man of letters-cum-*dévot*, but a Parisian insider now thrust among faraway provincials "*sans jugement.*" His affection and allegiance were divided, as expressed in these lines: "I leave you, pleasant abode / for a stay in the wilds where my duty calls me. / Paris has my respect and Grasse my love."[90] Like Balzac and the Jansenist Arnauld, both of whose self-exile has been called a "noisy solitude," Godeau used the Rambouillet salon to buttress his position as Bishop of Grasse, noisily asserting his association with the help of Chapelain and the salon.[91]

Balzac, Rambouillet, and Rome

Guez de Balzac, the most important prose writer of his generation, maintained a geographically distant though still constant relationship with the Rambouillet salon throughout his career. After the publication of *Le Prince* in 1630 failed to secure him Richelieu's favor in the form of a high ecclesiastical or governmental position, he retired to his ancestral home in Charente, where, except for one or two visits to Paris, he remained for the rest of his life, growing more disillusioned, even bitter, about the cardinal's rule, France, his century, and virtually everything else. Although he apparently never entered the precincts of the salon, he was a still a force in its life.[92] Chapelain read his letters and other writings aloud at the gatherings, and, as we have noted, his commentary on quarrels and literature was considered definitive. The Rambouillet salon was his first and most important public: in securing the attention and approval of Mme de Rambouillet and her guests, he reached the people in Paris who truly mattered.

A sense of retirement infuses his later writings, as if his physical retreat was something of a living metaphor for his general outlook. This is evident in the four "Dissertations politiques" addressed to Mme de Rambouillet, published in 1644 but written several years earlier.[93] These were styled as conversations between the writer and the *salonnière*, although the latter has no voice in the text. (He does repeatedly address her directly with "Madame," however, thus dramatizing her role as his interlocutor.) Balzac's esteem for her is evident throughout: she serves as an implicit foil for the corruption and decline of contemporary France; as a descendent of Roman aristocracy, she embodies those bygone virtues that characterized

---

[90] Cited in Pascal A. Jannini, "A. Godeau et G. Colletet: De l'avant garde des Illustres bergers à l'Académie," in Yves Géraud, ed., *Antoine Godeau (1605–1672): De la galanterie à la sainteté* (Paris, 1975), 78.

[91] Rémi Mathis, "'Une trop bruyante solitude': Robert Arnaud d'Andilly, solitaire de Port Royal, et le pouvoir royal (1643–1674)," *Papers on French Seventeenth Century Literature*, 37/73 (2010), 337–52.

[92] Tallemant des Réaux, *Historiettes*, II: 47.

[93] Jean-Louis Guez de Balzac, *Oeuvres diverses (1644)*, ed. Roger Zuber (Paris, 1995). All page numbers in the notes refer to this edition.

the Romans in the days of the late Republic and early Empire. "Your ancestors were heroes," he writes; later he adds, touching upon the theme of the *Discourse*, "La conversation des romains," "even in the smallest of things."[94] The greatness of Rome, especially the reign of Augustus, is a theme running throughout the texts. But his admiration is tempered by an even more pronounced wistfulness that the glories of Rome belong only to the past, that even for Romans their greatness was fleeting, and that, finally, historical circumstances have rendered Rome's example virtually irrelevant to contemporary Frenchmen and women, except as a lesson in irretrievable virtues. In addressing himself to Mme de Rambouillet, he was exploiting her reputation as a means of evoking a willing and agreeable audience for his often severe, even tragic, commentary, thus legitimizing his whole enterprise.

Balzac's admiration for Augustus allows him to deliver a remarkable commentary on his own times disguised as a panegyric for the reign of this "Caesar." In just a few pages he offers a crisp analysis of the particular circumstances created by the pacification of Rome after the civil wars, pages that could only have been read as referring to France's own passage from civil conflict to domestic peace in the late sixteenth and early seventeenth century. This analysis crystallizes what might be considered the "absolutist pact" as articulated by commentators from Tacitus to Reinhart Koselleck. Balzac's version celebrates the benefits of peace that come with the sacrifice of liberty, despite his acknowledgment that loss is as much a part of the equation as gain. The third discourse, "Maecenas," begins with a description of Augustus's reign, during which, he writes, "the Romans began to learn the design of Providence," as if their history heretofore, which is to say the experience of the Republic, was merely a passage to a greater glory that was the Empire. He refers to "the fatal illness of their old Republic." From their tumultuous recent past, the Romans learned that "they prefer a steady Master and a peaceful Servitude to the constant changes and perpetual fear of Civil War." Balzac's apology for the ethos of *otium* is here not only linked to the historical circumstances of a post-bellum culture but also framed in terms of a loss of "liberty," meaning access to the political realm, which had been, of course, fundamental to the Republic. "Repose, which they believed to be an essential good, took the place of liberty, which now seemed only a pleasant fantasy," he writes. "After such disturbances, everyone was happy to embrace leisure, the comfort of which penetrated their souls so agreeably that they would have nothing of their previous condition.... They were finished with intrigues and factions, now recognizing as a benefactor he who had removed from them the burden of self-governance, blessing the usurpation that had rescued them from their bad conduct."[95] It is difficult to read these lines in the light of modern history, and especially the oft-evoked warnings of "an

---

[94] "Le romain," in *Oeuvres diverses (1644)*, 57; "La conversation des romaines," in *Oeuvres diverses (1644)*, 85.

[95] *Oeuvres diverses (1644)*, 138.

escape from freedom," without concluding that Balzac was indulging in a bit of covert criticism of the "absolutist pact." But while Balzac was certainly capable of irony—and while he did in fact harbor growing misgivings about Richelieu's rule—there is no reason to believe that he was less than sincere in celebrating this version of the absolute settlement. Quite the contrary: as he reveals in *Le Prince* (see Chapter 7), he passionately believed in the rightness of royal supremacy; it was not only a historical necessity, given the fractiousness that its absence virtually guaranteed, but something dictated by human nature, which Balzac, like many of his contemporaries under the sway of Augustinianism, understood as innately disposed to waywardness.

Earlier, Balzac had harbored political ambitions; as demonstrated in his *Lettres*, he relished his privileged position as counselor to the "great," and it is likely that he aspired to something greater, perhaps even at a ministerial level or as a prelate of the Church. By the time he wrote these "Discourses," however, these ambitions had long since waned. Embittered and disappointed, he was more inclined to meditate on the virtues of a life of *otium cum dignitate* than to make a show of engaging with the affairs of the world. This he does in the second discourse addressed to the marquise, "La conversation des romains," the one among the four that most directly appeals to the values of the salon. Having in the first discourse provided an idealized portrait of the Roman hero, the military leader possessed of a charismatic power that requires barely a word for him to command legions, he next turns to a very different sphere of Roman life, imagining a Rome more proximate and accessible to his contemporaries. His discussion is prompted by Mme de Rambouillet's curiosity: "You would like, Madame, for me to show you the Romans when we normally cannot see them, to open the door of their cabinets. After having seen them in ceremony, you would like to see them conversing; and to know from me if that greatness, so justified and so elevated, could adapt itself to ordinary life, could be brought from great affairs and concerns down to games and diversions."[96]

That he puts such a question in the mouth of the leading *salonnière* suggests an affinity between Balzac's own valuation of private life and the salon's embodiment of "ordinary life" at its most cultivated. She "asks" him to "open the door of their cabinets," and to show them "conversing"—a request that readers surely recognized as a desire to see her own milieu in a distant mirror. Balzac's answer comprises a justification of civil society and of the pastimes, the entertainments, even the sensual delights that make up life away from the realm of politics. "The Senate, the campaign, civil affairs, and military actions have their seasons; conversation, the theater, poetry have theirs." Princes need respite from their travails, relief from the burdens of office. "Sometimes they must be men."[97] And in the privacy of

---

[96] *Oeuvres diverses (1644)*, 75.   [97] *Oeuvres diverses (1644)*, 75, 78.

their cabinets, away from the pressing demands of the court: this is when they should have the wise and diverting conversation with their muses. A better description of the salon as a retreat for harried aristocrats and weary warriors could hardly be imagined.

Trained in his youth by the Jesuits, Balzac hewed to the example of Rome, both ancient and modern; he idealized Roman greatness, whether that of Augustus or the Barberini.[98] Rome's martial and political accomplishments were glorious; and these we know from the copious sources that have survived. The way they enjoyed themselves at leisure—those "sweet" diversions, pastimes, games, "frank" conversations, and other "chaste and innocent" pleasures (*voluptes*)—these we can only imagine. And this is what Balzac offers in "La conversation des romains": a fully imagined version of Roman life beyond the battlefield and Senate, a fiction of the Romans "at home" in the time of Augustus. Here is where he elaborates on his own version of *honnêteté*—the "urbanity" discussed in Chapter 2—using the marquise as his foil and reference.

What perhaps is most telling in his own version of this ethos is how he relates it specifically to the realm of ordinary life, as a marker of the passage from public to private. "We cannot doubt that, when among themselves, they were capable of negligent graces and artless ornament, which our doctors do not know and which rise above rules and precepts," he writes. "I don't doubt that, after having seen them thunder and overturn heaven and earth on the tribune, it was quite a relief to consider them under a more human aspect. Once they had removed their enthymemes and their rhetorical figures, their feigned exclamations and their artificial ires, they appeared in what we may assume was their true self." Balzac concludes on a remarkable note: "It was then, Madame, that Cicero was no longer a sophist nor a rhetorician; neither extolling this, nor furious against that; neither of one party nor of the other. *He was then the true Cicero, and he mocked in private what he had adored on the public forum.*"[99]

For Balzac, the salon was a milieu where a select group of contemporaries could be, like their Roman forebears, the ancestors of Mme de Rambouillet, "among themselves." But what did this imply? If his description of the nature of Roman domesticity and retreat is any guide, it was hardly to be celebrated in unambiguous terms. For one thing, Balzac rarely lets us forget that the realm of repose and conversation exists at a remove from another world, a world that, while perhaps burdened by bombast and falsehood and inimical to expressions of authentic selfhood, is still the only world where true glory can be achieved. Second, as his commentary on Cicero implies, there is a degree of duplicity in this place of

---

[98] Roger Zuber, "Preface," in *Oeuvres diverses (1644)*, 22.
[99] "La conversation des romains," 83. I have used the translation of Elena Russo, *Styles of Enlightenment: Taste, Politics, and Authorship in Eighteenth-Century France* (Baltimore, 2007), 19; the emphasis is mine.

refinement and urbanity. How else to understand his assertion that the Roman orator "mocked in private what he had adored on the public forum"? Balzac echoes a trope found in such writers as Montaigne, Charron, and their acolytes, who acknowledged, not without some misgivings, that their age required a two-faced attitude toward being in their complex world—one shown to the public, the other reserved for the private realm of friends and intimates. Indeed, as presented by Balzac, Cicero is an *esprit fort*, the strong-minded individual who, while outwardly conforming to conventional beliefs and standards of behavior, inwardly and privately is a very different man. According to Balzac, he would be perfectly "at home" at the Hôtel de Rambouillet.

To what extent did Balzac mean to address not only the marquise, but her salon as well? In these passages, at least, the reference seems clear. He was not always scrupulous in paying court to the Rambouillet milieu; on at least one occasion, Chapelain had to prod him to send his letters to the *hôtel* on rue Saint-Thomas-du-Louvre. He was not a man to attend to social niceties and found it quite hard to pander for favors. He probably had very little personal regard for most of the salon's habitués and certainly harbored few illusions concerning their capacity for virtue, political or other. But he surely realized that a series of conversations addressed to the marquise would implicate her salon, at least in most readers' minds. After all, Mme de Rambouillet had no other reputation apart from the *hôtel* she so deftly hosted: to say one was to say the other. In an age when, under the aegis of Richelieu, the so-called absolutist state was taking shape, Balzac was engaged in the heroic task of trying to reintroduce notions of virtue, self-sacrifice, and patriotism into the language of contemporary politics. One can only guess whether, in his mind, the salon was crucial in the fashioning of this language. In any case, his *Dissertations politiques* serve to undermine the image of an entirely apolitical, frivolous community, suggesting that it was more receptive to high-minded political matters than we commonly assume.

* * *

While I have framed the salon as a space of *otium*, it hardly qualifies as a diminutive hideaway. In size, prestige, and visibility it was as "public" as any institution—a veritable court outside the court, assembling the cream of the Parisian elite and the leading lights of the new literary culture in a venue that served as a model for aristocratic refinement for generations to come. Its status as a place apart, a refuge for refined leisure or "dignified retreat," is justified rather by its distinction from official institutions such as the Louvre, the Sorbonne, the Church, and the magistracy, which traditionally channeled the nation's cultural and intellectual energies. Like the many other informal associations in the city, from private academies and cabinets to the entourages of great noblemen or the friends of a charismatic writer, the Rambouillet salon contributed to a varied Parisian *monde* that redefined elite culture. It may be an optical illusion created by the testimony of writers, which is all we have to rely on, but their presence meant that language and literature—a robust and refined vernacular and the emerging literary culture—seemed to dominate the salon's agenda of concerns.

Several features set the Rambouillet circle apart from other contemporary Parisian groups. Literary matters were not only a passing fancy but fundamental to its life; the salon itself served as a staging ground for performances and quarrels, drawing its habitués into the very heart of the emerging literary culture. It thus participated in the movement to foster a truly national language and literature. It also clearly functioned, literally, as a refuge for warrior noblemen home from the front, providing an asylum of sorts where they could rehabilitate the *galant* half of their personalities. For writers and, more significantly, for wannabe writers, the salon was both a proving ground for their capacity to shine and demonstrate their virtuosity and a meeting place where they could engage with potential aristocratic supporters. It was, in short, the premier public for *mondain* writers. And, of course, it was unique in fostering relationships between the sexes, where women were prominent, and where the likes of the marquise and her daughter Julie could attain heights of renown and influence unknown elsewhere for those of their gender.

As a meeting place for *gens de lettres* and Paris's cultivated elite, it is unlikely that conversation in the salon did not take a political turn from time to time. After all, we know that at least at one point Richelieu attempted to introduce a spy into its midst. And well he might have, with such once and future conspirators—Gaston, Condé, Epernon—among its frequenters.[100] In literary matters, the salon did not always toe the line: it hosted the staging of a play by Théophile just after his release from prison, and sentiment at the *hôtel* apparently ran in favor of Corneille's *Le Cid*. But this hardly suggests that the salon was anything but generally conformist in its outlook. And how could it have been otherwise, with such stalwart habitués so closely linked to Richelieu as Chapelain and the cardinal's niece, the Duchesse d'Aiguillon? Just as other institutions, such as the Académie française (or the Royal Society in London), imposed formal restrictions on what topics could be broached among their members, so the Rambouillet salon operated under a tacit understanding that *bienséance*, discretion, even a degree of self-censorship similarly restricted the limits of conversation. This is why the few shreds of evidence suggesting political views are so interesting. In turning now to the Dupuy cabinet, in many ways the polar opposite of the Rambouillet salon, we shall see that such views, while also handled with circumspection, are more in evidence.

---

[100] See Richard Bonney, *Political Change in France under Richelieu and Mazarin, 1624–1661* (New York, 1978), on these and others.

6
The Dupuy Cabinet
"An Innocent Refuge"

THE PRECISE DATE of the founding of the Dupuy cabinet is unclear. Peiresc writes about visiting the library in 1616–7; by the early 1620s, it was certainly well-established as a flourishing haven of intellectual activity and learned sociability, at precisely the same time its cross-town rival, the Rambouillet salon, was attracting a very different crowd of acolytes. The cabinet's origins are indisputable, however. When he died in 1617, the famous historian, magistrate, and *politique* Jacques-Auguste de Thou bequeathed his extensive library to his nephews, Pierre and Jacques Dupuy, who transformed its well-provided inventory of books and manuscripts into a center of scholarship and fellowship. Soon their *hôtel* on rue du Poictevins was the premier arena of French erudite life and one of the headquarters of the emerging Republic of Letters. Later, in 1645, when Pierre became the king's librarian, the brothers transferred their quarters to the rue de la Harpe. In the course of its over thirty-year history, virtually every scholar of note in Europe made a pilgrimage to the Académie putéane, as it was called, and those few who could not, cultivated their contacts with the Dupuys through sustained correspondence—reminding us of the crucial role of letter-writing in this age of print in constituting the Republic of Letters. The Dupuy cabinet functioned something like a research center, especially in matters relating to Gallicanism, serving as a clearinghouse for ideas, opinions, and discoveries; the library contained over ten thousand books and over a thousand manuscripts.[1] Along with the Bodleian and the Vatican collections, it was one of the great European libraries of the day.[2]

Like the salon, the Dupuy cabinet provided a refuge for kindred spirits, for the savants, men of letters, magistrates, diplomats, visiting dignitaries, and others who shared the intellectual tastes and values of the Adelphes, as the brothers were sometimes called. And men it was, for the cabinet, unlike the salon and other

---

[1] Isaac Uri, *Un cercle savant au XVIIe siècle: François Guyet, 1575–1655, d'après les documents inédits* (Paris, 1886), 103.
[2] There is a large literature on the Dupuy cabinet, but no work that is definitive. René Pintard, *Le libertinage érudit dans la première moitié du XVIIe siècle* (Paris, 1943), is still fundamental—an exhaustive source for the whole period. More recent is the deeply researched thesis by Jérôme Delatour, "Les frères Dupuy (1582–1656)," 3 vols. (Ecole des Chartes, 1996). See also Antoine Coron, "'Ut prosint aliis': Jacques-Auguste de Thou et sa bibliothèque," in Claude Jolly, ed., *Histoire des bibliothèques bibliothèques françaises*, vol. 2: *Les bibliothèques sous l'Ancien Régime, 1530–1789* (Paris, 1988), 101–25.

venues of literary sociability, maintained a distinctly masculine, if not necessarily anti-female, tone. Even Marie de Gournay, La Mothe le Vayer's erudite friend and patron, who had only scorn for the *mondain* literary culture of the salon, never was welcomed in their midst.[3] There was a cachet to being accepted into its precincts, as well as great pressure to prove equal to the intellectual and personal standards maintained by the Dupuys. Some failed the test or proved unable to trim their eccentricities or boorishness and were discreetly banished or never admitted in the first place. Pierre de Montmaur, for example, a professor of Greek at the Collège Royale, who had a reputation as a parasite and a pedant, was refused entry despite his excellent credentials.[4] And there were others, like the young savant Jean-Jacques Bouchard, who, despite his considerable learning and contacts, was ultimately banished from the select company because of his naked ambition and suspect morals. But those who managed to gain entrance were rewarded with the public distinction of membership in the most erudite and distinguished society in all of Europe. Like the Rambouillet salon, the cabinet served to fashion a certain elite.

We can situate the Dupuy group in several overlapping intellectual and cultural contexts—although each one must be qualified. Perhaps first among these is humanism; it was one of the last refuges of erudition, with a deep respect for ancient languages, texts, and history, that marked Renaissance learning, and which was waning in the face of contemporary trends, especially science, anti-Aristotelian thought, and the cult of the moderns. To a large extent, then, the linguistic culture of the Dupuys' circle was Latinate in an age when, as we have seen, vernacular literature and modern languages were gaining primacy. Some of their most notable works, however, were in French, a concession to the modern vogue, and an indication that, despite their intellectual elitism, they aspired to reach a wider readership beyond the Latin-reading public.[5] Many historians also place them at the center of the emerging Republic of Letters, the European-wide community of scholars and other *gens de lettres* that encouraged comity and exchange across linguistic and confessional barriers. But alongside this international context was a more local one, without which the cabinet simply could not have functioned. Though its habitués came from many different sectors, the Dupuys were especially close to the Parisian milieu of the Parlement. The de Thous were a dynasty of *robins*, and Pierre Dupuy was himself a magistrate. Such prominent magistrates as Jérôme Bignon and Mathieu Molé were frequent visitors to the library, which also served as a repository and archive of important legal sources. But here, too, as Robert Descimon has pointed out about their uncle, the Dupuys seemed to

---

[3] Christina of Sweden did pay a visit to the royal library of the Dupuys. See Uri, *Un cercle savant*, 56.
[4] Uri, *Un cercle savant*, 17.
[5] Marc Fumaroli, "Aux origines érudites du grand goût classique: *L'Optimus stylus gallicus* selon Pierre Dupuy," in Pierre Aquilon, Jacques Chupeau, and François Weil, eds., *L'intelligence du passé: Les faits, l'écriture et le sens. Mélanges offerts à Jean Lafond par ses amis* (Tours, 1988), 185–95.

want to distance themselves from the official world of the sovereign court, preferring to identify with a wider learned culture that combined erudition with letters.[6] Their direct lineage as descendants of the *politique* party was yet another context. Not only was their intellectual patriarch, J.-A. de Thou, whose great *History of His Times* eventually landed on the Index, one of the foremost apologists for this position, but the cabinet proved particularly receptive to Protestants like Grotius, Saumaise, and Rivet, whose religious tendencies favored accommodation and compromise. The Dupuys' own religious affiliation, however, was decidedly Catholic, though Gallican, and this context is arguably the most important aspect of their academy's identity. Marc Fumaroli has called the cabinet a CNRS for Gallicanism, and this religious ideology, which had great implications for the political order, both domestically and in the European theater, endowed the Dupuys with a public profile and a level of engagement unusual for such informal circles.

The habitués of the cabinet are also classed among the so-called "libertines," a notoriously imprecise term with several different meanings and associations. In the seventeenth century, Garasse, the scourge of freethinkers and skeptics, included the charge of "libertinage" in his broadside against the disciples of Charron, among others, who indeed were intimates of the Dupuy circle. The great historian of this milieu, René Pintard, used the term, significantly modified by "erudite," to describe the kind of thinking that characterized the Académie putéane. He also acknowledged the other sort of libertines—those whose morals and behavior shocked even freethinkers and *esprits forts*. Some of these "true" libertines maintained ties with the Dupuys, most notably Bouchard, who left posterity a sheaf of pornographic writings, and who died in sordid circumstances—knifed in a Roman street. Others, like Théophile and Vanini, as well as other writers who haunted the margins of respectability, preferring the low-life venues of inns and taverns, never got anywhere near the austere quarters of the Dupuy cabinet.

By and large, the true intimates of the cabinet were merely libertines of the mind, if that, whose morals were for the most part above reproach, or who at least exercised sufficient discretion to parry the charge of loose living or heterodox thinking. They were well aware that these reproaches might be leveled at them—how could they not be in the wake of Garasse's notorious campaign?—but they were confident to the point of nonchalance that it was mere calumny. In a famous and oft-quoted passage, Guy Patin, an intimate of the Dupuys, recalls a recent retreat at Gentilly with some friends, including Gabriel Naudé and Pierre Gassendi. The tone of the letter is tongue-in-cheek, as if to both acknowledge and scoff at the charge of debauchery. Patin makes a point of the fact that his

---

[6] Robert Descimon, "Jacques Auguste de Thou (1553–1617): Une rupture intellectuelle, politique, et sociale," *Revue de l'histoire des religions*, 226/3 (2009), 485–95. See also Robert A. Schneider, "Gallicans Not Magistrates: The Dupuy Cabinet in the Age of Richelieu," in Barbara B. Diefendorf, ed., *Social Relations, Politics, and Power in Early Modern France: Robert Descimon and the Historian's Craft* (Kirksville, MO, 2016), 237–59.

friends have never touched even a drop of wine, while he drinks "very little." "Nevertheless," he adds, "it will be a debauch, but a philosophical one, and perhaps something more. For all three of us, being cured of superstition and freed from the evils of scruples, which is the tyrant of consciences, we will perhaps go almost to a holy place."[7] In short, "libertine" seems an unhelpful, imprecise, and unnecessarily pejorative term to use in conjunction with the Dupuy cabinet.[8]

Rather, the members of this circle were *esprits forts*: men without illusions, tending toward skepticism, contemptuous of popular opinion and religious enthusiasm, and discreet about their own deepest beliefs. This (as I have noted) was a contemporary term, which is loosely translated as freethinkers, but the true meaning of which is more precisely conveyed literally: those with strong minds.[9] An *esprit fort* thus often found himself living a dual life: outwardly, or publicly, he conformed to the conventions and pieties of the political and religious order; in private, he shared with his like-minded confreres an awareness that things were very much different from how they seemed. Like the *honnête homme*, the *esprit fort* referred to a mode of elite self-representation and identification, ideally suited to those who had the luxury of cultivating *otium cum dignitate*. For the Dupuys, this identity was compounded by the family legacy of Gallicanism.

The Legacy of J.-A. de Thou

Jacques-Auguste de Thou, the Dupuys' uncle, not only bequeathed them his impressive library and a venue that already had a reputation as a center of learning and erudite sociability; he was also a major architect of the *politique* Gallican position, largely through his authorship of the *History of His Times*, one of the most significant historical works of the period. A prominent member of the Paris Parlement, he was a major player during the religious wars, whose position was well known; but his views emerge with even greater clarity and forcefulness in his scholarship. Like his contemporary and friend Paolo Sarpi, the great Venetian Republican and historian, he gained even greater renown for his writings than for his public service. First published in 1604, de Thou's vast chronicle covering the period of the Wars of Religion and their aftermath, stretching over a hundred

---

[7] Translation from Richard H. Popkin, *The History of Scepticism from Erasmus to Spinoza*, 3rd ed. (Berkeley, 1979), 88. See other references later in this chapter, in the discussion of La Mothe le Vayer and *Mémorial*.

[8] *Mémorial de quelques conférences avec des personnes studieuses* (Paris, 1669), a text by La Mothe le Vayer that purports to reproduce the conversations in the Dupuys' library, presents a scene in which a "libertine" is banished from their midst. See also Paul Oskar Kristeller, "The Myth of Renaissance Atheism and the French Tradition of Free Thought," *Journal of the History of Philosophy*, 6/3 (1968), 233–43, for a view that contrasts with Pintard's notion of erudite libertinage.

[9] See Chapter 3 on Charron and the *esprit fort*.

volumes, was never finished in his lifetime.[10] It underwent a series of revisions and emendations following his death in 1617, most undertaken by the Dupuys and their associates. And after its initial publication provoked a storm of criticism, ultimately leading to its placement on the Index in 1609, de Thou vowed never again to venture into print, and continued to compile his *History* only for the sake of his friends in the Republic of Letters, who would read it in manuscript, and for posterity.[11]

He prefaced his *History* with an extended epistle to Henri IV, which amounted to both a fulsome homage to the king and the author's political testament. In a few pages, de Thou nails his colors to the mast.[12] He combines his encomium to Henri with a declaration of loyalty to a king who has "given peace to France, and at the same time united liberty and regal power, two things usually thought incompatible." He also praises him as the restorer of the "muses, driven from their ancient seats by the rage of war," a restoration made even more glorious by the appointment of the savant Isaac Casaubon, "that luminary of the age" (though, of course, a Huguenot), to the position of royal librarian. But self-interest also inflects his praise of Henri, for he frankly avows that "as I have undertaken a work full of dangerous hazard, I stood in need of powerful patronage to screen me from the calumnious and malevolent."[13]

His dedication amounts to an advertisement of those "hazardous" views. For him, the disasters of religious wars serve as a cautionary lesson that to combat heresy with violence is both wrong and ineffective—wrong because it contravenes fundamental Christian principles, ineffective because it only invites martyrdom and thus even more violence. "What the stoics boasted," he writes, "with so much parade, of their wisdom, applies with far more justice to religion. Affliction and pain have no power over the religious man." "In a word," he continues, "it must be acknowledged that the records of sacred antiquity afford no example to sanction the capital punishment of heretics." He goes even further: "those princes have acted with prudence, and, conformably to the institutions of the ancient church, who have judged it right to appease religious contests even upon disadvantageous terms, rather than repress them by force of arms."[14] De Thou implicitly claims

---

[10] Samuel Kinser, *The Works of Jacques-Auguste de Thou* (The Hague, 1966), 2.

[11] On de Thou's reluctance to have his work translated, see Kinser, *The Works of Jacques-Auguste de Thou*, 27. See also Hugh Trevor-Roper, "Queen Elizabeth's First Historian: William Camden," in Trevor-Roper, *Renaissance Essays* (Chicago, 1985), 121–48, on Camden's similar reluctance to publish; Camden was also in the wider orbit of de Thou. On de Thou's project as a whole, see Anthony Grafton, "Back to the Future, 1: De Thou Documents the Details," in Grafton, *The Footnote: A Curious History* (Cambridge, MA, 1997), 122–47.

[12] On this, see Robert Descimon, "Penser librement son intolerance le président Jacques Auguste de Thou (1553–1617) et *L'Épître dédicatoire des Historiae sui temporis* (1604)," in François Lecercle, ed., *La liberté de pensée: Hommage à Maurice Laugaa* (Poitiers, 2002), 73–86.

[13] Jacques-Auguste de Thou, *The Life of Thuanus, with Some Account of His Writings and a Translation of the Preface to His History*, trans. J. Collinson (London, 1807), 390, 436, 439.

[14] De Thou, *Thuanus*, 395, 400, 407.

Michel de l'Hôpital, the great reforming chancellor and a forerunner of the *politiques*, as a model, though he does not cite him by name. He extols the "peace of 63," the treaty engineered by l'Hôpital between the crown and the Huguenot rebels, which, "like the sun breaking forth after storms, diffused a serene calm throughout the land."[15] That respite of peace was short-lived, of course, and, in a sense, de Thou dedicated his whole life's work not only to demonstrating the senselessness of the subsequent generation of warfare, but also to identifying the culprits for the wars' prolongation. Like others who shared his Gallican sympathies, he preferred to blame the noxious meddling of foreigners, especially the Spanish and the Jesuits, rather than the actions of his countrymen. "From that time," he concludes, "deluded by foreign intrigues, we bent our thoughts to artifice and hostility."[16] His position was embodied in the very style of his writing: just as he counseled leniency toward heretics, so he "abstained from opprobrious language, and...made honorable mention of the Protestants, especially those who excelled in learning."[17] Above all, he is guided by "the sentiment of the ancients, that our country is a second God, and the laws of our country other deities."[18] If ever one needed an example of civic virtue, one need look no further than de Thou.

De Thou's *History* was placed on the Index, but not without a struggle. Like the more famous case of Galileo several years later, the Roman Curia did not base its condemnation on intrinsic intellectual or doctrinal issues alone. Politics and patronage also played a role. And like Galileo, de Thou found champions among Church hierarchs. He also had an agent in Rome in the person of Christophe Dupuy, Pierre and Jacques's brother, who served in the entourage of the Cardinal du Perron. Du Perron was one of de Thou's supporters who, along with the several Italian cardinals, formed a loose coalition that made the historian's case. As Alfred Soman has demonstrated, however, this coalition quickly unraveled, owing to circumstances that had little to do with de Thou's *History*.[19] Du Perron left Rome in the middle of the deliberations, and this, compounded by the death and absence of several other supporters, made defending the book against its many detractors, in both Italy and France, virtually impossible. Indeed, when news reached Paris that the *History* had been placed on the Index in 1609, Du Perron lamented that his presence in Rome might have prevented it.[20] Though de Thou harbored some hope that the decision might be reversed, after 1610 he essentially gave up the struggle, for the assassination of Henri IV, in reviving fears of a renewed religious conflict, only undermined the fate of a book that extolled the irenic cause.

---

[15] *Thuanus*, 410.   [16] *Thuanus*, 411.
[17] *Thuanus*, 423. Elsewhere de Thou writes: "I have aimed to acquire a plain and simple style, the image of a mind averse from vain and ostentatious ornament, equally free from asperity and adulation" (393).
[18] *Thuanus*, 430.
[19] Alfred Soman, *De Thou and the Index: Letters from Christophe Dupuy (1603–1607)* (Geneva, 1972), 18ff.
[20] Soman, *De Thou and the Index*, 20.

But not even de Thou's death in 1617 put an end to the campaign to win approval for the *History of His Times*. And here is where the story of this work joins that of the Dupuys, for the Académie putéane continued to labor at the task of making this massive chronicle both available and acceptable to a discerning readership. The Dupuys took up the de Thou legacy in ways that extended beyond their place as their uncle's heir, a fact that does not usually find its way into the accounts of the history of their cabinet. The brothers' activities on its behalf proceeded on several fronts. They continued to collect materials and documents, hoping to fill in the gaps and complete their uncle's unfinished work; and they also attempted to edit and modify his text in order to make it more acceptable. Whole volumes of the *History* remained unpublished. And so in 1620, Pierre Dupuy and Nicolas Rigault, with the cooperation of a German printer, had books 1–138, covering the years 1546–1607 in five volumes, clandestinely published in Geneva. The editors disguised their role in its publication, and the place of publication, the headquarters of international Calvinism, was obscured by an artful use of its Latin name, which could easily be confused with the Latin for Orléans.[21]

Beyond the considerable efforts and subterfuge that went into this undertaking, spanning several years and involving the conspiratorial cooperation of a number of scholars and printers across Europe, Pierre Dupuy also published at the same time (and also in Geneva) an *Apologie pour Monsieur le président de Thou sur son Histoire*. This text not only represents a further brief for his uncle's life work; perhaps more important for our purposes, it offers additional insight into the contemporary views of the Dupuy cabinet as well. On one level, it marshals arguments both in favor of removing the *History* from the Index and, more vociferously, against those forces that landed it there in the first place. The effectiveness of Dupuy's apology in fact lies in its association of the latter with the same culprits for a half-century of religious turmoil, as so copiously documented by de Thou. This is why the Jesuits, Spain, and the descendants of the League are joined in opposition to the *History*. "The League uncovered and discovered, as it is in this work, cannot please them," writes Dupuy. The "remains" of the League cannot abide a history that tells "what really happened"—one, moreover, written by a historian who has "penetrated into the most secret counsels."[22] In their campaign against him, these "*méchants*" cleverly play upon common people's natural propensity to "listen with pleasure to slanders and calumnies, even those furthest from the truth." Like the Inquisition, they are the "persecutors of the *beaux esprits*," a term that Garasse would contemptuously deploy in his diatribe as a synonym for freethinkers and atheists four years later. How can these critics object to de Thou's revelations when, argues Dupuy, the same facts have been revealed by

---

[21] Kinser, *The Works of Jacques-Auguste de Thou*, 26–8ff.
[22] Pierre Dupuy, *Apologie pour Monsieur le président de Thou, sur son Histoire* (Geneva, 1620), 4.

historians elsewhere, including Italy? "Italian historians have discovered enough of this garbage [*ordures*]. One must be stupid to believe otherwise."[23]

The "truth" of de Thou's history, according to Dupuy, amounts to a Gallican view of the Wars of Religion. Not only are Spain, the Jesuits, and the League to blame for their continuation and virulence, but he implicates the whole ultramontane conception of Church and State as well. Dupuy cites de Thou's accounts of the Jesuits' nefarious activities—their "crimes" against monarchs like Henri IV and the Prince of Orange (whose assassinations he lays at the doorstep of the society) and Queen Elizabeth (whose persecution of her Catholic subjects found justification in the Jesuits' conspiracies against her). The Jesuits and kindred spirits, he writes, "confuse the Church with the Court of Rome." Dupuy cites de Thou's evidence asserting French kings' legitimate rights over bishops and papal emissaries, and the Parlement as the defender of Gallican "liberties." And he also notes the long history of Rome's and the Church's interference in French affairs, the most egregious example being the Wars of Religion themselves.

Dupuy's text is a spirited and candid defense of de Thou's *History*, but it is more than an apology; it is also an intervention into the contemporary political arena using his uncle's work as a vehicle. His intervention takes place on two levels. First, it attacks those forces that continue to prevent the publication of de Thou's *History*: these are "the enemies of the *Patrie* and peace." Dupuy concedes that "satirical writings, filled with untruths, injurious histories against the King, the State, or the Great should be prudently prohibited." But to condemn a history that merely reveals the "bad actions of Princes and others" is like criticizing the Bible for showing Mary Magdalene as a prostitute, Saint Thomas as incredulous, or Saint Peter as momentarily weak. Dupuy's brief amounts to a defense of scholarly license against the forces of censorship and persecution. Moreover, he notes that in the age of print, such prohibitions are meaningless: "what cannot be written in Italy is published in Germany, and what Germans do not dare to publish, one can read in France and Spain."[24]

On another level, his text addresses contemporary events in the geopolitical contest between France and the Habsburgs, which he saw, like other Gallicans, as largely a continuation of the religious wars of the last century. Dupuy points to the conflict over the Valteline, where France and the Habsburgs were presently locked in a military campaign over this strategic passage in northern Italy, as evidence of "Spain's design to make itself monarch of the whole world under the pretext of religion."[25] For Dupuy, who saw Europe in the thrall of a Jesuit-Habsburg conspiracy, the lessons of his uncle's *History* were more timely than ever. His *Apologie* was in the first instance a vehement defense of his uncle, who

---

[23] Dupuy, *Apologie pour de Thou*, 4, 5.   [24] *Apologie pour de Thou*, 10.
[25] *Apologie pour de Thou*, 6.

was the spiritual and intellectual godfather of the Dupuy cabinet. But it was also a bold Gallican declaration emanating from the premier scholarly center in Europe.[26]

The Friends of Orasius Tubero

The community of the Dupuy circle was expansive and numerous, with different figures maintaining very different associations, both far and wide. Perhaps the closest to home was a subset of the cabinet that seemed to have an identity of its own. This was the so-called Tetrade, composed in its first incarnation of La Mothe le Vayer, Naudé, Gassendi, and Eli Diodati; Diodati would later be replaced by Guy Patin. We have already met La Mothe le Vayer as the defender of erudition in literary matters, the friend and executor of Marie de Gournay, and among Richelieu's stable of writers. Naudé, too, has appeared in these pages: a trained physician, he was an apologist for reason of state and served a series of great men as librarian. And so has Gassendi, a priest, a philosophical skeptic, and the major advocate of Epicureanism in the seventeenth century. A Protestant patron of savants, rather than a savant himself, Diodati was a friend and supporter of Francis Bacon and Galileo. Finally, Patin was another physician, who, despite his identification with these freethinkers and his own advanced views, scoffed at new medical theories regarding the circulation of the blood as the invention of "charlatans." He was a fierce Gallican and, unlike Naudé and many other *esprits forts*, became a severe critic of Richelieu and his policies, ultimately siding with the rebels during the *Fronde*. If La Mothe le Vayer was not the leader or spokesman of this group, he did, through his writings, present them as a coterie of like-minded men, true *esprits forts*, united by scorn for the opinions and views of the common people, and the realization that their own views must be guarded with great discretion.

After a series of travels that shaped his worldview, La Mothe le Vayer returned to Paris in the late 1620s, where he struck up his relationships with the other members of the Tetrade, as well as the many associates of the Dupuy circle. The result was a book that appeared in 1630, *Quatre dialogues faits à l'imitation des anciens*, followed soon after by another, *Cinq dialogues faits à l'imitation des anciens*, both by one "Orasius Tubero." Both volumes were issued in very limited editions, probably around thirty copies. Both listed their place of publication as "Frankfort," while the date of publication indicated for the first was 1506, for the second 1606. It is unlikely that many people were fooled by this rather transparent ruse, which nevertheless signals a desire to obscure the true provenance of this undertaking. And within certain circles—certainly the Dupuy cabinet, but

---

[26] One feature that might be expected in this sort of text was absent: the kind of irenic sentiments one finds with some of the Dupuys' fellow travelers, or that have been found in the milieu of the Stuart court. See especially the important work by W. B. Patterson, *King James VI and I and the Reunion of Christendom* (Cambridge, 1997).

others as well—the identity of the dialogues' author, although he never publicly avowed his paternity, was hardly a secret.[27]

In the first dialogues, the participants are given fictional names such as Aristenetus, Philoponus, and Hesychius. With the next set, however, La Mothe le Vayer populates his text with living figures endowed with pseudonyms, which, largely through the ingenious labors of René Pintard, have been identified as the Tetrade core surrounded by others of the Dupuy milieu. Pintard's key to these and other dialogues allows us to assemble a roll call of the intimates of the Dupuy circle: "Cassender" is Gassendi, "Télamon" is Naudé, and "Diodatus" is Diodati. "Marcellus" is Michel de Marolles, the memoirist and historian who was also an associate of Marie de Gournay, and himself the animator of another private academy. "Xenomanès" stands for François-Auguste de Thou, the son of the historian, who would be executed in 1642 for his involvement in the Cinq-Mars conspiracy. "Crates" is the redoubtable François Guyet, perhaps the most erudite of the Dupuy circle, a disciple of Scaliger, and one of the foremost Latin poets of the day. "Nigrinus" represents Jean-François Sarasin, a poet and historian, an intimate, like Chapelain and Balzac, of both the Rambouillet salon and the Dupuy cabinet. "Eleus" is François Luillier, a patron and boon companion of several savants, including Gassendi, and a magistrate in the Metz Parlement. The erudite bibliophile Ismaël Boulliau, who lived at the Dupuys' and also was an accomplished astronomer, appears as "Eubulus." The writer on language Gilles Ménage, another figure who shuttled between salon and cabinet, is indicated by the sobriquet "Menalcus." Hobbes's translator, Samuel Sorbière, who was also a physician and a promoter of the views of Gassendi, makes an appearance as "Bibulus." Among the high officials and men of state in attendance in the circle was Jean Bouchart de Champigny, *contrôleur général* and *surintendant des finances*, who is given the name "Castrucius." The royal librarian, Nicolas Rigault, whom the Dupuy brothers would succeed in 1645, is present in the dialogues as "Gyraldus." Jérémie Ferrier, a Catholic convert and an apologist for the crown's policies, makes an appearance as "Ferrarius," identified as Richelieu's spy. Other characters appear, including a few in their own name. Several of these sobriquets had a wider currency than La Mothe le Vayer's dialogues. Both Balzac and Chapelain, for example, refer to La Mothe le Vayer as "Monsieur Tubero" in their letters.[28]

Why the elaborate attempt at subterfuge? Were the ideas expressed in the dialogues so dangerous that their provenance had to be disguised? Descartes, in a letter to Mersenne, called the dialogues a "wicked book" (*méchant livre*), but this

---

[27] On La Mothe le Vayer's writings, see Pintard, *Le libertinage érudit*, 131–47, 505–39; Popkin, *The History of Scepticism*; Jean-Pierre Cavaillé, *Dis/simulations: Jules-César Vanini, François La Mothe le Vayer, Gabriel Naudé, Louis Machon et Torquato Accetto: Religion, morale et politique au XVIIe siècle* (Paris, 2002), chap. 3.

[28] René Pintard, *La Mothe le Vayer—Gassendi—Guy Patin: Etudes de bibliographie et de critique suivies de textes inédits de Guy Patin* (Paris, 1943).

likely reflected his aversion for skepticism as a *terminus ad quem* of philosophy.[29] It is true that aspects of the book made a strong case for both philosophical skepticism and religious relativism. The concern might have stemmed as well from a desire not to embarrass or implicate the Dupuy cabinet with the publication of the dialogues. The Dupuy brothers themselves, while well known for their Gallicanism, were not in the habit of venturing into the realm of belief or doctrine with their opinions. They were never suspected of "libertinage" and, unlike the Tetrade, remained aloof from philosophical, potentially inflammatory discussions regarding skepticism and religion. The attempt to disguise Tubero's dialogues thus might have been a means of erecting a firewall between the Tetrade and the Dupuys. The overall intent, however, was likely not protective or defensive but rather, paradoxically, a means of collective self-promotion. If nothing else, these dialogues publicize the existence of a coterie of privileged individuals, a sort of subculture of the select few who not only share a common intellectual outlook but also enjoy the companionship and conviviality of their discerning brethren.

In any case, the very form of the dialogues, as a multi-sided discussion in which participants offer various points of view on different subjects, allows for a degree of indeterminacy as to the author's real opinions. And the text itself, generously sprinkled with Latin and Greek quotations from the ancients, seems positively to revel in obscurantism and obfuscation. It was hardly a book for a wide readership. Despite the deliberate obstacles set in the reader's way, several positions emerge clearly and unambiguously. Perhaps the most salient is the defiant embrace of liberty as a guiding spirit for philosophy, though it is a spirit that must be guarded. In the "Lettre de l'auteur," La Mothe le Vayer proclaims, "The liberty of my style scorns all constraint, and…my purely natural thoughts are today contraband goods and ought not to be exposed in public."[30] In this way is made clear a central tenet of the so-called *esprits forts*: their disdain for common opinion and their wary attitude toward disclosing their views to a wider public. Although their major concern was for the uneducated, the undisciplined and wayward crowd, their intellectual condescension was not limited to the lower classes. "I beg of you," writes La Mothe le Vayer, "to reflect a little, not only on all the errors, idiocies, and impertinences of the vulgar (and this word includes in our opinion equally the knight, the magistrate, and the peasant), but also the tyranny of our age, the customs that they have established, and the invincible obstinacy with which they are so blindly followed." The conclusion, he cautions, is that "an honest man who loves truth" can only distance himself from the common sort that

---

[29] J. S. Spink, *French Free-Thought from Gassendi to Voltaire* (New York, 1960), 18; Antonio Negri, *Political Descartes: Reason, Ideology and the Bourgeois Project*, trans. Matteo Mandarini and Alberto Toscano (London, 2007), 123. On Descartes's view of skeptics such as La Mothe le Vayer, see Sylvia Giocanti, "Descartes face au doute scandaleux des sceptiques," *XVIIe siècle*, 2/217 (2002), 663–73.

[30] François de La Mothe le Vayer, *Dialogues faits à l'imitation des anciens* (1606), ed. André Pessel (Paris, 1988), 11.

makes up society.³¹ Thus, the author proclaims his intention to consign his dialogues to "the darkness of a friendly cabinet, rather than suffer the disturbance [*éclat*] and daylight of public exposure." But of course this is patently untrue: his dialogues *were* published, the proof of which is in readers' hands as they read this sentence. Was La Mothe le Vayer having a bit of sport, punning on the double meaning of "cabinet"? The Dupuy circle was a "friendly cabinet" indeed.

In one of La Mothe le Vayer's dialogues, "La vie privée," he presents arguments for and against a life of retreat from the world. The philosopher Hesychius puts forth the case for a total rejection of public life: a refusal to engage in any activity or commitment that would compromise his absolute independence. His interlocutor, Philoponus, apparently a magistrate of some sort, offers various objections, some practical, others purely moral and ethical. By and large, La Mothe le Vayer does not construct the dialogue entirely in Hesychius's favor. In fact, Philoponus seems to take a moderate position that at once recognizes the virtues of retreat but also forces the point that it is incumbent on a truly virtuous man to enter the fray of public life. His ideal is to combine the "speculative" and the "active" life rather than to identify with only one or the other. Besides, he argues, "What great worth can we grant this lovely repose if not only Caesar could deprive us of it at his whim but also the least bothersome crow, a beating drum, a fever, and a thousand other things encountered in life."³² Hesychius, though, remains firm, ultimately convincing Philoponus with a peroration on the sublime comforts of total retreat—for him, the only position worthy of a philosopher.

But along the way, Hesychius delivers a personal insult against his interlocutor by ridiculing the latter's insistence that his elevated status as a magistrate somehow distinguishes him from the "common sort." The philosopher's riposte is categorical:

> You indeed believe that your Magistracy greatly distinguishes you from the common sort of men, and yet you ignore the little difference from those of whom you speak, between your purple [robes] and the fabric that covers the vilest multitude of our artisans, *vulgus tam chlamydatos quam coronatos vocantes* (Seneca). You should realize that neither the highest dignities of State, nor the leading positions in the Louvre, nor the most important offices in the [Parlementary] Palace exclude a man from the ranks of the people; *togis isti non judiciis distant*, they say, these are all weak-minded, vulgar people, all in the same category.³³

This moment in the dialogue marks Hesychius's position as uncompromising: he will not accept even an elevated position in the realm's magistracy—an office of

---

³¹ *Dialogues faits*, 14.   ³² *Dialogues faits*, 121.
³³ *Dialogues faits*, 117.

great dignity and authority—as an exception to his belief that total disengagement from the affairs of the world is the sole path to wisdom. More than that, in this respect, at least, he sees no distinction between a high officer of the court and the "vile" populace—this when the repeated and punctilious assertion of strict hierarchical distinctions was the order of the day.

Beyond a personal affront disguised as a debating point, Hesychius's remarks also suggest an attitude on the part not only of La Mothe le Vayer but also of the Dupuys. This has to do with their relationship to the parlementary magistracy. As I have noted, Robert Descimon has argued that several "ruptures" marked their uncle de Thou's later career, including a break from the milieu of the Parisian officialdom. After he witnessed the League takeover of the city, with the complicit participation of the "bourgeoisie," he turned away "from the preoccupations of a vain people, but also from the professional practices proper to the magistracy." He resigned his office in the Parlement, which had been the basis of his family's prestige and authority for generations.[34] Moreover, this stance of detachment seems to have been passed on to the Dupuys. Revisiting Pintard's roster of the cabinet, one notices how few are associated with the parlementary society in particular or the magistracy in general. Many associates depended upon the patronage of noblemen, churchmen, or high officials; others had positions in the ecclesiastical establishment; a few seemed to benefit from the direct support of the Dupuys themselves. But members of the Parlement or other royal courts—institutions that gave rise to the de Thou-Dupuy dynasty—were few and far between.[35]

If, then, the Dupuys, following the example of their uncle, deliberately distanced their cabinet from the parlementary milieu, we should note how surprising this is; for the centrality of Gallicanism to the religious and political ethos of the Dupuys would suggest, rather, close ties between them and the magistrates—the traditional defenders of the "liberties of the Gallican Church." In this particular redoubt of Gallicanism, however, this association was no longer seen as crucial to either their identity or their collective efforts. It was another sign of their retreat into a realm all their own.

One of La Mothe le Vayer's publications purported to represent the discussions that took place in that realm—the "Bibliothèque du président de Thou." *Mémorial de quelques conférences avec des personnes studieuses* was published in 1669, but internal evidence suggests that it was written much earlier.[36] The text is organized

---

[34] Descimon, "Jacques Auguste de Thou (1553–1617)," 488.
[35] See especially Jérôme Delatour, "Le cabinet des frères Dupuy," *Revue d'histoire des facultés de droit et de la science juridique*, nos. 25–6 (2005–2006), 157–200. Also Pintard, *Le libertinage érudit*, 95ff. Among the few magistrates who appeared to frequent the sessions of the Dupuys were Jérôme Bignon and Mathieu Molé. Philippe Fortin de la Hoguette, a military man who maintained a long relationship with the cabinet, became a *conseiller* in the Parlement of Metz. See also Marc Fumaroli, *L'âge de l'éloquence: Rhétorique et "res literaria" de la Renaissance au seuil de l'époque classique* (Geneva, 1980), 589.
[36] La Mothe le Vayer, *Mémorial*, 13.

into a series of discussions, sixty-one in all, each taking a particular theme or subject. Some are what one would expect from a group of savants schooled in the traditions of Renaissance humanism: dialogues on love and sex, the virtues of *otium*, the nature of the good life. Several dialogues criticize the clergy. Twice Pope Paul II is recalled as an enemy of men of letters who was "accustomed to declaring heretics anyone who even mentioned the word Academy."[37] Crates calls into question the infallibility of the pope.[38] A theologian who "by chance" visits the cabinet and voices his offense at the sympathetic discussion of pagan philosophy is met by a severe riposte from Marcellus for failing to appreciate the virtues of non-Christians. Incas worship a single god as do other pagans, he notes. "This proves that the natural reasoning of the Gentiles does not lead them to atheism or unbelief, despite their otherwise extravagant ways."[39]

In general, a pronounced sense of discretion guides the conversations in *Mémorial*, which emerges as fundamental to the very ethos of the Dupuy circle. Reticence is prized rather than volubility; even writing or publishing too much earns the disapprobation of the group. Nigrinus's eagerness to see his works in print is met with the advice that they would be esteemed more if he wrote less. The confreres extol silence, not only because it is sometimes necessary, but also because it has the virtue of meaning many different things.[40] They squarely condemn lying, bemoaning it as all too prevalent among men, but disguise and even deception are somewhat different. After all, they observe, Jesus spoke in parables, and Saint Chrysostom commented that these fables serve "as veils for truths important to our salvation, goading us to seek what is hidden, just as it is better to look at the sun when it is eclipsed."[41] This disposition toward reticence and discretion emerges most starkly in discussions relating to statecraft. Some political issues could be dealt with frankly, especially if the discussion echoed official policy. The arrival of the Spanish ambassador in Paris, for example, gives rise to a spirited discussion of Spain's aggression across Europe, and especially its perfidious use of Franciscans and other religious as agents whose "habits cover their duplicity."[42] But by and large, political matters were treated at arm's length, reflecting a consensus among the Dupuy intimates to keep their refuge free of such concerns. Castrucius stormed into a séance one day, livid at the news that he had been "betrayed" in Richelieu's presence by Ferrarius, who divulged what he had said in the confines of the Dupuys' library. Like others, he was under the impression that it was a "cowardly crime to reveal to anyone what was said between them." Though those in attendance demonstrated their solidarity with Castrucius, vowing henceforth to ban Ferrarius from their acquaintance, the elder of the Aldephes took the matter a step further. As far as he was concerned, Castrucius

---

[37] *Mémorial*, 298–309; see also 218–27.   [38] *Mémorial*, 235–45.
[39] *Mémorial*, 276–85.   [40] *Mémorial*, 245–9.
[41] *Mémorial*, 334–41.   [42] *Mémorial*, 28–39.

was to blame even for speaking about the cardinal-minister in the cabinet's precincts. And so he took him aside and gently informed him never to visit the library again.[43]

Discretion, guardedness, and sometimes self-censorship characterize this milieu, as elsewhere in learned and elite circles in the early seventeenth century. But to put this ethos in purely negative terms—to emphasize the prohibition against disclosure or the imperative to silence—is to reveal only one side of it. More positively, it connotes the value of gentlemanly and learned sociability, where the cares of the world, the tumult and contentiousness of public life, are left behind. This is the model of *otium*, so often evoked by La Mothe le Vayer and his friends. It is an ideal cultivated in the Dupuy cabinet but also embodied by certain individuals who were seen as paradigms of the virtuous life according this ideal—none more so than Nicolas-Claude Fabri de Peiresc.

Peiresc, the Barberinis, and the Italian Connection

Despite the fact that the Republic of Letters was European in scope, Italy remained the source of much that was important to men of letters and erudition throughout the early modern period. In retrospect, and especially in terms of political and social history, this was the time of Italian decline, or at least its relative eclipse. But, as we have seen for the culture of the salon, the traditions associated with the Italian Renaissance remained robust and influential well beyond the Alps and well into the seventeenth century, and nowhere more so than in Paris. Moreover, this was the high point of the Counter-Reformation, when keeping abreast of the inner workings at the papal court was of utmost importance throughout the Catholic world. Most men of learning and even many noblemen considered the pilgrimage to Italy an obligatory experience, and many ambitious young men sought positions in the entourages of French ambassadors or churchmen stationed in Rome. The Dupuy cabinet, with its European-wide contacts, maintained especially close ties with Italy—the Italy of both the Renaissance and the Counter-Reformation. Like the Rambouillet salon, the Dupuys never ceased to look upon Italy as the true source of Christian culture.

The enduring importance of Italy is illustrated by the imbalance in traffic between the Dupuy circle and Italian savants and men of letters. True, prominent Italians often visited the cabinet. Perhaps the most notable was Tommaso Campanella, who found a welcome refuge there after his escape from a Roman prison was engineered in part by associates of the Dupuys. Several Italian scholars maintained a permanent presence at the Dupuys', like the antiquarian and poet

---

[43] *Mémorial*, 67–71.

Girolamo Aleandro.[44] And there were others, especially visiting Roman prelates, who made a point of appearing at the cabinet during their time in Paris. Cardinal Francesco Barberini, the nephew of the future Pope Urban VIII, spent much time at the Dupuys' during his Parisian sojourn in 1624–5. But by and large the flow of itinerancy pointed southward, with men like Naudé, Bouchard, Boulliau, Gaffarel, Jean de Montreuil, Lucas Holstenius, and others spending years on the Italian peninsula.[45] Though they had their own reasons and interests for being there—most were attached to French ambassadors, cardinals, or other high officials of either church or state—they also served the Dupuys as informal agents in this heartland of humanism and the cockpit of the Counter-Reformation. In the early years of the cabinet, the third Dupuy brother, Christophe, acted in this capacity, as seen in his involvement in and as an informant on the campaign to prevent the placing of de Thou's *History* on the Index.

The linchpin in the Dupuys' connection to Italy was Peiresc. Nicolas-Claude Fabri de Peiresc is acknowledged as one of the most prominent and admired figures in the world of early seventeenth-century humanism. And now that we have Peter Miller's splendid studies, we can appreciate why Pierre Bayle called him the "*Procureur Général*" of the Republic of Letters.[46] Peiresc maintained a network of friends and correspondents that reads like a roll call of the savant community of Europe, including many members of the Dupuy circle. In 1617 he was in Paris and spent time at the Dupuys', and for the rest of his life he maintained an intense correspondence with the Adelphes, the extent and constancy of which qualify him as a member of the circle despite his physical absence. His relationship to the Dupuys was crucial in connecting him to the wider world of European learning, for chronic illness kept him bound to his native Provence for most of his adult life. In a 1626 letter, he draws an analogy between the Dupuys and Galileo's telescope: like this newly invented instrument, they bring distant lands, like England and Holland, within his view.[47] During his student years, he managed to undertake a tour of France, Switzerland, and, most importantly, Italy. There, from 1599 to 1601, he stayed in Padua, then still a center of learning. He became friends with the jurist and antiquarian scholar Giovanni Vincenzo Pinelli and was admitted as a member of Pinelli's important academy, where he established ties with Galileo and Sarpi.[48]

---

[44] Josephine de Boer, "Men's Literary Circles in Paris, 1610–1660," *Proceedings of the Modern Language Association*, 53/3 (1938), 732; Zur Shalev, *Sacred Words and Worlds: Geography, Religion, and Scholarship, 1550–1700* (Leiden, 2012), chap. 5.

[45] For more on this theme, see Pintard, *Le libertinage érudit*, 102.

[46] Peter N. Miller, *Peiresc's Europe: Learning and Virtue in the Seventeenth Century* (New Haven, 2000); Miller, *Peiresc's Mediterranean World* (Cambridge, MA, 2015). For Bayle's comment, see Miller, *Peiresc's Europe*, 3.

[47] Nicolas Claude Fabri de Peiresc, *Lettres de Peiresc aux frères Dupuy, publiées par Philippe Tamizey de Larroque*, 6 vols. (Paris, 1888), I: 80, XXIV (1626).

[48] Miller, *Peiresc's Europe*, 20.

For the rest of his life, Italy was Peiresc's second home, despite his forced immobility, while his own home served as a way station for French savants en route to the peninsula. Naudé, Bouchard, Holstenius, François-Auguste de Thou, and others associated with the Dupuys were harbored in his Provençal house and furnished with letters of recommendation and lists of contacts as they continued on their travels southward across the Alps.[49] Peiresc was a keen follower of Italian intellectual and political affairs and was scrupulous in channeling information to the Dupuys. This was especially crucial during such episodes as the Venetian Interdict and the Galileo controversy, when the vicissitudes of papal policy and opinion among the Roman hierarchy were of crucial concern for these Parisian Gallicans. Peiresc was honored in many Italian circles, his name and learning esteemed among great churchmen and savants alike.

The most dramatic demonstration of his high standing there was the unprecedented ceremony that followed his death in 1636 at one of Rome's most prestigious assemblies, the Accademia degli Umoristi. Peiresc was an honorary member of this select body of writers, savants, churchmen, and amateurs of letters, as were Naudé, Voiture, Holstenius, and Scipion de Grammont.[50] No fewer than ten cardinals, including Peiresc's personal friends Francesco Barberini and Guido Bentivoglio, attended the funeral service in his honor. Bouchard delivered a long funeral oration in Latin. Gassendi, Peiresc's biographer, writes: "the most choyse wits in all the City, recited Verses in prayse of the deceased, in Italian, Latine, and Greek."[51] Peiresc was the only member who was not a high official or churchman, and the rare foreigner to be honored so lavishly. Further honors followed. Bouchard organized a publishing project, drawing on scholars and linguists from throughout Europe, some connected to the Dupuy cabinet, most affiliated with the Umoristi, who presented eulogies to Peiresc's memory in forty languages. Some writers scoffed at the grandiosity, not to speak of the unwieldiness, of this project. Balzac complained to Chapelain that "in order to reach forty, there will have to be twenty-three that Scaliger was ignorant of."[52] Nevertheless, the *Panglossia* was published in 1638 at the Vatican Press in Rome, testimony not only to Peiresc's renown among men of letters, but also to his particular stature in Italy. Its ostentatious display of erudition is emblematic of the values and intellectual proclivities of the savants of the Republic of Letters, for whom Peiresc was both a friend and a model. It begs to be compared with a very different literary act of homage

---

[49] Peiresc's wide contacts and investigations of all aspects of the Levant and the Mediterranean have now been lavishly documented in Miller's *Peiresc's Mediterranean World*. One thing apparent from this account is the close relationship between Peiresc and François-Auguste de Thou, the historian's son and the Dupuys' cousin.

[50] Pintard, *Le libertinage érudit*, 227.

[51] Pierre Gassendi, *The Mirrour of True Nobility and Gentility: Being the Life of the Renowned Nicolaus Claudius Fabricius, Lord of Peiresk...Englished by W. Rand* (London, 1657), 234.

[52] *Lettres de Jean Chapelain, de l'Académie française*, ed. Philippe Tamizey de Larroque, 2 vols. (Paris, 1880–2), I: 459 n. 1; see also 359, 464, 569.

produced at just about the same time, the "Garland for Julie," which we looked at in the last chapter, both performing the function of ritually acknowledging a sort of totemic figure of a special group.

One of Peiresc's most important contacts in Rome was with the Barberini clan, whose most prominent member, Maffeo, was elevated to the papacy in 1623. Urban VIII's long pontificate of more than twenty years has been called a "second Italian Renaissance," for it occasioned an extraordinary movement of liberality, artistic creation, humanistic learning, and, in general, cosmopolitanism that stemmed in large part from papal patronage.[53] Peiresc was particularly close to the pope's nephew Cardinal Francesco Barberini, who maintained an active presence in erudite and literary circles, including the several academies, and who was himself, like his uncle, an accomplished poet and an energetic patron of artists and scholars. Peiresc's relationship with the Barberinis was never more intense, or more vexed, than during the Galileo controversy. He had long been Galileo's appreciative supporter, and when the astronomer-mathematician's views were finally condemned, he expressed disbelief that such an ill-considered decision should have emanated from a Church controlled by his friends, the cultivated and cosmopolitan Barberinis.[54] But Peiresc's disappointment should not obscure the fact that the Barberinis, and in particular Francesco, were both supporters of some of the most interesting and adventuresome thinkers of the day—including Galileo and Campanella—as well as partisans of France and French culture. Urban's ultimate acquiescence in the condemnation of Galileo came only after prolonged struggles within the Roman Curia, where the forces of a "hard" Counter-Reformation ultimately prevailed—despite, not because of, the Barberinis' own inclinations. In any case, the fact that they were part of Peiresc's and the Dupuys' extended circle reminds us that France was not as isolated in the Catholic world as sometimes thought. At least in the first half of Urban's pontificate, Rome tilted toward France in the Bourbon-Habsburg contest. In Urban's Rome, too, the Jesuits were looked upon with trepidation and suspicion. French theological innovations were held in high regard: witness the unprecedented—and to the Jesuits and enemies of the French, provocative—move of raising Pierre Bérulle to the College of Cardinals in 1627.[55] The "second Italian Renaissance," in short, created what has been called a "marvelous conjuncture" that gave rise to a cosmopolitan, humanistic, tolerant Catholicism that the Dupuys wanted to cultivate.[56]

---

[53] Fumaroli, L'âge de l'éloquence, 202ff. See also Pietro Redondi, Galileo, Heretic, trans. Raymond Rosenthal (Princeton, 1989), 68–103.
[54] See Miller, Peiresc's Europe, 109ff.; and Jérôme Delatour, "Abeilles thuaniennes et barberines: Les relations des savants français avec les Barberini sous le pontificat d'Urbain VIII," in Lorenza Mochi Onori, Sebastian Schütze, and Francesco Solinas, eds., I Barberini e la cultura europea de Seicento (Rome, 2007), 155–72.
[55] Redondi, Galileo, Heretic, 106.
[56] Redondi, Galileo, Heretic, 60–103; Mario Biagioli, Galileo, Courtier: Practice of Science in the Culture of Absolutism (Chicago, 2006), 34.

Thus, in part through Peiresc, in part through their own efforts and contacts, the Dupuy cabinet maintained a foothold in Urban's Rome. The connection was personal: both Maffeo and Francesco Barberini had spent time in Paris, the latter at the head of the French legation—one of the largest ever—in 1625, and both had been welcomed into the cabinet's precincts.[57] Most importantly, habitués of the circle maintained a presence in Italy, especially Padua and Rome, reporting back to the Adelphes on recent publications, Church gossip, and current affairs, often bringing back valuable books, manuscripts, and artifacts to add to the cabinet's library.[58]

Jean-Jacques Bouchard: The Bad-Boy Savant

Bouchard was one of the Dupuys' agents in Rome. To many, including Chapelain, Balzac, and Peiresc, he was one of the ablest, most promising scholars of his generation. In other respects, his life is the stuff of the Jacobean stage. The author of a manuscript that rivals modern erotica in its frank treatment of childhood and adolescent sexuality; the target of an assassination attempt in the streets of Rome under mysterious and perhaps sordid circumstances, which ultimately led to his death; an inveterate traveler whose accounts paid keen attention to the comeliness of the young women in every locale; a devotee of street life, and especially the notorious dark corners of such cities as Rome and Naples, he was also, for a time, at least, the darling of the Vatican, an insider who nearly managed to install himself in the highest echelons of the Roman clerisy. René Pintard, who studied every scrap of surviving evidence, resorted to dividing his account of Bouchard's life into two sections: "La vie édifiante" and "La vie scandaleuse." His interpretation, it must be said, is marked by a rather outmoded moralistic tone that serves to dramatize his bifurcated view of the savant's character. For the great historian, he was not only an *esprit fort* like Naudé, La Mothe le Vayer, and other *libertins érudits*, but a "monster" of duplicity, hypocrisy, and deception. The theme of dividedness, dissimulation, and bifurcation has run throughout the present book; it is suggested in the trope of "retreat," in the stratagems of courtliness and *honnêteté*, in the culture of discretion, and in the theory and practice of reason of state. With Bouchard, it may have marked his character like a hidden scar.

---

[57] On the papal legation, see Redondi, *Galileo, Heretic*, 138; and *The Letters of Peter Paul Rubens*, trans. and ed. Ruth Saunders Magurn (Evanston, IL, 1991), 457 n. 2.

[58] See also examples of other agents in Rome, such as Bourdelot and Prioleau: Pintard, *Le libertinage érudit*, 219–20, 287–8. On Peiresc's beneficence, see Peter N. Miller, "The 'Man of Learning' Defended: Seventeenth-Century Biographies of Scholars and an Early Modern Ideal of Excellence," in Patrick Coleman, Jayne Lewis, and Jill Kowalik, eds., *Representations of the Self from the Renaissance to Romanticism* (Cambridge, 2000), 39–62.

Bouchard was born in 1606 in Paris to a family of magistrates and officers. His father was a *secretaire du roi*; on his mother's side he was related to Gilles Ménage, the noted scholar and lawyer, who was also affiliated with the Dupuys. Educated by the Jesuits, he quickly earned degrees in civil and canon law and at a very young age secured a commission from the Conseil du roi. Barely out of his adolescence, he apparently gained entry into the Dupuy cabinet, and then just as quickly departed for an extended sojourn to Italy in 1632. He never left, dying there from his wounds in 1641.

As with others of his ilk, his path to Rome took him first to Peiresc's refuge for traveling scholars. He clearly impressed the great Provençal patron of men of letters with his learning; his mastery of Latin apparently distinguished him even among the *érudits*. Grotius commented that no one could equal the "purity" of Bouchard's Latin prose.[59] But it was his skill in Greek that really singled him out. Peiresc charged him to copy certain Greek manuscripts from the Vatican Library. Does Peiresc's advice to the young scholar suggest that he was aware of his wayward proclivities? For he counseled him not only on how to dress, and how to economize his funds, but also to "never speak of either the Pope or God."[60] In any case, furnished with letters of introduction from not only Peiresc but also other associates of the Dupuys, including Gassendi, Bouchard arrived in Rome in 1632 ready to scale the heights of this citadel of piety, learning, and patronage.

For several years, his success was stunning. In short order, thanks to Francesco Barberini's close ties to both Peiresc and the Dupuys, he managed to attach himself to the Roman cardinal, who hired him to research Greek supporters of the early Church; soon he became his secretary. With such contacts he also found a place in a community of kindred spirits, several of them French, who made up the academic and scholarly world of Rome—men like Naudé and Holstenius, associates of the Dupuys, but also Italian savants and patrons of letters. In the fictionalized account of his travels, Bouchard notes that a friend put him in touch with "a number of Frenchmen he knew in Rome who were entirely "*deniaisés*"—a term that, even more than *esprit fort*, conveyed an all-knowing cynicism, free thought, and duplicity: it could be translated as "undeceived." In a short time, he had become more Roman than French; and when his ambition turned to securing a bishopric, his first choice was an Italian seat.[61]

Meanwhile, he continued to impress his Roman hosts. Barberini introduced him to the pope. When the cardinal wanted to mount a Latin comedy, it was Bouchard who drafted the script. He was elected to the prestigious Academy of

---

[59] Pintard, *Le libertinage érudit*, 239.   [60] Pintard, *Le libertinage érudit*, 210.
[61] The main source for Bouchard's writings is Jean-Jacques Bouchard, *Journal*, ed. Emanuele Kanceff, vol. I: *Les confessions; Voyage de Paris à Rome; Le carnaval à Rome*, and vol. II: *Voyage dans le royaume de Naples; Voyage dans la compagne de Rome* (Turin, 1976, 1977). The best source on Bouchard's time in Rome is Kanceff, "Introduction à Jean-Jacques Bouchard," in *Journal*, I: i–cxxvi.

Humorists (Umoristi); and, as noted, he took charge of the obsequies on the occasion of Peiresc's death. During Ascension in 1640, he was conferred the honor of delivering a Latin prayer before an assembly that included Urban. He often preached in various churches, in both French and Italian. And in 1641 he was elected by acclaim to the prestigious position of clerk of the Holy Consistory. With such support and visibility, it is no wonder that he firmly believed that a bishop's hat would soon be his.

But this is precisely where his ambition faltered—or rather got the better of him. It does not seem as though this was a matter of a betrayal of his true beliefs or the disclosure of his shadowy life. That would come later, after his death. For the moment, it was rather the growing impression that this was a bounder whose pretensions and arrogance knew no limits. Evidence on this score comes from the correspondence of Chapelain with Balzac and others. At first he is clearly their golden boy among young savants. But little by little, a tone of irritation and finally downright disapproval creeps into the letters. "He is a great man and can be loved," comments Chapelain in 1637.[62] "The Sire Bouchard is a man of spirit," he writes to Godeau. "[B]ut approach him with halter in hand," he adds, "for I have learned from several places that his behavior has not been good and that almost everyone is his enemy." In a letter to Balzac, he laments Bouchard's overreaching ambition but attempts to make light of it by blaming his long sojourn in Rome, where "it is difficult to breathe without at the same time taking in the bad air of ambition."[63] By the end of 1638, however, Chapelain is referring to his "infamous habit of seeking good by such cowardly means," and confides to Balzac, "with his ways and his baseness of heart, I doubt he merits your love."[64] Thereafter, Chapelain's letters contain only scorn for his erstwhile friend in Rome, especially because of his vanity—"which is more contemptible because it is groundless"— and his graceless ambition.[65] He ruminates on the obscure origins and indebtedness of his family and his transparent attempt to concoct a line of nobility. "Our Roman," he writes to Balzac, "is vain and ambitious, a philosopher of fortune and not of virtue.... God save us from these pseudo-philosophers."[66] Although he never made it back to Paris, Bouchard could not have looked forward to a very successful *rentrée*, for Chapelain and others had already concluded that he was unworthy in their midst. There was no prospect for him in either the French Academy or the episcopacy; he failed even to be named to the modest position of Canon of Verdun. In the Dupuy cabinet, reports Chapelain, "his name and his actions are looked upon as a kind of abomination, enough to lead one to believe that he would be considered there like something vomited forth or the plague."[67]

---

[62] *Lettres de Chapelain*, I: 195.
[63] *Lettres de Chapelain*, I: 257.
[64] *Lettres de Chapelain*, I: 317.
[65] *Lettres de Chapelain*, I: 494.
[66] *Lettres de Chapelain*, I: 535 n.
[67] *Lettres de Chapelain*, I: 555 n.

Ambitious yet unwilling to observe the procedures for advancement in the world of letters, Bouchard irritated those, like Chapelain and the Dupuys, who served as the arbiters of this world, and thus, despite talents testified by all, found himself frustrated, his reputation, in Paris, at least, in ruins.

And then there is the matter of the attack in the streets of Rome. The episode is shrouded in mystery and confusion; it is not even clear whether he was stabbed or merely beaten. The source of the attack was an agent of the French ambassador, Maréchal d'Estrées, a notoriously intemperate and difficult character. The background seems to have been a simmering quarrel between him and a prominent Roman clan, probably having to do with previous incidents in which their men had tangled in the streets over sundry affronts and provocations. We are in the Rome of bandits and gangs disguised as the entourages of great men. Bouchard was as much at home in this rough-and-ready world as he was in the corridors of the Vatican. Still, why he was laid low one night in 1640 has never been explained. Various commentators have hinted at insults directed at d'Estrées, or perhaps contretemps of a more sordid nature. More likely, it was a matter of d'Estrées's pique at the appointment of Bouchard to a position in the Holy Consistory over his own candidate.[68] Ultimately, none of this really matters, because the cast of Bouchard's posthumous reputation was determined not by how he died but by how he lived.

This hidden aspect of his life was revealed to a clearly startled Christophe Dupuy, a Carthusian monk in Rome (and Pierre and Jacques's brother), who was among Bouchard's closest friends and supporters. Bouchard died in his monastery, leaving Christophe to carry out his last testament and deal with his possessions. Among these was a "large collection of the most impious verses one could imagine in Latin, French, and Italian," recounted a horrified Christophe in a letter to his brothers in Paris. There were also bundles of letters to "the most infamous and outrageous and vicious people one had ever heard of in this country." And here too was a manuscript that remained unpublished until 1881: a fictionalized account of his childhood followed by a narrative of his travels in Rome and Naples. It may seem unfair to assume that his writings were a true reflection of his behavior; nevertheless, this is what Christophe Dupuy concluded: "I do not know how it is that a man, who seemed entirely correct, could maintain friendships with such monsters, and nevertheless despite all of this eagerly sought a prelature and believed that he had been wronged by not being awarded a bishopric."[69]

---

[68] For more precise explanations of the circumstances of the attack, as well as interesting documents relating to it, see Claire Biquard, "L'Assassinat execrable et horrible' de Jean-Jacques Bouchard: Une lettre inédite de Bouchard à Jacques Dupuy," in Patricia Harry, Alain Mothu, and Philippe Sellier, eds., *Dissidents, excentriques et marginaux de l'âge classique: Autour de Cyrano de Bergerac* (Paris, 2006), 299–305.

[69] For this letter, see Kanceff, "Introduction," ci.

What has come to be known as the "Confessions of Jean-Jacques Bouchard" is indeed remarkable for its sexual candor and irreverence, especially the first part. In these pages, the young protagonist, "Orestes," provides an account of his life after he abandons his studies, returns to the home of his parents, and then departs for Italy.[70] While at home—plagued by adolescent confusion and disgruntlement—he falls in love with his mother's chambermaid, Allisbée, whence begins a series of experiments and ruminations, mostly dealing with his amorous and sexual travails. A historian of erotic literature claims that this is the first time in European letters that the topics of childhood, adolescent sexuality, and in particular impotence had been addressed so directly.[71] Indeed, Orestes' impotence seems to be the crux of the matter. The reader is treated to a series of incidents: seductions, impotence, coitus interruptus, masturbation and mutual masturbation, attempted rape, and more. Finally, tired of his travails at home, he decides to leave. Thus begins another chapter in Orestes'/Bouchard's life—which, while less risqué than the first part of the "Confessions," still reveals a lively interest in street life, freethinking savants, and women.

Was Bouchard an outlier even among the so-called erudite libertines, a man with a secret life that would have shocked even his fellow *esprits forts*? Clearly he suffered from overweening ambition and an arrogant streak that, unlike others, he failed to learn how to disguise. For the moralistic Pintard, this was not enough: "Beneath his wisdom, the persistence of ancient vices; behind the appearance of the scholar, a maniac of intrigue; in the place of piety, the restless spirit of an infidel."[72] We do not have to go so far as Pintard while still acknowledging a level of duplicity that did indeed "shock" those who thought they knew him. Before that, however, we should recall that leading a "complicated" life—one way in private, very different in public—was sanctioned by various ethical codes in this period, as we have noted. Even a model *honnête homme* could not escape the charge of a level of duplicity disguised as dissimulation. In this sense, perhaps, Bouchard was merely different in the degree to which his self was divided—although the degree was rather great.

---

[70] On the so-called "Confessions of Jean-Jacques Bouchard"—this title was provided by posterity—see Martha M. Houle, "Naming the 'Confessions' of Jean-Jacques Bouchard," *Cahiers du dix-septième*, 9/2 (2005), 1–9, https://www.earlymodernfrance.org/2005-volume-ix-2/2005-volume-ix-2. There have been four published versions: *Les confessions de Jean-Jacques Bouchard, parisien, suivies de son voyage de Paris à Rome en 1630* (Paris, 1881); *"Mémoires révélateurs": Les confessions de J.-J. Bouchard* (Paris, 1930); *Les confessions d'un perverti* (Paris, 1960); and the 1976 version in Bouchard, *Journal*, ed. Kanceff, I: 3–135. For an interpretation that emphasizes Bouchard's sexual license as well as his possible atheism, see Jean-Pierre Cavaillé, "Jean-Jacques Bouchard en Italie: Athéisme et sodomie à l'ombre de la curie romaine," in Harry, Mothu, and Sellier, *Dissidents, excentriques et marginaux*, 289–98.

[71] Sarane Alexandrian, *Histoire de la littérature érotique* (Paris, 1995), 119, cited by Houle, "Naming the 'Confessions,'" 2–3.

[72] Pintard, *Le libertinage érudit*, 234.

Lucas Holstenius: The Dupuys' Man in the Vatican

Peiresc, Bouchard, Barberini: here was one of the axes connecting the Parisian Dupuys to the intellectual and patronage riches of Rome. Each of them maintained an independent relationship with the cabinet, but there were linkages between them as well, creating a dense network of personal ties running across the Alps. And insofar as one end of that was anchored in Rome, Lucas Holstenius, a German savant, was pivotal.

If Bouchard's sojourn in Rome ended in tragedy and disgrace, Holstenius's career could not have been more different. His was a success story from start to finish. But as with Bouchard, his intellectual career is not immune to the charge of duplicity, although it is surely without the same moral disapprobation. Born in Hamburg in 1596 to a prosperous owner of a cloth-dyeing enterprise, he was clearly a precocious student: at fourteen, he became the tutor of the son of a local physician. He completed his university studies in Leyden, served as secretary to a Dutch diplomat, and in 1622 spent time in the libraries of London and Oxford, where he conceived his plan to assemble an edition of Greek geographers. As with Bouchard, an expert knowledge of Greek was his strong suit, compounded by an ambitious streak that took him to virtually every corner of the emerging Republic of Letters. In 1624 he arrived in Paris, first serving, like Gabriel Naudé, as librarian to Henri de Mesmes, the first president of the Paris Parlement, and quickly establishing ties with members of the Dupuy circle. Sponsored by the Dupuys, by 1627 he was installed in Rome, where he would live out the rest of his life, first as secretary to a cardinal, then as Francesco Barberini's close aide, afterward as custodian of the Barberini library, and finally as the chief librarian at the Vatican Library.

Although his personal ambition probably distracted him from serving his erstwhile patrons assiduously—Claude Dupuy did not hesitate to denounce his egotism and ingratitude—Holstenius was crucial, along with Peiresc, in securing from Cardinal Barberini a much-coveted benefice for Jacques Dupuy. If, thanks to the Barberinis and their erudite servants like Holstenius, the lucrative patronage of the Church was made available to the Dupuys, the same should be said for the riches of Rome's inventory of ancient manuscripts. To the antiquarians of the cabinet, Latin and especially Greek sources were the sine qua non of their existence; their appetite for manuscripts was insatiable. Yet the most valuable treasures were hidden in the bowels of the Vatican Library or stored away in private collections like that of the Barberinis.[73] Savants such as Holstenius were instrumental in their gaining access to these manuscript sources. It was especially helpful to

---

[73] On Peiresc's requests to Holstenius, including that he examine various texts in Greek, Coptic, and Samaritan, see Peter N. Miller, "An Antiquary between Philology and History: Peiresc and the Samaritans," in Donald R. Kelley, ed., *History and the Disciplines: The Reclassification of Knowledge in Early Modern Europe* (Rochester, NY, 1997), 167.

Pierre Dupuy in his direction of one of the most ambitious scholarly enterprises of the period: the collection of histories of the Byzantine Empire, which drew on the erudition, cooperation, and energy of savants throughout Europe. Because by the time this project was underway, in the 1640s, Holstenius occupied a strategic position at the Pontifical Library, his service as a supplier of manuscripts found in its recesses made him a valued agent of the Dupuys indeed.[74]

Pierre Dupuy's letters to Holstenius offer an abbreviated but still revealing portrait of the changing relationship between the two savants, a relationship characterized by mutual obligations and service. At the start, in the 1620s, the German scholar is clearly the junior partner. He owes Pierre much: entry into the highest circles of Parisian intellectual life and, perhaps more importantly, a place in the entourage of Cardinal Francesco Barberini, then living in Paris. Even when Holstenius was established in Rome, expeditiously scaling the heights of the Vatican establishment, he relied upon Pierre's good graces in order to secure a benefice in Germany, from which he enjoyed a very comfortable living. But then the tables turned, or at least tilted slightly. Once ensconced as head of the Vatican Library, Holstenius had the greatest manuscript collection in Europe—especially the wealth of unedited Greek texts—at his disposal. For the Dupuys and their confreres—the likes of Peiresc, Saumaise, and others—who were eager to mine this precious vein, he was now the man in Rome to know. In his letters, then, Pierre was often the supplicant, urging his savant friend to send him manuscripts, gently reminding him what obligations his privileged office imposed upon him in service to the Republic of Letters.[75]

Pierre thus had a personal interest in cultivating Holstenius's cooperation in his project for the history of Byzantium. But the latter also acted as a broker for other savants, not only those in Paris but also throughout the Republic of Letters, who could not exercise the same leverage as the Dupuys in the hope of prying the needed manuscripts from the Vatican archives. Holstenius, however, had his own ambitions, perhaps too many. In a letter to Peiresc, Naudé acknowledged the German scholar's great talents, as well as his many projects, noting, with some exasperation, how disparate they were: "to print all the ancient geographies, to collect all the works of Platonic philosophers, to publish all the manuscripts of ancient authors who have written on the lives of Popes, as well as other similar projects."[76] And yet, by common account, Holstenius was notoriously unreliable, and, in fact, rarely accomplished the scholarly tasks he set before himself. He even

---

[74] Léon G. Pélissier, "Les amis d'Holstenius," *Mélanges d'archéologie et d'histoire*, 7 (1887), 80–1. This article contains the series of letters between Holstenius and Pierre Dupuy.

[75] In fact, Pierre Dupuy employs this term in the context of asking Holstenius to send some Greek manuscripts to his nephew, who, Pierre notes, "has a marvelous passion to have himself known in the world; when I say the world, I mean the *republicae litterariae*, as for the rest, he has little concern." Pélissier, "Les amis d'Holstenius," 109.

[76] Philippe Tamizey de Larroque, ed., *Les correspondants de Peiresc*, vol. XIII: Gabriel Naudé, *Lettres inédites écrites d'Italie à Peiresc, 1632-1636* (1887; reprint, Geneva, 1972),) 60.

exhibited retentive tendencies, deliberately withholding manuscripts when he was fully aware that other scholars were in desperate need of them. More to the point, as everyone acknowledged, Rome lacked the scholarly resources to take on the formidable editing and translating of Greek texts. In a letter from 1629, in an attempt to encourage Holstenius to furnish his Parisian friends with source materials, Pierre emphasized "the little knowledge there of the Greek language and the difficulty of getting those gentlemen to permit the publication of various things." The situation was changing, he averred: "Little by little this barbarism is fading away."[77] But in a later letter to Holstenius he underscored the importance of regarding Paris as the best venue for this kind of scholarship. Referring to his plan to assemble all the histories of Byzantium from Justinian to the Fall of Constantinople, he pleads: "If you have any manuscripts that fulfill this design, you should oblige the public and the men involved in this project to share them with them." And he reminds him that the Procopius he sent to the Elsevier press, the well-known printing house in Amsterdam, had yet to see the light of day. "I assure you that if we had the same here, we would print them happily."[78]

Holstenius was thus an important link in the Dupuys' scholarly network, a network that depended upon well-placed individuals, but also, therefore, suffered the occasional weaknesses of unreliable individuals. Still, the German was instrumental enough to be cultivated and valued. He boasted that it was because of him that Grotius's treatise *De maris libertate* (*On the Freedom of the Seas*), first published in Leyden in 1609, avoided the Roman censors. He often managed to deliver on his promised manuscripts.[79] He maintained his connections with Bouchard, Peiresc, Saumaise, Naudé, Rigault, and others within the Dupuys' orbit. By 1641—with Peiresc and Bouchard dead and Naudé back in Paris—along with their brother Christophe, he was their chief Roman contact.

A consummate and careful insider who knew on which side his bread was buttered, Holstenius converted to Catholicism while in Paris in the 1620s. But for all his courtier skills, he harbored interesting, possibly heterodox, views. These were not egregiously out of place in the early year of Urban's papacy, but they do mark Holstenius as one of those *esprits forts* who managed to accommodate an ambitious careerism with intellectual independence. His attraction to Platonist philosophy, for example, is clear. Writing to Peiresc in 1631, he confessed to a life-long "desire, first to know more, and then to use all my forces to bring such a divine way of philosophizing to mankind and to promote it." When, with the Campanella and Galileo affairs, Neo-Platonist philosophy began to take on a dangerous cast, Holstenius, ever the shrewd courtier, abandoned his plan to edit a series

---

[77] Pélissier, "Les amis d'Holstenius," 93.   [78] Pélissier, "Les amis d'Holstenius," 111.
[79] In a letter to him, Pierre Dupuy acknowledges this service, noting that Grotius "kisses his hand" in gratitude. Pélissier, "Les amis d'Holstenius," 94.

of ancient Platonist texts. His views on these adventuresome thinkers, however, and his identification with the new thinking then under siege in Counter-Reformation Europe never wavered. In another letter to Peiresc, he vented his dissatisfaction with the treatment of Galileo. "Surely, nobody can see without indignation how Galilei's book, and the entire body of Pythagoreic or Copernican knowledge is judged by men who have no idea of mathematics and of the course of the planets, and no interest in physics." He was not alone among savants as viewing this narrow-minded attitude as not only wrong but detrimental to Rome— the Rome in which he had placed his ambitious hopes. "Precisely where the authority of the Church is at stake," he wrote, "[it] will be seriously impaired by a wrong judgement."[80] Like others we have encountered, both in the Dupuy circle and beyond, Lucas Holstenius strove to defend his bona fides as an independent thinker and maintain his position as an insider in league with the powerful.

Gabriel Naudé: Stendhal of the Seventeenth Century

Perhaps the most energetic and constant of the Dupuys' agents in Italy was Gabriel Naudé, a member of the Tetrade and one of the most erudite and provocative writers of his generation. Naudé left for Italy in 1630 as the librarian and Latin secretary to Cardinal Bagni (also Bagi or Bagy), the former papal nuncio to France, and stayed for eleven years, during which time he immersed himself in the intellectual life of the Italian peninsula. Despite his considerable obligations to his patron, which, much to his dismay, entailed tedious sojourns in the countryside, he never neglected his ties to the Dupuys. Naudé's letters to Jacques Dupuy reveal a restless scholar, observer, and confidant at work. He kept abreast of political affairs, especially during the fractious tenure of Maréchal d'Estrées as France's ambassador in Rome, when conflict between Romans and French officials seemed to be constant.[81] Indeed, it is likely that his discreet observations, which the Dupuys certainly passed along to Richelieu, were instrumental in having the maladroit ambassador recalled. He made sure to keep his patrons informed on the shifting fortunes of various clergy, for prompt news of rising stars and fallen favorites within the intensely competitive and normally obscure Roman ecclesiastical establishment could prove quite useful in Paris. It was no doubt important, for example, for the Dupuys to be aware that Cardinal Mazarin's brother was about to be promoted; or that the Jesuits were increasingly at ease in Urban's Rome; or that speculation about the possibility of a French Church led by

---

[80] This paragraph from Peter Rietbergen, *Power and Religion in Baroque Rome: Barberini Cultural Policies* (Leiden, 2006), chap. 6, quote from 267.

[81] *Lettres de Gabriel Naudé à Jacques Dupuy (1632-1651)*, ed. Phillip J. Wolfe (Edmonton, AB, 1982), 11.

Richelieu as patriarch was being taken seriously in some quarters.[82] In the aftermath of the publication of the *Libertez de l'Eglise gallicane*, which the Dupuys anonymously compiled, they certainly wanted to be kept informed about the reception of this controversial book among Roman readers. Naudé was able to reveal that their role in its publication was no longer a secret there—even more: rumors were being spread that the publication was meant to prepare the way for a schism. In light of this mischievous speculation, which, he assured the Dupuys, he was able to deny to his Roman friends and especially to his patron, Cardinal Bagni, Naudé counseled them to be cautious, lest suspicion run amok. It is interesting to note that this letter, like others dealing with sensitive material, was coded, with the names of individuals and nations disguised.[83]

Most of Naudé's letters were not so dramatic; for the most part, they reveal him to be a tireless scholar and an obsessive bibliophile. His missives are crammed with titles, some recently published, some older but newly discovered, some ancient. Wherever he finds himself, he is constantly on the hunt; even when stranded in Romagna while his patron tends to family matters, he manages to ransack the local church in search of interesting finds. He not only provides the Dupuys with news of books, thus allowing them to keep current with Italian erudition and letters; he also includes capsule summaries and critiques, revealing a gifted practitioner of the new craft of literary and scholarly criticism. In one letter, for example, he cites the recent publication of a commentary on the Psalms by Cardinal Ginnasio, remarking that his "style is not modern but rather in imitation of the Fathers and Doctors of the Church, among whom...he might be placed one day because of his dignity, his age and the goodness of his life." He bemoans the captious tendencies of Roman readers who always find something to criticize, even in the works of Augustin Mascardi, a cardinal and celebrated man of letters held in high esteem among the Dupuy associates. Naudé lauds Mascardi's recent publication on the art of history for its "matchless elegance in language and for its judicious treatment of its subject." "All men of judgment value it," especially since the author also demonstrates the "impertinence of the new style...applauded by some ignoramuses [*ignorants*]." Here as elsewhere, Naudé, like others of the Dupuy milieu, shows his colors as a partisan of traditional erudition, as opposed to the more accessible, more literary style embraced by many contemporary men of letters and endorsed by a wider public.[84]

While Naudé's immersion in Italian culture has moved one historian to dub him the "Stendhal of the seventeenth century,"[85] he was hardly an uncritical observer. He could be quite scathing about the dismal quality of Italian scholarship and the unwarranted arrogance he often encountered, especially vis-à-vis French

---

[82] *Lettres de Naudé*, 76, 101.   [83] *Lettres de Naudé*, 88.
[84] *Lettres de Naudé*, 32.
[85] Henri Busson, *La pensée religieuse francaise de Charron à Pascal* (Paris, 1933), 487.

erudition. As with others among his contemporaries, Naudé's relationship to Italy was tinged with both admiration and rivalry; he was always eager to trumpet French learning and never missed an opportunity to call attention to the pitiful state of Italian libraries in comparison to Parisian collections. His rivalry extended to his scholarly writings as well, though scholarship put to patriotic purposes. After his first visit to Italy, where he spent most of his time in Padua, he published *Addition à l'histoire de Louys XI* (1630), a work that did for the fifteenth-century monarch what Voltaire would later do for the reign of Louis XIV. For Naudé held up Louis XI as a paragon of princely beneficence, whose wise efforts in cultivating learning and patronizing scholars had fostered the revival of classical letters. He cited the creation of the Royal Library under the direction of Robert Gaugin, mistakenly claiming that printing was then introduced into the realm. In short, he credited King Louis with the Renaissance. And by extension he not only affirmed the connection between princely patronage and the growth of learning that was axiomatic to many humanists, he also claimed that French kings as far back as Charlemagne had been particularly noted for their generosity and wisdom in this respect. He concluded with an ambitious charge addressed to Louis XIII: "It is now up to you, oh most victorious and triumphant of all our monarchs, to follow the road traced by your ancestors, and to place the last stone as you have the first upon this new Parnassus."[86]

There was a polemical aspect to Naudé's text, which challenged the Italian humanists' view of history and Italian primacy in the Renaissance as well. He argued that Louis XI surpassed even such great Maecenases as the Medicis and the Neapolitan king Alfonso in both his own learning and the sponsorship of learning.[87] He recalled that Louis, too, had welcomed Greek scholars to Paris after the fall of Constantinople, the moment humanists traditionally cite as the beginning of the era of the Renaissance, thus denying the Italians their exclusive claim to this action.[88] And he argued as well, *pace* Petrarch and others, that Italy was not the sole source of the revival of learning and ancient languages: France, too, had its share of virtuosi. Did not "those two great lights who dispelled the fog and barbarism, Dante and Petrarch, learn a great part of what has made them renowned to posterity" in France"?[89] Even more, he offered an alternative view of history that explicitly contradicted the dominant understanding of the past as elaborated by Petrarch and accepted virtually throughout the humanist world. For even as Naudé lauded Louis XI, he also lavishly praised Charlemagne, Philippe-Augustus, as well as Frances I, as sponsors and wise custodians of art and learning.

---

[86] Gabriel Naudé, *Addition à l'histoire de Louys XI* (Paris, 1630), 377. See also Hubert Carrier, "Un aspect négligé de l'italianisme de Gabriel Naudé," in Giorgio Mirandola, ed., *L'italianisme en France au XVIIe siècle* (Torino, 1968), 31–46.
[87] Naudé, *Addition à l'histoire de Louys XI*, 55.   [88] *Addition à l'histoire de Louys XI*, 184.
[89] *Addition à l'histoire de Louys XI*, 175.

Indeed, unlike the Italian humanists, whose judgment of the Middle Ages was usually critical, even contemptuous, Naudé's acknowledgment of the salutary role of these monarchs in fostering learning had the effect of revaluing this unappreciated period, at least in French history. In this he was not alone; as we have seen with Voiture and Chapelain (*La pucelle*), the positive view of the legacy of the medieval period was greatly appreciated among contemporary *gens de lettres*. Among these Frenchmen, at least, a humanist education did not mean a disavowal of this period of their country's history.

Closer to Home: Guyet, Fortin de la Hoguette, and Boulliau

The range and number of savants throughout Europe with ties to the Dupuys' cabinet was impressive, justifying in the eyes of many its designation as the capital of the Republic of Letters in the early seventeenth century. Their network extended well beyond the Italian connections I have focused on here, especially to England and the Low Countries. But the cabinet's local roots were no less important. While it maintained some distance from the *mondain* culture of the salons and other literary groups, it certainly benefited from the social synergy of a revived Paris in the period following the Wars of Religion. As important as the cosmopolitan reach of the European Republic of Letters was, then, it should not obscure the fact that it rested on local and particular associations—that in order for the Dupuys to maintain their cabinet as a de facto "headquarters" of this Republic, it had to attract and maintain the allegiance of the savants who populated their entourage. Here, then, are three insiders of the cabinet who suggest the range of its habitués: François Guyet, a consummate savant; Philippe Fortin de la Hoguette, a noble soldier and magistrate who was also quite learned; and Ismaël Boulliau, known throughout Europe as a leading astronomer, a supporter of Galileo.

François Guyet: The Savant

No one represented the erudite side of the Dupuy cabinet more than François Guyet, a scholar whose imposing learning and fierce critical sense made him a figure to be reckoned with, even within this intellectually selective milieu. La Mothe le Vayer noted Guyet's "dogmatic and assertive" spirit. He even managed to insult the beloved Peiresc. More a scholar than a writer, he left behind an archive of commentaries, mostly on ancient texts, which demonstrate that he was a worthy successor to Isaac Casaubon and Joseph Scaliger, two better-known classical scholars—who both also maintained ties with the Dupuys. Guyet was universally admired for his skill at Greek and Latin and feared for his sharp tongue. Balzac, who rarely acknowledged an intellectual equal, craved his approval and once giddily wrote to Chapelain how much he valued his esteem. They were friends at one time, both having benefited from the patronage of the Epernon family. But their relationship turned decisively sour when Balzac learned that Guyet had uttered some disparaging comments about his Latin. His gratitude then turned to bitterness: "Guyet is an old fool who, in his best hours, acts only by caprice and chance," he declared. "He excommunicates in the evening people he canonized that morning."[90] Guyet's early twentieth-century biographer likens the dispute between Guyet and Balzac to a real-life version of Molière's Alceste and Oronte. While it might be hard to imagine the prickly hermit of Charente as a suave *honnête homme*, it certainly is not difficult to see Guyet as yet another model for the Misanthrope.

François Guyet was born in Angers in 1575 into a noble family with deep roots in the region. Orphaned at an early age, he was consigned to the care of tutors, who apparently proceeded to squander his entire inheritance. Beyond this, we know nothing of the first twenty-four years of his life, not even how he managed to achieve mastery in classical studies at an early age. In any case, in 1599 he made his way to Paris, where he quickly gained entry into the circle around Jacques-Auguste de Thou. The capital did not keep him long. Like other young scholars he roamed about Europe, spending most of his time in Rome, where he entered the entourage of the Cardinal de Joyeuse. Back in Paris in 1610, he secured the favor of the Epernon family, serving as preceptor for the future Cardinal La Valette. The family rewarded him with an ecclesiastical benefice, which allowed him to enjoy the life of a scholar. He took up residence in the Collège de Bourgogne, not far from the Dupuys' library on the rue Poictevins. A daily fixture at the Dupuys', there, writes Pintard, "he reigned rather than sat."[91] Indeed, he seems to have lived out his long life within the narrow orbit of his college chambers and the Adelphes. He died in 1655 at the age of 85.

Descriptions of Guyet usually make a point of his arrogance and intellectual severity, his tendency to dispense with *ex cathedra* judgments that broached no criticism or contradiction. But this only points to what contemporaries most valued about him. For, at least within the Dupuy cabinet, there was no one as skilled in Greek and Latin, nor anyone who had the intellectual and linguistic confidence to engage in the kind of textual criticism of ancient texts that was at the heart of the humanist project. Here Guyet's erudition, along with his considerable temerity, was on full display. He undertook a thorough examination of a range of canonical ancient texts, reserving the right to rule on their legitimacy, accuracy, or provenance. While severe, his judgments were often well founded. One modern scholar concludes that Guyet's critical notes on some key phrasing in Hesiod's *Theogeny* are "astute," offering emendations that "make more sense as far as the meaning of

---

[90] Uri, *Un cercle savant*, 103.   [91] Pintard, *Le libertinage érudit*, 185.

the passage is concerned" than traditional versions of the text.[92] But many of his views exceeded the reach of his erudition. For example, he claimed to have proven that Latin derived solely from Greek, but when his notes on this subject were examined after his death, they were found to be a vast and disordered jumble of words that proved nothing of the kind. He was a radical critic, unafraid to denounce whole passages of canonical texts as fraudulent or fake. A contemporary commented, "He wields his pen like an exterminating sword."[93] Pierre Bayle wrote that he "struck out many verses in his Vergil, pretending that they were supposititious, and that the poems of that great poet were like those troops, among which there are many false musters; so that he acted like a rigid commissary, who musters none but true soldiers."[94] He discarded the first ode of Horace as not being by the Roman poet, eliminated whole scenes from plays by Terence, and corrected several passages in Cicero as well as other Latin writers.

For all his ceaseless labors, Guyet never published his critical commentaries; they were preserved by the efforts of his friend and fellow habitué of the Dupuys Gilles Ménage. Some found their way into print posthumously. The source of his reluctance might have been more fear than modesty, for it seems that Saumaise—one of the few in Europe who were his scholarly equal—was at the ready if he did. Comments Bayle, "[Saumaise] would have proved too hard for him; he would have printed a hundred sheets before Guyet had been able to send four to the press."[95]

It appears, however, that one of his works was published, although anonymously. *Gaeomemphionis Cantaliensis Satyricon* appeared in 1628, with no author or place of publication noted.[96] Scholars have attributed it to Guyet. It was written in a neo-Latin style that in the late sixteenth and early seventeenth centuries was cultivated by humanists such as Lipsius and Barclay, works that mimicked the Roman satirical genre, especially as conveyed in the *Satyricon*. These, writes Anthony Grafton, "were academic to a fault: written in deliberately difficult Latin, they followed the doings of characters whose polysyllabic Greek names did more to conceal than to reveal their allegorical meanings. They often explicitly parodied academic customs and follies. Many of them took shots at such sitting ducks as the professional textual critic, that doyen of obsessive pedants, or offered set-piece parodies of university lectures and disputations."[97]

Guyet's *Satyricon* conforms to type. The story follows the peregrinations of Gaeomemphion, a young scholar fresh from his studies, as he attempts to make

---

[92] Merek Wecowski, "Can Zeus Be Deceived? The Mekone Episode (Hes. theog. 535–561) between Theodicy and Power-Politics," *Klio*, 94/1 (2012), 47.

[93] Uri, *Un cercle savant*, 148.

[94] Quoted in Anthony Grafton, "Jean Hardouin: The Antiquary as Pariah," *Journal of the Warburg and Courtauld Institutes*, 62 (1999), 260–1.

[95] Grafton, "Jean Hardouin," 261.

[96] *Le roman satirique de Gaeomemphion du Cantal*, ed. and trans. Juliette Desjardins (Geneva, 1972).

[97] Anthony Grafton, "Petronius and Neo-Latin Satire: The Reception of the *Cena Trimalchionis*," *Journal of the Warburg and Courtauld Institutes*, 53 (1990), 243.

his way in the world. His name can be translated as "Scorner of the World," which is increasingly borne out as an accurate description of his disposition as his travails mount and his disillusionment grows. At the novel's start, no sooner does he set out from his bucolic mountainside village than he encounters a series of misfortunes, beginning with the theft of his savings by a fellow traveler on the very first night. Thus is set in motion a succession of mishaps, many burlesque in character, casting the book as inspired in part by Rabelais, in part by Cervantes, in part, too, by the Roman satirical tradition. At heart it is a sort of satirical *Bildungsroman*, the education of a young man as he learns that the world little appreciates either his intellect, or learning, or virtue. He encounters duplicity and falsehood everywhere he turns. And so, at the novel's end, his disillusionment with the world complete, he decides that retreat is the only virtuous course, returning him to his native village. Like Odysseus after escaping from the snares of his punishing travels, he would "tread again the haven of his rocky Ithaca."

Here again the theme of retreat, of the value of withdrawal from a vexed and heartless world. In Guyet's telling it is a move born of defeat. In one sense, it might be seen as a satirical commentary on the humanist dream: the failure of society to accommodate the virtue and learning of the young hero, who, as the novel makes clear at its outset, fully expects that his years of study and commitment to scholarship will be repaid with worldly success. The fault, however, lies as much with Gaeomemphion's hopeless naiveté, compounded by his upbringing in rustic isolation, as with the duplicity or viciousness of almost everyone he encounters. The moral of the story, then, is not so much that a virtuous life committed to learning cannot be sustained in the "world"—which does nothing more than repackage an age-old axiom—but rather that this expectation is nothing less than another form of ignorance. Balzac called the Dupuy cabinet an "innocent refuge." As usual, he exaggerated for effect: while hosts of a privileged milieu that cosseted the likes of the eccentric Guyet, the Dupuys were hardly "innocent" of the world and its many snares.

Philippe Fortin de la Hoguette: The Soldier

If Guyet was the stay-at-home *érudit* who rarely strayed from the confines of the cabinet, Fortin de la Hoguette was one intimate of this group whose intimacy was affirmed at a distance.[98] He rarely entered the precincts of this Parisian capital of the Republic of Letters, but nevertheless, over almost forty years, he maintained a steady and warm correspondence with the Dupuy brothers. His peregrinations,

---

[98] Giulini Ferretti is the best source on Fortin de la Hoguette. See his *Un "soldat philosophe": Philippe Fortin de la Hoguette, 1585–1668?* (Genoa, 1988) and *Lettres aux frères Dupuy et à leur entourage, 1623–1662* (Florence, 1997).

however, were hardly the undertakings of a man of leisure, for La Hoguette led the life of a soldier, active in several combat arenas. Unlike the Rambouillet salon, which, as we have seen, served as a sort of refined refuge for war-weary aristocratic warriors home from the front, the Dupuys had virtually nothing to do with military men. La Hoguette was the exception. But as much as his adult life was punctuated by extended bouts of campaigning, he never neglected his commitment to letters and his ties to this savant society. In him—as with Georges de Scudéry and Honoré d'Urfé—arms and letters are present in equal measure.

Philippe Fortin de la Hoguette was born in 1585 in Falaise (Normandy), to a family of Robe officers: his father was *président de l'élection*. He received a solid education as a youth, but early on, and apparently contrary to the wishes of his parents, he decided to take up the profession of arms. His first travels led him to Holland, where he studied at the military school of Prince Frederick Henry of Nassau. He fought at the Siege of La Rochelle (1627–8) and in subsequent campaigns in Italy (1629–30). Following this, he purchased the position of lieutenant, which he then sold in 1634. After a period of retirement, he again entered the ranks in 1639, serving in the flotilla of Cardinal de Sourdis, archbishop of Bordeaux, in its expedition against the Spanish in Galicia. This would be his last bout of military service. In 1641, at the age of 56, he married Louise de Péréfixe, sister of Hardouin, Richelieu's *maître de chambre*. Although early on he was a member of the queen's party, joining many in opposing the power of the king's favorite, Luynes (which very well may have earned him a spell in the Bastille in 1620), he would remain a loyal follower of the cardinal, and of his successor Mazarin. This did not guarantee his success as a courtier. Despite his ties to Richelieu, in 1645 his candidacy as governor of the young Louis XIV was denied. It did not even help that that same year he published (anonymously) his *Catechisme royal*, a brief for monarchical supremacy, which also celebrated the alliance of nobility and crown along with the virtues of Mazarin.

In 1622, La Hoguette established ties with the Dupuys; he was then forever considered a member of their entourage, despite his physical estrangement from their Paris cabinet because of either military service or his self-imposed exile at his country estate in Saintonge, south of La Rochelle. It was largely an epistolary relationship; in the course of thirty-two years between 1623 and 1650, he wrote the Adelphes nearly five hundred letters, which reveal a soldier-philosopher with a keen sense of the varied, even provisional, nature of his life. In 1631, in a letter to Pierre, written when he was 46, he muses, "The actions of my life are so diverse that I do not have the leisure to commit myself to any one of them.... One day I am at court, another I am at battle, one day very busy, another doing nothing; and whenever I decide to conform to a particular task, something happens to make me take up something altogether different, as if I were condemned to a life of perpetual disorderliness."[99] Speaking for himself, La Hoguette's musings are those of the typical *honnête homme*—the nobleman whose ironic self-awareness is informed by the burdens of negotiating a world of many parts and commitments.

Although he published very little and spent as much time on the battlefield as in his library, La Hoguette's commitment to letters and learning is clear. Nothing demonstrates this more than his early championing of Francis Bacon. In 1622, the same year he "entered' the Dupuy cabinet, he conceived an interest in Bacon, especially his *Novum Organum*, just published (1621), and the *Essays*. Interest in the Lord Chancellor was keen in France: many of his works were translated into French, and most of these were dedicated to prominent figures, ranging from Mme de Rambouillet to ministers of state such as Sully and Richelieu. Savants, especially those close to the Dupuys, were devoted followers of Bacon; Peiresc, in particular, expressed great curiosity about his writings.[100] The Baconian consensus was not total, however: Mersenne criticized his views in *La vérité des sciences*, prompting La Hoguette to insist that the Dupuys ban "this monk" from their cabinet for the "crime of treason [*lèse majesté*]."[101]

La Hoguette took it upon himself to try to meet the Lord Chancellor; 1623 found him in London, where he wrote Pierre Dupuy that he had spent time with the English philosopher and seen the first part of his *Instauration*. When he left London for Paris, he bore with him a copy of the *De augmentis* and Bacon's portrait—a token of esteem among humanists. The editor of the Oxford edition of Bacon's writings, Graham Rees, claims that La Hoguette stole some other manuscripts, something he seems to confirm in a letter to Pierre Dupuy. Two of the essays, "Of Religion" and "Of Superstition," were translated with the help of Peiresc's brother. For some reason, La Hoguette hoarded the other trove of purloined manuscripts; they disappeared until they were discovered by a researcher among the Dupuy papers in 1985.[102]

La Hoguette's major publication is his *Testament*, written for his sons, a work republished well into the eighteenth century; it is, among other things, a consideration of the code of *honnêteté* (as we have seen in Chapter 2). In the middle of this text, he meditates on the virtues of retreat—and the difficulty of securing its comforts. There is no peace, not even true "society," among the many. In the "multitude, the faces of men one meets make as little impression on us as those one sees

---

[99] Ferretti, *Lettres aux frères Dupuy*, 14.

[100] On interest in Bacon in France in the early part of the seventeenth century, see Michèle Le Doeuff, "Bacon chez les grands au siècle de Louis XIII," in Marta Fattori, ed., *Francis Bacon: Terminologia e fortuna nel XVII secolo* (Rome, 1984), 155–78. Mersenne, however, objected.

[101] On this, see Stéphane Garcia, *Élie Diodati et Galilée: Naissance d'un réseau scientifique dans l'Europe du XVIIe siècle* (Florence, 2004), 212.

[102] *The Oxford Francis Bacon*, ed. Graham Rees, vol. XIII: *The Instauratio magna: Last Writings* (Oxford, 2000), liii; see also La Hoguette's own admission, lvii; Ferretti, *Un "soldat philosophe,"* 17–18; Ferretti, *Lettres aux frères Dupuy*, 96–108.

in a dream. The sound of their words is hardly more articulate than the noise of a torrential rainfall."[103] He does, however, acknowledge that the virtues cultivated in retreat are "imperfections in the order of civil society, which requires that each maintain the rank of his mind and condition," and in this sense, as befitting a man whose commitments were divided, his *Testament* affirms the contradictory nature of such a life. But his preference for retreat is clear. However, while flight from the many is desirable, solitude is not. A just mean must be found, "composed of a choice of some particular people with whom one can communicate in order to avoid the disadvantages of the multitude."[104] And here is where La Hoguette indulges in an extended encomium to the Dupuy cabinet, which serves as the model for his ideal of like-minded friends enjoying the privilege of dignified retreat.

In a work almost entirely devoid of autobiographical references, these pages are marked by specific allusions. "God granted me the grace, being at court, of having been received for thirty years in the society of two brothers of renown and an illustrious life, who are the Messieurs Dupuy," he writes. As Marc Fumaroli has noted, in this sentence, which discreetly yet pointedly underscores the antinomy between his courtly commitments and social attachments, La Hoguette frames the cabinet as a place of retreat.[105] He then launches into a description of the gatherings each evening at the Dupuys', which are distinguished by their "harmony," "gentleness," and "discretion." Everyone brings the best of himself to this "honest society." Beyond "calming our passions," the conversation "also illuminates our understanding," he continues, in a vein that both echoes and modifies Montaigne's "De la conversation." Like the sixteenth-century essayist, he considers solitary thinking or pure meditation as inadequate for producing ideas of substance. It is only in the back-and-forth of conversation that our thoughts are endowed with body and substance. Productive thinking requires intellectual sociability, especially among like-minded men committed to serious discussion—exemplified by his friends in the Dupuy cabinet. But he does not endorse the rough-and-ready jousting that Montaigne preferred. For La Hoguette, it is rather the comity and civility of these exchanges—the "sweetness" that, he asserts, particularly characterizes the milieu of the Dupuys—which distinguishes them from the banal, empty conversation of most people. His *Testament*, among other things, offers a sustained celebration of friendship—not the traditional idea of friendship as a model of society or a template of the Republic, but the more restricted notion that sees it as a privileged relationship between the virtuous and like-minded few. This is the kind of friendship found among the Dupuys, an affection that can be

---

[103] Philippe Fortin, sieur de La Hoguette, *Testament, ou, Conseils fidèles d'un bon père à ses enfans* (Paris, 1698 ed.), 269. Page numbers in the notes refer to this edition.
[104] La Hoguette, *Testament*, 269.
[105] Marc Fumaroli, "La 'conversation' au XVIIe siècle: Le témoignage de Fortin de la Hoguette," in Louis van Delft, ed., *L'Esprit et la lettre: Mélanges offerts à Jules Brody* (Tübingen, 1991), 99.

cultivated only between "good men, whose actions are uniform in the sense that they are all guided by what is virtuous."[106]

For all his emphasis on virtue, La Hoguette's blending of Christianity and Neo-Stoicism comes through in a pronounced note of resignation and submission, especially with respect to the political realm. Unlike the Dupuys and several others affiliated with their cabinet, he never wavered in his loyalty to the crown, Richelieu, and later Mazarin. At least to his children, he explains this stance with a prolonged acknowledgment of the gap between ordinary men and those who hold authority. The actions of the great are simply beyond our understanding and deserve not our censure but veneration. "Instead of complaining of our public miseries, let us renounce our particular interests, and regard with respect the visible arms that create such desolation [in service to] an invisible power that wishes it so."[107] It is possible that this passage is not untouched by irony. He writes, for example, that we should honor the qualities of conquerors, "even though they depopulate the world"; and after offering a list that includes Cyrus, Alexander, Caesar, Attila, and the "last king of Sweden," he adds—in a likely reference to Louis XIII, Richelieu, and Mazarin—"and several others on whom I will remain silent." In any case, these "conquerors" deserve our respect and admiration. We should look upon their actions as "tempests of the earth that serve to cleanse it...and admire the grandeur of God in the excellence of Ministers of his justice." He concludes: "the best recourse is to speak with modesty of those who are responsible for them, and to thank God for not having chosen us for a task so contrary to the softness of our inclinations [*douceur de nos sentiments*]."[108] At least in this public declaration of his values and beliefs, his most precious legacy to his children, Fortin de la Hoguette presented a case for quiescence, resignation, and submission to authority that may have struck some within the Dupuy orbit as unworthy of a true *esprit fort*.

Ismaël Boulliau: The Astronomer

The Dupuys' librarian for much of his career, Ismaël Boulliau also spent time abroad, sometimes in the company of Naudé, and like him usually in the service of the brothers and other savants. He is best known as an astronomer, a promoter of the Copernican view of the solar system, a defender of Galileo, and an accomplished mathematician who employed his geometrical expertise to refine Kepler's

---

[106] La Hoguette, *Testament*, 361. Changing notions and practices of friendship in early modern Europe have recently attracted considerable scholarly attention. On this see, for example, Ulrich Langer, *Perfect Friendship: Studies in Literature and Moral Philosophy from Boccacio to Corneille* (Geneva, 1994); Peter N. Miller, "Friendship and Conversation in Seventeenth-Century Venice," *Journal of Modern History*, 73/1 (2001), 1–31; and the essays in Lewis C. Seifert and Rebecca M. Wilkin, eds., *Men and Women Making Friends in Early Modern France* (Burlington, VT, 2015).
[107] La Hoguette, *Testament*, 293.   [108] *Testament*, 293.

view of planetary ellipses. Born in 1605 in Loudun to Calvinist parents, Boulliau converted to Catholicism when he was 21 and entered the priesthood in1631. He moved to Paris in the early 1630s,[109] and by 1636 had taken charge of the Dupuys' library, remaining the custodian of their prestigious collection for the next thirty years. It is likely that Mersenne and Gassendi, with whom he shared scientific interests, sponsored his entrée into this privileged domain, aided by the efforts of Luillier, the magistrate and patron of savants.[110] Before Boulliau was installed at the Dupuys', he was considered a "domestic" in the household of their cousin Jacques-Auguste de Thou, serving as his confessor and the tutor to his children.[111] Both Pierre and Jacques left him considerable sums in their wills. While he had other patrons in the course of his career, he acknowledged his debt to the Dupuys. Like others, he appreciated the privileges—both material and intellectual—of their protection. Enjoying the support of what amounted to a seventeenth-century version of an independent think-tank, he was able to turn down several offers of university positions, much to his relief (something he also advised Gassendi to do).[112] "Their favor and kindness has given me the opportunity to study at my leisure and in peace and to learn with ease so many things that I would never have been aware of otherwise," he wrote to his sometime patron, the French ambassador to Venice.[113] But his reputation went well beyond the confines of their cabinet. Contemporaries acknowledged his stature, especially after the publication of his major astronomical study *Astronomia philolaica* in 1644.[114] He was one of the few foreigners to be elected to the Royal Society of London, in 1667. His relationship with the Dupuys ended with Jacques's death in 1656, after which he followed de Thou throughout Europe on various diplomatic missions. He spent the last years of his life bereft of patrons, serving as a priest and then retiring to the Abbey Saint-Victor in Paris. He died in 1694.

Boulliau's espousal of Copernicanism and his support of Galileo did not necessarily distinguish him among those associated with the Dupuy cabinet; but he was one of the few whose own investigations brought him directly into the fray over the new astronomy. And like others, he found it necessary to exercise caution in expressing his views. On one level, however, he was convinced that he had nothing to fear from agents of the Holy See, for he assumed that because neither French ecclesiastical authorities nor the Sorbonne had been notified of the judgment against Galileo, it simply did not apply in France. Perhaps this was the wishful thinking of a convinced Gallican. In any case, Boulliau took care to publish

---

[109] Henk J. M. Nellen, *Ismaël Boulliau (1605–1694): Astronome, épistolier, nouvelliste et intermédiaire scientifique: Ses rapports avec les milieux du "libertinage érudit"* (Amsterdam, 1994), 44. Nellen's biography is as close to exhaustive as any study of such a figure is likely to be. I have primarily relied upon it throughout.
[110] Nellen, *Boulliau*, 87. [111] Nellen, *Boulliau*, 49. [112] Nellen, *Boulliau*, 185.
[113] Nellen, *Boulliau*, 46 n. 50. [114] Nellen, *Boulliau*, 57.

his views only abroad and anonymously.[115] His friends Gassendi, Grotius, and Saumaise warned him to be circumspect, especially as Théophraste Renaudot, also a native of Loudun (and whom Boulliau undoubtedly knew), was apparently eager to "out" Parisian followers of Galileo in his *Gazette*.[116] Like others of his milieu, he learned to play a double game, making sure to keep his true opinions to himself and his friends. "I have learned not to get myself caught, and sometimes I appear to accept common thinking so as not to stand out as unconventional even though I think otherwise," he wrote Jacques in 1646. "Events have taught me," he concluded, that in these matters, "*spesso la moltitudine s'inganna*"—"often the masses are angry."[117]

Boulliau's hometown of Loudun figures in a revealing aspect of his intellectual biography. He was certainly not alone in taking an interest in the notorious case of the "devils" of Loudun—the trial and execution of Bishop Urban Grandier, accused of witchcraft for supposedly casting a spell over the Ursuline nuns of the town in 1634. But he personally knew Grandier, and this fact undoubtedly compounded his interest. He shared the view of his circle that the prosecution of the bishop was both politically motivated and represented yet another unedifying example of religious fanaticism and churchmen gone wrong. "You see," he wrote to Gassendi, "where the madness of these exhausted brains leads us, to the ruin of humankind and the Catholic religion."[118] He was a debunker of miracles and a skeptic when it came to many of the lives of the saints.[119] A churchman himself, he knew he had to remain circumspect in his criticism. In point of fact, his fundamental allegiance to his faith never wavered, even as he conducted respectful and spirited correspondences with Lutherans and Socinians, rabbis and Muslim clerics alike. If they attacked the dogmas of the Church, however, then "he showed his claws."[120]

Boulliau's religious views were in line with the Gallicanism that characterized the Dupuy circle. He was vocal in his support of Jacques-Auguste de Thou's *History*, which (as we have seen) was placed on the Index. Debating a German Jesuit who insisted that de Thou's writings undermined the authority of the pope, Boulliau responded that the historian had only observed the long-acknowledged fundamental laws of the Gallican Church.[121] He was unsparing when it came to the Jesuits, not so much on theological grounds but rather for what he considered their heavy-handed tactics. "Except for the Fathers Petau and Sirmond, that company has no one worth anything," he wrote to Jacques Dupuy.[122] He called for the reform of religious orders. He denounced the bigotry of the Parisian *dévots*. His support of Galileo was not simply a matter of his acceptance of Copernicanism; it

---

[115] Nellen, *Boulliau*, 57–64. [116] Nellen, *Boulliau*, 56; Pintard, *Le libertinage érudit*, 299.
[117] Nellen, *Boulliau*, 348. [118] Nellen, *Boulliau*, 42.
[119] Pintard, *Le libertinage érudit*, 290. [120] Pintard, *Le libertinage érudit*, 288.
[121] Nellen, *Boulliau*, 195. [122] Nellen, *Boulliau*, 115.

was also based on the assertion—echoing Galileo himself—that the Holy See had jurisdiction in spiritual matters or concerns of salvation alone, not over the workings of nature. The whole controversy only heightened his Gallican suspicion of the overreaching power of the papacy into French affairs. His critique of fellow Catholics drew upon his observations in Constantinople during his time there in the 1640s: he came away from his visit with a great appreciation for the dignity and concentration of Muslims in their devotions, favorably comparing their comportment to the lack of decorum he bemoaned among his Catholic co-religionists. His admiration for what he witnessed in the Ottoman capital extended to an appreciation for the religious politics of the sultan, who, he averred, tolerated a variety of faiths, while managing to avoid the bloody Wars of Religion that blighted Christian Europe. In so many words, then, Boulliau held the view that forbidding the free exercise of religion was a sure route to a prince's ruin.[123]

In 1645 Boulliau left Paris for Italy, on a mission not only to find books and manuscripts for the Dupuys but with special orders from Diodati, Gassendi, Guyet, and others as well. His quest was mostly successful, although he could not match his sometime companion Naudé, who, financed generously by Mazarin, proceeded to wipe out entire bookshops. He was pleased at the prices for Greek and Latin books in the shops near the Rialto bridge in Venice. Something of a bargain hunter, he passed up a copy of Vasari's *Lives of the Artists* when he heard that a cheaper edition had just appeared in Bologna. He was disappointed, however, when his request to copy manuscripts at the Library of Saint Marks was denied: "They are guarding this library for the rats, the mice, and perhaps even for the Turks."[124] And he expressed outrage at the shoddy state of the local libraries, with their books lying flat and chained to the shelves. (The Dupuys, apparently, had already liberated their books from their chains.)[125]

Boulliau maintained a steady correspondence with Jacques Dupuy during his travels. He usually attached something of a newsletter to his letters, meant for circulation among his friends. These *foglietti*—about twenty-five in all—offered his views on European politics from the perspective of a Frenchman in northern Italy. Here he mostly proved himself to be a defender of French interests and the aggressive policies of Mazarin. This was not a knee-jerk reaction by a political toady. During Richelieu's ministerial reign, he condemned, though discreetly, the cardinal's policies as detrimental to France and accused him of manipulating Louis XIII to his wrong-headed purposes.[126] (When it came to discussing politics in his letters, like others, he often resorted to code.[127]) More generally, he expressed some dissatisfaction with what he saw as Christian Europe's lack of success

---

[123] Nellen, *Boulliau*, 63.
[124] Jack A. Clarke, "A Book Buying Tour in 1645: A Note on Ismael Boulliau in Italy," *Journal of Library History*, 4/4 (1969), 334.
[125] Clark, "A Book Buying Tour," 335.   [126] Nellen, *Boulliau*, 197–8.
[127] Nellen, *Boulliau*, 348.

in the confessional and geopolitical conflict between Islam and Christendom. He expressed downright impatience with the French-Habsburg conflict, despite his professed support for Mazarin's campaigns in Italy. For all his sympathy and genuine interest in Ottoman culture and Islam, then, Boulliau was among those Europeans who pointed to the divide between the Ottoman Empire and Europe as fundamental—so much so that it now should supersede the conflicts within Europe. He endorsed the formation of a Christian alliance against the Turks, even though he conceded that France itself was hardly at risk from the Ottomans. In "Conseil de la paix," a communication to Mazarin written somewhat after the period of our concern, in 1656, he urges an end to the infighting among Christian nations in favor of a European united front against the Turks, offering a vision of "Europe" that was as much geographical as it was religious. Indeed, his vision of an ideal continental unity, based on a range of commonalities transcending the century-long conflict between both Protestants and Catholics and France and the Habsburgs, begins to resemble the conception of a civilization. One of the takeaway points of Mark Greengrass's panoramic *Christendom Destroyed* is that Europe's conflict with the Ottoman Empire fostered a heightened sense of "Europe" as a civilizational unit.[128] Boulliau, this Gallican who otherwise displayed such admiration for Ottoman culture, might be considered an early advocate of a "clash of civilizations." As with the Dupuys, Boulliau's liberal stance on religious matters and his general openness to new intellectual trends did not preclude a steely attitude when it came to fundamental political matters.[129]

A Gallican Think-Tank

Whatever else characterized the Dupuy brothers and those who gathered around them, the values most central to their intellectual and political identity were those associated with the "liberties of the Gallican Church," or Gallicanism; they were identified with its cause for their entire lives. Unlike some other partisans of this religious ideology, however, for the most part they refrained from turning this identification into an openly critical stance toward either the crown or the papacy. For one thing, as should be clear, the Dupuys' ties with Rome and the Holy See under Urban VIII were deep—and extremely important to their whole enterprise. For another, by the 1630s, largely through Richelieu's clever cooptation of a flashpoint in the history of Gallicanism—the Santarelli affair—there emerged a *via media* offering a rapprochement between at least some ultramontanes and

---

[128] Mark Greengrass, *Christendom Destroyed: Europe, 1517-1648* (New York, 2015).
[129] For an interpretation of Gallicanism that emphasizes its realist embrace of monarchical power as opposed to irenicism, see Jonathan Powis, "Gallican Liberties and the Politics of Later Sixteenth-Century France," *The Historical Journal*, 26/3 (1983), 515-30.

Gallicans.[130] And it was a position that was largely congenial to the Dupuys. Finally, the Dupuys, like most savants and *gens de lettres*, observed the self-imposed imperative of discretion when it came to giving voice to their critical views. They were loath to go public.

Nevertheless, their most important publishing effort risked doing just that: the two volumes of Gallican texts titled *Traitez des droits et libertez de l'Eglise gallicane* and *Preuves des libertez de l'Église gallicane* both appeared in 1638, published anonymously and without permission. The history of this publication is complex and somewhat shrouded in mystery. William Church suggests that Richelieu accorded his tacit permission for it.[131] And yet, these volumes risked reviving a militant Gallicanism that had supposedly been laid to rest. Of course, this was precisely the leverage Richelieu might have been seeking: the cardinal was presently engaged in a struggle with the French clergy over fiscal matters, and thus to assert the supremacy of the crown over the secular affairs of the Church could have only strengthened his hand. There was also the persistent rumor, already noted, that he planned to set himself up as the patriarch of a Gallican Church, a rumor that Richelieu might have found useful to tolerate or even foster, if only to frighten Rome. The Dupuys' volumes would certainly have been helpful in this respect. Jerôme Delatour, however, argues that the cardinal played no role in sanctioning this publication. "It had the effect of a bomb. No one saw it coming," he writes.[132] Were the Dupuys playing a dangerous game of provoking Richelieu's hand to move decisively on the Gallican front by publishing a work they knew would cause a controversy?[133]

If they were, Richelieu was ahead of them: he had the royal council pass an interdiction against the publication on the grounds that it had appeared without royal permission. In short order, it was denounced by eighteen bishops meeting in Paris—only one measure of its impact on the clerical establishment. Pierre Dupuy responded by charging that the bishops' actions represented a serious challenge to royal sovereignty. In turn, the Parlement of Paris condemned the bishops' letter. What followed was series of publications, several commissioned by Richelieu, which turned the controversy into a full-scale rehearsal of the conflict between Gallican and ultramontane positions. The final salvo, *De concordia sacerdotii et imperii*, a treatise by Pierre de Marca, who was both a bishop and a royal official, provided a belabored version of Richelieu's moderate Gallicanism, which

---

[130] On this, see especially Sylvio Hermann De Franceschi, "La genèse française du catholicisme d'Etat et son aboutissement au début du ministériat de Richelieu: Les catholiques zélés à l'épreuve de l'affaire Santarelli et la clôture de la controverse autour du pouvoir pontifical au temporel (1626–1627)," *Annuaire-Bulletin de la Société de l'histoire de France* (2001), 19–63.

[131] William Farr Church, *Richelieu and Reason of State* (Princeton, 1972), 405.

[132] Delatour, "Les frères Dupuy," II: 337.

[133] On this publication, see Gabriel Demante, "Histoire de la publication des livres de Pierre Du Puy sur les libertés de l'église gallicane," *Bibliothèque de l'Ecole des Chartes*, 5 (1843–4), 585–606.

emphasized, along with the principles of divinely authorized royal supremacy, the need for reconciliation and harmony of Church and State.[134] In all of this the Dupuys seem to have been relegated to the sidelines, stung by the officially sanctioned condemnation of their work, but forced to witness a campaign in defense of their cause, also officially orchestrated. Vindication for their publication would come only in 1651, when, during the *Fronde*, the *Traitez* and the *Preuves* were republished, this time with permission.

On one level the Dupuys were likely convinced that they were simply serving the venerable Gallican cause, a cause, moreover, that Richelieu shared. Indeed, the volumes merely collected documents that had long been in the public domain.[135] On another level, however, their labors revealed that the Gallican case still had teeth, and that the modus vivendi supposedly engineered in the course of the Santarelli affair was not very stable. If in fact Richelieu was complicit in their project, it amounted to sanctioning positions he otherwise did not embrace. This is most evident with the issue of the canons and decrees of the Council of Trent. At the Estates General in 1614, in a discourse that helped make his reputation, Richelieu had himself called for their acceptance in France.[136] A rejection of Trent, however, had been a staple of the Gallican cause since the mid-sixteenth century— ever since Henri II had brought France to the brink of schism over Pope Julius III's reconvening of the council in 1550. Pierre Dupuy had also participated in the controversy at the Estates General by writing a tract that vehemently rejected

---

[134] On this and the above, see Church, *Richelieu and Reason of State*, 404–11.

[135] Despite the controversy it provoked, the Dupuys' publication was hardly marked by originality. It relied heavily on previous Gallican scholarship, especially as accumulated by such sixteenth-century *érudits* as Charles Dumoulin, Jean du Tillet, and Pierre Pithou. Indeed, the Dupuys' two volumes picked up where Pithou's labors had left off. Like Pierre Dupuy, Pithou had access to the royal archives: under Henri IV he was charged with making the royal case against feudal and ecclesiastical challenges through the mobilization of documentary evidence. Though he died in 1596, only two years after his appointment as *procureur général*, a position that gave him full access to the unmatched treasure of royal sources, he left an archive of notes, inventories of documents, extracts from official registers, copies of manuscripts, as well as legal and historical commentaries on French customary law, all of which passed into the hands of the Dupuys. Much of his research aimed to shore up royal authority against feudal customary law, but it was his work on the crown's power in religious affairs that proved most fruitful. As with others of his generation, his royalist and *politique* sentiments were sharpened by the threat of ultramontanism, and in particular the challenge represented by the Council of Trent. In 1594 he published a tract, *Les libertez de l'Eglise gallicane*, which pithily summarized the fundamental principles of Gallicanism as it had evolved in the course of the sixteenth century. Composed of eighty-three propositions, it was based on two principles: "that the pope enjoyed no temporal authority in France, and that his spiritual jurisdiction was limited by the ancient councils and canons recognized by the French monarchy." Donald R. Kelley, *Foundations of Modern Historical Scholarship: Language, Law, and History in the French Renaissance* (New York, 1970), 262. So important was Pithou's relatively short treatise that the Dupuys granted it privilege of place as the lead document in the *Traitez*.

[136] In that virtuoso discourse before the assembly, he evoked "the goodness of the thing, the authority of its cause, the sanctity of its goals, the fruits that its constitution would produce, the evil that would result with the delay of its reception, the example to other Christian princes, and the word of the late king your father." Victor Martin, *Le gallicanisme et la réforme catholique: Essai historique sur l'introduction en France des décrets du Concile de Trente (1563-1615)* (1919; reprint, Geneva, 1975), 376.

Trent as a tool of Spain and a threat to France's very existence. And this view was reflected in several documents in the *Traitez* and the *Preuves*.[137]

In fact, it would have taken a close reading of the *Traitez* and the *Preuves* to appreciate that the two volumes, crammed with hundreds of documents, contained passages critical of the Council of Trent; perhaps the airing of this particular issue was not what disturbed Richelieu and those in Rome who were alarmed by the publications. They were more likely reacting to what the volumes represented: a highly accomplished, erudite presentation of the Gallican case in all its historical, legal, and theological dimensions, assembled by two gentlemen savants whose position at the center of the Republic of Letters was unassailable. Recently, in the wake of subaltern and post-colonial studies, historians have become more aware of the contingent nature of the "archive," which is usually taken for granted by those of us who work in more established venues for historical research. Here, however, in this massive two-volume compendium of documents, we have a veritable Gallican archive—an authoritative demonstration of the historical case for the "liberties of the Gallican Church."[138]

Moreover, the way the affair unfolded to the discredit of the Dupuys drew Pierre out of his cover of discretion and self-censorship, transforming him from a cautious savant and librarian, a compiler of documents in service to the crown, into a polemicist willing to skirt the boundaries of permissible discourse.

While the controversy was still brewing, Pierre circulated in both French and Latin versions an "Apologie pour la publication des *Traitez* et des *Preuves des Libertez de l'Eglise gallicane*."[139] If the Dupuys had heretofore remained anonymous in their publishing careers, eschewing the fashionable first-person approach to writing associated with worldly *gens de lettres* in favor of the detached stance of a scholar, with this text Pierre now exhibited a change in tactics. His "Apologie" is a florid attack on the bishops and all those who share their rejection of the Gallican principles conveyed in the two volumes, a text at once scathing and scornful, dripping in sarcasm and outrage and drenched in hyperbole. At the very start he draws a line in the sand. All those who truly love France, he declares, have greeted the Dupuys' work with "applause," while the critics are those who "have long declared war on the secular powers and independent and sovereign princes."

---

[137] Those by Pithou, Coquille, Hotman, and Milletot, in particular. In "Discours de M. Guy Coquille des droits ecclésiastiques et libertez de l'Eglise gallicane" (originally published in 1607), in *Traitez des droits et libertez de l'Eglise gallicane* (Paris, 1639), the author refers to the many acts and papal rulings that the French Church had rejected over the centuries: "Some of these constitutions refused in France have been repeated and confirmed by the Council of Trent, which is in part the reason why the said Council has not been accepted in France, as derogatory of the rights of the king and of the liberties of the church" (192).

[138] For two model studies of the place of the archive in post-colonial cultures, see Ann Laura Stoler, *Along the Archival Grain: Epistemic Anxieties and Colonial Common Sense* (Princeton, 2009); and Kirsten Weld, *Paper Cadavers: The Archives of Dictatorship in Guatemala* (Durham, NC, 2014).

[139] Delatour, "Les frères Dupuy," II: 341; Pierre Dupuy, "Apologie pour la publication des *Traitez* et des *Preuves des Libertez de l'Eglise gallicane*" (1731).

The bishops, whom he calls "Charlatans," have found heresy where there is none; they probably did not even read the works, he suggests. And he wonders how it is that their "censure" has been allowed to go unopposed (in fact, the Parlement ruled against it), using language that conveys a not too subtle critique of Richelieu: "How is it that those who govern France so absolutely have thus abandoned the authority of their master in Paris, while supporting it in Rome?" Perhaps, he muses, it would be wiser not to respond to the bishops, referring to an ancient parable about not prosecuting the Bacchantes, the "deranged women," for fear of only enraging them more; or, more tellingly, the advice given to Brutus as he contemplated the plot against Caesar, that it was hardly right for a "prudent man to cause himself grief for the sake of the mad and ignorant." Comments Dupuy, "Certainly it seems that the conduct of our State, such as it is today, is hardly worthy of such efforts." For an elite savant, this question, which struck at the heart of the quixotic attitude of *esprits forts* toward the public realm, was apposite indeed. Clearly, however, he felt that this cause warranted venturing where he and his confreres had theretofore not deigned to go. Despite their lack of reason, someone had to respond to those who "had abandoned their country, rendering it enslaved and tributary."[140]

His outrage is justified, he asserts, by the outrageousness of the bishops' censure. "What impertinence!" he exclaims. "They condemn these books which contain, they say, as many heresies as there are lines." Their censure is thus tantamount to a condemnation of centuries of papal and ecclesiastical history: "25 or 30 papal bulles, 30 or 40 ancient councils of the realm"; for these are the rulings that created the principles of Gallicanism. The bishops arrogantly believe that they constitute the Gallican Church. They may be its "principal ministers," concedes Dupuy, but in a statement that plays on the theme of a unified "body" of the Gallican Church, he writes, "all of France, that is to say, all French Catholics, compose the ensemble of bodies of this Church."[141]

Much of Dupuy's "Apologie" is taken up with summarizing the Gallican position, and especially the point that true royal sovereignty cannot coexist with assertions to ecclesiastical or papal authority over a king's subjects, whether clerical or lay. Such pretensions not only undermine sovereignty; they threaten the entire social and political hierarchy, and even invite subjects to revolt. Why would they not, he asks, when they see that in the eyes of the pope there is no difference between them and their kings?[142] And he adds the novel and provocative argument that, given Rome's intrusion into the temporal affairs of Catholic countries, what would be the incentive for "kings and free republics who have separated from the Catholic Church" to rejoin the faith, knowing that they could hardly expect better treatment than that accorded to "the very Christian king, the eldest

---

[140] Dupuy, "Apologie pour la publication," 3. [141] "Apologie pour la publication," 5, 4.
[142] "Apologie pour la publication," 6–7.

son of the Church?"[143] Like other seventeenth-century Gallican texts, Dupuy's "Apologie" looks back to the Wars of Religion and especially the League in support of its defense of Gallican liberties. He refers to the League twice, the first time tying it both to Spain and to the pope, the second time alluding to the League as an example of how the papacy uses religion as a "mask" to disguise its political ambitions.[144]

The last pages of the "Apologie" amount to a call to battle for the partisans of the Gallican Church against Rome. But here his tone turns plaintive, as if he doubted that France's leaders had the resolve to pursue the fight. Indeed, he repeats the charge of "cowardice" and "weakness" with rhetorical effectiveness. "We are afraid of offending Rome, but Rome does not fear offending God." And he drives home the point that the defense of Gallican liberties is linked to the present European war. "What weakness of State! There, can we imagine afterward what advantages this will give to the Empire and Spain? What will remain for us but cowardice?"[145]

In point of fact, the "Apologie" contains a brief for a politics guided by interest, with whole passages that might have been lifted from the reason of state treatises that abounded in the period. Playing on the well-known trope of "the useful and the honest," he writes, "Princes sometimes do things that are shameful, which cannot be blamed when they are useful to their states; for the shame is covered by the gain, which is then called wisdom." Similarly, he asserts the distinction between ethics for princes and for ordinary Christians: patience is "praiseworthy" for Christians in their private lives, but for statesmen it is "a vice, a sign of cowardice, which is the inevitable ruin of the most powerful monarchies."[146] For Dupuy, Rome is just another government. We should not be surprised if it tries to increase its power, nor if, like other states, it takes advantage of weakness in others. "They are men attached to their interests like others," he notes laconically. The difference is that Rome acts under the pretext of religion. Pierre Dupuy, this *esprit fort*, writes as a *déniaisé*, as one who is "undeceived" by the masks and pretenses of the world. What is interesting about his "Apologie" is that for once he let his own mask fall.

The Execution of F.-A. de Thou: Pierre Dupuy on Richelieu as Tyrant

If the Dupuys' destiny was set by the example, influence, and legacy of their uncle Jacques-Auguste de Thou, a turning point in their lives surely came with the death of the great historian's son, François-Auguste de Thou. In 1642 this young de Thou, the Dupuys' cousin and an intimate of their circle, was executed along with the infamous Cinq-Mars, Louis XIII's erstwhile favorite. The story of the Cinq-Mars conspiracy has been told many times: essentially it was the last in a long line of

---

[143] "Apologie pour la publication," 6. [144] "Apologie pour la publication," 10.
[145] "Apologie pour la publication," 9, 10. [146] "Apologie pour la publication," 10, 11.

plots against the cardinal, most inspired, if not led, by the king's brother, the Duc d'Orléans. Because of his proximity to the throne and royal blood, Monsieur knew that he would be spared the fate of his co-conspirators, which made it unconscionably easy for him to draw more vulnerable noblemen into his plans. With only non-royal blood coursing through their veins, these hapless fellow travelers risked ending their lives on the scaffold.[147]

Cinq-Mars was no exception. At first promoted by Richelieu as a confidant and boon companion to the weak-minded king, a favorite the cardinal thought he could control, the young, handsome, and headstrong Cinq-Mars soon tired of his patron, chafed at the constraints of court life and his designated role as Louis's playmate, and cast about for ways to exercise more influence. It did not take long for his ambition to lead him to those plotting against the cardinal. In 1641, his involvement in the Count of Soissons's rebellion narrowly escaped detection. The next year he again plunged into a full-scale conspiracy with Spain, designed to culminate in the assassination of Richelieu and the reversal of France's anti-Habsburg policy. It turned out, however, that in at least one respect the cardinal's critics were right: he had spies everywhere, and this master of secrecy knew how to penetrate the secrets of others. Informants presented Richelieu with news of the plot and even a copy of the proposed treaty with Spain. In short order, Cinq-Mars was arrested, tried, and executed.

Following him on the scaffold was François-Auguste de Thou. De Thou was an admired figure among the French nobility and, of course, the Dupuys' favorite cousin and an intimate of their circle. There is very little linking him directly to the Cinq-Mars conspiracy, at least as a participant. It is, however, virtually certain that he was aware of the plot; he was very close to the king's favorite. Perhaps a scrupulous sense of honor prevented him from informing on the noble conspirators; like many of his class, he was surely sympathetic to their goals, and he would not have mourned the demise of the powerful cardinal and an end to the war with Spain. In any case, he was caught in Richelieu's snare. Although a couple of judges balked at rendering a sentence of death for his tangential involvement in the conspiracy, Richelieu's agent, Chancellor Séguier, had his orders: de Thou was to be found guilty of a capital offense. Moments after Cinq-Mars was mutilated on the block, the same blunt axe wielded by the same inexperienced executioner severed de Thou's head from his body, though it took several blows.

Many mourned de Thou's passing, but no one more than the Dupuys and their circle. Ultimately they had their revenge. Like many "insider" contemporaries, they had been of two minds about the great cardinal-minister—at once cognizant of his brilliance and largely supportive of his policies, but increasingly wary of his power and doubtful whether his bellicose tendencies could ever be curbed.

---

[147] An account of this episode can be found in the standard histories of the period. For a fresh and revealing look at the trial, focusing especially on de Thou, see Jérôme Delatour, "'Les armes en main et les larmes aux yeux': Le procès de Cinq-Mars et de Thou," in Yves-Marie Bercé, ed., *Les procès politiques (XIVe–XVIIe siècle)* (Rome, 2007), 351–93.

De Thou's execution tipped the scales of their judgment. Pierre Dupuy wrote a long *Mémoire* in defense of their cousin, which, though not published until the early eighteenth century, certainly circulated in manuscript.[148] At least one historian believes that this text is evidence that the Dupuys sided with the *Frondeurs* during France's civil war in 1648–53.[149]

This must remain a matter of speculation. In any event, the *Mémoire* confronts the accusations and judgment against de Thou, with long, tedious passages citing legal precedents and royal history that served to undermine the legitimacy and legality of the case. Then it proceeds to a vociferous condemnation of Richelieu, denouncing him in the most scathing terms. There is hardly any crime, sin, misdeed, character flaw, or excess of which he is not accused. He is guilty of "insatiable avarice." He has surrounded himself with "corrupt, mean men, born only for servitude." No element of the realm—from the king and queen and the entire royal family to the smallest province—has escaped the ravages of his rule. He has left a trail of suffering in his wake: thousands of innocent people imprisoned, banished, unjustly condemned, even poisoned. Through his wiles, the king has been duped, isolated, deprived of good counsel and favorites, cleverly distracted by the hunt and other frivolous pastimes. Dupuy even accuses him of deliberately hastening the king's death by "forcing" him to lead the military campaign in Roussillon in 1641. Truly virtuous people—like de Thou—always saw the cardinal for what he was. "His bad qualities naturally made him an enemy of good people [*gens de bien*] and generous souls who live by honor and virtue."[150] Dupuy's Richelieu is, in short, not just an evil minister but a monster who has left France in ruins. No wonder, he muses, that the king's brother was driven to conspire against him.

How long had the Dupuys harbored these views? It is pointless to ask. They were certainly not the only Frenchmen to have started out admiring the talented and savvy cardinal as he consolidated his power after 1630, especially after so many years of indecisiveness and rivalry at court, only to have grown weary and wary of his rule as his power grew more imperious, his deviousness more apparent, and his foreign policy more humanly and fiscally costly. After all, they maintained close relations with men like Grotius, Saumaise, and others who made no secret of their distaste for Richelieu. And their brand of Gallicanism, while clearly in support of royal authority, though not "absolutism," represented a religious position that Richelieu was happy to exploit but in actuality found extreme and possibly dangerous, going far beyond his vision of the French Church and its relations with Rome.[151]

---

[148] Pierre Dupuy, *Mémoires et instructions pour servir à justifier l'innocence de messire François-Auguste de Thou*, in *Histoire universelle de Jacques-Auguste de Thou depuis 1543 jusqu'en 1607*, vol. XV: *1607–1610* (London, 1734). The text of Dupuy's memoir is separately paginated at the end of this volume of de Thou's history. Page numbers in the notes refer to this edition.

[149] Ferretti, *Un "soldat philosophe*," pt. IV.   [150] Dupuy, *Mémoires et instructions*, 28.

[151] On the Dupuy cabinet as a venue for the sharing of views critical of the regime's policies, see Klaus Garber, "A propos de la politisation de l'humanisme tardif européen: Jacques-Auguste de Thou

There are, on the other hand, many reasons why the Dupuys and their circle not only publicly sided with Richelieu and his policies but also did so out of genuine approval. They continued to serve as the king's librarians even after the cardinal's death. While during the *Fronde* there are indications that they were supportive of the revolt, as always, their partisanship remained muted. Moreover, they failed to signal any displeasure with Richelieu's chosen successor, Mazarin, and the continuation of his policies, especially France's engagement in the European war. Indeed, one of the Dupuys' closest intimates, Gabriel Naudé, remained a stalwart supporter of Mazarin, even going so far as to rescue much of the contents of his celebrated library from a pillaging *Frondeur* crowd. The fact is, like many of their contemporaries, especially those of the Parisian elite of literati and savants we have been examining, the Dupuys were in all likelihood Janus-faced with regard to both Richelieu and the political values he embodied. That these men of letters and "intellectuals" were plagued by a divided conscience, torn between idealism and the "realistic" demands of a dangerous, complex world, should not be surprising.

The Cabinet and the Republic of Letters

Although the term "Republic of Letters" did not have the currency then that it would have later in the century, the Dupuys were clearly at the center of a community of savants who embodied this republic in embryo, perhaps even at its very best. Jerôme Delatour, the cabinet's premier contemporary historian, has assembled a list of the brothers' correspondents; out of the nearly 7,000 letters that have survived, about 1,500 are from outside France, with most originating in Italy, the Low Countries, and England. Very few are from Spain, and only a handful come from correspondents situated in Germanic lands. The provenance of their correspondents certainly describes the Republic of Letters in the early seventeenth century, with the traditional breeding ground of humanism running from Rome to northern Italy, in particular Padua, cutting through France by way of Aix-en-Provence (Peiresc), carving out an arc into northwestern Europe, especially through the intellectual centers of Leyden and Amsterdam, then across the Channel into the British Isles with its great universities of Oxford and Cambridge. At its heart in Paris was the Dupuy cabinet, linking the northern and southern components of the Republic, serving as its unofficial capital, clearinghouse, way station, and gathering spot. Although the Dupuys were servants of the French crown, their interests, their friendship networks, and perhaps their allegiances were certainly cosmopolitan in reach.[152]

et le 'Cabinet Dupuy' à Paris," in C. Lauvergnat-Gagnière and B. Yon, eds., *Le juste et l'injuste à la Renaissance et à l'âge classique* (Saint-Etienne, 1983), 157–77.

---

[152] Delatour, "Les frères Dupuy," III: 427.

But we should be cautious in casting the cabinet solely in a cosmopolitan light. Anthony Grafton describes the Republic of Letters as "a new kind of virtual community: one sustained not by immediate, direct contact and conversation so much as by a decades-long effort of writing and rewriting... it had no borders, no government, no capital."[153] Lorraine Daston also notes that the "cosmopolitanism" especially of the scientific communities that were at the core of the Republic of Letters distinguished them from "their literary and artistic counterparts."[154] If the Dupuys' network seemed to embody a version of this "lost continent," however, this still fails to account for what sustained them. Many other *gens de lettres* toiled outside this lofty "strange imaginary land."[155] Alongside—or perhaps beneath—the cosmopolitan networks of the Dupuys, Mersenne, Peiresc, or Diodati, we should also acknowledge a sort of local infrastructure of relationships without which something like the cabinet could not have functioned. This can be illustrated by the figure of Louis Jacob de Saint Charles (1608–70), a Carmelite monk who was a frequenter of the cabinet and a friend of the likes of Naudé, Patin, and Colletet, as well as Marie de Gournay. Jacob was perhaps the most prolific bibliographer of his times, producing over thirty bibliographies, many of which identified books and manuscripts in Parisian public and private libraries. These volumes not only contained lists of titles but suggested a sort of ethnography of the savant culture of the city. His *Traicté des plus belles bibliothèques publiques et particulieres qui ont esté et qui sont à présent dans le monde* (1644) describes a savant urban culture rich in libraries, private collections, and other resources that the Dupuys, and others of their intellectual ilk, depended upon. Jacob claimed that seventeenth-century Paris had more of these venues—spaces not only for books and manuscripts but for scholarly exchange and intellectual sociability—than all of Spain and Germany combined.[156] We should imagine the Dupuy cabinet, then, rooted in the rich Parisian soil of varied associations—the libraries, academies, and gatherings of those such as Mersenne, Bourdelot, Bourbon, and others—just as we saw the *mondain* literary groups in the first chapter. From below, this cosmopolitan, European-wide Republic of Letters looks like it was held aloft by an array of local supports and supporters.

Beyond its celebrated cosmopolitanism, the Republic of Letters in this period is often viewed as essentially quiescent and politically conformist—as having forsaken a political profile in exchange for a certain independence of thought and liberty of expression, as long as the thinking and expressing remained free of

---

[153] Anthony Grafton, "A Sketch Map of a Lost Continent: The Republic of Letters," *Republics of Letters*, 1/1 (2009), 10, 1.

[154] Lorraine Daston, "The Ideal and Reality of the Republic of Letters in the Enlightenment," *Science in Context*, 4/2 (1991), 367–86.

[155] Grafton, "A Sketch Map," 1.

[156] Ian Mclean, "Louis Jacob de Saint-Charles (1608–1670) and the Development of Specialist Bibliography," in Mclean, *Learning and the Market Place: Essays in the History of the Early Modern Book* (Leiden, 2009), 403–45, on 417.

political contentiousness or even commentary. This view, in a sense, recapitulates the more general assumption about intellectual culture in the late sixteenth and early seventeenth centuries: that it was defined by a withdrawal from political concerns and cultivated instead private matters in keeping with the spirit of *otium* that characterized the period. For Françoise Waquet, inspired by the work of Reinhart Koselleck, this was an essential condition for the liberty of the Republic of Letters—indeed, it allowed for it to flourish as a "republic." The members of the Republic embraced the absolute authority of the crown as a part of an implicit bargain that defended their "liberty of thought," but within prescribed limits.[157]

Does this describe the Dupuys? They certainly sometimes took care to avoid extreme, dangerous, or otherwise objectionable publications or commentary. Witness Pierre's great efforts, as editor and publisher, in suppressing and smoothing over the more contentious aspects of Pierre de L'Estoile's *Mémoires*, whose criticism of the Jesuits, Rome, and the League risked reviving the tensions of the last century (discussed in Chapter 3). But as discreet and careful as they were—and the cabinet was scrupulous in exercising caution and self-censorship—they nevertheless consistently cultivated a Gallican perspective and made sure that that position found effective outlets. In their great two-volume publication on "Gallican liberties," in their perpetuation of the work of their uncle Jacques-Auguste de Thou, and in Pierre's vehement defense of François-Auguste de Thou, which was as much an attack on Richelieu as a response to their cousin's trial and execution, they made their political positions clear. They were not opposed to royal authority and, of course, served the crown on several different fronts. But this did not mean that they were, as Michelet judged them, "servile."[158] Nor were they hypocritical, serving a king and a minister with whom they differed over policy in fundamental ways. Their work illustrates that support for "absolutism" could accommodate a range of political visions. Their vision was of a France firmly committed to a Gallican tradition, a tradition that put it not only at odds with the Spanish Habsburgs but also opposed to the pretensions of Rome. They were thus of one mind with Richelieu on the first count, but only partially in sync on the second, for the cardinal-minister's embrace of Gallicanism was more tactical than thoroughgoing. For the Dupuys, however, the "liberties of the Gallican Church" were at the heart of the French nation, its history, and its place in Europe. Moreover, this difference with Richelieu was compounded by a growing dislike for his style of rule, a style that eventually, like others, they regarded as tyrannical

---

[157] In the words of one writer in 1684, "Savants should have the liberty to examine things on their own in the cabinet, to think of them as they please and to discuss among themselves in a friendly manner, with a pleasing liberty, without getting angry with each other if their thoughts are not in agreement, and without bringing their disagreements into the theater of the public." Françoise Waquet, "Qu'est-ce que la République des Lettres? Essai de sémantique historique," *Bibliothèque de l'Ecole des chartes*, 147 (1989), 500.

[158] This would be to follow in the interpretation of humanism offered by Anthony Grafton and Lisa Jardine, *From Humanism to the Humanities: Education and the Liberal Arts in Fifteenth- and Sixteenth-Century Europe* (London, 1986).

and dangerous. As leaders of a community of savants that constituted an early Republic of Letters, they clearly believed that the knowledge they so painstakingly cultivated and disseminated had a role in shaping the destiny of France and a Europe it aspired to lead.

It is thus misleading to define the Republic of Letters primarily in terms that vaunt its supposed distance from confessional strife and the affairs of state. These savants were not so removed from such worldly, partisan, and messy matters. "The almost universal solution," proposed to the problem of partisan strife was distance, both literal and figurative," observes Lorraine Daston regarding the members of the Republic of Letters' relationship to the religious conflicts of the day.[159] Though ensconced in an informal institution, their cabinet, which provided them a measure of autonomy as well as a community of like-minded *gens de lettres*, they were at home in the inner precincts of France's foreign policy "establishment," and certainly not above exploiting scholarship toward pragmatic, political ends. In other ways, however, they managed to make known their criticisms of certain policies and state actions, especially of the minister responsible for them. It was probably only Richelieu's death in 1642, shortly after Pierre Dupuy drafted his unsparing denunciation of him, that thwarted a sort of reckoning between the cabinet and the cardinal-minister.

If there are some aspects of the Dupuys' cabinet that do not jibe with a rather elevated, idealized conception of the Republic of Letters, there are others that confirm the view of an "innocent refuge" of the learned few. And this is most apparent when we consider the cabinet in comparison with the Rambouillet salon, the other great gathering of the privileged in early seventeenth-century Paris. There, as we have noted, while certainly limited to an elite, the *ruelle* was still populated with a mix of women and men, many of the latter noble warriors. In this sense, it more accurately mirrored the social and vocational profile of the nobility. By contrast, the Dupuy circle was not only a bastion of male-only sociability, it also was lacking in the participation of warriors—those with direct experience on the front lines of France's geopolitical struggles.[160] Which, then, was more engaged with the realities of the day? The Dupuys more actively—or rather intellectually—grappled with great affairs of Church and State; the denizens of the salon seemed more content with pastimes and diversions of a less public nature. The ethos of retreat characterized both, but also in different ways, they each managed to address contemporary concerns—the salon providing a hospitable space for the literary field, the cabinet as a player in the conflict over Gallicanism.

Spaces of retreat, neither the salon nor the cabinet obstructed outlets for their frequenters to engage with the world beyond. On the contrary, they provided them a haven from which they could enter the world on their own terms.

---

[159] Daston, "The Ideal and Reality," 380.

[160] The only noble soldier associated with the Dupuys was Fortin de la Hoguette, and his relationship was largely epistolary.

7
Writing *Otium*
Retreat as a Mode of Engagement

"Reculer Pour Mieux Sauter."—Old French Expression

Jean Chapelain, perhaps the consummate man of letters of his time, derived his status from multiple roles and associations—as an intimate of Richelieu's cabinet, a frequenter of the Hôtel de Rambouillet, a friend and supporter to numerous writers and aristocrats alike, a literary critic, a privileged client of the powerful Longueville family, and Balzac's unique *compagnon de route*. But he also affirmed this status in more subtle ways, with a mode of self-presentation, a self-fashioned identity that, as Christian Jouhaud argues, rested on "the fiction of retreat from the world and from action."[1] This fiction was both protective, allowing him to assert his distance from the messy affairs of the world, and strategic, providing him a pretext for engagement on his own terms. His example thus demonstrates that retreat, or *otium*, and action were not antithetical—that a rejection of the *vita activa* could serve as a useful pose, especially for men of letters who wanted to preserve or assert their status as uniquely detached from the world while at the same time claiming a license to enter it as they wished.

This "fiction" also characterized some texts, even those that were not themselves works of fiction. In this chapter I will discuss four full-scale works. The first two are usually considered major expressions of *raison d'état*, even though their authors, Balzac and Naudé, clearly had more on their minds than a narrow concern for statecraft. The other two are works of imagination, in fact two of the best-sellers of the day: *L'Astrée* by Honoré d'Urfé, and the lesser-known neo-Latin political romance *Argenis* by John Barclay. Conveniently, following the last two chapters, we can associate these works (in pairs) with two distinct milieus and their wider circles, the Rambouillet salon and the Dupuy cabinet. Balzac addressed his *Le Prince* to the habitués of the salon, or those who identified with this refined urban elite of men and women—that is, people familiar with the emerging "worldly" literary culture that Balzac was so instrumental in fostering. And, as is well known, *L'Astrée* was avidly read by these same *honnêtes gens* as a sort of behavioral and conversational script for living in a privileged *monde*. Naudé and

---

[1] Christian Jouhaud, "Sur le statut d'homme de lettres au XVIIe siècle: Le correspondance de Jean Chapelain (1595–1674)," *Annales: Histoire, sciences sociales*, 49/2 (1994), 344.

Dignified Retreat: Writers and Intellectuals in the Age of Richelieu. Robert A. Schneider, Oxford University Press (2019).
© Robert A. Schneider. DOI: 10.1093/oso/9780198826323.001.0001

Barclay, on the other hand, both identified with the savants who orbited around the Dupuy brothers. Naudé's *Considérations politiques sur les coups d'états*, a work by an *esprit fort* for *esprits forts*, a "libertine" text by a self-professed *déniaisé*, is crafted to disclose mysteries of statecraft only to those capable of handling such dangerous knowledge. Barclay wrote his romance *Argenis* for a readership of the Republic of Letters; his closest friends and supporters were Guillaume du Vair, Peiresc, and Grotius.

Despite these differences, as I will argue in this chapter, all four works display features of *otium*, primarily in two respects. The first is stylistic or generic. In the case of *L'Astrée* and *Argenis*, the genre of fiction serves as a technique that establishes a distance between readers and the world, in the simple sense that every work of the imagination creates another world for its readers to inhabit. And, as I hope to show, Balzac's and Naudé's works on *raison d'état*, though certainly not fiction, are also inflected stylistically and rhetorically in ways that accomplish virtually the same effect. In addition to these features, all four works disclose their authors' desire to insulate or distance themselves from the contretemps and compromising realities of contemporary life. Even as they prescribe political stratagems or celebrate political figures or otherwise offer political commentary, they leave themselves a way out, so to speak, signaling to the knowing reader that one enters the vexed stage of public life at one's peril.

Writing Reason of State

Jean Bodin, perhaps the most significant French political thinker of the sixteenth century, had very few followers in the seventeenth. Political writings continued to appear, of course, but they mostly adhered to the theme of *raison d'état*, a stance that largely dispenses with the social order and the constitutional basis of authority, and certainly does not lend itself to authoritative expositions like Bodin's *Six Books of the Republic*.[2] Reason of state put a premium on statecraft, the "art" of politics, and the exercise of power guided by a state's interests rather than considerations of morality or religion.[3] It thus was narrow in scope, fixated on circumscribed ends. As formulated by Michel Foucault, the "most typical feature" of this discourse of statecraft is that "there is no prior, external purpose, or even a purpose subsequent to the state itself.... The end of *raison d'Etat* is the state itself."[4] While true, this feature can be explained by the circumstantial basis of these texts: most French writings in the reason of state genre were occasional publications,

---

[2] A notable exception is Cardin Le Bret, *Traité de la souveraineté du roy* (Paris, 1632).
[3] Maurizio Viroli, *From Politics to Reason of State: The Acquisition and Transformation of the Language of Politics, 1250–1600* (Cambridge, 1992).
[4] Michel Foucault, *Security, Territory, Population: Lectures at the Collège de France, 1977–1978*, ed. Michel Senellart, trans. Graham Burchell (New York, 2009), 258.

often pamphlets issued at the behest of Richelieu in defense of his controversial foreign policy. It cannot be said, then, that there is much profundity or even originality to them. Rather, they offer variations on the same theme. Their authors are apologists, whose originality, such as it is, consists not in the speculative or philosophical treatment of political questions, but rather in the novelty of their way of explaining or justifying an already well-established manner of statecraft embodied in the political practice of the cardinal-minister.[5]

The works of Balzac and Naudé are exceptions, for while they certainly sounded the main themes of reason of state, they did so to their own tune—with an originality in style and interpretation that identified them as "authors." As Charles Sorel noted in arguing for a program of "civic history," hacks are not sufficient. "We need true authors, that is, men who are accustomed to writing things that are of their own invention, or at least take an original form which only their imagination can create."[6] As "true authors," Balzac and Naudé exhibit the tension between giving voice to a perspective identified with Richelieu and remaining faithful to their own identities as men of letters. Unlike the output of hired pens or anonymous tracts, their writings are personal, endowed with individual perspectives going beyond the narrow concerns of reason of state, and characterized as well by a style that made each distinctive. As writers ostensibly approaching their controversial subjects from beyond the corridors of power—as outsiders—they self-consciously styled themselves as removed from the realm of politics. Even when they assumed knowledge of hidden practices and "mysteries" of state, they did so with a sense that their access was special, perhaps even untoward, and that readers were being shown something that, in truth, should not be unveiled.

Balzac's *Le Prince*: The "Galant" as Political Sage

In 1631, the world was full of possibilities for France, according to Balzac, and, he hoped, for himself as well. Flush from the spectacular success of his *Lettres* in 1624, a literary sensation that had the added value of provoking one of the great quarrels of the era, he could be confident of his stature on the new literary scene. In *Le Prince* he extols Louis XIII as embodying all the heroism and grandeur that, in his *Lettres*, he had once reserved for the nobility. But just as evident as his

---

[5] For a survey of the legacy of political thought, see William Farr Church, *Constitutional Thought in Sixteenth-Century France: A Study in the Evolution of Ideas* (Cambridge, MA, 1941). See the comment of Orest Ranum, *Paris in the Age of Absolutism: An Essay* (revised and expanded ed., University Park, PA, 2002), 196: "Indeed, medieval conceptions so limited the imaginations of Frenchmen that political philosophy in France died immediately after the civil wars. Between Bodin in the 1560s to 1580s and Montesquieu in the 1720s to 1740s, we encounter no political philosophy of the speculative sort, but only elaborations and emendations of the medieval tripartite conception of society."

[6] Quoted in Christian Jouhaud, "Roman historié et histoire romancée: Jean-Pierre Camus et Charles Sorel," *XVIIe siècle*, 215/2 (2002), 310.

desire to elevate Louis is his eagerness to raise himself to new heights—both literary and political—an aspiration evident in the personal tone, the audaciousness, and the hyperbole that characterize the work.

Le Prince argues that because of this perfect king, France has been reborn, turning away from a past marred by internecine conflict and decline. The theme of reform and renewal runs throughout the work. It is infused with a sense of patriotic commitment; only a portion of his text serves to justify reason of state. One reason for the exuberant tone—and the general sense of hopefulness that runs through Balzac's book—is that the interval between the religious wars and the present had witnessed not only a restored royalty but also a "moral revolution." The two are related, with the monarchy deserving credit for the transformation. Balzac can scarcely believe his eyes when he compares the France of today with that of yesterday. "It is no longer the France of before, so torn, so sick, so dilapidated. It is no longer the French, such enemies of their country, so indolent in the service to their Prince, so disparaged among foreign nations.... There has been a moral revolution [*révolution Morale*], a change of spirit, a sweet and pleasant passage from bad to good. The king has restored the reputation of his subjects, has communicated his force and vigor to the Republic, has corrected the faults of the past century, has driven out all weakness and temerity in the administration of affairs."[7] While largely in praise of his king as the *deus ex machina* of France's salvation and promise, Balzac also clearly wanted to convey, perhaps in muted terms, an appreciation of a more general transformation among his countrymen. With this extended encomium to Louis, he also addressed a literate French public he wanted to arouse—a public he was in no small part responsible for creating.

The pronounced literary quality of *Le Prince* hardly surprises from a writer like Balzac, who presented himself as a master stylist for a generation that would witness the fashioning of the vernacular to a standard that could rival the ancients and surpass the Italians. As well, it seems that after the controversy over the *Lettres*, in which critics charged him with failing to strike a note of true eloquence, he was keen to prove that he could achieve the grand style characteristic of the ancient orators. Indeed, much of *Le Prince*, especially the "Advertissement" and the first pages of the body of the work itself, is taken up with a riposte to his critics—those responsible for "the cruelest persecution of an individual ever recollected by men."[8] In this work, his anonymous booster (or Balzac himself—it is not clear) proclaims, "He praises very grandly, he deliberates exactly, he accuses with great vehemence. In brief, he accomplishes effectively all the duties of an Orator."[9]

---

[7] Jean-Louis Guez de Balzac, *Le Prince* (Paris, 1632 ed.), 165–6.
[8] Balzac, *Le Prince*, 11, "Advertissement," separate pagination.   [9] *Le Prince*, 9.

This reference to the "Orator" is hardly otiose, for in this text Balzac self-consciously strikes a high rhetorical tone and a particular mode suited to his purposes. As Eric Méchoulan has noted, this is the epideictic, which since antiquity had been considered appropriate for public, often ceremonial occasions, contrasting with the deliberative and forensic styles more suited to practical and immediate contexts, such as law and politics.[10] Unlike these, which aim to promote action or decision, the epideictic, especially as articulated in Aristotle's *Rhetoric*, either praises or blames; there is an element of display or show, often characterized by a declamatory manner in the fashion of a harangue. It prized, or at least allowed for, ornamentation and virtuosity; often it was marked by amplification and hyperbole. In this respect, it has often been demeaned as "mere rhetoric." But in antiquity its purposefulness was evident in encomia, eulogies, and funerals, and on other public occasions. And during the Middle Ages and the Renaissance, it was no longer confined to the oratorical context; according to Brian Vickers, "all literature became subsumed under the epideictic, and all writing was perceived as occupying the related spheres of praise and blame."[11]

In adopting this rhetorical mode, then, Balzac was able to address public and political matters—the nature of kingship, the character and wisdom of Louis XIII, the legacy of the Wars of Religion, France's recent victory over the Huguenots at La Rochelle and the potential threat from Calvinists more generally, the menacing role of Spain in European affairs, the quarrelsome nature of France's *grands*, the traitorous *dévots*—all while maintaining a discursive distance conjured by this self-conscious literary style.

That Balzac knowingly cast his text in the epideictic mode is confirmed by the fact that the goals of praise and blame largely configure *Le Prince*. As an extended encomium, it extols the virtue and character of Louis XIII in the most superlative terms. He is responsible for nothing less than stemming the disastrous tide of French history, from the religious wars to the latest rounds of noble fractiousness. He has resolved all discord and difference, not only between Catholics and Protestants but also between the "vulgar" and "sages."[12] He is possessed of a magnetic force—we would have no trouble calling it charisma—that draws the people toward him. Louis is nothing less than a paragon of Neo-Stoic virtues: unlike

---

[10] Eric Méchoulan, *Le livre avalé: De la littérature entre mémoire et culture, XVIe–XVIIIe siècle* (Montreal, 2004), chap. 5. See also, Hélène Merlin-Kajman, "Eloge et dissimulation: Eloge du prince au XVIIe siècle, un éloge paradoxal," in *L'Eloge du prince*, eds. I. Cogitore et Fr. Goyet, (Grenoble, 2003), 317–353; Christian Jouhaud, "Une 'religion du roi equivoque: *Le Prince* de Jean-Louis de Balzac," ed. Ran Halévi, *Le savoir du Prince. Du Moyen Age au Lumières* (Paris, 2002), 175–196; and Mathilde Bombart, *Guez de Balzac et la querelle des Lettres* (Paris, 2007), 42.

[11] Brian Vickers, *In Defence of Rhetoric* (Oxford, 1988), 54, and more generally chap. 1. Also helpful on the epideictic is J. Richard Chase, "The Classical Conception of Epideictic," *Quarterly Journal of Speech*, 47/3 (1961), 293–300; Cynthia Miecznikowski Sheard, "The Public Value of Epideictic Rhetoric," *College English*, 58/7 (1996), 765–94. Aristotle, *Rhetoric*, 1366a–1368b, in *The Rhetoric and the Poetics of Aristotle*, trans. W. Rhys Roberts and Ingram Bywater (New York, 1954).

[12] *Le Prince*, 36.

other men, he is moved solely by reason and an extraordinary "love of the public," whose "spirit has so much destroyed his body that the interests of his state today have taken the place of the passions of his soul."[13]

Even given the kind of hyperbole common when speaking of royalty, these sorts of passages undoubtedly struck some readers as a bit much. For frequenters of the court and members of the Parisian *monde*, the orbit of monarchical power was rather small. For these insiders, Louis was no mystery at all. Many at least knew what Louis was all about—a reticent, stuttering, shy, clearly indecisive young man (he was about 30 at the time) burdened by a headstrong mother and overshadowed by a brilliant, extraordinarily self-possessed and eloquent chief minister. Was Balzac taking advantage of the epideictic, which allowed not only for exaggeration but also sometimes for irony, to wink at his more knowing readers? The gap between Balzac's panegyric and the real king was so great, Jouhaud suggests, that the author's purpose was to hint to readers that Louis simply did not measure up.[14]

Balzac adds audacity to hyperbole. He argues, for example, that Louis was incapable of sin, that he preserved the innocence of his baptism, and that his taking of the sacrament of confession was merely to "refresh him and not for cleansing," his having no need.[15] Such a claim not only was novel and certainly dubious, it was also blasphemous, at least according to the Doctors of the Sorbonne, who censured Balzac for asserting it. Balzac must have known that he ran this risk: he was well versed in theological matters. But it is likely that, swollen with the success of his *Lettres*, he was ready to provoke.[16]

If Balzac stirred the theologians' ire, his license also risked provoking Richelieu on His Majesty's behalf. In praising Louis's severity against rebels and heretics, he editorialized that the king "has taken Royal Authority as far as it could go without Tyranny." Richelieu was known to have objected to the presumption of a mere man of letters to air publicly the question of royal limits—even worse, to suggest that tyranny was within reach.[17]

But this was in keeping with the invitation to overstatement inherent in the epideictic mode of expression. Perhaps his most stunning assertion, the passage in *Le Prince* most often cited, justifies some rather commonplace tenets of reason of state—preventive detention, the violation of the life and liberty of individuals, selective violence—but does so in a manner that displays a highly presumptive view of princely prerogative. Addressing the issue of threatening plots, he first offers, quite reasonably, "The people will not believe that a conspiracy against a

---

[13] *Le Prince*, 119–20.
[14] Christian Jouhaud, *Les pouvoirs de la littérature: Histoire d'un paradoxe* (Paris, 2000), 349–50.
[15] *Le Prince*, 117.
[16] Jean Jehasse, *Guez de Balzac et le génie romain, 1597–1654* (Saint-Etienne, 1977), 234–6.
[17] Jehasse, *Guez de Balzac*, 228–9.

king has occurred until he is dead." Thus, rulers "may forestall the danger, even by executing those whom they suspect; it is an excusable severity." He then continues:

> Upon a mere suspicion, a minor misgiving, a dream that the prince may have had, why should he not be permitted to detain his rebellious subjects and put his mind at ease merely by punishing them with their own safety? Why should not a faithful servant joyfully suffer detention which, by providing proof, would demonstrate his fidelity, contradict the calumny of his accusers, and appease the anxiety of his master?[18]

The notorious "dream" passage was in fact derived from Seneca's *De clementia*, a model panegyric.[19] Nevertheless, Balzac's presumptuous temerity was again on display: how dare he, Richelieu was known to muse, enter the dream life of a king? And, under the (erroneous) assumption that Balzac was Richelieu's mouthpiece, this passage was seized upon by the opposition pamphleteer Mathieu de Morgues as proof of the cardinal-minister's insidious tyranny, giving ammunition to his critics.[20] Clearly, the rhetorical style adopted by Balzac, a style that lent itself to the kind of "ornamentation" and exaggeration he readily indulged in, did not conform with the cardinal-minister's expectation of how matters of state should be treated in print.

If Richelieu was less than pleased with Balzac's presumption and rhetorical indulgence, he certainly could not have objected to the "blame" portion of *Le Prince*, where he takes aim at those forces and elements that have threatened France and challenged the king's supreme rule. Balzac lines up the usual suspects and dispatches them with relish. Here, too, however, he allows himself rhetorical flourishes and hyperbole, never letting the reader ignore his strong authorial voice. First up are the Huguenots. It was not simply that Louis had rendered them a decisive blow at La Rochelle; he now had decided to treat them as something like domesticated animals, or privileged prisoners, enlarging the "circumference" of their captivity. "He holds them on longer chains...and in allowing them to live among the rest of his subjects, he is only increasing the number of guards."[21] The great aristocracy, whom Balzac had celebrated in his *Lettres* for their heroism and stature, here are cast as petty tyrants, disrupters of the public order, and a standing threat to monarchical rule. The *dévots* come in for particular scorn, mocked for their "false devotion."[22] Even more than the Huguenots, they are the true enemies of France: "they are cruel, they are incestuous, they are sacrilegious, and do not stop with being *dévots*."[23] The Spanish not only threaten France without,

---

[18] *Le Prince*, 199–200.   [19] Jehasse, *Guez de Balzac*, 319.
[20] Etienne Thuau, *Raison d'Etat et pensée politique à l'époque de Richelieu* (Paris, 1966), 121.
[21] *Le Prince*, 42–3.   [22] *Le Prince*, 84–5.   [23] *Le Prince*, 92–3.

306   DIGNIFIED RETREAT

they are the "enemy within"—surely an aspersion meant to implicate the *dévot* party: "We have received their garrisons in our cities, and their ministers in our counsels," he writes with typical hyperbole. "Most of our people, if they were born in Madrid or Toledo, couldn't be better Spaniards than they are."[24] There is something perverse and unnatural about Spain's very configuration. His language, cast in the metaphorical terms of the body, evokes the argument that Imperial Spain—a political entity of parts and great extension—is fundamentally unnatural, a monstrous thing: it is "a body composed of separated parts connected rather by cords than by nerves. It has many members, but it is neither well-proportioned nor well-constructed. The arms cannot reach the head; the stomach is exposed while the extremities are covered, and if it manages to move, it leaves the rest paralyzed."[25] Finally, he turns again on his old critics, using the cover of his panegyric to indulge in a bit of intramural skirmishing against those savants who had heaped scorn on his *Lettres*. In paying them back in kind, he also claims the high ground of civic virtue. These learned scholars are like "members cut off from the common society," he adds. "They are superfluities of the Republic, and to use terms from ancient Greece, they are worthless except to inhabit the desert and other solitary places."[26] In passages like these, the reader is correct in concluding that Balzac cares as much for scoring points against his critics as he does for praising his king—possibly more.

We see in *Le Prince*, then, an author on full display, exercising his rhetorical skill and offering his opinions with some abandon, or at least with little regard for the restraints and niceties that normally governed political discussion. That the reader will be treated to a personal view of a political subject is made clear from the outset of the book. Here Balzac begins with an extended first-person rumination—a series of reflections on the physical setting in his bucolic retreat in Charente, far from Paris.[27] For several pages he indulges in a rhapsodic description that plays on well-worn pastoral tropes. He expostulates with pleasure on finding himself now "liberated" from his "captivity" in the capital. In his rural retreat, enjoying the "smiling face of the countryside," he is able to take in the pure air, "giving him such sweet and peaceful thoughts." Here there is "no more suspicion, defiance, or jealousy," no "envy and hatred." Here all is calm, and everyone enjoys the daily pleasure of familiar conversation; they talk of their orchards, crops, and vineyards rather than "affairs of state, the controversies over religion, philosophical questions." After a midday meal, while others go about their pastoral duties, he retires to his room, where he falls asleep over a book—"as little serious as their conversation." In the afternoon he leaves for a walk along the banks of the Charente, which again provides him with an opportunity to praise the bucolic

---

[24] *Le Prince*, 170–1.   [25] *Le Prince*, 374.   [26] *Le Prince*, 153.
[27] Nicolas Faret, *Recueil de lettres nouvelles*, 2 vols. (Paris, 1627), II: 83 (letter of Faret) on Balzac's self-exile, which was apparently well known among readers.

beauty of his native country. "These are charms unknown to the ambitious and to the greedy, who amidst the abundance of precious things miss those that cost nothing, which is to say those gained from leisure, who burden themselves with matters of civic life, leaving them no time for the tasks of human life."[28]

Prolonging his walk along the riverbank, taking a moment to revel in the bounty of the sun but also to share with us his tendency to melancholy when he is not warmed by its rays, he comes upon a vision—something in blue and yellow—which he likens to the appearance of Tiberinus to Aeneas (in Book VIII of the *Aeneid*). In fact, in what might be a reference to a passage in Petrarch's "Ascent of Mont Ventoux," Balzac tells us that just at that moment he had opened his copy of Virgil's epic to exactly that passage. "Was this the god of our river?" he asks.

Somewhat abruptly, then, the account becomes eventful. First, as if to prepare us for an intrusion into his idealized account, he mentions that this is the day when news of France's victory over the Huguenot stronghold of La Rochelle has reached Charente. Then he perceives the true nature of the "vision" that has just caught his eye: it is a Flemish gentleman, recently escaped from captivity in Algeria, who proceeds to tell Balzac of an incident he witnessed among his fellow prisoners.

So we have a story within a story—first Balzac's, then this Flemish stranger's. One day, news of the French victory at La Rochelle reaches the prisoners (the chronology here is a bit confused); a Spaniard among the captives then provocatively boasts that the French could not have won without his country's aid. Upon hearing this, a Frenchman responds by challenging the Spaniard to a fight, killing him. Balzac comments: "I was delighted to learn that despite the advanced age of the world and the decline of all things, France still bears children worthy of the original vigor of their mother."[29] Like this French prisoner, Balzac is moved to take up his monarch's defense. "It is impossible for me to resist the inner force which pushes me: I know not how to stop myself from speaking of the king, his virtue…and to ask of all people and of all times whether they have ever seen anything like him."[30] From the very start of *Le Prince*, then, Balzac himself is part of the text—his "I" is present throughout, framing his praise and criticism in the personal terms of an author who manages to convey intense involvement with his subject—which is, after all, the fate and destiny of his country—while maintaining a certain authorial distance in his rural retreat. Here as well, in mimicking the heroic French prisoner, Balzac styles himself as a *galant*, ready now to take up his pen in chivalric service to his king.

But *Le Prince* was a failure, at least as a vehicle for Balzac's promotion to a bishopric or a high position of state. In several respects, as noted, he proved obtuse to the limits of discretion that should guide commentary on political matters. Richelieu was especially angry at his commentary in the two appended letters

---

[28] *Le Prince*, 2, 5, 7.   [29] *Le Prince*, 26–7.   [30] *Le Prince*, 32.

addressed to him on the cardinal's messy contretemps with the Queen Mother during the infamous Day of Dupes. How could he have erred so blatantly? How could a man who exhibited such exquisite sensitivity when it came to describing the politics of *arcana imperii* have violated its central tenet?

The answer takes us back to the literary quality of Balzac's text, despite its political subject. Jouhaud argues for the "literalization" of politics in this period (as well as the "politicization" of literature), and *Le Prince* certainly illustrates his point. In the bucolic state of rural retreat from which he addresses the reader, in the legend-like story that opens the text, in the panoramic passages in which he sweeps across time to clinch an argument, in his own musings disguised as analysis, in the hyperbole that characterizes both his praise and his condemnations, and, most notably, in the way he intrudes into the text with a voice and perspective that is unmistakably his, this is a work in which, as with the *Lettres*, Balzac the author risks obscuring its ostensible subject. Perhaps this, then, is why the book was considered a failure, at least in terms of securing Balzac's favor with Richelieu: it was simply too literary. And in this sense, it demonstrates that turning politics into literature could go too far.

But while perhaps excessively personal for an essentially political work, *Le Prince* manages nevertheless to convey a tone that likely resonated with Balzac's readers, especially the denizens of Parisian salons. Like his enormously successful *Lettres*, this text manages to be both profuse and seductive, offering over-the-top praise of his king while augmenting his own presence in the text as a man with great affections, strong views, and large ambitions both for himself and for his country. One might thus consider it a work of literary *galanterie*, for here Balzac reveals himself as something of a *galant*, the embodiment of a true *bon françois*, whose love for his king and country ultimately depends not on the cold interests of raison d'état but on an affection and loyalty that is both old and new. In *Le Prince*, Balzac brings the same playful eloquence and chivalric romance to his Prince as one would expect to be expressed for a lady. As Noémi Hepp notes, it is the grand gesture that defines gallantry just as it marked chivalry, only in the former the jest was rhetorical, not one of physical prowess. If nothing else, *Le Prince* is a work bristling with great rhetorical gestures.[31]

Naudé's *Considérations politiques*: The Undeceived Outsider Looking In

Gabriel Naudé was a well-known mainstay of the so-called Parisian "libertines," a designation, as noted, that has proven more confusing than enlightening. It does not mean that he led a morally questionable life; he was, rather, a philosophical

---

[31] Noémi Hepp, "La galanterie," in Pierre Nora, ed., *Les lieux de mémoire*, 3 vols. (Paris, 1992), III, pt. 2: 745–83.

skeptic, an adventuresome polymath, and an obsessive bibliophile. He may have been more of a freethinker than most of his confreres in the orbit of the Dupuy cabinet, perhaps even an atheist. Like most of these other *esprits forts,* however, he was outwardly conformist with regard to religion and certainly embraced the cause of royalism. Both his first publication, *Le Marfore, ou, Discours contre les libelles* (1620), and his last, *Mascurat, ou, Jugement de tout ce qui a été imprimé contre le cardinal Mazarin* (1650), were written in defense of the king and his ministers. Though trained as a physician, and holder of the office of *médecin ordinaire du roi,* for most of his life he served as librarian to a succession of great noblemen, prelates, ministers, and a queen (Christina of Sweden). He spent many years in Rome as Cardinal Bagni's librarian, and it was there, in 1639, that he published *Considérations politiques sur les coups d'état,* dedicated to the cardinal.

The publishing history of this, his most famous book, is shrouded in mystery, compounded by his own likely disingenuous account of its composition and publication. In fact, this account takes the form of a series of vignettes, which lends it a literary quality that serves only to heighten the mysterious nature of the whole work. He asserts that it "was not written to please everyone," but merely as a courtesy to his patron, Cardinal Bagni. And he consigned it to a press only because the prelate "cannot read anything with pleasure unless it is printed."[32] On the face of it, this is an unlikely justification (although perhaps understandable today, when so many of us insist on printing out longer texts rather than reading them on the screen). In any case, he claims that only twelve copies were printed. Peter Donaldson, however, insists that this account is deceptive, a deliberately contrived subterfuge to reinforce its air of mystery. And evidence indicates that its print run was certainly in excess of the twelve copies cited in the preface.[33]

Naudé pursues the theme of the problematic, even dangerous, nature of his book in the first chapter, "Objections Which One Might Make against This Discourse, with the Necessary Responses," which dwells on his own concerns and fears, anticipating those of others. Throughout this chapter (and it is a whole, stand-alone chapter, not the sort of prefatory remarks or dedicatory pages one routinely finds), Naudé the author maintains an assertive presence. Toward the end he even provides a sort of *curriculum vitae,* complete with a bibliography of authors, ancient and modern, who have most influenced him, to justify broaching such a vexed topic. Like Balzac's book, the chapter begins with a personal reflection, here taking the reader into the intimate space between him and his patron. We are treated to a moment of *res media,* where the author seems to perform an act of hesitation, wondering whether he should even proceed with his writing: "Hardly

---

[32] Gabriel Naudé, *Considérations politiques sur les coups d'état* (1639), ed. Louis Marin (Paris, 1988), 69.
[33] For one thing, he argues, it was certainly not published in Rome; the printer's mark, a device found in books printed by a branch of the Plantin Press, indicates that the place of publication was likely Leiden. Peter S. Donaldson, *Machiavelli and Mystery of State* (Cambridge, 1992), chap. 5.

had I, Monseigneur, drawn the first lines of this discourse, than I found myself confronted with two difficulties." What follows is a chapter-long elaboration of his concerns: repeated declarations of his anxiety at undertaking such a "dangerous" enterprise. Three times he wonders aloud whether he should "be so bold as to intrude into the Cabinets of the great." He cites lines from Horace warning about venturing "[w]here treacherous cinders hide the lurking fires."[34] Significantly, this was with regard to Horace's friend Pollio's plan to write a history of the civil wars.

It was, of course, a commonplace of writings on reason of state for authors to declare their reluctance to disclose the "springs" of statecraft—mysteries of state (*arcana imperii*) that ought to remain hidden. In actuality, as they often confirmed, it seems as if these were something of an open secret. Giovanni Botero, considered to be the originator of the reason of state tradition, remarked that he was moved to write his book precisely because, in his many travels, "I have been greatly astonished to find Reason of State a constant subject of discussion."[35] Contemporary comment often observed that reason of state was, shockingly, the stuff of public discussion: shoemakers and peddlers, even women, dared to debate its virtues and meaning in the city's streets and squares.[36] Antoine de Laval, writing in 1612, deplored the fact that the term is "frequently in everyone's mouth," and noted with displeasure that "there is scarcely the smallest man who doesn't say, when something occurs beyond his understanding: that happens because of reason of state."[37] Naudé, despite his professed anxiety that he was venturing where he should not tread, ultimately concludes that "monarchs' great secrets, the intrigues of the court, the cabals of factions" are really nothing of the sort, for they are to be discovered in the "relations, *mémoires*, discourses, instructions, libels, manifestos, pasquinades, and other similar secret pieces that come to light every day."[38]

---

[34] Quotations from Naudé, *Considérations politiques*, 73, 74.

[35] Giovanni Botero, *The Reason of State*, trans. P. J. Waley and D. P. Waley (New Haven, 1956), xiii.

[36] In 1621, the Venetian writer Lodovico Zuccolo observed that even "barbers...and other artisans of the humblest sort, in their shops and meeting-places, make comments and queries on reason of state, and pretend that they know which things are done for reason of state and which are not." Quoted by Noel Malcolm, *Reason of State, Propaganda, and the Thirty Years' War: An Unknown Translation by Thomas Hobbes* (Oxford, 2007), 93.

[37] Antoine de Laval, *Desseins de professions nobles et publiques* (Paris 1612), cited in Marcel Gauchet, "L'Etat au miroir de la raison d'Etat: La France et la Chrétienté," in Y. Ch. Zarka, ed., *Raison et déraison d'Etat au XVIe et XVIIe siècles* (Paris, 1994), 195–6. "You may perhaps wonder," apologized Estienne Molinier to the readers of his *Mirror for Christian States*, a work that took issue with the doctrine of reason of state, "to see mee adde this little abortive to the importunate spawne of so many Bookes, which (as the Souldiers of Cadmus) rise up, and iusle each other, appearing and perishing in a moment." Quoted in Peter N. Miller, *Defining the Public Good: Empire, Religion and Philosophy in Eighteenth-Century Britain* (Cambridge, 1994), 27 n. 31. Michel Foucault cites the German lawyer Bogislaw P. Chemnitz, who during the negotiations over the Peace of Westphalia wrote: "Every day we hear an infinite number of people speaking of *raison d'État*. Everyone joins in, those buried in the dust of the schools as well as those with the responsibilities of public office." Foucault, *Security, Territory, Population*, 240.

[38] Naudé, *Considérations politiques*, 83.

Still, a sense of anxiety prevailed, underscoring the default position that the mysteries of statecraft ought not to be traduced, a prohibition extended to the mystique of kingship itself. Balzac advised "respect for that Majesty that is hidden.... Let us adore the veils and clouds that are between us and it."[39] A Breton nobleman, Julien Furic du Run, in his *Réflexions politiques* of 1640, began his defense of Richelieu tentatively, as if even to broach the subject was to violate a taboo. "How," he asks, "might this be permitted to me, who has never had the honor of entering the Cabinet, and who is not at all capable of the secrets or the great mysteries that are dealt with there?"[40] Daniel de Priézac, a devout defender of reason of state and a member of the French Academy, offered perhaps the most rhetorically stunning assertion of the essentially ineffable nature of kingship, which expresses the common assumption that majesty demands silence. He writes: "[I]t seems that the same band which so gloriously encircles the monarch's head also ties our tongues in order to prevent our speaking of it.... and it is not with imperfect speech but with religious silence that one should respect the features that the divine Hand imprints on the foreheads of those with whom He deigns to share his power."[41]

Attempting to enforce silence as the appropriate approach to political affairs, however, reproduced a similar contradiction evident in other domains where the principle of prudential self-censorship also prevailed. In the writing of history and the theater (as we saw in Chapter 3), strains emerged between the imperative of discretion, on the one hand, and the creative impulses and ambitions of certain practitioners, on the other. In the political realm a contradiction is also apparent, but it stemmed from the very nature of reason of state. Marcel Gauchet formulates the problem well on a theoretical level: "The more the State acts according to reason of state, the more its action is in principle open to investigation, assumed to be predictable and decipherable, exposed for the appreciation of the 'public.'"[42] An aspect of the novelty of reason of state, in other words, resided in its appeal to a set of interests that could be articulated in a rational, objective manner. Witness

---

[39] Guez de Balzac, *Oeuvres complètes*, 2 vols. (Paris, 1665), II: 11–13; quoted in E. B. O. Borgerhoff, *The Freedom of French Classicism* (Princeton, 1950), 20.

[40] Julien Furic du Run, *Reflexions politiques* (Paris, 1640), 3.

[41] Daniel de Priézac, *Discours politiques* (Paris, 1652), 142, quoted in William Farr Church, *Richelieu and Reason of State* (Princeton, 1972), 451–52. Many of these writings were printed missiles in France's propaganda war against the Habsburgs and in defense of a foreign policy that alarmed Catholic *dévots* both at home and abroad. They were thus likely both to exaggerate the costs of making matters of state public and cynically to turn a pragmatic attempt to stifle criticism into a time-honored principle. Such was the case with an important text of the period, *Le Catholique d'Estat*, written in 1625 by a committee of Richelieu's advisors, including Hay du Chastelet, Pierre de Bérulle, and Père Joseph. It argued that to presume to lift the veil from the realm of statecraft was to court disaster, indeed to threaten the very order of the cosmos: "As soon as one incites this frenzy [of speculation] the whole order of the universe is shaken, states destroy themselves." Jérémie Ferrier, *Le catholique d'Estat, ou, Discours politique des Alliances du Roy très-Chréstien contre les calomnies des ennemis de son Estat*, in Paul Hay du Chastelet, *Recueil de diverses pièces pour servir à l'histoire* ([Paris], 1640), 95.

[42] Gauchet, "L'Etat au miroir," 237.

Henri, duc de Rohan's *De l'interest des princes et Estats de la Chrestienté* (1638), with its transparent, logical exposition of the interests of various European states: "[P]rinces rule people, and interest rules princes.... The prince may be deceived and his council may be corrupt, but interest alone is forever sure."[43] On a more practical level, the problem was exacerbated by the need for statesmen like Richelieu to justify and defend their controversial policies in the court of European opinion. Thus, the early decades of the seventeenth century were marked by a remarkable outpouring of pamphlets and treatises, many authorized and encouraged by the crown—writings openly discussing an approach to statecraft while simultaneously vaunting secrecy and silence as defining principles.

This contradiction between two imperatives—to disclose these secrets and to respect their secrecy—was never really resolved, at least in most cases. And, to return to Naudé's *Considérations politiques*, it runs through this text like red thread. Even after providing all sorts of justifications for proceeding with his enterprise, Naudé concludes that "if I knew that the little I will say about these matters might cause some abuses or disorder... I would throw this pen and paper into the fire, and make a vow of eternal silence."[44]

It may be, however, that several deft moves go a long way toward rescuing Naudé's book from the snares of this contradiction. For one thing, more than any other writer in the reason of state tradition, he declares—repeatedly—his anxiety in "penetrating" the secrets of statecraft; indeed, "penetrate" or "intrude" is the action he pointedly evokes. What this suggests is a spatial aspect to his positioning: he stands *outside* the place where statecraft is conducted ("the Cabinets of the great"); he observes the machinations of princes, kings, and ministers from a distance; or he learns about the "intrigues" and "mysteries" from their being disclosed in the public realm, through publication. This sense of distance that informs his text contrasts with the discursive nature of Jean Bodin's *Six Books of the Republic*. As Ellen McClure argues, "Bodin dreams of an authoritative treatise whose language would mirror the object described."[45] No authorial voice intrudes into Bodin's text; it is absent any sense of anxiety; there is no distance between "discourse" and subject matter—all features of *Considérations politiques*, features signaling to readers Naudé's position at a remove from the sphere of statecraft.

Naudé further affirms this position in the course of his extended apologia for the work he has boldly chosen to pursue. On the one hand, he confidently insists that, with his education and wide reading, he is equipped with the requisite knowledge to undertake this perilous project. But he also makes it clear that he will remain committed to the "contemplative life for the rest of my days... without getting

---

[43] Henri, duc de Rohan, *De l'interest des princes et Estats de la Chrestienté* ([Paris], 1639 ed.), 104. For the publishing history of this work, see Church, *Richelieu and Reason of State*, 352–4.
[44] Naudé, *Considérations politiques*, 85.
[45] Ellen M. McClure, *Sunspots and the Sun King: Sovereignty and Mediation in Seventeenth-Century France* (Urbana, IL, 2006), 26.

myself entangled in the active."[46] While he is keen to disavow any truck with pedantry, he is nevertheless frank in defending his bookish perspective, arguing that his considerable learning can easily compensate for his lack of political experience. "I have not had the kind of experience in the world to learn directly about the tricks and wickedness that abound, but I have observed a great number of them in histories, satires, and tragedies."[47] But not only learning, which might smack of pedantry: he also offers a brief for the role of the imagination as his guide, citing the examples of Gerolamo Cardano and Tommaso Campanella, who conceived a "perfect idea" of their subjects using only their "wits" and "imagination"; or actors who employ that "faculty of the imagination" to create their characters on the stage. "For myself," he concludes, "when I treat or write about any subject well and profitably, I will be content to rely upon these imaginings."[48] In short, Naudé's self-presentation is of an author claiming an equal footing to those who frequent the corridors of power—at least in terms of political wisdom—all the while insisting on his identity as a man of letters who inhabits a very different world.

But Naudé's status, as we are meant to infer, is not simply that of a man of letters; nor, as we are reminded several times, is his relationship to "the Cabinets of the great" merely an abstraction. Naudé is the secretary to a powerful cardinal, touted as a possible future pope; and it is this particular relationship of a privileged servant to a consummate Roman insider that has generated the secret knowledge which he imparts in *Considérations politiques*. "You are, as much as I, the author of this book," he declares in a sentence that suggests a fiction of shared responsibility for disclosing the secrets of statecraft.[49]

Another aspect of *Considérations politiques* fosters a different sense of distance, although here between text and readers. For the book raises considerable linguistic and intellectual barriers for a broad readership, thus serving to reduce the risk of disclosing what should remain hidden. Like the works of La Mothe le Vayer, it is characterized by what has been called a "shower of citations" in Latin and Greek. These remained untranslated until the 1667 edition, when the publisher decided that they rendered this "curious piece, a treasure of the cabinet of the very few," out of reach for most.[50] He was right. Recall that Marie de Gournay translated the many passages in Latin and Greek in her 1610 edition of Montaigne's *Essais*—a concession to a broader, *mondain* readership. Naudé, however, was loath to make such a concession for a book that "was not written to please everyone." If he had wanted to, he added, "he would not have written it in the style of Montaigne and Charron, which, he knows, puts off many people

---

[46] Naudé, *Considérations politiques*, 82.   [47] *Considérations politiques*, 81.
[48] *Considérations politiques*, 84–5.
[49] Quoted in Louis Marin, "Pour une théorie baroque de l'action politique," in *Considérations politiques*, 36.
[50] *Considérations politiques*, "Au Lecteur" in the 1667 ed.; 68 in the 1988 Marin ed.

because of the great number of Latin citations."[51] He raised the bar even higher for the common reader with the plethora of examples, mostly from antiquity, and references to authors and figures that fill his pages to the brim. On one page alone (chosen virtually at random), he mentions Diogenes Laertes, Pythagoras, Plutarch, Hercules, Jupiter, Socrates, Plotinus, Porphyry, Brutus, Scylla, Apollonius, Pico della Mirandola, Cecco d'Ascoli, Ermolao Barbaro, Savonarola, Agostino Nifo, Guillaume Postel, Gerolamo Cardano, Tommaso Campanella, Virgil, Agrippa von Nettesheim, Marsilio Ficino, Giordano Bruno, Pierre-Ange Manzolli (Palengenius), Johann Reuchlin, the fables of Numa Pompilius, Zalmoxis, and Minos, and several archangels (Raziel, Jophiel, Zadkiel, Raphaël, and Metatron).[52] This was a book designed to delight and educate the very few and trip up the many.

Finally, *Considérations politiques* manages even to distance itself from its ostensible subject. Curiously, it does not convincingly convey the sense that it really means to be a book about statecraft, or at least to be instructive in the "art of governing." To be sure, there are long passages arguing for the wisdom of certain stratagems, and more generally on the nature of prudential statecraft. And here he proposes some fundamental distinctions between what he calls the science of politics, found in the works of Plato, Aristotle, and Cicero, among others, and "maxims of state," which he defines as "a violation of common law for the benefit of the public good." Distinct from both of these are "coups d'état": "daring and extraordinary actions which princes are forced to carry out in difficult and even desperate situations, against the public law, without even respecting either the order or forms of justice, putting at risk particular interests for the benefit of the public good."[53] There is thus some overlap between maxims of state and coups d'état. The difference is that the former are not secret; they can be discussed and contemplated before they are acted upon. With a coup d'état, however, silence and secrecy are paramount; they are made known only with their execution. As Naudé writes, vividly evoking their dramatic nature in language that pulls no punches with regard to the extraordinary and deadly nature of what English translators called "master strokes":

> [O]ne sees the thunderbolt before one hears it groaning in the clouds, it strikes before the flame shines forth, here Matins are said before the bells have rung, the execution precedes the sentence, everything is done in the Jewish fashion—one is taken, according to the French proverb, unripe and unsuspecting, he receives the stroke who thought to give it, he dies who thought himself quite safe, one suffers what one never expected, all is done at night, in obscurity, in fog and darkness, the Goddess Laverna [the patron of thieves] presides.[54]

---

[51] *Considérations politiques*, 69.   [52] *Considérations politiques*, 94.
[53] *Considérations politiques*, 101.
[54] *Considérations politiques*, 101. I have relied upon the translation in Donaldson, *Machiavelli and Mystery of State*, 168, though with some changes.

As this passage suggests, there is an occult quality to his conception of statecraft, which pertains especially to decisive political moments, when the very existence of the state, or at least the regime, is in question. His most shocking endorsement is of Saint Bartholomew, which he discusses at length. Naudé approved of the massacre as a legitimate act of state, calling it the "most daring *coup d'état* and the most subtly conducted that has ever been staged in France or any other place." In fact, his only criticism is that it was not pursued to the end. One must appreciate the enormity of this act of political violence—how it lived on as a traumatic memory for Gallicans, in whose ranks, in fact, Naudé belonged—to measure the likely impact of his cold-blooded analysis. "We must," he writes, "imitate expert surgeons who while a vein is open let blood to the point of having the patient faint, in order to purge the body of its bad humors."[55] Here, as elsewhere, Naudé's coup d'état would seem to be the perfect antecedent to Carl Schmitt's "state of exception."[56] They are extraordinary actions that, in Naudé's understanding, evoke a fundamental element of princely politics—foundational moments that reveal the hidden "springs" of statecraft at its most basic and violent.

While he devotes much of his book to the various contexts of different "coups," citing many examples and texts, both ancient and more contemporary, to illustrate and justify this extraordinary measure, it is not clear that Naudé meant *Considérations politiques* primarily as a guide to political action. Despite the plethora of examples—or perhaps because of the sheer surfeit of them—the reader is left at a loss as to what could be gleaned as a guide for political action. And this is acknowledged by Naudé, who likens "political prudence" to Proteus, "of whom it is impossible to have any certain knowledge, even after penetrating the secrets of that old man and having contemplated with a fixed and confident eye all his different movements, figures, and metamorphoses," leaving us horrified and confused by his various appearances.[57]

Ultimately, then, the political prudence that Naudé strives to impart is less a matter of technique and more a function of the character, intelligence, and position of the political actor. Clearly, he must be an *esprit fort*, with qualities personified by his patron, Cardinal Bagni, but also by Richelieu, who "was pulled from the depths of his library to govern France."[58] The library, a classic space of *otium*, serves as an antechamber for the accomplished minister. Another space is evoked at least metaphorically: an elevated position allowing the statesman to "see with a firm and assured eye, as if from the high tower of a donjon, all of this world, perceiving it as one would a badly organized theater, full of confusion, where some perform comedies and others tragedies." His charge is to intervene in this world "like a divinity from a machine as often as he pleases or when the variety of

---

[55] *Considérations politiques*, 121.
[56] Carl Schmitt, *The Concept of the Political*, trans. George Schwab, (Chicago, 1996).
[57] *Considérations politiques*, 75.   [58] *Considérations politiques*, 158.

occasions prompt him."⁵⁹ Just as Naudé the author positions himself at a remove from the political realm, so his prudent statesman, his Neo-Stoic hero, becomes master of his world only by distancing himself from the world's noxious vicissitudes. "I want him to have the good principles of philosophy in his head and not only on his lips, to know nature in its entirety and not only in some part, to live in the world as if he were outside it, and under heaven as if he were in it."⁶⁰

A consummate political observer who rarely strayed from political or public matters in his writings, Naudé acknowledged the slippery nature of maintaining one's virtue in this divided world and the need to distance oneself from the sphere of public affairs. This is evident, as I argue, in the text of *Considérations politiques*, even as it plunged into the secret realm of statecraft at its most morally compromised depths. And this ambivalence seemed to mark his more general outlook, at least as represented by his friend and fellow *esprit fort* La Mothe le Vayer. In his dialogue "Traictant de la politique sceptiquement," Orasius Tubero (La Mothe le Vayer) argues with Telamon (acknowledged to be Naudé) about the highly vexed nature of politics. The dispute is over the age-old question of whether a wise man should commit himself to its demanding burdens and forced compromises. "Orasius" cites the examples of Ulysses, who wished to be reborn into a life removed from the cares of public service, and Socrates, whose "demon" warned him about the dangers of a political calling. By the end of the dialogue, "Telamon" appears convinced by his fellow member of the Tetrade. Together they celebrate the pleasures and virtues of the contemplative life, and pledge to "try to remain that small number of the elect," keeping their happiness hidden, "imitating those animals who seek food and tranquility out of sight." Naudé, this undeceived exponent on the dark art of "master strokes," would seem, then, to be a man who, like many others, cast a jaundiced eye on politics from the refuge of *otium cum dignitate*.⁶¹

Two Fictions of France

THE WARS OF RELIGION ended, and the aristocracy turned from mutual slaughter to reading novels. If this is something of an exaggeration, it also contains a grain of truth, for it cannot be denied that in terms of both production and consumption, the early seventeenth century witnessed the takeoff of the French novel. By one count, nearly six hundred were published between 1600 and 1660.⁶²

---

⁵⁹ *Considérations politiques*, 81.   ⁶⁰ *Considérations politiques*, 160.

⁶¹ François de La Mothe le Vayer, "Dialogue traictant de la politique sceptiquement, entre Telamon et Orontes," in La Mothe le Vayer, *Dialogues faits à l'imitation des Anciens* (1606), ed. André Pessel (Paris, 1988), 387–451, especially 445.

⁶² *Dictionnaire des lettres françaises: Le XVIIe siècle* (Paris, 1951), 1106. H. J. Martin states that there were half a thousand titles published between 1601 and 1640, 282 of these in Paris: Henri-Jean Martin,

Writers like Honoré d'Urfé, Marin Le Roy de Gomberville, Charles Sorel, Paul Scarron, and Madeleine de Scudéry established the form as an acceptable literary genre, while an aristocratic reading public, avid for books that would both entertain and edify—and written in French—ensured the popularity of their works. Of course, we should not overestimate the reading capabilities of aristocrats, not to speak of their mental concentration. H. J. Martin has commented on the very configuration of the text in these early novels—the large print, the run-on sentences devoid of punctuation, the lack of paragraph breaks—suggesting that they were probably read very slowly or out loud by people not really very practiced at the silent, solitary experience of keeping one's nose in a book.[63] Certainly the *"mondain"* aristocrats, those who consumed the new novels, were judged woefully ignorant by contemporary commentators of various stripes, especially those savants who insisted on the primacy of ancient languages and still defended the encyclopedic tradition of the Renaissance. Even Vaugelas, a keen and sympathetic observer of the reading habits in the salon milieu he inhabited, rather condescendingly mentions seeing ladies stop in the middle of reading something engrossing simply because they failed to understand a relatively common word.[64]

Despite these limitations, it is striking how bookish certain aristocratic circles seemed to be. And nothing underscores this disposition more than the extraordinary popularity of one sprawling novel, Honoré d'Urfé's *L'Astrée*, the four volumes of which were published between 1607 and 1627. Embraced by a reading public that, if not exclusively aristocratic and courtly, largely thought of itself in these terms, this was a book that was not simply read—it was lived. What follows will consider this pastoral novel as a quintessentially French literary product, and especially how it resonated with contemporary notions of being French in a postbellum age. In conjunction with *L'Astrée,* I will look at another novel that, like *L'Astrée,* spoke to French elites and also evoked questions of civil war and French unity: *Argenis* by John Barclay, first published in Latin in 1621, then quickly translated into several European languages. While *L'Astrée* dealt endlessly with love and amorous conversation, *Argenis* addressed political and historical issues against a fictionalized backdrop of France during the recent Wars of Religion.

Livre, pouvoirs et société à Paris au XVIIe siècle (1598-1701), 2 vols. (Geneva, 1984), I: 293. (Martin cites the work of Ralph Copleston Williams, *Bibliography of the Seventeenth-Century Novel in France* [London, 1964], 109-77.) Kathleen Wine, *Forgotten Virgo: Humanism and Absolutism in Honoré d'Urfé's "L'Astrée"* (Geneva, 2000), 114. Novelistic production was virtually nonexistent during the religious wars, reappeared during the years 1589-99, and quadrupled between 1600 and 1610. See Maurice Lever, *Le roman français au XVIIe siècle* (Paris 1981), 12.

[63] Henri-Jean Martin, "La vie intellectuelle au temps de Richelieu," in *Richelieu et le monde de l'esprit* (Paris, 1985), 183-92.
[64] Karl August Ott, "La notion du 'bon usage' dans les *Remarques* de Vaugelas," *Cahiers de l'association internationale des études françaises*, 14/1 (1962), 92.

The task in what follows will be to read these two texts as evidence of what values and concerns were close to French *gens de lettres* as they participated in the fashioning of contemporary literary culture. As writers who addressed this public, they also appreciated the imperative to entertain, amuse, and divert, but not frivolously or vacuously. For like the aristocrats and other elites whose attention and readership they strove to attract, they believed that there was virtue in *otium*—in the privileged retirement from the sordid world of *negotium*—and that the pursuit of letters was an edifying and worthy way to fill that privileged leisure. It might be said that "literature" itself emerged as part of the embrace of the ethos of *otium*, that its very existence as a self-sustaining "field" resulted from a move of "dignified retreat" into a cultural space that, precisely because of its distance from the world of public or political affairs, allowed for a wide range of concerns.

One way to dignify leisure, indeed, was in the beguiling and flattering charge of asking readers to consider what it meant to be French; not only to reflect on larger aspects of being French, but being French in their own time. Thus, in different ways, these works address a particular readership at a particular time, which is to say, the present moment of the early seventeenth century. Somewhat paradoxically, the two authors convey this present-mindedness through stories situated in times quite far from the present—the fifth century (*L'Astrée*) and a vague pre-Roman antiquity (*Argenis*). In part, these works refracted—with contrasting optics of both focus and distortion—the Wars of Religion, offering different ways of engaging with this experience through the genre of literature, that is, fiction. They were also meditations on living in fealty to an all-powerful French monarch, with all of the historical and moral resonances that this entailed. They were, then, about the age-old quandary of maintaining virtue in the face of power. "Literature" and "power"—to use Christian Jouhaud's terms—were intertwined in the Age of Richelieu. How they were intertwined—the varieties of how that relationship was imagined—can be demonstrated only by the texts themselves. Just as the expressions of reason of state we have examined seemed to fictionalize power, or at least endowed their presentation of this form of statecraft with literary qualities, so these works of fiction are imbued with strong visions of the political nation that was France in the seventeenth century.

D'Urfé's *L'Astrée*: A Pastoral Mirror for France

Upon the publication of its first volume in 1607, *L'Astrée* was an immediate success. Henri IV had portions of it read aloud to him. The entire four volumes went through ten editions in the seventeenth century and had, according to the premier historian of the book in the period, thousands of readers.[65] Marie de Gournay

---

[65] Martin, *Livre, pouvoirs et société*, I: 295.

called it "the breviary for ladies and *galants* of the court."⁶⁶ Not only did the epic novel have many readers; it fostered a cult of imitators who adopted it as a kind of script for aristocratic behavior, even beyond France. Cardinal de Retz recalled in his memoirs how in his youth he and his friends often re-enacted scenes from the pastoral novel and tried to identify particular characters and situations.⁶⁷ The Rambouillet milieu was infused with the spirit of *L'Astrée*: the country outings undertaken by the salon's habitués frequently became ritual imitations of the novel; and the only portrait of Julie d'Angennes, Mme de Rambouillet's daughter, depicts her as the book's female protagonist.⁶⁸

What explains the appeal of this epic, each of whose four volumes ran to over a thousand pages crammed with a head-spinning tangle of stories and characters?⁶⁹ How is it that several generations of well-born readers embraced a book filled with interminable conversations on the vicissitudes of love in all its (mostly) edifying forms, interspersed with sometimes abstruse ruminations inspired by Neo-Platonism?

It is of some importance to note at the outset that readers undoubtedly knew something about the author and realized that he was a well-placed aristocrat whose biography summarized the experience of a generation. Honoré d'Urfé was one of them. Moreover, it was widely believed that the novel was autobiographical. D'Urfé confided to Pasquier that *L'Astrée* was the "story of my youth," while many readers assumed that the main account of the quest for love was inspired by his early passion for his brother's wife, Diane, whom he later married. Although he strenuously denied that his work was a *roman à clef*, readers undoubtedly convinced themselves that they were reading a true-life romance.⁷⁰

D'Urfé was born into an old family of Forez in 1567; his mother came from the princely house of Savoy. As a youth he was educated by the Jesuits and partook as well of the Italian influences present in the courtly atmosphere of his household. Like others we have met, such as Georges de Scudéry and Montausier, d'Urfé was a learned gentleman but also an experienced warrior; he too combined arms and letters. He seems to have spent much, if not most, of his adult life on the battlefield. He fought for the League and remained loyal to the Duc de Nemours, the Leaguer chief in the province, even after its defeat. By the end of the century,

---

⁶⁶ Antoine Adam, *Histoire de la littérature française au XVIIe siècle*, 3rd ed., 3 vols. (Paris, 1997), I: 133; and Maurice Magendie, *La politesse mondaine et les théories de l'honnêteté en France au XVIIe siècle, de 1600 à 1660* (1925; reprint, Geneva, 1970), 126.

⁶⁷ J. M. H. Salmon, *Cardinal de Retz: The Anatomy of a Conspirator* (New York, 1970), 35; Magendie, *La politesse mondaine*, 141–2.

⁶⁸ David Maland, *Culture and Society in Seventeenth-Century France* (New York, 1970), 51. On Julie as Astrée, see Roger Zuber, "Le temps des choix (1630–1660)," in Jean Mesnard, ed., *Précis de littérature française du XVIIe siècle* (Paris, 1990), 142.

⁶⁹ The 1633 edition of five volumes came to more than 5,500 pages. *Astrea, Part One*, trans. Steven Rendall (Binghamton, NY, 1995), ix.

⁷⁰ See d'Urfé's own warning not to assume that characters' identities are so apparent.

however, he had rallied to the crown; in 1603 he was named *gentilhomme ordinaire du roi*. He frequented the Parisian *monde*, appearing both at court and at the Hôtel de Rambouillet. At his death in 1625, from pneumonia while campaigning in northern Italy, he left *L'Astrée* unfinished, having published three volumes.[71]

The story of *L'Astrée* is really incidental to its success, and probably to its meaning as well. The main narrative thread, in fact, is not terribly original, having been lifted almost wholesale from Jorge de Montemayor's *Los siete libros de la Diana*. But the setting and larger context are crucial. D'Urfé situates the novel in fifth-century Forez, his native *pays*, which he endowed with enough geographical detail to convince readers that it was a real place, and not some mythical Arcadia.[72] The period in which the action takes place probably counts as much as its physical context, for it is a time of general warfare, of armies marauding throughout Europe—except for Forez, a peaceful refuge in a world at war. In this sheltered country live a race of shepherds, descendants of a rich and cultivated people who had fled Roman domination and the royal court to take up a life of pastoral simplicity. Though they are rustic settlers, their lives are hardly difficult; though they are called *bergers* and *bergères*, they are not. Few sheep are tended; little labor is exerted. D'Urfé frankly acknowledges that his characters are not meant to represent actual social types, let alone shepherds. Rather, they are ideal creatures— uncorrupted by the ways of court and city, unencumbered by possessions, pure in mind and body.

This main story of the love and contretemps between the protagonists, Céladon and Astrée, occupies only a small portion of the epic's several thousand pages. *L'Astrée* has been called a French *Thousand and One Nights,* and its narrative complexity, leisurely pace, fondness for digressions, and variety of characters easily rival the most convoluted epic in the canon. There are stories within stories— sometimes stories within stories within stories.[73]

One of the reasons this unwieldy text appealed to aristocrats is that it presented them, in leisurely and spacious terms, an idealized world they were happy to recognize as their own. The social order of fifth-century Forez is cozy and attractively limited—a purified *haut monde*. There are kings and queens, but they play a distinctly minor role; the action does not depend upon the initiative of a charismatic prince.[74] It may be that readers associated their rural vocation with the image of

---

[71] A fourth, completed by his secretary, Balthazar Baro, and based on his extensive drafts, appeared posthumously in 1627. There are two versions of a fifth and final volume, one by Baro (1627) and another by Borstel de Gaubertin (1625).

[72] Details on the region and its history come mostly from Claude Fauchet, *Recueil des antiquitez et histoires gauloises et françoises* (Paris, 1579); on Fauchet and other historical sources d'Urfé consulted, see Maxime Gaume, *Les inspirations et les sources de l'oeuvre d'Honoré d'Urfé* (Saint-Etienne, 1977), an indispensable source.

[73] Erica Harth, *Ideology and Culture in Seventeenth-Century France* (Ithaca, NY, 1983), 34–48.

[74] Marc Fumaroli, "Sous le signe de Protée, 1594–1630," in Mesnard, *Précis de littérature française*, 21–108.

the country seigneur, the self-sufficient, virtuous nobleman who maintained the traditional ways of this class, in a conscious rejection of the venal, corrupt, and dependent ways of the courtier. In this sense *L'Astrée* might be seen as expressing a Gallic version of the "country" ideology that has been found lacking in France, unlike in England, where its place in seventeenth- and eighteenth-century political culture has long been acknowledged.[75] D'Urfé places particular emphasis on the city-country opposition that magnified the moral valence of *L'Astrée*'s setting. "There is nothing in cities," comments one character, "that equals the freedom and liberty of these villages." Those fortunate to call Forez their home enjoy a "virtuous liberty."[76] Virtually everyone in *L'Astrée* is cultivated and endowed with an effortless grace that marks them as naturally noble. And to a one they are beautiful; ugliness has been banished from fifth-century Forez.[77] In short, the social world of *L'Astrée* is an aristocratic paradise.

A more capacious way to understand this aspect of Forez is in terms of the theme we have sounded throughout this study—as a place of *otium cum dignitate*. This is the way Céladon explains the origins of the shepherds and shepherdesses whose long-ago ancestors decided that happiness could be found only in retreat from the cares of the Roman world. "[O]ut of mutual consent [they] vowed that they would all flee forever all kinds of ambition, because this alone is the source of so much trouble, to live...in the peaceful guise of the shepherd."[78] This physical withdrawal is affirmed in the dress of the shepherds and shepherdesses. Although they tend no sheep, and do not even labor in any recognizable way, d'Urfé repeatedly calls attention to the fact that they carry staffs and are garbed in simple pastoral apparel. Jean-Pierre van Elslande sees this dress, which significantly renders the shepherds as virtually alike in outward appearance, as comparable to the habit of a religious order.[79] Isolation, withdrawal, common dress—these are the conditions that mark the novel's characters and their place of residence as a liminal space, the specificity of which can be appreciated only in its fundamental difference from the actual world of d'Urfé's readers.

D'Urfé's dream world, deliberately set apart from a Europe at war, surely appealed to a war-weary generation and those that followed, alert as they were to the cost of civil war and to the possibility of its recrudescence. The very geographical configuration of Forez speaks to this sense of withdrawal and separation. It was an island of Gauls at peace, surrounded by a Roman theater of constant warfare and invasion. The country was divided by the Lignon River: on one side lived

---

[75] On its lack in France, see Jonathan Dewald, *Aristocratic Experience and the Origins of Modern Culture, 1570–1715* (Berkeley and Los Angeles, 1993), 16–17.

[76] Jean-Pierre Van Elslande, "Roman pastoral et crise des valeurs dans la France du premier XVIIe siècle," *XVIIe siècle*, 215/2 (2002), 217.

[77] Magendie, *La politesse mondaine*, 61.

[78] Quoted in Jean-Marc Chatelain, "Institution civile et pensée constitutionnelle: Pour une lecture politique de *L'Astrée*," in Delphine Denis, ed., *Lire L'Astrée* (Paris, 2008), 198.

[79] Van Elslande, "Roman pastoral et crise des valeurs," 212.

royalty and nobles of the court—the nymphs—whose lives were consumed by political and military strife; on the other was the land of the shepherds and shepherdesses, almost entirely preoccupied with matters of the heart.

One view of this aristocratic idyll is that it exhibits an undercurrent of disappointment and decline. For Norbert Elias, the novel reads as a sort of ideological testament of "an aristocratic middle stratum," neither courtly nor marginal, neither great nor impoverished. Its author is a spokesman for his class: "even though d'Urfé, having fought vainly against the man who is now crowned and at the centre of the court and probably against the growing power of the monarchy as well, lays down his sword and creates a dream image of peaceful and simple pastoral existence for war-weary people, nevertheless, on the ideological level he continues the struggle in his novel."[80] For Erica Harth, the novel offers an artful form of consolation for the traditional aristocracy as a whole. Challenged from almost every side, aristocrats sought refuge in art and love from a reality that was increasingly hard to bear. For both critics, *L'Astrée*'s meaning emerges in relationship to a social group whose hard-pressed fortunes transformed the rather inchoate options of withdrawal, escape, passivity, and rural retreat, now artfully projected onto the novel's pastoral canvas, into a compelling ideology.[81]

I would suggest, however, that the meaning of *repos*, or *otium*, here reflects not a sense of withdrawal in defeat but something quite different: not the social conditions or psychological disposition of a ruling class, or a portion of it, but rather a specific historical conjuncture associated with a restored monarchy. For this aristocratic idyll, the shepherds and shepherdesses' endless pleasures, even their vexatious love lives, were possible only because *L'Astrée*'s residents were blessed with a country at peace. In this sense, the so-called civilizing process—if that is what it was—required a post-bellum settlement, and thus the political developments that guaranteed it. These circumstances are not merely peripheral or ancillary to the story. *L'Astrée* celebrated peace: the conventions of the novel were deliberately cast against those of the chivalric tradition; the setting was an island of peace in a Europe at war; the dedication (which first appeared in the 1610 edition) extolled Henri IV as a Prince of Peace. "So therefore accept her (Sire), not as a simple shepherdess, but as a work of your own hands: for truly one can say you are the author, since it is to Your Majesty that all Europe owes its peace and tranquility."[82] The very figure of Astrée, or Astraea, suggested the importance of the theme of peace to the novel: she was the just virgin of the Golden Age who left earth when men turned to war, and whose return, once they renounced it, would

---

[80] Norbert Elias, *The Court Society* (Oxford, 1983), 256.

[81] "The seventeenth-century reader, then, saw a reflection in the metaphorical mirror of d'Urfé's pastoral. What we see instead is a projection, a literary image created not in reflection of any social reality but as a vehicle for the hopes, dreams, and fantasies of a class whose ideology was embarking on its long descent into obsolescence." Harth, *Ideology and Culture*, 47–8.

[82] *Astrea, Part One*, 1.

usher in an era of peace. The illustrated edition of the novel includes a picture of Astrée complete with stalks of grain in her hair—symbols of the goddess's virtues.[83] And Adamas suggests to Céladon that he erect altars in worship of his beloved Astrée. At one point the Druid priest intones a prayer—not coincidentally before one of these altars—beseeching their god Teutatès to return "this goddess Astrée by whose presence we hope all kinds of blessings."[84]

The importance of Astraea in the Renaissance has been demonstrated by Frances Yates, who refers mostly to the deity's association with the cult of Elizabeth I.[85] But Henri IV also benefited from this association, just as his reign, too, was invested with the hopes of many for the dawning of an era of peace and religious harmony in Europe. That d'Urfé dedicated his novel to Henri, a man he once fought against, underscores the work's role as one device in fostering this political cult. Like others, he was willing to revere his valiant king, a man of war whose reign promised peace and unity after several generations of civil war. As with other contemporary works, readers of *L'Astrée* could hardly have ignored the relevance of this conflict for the story. Its context is infused with the air of a postbellum society—now at peace, but a peace only recently secured after a long period of conflict and internal strife. For example, the Gauls appreciate that the reason for their former subjugation to Roman rule lay not in Rome's superiority in arms but in their own fractiousness. As with Spain's meddling in French affairs during the religious wars, Rome took advantage of their internal disarray to invade and conquer.

Thus, the circumstances of peace in fifth-century Forez were rather specific and evoke the novel's participation in the creation of a veritable *lieu de mémoire* for seventeenth-century French readers. Forez is inhabited by Gauls, who are surrounded by Romans. Like many of his learned contemporaries, d'Urfé was steeped in the mythology of Celtic history. The second half of the sixteenth century saw an efflorescence of scholarly work on the history of the Gauls, a savant movement that overlapped with an attempt to find the sources of French law not in Roman antiquity but in a more native past. Our erudite author clearly digested the learned histories of Haillan, Fauchet, Du Moulin, Pasquier, and others.[86] Unlike Ronsard, whose *Franciade* depended upon classical antiquity for the mythological origins of France, casting Hector's son Francus as the source of French dynastic history, d'Urfé turned away from the entire Greco-Roman legacy. This move was not only a rejection of the classical legacy but also a blow to Italian primacy as the source of European civilization. For d'Urfé the Romans are the invaders;

---

[83] Frances A. Yates, *Astraea: The Imperial Theme in the Sixteenth Century* (London, 1975), 86, 210. On this, see also Jean Lafond, "Preface," in Lafond, ed., *L'Astrée* (Paris, 1984), 20–1.

[84] *L'Astrée*, III, pt. 9; quoted in Lafond, *L'Astrée*, 21.   [85] Yates, *Astraea*.

[86] As well as the more suspect writings of the late fifteenth-century writer Annius of Viterbo, whose views of a Europe founded by Noah and his immediate progeny were based on forged documents. Wine, *Forgotten Virgo*, 88–9.

the people of Forez are the exceptional preservers of the culture and religion of the Gauls. Most interestingly, the Franks, who have just recently conquered Gaul, are discovered originally to have been Gauls themselves, and thus the liberators of their own ancestors. Says Adamas: "And now that the Franks have brought with them their druids, revealing that they were once known as Gauls, it seems that our authority and our holy customs can return to their former splendor."[87] As Jean Chatelain points out, this tendentious historical interpretation depended upon d'Urfé's very selective reading of the historians he routinely consulted.[88] While he might have found support for this view in some passages in the works of Guillaume Postel or Jean Bodin, others, especially the writings of Pasquier and Haillan, belie it. This suggests, in turn, the importance to the historical frame of his novel of the supposed merger of Franks and Gauls: it was so important that he was willing to ignore sources he otherwise depended upon. And it is this fictitious conflation that defines "French" history at its very start.

For the union of the Gauls and the Franks speaks to the propitious, even unique, nature of this historical origin of a people. In *L'Astrée*, as well as in the antiquarian histories d'Urfé consulted in writing his pastoral, two distinct sets of virtues mark the Gauls and Franks. The Franks are conquerors, endowed with a martial spirit that will bequeath to the French nobility essential traits as a warrior class. The Gauls, on the other hand, are possessed of very different qualities: natural eloquence, gentleness, and a civilized knowledge of the arts and sciences. "If the Franks liberate the Gauls from their Roman occupiers, it is the mature and urbane Gauls whose civilizing influence authorizes the Franks to wield their newly won power," writes Kathleen Wine.[89] In this union, we have the perfect confluence of arms and letters, endowing France with a noble birthright in both domains. The fifth century, when d'Urfé situates the story, was the era of the founding of the Merovingian monarchy, the first dynasty of French kings. It was in this period, he notes as well, that France gained its name. The Frankish kingdom erected by the Merovingians in the fifth century thus becomes, in d'Urfé's novel, a restoration of Celtic Gaul. It was then, as the contemporary historian Claude Fauchet argued, that the "French" were born. Significantly, d'Urfé makes this advent a self-conscious aspect of his novel, having his Gauls comment, "Until this name we were called Gauls, but little by little we changed our name, taking on that of France for the future."[90] While crucial passages in the text celebrate the monarchy—from the Merovingians to Henri IV—the story's temporal context in

---

[87] *L'Astrée*, II, pt. 8, quoted in Wine, *Forgotten Virgo*, 25. Adamas also recounts that the Gauls were conquered not by Roman superiority, but rather because of internal divisions that weakened them. As Louise K. Horowitz notes, this view, derived in all likelihood from Pasquier's writings, also suggested to readers a connection between the novel's context and the religious wars. Horowitz, *Honoré d'Urfé* (Boston, 1984), 4–5.
[88] Chatelain, "Institution civile et pensée constitutionnelle," 194–5.
[89] Wine, *Forgotten Virgo*, 95.   [90] Quoted in Wine, *Forgotten Virgo*, 93.

the deepest recesses of Franco-Gallic history suggests that France's virtues and strengths cannot be ascribed to kings alone. These, rather, are rooted in history—in the history of a people whose special traits are the gift of a propitious blending of two races.[91]

This pastoral tale, then, so often described in terms of retirement, withdrawal, and passivity, even defeat, had much to say about French history and French identity. In its very title and its main female protagonist, it called to mind an ancient Golden Age, suggesting the hope that the present era might witness its return. It celebrated the French monarchy: there is even the suggestion that Céladon and his epic quest were meant by d'Urfé to make readers think of Henri IV and his long campaign to the throne. The historical context of *L'Astrée*, based upon several generations of historical research into France's Gallic past, which d'Urfé deftly deployed for his unlearned readers, created a usable past in literary guise—an orienting point in French history that fixed the essence of their identity in a recoverable past. Finally, it presented its readers with a distant mirror of another post-bellum era, reminding them of their own very recent return to peaceful times following several generations of civil strife.

Barclay's *Argenis*: A Civil War Romance

John Barclay's *Argenis* tells the story of how that peace was won and offers as well a primer on what forces still threatened it. Published in Latin in 1621, the novel offered a political vision that very well may have guided Richelieu once he ascended to power three years later. It was one of the cardinal's favorite books

---

[91] The political meaning of *L'Astrée* is to be found not only in Forez's remove from the royal court or in its insulation from a Roman world perpetually at war, but more fundamentally in its very constitution. As Galathée explains to Céladon, even Alaric, king of the Wisigoths, when he conquered all the lands beyond the Loire, stopped short of imposing his authoritarian rule on the Forezians. He "recognized our statutes and confirmed our privileges, and without usurping our authority, left us with our ancient liberties." *L'Astrée*, ed. Hugues Vaganay, 4 vols. (Lyon, 1925–8), I: 46. Chatelain, "Institution civile et pensée constitutionnelle," 193. Related to this, it has been suggested that d'Urfé's imagined ancient country actually embodied the principles enunciated by the Catholic League during the Wars of Religion, in particular the noble League of Peronne of 1572, which, like other rebels both before and after, saw in France's supposed ancient liberties a template for their own program. But, as Chatelain correctly observes, this interpretation is too narrow. The embrace of fundamental liberties as enshrined in France's unwritten constitution was part and parcel of a whole trend of "constitutional" thought, from a royal jurist like Claude de Seyssel, to a Protestant such as François Hotman, to Gallican savants; it was hardly the special ideology of noble Catholic militants. Comments Chatelain, "Such a declaration shows...that the 'repose' of its shepherds...is not only constituted by pastoral conventions of a life of leisure: it is also based on the perpetuation of rules of an ancient common life which defines these 'liberties.'" Chatelain, "Institution civile et pensée constitutionnelle," 193. In *L'Astrée* the spirit of constitutionalism is transferred from the dry tomes of legal scholarship to the pages of a pastoral romance. In Jean-Marie Constant's account of aristocratic notions of "liberty" in the seventeenth century, this was an ideology that was close to that of the League and Protestants, but beyond this it was also rooted in an image of the ancient Gauls as the mythic embodiment of a true France. Constant, *La folle liberté des baroques (1600–1661)* (Paris, 2007), 72ff.

(it is said), always on his nightstand.[92] And no wonder: *Argenis* offered a sustained brief for the virtue, indeed necessity, of supreme monarchical authority, and the terrible cost of its violation.

But it did so via the medium of a literary form, the romance, which Barclay enlarged beyond the genre's stock account of the travails of star-crossed lovers into a tale of high statecraft—a patently transparent depiction of France and Europe during the religious wars of the sixteenth century. His reworking of this genre, however, was more than simply a matter of endowing it with a political narrative. Barclay himself proclaimed it a "new genre of literature, not perhaps hitherto seen."[93] Contemporary scholars agree. Indeed, with *Argenis*, Barclay led the transformation of this established literary genre: "From being an attractive but untrustworthy alternative to the serious, romance itself came to be redefined as serious, as a way of perceiving history and even a means of influencing it," writes Annabel Patterson.[94] According to Paul Salzman, Barclay's adaptation of the romance allowed him to comment on crucial and controversial contemporary matters while disguising his "social critique."[95]

This strategy is articulated by the character of Nicopompus, acknowledged to be speaking for Barclay himself. Early in the book he announces his intention "with a free hand [to] guide my Pen," to write a book about "the king's errors," the seditious actions of "the great Ones," and "the folly of [the people's] credulity." Nicopompus's interlocutor, a priest, greets this proposal skeptically. "If thou wilt be advised by me, thou shalt repress this rage," the priest advises. Better he should express his criticisms to the king in private. To "divulge by thy writings" would only be to give "the vulgar" reason to resist or oppose him.[96] But Nicopompus has a strategy to avoid this "public trial." Barclay, then (as Nicopompus), essentially adumbrates a mode of critique disguised by the technique of fiction—both the veil of allegory and seduction by way of the fabulous. Have no fear, he announces, "I will lead them, ignorant of my intention, about with so delightful mazes, as even themselves shall be pleased to be blamed under other names.... I will write a Fable like a History.... They will love me, as they do the shows of the Theater or the Tilt-yard. So having won their liking to the Potion, I will also add to it wholesome herbs." True, some may recognize their own misdeeds portrayed: "To disguise them, I will have many inventions, which cannot possibly agree to those that I intend to point at. For this liberty shall be mine, who am not religiously tied

---

[92] Michael Meere, "The Politics of Transgenericity: Pierre du Ryer's Dramatic Adaptations of John Barclay's *Argenis*," *Studia Aurea*, 10 (2016), 328.

[93] This is in the dedication to Louis XIII. See "Introduction," in John Barclay, *Argenis*, ed. and trans. Mark Riley and Dorothy Pritchard Huber, 2 vols. (Tempe, AZ, 2004), I: 12.

[94] Annabel Patterson, *Censorship and Interpretation: The Conditions of Writing and Reading in Early Modern England* (Madison, WI, 1984), 168.

[95] Paul Salzman, *Literary Culture in Jacobean England: Reading 1621* (New York, 2002), 77, 81.

[96] *John Barclay, His Argenis, Translated out of Latine into English*, trans. Robert Le Grys (London, 1628), 129, 130. I have sometimes modernized the spelling from Le Grys's translation.

to the truth of a History." What Nicopompus is describing, of course, is the novel in the reader's hands.[97]

Here Barclay echoes the common contemporary imperative we have often noted: the need for discretion, indirection, even secrecy when dealing with potentially sensitive political matters. But as well this passage suggests a larger claim; indeed, it offers a striking confirmation of the assertion that "literature," exemplified in this case by a text deliberately fashioned to "delight," "stir," "perplex," and in general beguile readers, was uniquely capable of conveying views and ideas that it might be indelicate to disclose otherwise.[98] Whatever the meaning of "fiction" in what we could consider the pre-history of the modern novel, the development of this genre of literary expression allowed for a thoroughly convincing presentation of a historical reality that was, however, "unreal."

This does not mean that Barclay's readers remained in the dark as to the historical analogues of his characters. In fact, his allegory was not terribly successful in ensuring that, as Nicopompus promised, "there shall be no man's picture to be plainly found there."[99] The English translation included the key as an appendix. In it we find that the main characters are meant to represent the leading rulers of the sixteenth century, the whole novel being a slightly veiled depiction of the French Wars of Religion. Meleander is Henri III; his daughter Argenis represents the French crown. Catherine de Medici has a role as Selenissa. Poliarchus, the novel's hero, is listed in the English key as Henri IV, but he likely was meant as an idealized composite of the first Bourbon and his son, Louis XIII. The rebellious Licogenes is most certainly modeled on the Guises, while the Lydian couple is unmistakably Concini and his wife, Leonora Dori. Foreign monarchs are represented in the book, among them Philip II and Philip III of Spain as, respectively, Radirobanes and Hippophilus, and Queen Elizabeth as Hyanisbe. Pope Urban VIII makes an appearance as Ibburranes.

John Barclay (1582–1621) was Scottish by parentage and Catholic by both upbringing and conviction. Although he lived in England and Rome for a time, his primary allegiance was to France. His father, the well-known jurist William Barclay, was professor of law at the University of Pont à Mousson in Lorrain, where John was born. In 1609 the son published his father's *Tractatus de potestate papae*, a strongly worded anti-papal text that took aim at the ultramontane arguments of Cardinal Bellarmine. Though he was educated by the Jesuits and even became a novice, he shared his father's Gallicanism. In 1614 he published *Icon animorum*, dedicated to the young Louis XIII, which gave expression to his anti-papal, anti-Jesuit views, as well as his Francophilia. Like many in the Republic of Letters in the early seventeenth century, he saw a restored France under the Bourbons as embodying the hopes for European peace and a cultural

---

[97] *Argenis*, 131. [98] *Argenis*, 130, 131. [99] *Argenis*, 131.

rebirth, especially if the claims of imperial Spain and the ultramontane Church could be resisted.

In a sense, *Argenis* presents the political preconditions for such a French restoration. Though a champion of French supremacy, Barclay served several princes. He found favor with James I, who especially appreciated his writings in defense of the inviolability of kings. It was in the Jacobean court that Barclay met Peiresc, whose friendship would prove invaluable in the editing and publishing of *Argenis*. Royal protection did not mean financial comfort; no less a witness than Grotius testified to Barclay's impoverishment in London.[100] And so he sought a position in Rome, despite the fact that all his books had been placed on the Index. But it was only after writing a letter of apology to Paul V, in which he essentially disavowed the anti-papal and anti-Jesuit nature of his previous writings, that he found welcome in Rome in 1615. He served in the papal court as an advisor, and grew close to Cardinal Barberini, who stood as godfather to his second son. His primary allegiance, however, was still to France. Through his friends in Paris, Peiresc and the magistrate Guillaume du Vair, he sought a royal pension in return for lobbying for French interests at the papal court. It was granted too late: after watching seven of his nine children die of illness, two in 1621 alone, he himself succumbed later that same year. *Argenis* was published several months afterward.

The writing and publishing of *Argenis* involved the collaboration of several of Barclay's French friends. Balzac apparently read portions of it in draft while he was living in Rome. The manuscript circulated in Paris, where it was read with approval at court. Grotius and Du Vair both commented on the work in progress. But it was Peiresc who served as the novel's godfather. He encouraged Barclay when the project was merely an idea, advised him on the wisdom of certain passages, and went to enormous lengths to have it published. Once it appeared, he had specially bound copies distributed at court and among a select group of important men. He also took steps to arrange a French translation. Malherbe and Faret both considered the project, but it was ultimately taken up in 1624 by a rather unsavory character of impecunious means, Pierre de Marcassus.[101] One indication of the appeal of *Argenis* beyond France is that James I commissioned Ben Jonson to translate it into English, a translation that unfortunately has not survived.

Because *Argenis* is fundamentally a political novel concerned largely with monarchical authority, many of its passages deal explicitly with this theme. At times the story itself is cast to impart a particular lesson; but as is often the case in this kind of literature, the characters sometimes merely discourse on the subject, squarely setting out differing opinions like one would find in a dialogue. Much of

---

[100] Albert Collignon, *Notes historiques, littéraires et bibliographiques sur L'Argenis de Jean Barclay* (Paris, 1902), 11.
[101] Collignon, *Notes sur L'Argenis*, 96.

the discussion is devoted to the nature of kingship, and especially the need for a strong monarchy acknowledged as supreme over all other elements of the political order. Here the depiction of Meleander serves as an example of all that kings should not be. At the start of the novel, Poliarchus draws his portrait in only mildly critical strokes: "a man of a most sweet and mild nature, but who not rightly judging of this Age, or the manners of men in it, doth so trust the faith of strangers."[102] This explains the ease with which Meleander was taken in by the show of friendship offered by the faithless Licogenes. In the same breath, Poliarchus wonders whether he "might be silent, and these things concealed"[103]—thus echoing the concern that matters of royal authority and prestige be treated with circumspection, if not complete silence; but he ultimately decides that circumstances require an airing of his criticisms. Later there arises the question of whether Meleander should take a public oath of reconciliation with Licogenes. "Shall he then descend to make a league with his subject? And this in public?" In fact, the whole discussion evokes two separate questions: not only whether a monarch ought ever to treat with a subject, to thus "descend," but also whether "to call the people to witness it," again raising the issue of public disclosure.[104] This second concern surfaces later, when a wandering stranger from Africa appears at the Sicilian court claiming knowledge of the heavens. The narrator interjects: "As yet it was not made a capital crime to enquire by the observation of the Stars concerning the fate of Princes themselves."[105] Here again, the concern represents another variation on the theme of the danger of penetrating into the royal preserve—the *arcana imperii*.

The king must be able to act alone and without consulting his people: so argues Barclay in a passage that amounts to a clear defense of absolute monarchy. In Book Four, an invasion threatens the queen of the Gauls, Hyanisbe, but she is unable to raise an army without the people's consent. Poliarchus, "being bred in a free Monarchy," is dumbstruck: is this, he asks, the time to call on "the States of the whole Nation"? "Shall then, forsooth, the sinews of the Empire that is the treasury be in the power of the people?" This hardly accords with the "title of an absolute monarchy."[106] Poliarchus presses the case by pointing to the need for secrecy in the conduct of royal affairs. Often, he asserts, "[i]t is necessary that neither he [the enemy], nor any of thy Neighbors, know at all of thy purpose... but if (as it ought to be) thou keepest the design secret to thyself, what reason wilt thou give to the people for thy demand of a tribute?"[107]

Scattered throughout the novel are arguments in favor of a strong and decisive monarch, willing and able to act on his or her own. When Licogenes, joined by several cities, revolts for a second time, the action is blamed on the king's reputation for weakness: "Neither were they slow in rebelling against this excellent King,

---

[102] *Argenis*, 6.   [103] *Argenis*, 6.   [104] *Argenis*, 76.   [105] *Argenis*, 141.
[106] *Argenis*, 354.   [107] *Argenis*, 360.

330 DIGNIFIED RETREAT

who had grown up by his mild gentleness."[108] Ultimately Meleander seeks out an old courtier, Cleobulus, for advice on how to secure peace. Cleobulus affirms, "Thy mildness...the malevolence of the destinies hath abused to the misfortune of thee and the Country." But then he turns to discussing the aristocracy, "the great Ones," whose lack of respect for royal authority clearly strikes at the heart of the problem.[109] First, he proposes, the aristocracy must be disarmed. Their weapons, after all, are really the king's to begin with.[110] The number of "Forts, Castles, and Garrisons" must also be limited.[111] In addition, they must be deprived of certain offices and positions. Governorships should not be granted for life; nor should they be permitted in "thy most secret counsels."[112] Finally, the king should act decisively and severely to end all quarreling and faction.[113] Meleander responds by expressing a concern for the limits of royal severity. He has already executed his enemies, he declares—should he go further and strike merely on the pretext of suspicion? "But shall I put out those clear lights, or only darken them? What? All of them? Yet that were inhumane and perhaps more than the power of a King can compass.... Shall I live like a wild beast alone, or rather fill my Court with men of no note or birth?"[114]

In answering the king, Cleobulus addresses the problem in a way that mirrors the views of those contemporaries, most notably Richelieu, concerned with both imposing order and reforming aristocratic behavior. Severity was not in itself sufficient; the very language of political action had to be transformed. The act of challenging the crown should be known by "the dishonor of the true name of it, by styling it Rebellion, Conspiracy, and Perfidiousness: not as it used to be termed, Greatness of Spirit, Wisdom, Consortship, and care of the Common good."[115] The point was not an idle one in an age that often celebrated the heroic rebel as the paragon of aristocratic virtue. Nor were readers likely to miss the reference to the routine practice, clearly bemoaned by Barclay—and consistently opposed by Richelieu—of allowing aristocratic rebels to escape with their pride and status intact. They should "be at least made to stoop to the humility of begging, and with all submissiveness, thy Pardon." But Cleobulus acknowledges that there should be limits to royal severity as well. Like most commentators, he strove to strike a balance between an appreciation for the aristocracy's essential role in the constitution of the monarchy and an insistence that it change its headstrong ways. The words Barclay puts in Cleobulus's mouth summarize well the position: "But it is a cruel thing to dim the light of these Stars," he proclaims, referring to aristocrats. "[T]hey must neither be extinguished, nor yet governed without humanity. Let them shine (O King) so that they remember to what Sun they owe their light, and do not eclipse thy Orb."[116]

---

[108] *Argenis*, 139.   [109] *Argenis*, 191.   [110] *Argenis*, 192.   [111] *Argenis*, 205.
[112] *Argenis*, 208, 193.   [113] *Argenis*, 196.   [114] *Argenis*, 195.   [115] *Argenis*, 196.
[116] *Argenis*, 196.

Like most commentators, even those who bitterly complained about the comportment of the aristocracy, Barclay was fundamentally traditional in his view of society. But this view was compounded by an emphatically negative assessment of the lower classes, which, though common among contemporary commentators, exceeded the typically condescending though milder views of earlier generations (see Chapter 3). Criticism of the people's foibles and follies appears as a recurring leitmotif throughout *Argenis*. If a rebellious aristocracy combined with a weak king is primarily to blame for the civil wars, the people are not far behind. Certainly it is they who are responsible for much of the excess that characterizes the conflict: "The multitude was enraged, and had filled the palace with a tumultuous assembly, ready to follow as their Leader any of the most headstrong of the company."[117] In a discussion over the comparative merits of aristocracy and democracy, the latter is condemned because "the levity of the people do bestow the offices of State upon ignorant and worthless men,... with factious envy and passion, the vulgar sort are furiously transported."[118] Barclay employs the common disparaging metaphor for the people—noted at length in Chapter 3—when, discussing the merits of a standing army, he notes that it is "more fit to be opposed to that many-headed monster."[119] And he later justifies increased taxation as a device to prevent the people from wallowing in the "slothfulness" that is their natural state, as a goad to spur them to labor, if not for themselves, at least for the good of the king and kingdom.[120]

Some of the political counsel contained in the novel derived, not purely from Barclay's fixed principles, but from the advice he received from his friends, especially Peiresc, who was particularly sensitive to how the book would be read in Paris in the light of contemporary events. He convinced Barclay, for example, to modify his view of how the crown should deal with religious heresy. An early draft had the Calvinists repressed severely, a policy that was certainly appealing given the renewed threat of religious rebellion by the French Protestants in 1620–1, just as *Argenis* was in its final stages. But Peiresc advised his friend to temper his counsel by "adding another character who speaks of this matter in a different sense than someone who only wants to wage war."[121] And indeed, in the final version, Ibburranes—who was meant to be, recall, Pope Urban VIII—counters Archombrotus's insistence that the heretics be exterminated with the view that prudence and patience ought to guide their actions. As long as they do not threaten him with war, he argues, the king should attempt to win their allegiance and secure their religious conformity with favors, honors, and other various "seductions."[122]

---

[117] *Argenis*, 47.
[118] *Argenis*, 61. Kings cannot even allow their people to support them with voluntary offerings, for "they dislike the right ways of government, and are pleased to be abused with false virtues, or specious vices; that in fine, they may divert all their Princes' thoughts from the common good." *Argenis*, 358.
[119] *Argenis*, 286. [120] *Argenis*, 358.
[121] Letter of July 1621, quoted in Collignon, *Notes sur L'Argenis*, 68. [122] *Argenis*, 94–5.

We should appeal to their interests, rather than provoke their fears. With some exceptions, this is the policy pursued by the crown vis-à-vis the Huguenots; and it was certainly the one preferred by Richelieu, despite his role in the forced submission of La Rochelle.

Barclay's choice of the religious wars as the novel's theme was in itself significant. He was of the generation born in the last years of the wars: old enough to remember them, too young to have been direct participants, this was a generation that represented the last living link to this traumatic era in French history. The memory of the wars permeated contemporary religious and political culture; but as with any contentious period, the memory itself was subject to varied, often contrasting, reconstructions. Some wanted to sink them into the black hole of *oubliance*.[123] Barclay would have none of this, as he makes clear in *Argenis*: when Meleander concludes a truce with Licogenes and proposes "[t]hat not only all dislikes must be laid away, but also all memory of them," he snidely comments on this "feigning," which in any case amounts to a hollow and short-lived peace.[124] Whatever the contrasting views of the Wars of Religion, virtually every commentator in the seventeenth century agreed that their recurrence must be avoided at all cost. Thus, when the specter of civil war threatened, as it often did in the early decades of the century, the memory of the Wars of Religion was readily evoked as a cautionary lesson.[125]

Barclay's somewhat nuanced treatment of Henri III, as well as his depiction of other major actors on the sixteenth-century stage, permits him largely to relieve France of responsibility for the wars themselves. It is true that Licogenes, the main rebel, is Sicilian (which is to say, French); but, except for the aid of the people—whose fickleness and proclivity toward violence are pathological constants—he acts alone; there is no consortium of aristocrats, certainly no factions or parties of native warring aristocrats, in view. And because the wars have been drained of their religious content, the generalized passion that fueled the conflict is absent as well. The other major villain of the novel, Radirobanes, is foreign; the king of Sardinia, he is listed in the key as representing Philip II of Spain. It is arguable, in fact, that Radirobanes was meant to arouse readers' animosity even more than Licogenes, for the former's conspiring and outright warfare against Meleander persists longer than the latter's; and his deeds are more devious and heinous as well. Only he makes a direct attempt on the king's life; and at one point he nearly rapes Argenis.[126] He insinuates himself into the sanctum of Argenis's household by corrupting Selenissa, her noble companion, and turning her into his spy. Selenissa herself proves to be another villain of the piece: "she turned herself to

---

[123] On *oubliance*, see Chapter 3.   [124] *Argenis*, 58.
[125] On considering the religious wars as persisting into the seventeenth century, see the fundamental work of Mack Holt, *The French Wars of Religion, 1562–1629*, (Cambridge, 1995).
[126] *Argenis*, 263.

the malice and mischiefs which are familiar in Courts."[127] Ultimately, she dies by her own hand. The key reveals her as Catherine de Medici. The Italian-born queen thus adds to the novel's message that France's ills of the last century had a foreign provenance.

But what of Poliarchus, this young hero who hails from a province of "Gaul"? He clearly was drawn to evoke the valiant, headstrong Henri IV. The first of the Bourbons, however, was more than a decade dead at the novel's publication. Many hoped that his successor was possessed of his same qualities. Hopes were indeed high for Louis XIII, who had already deposed the Concinis and faced down his mother (not for the last time). Men of letters, in particular, harbored great expectations for the reign; some predicted that the young king would preside over a flourishing of arts and letters comparable to that under his illustrious forebear Francis I. That he would soon disappoint them could not be known in 1621. Rather, Barclay and others found it easy to idealize Louis XIII, just as they invested France with their hopes for a revived Europe at peace. Poliarchus's valiance and incorruptibility, combined with his innate understanding of reason of state, conform to the image of a young monarch poised to inaugurate a new era in his country's history. His origins in Gaul also suggest a reference to France's pre-Roman history; as in *L'Astrée*, this was likely a patriotic evocation of a mythological national past. And is not the fact that, in order to identify him, his mother had him scored as an infant with images of shafts of wheat on his neck and right leg an oblique reference to the symbols of fecundity and peace worn by the goddess Astraea?[128] Furthermore, the marriage of Poliarchus, the nephew of Hyanisbe, understood to represent Elizabeth, with Argenis symbolizing France, could only have prompted knowing readers to think of the emerging Anglo-French alliance—soon to be secured with the marriage of Louis XIII's sister to the Prince of Wales—as the linchpin of a restored Europe now secure against the imperial threat of the Habsburgs.

A political novel through and through, *Argenis* cannot be reduced to an ideological or policy statement with a fictional gloss. Its characters are as important as the positions they represent. And except for the villains of the novel, they are entirely high-minded, largely admirable figures endowed with characteristics that can only be described as heroic. The mode of fiction allowed Barclay to create a panegyric vision of politics that offered statecraft as the summit of human activity. *Argenis* thus revived the spirit of an earlier humanism that vaunted the virtues of the *vita activa*. That the novel was an unusual example of this position in an era when, in the aftermath of the Reformation and the Wars of Religion, the civic aspect of humanism was much less confidently espoused than before, did not diminish its effectiveness. No less a figure than Balzac, it is said, was moved to

---

[127] *Argenis*, 84.   [128] *Argenis*, 309.

enlarge his own vision beyond the individualistic ethic of Pierre Charron after reading *Argenis*.[129]

But Barclay acknowledged in the novel what he and his kindred savants often expressed about the commitment to the public life of politics: it was a mixed blessing, so potentially full of pitfalls for those interested in pursuing the virtuous life that another, entirely different course—more private, less active—might be advised. On several occasions the familiar anti-court motif is iterated: "[I]t is almost grown a sign of a brave disposition, to be discarded out of the Court, or to lie neglected in it: so do the dastardly or barbarous vices of those that are great love to disarm virtue."[130]

The most telling passage in the novel testifying to Barclay's ambivalence about political action comes toward the end, when Poliarchus encounters Aneroestus, the long-lost king of his native land. Moved by his modest circumstances and fallen state, Poliarchus proposes to restore this now-wizened man to his throne. His gesture is rebuffed; and what follows is a long discourse detailing the moral pitfalls and liabilities of the engaged life. Aneroestus in fact seems to belong to a special "Order," composed of men who have vowed to shun society and seek solitude—the only way, he submits, the virtuous can preserve themselves from the evils and dangers of the world. Those of this Order certainly keep themselves far removed from the realm of statecraft, which Aneroestus proceeds to criticize in a manner that amounts to an unmistakable critique of *raison d'état*. When confronted with adversity or misfortune, he asserts, "[t]hen to dissemble, to deceive, and to falsify their promise and word is held an excellent thing in Kings." These are simply "vices and crimes."[131] He continues by listing the various misdeeds and injustices princes commit in pursuit of their interests: the bribes and corruption, the persecution and punishment of the innocent, the neglect of the common people, and so forth. Aneroestus hastens to exclude his princely interlocutors, Poliarchus and his companion, from his condemnation of the behavior of kings: "I do not condemn your quality. It is the part of brave spirits, and such as are like yourselves, with the sacred bridle of virtue, to govern the lusts of a fortune that is excessive and striveth to run astray."[132] And he admits that his Order is only for the few, their choice of solitude and withdrawal an impractical and even dangerous model for others. "For who should then serve in a religious war against the wicked? Who should govern the Commonwealth?" And he adds: "What can there be more excellent than a valiant and prudent King? If by his example, if by his Laws he do make the Age in which he lives anything better."[133] Thus the interview with Aneroestus ends with an avowal of the dignity and value of the engaged life in general and the princely vocation in particular, but not before a strong case has been made for the essential irreconcilability of virtue and political pursuits. If on

---

[129] Jehasse, *Guez de Balzac*, 279.   [130] *Argenis*, 41.   [131] *Argenis*, 452.
[132] *Argenis*, 452.   [133] *Argenis*, 454, 455.

balance *Argenis* conveys a positive image of high statecraft, framing monarchical politics in the most heroic terms, it nevertheless also acknowledges this other position. And in this sense, the novel reproduces the ambivalence expressed by many men of letters (as we have just seen with Gabriel Naudé) as they contemplated the choice between public and private realms, between engagement and *otium*. That the novel concludes shortly after this discussion suggests that Barclay wanted to leave the reader with the sense that his edifying political tale does not tell the whole story.

* * *

The memory of the religious wars hangs over all four of these works, explicitly in the case of those of d'Urfé and Barclay, with accounts of civil strife or references to warfare written into the texts; somewhat obliquely in the case of those of Balzac and Naudé, insofar as reason of state implied both elevating and obscuring monarchical statecraft as a means of avoiding a repeat of the wars. But beyond echoes of the conflict, these works also exhibit a sense of ambivalence or alienation with regard to the realm of politics and statecraft. And this, too, suggests the aftereffects of the religious wars and the continued threat of civil strife. I use the word "sense" advisedly, because, as I hope is clear, much of what I have been discussing has to do with postures of retreat rather than actual (or definitive) stances of withdrawal from or rejection of public or political matters. We might think of this posturing as realizing the impossible task of being in two places at the same time—at once ensconced in Montaigne's "back of the shop," while ready and able to engage with the world beyond. The works we have looked at in this chapter suggest how this was often made possible between the covers of a book.

Conclusion

IN THE MIDDLE of his history of the French Academy, first published in 1653, Paul Pellisson breaks off from his series of capsule biographies of the first generation of academicians for a personal account. Discussing Jean Sirmond, he declares that the works of this writer were "among the first that gave me a taste for our language." A short autobiographical vignette follows: "I was fresh out of *collège*. I was given I don't know how many novels and other new works which, because I was so young and childish, I couldn't help mocking, always returning to my Cicero and my Terence, which I found much more reasonable." Then several books virtually fell into his lap, including an edition of Balzac's *Lettres*, Sirmond's *Coup d'Etat*, the French translations of Cicero's orations, and the *mémoires* of Marguerite de Valois. The last he read twice during a long night of enthralled wakefulness. "From that time," he continues, "I not only ceased to hold the French language in contempt, but came to love it more passionately, to study it with care, and to believe, as I do to this day, that with inventiveness, time, and work, we may be able to render it capable of anything."[1]

Pellisson's confession suggests one of the main themes of this book—how a generation of *gens de lettres* rode the crest of a movement for the reform and refurbishment of French into the heart of aristocratic culture and the centers of power. His story relates a conversion experience—including even a nocturnal vigil that produced his awakening. From a youthful, dogmatic partisan of the ancients, who looked with undisguised condescension on modern literary works, he was suddenly transformed into a passionate advocate for the vernacular, confident in its potential and committed to its future development. It was a conversion that set him on the path to becoming a professional man of letters, confidant to the great, and ultimately a member of the French Academy.

But this book has had another theme: the importance of Gallicanism for many of these writers, especially the savants associated with the Dupuy cabinet. While I have looked at the writings and activities of these *érudits*, it cannot have escaped notice that they have played a secondary role in these chapters. And it seems to me that this imbalance suggests something of a corrective to the impression conveyed in most recent intellectual histories of the period. Owing to the remarkable work of A. D. Momigliano and his followers, especially Anthony Grafton, we are

---

[1] Paul Pellisson and Pierre-Joseph Thoulier d'Olivet, *Histoire de l'Académie françoise, par Pellisson et d'Olivet*, 3rd ed., revised and enlarged, 2 vols. (Paris, 1743), I: 281–2.

now quite aware of the vitality of humanism in the seventeenth century, and in particular the robust and creative tradition of antiquarianism, which, far from embodying the oft-decried "mere pedantry," gave rise to important advances in natural philosophy, history, jurisprudence, and other areas of scholarship. There can be no disputing that, notwithstanding the critique of Aristotelianism and the advances of the "new science," humanistic erudition was alive and well not only among professors and savants but also in the amateur world of gentlemen scholars. It may be, however, that our view of this scholarly culture exaggerates its importance—at least for contemporaries. In terms of numbers and impact at the time, the new community of *gens de lettres* eclipsed the savants of the Dupuy cabinet in the context of France's intellectual and cultural life. Their integration into Parisian elite circles, their domination of the ranks of the Académie française, their role in fashioning a robust vernacular and in fostering a truly French literature, as well as the rich social world they created, all lead to the conclusion that this *mondain* culture constituted the order of the day. Peter Miller's splendid studies of Nicolas-Claude Fabri de Peiresc illuminate an expansive and richly varied intellectual world of which this Provençal humanist antiquarian was the center; but it was, as the title of one of his books, *Peiresc's Europe*, aptly denotes, a cosmopolitan, *European* world. A book on "Balzac's France" or "The France of Chapelain" would arguably carry less intellectual weight than Miller's study (that is a separate consideration), but it would document that the world of these men of letters overshadowed the savant corners of France's intellectual life. In history, the opinion of contemporaries and the judgment of posterity are often at odds. Jean Chapelain is probably not worthy of canonical status, but his stature in his day was at least as high as those, such as René Descartes and Hugo Grotius, who certainly are.[2]

Another perspective, however, suggests a somewhat different assessment. I have tried to discover expressions of critique of the prevailing political order and its policies from these writers and savants. These have not been readily apparent, for such views were for the most part muted, expressed obliquely, ambiguously, or in ways that ensured that only those "in the know"—the *esprits forts*—would discern their meaning. The discretionary and guarded nature of contemporary discourse has been another theme of this book. I have argued that this disposition was rooted in part in a particular understanding of the Wars of Religion and the ever-present threat from a wayward and capricious populace, in part in *gens de lettres'* close association with the social and political elite. But when it was expressed, the usual provenance of this critique is noteworthy: the Dupuy cabinet. While most writings of this nature circulated in manuscript only—itself an act of both

---

[2] I have addressed this question in Robert A. Schneider, "Friends of Friends: Intellectual and Literary Sociability in the Age of Richelieu," in Lewis C. Seifert and Rebecca M. Wilkin, *Men and Women Making Friends in Early Modern France* (Burlington, VT, 2015), 135–60.

caution and discretion—the attacks were sometimes vehement and unambiguous, especially when it came to Gallicanism and Richelieu's authoritarian style of rule. It is perhaps surprising that these most traditional of savants, humanist guardians of a culture of erudition, should prove willing to put forth critical views, while the innovators of the day, the creators of a new literary field, were characterized mostly by quiescence and conformity. But this is not, I would suggest, as paradoxical as it might seem, for it was precisely because these savants remained faithful to the discursive protocols of erudition, rather than the more accessible ways of *mondain* literature, that they were able to stray, though tentatively, into the dangerous realm of criticism.

To restrict our assessment of *mondain* writers to the terms of conformism is, however, to settle for a rather impoverished view of the culture they created. It may be satisfying or even imperative for some to track our understanding of historical actors along divergent judgmental lines—"good" if critical or opposed to the status quo, "bad" if aligned with the powers-that-be or simply indifferent to social or political matters. But this has not been the approach here. It is true, of course, that, especially in the case of *mondain* writers, their identification with and reliance upon their social betters of the privileged elite goes a long way toward explaining their conformism and, in some respects, quiescence. For the most part, they strove to appeal to the traditional nobility, even to the point of fashioning the code of *honnêteté* in service to an expanded elite's sense of class consciousness.

But I do not think that these writers' position and attitudes can be ascribed solely to craven interests. I have tried to understand the pressures and concerns that worked upon them, especially those stemming from the memory of the Wars of Religion and the collective desire to avoid the conditions that perpetuated this terrible chapter in French history. Perhaps this has led me to give them the benefit of the doubt and thus to underestimate the element of opportunism in their willing submission to both domestication by an appreciative aristocracy and the overtures of a determined cardinal. If so, my defense—beyond an excess of sympathy for the historical actors I have long studied—is that their activities, regardless of their precise motivations, did more than merely offer cover for ruling elites. As I hope I have shown, they were engaged in a movement for linguistic reform and literary innovation that opened up the cultural vistas for an expanding elite.

More generally, there is something fundamentally reductive about the very concept of conformism, which suggests a kind of slavish falling into line associated with courtiers, party apparatchiks, high school cliques, street gangs, and boardroom yes-men. To be sure, the Ancien Régime is known for its cloying panegyric literature, courtly sycophancy, and tyranny of fashion; and we have certainly witnessed examples of this in the writings of Balzac, Silhon, Chapelain, Georges de Scudéry and others. However, if we think of conformity not simply as a position or stance, but rather more discursively as something that must be expressed and articulated, then we might appreciate the possible nuances, variations, creativity, even ambiguity that representations of conformity often contain.

There is as well a particularly modern assumption that the "writer" and the "intellectual" are endowed with both independence and a critical disposition intrinsic to their very vocation. As we have seen, neither of these qualities defined the nature of literary and intellectual culture in the seventeenth century. Did the lack of the first constrain the latter? That is, was their conformity a necessary result of their lack of independence? This was surely a factor, but it seems a bit a priori to assume that the process worked in only one direction. It is hardly unthinkable that *gens de lettres* had their own reasons and motivations for aligning themselves with social and ruling elites. They not only had a lot to gain; they also saw the stability of the social order, the prestige of French language and letters, and the glory of the French king and nation as positive values they were eager to adopt, and interpret, as their own. In addition, they had the opportunity to do what intellectuals and writers have long sought—influence people with power and shape the dominant culture.

The question of conformity suggests an additional observation on the literary and intellectual culture of the seventeenth century. And it can be elucidated by borrowing concepts devised by the economist Albert Hirschman in his famous book *Exit, Voice, and Loyalty* (1970). With these terms, Hirschman lays out the options in (for the most part) political or economic contexts, where the choices are to accept the status quo (loyalty), criticize it (voice), or opt out, refusing the choices offered by the system (exit). Interestingly, the historical moment we have examined suggests not only that the options of loyalty and exit were both simultaneously operative, but that voice was possible as well—and by the same historical actors. This insight returns us to where we began—to the *otium* and sense of withdrawal or retreat that characterized the moral outlook fashioned by humanists and other commentators. While enjoying the privilege of "exit" in the realm of *otium*—a space as well as a cast of mind they cultivated and cherished—they nevertheless maintained a posture of "loyalty" to the established order, often serving it with their pens. "Voice," too, was an option—not the public critical voice envisioned by Hirschman (or by Habermas, for that matter), but the muted, sometimes discreetly coded or otherwise cautiously targeted expressions of discontent, opposition, or non-conformity. Thus the Dupuys: loyal servants of the crown, while also circulating texts critical of Richelieu, pushing the bounds of permissible Gallicanism; La Mothe le Vayer: member of the Académie française and pamphleteer at Richelieu's service, publishing dialogues that embody the freethinking spirit of *le libertinage érudit*; Boisrobert: Richelieu's closest literary advisor, who was his agent to the world of letters, notorious for his sexual adventures. Here too is Vincent Voiture, as described by Chapelain to Balzac in terms that might seem to epitomize hypocrisy yet clearly only elicit the approval of these two leading *hommes de lettres*: "In writing his licentious and lascivious epistles, he was no less a good Christian," writes Chapelain admiringly. "He discovered how to live at the same time in the world and according to the Evangelists; to go dutifully to Mass in the morning for sincere devotion and then to enjoy himself [*galantier*] after dinner with an inveterate spirit of corruption."[3]

Plenty of moralists, then and now, would judge Voiture severely for duplicity, dishonesty, and worse. Certainly the Jansenists' own move to withdraw from "society" amounted to a critical commentary on the moral compromises and self-serving ethical subtleties that Voiture, like many of his contemporaries, seemed to embody. I believe, however, that such moralism limits our understanding of the cultural conditions that governed elite society in this period. Voiture operated under an aristocratic code that, as a man of letters deeply entrenched in Parisian elite circles—and despite his modest origins—he helped fashion with his literary talents. Of course, the freedom enjoyed by aristocrats had long entailed the privilege to govern themselves with a license that would prove costly, if not unthinkable, to the lesser-born. Arguably, however, this disposition for license (and licentiousness) was changing, especially in the *mondain* milieu of Paris, where it was to be channeled within the bounds of discretion and *bienséance*. In the minds of some, these bounds could be stretched to contain the kind of duplicity embodied by Voiture; for others, such elasticity made a mockery of the assumption that virtue was still at the heart of *honnêteté*—that it was not only about the "art of pleasing." But this only reminds us of the contradiction at the heart of *honnêteté*, "a form of behaviour that combines prudence with politeness, the morally correct with the socially pleasing," notes Richard Scholar. "The tension between those two principles," he adds, "often comes to the surface...accompanied by the suspicion that *honnêteté* is no more than a self-interested aesthetics."[4]

The ambiguous nature of *honnêteté* suggests a connection to the political realm that challenges the assumption that the seventeenth century lacked an overarching ethics bridging the personal and the public.[5] Recall that at the start of this book I referred to this separation as an aspect of the prevailing view of the period, especially in the wake of the sixteenth-century religious wars and the rise of "absolutism." But if we think of *honnêteté* as a complex worldly ethics driven by short-term considerations of succeeding by pleasing, it begins to look very much like reason of state. There, too, prudence, self-interest, situational ethics, adaptability, and dissimulation are paramount. Like the *honnête homme*, the statesman confronts a sometimes dangerous or at least morally compromised world and a range of situations; he has no choice but to act in response to unpredictable

---

[3] Pellisson and d'Olivet, *Histoire de l'Académie*, I: 274 n. 4.
[4] Richard Scholar, "*Moraliste* Writing in the Seventeenth Century," in William Burgwinkle, Nicholas Hammond, and Emma Wilson, eds., *The Cambridge History of French Literature* (Cambridge, 2011), 318.
[5] Nannerl O. Keohane, *Philosophy and the State in Early Modern France: The Renaissance to the Enlightenment* (Princeton, 1980).

challenges, not according to a set of fixed principles but in a way that defends and promotes the interests of his king and state while preserving the impression that he is guided by virtuous and timeless values. Intellectually, too, reason of state resonates with a central trope of *honnêteté*: the abhorrence of pedantry. Wisdom in this sort of statecraft could not be learned from books, certainly not from those that attempt to promote a stable, timeless understanding of politics as a set of "maxims." Finally, writings on both reason of state and *honnêteté* ultimately rely on qualities and virtues of the individual, whether the statesman or prince, courtier or ordinary nobleman. As we have seen, there is an element of mystery in reason of state—the notion that statecraft of this sort requires a rare or even esoteric intelligence far beyond the grasp of most. While *honnêteté* is not a discourse of arcana, there is an element of the *"je ne sais quoi"*—that nescioquiddity that says either you have it or you don't.[6]

The confluence of *honnêteté* and reason of state has been, then, a muted theme running throughout this book. They are codes that mirror each other in several ways. The first two are variations on the same theme: the ineffable quality of *sprezzatura* reflects the mystery that surrounds the "absolute" prince, and the reticence and discretion of the *honnête homme* suggests the refusal to disclose or consult implicit in this concept of statecraft. Another, however, takes us into the discursive aspect of contemporary culture, that is, the particular language that was conducive to both the literary and the political realm. As has been observed, "reason of state" lacked "final ends"; it was never systematic in its presentation; and it could, consequently, be deployed to justify or support any given number of policies, decisions, or actions. Likewise, the "literature" that emerged from the dense society of *gens de lettres* we have been examining was characterized by an emphasis on wit, brevity, an aversion for pedantry, and a lightness of touch. Perhaps most crucially here, its eclecticism made it suitable for the vicissitudes of aristocratic sociability that, unlike the corporate ecclesial, judicial, and scholastic worlds, was free of prescriptions and purposes, save for the obligation to stay within the bounds of *bienséance*.

But, as I have insisted throughout these chapters, this did not mean a lack of commitment to values, interests, or collective identities on the part of writers and intellectuals in the Age of Richelieu, who are all too readily depicted as merely servants, sycophants, or otherwise in thrall to aristocratic and monarchical power. An investment in the status and vitality of the French language, an interest in the historical roots of the French nation, a keen concern for its fortunes amidst the European conflict of the day, an identification with the Gallican tradition, a desire to preserve the religious settlement that ended the Wars of Religion: these

---

[6] Richard Scholar, *The Je-Ne-Sais-Quoi in Early Modern Europe: Encounters with a Certain Something* (Oxford, 2005).

are some of the causes that stirred their passions and galvanized their creative energies. It may have been that their allegiances were mixed or conditional: in Neo-Stoicism, which qualified every commitment, their patriotic identification with France was modified by a belief that they were really citizens of the world; as disciples of Montaigne and Charron, they certainly valued the virtue of withholding in reserve an essential aspect of the self from the vicissitudes of public affairs; as *esprits forts*, they understood the need for duplicity in mouthing pieties in public that they mocked in private; as *honnêtes hommes*, they were willing to trim their sails to the prevailing winds of convention; influenced by skepticism, they tempered their religious faith and fidelity to the Church with doubt; and as courtiers, clients, and servants, it is true, they often demonstrated a degree of accommodation that makes one suspect that their writings were nothing more than well-turned translations of their masters' tastes, interests, or wishes. Do these qualifications warrant the conclusion that they were merely cynics, committed to nothing more than their own personal interests, that their professed love of king and country was unfounded, or that their activities in promoting French culture and literature were merely "service"? This book has argued to the contrary. And in a sense, these sorts of conclusions are plausible only if some impossibly idealistic notion of commitment—a commitment exemplified by the passion of saints or martyrs, the sacrificial patriotism of martial heroes, or the love of parents for their children—is held up as a standard by which everything less unambiguous or conditional is found lacking. It may have been that their sense of "virtue" was less infused with public-mindedness than that of their forebears of the sixteenth century, some of whom, at least, professed a republican identification with the polis that was total and all-consuming. And they would be the first to admit to disavowing the kind of passionate religious engagements that led to the endless confessional strife of generations past. Tempered by skepticism, conditioned by the lessons of recent history, their commitments were stretched across the divide of the personal and the public, the private and the political. In the light of modern history, is this so unusual?

Still, an argument can be made that this generation of writers and intellectuals harbored rather diminished intellectual ambitions, especially when compared to the aspirations, visions, and speculative thinking of the sixteenth century. The Renaissance yearning for encyclopedic knowledge, occult wisdom, and mystical spirituality had few emulators in the seventeenth century. And in this sense, it is hard to deny the legitimacy of Frances Yates's judgment (cited in Chapter 4) that the program of the Académie française, which was largely restricted to concerns with the French language, represented a step down from the interests and activities of the sixteenth-century palace academies in France or those of northern Italy, which cultivated the whole gamut of arts, letters, and sciences. If *gens de lettres* of the late sixteenth and early seventeenth century did indeed engage in a collective act of lowering their expectations, then the reason is to be found, not in their lack of ambition or imagination, nor, it seems to me, in the limitations imposed upon them by their aristocratic and royal masters, but rather in the lessons they were forced to learn about the cost of excessive expectations of an earlier era. In the next four centuries, it is a lesson that would be forgotten and relearned again and again.

Selected Bibliography of Primary Sources

Aristotle, *Rhetoric and Poetics*, trans. W. Rhys Roberts (New York, 1954).
Arnauld d'Andilly, Antoine, *Mémoires de l'abbé Arnauld: Contenant quelques anecdotes de la cour de France depuis 1634 jusqu'à 1675*, in Joseph François Michaud and Jean Joseph François Poujoulat, eds., *Nouvelle collection des mémoires pour servir a l'histoire de France depuis le XIIIe siècle jusqu'à la fin du XVIIIe siècle*, 2nd series, vol. IX: *Mémoires du cardinal de Richelieu, Arnauld d'Andilly, l'abbé Arnauld, la duchesse de Nemours, Gaston, duc d'Orléans* (Paris, 1838), 481–556.
Aubignac, François Hédelin, abbé d', *La pratique du théâtre* (Amsterdam, 1715), reproduced in Hans-Jörg Neuschäfer, *"La pratique du théâtre" und andere Schriften zur "Doctrine classique"* (Munich, 1971).
Bacon, Francis, *The Oxford Francis Bacon*, ed. Graham Rees, vol. XIII: *The Instauratio magna: Last Writings* (Oxford, 2000).
Balzac, Jean-Louis Guez de, *Oeuvres diverses (1644)*, ed. Roger Zuber (Paris, 1995).
Balzac, *Les premières lettres de Guez de Balzac, 1618–1627*, ed. H. Bibas and K.-T. Butler, 2 vols. (Paris, 1933-4).
Balzac, *Socrate chrestien* (1662), ed. Jean Jehasse (Paris, 2008).
Barclay, John, *John Barclay, His Argenis, Translated out of Latine into English*, trans. Sir Robert Le Grys (London, 1628).
Bardin, Pierre, *Le lycée du Sr. Bardin, ou, En plusieurs promenades il est traité des connoissances des actions et des plaisirs d'un honneste homme* (Paris, 1632).
Barthélemy, Ed. de, and René Kerviler, eds., *Un tournoi de trois pucelles en l'honneur de Jeanne d'Arc: Lettres inédites de Conrart, de Mlle de Scudéry and de Mlle du Moulin* (Paris, 1878).
Bodin, Jean, *Colloquium of the Seven about Secrets of the Sublime* (1588), trans. and ed. Marion Leathers Kuntz (Princeton, 1975).
Bodin, *The Six Bookes of a Commonweale* (1606), ed. Kenneth Douglas McRae (Cambridge, MA, 1962).
Botero, Giovanni, *The Reason of State* (1589), trans. P. J. and D. P. Waley (New Haven, 1956).
Bouchard, Jean-Jacques, *Les confessions de Jean-Jacques Bouchard, parisien, suivies de son voyage de Paris à Rome en 1630* (Paris, 1881).
Bouchard, *Les confessions d'un perverti* (Paris, 1960).
Bouchard, *Journal*, ed. Emanuele Kanceff, 2 vols., I: *Les confessions; Voyage de Paris à Rome; Le carnaval à Rome*, and II: *Voyage dans le royaume de Naples; Voyage dans la compagne de Rome* (Torino, 1976, 1977).
Bouchard, *"Mémoires révélateurs": Les confessions de J.-J. Bouchard* (Paris, 1930).
Bourzeys, Amable de, *Le discours sur le dessein de l'Academie et sur le différent génie des langues* (1635), in James Dryhurst, "Les premières activités de l'Académie française: Le Discours sur le dessein de l'Academie et sur le différent génie des langues, de Bourzeys," *Zeitschrift für französische Sprache und Literatur*, 81/3 (1971), 225–42.
Campion, Henri de, *Mémoires de Henri de Campion (1613–1663), suivis de trois entretiens sur divers sujets d'histoire, de politique et de morale*, ed. Marc Fumaroli (Paris, 1967).

Camus, Jean-Pierre, *Conférence académique sur le différent des belles-lettres de Narcisse et de Phyllarque, par le sieur de Musac* (Paris, 1630).
Chapelain, Jean, *De la lecture des vieux romans*, ed. Jean-Pierre Cavaillé (Paris, 1999).
Chapelain, *De la lecture des vieux romans*, ed. Alphonse Feillet (Paris, 1870).
Chapelain, *Lettres de Jean Chapelain, de l'Académie française*, ed. Philippe Tamizey de Larroque, 2 vols. (Paris, 1880–2).
Chapelain, *Opuscules critiques*, ed. Alfred C. Hunter (Paris 1936).
Chapelain, *La pucelle, ou, La France délivrée*, ed. Emile de Molènes, 2 vols. (Paris, 1891).
Chapelain, *Les sentimens de l'Académie françoise sur la tragi-comédie du Cid* (1638), ed. Georges Collas (1912; reprint, Geneva, 1968).
Charron, Pierre, *Of Wisdome: Three Books Written in French by Peter Charro[n], Doctr of Lawe in Paris*, trans. Samson Lennard (1608; London, 1630).
Charron, *De la sagesse* (1604), ed. Barbara de Negroni (Paris, 1986).
Charron, *Les trois veritez contre tous athées, idolâtres, juifs, mahumetans, hérétiques et schismatiques* (Paris, 1594).
Civardi, Jean-Marc, *La querelle du Cid (1637–1638): Edition critique intégrale* (Paris, 2004).
Colletet, Guillaume, *Discours de l'éloquence et de l'imitation des anciens* (Paris, 1658).
Deimier, Pierre de, *L'académie de l'art poétique* (Paris, 1610).
Descartes, René, *Descartes: Philosophical Letters*, ed. Anthony Kenny (Oxford, 1970).
De Thou, Jacques-Auguste, *The Life of Thuanus, with Some Account of His Writings and a Translation of the Preface to His History*, trans. J. Collinson (London, 1807).
Du Bellay, Jacques, *La deffence et illustration de la langue françoyse* (1549), ed. Henri Chamard (Paris, 1904).
Du Bosc, Jacques, *L'honnête femme: The Respectable Woman in Society and the New Collection of Letters and Responses by Contemporary Women*, ed. and trans. Sharon Diane Nell and Aurora Wolfgang (Toronto, 2014).
Dupleix, Scipion, *Liberté de la langue françoise dans sa pureté* (Paris, 1651).
Dupuy, Pierre, *Apologie pour Monsieur le président de Thou, sur son Histoire* (Geneva, 1620).
Dupuy, *Mémoires et instructions pour servir à justifier l'innocence de messire François-Auguste de Thou*, in *Histoire universelle de Jacques-Auguste de Thou, depuis 1543 jusqu'en 1607*, vol. XV: *1607–1610* (London, 1734).
Dupuy, and Jacques Dupuy, *Preuves des libertez de l'Eglise gallicane* (Paris, 1639).
Dupuy, *Traitez des droits et libertez de l'Eglise gallicane* (Paris, 1639).
Du Vair, Guillaume, *De la constance et consolation es calamitez publiques*, in *Les oeuvres politiques, morales et meslées du sieur Du Vair, premier président au Parlement de Provence* (Cologny, 1614).
Du Vair, *De l'éloquence françoise* (Paris, 1594).
Du Vair, *De l'éloquence françoise et des raisons pourquoy elle est demeurée si basse* (1606), in *Les oeuvres de messire Guillaume du Vair* (Paris, 1641 ed.).
Du Vair, *Philosophie morale des stoïques* (Paris, 1585).
Faret, Nicolas, *L'honnête homme, ou, L'art de plaire à la cour* (1630), ed. Maurice Magendie (1925; reprint, Geneva, 1970).
Faret, *Projet de l'Académie, pour servir de préface à ses statuts*, ed. Jean Rousselet (Saint-Etienne, 1983).
Faret, *Recueil de lettres nouvelles* (Paris, 1627).
Faret, *Recueil de lettres nouvelles, dit "Recueil Faret,"* ed. Eric Méchoulan (Rennes, 2008).
Faret, *Des vertus nécessaires à un prince pour bien gouverner ses sujets* (Paris, 1623).
Ferrier, Jérémie, *Le catholique d'Estat, ou, Discours politique des Alliances du Roy très-Chrétien contre les calomnies des ennemis de son Estat* (1625), in Paul Hay du Chastelet, *Recueil de diverses pièces pour servir à l'histoire* ([Paris], 1640), 90–154.

Fortin de la Hoguette, Philippe, *Lettres aux frères Dupuy et à leur entourage, 1623-1662*, ed. Giuliano Ferretti, 2 vols. (Florence, 1997).
Fortin de la Hoguette, *Testament, ou, Conseils fidèles d'un bon père à ses enfans* (Paris, 1648).
Furetière, Antoine, *Nouvelle allégorique, ou, Histoire des derniers troubles arrivez au royaume d'éloquence* (Paris, 1658).
Furetière, *Nouvelle allégorique, ou, Histoire des derniers troubles arrivés au royaume d'éloquence*, ed. Mathilde Bombart and Nicolas Schapira (Toulouse, 2004).
Furetière, *Nouvelle allégorique, ou, Histoire des derniers troubles arrivés au royaume d'éloquence*, ed. Eva Van Ginneken (Geneva, 1967).
Furic du Run, Julien, *Reflexions politiques* (Paris, 1640).
Garasse, François, *La doctrine curieuse des beaux esprits de ce temps, ou prétendus tels, contenant plusieurs maximes pernicieuses à l'Estat, à la Religion et aux bonnes moeurs* (Paris, 1624).
Gassendi, Pierre, *Pierre Gassendi (1592-1655): Lettres latines*, ed. and trans. Sylvie Taussig, 2 vols. (Turnhout, 2004).
Godeau, Antoine, *Discours sur les oeuvres de Mr de Malherbe* (1630), in *Oeuvres de Malherbe*, ed. Ludovic Lalanne (Paris, 1862), I: 365-85.
Gournay, Marie de, *Oeuvres complètes*, ed. Jean-Claude Arnould, 2 vols. (Paris, 2002).
Guyet, François, *Le roman satirique de Gaeomemphion du Cantal*, ed. and trans. Juliette Desjardins (Geneva, 1972).
Hay du Chastelet, Paul, *Recueil de diverses pièces pour servir à l'histoire* ([Paris], 1640).
La Mothe le Vayer, François de, *Considerations sur l'éloquence françoise de ce tems* (Paris, 1638).
La Mothe le Vayer, *Dialogues faits à l'imitation des anciens* (1606), ed. André Pessel (Paris, 1988).
La Mothe le Vayer, *Mémorial de quelques conférences avec des personnes studieuses* (Paris, 1669).
Laval, Antoine de, *Desseins de professions nobles et publiques* (Paris, 1612).
Le Bret, Cardin, *Traité de la souveraineté du roy* (Paris, 1632).
Lipsius, Justus, *Deux livres de la constance de Juste Lipsius: Mis en françois par de Nuysement* (Leiden, 1584).
Lipsius, *Two Bookes of Constancie, Written in Latine by Justus Lipsius, Englished by Sir John Stradling* (1595), ed. Rudolf Kirk (New Brunswick, NJ, 1939).
Luillier, François, *Lettres inédites, écrites de Paris à Peiresc, 1630-1636*, vol. XVI of Philippe Tamizey de Larroque, ed., *Les correspondants de Peiresc* (1889; reprint, Geneva, 1971).
Machiavelli, Niccolo, *The Essential Writings of Machiavelli*, ed. and trans. Peter Constantine (New York, 2007).
Mairet, Jean, *La Sophonisbe*, ed. Charles Dédéyan (Paris, 1945).
Mairet, *Sophonisbe*, in Lacy Lockert, ed. and trans., *The Chief Rivals of Corneille and Racine* (Nashville, TN, 1956), 1-54.
Marmet, Lord of Valcroissant, *Entertainments of the Cours; or, Academical Conversations, Held upon the Cours at Paris, by a Cabal of the Principal Wits of That Court* (London, 1658).
Marolles, Michel de, *Mémoires de Michel de Marolles, abbé de Villeloin*, 3 vols. (Amsterdam, 1755).
Ménage, Gilles, *Le Parnasse alarme; ou, La requête des dictionnaires* (Paris, 1649).
Mersenne, Marin, *Lettres inédites écrites de Paris à Peiresc, 1633-1637*, vol. XIX of Philippe Tamizey de Larroque, ed., *Les correspondants de Peiresc* (1892; reprint, Geneva, 1971).
Monluc, Adrien de, *Oeuvres*, ed. Michael Kramer (Paris, 2007).
Montaigne, Michel de, *The Complete Essays of Montaigne*, trans. Donald Frame (Stanford, 1958).
Naudé, Gabriel, *La bibliographie politique du sieur Naudé* (Paris, 1642).

348 SELECTED BIBLIOGRAPHY OF PRIMARY SOURCES

Naudé, *Considérations politiques sur les coups d'état* (1639), ed. Louis Marin (Paris, 1989).
Naudé, *Instruction à la France sur la verité de l'histoire des Frères de la Roze-Croix* (Paris, 1623).
Naudé, *Lettres de Gabriel Naudé à Jacques Dupuy (1632–1652)*, ed. Phillip Wolfe (Edmonton, AB, 1982).
Naudé, *Lettres inédites écrites d'Italie à Peiresc, 1632–1636*, vol. XIII of Philippe Tamizey de Larroque, ed., *Les correspondants de Peiresc* (1887; reprint, Geneva, 1971).
Ogier, François, *Jugement et censure du livre de la Doctrine curieuse, de François Garasse* (Paris, 1623).
Pasquier, Etienne, *Choix de lettres sur la littérature, la langue et la traduction*, ed. D. Thickett (Geneva, 1956).
Peiresc, Nicolas-Claude Fabri de, *Lettres à Naudé*, ed. Phillip J. Wolfe (Paris, 1983).
Pellisson, Paul, and Pierre-Joseph Thoulier d'Olivet, *Histoire de l'Académie françoise, par Pellisson et d'Olivet*, 3rd ed., revised and enlarged, 2 vols. (Paris, 1743).
Priézac, Daniel de, *Discours politiques* (Paris, 1652).
Racan, Honorat de Bueil, seigneur de, *Vie de monsieur de Malherbe*, ed. Marie-Françoise Quignard (Paris, 1991).
Richelieu, Armand Jean du Plessis de, *The Political Testament of Cardinal Richelieu*, trans. Henry Bertram Hill (Madison, WI, 1961).
Rohan, Henri, duc de, *De l'interest des princes et Estats de la Chrestienté* (Paris, 1639).
Rubens, Peter Paul, *The Letters of Peter Paul Rubens*, trans. and ed. Ruth Saunders Magurn (1955; Evanston, IL, 1991).
Sainct-Clément, René de, *Lettre du sieur de St-Clément à monsieur d'Hozier... sur les prédications faictes à Grenoble par le sieur de Gaffarel* ([Paris], [1642]).
Saint-Evremond and comte d'Etelan, *La comédie des Académistes et Saint-Evremond: Les académiciens*, ed. Paolo Carile (Milan, 1976).
Saumaise, Claude, *Le dernier voyage à Paris et en Bourgogne, 1640–1643, du reformé Claude Saumaise*, ed. Pierre Leroy (Amsterdam, 1983).
Scudéry, Georges de, *Le cabinet de Monsieur de Scudéry* (1646), ed. Christian Biet and Dominique Moncond'huy (Paris, 1991).
Scudéry, *Le cabinet de Mr de Scudéry, gouverneur de Nostre Dame de la Garde* (Paris, 1646).
Silhon, Jean de, *Le ministre d'Estat, avec la véritable usage de la politique moderne* (Paris, 1641 ed.).
Sorel, Charles, *La bibliothèque française* (Paris, 1667).
Sorel, *La bibliothèque française*, édition critique, ed. Filippo d'Angelo, Mathilde Bombart, Laurence Giavarini, Claudine Nédelec, Dinah Ribard, Michèle Roselllini, and Alain Viala (Paris, 2015).
Sorel, *Histoire comique de Francion*, in Antoine Adam, ed., *Romanciers du XVIIe siècle* (Paris, 1958).
Sorel, *Rôle des présentations faictes au Grand Jour de l'éloquence françoise* ([Paris], 1634).
Tallemant des Reaux, Gédéon, *Historiettes*, ed. Antoine Adam, 2 vols. (Paris, 1960).
Urfé, Honoré d', *Astrea, Part One*, trans. Steven Rendall (Binghamton, NY, 1995).
Urfé, *L'Astrée: Nouvelle édition*, ed. Hugues Vaganay, 5 vols. (Lyons, 1925–8).
Vaugelas, Claude Favre de, *La préface des "Remarques sur la langue françoise,"* ed. Zygmunt Marzys (Neuchâtel, 1984).
Voiture, Vincent, *Lettres (1625–1648)*, ed. Sophie Rollin (Paris, 2013).
Urfé, *Oeuvres de Voiture: Lettres et poésies*, ed. Jean-Henri-Abdolonyme Ubicini, 2 vols. (1855; reprint, Geneva, 1967).

Index

Note: Tables and figures are indicated by an italic '*t*' and '*f*', respectively, following the page number.

For the benefit of digital users, indexed terms that span two pages (e.g., 52–53) may, on occasion, appear on only one of those pages.

Ablancourt, Nicolas Perrot d' 30*t*, 130–1
   as translator of ancient authors 78–80
Absolutism 4–5, 7–8, 16, 81–2, 141–2, 173, 294, 297–8, 341–2
   critique of the term 5–7
   and French Academy 28–9, 174
   and French language reform 43
   and the public sphere 161
Académie Française. *See* French Academy
Amyot, Jacques 77–8, 180
Ancient Rome 3–4, 11–12, 17, 24–5, 40, 60–1, 114, 139–40, 157, 175–6, 196, 224–6, 321–5
   as source of *honnêteté* discourse 114
   as source of political and moral ideals 134, 241–5
   literary traditions of 278–9
   oratorical model 69
Ancien Régime 4–5, 18–19, 29–37, 213, 339–40
Angennes, Julie d' 169, 179–80, 216–19, 222–3, 235, 237–8, 318–19
   role in the Rambouillet salon 215, 220–2, 224–5, 246
   relationship with marquis de Montausier 227–31
Ariosto, Ludovico 221–3
Aristotle 41–2, 68–9, 73–4, 127, 156–7, 303, 314
   and *otium* 2
   honnêteté and the rhetoric of 113–14
Arnauld family 74, 92, 220–1, 224–5
   and Jansenism 2, 207–8, 217
   at the Rambouillet salon 225, 229
   Arnauld d'Andilly, Robert 30*t*, 217, 224–5
   Arnauld, Antoine 2, 220–1, 239–41
   Arnauld, Pierre Isaac de Corbeville 217, 220–1
Aubignac, François Hédelin, abbé d' 30*t*, 148–9
Auchy, Charlotte des Ursins, Vicomtesse d'Auchy 48
   her salon 13*f*, 73–4
Auerbach, Ernst 121–2

Balzac, Jean-Louis Guez de 9–10, 30*t*, 40–2, 45–6, 53–4, 57–8, 105–6, 165–88, 339–40
   and Cardinal La Valette 93–5, 97–8, 106
   and Garasse 152
   and the Rambouillet salon 241–5
   and Richelieu 165–6, 181–2
   criticism of 60–2
   on French Academy 172
   on *honnêteté* 114, 116
   on de Viau 153–4
   on women 110–11
   Lettres de Monsieur de Balzac 54–7, 66–7, 75–6, 81, 90–1, 154–5, 221
   on reason of state 300–1
   Le Prince 301–8
Barberini family 101–2, 244, 261–76
   Barberini, Francesco 261–7, 270–1, 328
Barclay, John 30*t*, 138–41, 278, 299–300, 314, 317, 325–35
   Argenis 138–9, 299–300, 317–18, 325–35
Bardin, Pierre 30*t*, 81–2, 111–12
   on women and *bienséance* 108
   on *honnêteté* 114–15, 118–21, 130
Baro, Balthazar 30*t*, 103, 320n.71
Baudoin, Jean 30*t*, 80–1, 138–9
Bautru, Guillaume 30*t*
Bellay, Joachim du 42–3, 58, 83–4.
   See also Pléiade
bienséance 70, 122, 126, 150, 220–1, 246, 341–2
   as value for literary French 41–2, 124–6, 156, 215–16, 223
   and women 108
Bignon, Jérôme 13*f*, 248–9
Blocker, Deborah 48n.23, 107
Bodin, Jean 14, 173, 312, 323–4
   on oratory 14–16, 143–5
   on social order 139–40, 142–3, 300–1
Boileau, Nicolas 46–7, 188n.91
Boisrobert, François Le Metel de 30*t*, 51, 55–8, 72–3, 76–7, 104–5, 151–2, 156, 166, 170–1, 179
   and Richelieu 92–3, 106, 154, 167–9, 173–4, 182–6, 203, 340–1
   sexuality 185–6, 340–1

Boissat, Pierre de 30*t*, 72–3, 76–7, 103, 179
Bouchard, Jean-Jacques 30*t*, 204, 247–9, 261–70, 272
  "Confessions" 269
  reputation 265, 267–8
  assassination attempt on 268
Boulliau, Ismaël 30*t*, 79, 130n.24, 256, 261–2, 283–7
  critique of French Academy 171–2
  critique of Jesuits 285–6
  critique of Richelieu 286–7
  supporter of Galileo 276, 284–6
Bourbon, Nicolas 13*f*, 30*t*, 296
  academy of 75–7
Bourdelot, Pierre Michon 13*f*, 30*t*, 75–6, 89–90, 103–4, 296
Bourdieu, Pierre 44–5, 108–9
Bourzeys, Amable de 30*t*, 180–1
Brun, Antoine 13*f*, 30*t*, 72–3, 76–7
Brunot, Ferdinand 44–5, 47
Bureau d'adresse. *See* Renaudot, Théophraste
Bury, Emmanuel 79–80, 107, 113n.108

Caldicott, Edric 181–2
Calvinism 6, 22–3, 127–8, 130–1, 199, 202, 253, 303, 331–2
Campanella, Tommaso 203, 261–2, 264, 272–3, 312–14
Camus, Jean-Pierre 30*t*, 45–6, 54–62, 67, 124–5
  on writers 59–62
  Conférence Académique 1–2, 12, 60–2, 154–5
Cardinal Richelieu. *See* Richelieu, Armand Jean du Plessis, Duc de
Castiglione, Baldassare 108–9, 116, 124, 228–9
Catholic League 3–4, 21–2, 134, 142n.68, 148, 218n.15, 259, 297–8, 319–20
  role in the Wars of Religion 38, 138–41, 253–4, 291–2, 325n.91
Cerisiers, René de 30*t*
Chapelain, Jean 16–17, 23, 30*t*, 40, 44, 71, 74, 78, 83–4, 89–90, 104–5, 107–8, 167–72, 179, 182–3, 193, 195–6, 202, 207–8, 212, 216–17, 229, 237–41, 266–8, 299, 337–41
  and his patrons 91–3, 106
  in the Rambouillet salon 219–23, 241, 246
  on women 110–11
  on common people 140
  on writing of history 147–8
  and *Le Cid* controversy 149–50, 155–7
  and Richelieu 186–91, 246
  La pucelle 188–91, 197, 223–4, 275–6
Charron, Pierre 3–4, 19–20, 30*t*, 143, 207, 342–3
  on common people 134–5
  on reason of state
  De la sagesse 131–44, 152–3

Chauveau, François 13*f*
Chevreau, Urbain 30*t*
Christina, Queen of Sweden 100, 199, 248n.3, 308–9
Cicero, Marcus Tullius 2, 42–3, 54–5, 65–7, 69, 78–80, 125–6, 136, 144–5, 152–3, 179–80, 207–9, 244–5, 337
  and *otium* 2, 9–10
  and reason of state 314
  as source of *honnêteté* discourse 113
Cinq-Mars conspiracy 200, 256, 292–3
Coëffeteau, Nicolas 30*t*, 62–3
  his academy 70
Colletet, Guillaume 17, 31, 37, 51, 71–3, 76–8, 80, 128, 140, 180–1, 183, 229, 296
Colomby, François de Cauvigny de 30*t*, 48
Compagnie du Saint-Sacrement 21–2, 168. *See also dévots*
conformity 23–4, 338–41
Conrart circle 13*f*, 30*t*, 72, 76–7, 152, 167–9, 172–4
Conrart, Valentin 30*t*, 40, 44, 90–1, 130–1, 151–2, 157, 220–1, 229–30
  as patron of translation projects 78, 82–3
  and Richelieu 203
Corneille, Pierre 56, 62, 85, 104–5, 106n.83, 148–50, 178, 182–3, 219, 223–6
  Le Cid controversy 81, 149–50, 155–6, 168, 221, 224–5, 246
Cotignon de la Charnaye, Pierre 30*t*
Council of Trent 289–90
Counter-Reformation 8, 22–5, 88–9, 127–8, 130–1, 150, 152–3, 203, 261–2, 264, 272–3
Cremonini, Cesare 26–7
Croisilles, Jean-Baptiste de 30*t*, 71–2
Cureau de la Chambre, Marin 30*t*
Curtius Rufus, Quintus 63, 77–80

D'Orléans, Gaston, duc d'Orléans 13*f*, 30*t*, 95, 106, 168, 216–19, 233, 235–6
  court of 102–3
  role in Cinq-Mars conspiracy 292–3
Dante Alighieri 62, 65–6, 275–6
Day of Dupes (1630) 147–8, 154, 168, 182–3, 229, 307–8
Deimier, Pierre de 48–9
des Loges, Marie Bruneau 13*f*, 53n.45, 185–6
Descartes, René 2, 30*t*, 37–8, 64, 107–8, 123, 128–30, 193, 256–7, 337–8
  on *otium* 9–10
  on Balzac's *Lettres* 55–6
  on pedantry 73
Descimon, Robert 140–1, 248–9, 259
Desmarets de Saint-Sorlin, Jean 30*t*, 168–9, 179, 223–4, 229

Desportes, Philippe 46-8
dévots 22n.43, 23-4, 58-9, 168, 236-7, 285-6, 303, 305-6, 311n.41
  and the Day of Dupes (1630) 229
Dewald, Jonathan 90-1
Diodati, Eli 30*t*, 76-7, 129-30, 255-6, 286, 296
discretion 12, 28-37, 122, 126, 131, 152-5, 157-8, 246, 260-1, 265, 338-9, 341
  as virtue 124-8, 136, 143, 311-12
    in *honnête homme* 161, 342
  in fiction and theater 123, 150-1
  as concern of historical writing 146-8
  tension between openness and 161-2
dissimulation 25-39, 117-20, 143, 174-5, 212-13, 265, 269, 341-2
  association with reason of state 26-7, 116-19
Du Bosc, Jacques 30*t*, 109-10
  on *honnêteté* 115-16
  and women 108, 114-15, 117-20
Du Chastelet, Paul Hay 30*t*, 179-83, 311n.41
Du Duc, Fronton 30*t*
Du Perron, Jacques Davy 50-1, 53, 62, 133, 180, 252
Du Ryer, Pierre 13*f*, 30*t*, 78-80
Du Vair, Guillaume 30*t*, 46, 106, 126, 140-1, 299-300, 328
  on eloquence 45n.13, 67, 69
Dubois, Claude-Gilbert 24
Duchesne, André 30*t*
Dupleix, Scipion 30*t*, 147-8
Dupuy Cabinet 13*f*, 30*t*, 37, 42, 66-9, 75, 107-8, 110, 158-9, 187, 202, 222, 237-8, 246-50, 254-7, 261, 266-8, 276-8, 281-5, 299-300, 308-9, 337-9. *See also* Dupuy, Christophe; Dupuy, Jacques; Dupuy, Pierre
  origins of 247
  contemporary views of 253-4, 279
  on French Academy 171-2
  Italian connections 261-76
  criticism of Richelieu 293-5
  and the Republic of Letters 295-8
Dupuy, Christophe 252, 261-2, 268, 272
Dupuy, Jacques 30*t*, 79, 171-2, 191-2, 247, 273-4, 283-7
Dupuy, Pierre 23, 30*t*, 146-8, 191-2, 270-2, 281, 288-90
  Defense of J.-A. de Thou 253-5, 291-2
  on Richelieu and F.-A. de Thou 292-5

Edict of Nantes (1598) 6, 8, 21-3, 38-9, 131, 144-6
Elias, Norbert 11-12, 322
  "civilizing process" 26-7, 112-13, 121-2, 214

Epernon, Louis de Nogaret de La Valette (Cardinal La Valette) 54-5, 93-7, 216-19, 237-8, 277
  and Balzac 93-5, 105-6
  and Voiture 95-7
Epicureanism 11-12, 98-9, 255
Erasmus of Rotterdam 14, 47
  Ciceronianus 42-3, 180
esprit fort 11-12, 23, 25-7, 66, 119-20, 130, 135-6, 142-3, 159-61, 249-50, 257-8, 266, 290-1, 299-300, 308-9, 315, 337-8, 342-3

Fancan, François Langlois, sieur de 30*t*, 182-3
  in Richelieu's inner circle 184-6
Faret, Nicolas 16-17, 30*t*, 57-8, 166-8, 185-6
  on *honnêteté* 41-2, 113-21, 124, 130
  appreciation of the salon 212-13
  on elite education 87-8
  on Richelieu 166, 168
  Projet de l'Académie 174-80
  on French vernacular 176-7
Faudoas-Averton, François de 104-5
Female aristocrats. *See* Women
Ferrier, Jérémie 30*t*, 184
  as apologist for royal foreign policy 182-3, 256
Fortin de la Hoguette, Philippe 30*t*, 116-17, 259n.35, 276
  on *otium* 119-21
  on *honnêteté* 281-3
  in the Dupuy cabinet 279-83
Foucault, Michel 11-12
  on reason of state 300-1, 310n.37
Franks
  in d'Urfé's *L'Astrée* 323-5
French Academy 13-14, 16-17, 30, 40-2, 44, 66, 71-2, 76-7, 79-83, 114, 128-31, 161-3, 166, 169-70, 179, 219, 233, 238, 246, 267-8, 311, 337-8
  founding of 28-9, 43-4, 71, 77-8, 81-2, 111-12, 164-5, 167, 169, 173-8, 186-7
  critiques of 172-3
  satires 51
  on Corneille's *Le Cid* 155-7, 178
  on eloquence 179-82
French vernacular 24-5, 55-6, 71, 169-70, 180-2, 245-6, 248-9, 302
  as literary language 27-8, 40-1, 43, 61-2, 67, 81-3, 161-2, 222-3, 337-8
  and classicists 165
  regulation and usage of 62, 64-6
  ancient authors translated into 77-81, 143-4, 157-8
French Protestants 189-90, 331-2. *See also* Huguenots

INDEX

French Revolution (1789) 4–5
   and French language 43–4
Frénicle, Nicolas 30*t*, 76–7
   and *Parnasse satyrique* 37, 128
Frisch, Andrea 145–6
Fronde (1648–1653) 70, 228, 255, 288–9, 293–5
Fumaroli, Marc 7–8, 44–5, 84, 173, 248–9, 282–3
Furetière, Antoine 30*t*, 44, 80–1
   on eloquence and pedantry 40–2
   on common people 138–9

Gaffarel, Jacques 30*t*, 159, 203, 261–2
   study of the Kabbalah 204–6
   in service to Richelieu 204, 206
galanterie 214, 218–19, 235, 238, 308
   attempts to define 231–2
Galilei, Galileo 100, 255, 262, 276, 283–6
   discoveries 54–5, 57–8, 152–3
   controversy 129–30, 252, 263–4, 272–3, 284–5
Galimatias. *See* Furetière, Antoine
Gallicanism 184, 188–90, 327–8, 337–41
   variations of 38–9, 58–9
   Wars of Religion and 39
   irenic Christianity and 202
   Dupuy cabinet and 247–50, 257–9, 285–92, 298
Garasse, François 30*t*, 204–5
   criticized 152–4
   attacks on Gallicanism 25–6, 118–19, 253–4
   against Théophile de Viau 127–9, 151–2
   against Pierre Charron 131–3, 207–8
   and his disciples 249–50
Garnier, Claude 30*t*
Gassendi, Pierre 30*t*, 37–8, 129–32, 157, 283–4
   on *otium* and *negotium* 11–12
   in the Dupuy cabinet 255–6, 266
   and his patrons 97–101
Gauls 11–12, 14–16, 24–5, 329
   as source of French pride 175–6, 333
   in d'Urfé's *L'Astrée* 321–5
   and French eloquence 65
Giry, Louis 30*t*, 78
Godeau, Antoine 30*t*, 44, 57–8, 72, 166, 170–1, 197, 222, 267–8
   and the Conrart circle 71, 169
   and the Rambouillet salon 110–11, 169, 219–21, 237–41
   praising Richelieu 168, 193
   on eloquence 179–80
Godefroy, Théodore 30*t*
   working for Richelieu 191–2
Goldmann, Lucien 4–5, 21–2
Gombauld, Jean Ogier de 30*t*, 40, 71, 103–4, 168–9, 179

Gomberville, Marin Le Roy de 30*t*, 72–4, 169, 316–17
Goulu, Jean 30*t*
   polemic with Balzac 60–1, 154–5
Gournay, Marie de 13*f*, 30*t*, 45–6, 50–1, 58–60, 72–4, 76–7, 89–90, 109–10, 247–8, 313–14
   as critic of Malherbe and purists 50–4, 103, 124–5
   on *L'Astrée* 318–19
   criticized in contemporary fiction 170–1
Grafton, Anthony 110, 278, 296, 337–8
Greenblatt, Stephen 124
Grotius, Hugo 30*t*, 126, 266, 272, 284–5, 294, 299–300, 328, 337–8
   and Richelieu 131, 198–9, 201–3
   and the Dupuy cabinet 212–13
   on Church schism and irenic ideal 201–3
Gustavus Adolphus, King of Sweden 228–9, 235
Guyet, François 30*t*, 157, 223n.29, 256, 279–80, 286
   in the Dupuy cabinet 276–9
   Satyricon 278–9

Habermas, Jürgen 121–2, 161, 340–1
Habert, Germain 30*t*, 72, 104–5, 168–9
Habert de Montmor, Henri Louis 30*t*, 100
Habert, Philippe 30*t*, 72, 168–70, 218
Habsburgs 23–4, 199, 201, 297–8, 333
   rivalry with France 21, 23–5, 182–3, 191–2, 199, 237, 254–5, 264, 286–7, 293
Hardy, Alexandre 30*t*, 70, 103, 150
Harth, Erica 107–10, 113
Henri II, prince de Condé 75–6, 90–1, 196–8, 200, 216–17, 246
Henri III, King of France 134, 138–9, 167, 327
   treatment by later authors 24–5, 148, 332–3
Henri IV, King of France 16, 90–1, 101–2, 101n.55, 148, 173–4, 215–16, 318–19, 324–5
   assassination of 252, 254
   depicted as model king 14, 83, 141–2, 189–90, 251, 322–3, 327, 333
   role in rebuilding Paris 85–6
Hercules 141–2, 313–14
   as symbol of eloquence 14–16, 49
   Richelieu as 197
Hirschman, Albert 340–1
Holstenius, Lucas 30*t*, 261–4, 266
   in the Dupuy cabinet 270–3
honnêteté 25–39, 41–2, 81–2, 123–5, 130, 212, 223, 244, 265, 281–2, 339, 341–2
   origins of 112–22
     ancient roots of 113–14, 121
   and women 108–9, 115
   inclusiveness beyond aristocratic elites 217

and dissimulation 116–18
and *galanterie* 232
and pedantry 41–2, 341–2
and reason of state 342
in fiction 123
Huet, Daniel 107–8, 231
Huguenots 130–1, 184, 202, 206, 228, 251–2, 307.
    See also French Protestants
Humanism 48–9, 88, 171–2, 191–2, 259–62, 295, 333–4
    and erudite knowledge 42–3, 48–9, 81–2, 248–9, 337–8
    and preference for ancient languages 83–4

Illustres bergers 13*f*, 30*t*, 72, 76–7, 237–8
Index Librorum Prohibitorum
    John Barclay and 328
    Pierre Charron and 132, 134
    Jacques-Auguste de Thou and 146–7, 249–54, 261–2, 285–6

Jacob de Saint-Charles, Louis 30*t*
Jansenism 2, 21–2, 207–9, 240–1
    and *otium* 4–5, 21–2, 341
    and mainstream Catholicism 207–8
    view of paganism 208–9
    support for among French elites 207–8, 217
Jesuits. *See* Society of Jesus
Jouhaud, Christian 19–21, 44–5, 56–7, 92, 105, 187–8, 213, 299, 304, 308, 318

Koselleck, Reinhart 4–6, 8, 242–3, 296–7

L'académie Le Pailleur 13*f*
L'Estoile, Claude de 30*t*, 76–7, 182–3, 219n.20
L'Estoile, Pierre de 140–1, 148, 297–8
La Mesnardière, Hippolyte-Jules Pilet de 30*t*, 138–9, 163–4
La Milletière, Théophile Brachet de 30*t*, 200–1
La Mothe le Vayer, François de 13*f*, 26–7, 30*t*, 40, 79, 129–30, 157–9, 276–7
    and Richelieu 207–11
    and the Dupuy circle 255–60
    critique of Jansenist stance on pagans 208–11
    on *otium* 11–12, 261
    as critic of purists 66–9, 125–6
    on eloquence 69
La Rochelle 280–1
    siege of (1627–1628) 1, 193, 280, 303, 305–7, 331–2
Le Bret, Cardin 30*t*, 191–2, 300n.2
Lesclache, Louis de 30*t*, 73–4
Liancourt, Roger du Plessis, Duc de 13*f*, 74, 106

Lipsius, Justus 15–16, 47, 51, 54–5, 143–4, 157–8, 174–5, 230–1, 278
    as popularizer of Neo-Stoicism 3–4, 125–6
Lorrain, Henri de, Count of Harcourt 13*f*, 92–3, 103–4, 106, 218n.15
Louis XIII, King of France 7, 20, 82–3, 101–2, 141–2, 147–8, 151, 180–1, 192, 286–7, 292–3, 327–8
    in contemporary writing 189–90, 196–7, 274–5, 283, 327, 333
    in Balzac's *Le Prince* 301–4
Louis XIV, King of France 37, 88–9, 101–3, 228, 274–5, 280
Loyola, Ignatius 84
Loyseau, Charles 87–8, 143
    on social order 139–40
Lucian of Samosata 14, 79–80
Luillier, François 30*t*, 99–100, 256, 283–4
    and Gassendi 100–1
Lusson, Guillaume 30*t*
Lyons, John 116–17

Machiavelli, Niccholo 9–10, 139–40, 147–8, 174–5
Mairet, Jean 30*t*, 103–5, 224–7
    Sophonisbe 224–7
Malherbe, François de 13*f*, 30*t*, 40, 83–4, 90–1, 124–5, 142–3, 165–6, 181–2, 237–9
    on language 13–14, 16, 24–5, 46–50
    "Doctrine" 40–1, 46–9, 71, 76–7, 82–3, 219, 222–3, 233–4, 238
Malleville, Claude 30*t*, 72, 76–7, 103–4, 168–9
    in the Rambouillet salon 221n.24, 229
Marbeuf, Pierre 30*t*
Marcassus, Pierre de 30*t*, 328
Marino, Giambattista 62–3, 195–6, 216–17
Marolles, Michel de 13*f*, 30*t*, 51, 76–7, 150n.109, 256
Marot, Clément 49, 56–7, 233–4
Maucours, Piat 13*f*, 71, 76–7
Mauduit, Louis 30*t*
Mauléon, Auger de, seigneur de Granier 13*f*
Maynard, François 30*t*, 48, 72–3, 103–4, 112, 169
Medici, Catherine de 24–5, 327, 332–3
Medici, Marie de 104–6, 168
Ménage, Gilles 30*t*, 76n.136, 78, 200–1, 229, 256, 266, 278
Merlin-Kajman, Hèléne 8–9, 21, 44–5, 56, 173–4
Mersenne, Marin 13*f*, 30*t*, 75–6, 97–101, 128–9, 151–2, 204, 256–7, 281, 283–4, 296
    critique of "libertinage" 152–3
    argument with Gaffarel on Kabbalah 204–6
Mesmes, Henri de 13*f*, 100, 270
Mézeray, François Eudes de 30*t*
    writing a history of France 147–8

Méziriac, Claude-Gaspar Bachet de 30t
   on translation of ancient authors 77-8
Molière (Jean-Baptiste Poquelin)
   Les femmes savantes 62, 108-9
   The Misanthrope 123, 231, 276-7
Molière d'Essertines, Hugues Forget 30t, 71-2
monde 20-1, 27-8, 88, 91, 101, 161, 213-14, 233, 238, 245-6, 320
   composition of 17-18, 107-8
   predominantly unofficial nature of 102, 107
   and honnêteté 27-8
   embrace of otium 102, 107
   literary culture of 121-2
   sociability in 220, 299-300
   and Louis XIII 304
Monluc, Adrien de 30t, 90-1, 103
Montaigne, Michel de 50-1, 53-4, 58, 114, 124-5, 130-2, 153-4, 157, 207, 244-5, 282-3, 313-14, 335, 342-3
   and the idea of otium 2-4, 9-10
   suspicion of oratory 15-16, 143-4
   on pedantry 42-3
   literary style 54-5
   and French vernacular in literature 65-6
   on formal education 87-8
   and the origins of honnêteté 112-13
   on common people 139-40, 143-4
   on memory 145-6
Montausier, Charles de Sainte-Maure 30t, 92, 112, 130-1, 189-90, 319-20
   in the Rambouillet salon 216-21, 227-33, 237-8
   "Guirlande de Julie" 228-32, 235
   marriage to Julie d'Angennes 219
Montmorency, Henri, duc de 13f, 37, 71-2, 104-6, 127-8, 197-8, 224-5
   court of 103-4
   rebellion (1632) 88-9
Morel, Fèdèric 30t
Morgues, Mathieu de 30t, 128-9, 172, 182-3, 305

national identity 23-4
Naudé, Gabriel 11-12, 13f, 24-5, 30t, 158-61, 255, 273-6
   on dissimulation 26-7
   on common people 138-9, 157
   on reason of state 301, 308-16
   on history 275-6
negotium 2, 11-12, 97, 318. See also otium
Neo-Platonism 204-5, 230-1
   and L'Astrée 319
Neo-Stoicism 46, 97, 126, 227, 283
   and otium 3-4
   and patriotism 39, 342-3
   and the ethos of self-restraint 125-6

Ogier, François 30t, 61, 72
   his defense of Balzac over Lettres 76n.136, 152
otium 2-5, 70, 75-6, 104-5, 107, 178, 181-2, 215-16, 245-6
   positive valence of the term 8-12
   differences in framing of 11-12
   as engagement 81, 159
   and female aristocrats 111-12
   and fashioning of the self 214
   spaces of 245-6, 315-16

Pasquier, Etienne 14, 127-8, 189-90, 319, 323-4
   on common people 138-40
Patin, Guy 13f, 23, 30t, 37, 76-7, 130, 203, 249-50, 296
   in the Dupuy cabinet 255
patronage 28, 70
   common characteristics of in 17th century France 18-21
   and absolutism 81-2
   writerly legitimacy and autonomy and 105-6
   importance for mondain writers 130-1
Patru, Olivier 30t, 78
Pedantry 13-14, 27-8, 40, 61-2, 82-3, 113-14, 121, 170-1, 230-1, 239, 312-13, 337-8
   critiques of 41-3, 47, 63-4, 73-4, 107, 124, 341-2
   as source of division 135
Peiresc, Nicolas-Claude Fabri de 30t, 40, 99-100, 129-30, 157, 265, 337-8
   as liaison between Dupuy cabinet and Italy 262-6, 270-1
   role in publishing Argenis 328, 331-2
Pellisson Fontanier, Paul 30t, 103, 105-6, 156, 233-4
   historian of French Academy 167-8, 172-4, 177-8, 184-5, 337
   on otium 71
Pétau, Denys 30t, 285-6
Petrarch 2, 47, 275-6, 307
Pinchesne, Etienne Martin de 13f, 30t, 73n.125
Pintard, René 25-6, 249, 256, 265, 269, 277
Plantin, Christopher 15-16, 309n.33
Pléiade 47n.17, 49-53, 153-4, 219. See also Bellay, Joachim du; Ronsard, Pierre
   and French vernacular 83-4
political culture 5-7, 43-4, 161-2
politiques 127-8, 140-1, 247, 249-52
Popkin, Richard 132-3, 208-9
Porchères-Laugier, Honorat de 30t, 179
Poirier, Hélie 30t

Rabelais, François 2, 4-5, 51, 278-9
   and libertine writers 124-5

INDEX 355

Racan, Honorat de Bueil 30t, 48, 57–8, 62–3, 112, 166, 169, 179, 219
  on Malherbe 41–2, 47–50
raison d'etat. See reason of state
Rambouillet salon 13f, 30t, 62–3, 74–5, 161–2, 169, 193, 212
  founding of 215
  distinguishing features of 246
  writers attached to 219–23, 227–41
    corps and anti-corps 220–1
  as staging ground for plays 223–7
Rambouillet, Catherine de 9–10, 109–10, 114, 197, 215
Ranum, Orest 156–7
reason of state 8, 20, 23–4, 26–7, 136, 236–7, 265, 299–300, 308, 318
  and *honnêteté* 341–2
  and secrecy 310, 312, 342
  justifications for 159–60, 182–3, 192, 255, 292, 308–16
  critiques of 174–5, 227, 334–5
  ethics of 116–17
  in fiction 333, 335
  Richelieu and 201
Regnier, Mathurin 103–5, 141–2
Reiss, Timothy 143–4
Renaissance 2, 14, 56–7, 108–9, 124, 164–5, 204–5, 303, 323, 343–4
  educational traditions of 167, 259–60
  erudite learning 248–9, 316–17, 343–4
  Louis XI and 274–6
  in Italy 261, 264, 275–6
Renaudot, Théophraste 13f, 30t, 37, 75–6, 284–5
  and Richelieu 130–1, 158–9, 164–5
Republic of Letters 8, 24–5, 29, 51, 54–5, 59–60, 68–9, 99–101, 250–1, 262–4, 270–2, 299–300, 327–8
  self-censorship as practice within 158–9
  cosmopolitanism and localism of 296
  and political conformism 296–7
  Dupuy cabinet as center of 75, 191–2, 247–9, 276, 279–80, 290, 295–8
  letter-writing as basis for 247
  Italy and 261
Revol, Louis de 30t
Richelieu, Armand Jean du Plessis, Duc de 67, 126–30, 154, 161–2, 340–1
  The "Age" of 5–6, 8, 12, 37–8, 56, 81–2, 124, 318, 342–3
  and monarchical authority 6–7
  and writers 19–20, 44, 51, 76–7, 92–3, 130–1, 136, 163–6, 182–211, 193–8, 203–11, 237–8
  and French Academy 167–82
  French theater and 148–9, 151, 155–6

  foreign policy of 23–4, 188, 199, 229, 235–7
  on the royal court 101–2
  and Jansenism 207–8
  and Gallicanism 199, 202, 273–4, 288, 338–9
Rigault, Nicolas 30t, 45n.13, 253, 256, 272
Robe nobles 37, 217, 248–9
  competition with traditional nobility 87–90
robins. See Robe nobles
Romans. *See* Ancient Rome
Ronsard, Pierre de 49, 53–4, 197–8, 323–4
  as literary model 51, 72, 125–6, 176–7, 180, 197
  critiques of 48–9, 56–7, 83–4
Rosset, François de 48, 58–9
Rotrou, Jean de 30t, 104–5, 182–3

Sablé, Madeleine de Souvré, marquise de 13f, 216–17
Saint-Amant, Antoine Girard 13f, 30t, 72–4, 76–7, 103–4, 106, 112–13
Saint-Evremond, Charles de 103–4, 225
Sales, François de 1, 11–12, 58–9, 61–3, 179–80
salonnières
  as cultural arbiters 12, 52, 107–10
Sarasin, Jean-François 30t, 103–4, 256
Saumaise, Claude 30t, 130–1, 202, 248–9, 271–2, 278, 284–5, 294
  relationship with Richelieu 198–201
Scarron, Paul 29–37, 30t, 40, 104–5, 316–17
Schapira, Nicolas 44, 78, 128, 213–14, 229–30
Scholar, Richard 116, 341
Scudéry, Georges de 30t, 104–5, 112, 138–9, 189–90, 195–8, 222, 229, 279–80, 319–20, 339–40
  and the *Cid* controversy 155–7, 178
  on Richelieu 197–8, 211
Scudéry, Madeleine de 30t, 104–5, 222, 316–17
  as author 109–10, 112, 215–16
Seneca, Lucius Anneus 46, 94–5, 159–60, 208–10, 258, 305
  on *otium* 2, 9–10, 119–20
Serisay, Jacques de 30t, 71, 168, 170–1
Servien, Abel 30t
Shoemaker, Peter 20–1, 56, 58–9, 105–6
Silhon, Jean de 30t, 57–8, 83–4, 133, 170–1, 339–40
  and Richelieu 92, 130, 165–6, 182–3
  Le ministre d'Estat 193–5
  on common people 138–41
Sirmond, Jacques 30t, 285–6
Sirmond, Jean 30t, 337
Society of Jesus 51, 58, 73–4, 148, 152, 179–80, 188, 264, 273–4, 285–6, 297–8, 328
  and ultramontanism 22–3, 131, 207–8, 251–5
  as educators 84, 89, 95, 126, 244, 266, 319–20, 327–8

Socrates 2, 114, 139–40, 210, 313–14, 316
Sorbière, Samuel 30t, 256
Sorel, Charles 29–37, 30t, 50, 54–5, 71–2, 80–1, 88–9, 103, 142–3, 173–4, 203, 301, 316–17
    Francion 2, 90–1, 124–5
Spain 184, 194–5, 254, 280, 295, 305–6, 327–8
    rivalry with France 21, 184, 191–2, 235–6, 254–5, 259, 289–90, 292–3, 303
    role in Religious Wars 254, 291–2, 323
    role in Cinq-Mars conspiracy 293
sprezzatura 108–9, 116, 342. *See also* Castiglione, Baldassare
St. Bartholomew's Night Massacre 140–1, 194–5
    justified through reason of state 315
Stanton, Domna 214, 231–2

Tacitus, Publius Cornelius 15–16, 79–81, 105, 113–14, 140–1, 146–8, 174–5, 242–3
Tallemant des Réaux, Gédéon 30t, 54–5, 96, 103–5, 215–16, 224–5, 237–8
    on the Rambouillet salon 217, 219, 231, 233–4
Tetrade 129–30, 255–7, 273–4, 316. *See also* Diodati, Eli; Gassendi, Pierre; La Mothe le Vayer, François de; Naudé, Gabriel
Thirty Years' War 39, 199, 217–18
    France and 227–9, 237
Thou, François-Auguste de 30t, 201, 263, 277, 283–4
    execution of 199–200, 256, 292–5, 297–8
Thou, Jacques-Auguste de 23, 30t, 145–6, 247–55, 259–60, 292–3, 297–8
    History of His Times 146–8, 250–4, 261–2, 285–6
Tristan l'Hermite, François 30t, 72–3, 76–7, 89–90, 102–3, 106

Ultramontanism 22–3, 38–9, 89, 131, 192–5, 199, 202, 254, 287–9 327–8
Urban VIII 251, 262, 264, 327, 331–2
Urfé, Honoré d' 58–9, 112, 197, 316–17, 335
    L'Astrée 11–12, 24, 68–9, 72, 197, 299–300, 317–25
    and *honnêteté* 118–19

Valois, Adrien de 30t
Valois-Angoulême, Louis-Emmanuel de
    relationship with Gassendi 97–101
Vanini, Lucilio 29–37, 30t, 88–9, 103–4, 118–19, 132, 249
    conviction and execution of 127–8, 157–8
Vaugelas, Claude Favre de 16, 30t, 45–6, 53–4, 62–9, 102–3, 107–8, 178, 268
    on French language 63–6, 82–3, 125–6
    on *galanterie* 231–2
    as translator 77–80
Viala, Alain 18–21, 40–1, 44–5, 104–5, 188, 231–2
Viau, Théophile de 13f, 29–37, 30t, 51, 71–3, 76–7, 88–91, 103, 106, 153–4, 157–8, 170–1, 197–8, 219, 246, 249
    controversy and imprisonment 81, 127–30, 151–2, 224
Villeneuve, Jean César de 30t
Villers-Cotterets Ordinance (1539) 43–4
Vion, Charles, sieur Dalibray 30t
virtue 26–7, 61, 68, 87–8, 97–9, 110, 118–19, 122, 126, 142–3, 170, 174–5, 214, 228–9, 231–2, 241–2, 245, 283, 318, 324–5, 330, 333–5
    civic 251–2, 305–6
    and *otium* 2–4, 9–10, 107, 120–1, 243, 258, 281–2, 316, 318, 342–3
    and *honnêteté* 112–14, 116–18, 121, 124, 212, 341
    and pagans 208–11
    Ciceronian 69
    Neo-Stoic 94–5, 215–16, 227, 303–4
    of rulers 193–4, 280, 303–4, 307, 325–6
Voiture, Vincent 30t, 40, 67–8, 97–8, 102–3, 157, 169, 172, 207–8, 237–8, 263–4, 275–6, 340–1
    and Cardinal La Valette 95–7, 218–19
    in the Rambouillet salon 219–23, 233–7
    on women as readers 107–8

Wars of Religion 3–6, 8, 14, 21–4, 27–8, 43–4, 70, 76, 84, 125–6, 170, 276, 285–6, 316–17, 342–3
    histories and memories of 144–8, 250–2, 254, 291–2, 332
    as moral lesson for writers and intellectuals 28–39, 127–8, 131, 134, 136, 140–3, 303, 338–9
    in fiction 318, 327, 332–4
    discourse on popular passions and 138–41
    and nobility 88
Women 52, 55–6, 114–15, 117–20, 217, 310
    as part of *monde* 17–18, 38–9, 44–6, 48–9, 63–4, 96, 107, 238, 299–300
        through the salon 74, 110–11, 189–90, 212–15, 246, 298
    as readers 55–6, 108
    relationship with male writers 107–22
    as writers 74
    and French vernacular 63–4
    and *galanterie* 231–2
    education of 51, 73–4, 77–8
Wootton, David 133–4, 136

Yates, Frances 49, 167, 170, 173–4, 323, 343–4